Political Geography

Political Geography

Sudeepta Adhikari

RAWAT PUBLICATIONS
Jaipur • New Delhi • Bangalore • Guwahati • Kolkata

Dedicated to my father
Late Baidyanath Adhikari (1898-1968)
who infused my faith in the honest and dedicated
pursuit of learning to strengthen humanism.

ISBN 978-81-7033-374-6 (hardback)
ISBN 978-81-7033-375-3 (paperback)

Reprinted, 2022

Published by
Prem Rawat for **Rawat Publications**
Satyam Apts., Sector 3, Jawahar Nagar, Jaipur - 302 004 (India)
Phones: 0141 265 1748 / 265 7006
E-mail: info@rawatbooks.com
Website: rawatbooks.com

New Delhi Office
4858/24, Ansari Road, Daryaganj, New Delhi 110 002
Phone: 011-23263290

Also at *Bangalore*, *Guwahati* and *Kolkata*

Typeset by Rawat Computers, Jaipur
Printed at Nice Printing Press, New Delhi

Contents

Acknowledgement

I express my deep indebtedness to Y.M. Goblet, W.A. Douglas Jackson, Charles A. Fisher, Norman J.G. Pounds, Harm de Blij, Robert E. Norris, L. Llyod Harring, R.D. Dikshit, R.L. Dwivedi, R.J. Johnston and Peter J. Taylor, whose books and other works have provided the necessary source material for the book.

I express my sincere gratitude to Prof. P. Dayal, Founder-Head of the Department of Geography, Patna University, Patna, for giving me an opportunity to develop an everlasting interest in Political Geography.

I am equally grateful to Prof. R.N.P. Sinha, former Head of the Department of Geography, M.S. University, Baroda, who taught me Political Geography for years. I wish to express my thanks to Dr. (Sister) Violita A.C., Head of the Department of Geography, Patna Women's College, Patna, who has gone through the entire manuscript, and made necessary corrections.

I am thankful to Dr. K.K. Maltiar, Reader in Geography, B.N. College, Patna University and Dr. A.R.K. Sinha of the same department, and Dr. A. Kumar, Reader in Geography, Maharaja College, Veer Kuer Singh University, Ara, for their constant encouragement, advice and support.

I am grateful to Mr. Lakhan Prasad of the Department of Geography, Patna University and Mr. Devendra Nath, a research scholar of the same department, who have done the cartographic work for the book. I am also grateful to Mr. Sudhir Kumar, another research scholar of the same department.

Lastly, I express my sincere gratitude to Mr. Pranit Rawat for taking pains in getting the book published.

Sudeepta Adhikari

Preface

Political Geography, which was in the pre-paradigm phase in the 1950s and the 1960s, has moved on to the professionalism phase in the 1970s when it attained some kind of professional maturity. From the professionalism phase in the 1970s, it has entered the paradigm phase and finally established itself as a sub-discipline par excellence. Since the 1980s it continues to prosper. The world-systems analysis in political geography in the 1980s gives a new dimension to it and appears to have initiated a 'new' paradigm phase in it, as the world-systems analysis attempts to explain the convenient existence of three scales—imperialism, the state and the local state—and to understand their interrelations. It gives a holistic outlook to political geography. The cessation of Cold War and the superpower rivalries in the later 1980s and the early 1990s, do not seem to have reduced the relevance of geopolitics, rather it has increased its relevance as large number of semi-peripheral powers in Latin America, Africa and Asia have emerged. As a matter of fact, geopolitics in the present-day world has acquired a new dimension and responsibility. The question is: whether geopolitics or geopacifics?

In most parts of the world, a tendency has developed, particularly in the cleavage-ridden plural society that the people seek to perpetuate their ethnic distinctiveness and regional claims and demand that their territories be organized politically. This results in large scale emergence of nation-states in the present world. Such a tendency has, necessarily, caused the defederation of the Soviet Union, Yugoslavia and Czechoslovakia in the recent past, and now largely threatens the *raison d'etre* of some more states in the periphery of the world-systems.

A large number of landlocked states exist in Africa and Eurasia and they have the common problem of access to the ocean/sea. However, they are provided with the right to transit across their neighbours' territories. Landlocked states are, necessarily, peripheral in nature and to a greater extent, their destiny depends on their neighbours. Fall of socialism, disintegration of the Soviet Union and the cessation of Cold War have caused the decay of the buffer zones, and also made them irrelevant in the global power politics. In Africa, rapid 'Blackenization' of Southern Africa has done away with its buffer character in the recent past.

Population is an important index of national strength but it is the composition of population that largely determines the power potentials of the state. A homogeneous population provides greater sustenance to the state's stability rather than a heterogeneous population which often threatens the state's *raison d'etre.* Conflictual pluralism is a common phenomenon in the periphery of the world-systems, wherin each state is somehow involved in ethnic strife and civil war, e.g., Sri Lanka, Afghanistan, Ruwanda, and former Yugoslavia etc. The core states, on the other hand, seek to perpetuate their domination in the periphery, with an obvious eye on the resources of the region. Neo-colonialism, during the greater part of the Cold War period, provided a 'sustained paradigm' to the core states to interfere with the affairs of the states of the periphery.

The concept of frontiers and boundaries fits very neatly into the word-systems framework. With the rise of the world economy a frontier emerged between this system and the system it was supplanting. However, frontier everywhere has been replaced by boundaries. Boundaries are a necessary component of the sovereignty of territories. A world of sovereign states is a world divided by boundaries. Boundaries, therefore, are an essential element of the modern world economy.

The modern concept of resources, power and development is expressive of the core-periphery conflict for the domination of the resource-rich periphery. 'Resources' in political geography is defined as anything a state can obtain or can conjure upto support its strategy. The definition is relevant only to the states with the core strategy, where the processes help states to identify, utilize and obtain resources to furtherance their strategies.

The core model as the germinal area of the modern state is a very early process that contributed to the development of core process in the world economy and that have not been repeated in the periphery. There are three types of capital city: one the result of core processes, second the result of peripheral processes and a third reflecting semi-peripheral strategies. The first tends to produce the Eurocentric concept of a capital city and the third to the American concept of a capital city.

A federalism is the most geographical of state systems that necessarily results from the peripheral and semi-peripheral processes and strategies as most of the federations occur in the periphery and in the semi-perophery areas of the world-systems. However, federations in the periphery have not been much stable than those in the 'older' semi-periphery. In political geography elections play a key role at the scale of ideology in channeling conflicts safely into constitutional arenas. The quantitative revolutions in human geography has added a new dimension to electoral studies in political geography.

In this era of satellite geopolitics, the two-dimensional strategic thinking has given way to the three-dimensional strategic thinking. The global strategic models in the post-Cold War scenario have lost much of their relevance and credibility.

If the world organizations, like the League of Nations and the United Nations Organization (UNO), were an attempt on the part of the world community to perpetuate peace, freedom and stability in the world, the regional multilateral systems or organizations, then, were an attempt to harden political, social and economic cleavages between states, such as those of the EEC, NATO, CEMA, Warsaw Pact, etc. In fact, regional alliances were a part of the core-semiperiphery conflicts in Eurasia and elsewhere. Political regions are, in fact, larger geographical regions, wherein, political issues and phenomena are so deeply interwoven and interlinked in a general setting of geographical uniformity, as to have given a dominant political outlook to each of them.

All the above discussed aspects have been dealt with in the book in a holistic manner. Attempts have been made to give most recent examples in each chapter of the book with a view to make it worth-reading and useful to students and scholars. The book will be useful to the students of political science and international relations as well. It has been prepared in the hope of guiding graduate and post-graduate students to a better understanding of the fundamental principles and the changing nature of political geography, so that they require little expertise to understand the philosophy of the subdiscipline. The book will also be useful to those preparing for various competitive examinations.

However, the book makes no claim to be comprehensive. The aim is also to provide insights into current concern about the future of political geography. The author welcomes critical comments and suggestions on the book.

stable than those in the 'order'/'centre-periphery'. In political geography election play a key role at the centre of ideology in channelling conflicts safely into constitutional arenas. The quantitative revolutions in human geography has added a new dimension to electoral studies in political geography.

In this era of satellite geopolitics, the two-dimensional strategic thinking has given way to the three-dimensional strategic thinking. The global strategic models in the post-cold war scenario have lost much of their relevance and credibility.

The world organizations, like the League of Nations and the United Nations Organization (UNO) were an attempt on the part of the world community to perpetuate peace, freedom and stability in the world, the regional multilateral or treaty organizations; they were an attempt to harden political, social and economic cleavages between states, such as those of the EEC, NATO, CEMA, Warsaw Pact, etc. In fact, regional alliances were a part of the core-semi-periphery conflicts in Eurasia and elsewhere. Political regions are, in fact, larger geographical regions, wherein political issues and phenomena are so deeply interwoven and interlinked in a general setting of geographical attributes, as to have given a dominant political character to each of them.

All the above discussed aspects have been dealt with in the book in a lucid manner. Attempts have been made to give most recent examples in each chapter and the text with a view to make it worth-reading and useful to students and scholars. The book will be useful to the students of political science and international relations as well. It has been prepared with the hope of guiding graduate and post-graduate students to a better understanding of the fundamental principles and the changing nature of political geography, as their studies require the expertise to understand the philosophy of the subject matter. The book will also be useful to those preparing for various competitive examinations.

However, the book makes no claim to be comprehensive. The aim is also to provide insights into current concern about the future of political geography. The author welcomes critical comments and suggestions on the book.

Chapter 1

The Substance of Political Geography

Political geography has a long tradition of its existence on the academic horizon but not in an organized way, though in the past it has boasted some of the most renowned academic geographers and has contributed notably to the emergence of scientific geography during the past century. However, the origin of political geography can be traced back to the seventeenth century, particularly to the works of Sir William Petty whose *Essays in Political Arithmetick*, published posthumously, sought to underline the interplay between states and their geographical environment, and contained elements of true politico-geographical scholarship. His other works, viz., (i) *Treatise on Taxes*, published in 1662, dealt with the territorial and demographic bases of the power of states; (ii) *Political Anatomy of Ireland*, published in 1672, intrinsically dealt with the position and extent of Ireland—the two essential characteristics of the geographical domain of the state. It also dealt with the concept of the state's geographical sphere of influence, with the population density, capital cities, the principle of intensity and with distance, as a factor controlling man's political activities; and (iii) *Treatise on Ireland* which was not published until 1899, and which boldly expounded the theme of 'colonial utopias'. It was the very first plan for an experimental political geography based upon anthropo-geographical observations, and these were surprisingly exact for the time at which they were made and propounded.

Since Sir William Petty was not a professional in the subfield, his ideas could not get proper academic expression and recognition. However, it was not until the late nineteenth century that political geography was established and recognized as a 'subdiscipline' by the publication in 1897 of Friedrich Ratzel's *Politische Geographie*. The establishment of the subdiscipline was further strengthened by the publication of Sir Halford Mackinder's *Geographical Pivot of History* in 1904 which further developed into the Heartland Theory. Nevertheless, political geography, for the greater part of the early twentieth century remained incoherent with ill-defined scope, weak conceptual structure and confused objectives, and without working assumption and procedures. Thus, the political geography, in the greater part of the early present century, suffered from inherent inner weaknesses and contradictions which got further accentuated by contemporary geopolitik, environmentalism, loose speculation on world power distributions, and synoptic and descriptive studies of the form of states. It had been rightly observed by Carl Sauer in 1927, when he branded the contemporary political geography as the "wayward child of the geographical sciences". Nevertheless, Whittlesey, as early as in 1922, proposed a definition for political geogprahy as a "study of areal differentiation based on political phenomena".

It was not until 1935 when Richard Hartshorne came up with a reasonable definition for political geogprahy as "the science of political areas, or more specifically the study of the state as a characteristic of areas in relation to other characteristics of areas". This definition sought to make political geography a "legitimate child of geographical sciences". This initiated a regional tradition in political geography, providing the subdiscipline with more durable working assumptions and procedures, which hitherto, remained absent in it.

Political geography is that part of human geography which deals with those political complexes which have a territorial component (Goblet, 1955).

The internal and external life of political groups is conditioned by the geographical environment or milieu in which these groups evolve. Hence, the need in studying them is of critical geographical analysis which paves the way for a geographical exploration of their existence. It is the task of the political geographer to study by means of this critical analysis the territorial elements and complexes and the geographical forces and relationships which are at work in the formation, evolution and disintegration of most political organisms, notably of states (Goblet, 1955).

Meaning and Nature of Political Geography

"Political geography is concerned with politically organized areas, their resources and extent, and the reasons for the particular geographical forms which they assume. In particular, it is concerned with that most significant of all such areas, the state...the essence of the state is sovereignty. Each state is independent, each in greater or lesser degree is self-governing and each owes to other states and outside organizations only such obligations as it voluntarily assumes" (Pounds, 1972).

The state is the *raison d'etre* of political geography, or in other words, it is the central subject matter of the subdiscipline, notwithstanding the fact that it is the only one manifestation of political activity though, to be sure, the focus of our most intense loyalties, and, at present, of greatest political power.

The state, a politico-territorial or administrative unit, represents the organization of a particular area of the surface of the earth and of the people who presently reside there. Ordinarily, the state is conceived in terms of the 'nation-state' which is of relatively recent origin.

The state, national or otherwise, represents not only an independently organized piece of territory, but it is also a set of institutions involving a system of relationships, which men(must) establish among themselves (not necessarily in the democratic sense) to carry on the activities and to obtain the goals they desire. Statehood, therefore, involves a dual aspect—that which pertains to the organization of territory and that which consists of a system of relationships among the inhabitants of the territory. One aspect cannot exist without the other, nor can one aspect be studied without an appreciation for the nature of the other. All political-territorial units (presumably of the same order and function) have this in common. Yet, at the same time, we know that the surface of the earth is highly differentiated physically, sustaining a great variety of human cultures, while the established political units vary in size, shape, resources, population, level of economic development, and finally, in political power.

In their study of the state, the political geographers have often been aware of the duality of statehood, but, while proceeding to deal 'geographically' with the territorial unit, have often seemed perplexed as to what they should do, if anything, about the institutional relationships. For insight and deeper understanding of their subject matter, they have turned to political science, the related discipline. According to Hans Morgenthau, the noted political scientist, however, there is a common denominator which unites the field; it is a common subject matter defined in most general terms, an orientation towards the nature and activities of the state and toward activities which have in turn a direct bearing upon the state. Clearly, this sharing of interest in the state serves as a major link between political science and political geogprahy. Indeed, in many respects, the subject matter of both disciplines is similar but in either case the aspects of the subject matter may be quite different and what is essentially different is the point of view, the core of interest, and consequently, the emphasis.

However, to Edward F. Bergman (1975): "politics is people coming together to deal with common problems. Whenever and wherever people engage in cooperation and conflict to organize themselves and their resources in order to insure their welfare, political processes are at work and political decisions are made. The extent of population engaged defines the scope of the political organization. Political science deals with the ways men organize and create the machinery and institutions of government. The field of political geography concentrates on three other themes essential to understanding political processes: the geographic factors considered during the making of political decisions, the geographic factors which influence the outcomes of political decisions, and the geographic consequences of political decisions and actions".

"Most political geographers have traditionally focused their attention on the organizational level of the state, or nation-state, which is today the ultimately sovereign level of political authority. They have studied the evolution of states' boundaries, states' distinctive vocational characteristics, and the various ways states differ in size, resources, power, internal cohesion, and other selected characteristics. Political science also tends to focus on the state level of political processes. The state, however, is not the exclusive concern of either political geography or of political science. Politics occurs on all levels from a neighbourhood action committee to large groupings of sovereign states. Political processes and political geogprahy can be studied at any organizational level."

To Jackson (1964), "...political science is concerned mainly with the system of relationships and institutional structure...Political geography, because of its interest in political phenomena, must also be concerned with the institutional structure, but essentially as the institutional structure makes itself evident, and is involved, in the formation of geographic patterns and relationships."

Hartshorne (1954), while clarifying the nature of political geography, in terms of the relationships between political geography and political science, remarks: "The geographer, concerned with regions...has found in the political unit an example of an area that is homogeneous and cohesive in political terms, yet heterogeneous and perhaps not even cohesive in other terms. He studies the structure and functions of that area as a region homogeneous in political organizations, heterogeneous in other respects. The political scientist, concerned with political processes, has found that he must do more than develop generalizations independent of differences in different areas; the processes, which can only be partially described and analyzed in generalization, must be studied as they operate in particular areas; he has been led increasingly to the study of what may be called regional politics."

Jackson further concludes: "...while recognizing that the state is the centre of political geographical study, since it—or at least the nation-state—is the embodiment of contemporary political activities, this interest must be kept in perspective. Political institutions, activities, their interactions and interrelationships with other phenomena, political patterns—all these existed in the pre-nation-state period on a pre-nation-state level. These may, in future, moreover, be propelled to a supra-state level as well . At whatever the period in history or whatever the level, the real core of political geography is the study of the spatial (territorial) variations and interrelationships of political activities and systems."

Contemporary Geographical Traditions

Thus, all the major successive definitions of political geography have necessarily emphasized the state being the *raison d'etre* of the subdiscipline. Further, these definitions tend to reflect the major geographical philosophies of their times, or implicit/inherent in the definitions, are the major contemporaneous geographical paradigms and traditions, such as environmentalist tradition, possibilist tradition, regionalist tradition, topical-specialism or systematic tradition, and the Marxist tradition. These traditions, epistemologically* seem to be opposed to one another, and that necessarily create 'dichotomy' or 'dualism' in political geography.

Environmentalist Tradition

The basic philosophy of this tradition is that 'the environment controls the course of human action'. It received its modern credentials largely through the influence of Darwin, whose ideas made it "inevitable that geographers, along with other scientists, should begin to see in the differentiation of man, the operation of natural laws". In political geography, there is a long-standing interest in the relationship between the environment, both in its natural state and as modified by man, and man's political activity, including all aspects of political structure, process and behaviour. The relationship is seen mainly in terms of a one-way cause and effect, with political activity of man assumed, in large measure, to be strongly influenced by aspects of the physical environment. Friedrich Ratzel carried forward this tradition to his *Politische Geographie* in 1897 when political geography was first established as a subdiscipline.

Political geography in the early part of the present century was viewed primarily as "the study of the relations between man's political activities and organizations...and the natural environment or earth conditions, whether stated directly (i.e., in terms of 'controls' or 'influence') or conversely (i.e., in terms of adjustments) (Hartshorne, 1935).

Camile Vallaux, the French geographer, observed that the "essential problem of political geography was to determine whether the life of political societies is determined, in part at least, by the natural frame in which they develop, in what manner the soil, air and water...relate themselves to the collective action of men" (quoted in Hartshorne, 1935). Vallaux's observation

* Refers to the study of knowledge and justification of belief.

was expressive of crude environmental determinism that political societies were an outcome of the operation of natural laws, influencing their birth and distribution. Political societies, in terms of Vallaux's observation, seemed to be subordinate to the environment.

"Political geography is the study of the extent to which the nature of states together with their organizations and interrelations is influenced by and adjusted to conditions of geography" (Fitzerald, 1946). According to Moodie (1957), "...the major objective of political geogprahy is to analyze interstate relationships and internal adaptations to environmental conditions". "...the aim of political geography is to determine how political organizations are influenced by and adjusted to physiographical conditions and how these factors affect international relations" (Weigert et al., 1957).

These definitions, intrinsically use words like 'influenced by', 'adaptation', 'adjusted to', and 'affect', etc., which necessarily reveal that political space relationships, both internal and external, are, to a large extent, conditioned by the physical environment. Words like, 'adaptation', 'adjusted to' and 'affect', etc., necessarily reveal "human responses (political) to the natural laws, or to the items of inorganic conditions that constitute the physical environment", i.e., how man's political activity responses/reacts to nature's dominance. Nature or the physical environment in these definitions is regarded as dominant with man being subordinate to it; therefore, the political phenomena and political landscapes are largely a manifestation of the operation of the natural laws.

As Goblet (1955) puts it: "The internal and external life of political groups is conditioned in large measure by the geographical environment (land, water and climate) in which these groups evolve. Hence, the need in studying them is of critical geographical analysis which paves the way for a geographical explanation of their existence. It is the task of the political geographer to study by means of this critical analysis the territorial elements and complexes and the geographical forces and relationships which are at work in the formation, evolution and disintegration of most political organisms, notably of states."

Possibilist Tradition

Reaction to the generalizations of the environmental determinisms led to the development of a counter-thesis, that of possibilist, in which man was presented as an active rather than a passive agent. Led by the French geographer, Vidal de la Blache, and other geographers, followers of the historian Lucian Febvre, the possibilists presented a model of man perceiving his freedom to choose. For them the pattern of human activity on the earth's surface is the result of the initiative of man operating within a framework of natural forces.

Without denying the limits every environment sets to man's ambition, they emphasize the scope of man's action rather than these limits.

The political system can be fashioned to emphasize hitherto inert qualities which in turn can modify some of the effects of the physical environment. Political way of life explicitly manifests man's choices of political activity in the realm of 'possibilities', that which of the systems is best fitted to his political disposition. The same environment has different meanings for people with different political ways of life, for it is a basic factor in determining which of the various possibilities offered by nature, a particular human group will select for its political identification, political structure and system. Montesquieu is believed to be the earliest possibilist political geographer (Kriesel,1968).

States are largely a creation of man's choices of political activity, and the types of political structure necessarily reveal his discretion to select/choose which of the political structures is best suited to his political identification, credential, and political expression and disposition. Derwent Whittlesey, as early as, in 1922, attempted to incorporate the possibilist tradition in political geography when he defined the subdiscipline as "a study of areal differences based on political phenomena".

Political phenomena are largely a manifestation of *genres de vie** of the people, being carved out on the physical environment. Each human group has its own *genres de vie* which is reflective of its political identification, credential and political expression, and which, together with other factors, lead to the distinctiveness of the political phenomenon. Since *genres de vie* are variable, human qualities also are variable and, therefore, it is quite natural that political phenomena associated with them are variable, distinct and distinguishable, creating areal differences, expressing distinctiveness in political character.

Hartshorne's (1935) definition of political geogprahy also emphasizes the possibilist tradition in the subdiscipline. Accordingly, "...political geogprahy is the science of political areas, or more specifically the study of the state as a characteristic of areas in relation to other characteristic of areas"

Each state is distinguishable from other, in terms of its political structure, feature, process, political character, system and organization, and politiy as well. No two states will have the same political character and phenomena. States are necessarily a creation of man's choices of effort and activity, in the realm of possibilities that the nature offers and provides. Each state, or political area, is characterized by its human groups which, through its *genre de vie*, carves out the political landscape, making it distinguishable.

---

* Stands for the complex of institution, tradition, attitudes, purposes, heritage, political institutions and organization, technical and political skill of a people.

The dichotomy in political geogprahy was clear between the environmentalist tradition and the possibilist tradition in the pre-war period as the state was conceived of both as an outcome of the operation of the natural laws and a manifestation of man's choices of effort/activity. This dichotomy seemed to have endangered the unity of political geography, and the need was felt to maintain the unity of the subdiscipline through the concept of a chorological science, i.e., a subject which studied things which are mutually coordinated and integrative, not subordinated, in space. Bowman provided a chorological interpretation when he remarked that geography had political implications because it helps to provide an understanding of the adaptation (mutually coordinated) of group life to the environment of a given area of political control, and it sought to indicate the scope of national limitations and possibilities.

Regionalist Tradition

One of the major consequences of the possibilist tradition vis-a-vis the chorological science was the birth of the regionalist tradition in geography, i.e., the study of the geography of regions, classically through chorology; an analysis of areal differentiation, in which the purpose of the study is to clarify a specific situation in a particular locality. Classically, a region is "a differentiated segment of earth surface".

"The fundamental idea was that the small area would legitimately be expected to show some distinct individuality, if not necessarily homogeneity, through a study of all its geographical features—structure, climate, soils, vegetation, agriculture, mineral and industrial resources, communications, settlements and distribution of population. All these...are united in the visible landscape, linked into one whole and dependent on one another. And more, every area...has been influenced, developed and altered by human activity, and therefore, the landscape is an end-product, moulded to its present aspect by successive generation of people." A region is, therefore, a manifestation of such an intimate relationship between man and nature which has developed through centuries. That is why a region is unique and particular.

Political geography was no exception to the contemporary regionalist paradigm. In general geography, state was conceived of a unique political region. Each state is distinguishable, in terms of its specific situation in a particular locality, political structure and system, political identity and phenomena, and distinctiveness. All observable political phenomena and features in a state seem to be so closely interwoven and united in the visible political landscape, linked into one whole and dependent on one another that the whole state becomes politically homogeneous, thus, creating areal differentiations and variations on the political space of the earth's surface.

Richard Hartshorne is credited with having carried forward the regional paradigm in political geography that the subdiscipline is methodologically distinct as it is concerned with the study of the political region, i.e., the state, which is 'unique' and 'particular'. The tradition is closely associated with exceptionalism* (Kantianism) which calls for an idiographic** geography.

To Hartshorne, "...the geographer analyzes the area concerned by the regional method. On the basis of a series of criteria relevant to political problems, he determines the regional differences and similarities within the area and, by comparative study of the different regional systems revealed by each criterion, seeks for evidence of accordant areal relationships. By studying in historical geography he seeks the cause-and-effect relationships that are suggested by the application of the regional method..."

"Political geography, then, may be defined as the study of areal differences and similarities in political character as an interrelated part of the total complex of areal differences and similarities. The interpretation of area differences in political features involves the study of their interrelations with all other relevant areal variations, whether physical, biotic, or cultural in origin" (Hartshorne, 1954).

Norman J.G. Pounds (1972) also defined political geography in terms of exceptionalism or idiographic tradition. Accordingly, "political geography is concerned with politically organized areas, their resources and extent and the reasons for the particular geographical forms. In particular, it is concerned with the most significant of all such areas, the state." The use of word 'particular' is significant in the definition as it relates to the accordant areal relationships that tend to make a state 'unique' and 'distinguishable' in its totality. Each state is, therefore, unique and particular, making the political space of the earth's surface variable, in terms of political character and landscape.

However, the regional paradigm or regionalist tradition was dominant in the years before and just after the Second World War. Its main focus was on areal differentiations, on the varying character of the earth's surface (basically, the inhabited parts of the earth's surface), and its picture of that variation was built up out of parallel topical studies of different aspects of the physical and human patterns observed. By the 1950s, the disillusionment with the empirical philosophy of the regional paradigm was growing. Slowly, the

---

* Refers to the belief that geography and history are methodologically distinct from other sciences because they are particularly concerned with the study of unique and particular.

** Concerned with the unique and particular, as well as, distinct areal characteristics and relationships.

topical specialism grew in dominance and the regional synthesis was weakened considerably; eventually a full revolution was launched that replaced the regional paradigm by a new paradigm.

It was K.K. Schaefer who is credited with having initiated the theoretical and methodological revolution in geography. Schaefer in his paper "Exceptionalism in Geography: A Methodological Examination", published in 1953, in the *Annals of the Association of American Geographers*, challenged the exceptionalist claims of Hartshorne, made for regional geography, and argued for a nomothetic geography to adopt the philosophy and methods of the positivist school of science. According to him geography must be "conceived of as a science concerned with the formulation of the laws governing the spatial distribution of certain features on the earth's surface". It is these spatial arrangements of features and phenomena themselves, above which geographers should be seeking to make law-like statements.

However, political geography remained very little affected by the conceptual or theoretical revolution in the 1960s. In fact, the subdiscipline was failing to attract its share of the lastest 'new geography'. Political geography in the 1960s seemed to have been trapped in between the 'failing' regional paradigm and the 'growing' positivist (quantitative-systematic) paradigm, and the subdiscipline, therefore, seemed to have lost way, which probably led Brian Berry in 1969 to remark about political geography being 'a moribund backwater'.

Systematic Tradition or Topical Specialism

Notwithstanding the subdiscipline being called 'a moribund backwater', there have been some attempts for a new interpretation of political geography in the light of the growth of systematic and theoretical geography as a result of the methodological revolution.

Douglas Jackson (1964) is believed to have first attempted for a systematic interpretation of political geography, when he defined it "...as the study of political phenomena in their areal context, whether that involves an analysis of boundaries, the geographical patterns resulting from the application of governmental authority, or the political viability of new state units." The same tradition of topical specialism is explicit in the definition of Kasperson and Minghi (1969) when they defined political geography as "...the study of the spatial and areal structures and interactions between political processes and systems, or simply, the spatial analysis of political phenomena".

"The definition", they argue, "is sufficiently broad to comprehend the pluralistic nature of the field and to involve political geography in the mainstream of current social science theory and research. The emphasis on inclusiveness rather than exclusiveness draws attention to the important interdisciplinary contributions originating at the peripheries of the field or even outside the discipline completely."

The above definitions reflect a change from the contemplation of the unique to the adoption of the more rational scientific methodology, and the particular political phenomena must be analyzed in terms of the relation of its areal differentiation with the others. Each particular political phenomenon or phenomenon-complex that is spatially significant, is studied in terms of its relations to the total differentiation of areas as it varies from place to place over the world or any part of it. The spatial analysis of political phenomena is used as a synonym for locational analysis, the positivist approach to the identification of spatial order in political affairs. More specifically, spatial analysis refers to the quantitative procedures and techniques applied in locational analytic work, although such procedures and techniques are not particular to the philosophy of positivism.*

Notwithstanding the approaches of Jackson, and Kasperson and Minghi, the contemporary political geography lacked in methodological approaches by which general theory and hypotheses can be developed and tested. There was an intrinsic requirement in the 1970s for specific methodological directions which could be used in theory building. And Cohen and Rosenthal (1971) provided a more positivist model for political geography when they defined the subdiscipline in the following words: "... it is concerned with the spatial attributes of political process".

The term 'spatial' is defined here as the distributional patterns of political processes (political process refers to the sucession of events, actions, or operations that man employs to establish, to maintain, or to change a political system) and the spatial relations of these patterns with pertinently related phenomena, using space in its sense as a boundless medium. Such patterns and relations form unique political action area, or field of actions.

The methodology, which they suggest, seeks to link effectively political process and its spatial attributes—a methodology that, having identified a specific political process, can pinpoint spatially significant phenomena which relate to this process, and can observe the impact of these phenomena within some control context, and can correct the one process or parts thereof to another.

Another positivist interpretation/definition of political geography was given by Norris and Haring (1980) which sharply contradicts the idiographic

* It is a philosophy whose primary purpose is to distinguish science from both metaphysics and religion. It is concerned with the naturalistic-pragmatic trend in modern thought, and in some connection called empiricism that science can only be concerned with empirical questions.

interpretation of the subdiscipline but necessarily concerns itself with the nomothetic* tradition of the contemporary basic paradigm of geography. According to them, "political geography...as the scientific study of the relationship between politics and terrestrial space".

A scientific study implies a systematic knowledge based on observation, description and analysis. Politics includes political behaviour at all levels of human area centered on the earth's surface in which all material things are contained. Thus, the tasks of political geographers are to observe, describe, and analyze the relationships between political behaviour and spatial distribution, and to formulate generalizations (empirical).

Thus, the dichotomy between regional political geography and the systematic political geography was clear, with the former concerned itself with the 'unique' and 'particular' character of the political region, and the latter concerned itself with the topical specialism, involving scientific enquiry, formulation of empirical laws/generalizations and, analyzing political problems/phenomena by comparing and contrasting political regions.

Nevertheless, political geography must be both idiographic and nomothetic. There is a continuous transfusion from one to the other, and most recent research in the subdiscipline contains of both. An integration of both regional political geogprahy and systematic political geogprahy is one of the tasks which justify the *raison d'etre* of the subdiscipline. The dichotomy is only expedient on strictly practical grounds, one merges into the other. Both should generally be used in the same scientific analysis. It is through the formulation of empirical generalizations or laws, with regard to the spatial analysis of political phenomena that the 'uniqueness' of the political regions is tested and analyzed, leading to the improvement of subsequent theories. Therefore, the dichotomy seems to be illogical and meaningless.

Marxist Tradition

The contemporary political geograhy also underwent Marxist interpretation which sought for a new paradigm for the subdiscipline. Marxist geography, as a matter of fact, provides a new perspective within 'historical materialism' centrally concerned with the ways in which the production of space, place and landscape is complicated in the reproduction of specific social formulations. It was R. Peet who carried forward the Marxist tradition in geography, and proposed a 'spatial dialectics' which tended to conceive of "social process and

---

* Concerned with the universal and the general and geography should be concerned with the formulation (rather than simply the application) of scientific laws which tend to contribute the nomothetic approach.

spatial forms" as two components of a dialectical unity. Marxist geogprahy, then sought to disclose "social process which tended to originate spatial appearance and which in turn led to an input into the continuing social process".

There has been some merger between political geography and Marxist geography. Marxist theories in imperialism, the state and the local state are applied within the three-scale framework in political geogprahy. Marxist geography must offer much more than a critical analysis of contemporary imperialism and capitalism and it must also seek to define a political project that sees the transition from capitalism to socialism in historical-geographical terms. This depends upon an appropriation of political geogprahy and upon the formulation of coherent political strategies; with the greater emphasis on the capitalist state in terms consonant with modern historical materialism.

Thus, the Marxist political geography seeks to deal with "the interrelationship between socio-political processes on the one hand and spatial processes on the other hand, necessarily in terms of historical-geographical materialism".

However, the Marxist tradition in political geography was not much popular, even in the erstwhile Socialist Block. Only a handful of Anglo-American geographers subscribe to this tradition as a part of their radical approach to the contemporary socio-political problems. However, modern political geography which is particularly concerned with the global heritage, necessarily emphasizes the 'holistic tradition' in it.

Political geography, therefore, no longer remains 'a moribund backwater'. It has now become "technically more capable, substantively more Catholic, philosophically mature, internationally more merged, socio-politically more relevant and more linked to other disciplines, which in the coming days will lead to a continued plurality of approaches".

Scope of Political Geography

State is the *raison d'etre* of political geogprahy, notwithstanding the subdiscipline's concern with the global heritage. It exists, as Pounds (1972) says, "to perform a particular function, and in most instances this function is to protect, foster and give political expression to that body of ideas and ideals which characterizes the nation... But for the nation-states, which constitute the great majority of states...the objective of the state is the welfare and integrity of the nation or nations of which it is the political expression."

Pounds (1972) refers to the following six aspects of the state, to be taken into consideration in the politico-geographic study of the state (Fig. 1.1):

1. The geographical coincidence of state and nation. This raises the question of political boundaries and claims to territory, of dissident groups within and of related groups outside the limits of the state.

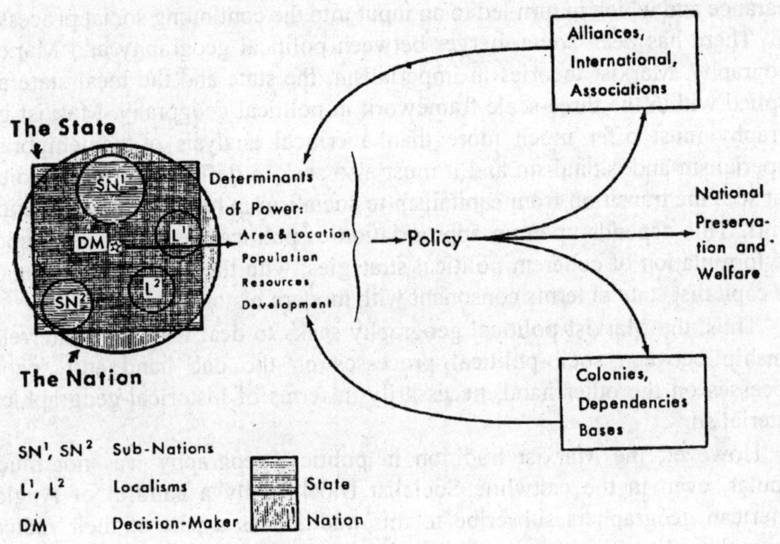

Figure 1.1: The Relationship of State, Nation, Policy and Power: Politico-Geographic Study of the State (After N.J.G. Pounds, 1972)

2. The resources which the state can command in the pursuit of its objective, the well-being and integrity of its people. These resources consist of the location, size, and shape of the state, which influence its strategy and defense and, through communications and transportations, its cohesion; second, the population, its structure, competence, and skills; and, lastly, naturally occurring resources, their utilization, and the degree of industrial and technical development.
3. The social cohesion of the population. Since this is in all respects an important factor in national power, the focus of loyalties within the state and the division of the state for administrative purposes acquire in some instances a political importance. In some respects the social cohesion within a state is reflected in the geographical patterns of voting habits, which thus become an important element in the study of political geography.
4. The state does not rely wholly on its own internal resources. It is likely to have allies and dependencies which in varying degrees support it in the pursuit of its primary objective. The geographical pattern of the alliances,

the distribution of colonies, dependencies, and bases, and the division or joint use of resources are all factors in the power of a state.

5. Every state carries on trade, however, limited in scope this may be in some instances. Trade may be a source of strength, or excessive dependence upon certain goods and markets may spell weakness. Trade can be, and sometimes, has been, used as an instrument of policy, and an evaluation of the significance of trade in the power potential of the state is necessary.
6. The ways in which the citizens of the state perceive not only their country and the component parts but also their friends and neighbours is also important. Perception and, in consequence, voting and decision making are likely to be influenced by preconceived ideas. The traditional enemy or friend, stereotyped views of other groups, and the role of environment are all of significance in shaping decisions.

The above model of Pounds, dealing with the scope of political geography, is shown in Figure 1.1. However, the model, dealing with the factors and relationships, and illustrating the scope of political geography, intrinsically reveals the regional approach with the 'state' as 'unique' and 'distinguishable' and 'particular'. All the six factors and their interrelationships tend to make the state 'unique and particular'. The model was applicable only to the study at the scale of the individual state.

However, the modern political geogprahy does not confine itself merely to the study of the individual state, rather, political geographers now emphasize the study of political phenomena at scales/levels both higher and lower than the state. In fact, the modern political geography is more concerned with global phenomena. However, it does not mean that the model of Pounds has lost its relevance. It is still relevant, given the scale/level of analysis and study.

A New Perspective: Scope Redefined

Cox and Reynolds (1975) attempted to redefine the scope of political geography in the light of a new paradigm shift in human geography that which necessarily concerned itself with the 'critical revolution', as opposed to the 'quantitative revolution'. In political geography, the application of the new paradigm was mainly related to 'conflict resolution' in different ways. It was felt that "a locational consideration of basic importance in the analysis of political system concerns the feedback relationships between the allocational outputs (locational decision) of political systems and the generation of new conflicts, demands and expectations with which the system must cope". The philosophy behind the new paradigm shift in geography and particularly in political geography was: who gets what, where and how.

The 'who' refers to the population of the area under review (a political system), subdivided into groups on the basis of class, race or other relevant characteristics. The 'what' refers to the various goods (and bads), enjoyed or enduced by the population, in the form of commodities, services, environmental quality, social relationships and so on. The 'where' reflects the fact that living standards differ according to area of residence. The 'how' refers to the process whereby the observed differences arise. The primary concern of the geographers in this context is to determine the impact of a benefit or cost at a given location as compared to other alternative locations. Cox and Reynolds (1975) redefined the scope of the subdiscipline as a study of 'conflict resolutions' in the following way: "Political systems*, in an aspatial sense can be defined as systems of interaction between and within sets of individuals for the allocation of scarce public resources to preferred public ends. Since conflict is endemic in scarcity, therefore,...political systems are conflict resolving mechanisms."

"Political systems, however, are spatial systems. Individuals and populations of individuals constituting the political systems all have geographical locations relative to each other and to the environment of public resources applicable to public ends. These geographical locations are of critical significance for the preferences expressed for public goods, for the allocational conflicts engendered, for the mechanism of conflict resolution selected, and for the allocation of public goods ultimately arrived at." In other words, the inputs, the outputs and the allocational mechanisms of political systems have a clear locational expression.

"The political geographer begins with the study of the state in the traditional context (1). The student initially assumes that the individuals in the political system have preference schedules (2) indicating the consumption levels of various public goods which must be attained before the individual is satisfied. Given the variable locations of individuals in the political system and the strictly localized character of most public goods, it is clear that the preference schedules of individuals find political expression as 'revealed preferences' for certain locational policies regarding the allocation of costs and benefits associated with public goods and services. Preference schedules can only be understood in terms of the locational context of those holding preferences."

"Locational context is a critical variable in the formation of these preferences. Similarly, the satisfaction of preferences for public goods (3) can also be interpreted as a function of the individual's location. This is because public

---

*** Political systems are frameworks for the generation and allocation of power, authority and responsibility to identify and to pursue the members' goal.**

goods supplied by governments are (a) not equally available to all consumers, and (b) some consumers (i.e., those living outside an administrative area) can be excluded from consumption. This is equally true both for local/regional politics as well as for national politics where an intense inter-state competition for the location of federally supported facilities and programmes is a usual feature."

"Disparities between preferences for public goods and satisfaction, as related to location, give rise to conflicts (4) which are essentially locational in nature. While some conflicts are fundamentally locational in nature such as conflicts relating to location of public facilities and installations, there are many conflicts which are derivatively locational. These relate to conflicts arising from attempts to allocate between groups defined in social or ethnic terms. But these groups are themselves often locationally distinctive "so that the conflict can be transformed in the politicization process from one which is social in character to one which is locational in character".

It is also observed that a "major function of the political system is to manage all such conflicts and to resolve them. Given the locational nature of the conflicts, it is logical to expect the resolving action from which choice is made (5) to be likewise locational in character. An alternative strategy to the resolution of locational conflict is some form of collective action (6). The dissatisfied may combine to form a neighbourhood association, regional political party or to organize a local petition and provide pressure for an alteration in policy with respect to their locality or region. The policies propounded by such local pressure groups are explicitly spatial in character. These may often relate to territorial policies designed to manipulate boundaries for some locational or regional purposes. In all this some relocation (7) is involved. All these are, therefore, part of the task of the geographer".

"Given the inputs of a political system and its allocational mechanisms, two types of spatial product or output can be considered: (i) the actual allocation pattern of public goods and public bads (8), and (ii) spatial organization of the political system designed to facilitate that allocation (9). Thus, the actual geographical allocation of public goods in the form of educational expenditures per pupil, subsidies to the private economy, desirable social contacts, highway investments, etc., is conceptually distinct from the spatial organization to the political system in the form of boundaries, territories, land uses, etc., designed to facilitate allocation. The former are included under the head "allocation of public goods over space" (8) and the latter under the head "spatial organization of the political system" (9) (Fig. 1.2).

"Steps (1) to (9) are closely interconnected through an effective feedback. The allocation of public goods (8) and the spatial organization of the political system (9) designed to facilitate that allocation at a particular time

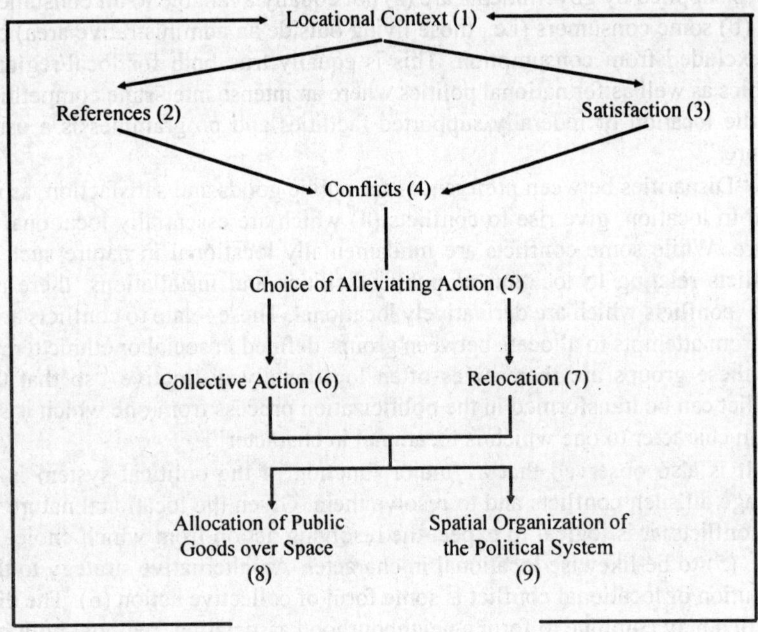

Figure 1.2: The Political System in a Locational Context: State as a Conflict Revolving Mechanism (After K.R. Cox and D.R. Reynolds, 1974)

period affect the locational context (1) in ensuing time periods. Allocations of public goods across space results in new source of dissatisfaction and, therefore, of conflicts...Feedbacks also occur through the effects of the locational context upon preferences. Changes in spatial organization affect the pattern of interpersonal contacts and therefore the influences to which the individual is subject. Likewise...relocation tends to induce a congruence between the party political preference of this relocate and those of the individuals in the neighbourhood to which he has relocated."

Bergman (1975) observes: "Political systems provide a new unit of analysis in political studies, and when we analyze system's activity, we gain a new understanding of processes motivating the creation and dissolution of political structures such as states."

Measurement of Political Systems: Prerequisites

Political systems can be measured by four functional prerequisites which are intrinsic for the continuance of any social system. These are: goal attainment, pattern maintenance and tension management, integration, and adaptation. These are the dynamics of negentropy. "While Parsons defined these functional criteria for social systems without regard to territory, we can easily extend their application to the political-social system as a territorial entity as well."*

Goal Attainment

"In social systems, particularly political systems, however, the system must have a goal beyond its own survival. The maintenance of a political system for its own sake would be tyranny: political systems are only means to achieve public ends; every political system, then, must have objectives (*raison d'etre*), and often these objectives themselves define the most suitable constituency and territory to organize to achieve them."

"The concept of political-spatial organization or a means to achieve public ends is not new to political geography. In the 1890s the German geographer Friedrich Ratzel noted that a state comprises a section of land and a section of humanity organized to a particular distinctive idea, or *raison d'etre* (reason for existing)... In the most mature political structures the *raison d'etre* is related to the general welfare of the group and is shared among all the people. Most states proclaim their citizen's welfare as their *raison d'etre*... Political systems at all levels, not only at the state level, must have defined goals. The state remains the most powerful and ultimately sovereign level of political systems in the world, but supranational political systems, however weak, have arisen. Military or economic blocs of states represent joint pursuit of common goals, and international organizations such as the League of Nations and the United Nations have tried to achieve peace and prosperity for all mankind."

"The continuance of any political system requires not only that its goal be defined and be accepted by the system's constituents, but also that the constituents feel that the goal is being actively pursued. The goal need not necessarily be attained, but if the public feels the system is not pursuing its stated goal, support for the system will fall away.... Sometimes a political system can fully achieve its goals, but may persist in order to safeguard the goal's achievement. If a political system's goals are of a one-time nature, such as the completion of a public construction project, the system may dissolve after the achievement of that goal. While cases such as these emphasize systems' ad hoc nature, most political systems represent ongoing efforts to achieve the

---

* The tendency of systems towards disintegration is today called *entropy*, and the ability to stave off entropy and to maintain pattern integrity is called *negative entropy* or *negentropy*.

constituents' goals. Investigation of a system's goals, of the population's dedication to those goals, and of efforts to achieve the goals is an important part of any political or geographic analysis."

Pattern Maintenance and Tension Management

"At any level of political organization leaders must be chosen, plans laid and programme executed, rules made and adjudicated, and competing interests balanced and reconciled. Every system must be able to regulate its members in order to achieve the public goals. These functions necessitate the creation of machinery and institutions of government, which formalize and stabilize the system. Institutionalization of political systems as instruments takes place at all levels of political organization. Total breakdown of political systems, is a state of entropy in human affairs...".

"Local governments are established and formally recognized, but even within local governments, groups of citizens can organize themselves into a pressure group or bloc to sway the government on various issues.... At the higher end of the scale of human organization, the regulatory power of international systems is limited. These organizations cannot enforce their wishes or decisions upon the sovereign states. Thus international systems exemplify subsystems, dominant systems...".

"The study of these political processes is the essence of political science, but political geography enters here when the interests to be reconciled are regional. Political geography examines the roots of differences among regional interests, and the system's success or failure in reconciling them. Also, political decisions and actions may have differing regional impacts of interests to political geographers. Support for the creation of a metropolitan-aide sewerage district, for example, will vary among metropolitan areas on the basis of existing installations. Some upstream areas or suburbs may already have what they feel to be adequate sewage treatment facilities, but downstream communities which draw their drinking water from the river may not agree... At the level of states, failure to reconcile regional interests may lead to secession or civil war, while successful reconciliation of competing regional interests helps to integrate the population and the territory.... The degree of centralization or decentralization of power in a political system and throughout its territory is another important factor in the management of tension."

"All political systems but the very smallest, however, must subdivide and distribute power and authority, and the degree of centralization or decentralization can influence the system's ability to manage tension and to survive. Even the most centralized governments find it necessary to decentralize some authority in order to unburden the central government, to mobilize local initiative, responsibility and support, to learn about local needs and discontent, and to translate the system's goals into local terms. Excessive decentralization, however, may lead to dissolution of the system. The central government may not be in complete control of the territory's farthest reaches; the ability of the centre to exert power may diminish with distance. Excessive concentration of power, on the other hand, may result in inflexibility, and lay the foundation for local discontent to grow into rebellion. The achievement of an appropriate balance between centralized and decentralized power is one of the finest points in the art of politics."

"...international systems as subsystems dominant: They exist and function only at the pleasure of the sovereign states. Each sovereign state, however, has a different internal division of power between its central government and its subunits. A unitary government is one in which all power and authority are concentrated in the central government, and all subunits are its creatures... In federal states, the balance of power between the federal government and the various states may vary between a concentration of power at the federal level, as in India and Brazil, and the retention of considerable power by the internal states, as in Australia and Canada. In the (erstwhile) Union of Soviet Socialist Republic power is (was) theoretically divided between the union government in Moscow and the governments of the fifteen republics, but power is (was) in fact highly concentrated in Moscow."

"The political and territorial subdivision of power can be studied even on the level of a large city."

"The management of tension within political systems through the balancing of power and the reconciliation of interests thus may stem partly from regional interests, have different impacts in different regions, and take place within a framework of centralized or decentralized power."

Integration

"To a political geographer integration means both the integration of a political region as a spatial entity and the integration of population as a social entity."

Spatial Integration

"Spatial organization and integration evolves with transportation and communication networks. Facility of movement of people, goods and ideas and formation allows differentiation of land use and exchange among regions, as well as differentiation of human social roles and the division of labour in a society. Transport networks do not in themselves catalyze interaction, but there could be no interaction without them. A transport and communication network pattern, density, and even adequacy can be measured on any scale of region from the streets and the presence of or absence of a radio station in a small town up to analysis of international communications, migration and trade."

"Other measures of the integration of a political region are the degree to which the populations of the various subregions participate in the political system and, conversely, whether or not the system's decisions and actions apply uniformly throughout the space. In a large city, voter turnout varies greatly by electoral district, usually depending on district population's socio-economic-educational levels. High voter turnout and degree of participation usually feeds back as a high level of city services. Politically unorganized schemes receive less attention from city hall. Most independent states contain regions where central government influence reaches only weakly..."

Social Integration

"The integration of the political system itself as a social entity depends ultimately upon the degree and durability of support it receives from the population. Therefore, a political geographer must be concerned with what we might call the psychological integration of the population. 'Cognitive integration', 'effective integration', 'sense of community', and 'geographical proximity', are some of the basic ingredients, intrinsic for the social integration.

"Some social scientists have measured densities of human interaction among both proximate and separate groups as a key to community formation...Of more importance than proximity or quantity of interactions alone may be mutual perception and favourable or unfavourable prejudices. Even when interaction is mutually interdependent, as in trade, effective integration does not necessarily follow."

"The idea of egocentrically expanding levels of cognitive and effective integration does not describe psychological integration completely. Individuals also grow to recognize and appreciate the independent integrity of other individuals or groups, to comprehend and even to respect the points of view of others. Psychologists call this reciprocity... Thus, a very important part of intellectual maturation consists of steadily widening one's level of cognitive and effective integration, with an appreciation of reciprocity at each level. Each level of integration is recognized as one of several collateral subsystems of the next higher system all the way up to all mankind, or even all life. ..Since the nation is today often the level of strongest integration, however, and since it is the ultimate level of political sovereignty, individual patriots only with great difficulty recognize the legitimacy of other groups patriotism, or respect them, if indeed they ever do..."

"At each level of political integration, from the smallest to the most inclusive, there are three potential objects of political support. The most general of these is the *political community* which is simply the sense of community within the political sphere of activity. Whenever people collaborate, we have, *ipso facto*, a political system, but political community involves more than just working together: it necessitates a sense of commitment to continue working together. *Nationalism* is a sense of political community...A *political regime* is a more specific object of political support. A regime is the set of legal-political arrangements within a political system—the constitutional principles or rules of the game. The third object of support is the *government*, the actual administration in power... New political structure may emerge through chronological development of a political community, a regime and then a government."

"In other cases, a government may chronologically precede a political community. In many states, recently emerged from colonialism, the government represents the legally legitimate successor to the colonial administration, but it has yet to win the allegiance of the people and to weld them into a national political community. A nation may antedate and demand a state, or a state may forge a nation...changes in governments are common, but constitutional crises are less so, and the dissolution of the political community itself can result in civil war."

"A society's appreciation of the differentiation among political community, regime, and government will be reflected in the society's ability to cope with dissent. A politically matured society recognizes that a segment of the population may disagree with the policies of the government, but still remain loyal to the regime and political community. That society will recognize such a group's right to offer constructive criticism and to attempt to sway the majority to its point of view. The dissenting group is known as the *loyal opposition*, and without a loyal opposition any government becomes highly tyrannical and stagnant. A politically immature society often interprets every dissension from the government or the regime as a threat to the political community itself."

Boundary Maintenance

"Boundary maintenance is a function common to all systems. Social systems, for instance, must define their membership. Sharing an iconography helps differentiate insiders from outsiders and thus defines the boundary of the political community..." The importance of boundary maintenance in the geography of politics derives from the simplicity of Jordan's theorem in topology which states that every closed curve in a plan which does not cross itself divides the plane into one inside and one outside. Every government must delimit its jurisdiction by differentiating the inside from the outside and by making the distinction meaningful." "Efforts directed toward spatial integration and boundary maintenance have, of all political decisions and actions, some of the most profound effects in geographical patterns."

Adaptation

"...political systems must adapt to their physical, biological, social, and psychological environments. The social and psychological environments in which decision makers act include the attitudes and ideas of their constituencies, as well as the attitudes and ideas of other constituencies which might react to any action. Thus, we speak of the mood of the electorates, and both internal and political pressures and of international pressures. Any political decisions, action or process causes social and psychological responses which in turn affect new decisions."

"The process of political organizations' adaptation to the physical environment has been a point of argument among political theorists... Many theories have unfortunately viewed this topic as the sole concern of political geography. Before examining this question, we must differentiate the important geographic terms and ideas, site and situation. Site factors refer to the local attributes of a place/its climate, soil, local resources, population and so forth. Situation characteristics refer to the location of a place relative to other places, its accessibility or distance and direction from other sites. Both site and situation factors and their perception may affect political decisions on their outcomes."

"Idea of a political system's adaptation to the physical environment is thus complex, involving perception and evaluation of resources, the definition of goals, decisions on the allocation of effort, mobilization of effort and exploitation of resources, and the site' s influences on the outcomes of political decisions. Situational factors, especially accessibility, also influence policy or goal attainment by allowing intrusion upon internal affairs."

"Goal attainment, pattern maintenance and tension management, integration, and adaptation must all be satisfied for the continuance of a political system. If the system proves unable to sustain any of these functions, it will disintegrate. Failure of goal attainment leads to loss of support. Inability to maintain the patterns of human interaction and to manage tension results in the war of all against all. A system dissolves without adequate integration, and no system can survive if it fails to adapt to its environments."

"While these functions were originally defined as requisite without reference to space and territory, our exposition of them has revealed both significant geographic influences upon them and significant influences they exert in geographic patterns. Political systems can be depicted by flow charts, with demand and support inputs, authoritative outputs and feedback without reference to spatial variables. Each actor within a political system, however, does have a location, both site and situational attributes of which affect his behaviour and, in turn, that of the system. Conversely, locational attributes of the system as a whole may influence the behaviour of the system's individual members. The relationships among geography and political processes uncovered and studied by political geography affect all levels of political organization, and political geography thus contributes significant insights into both political affairs and into other aspects of geography."

Recent Trends in Political Geography

Political geography in the late 1920s was defined as the "wayward child of geographical sciences",though its legitimacy was recognized in the early 1920s itself when the subdiscipline was defined as "a study of areal differentiation in political phenomena" Political geography in the mid-1930s moved into the realm of the contemporary regional paradigm which was then current in general geography.

In the early post-Second World War period, political geography retreated into the safer realm of study at the scale of the individual state. Although publicly overshadowed by the more spectacular geostrategic studies, state-scale analysis had always been a major component of the subdiscipline, the most notable pre-Second World War example of this 'genne' being Derwent Whittlesey's: *The Earth and the State* of 1939. By the early 1950s there began a quickening of the trend towards shedding some of the environmental baggage of political geography and making the subdiscipline more narrowly systematic in character. Hartshorne, Gottmann and Jones in the 1950s attempted to provide a new rigorous framework for analyzing the geography of political areas and the modern state in particular. Basically, these amounted to a theory of the geographical integration of states as a balance between centrifugal and centripetal forces.

It was from this point, until about 1970, just after Brian Berry's (1969) oft-quoted remark about political geography being 'a moribund backwater' that the subdiscipline seemed to lose its way. As a 'logical' division of human geography, it continued to be widely taught in universities but there was a dearth of research to back up the teaching. Just as human geography as a whole was going through a major and exciting expansion phase usually referred to as the quantitative revolution, political geography was failing to attract the share of the latest 'new' geographers. It seemed to many to be stodgy and old-fashioned. The subdiscipline, then, consisted of the geography of different bits of politics—boundaries, capital cities, territories, administrative areas, elections, geostrategy, etc., but with no particular coordination of these parts. In shedding the environmental basis, the traditional political geography would seem to have lost its coherence and it is this which is the real cause of the post-war demise of political geography.

Although political geography was in the doldrums in the 1960s, this was certainly not true of its related social science—political science. Hence, the most obvious solution to political geography's problems seemed to be to follow the example of human geography's other subdisciplines and borrow heavily from the theories of the relevant social science. This approach was adopted but without much success. Quite simply, political science was not able to furnish any location theory equivalent to that available in economics and sociology. Furthermore, political geography's continued emphasis at the scale of the state was out of step with intra-state and largely urban concerns of the new human geography. Hence, even the most sophisticated application of systems theory to political geography (by Cohen and Rusenthal in 1971), although briefly influential, could not overcome the subdiscipline's handicaps. Systems theory became widely advocated but rarely applied in a constructive manner; and in the end the subdiscipline's revival came about more because of external influences than the efforts of the political geographers themselves.

The political events of the Cold-War period, particularly of the late 1960s in Europe, Asia and USA, had a profound effect on all social sciences. In human geography, it brought the political dimension to the fore. This was expressed in three distinctive ways. First, economic geography and social geography included political variables in their analysis and interpretations. Second, as geography became more politicized, radical geography was created, firmly establishing a Marxist geography. Third, there was the revival of political geography. The first two trends are important for understanding modern political geogrephy because very often they covered subjects which were also dealt with in political geography itself producing, as it were, 'political geographers'. The distinctions between the subdisciplines of human geography were becoming extremely fuzzy in the wake of the criticism of positivism in geography.

Initially two main research areas came to dominate the growing political geography of the 1970s. First, urban conflicts became a very common topic in human geography generally and in political geography, location of 'goods' and 'bads' with their respective externalities became an important part of a new urban political geography. This has developed into a welfare geography (critical geography) approach to political geography, and Cox and others have, in fact, carried forward the welfare paradigm to political geography.

The second growth was electoral geography where the techniques of quantitative revolution were, at last, comprehensively applied in political geography. The areas of interest identified were: (i) the geography of voting; (ii) geographical influences in voting (neighbourhood effect); and (iii) the geography of representation (Cube Law; Gerrymandering and Malapportionment). But this research growth did not overcome the uncoordinated nature of political geography, if anything, it enhanced the lack of coherence. The general reaction was to order political geography information into three separate scales: for teaching and research; international or global; national and intra-national or urban. This framework has become almost ubiquitous among political geographers of all persuasions.

Political geography continued to prosper in the 1980s as most reviewers proclaim its remakrable resurgence. Three groups of political geographers may be identified:

(i) The status-quo group largely accept current institutions and society and continues to research many of the topics of traditional political geography. Their ultimate concern is for political order and stability and this viewpoint has been recently expressed by Gottmann (1982) in his paper: "The basic problem of geography: the organization of space and research for stability."

(ii) The reformist group is dissatisfied with current institutions and society and advocates limited change. From order as the key issue to welfare and common tool for improving society is social-choice theory. This standpoint can be found in the works of (a) Archer, *Public choice paradigm in political geography* (1981), Hall, *The new political geography-seven years on* (1982), and Reynolds, *The geography of social choice* (1981), and

(iii) Finally, there has been some merger between political geography and radical geography among political geographers who neither accept nor wish to reform the existing social and political order. Marxist theories of imperialism, the state and the local state are applied within the three-scale framework. This point has been explained by Short, in his book, *An Introduction to Political Geography*, published in 1981.

Alternatively, the world-systems analysis, a new paradigm, advocated by Wallerstein, has been adopted in political geography to attempt to explain the convenient existence of these three scales and to understand their interrelations, because "geographical scale is itself political" (Taylor, 1985).

Chapter 2

Organic State, Geopolitik and Geopolitics

The metaphor of society or of the state as an organism dates back at least to the French encylopedists. Later Rousseau, in his *Discourse on Political Economy* (1775), compared the body politic to "an organized living body, resembling that of man ", although he admitted the inaccuracy of the simile. Throughout the nineteenth century, however, theories of the state suffered increasing entanglement with biological analogies. Carl Ritter, in his *Comparative Geography*, developed, by analogy with physical organism, a cycle theory of state growth. Human cultures and political units were natural organic entities, each going through a natural cycle of birth, maturity, and death. This idea of a developmental stage of a culture gave Ritter a new independent variable for more sophisticated analysis and theory building when coupled with the other variable, the physical environment, about which far more was known than in the times of earlier writers. Furthermore, armed with a clearer understanding of the role of nature that this developmental stage idea provided, Ritter went on to suggest that prediction was now possible.

At the global scale, cultures were seen in continental proportions, each continent representing an organ in the 'living world'. In this scheme, Ritter, as Montesquieu before him, saw Europe as naturally gaining precedence over all the other 'organs'. Its comparatively compact size and shape, its location in the temperate zone and its complexity of national entities equipped the continent for the most successful growth by immigration and cultural development, for Ritter believed that, given favourable environmental circumstances, 'strong cultures' had the ability to 'guide' their destinies. The notions about the workings of nature on the evolution of cultures, their implications for prediction and for global structure models, and their application in statecraft, were to lead, a generation later, to the theory of the organic state.

Auguste Comte, the French father of sociology, described society as a 'collective organism' with social institutions as its organs. "Foree", he wrote, "answers in sociology to tissue in biology: it is the cement of the social organism." Evolution or progress was characterized by increasing specialization of social institutions as organs.

Spencer and Schaffle and Concept of Organic State

Charles Darwin's and Alfred Wallace's theories of biological evolution stimulated the elaboration of social organismic theories by Herbert Spencer in England and Albert Schaffle in Germany. Spencer introduced the phrase "survival of the fittest", translated the biological competition among the species into competition among human societies. This was known as 'Social Darwinism'. In his book *The Principles of Sociology* (1896), he emphasized the fact that the strong against the weak as a law of nature both among societies and among animals: "Tribes which are larger, or better organized, or both, conquer adjacent tribes and annex them...and as political evolution advances, it becomes a trait of the larger and stronger societies that they acquire appetites prompting them to subjugate and incorporate weaker societies...Thus, then, with social organisms as with individual organisms. It is through the struggle for existence, first, by appropriating one another's means of growth, and then by devouring one another, that there arise those great aggregates (of) high organization."

Schaffle in Germany advanced beyond Comte in his analysis of both the structure and the development of the social body, as had Spencer but Schaffle saw the family rather than the individual as the basic social unit. Beginning with the family, Schaffle posited an entelechy or life force of development to ever-higher social forms with increasing differentiation and integration of the social body. Comte had seen force as the cohesive element in the social organism: for Spencer society remained a mechanical puzzle, but Schaffle emphasized society's psychial unity, the spiritual life and development, but he also noted the need for defence as an important element lending cohesion. In his major work, *Structure and Life of the Social Body* (1875-78), Schaffle writes: "At the very summit of life on earth stands human society—the social body and its private and national institutions. Built up out of matter and impelled by forces of the organic and inorganic world, it is nevertheless a living body of peculiar kind. Human and civil society, a far higher structure than the societies of animals, is a purely spiritual result, an indivisible social life of organized individuals wrought out through the force of ideas and achievements of arts."

Friedrich Ratzel (1844-1904) and the Organic State

Friedrich Ratzel is credited with having carried forward the tradition/heritage of his predecessor Carl Ritter with respect to the concept of the organic state.

Though he conceptualized the heritage of Carl Ritter, he drew upon the works of Herbert Spencer and Albert Schaffle to define his own use of the organismic analogy in his monumental *Politische Geographie* (1897), which is often described as the first book on modern political geography. He is rightly called the 'founder' of political geography and is certainly recognized as the "father of modern political geography". He gave a systematic treatment to this subdiscipline. He had a number of articles/papers to his credit, particularly in the field of political geography. These include: "People and Spaces" (1894), "The State and Its Land Geographically Considered"(1896), "The Territorial Growth of States: A Contribution to Scientific Political Geography" (1896), "Concerning Living Space" (1897), and "Living Space"(1901). Ratzel maintained that states are involved in an endless struggle for space. All living organisms are in a fight for space, he believed, and the most powerful will have the largest spaces (reflection of Social Darwinism). States with high population density have a more valid claim to empty land than those with a low density. Thus, to become politically powerful, people should multiply themselves as rapidly as possible, and take over empty land. People of all states should develop a space conception or space consciousness, for the decay of every state is caused by a declining space conception.

For Ratzel an 'organism' was primarily a framework or structure cohesion occurred in the division of labour and specialization of functions. This was more abstract than a literal analogy with biological organisms. He used the word 'organism' largely because it was so widely used in his days, but he frequently warned against using the image too strictly. He applied alternative words, like, 'organized existence', 'structure', 'model', 'form' and even 'system'. There is much about Ratzel's use of the word 'organism' that actually approaches today's meaning of the world 'system'. Certainly Ratzel would have appreciated Anatal Rapaport's recent clarification that "the difference between 'living' and 'non-living' becomes obscure. Systems that are 'living' in the common sense or biological sense of the word, share many features with systems that are not; and these common features derive from the way systems are organized.This suggests a generalization of the concept of 'organism' to the concept of 'organized system' Organized systems include organisms."

While using the organismic metaphor, Ratzel inquired what sort of organism that state might be. Both states and biological organisms are frameworks for the division of labour and specialization of functions, but the state is an extremely 'incomplete' organism because the members do not surrender their autonomy or individuality. Men retain their freedom to exchange roles in the state or even to emigrate. Also, while the goal of a biological system is to live and to reproduce, states and societies as systems must have public ends as goals.

Ratzel blended these ideas with Schaffle's interpretation of the societal organism, but he added a geographic dimension.Thus, for Ratzel, it is the state, rather than the society as for Schaffle, which becomes "one of the most magnificent manifestations of life on earth". The state has two complementary aspects: the 'organic' which is the land, and the 'spiritual' which is the society and the society's sentimental or econographities to the land. Both aspects evolve.

The organic aspect evolves as greater occupation of space leads to its organization, the differentiation of land usage, and exchange among regions. Transport routes are the veins and arteries of the state organism, and the landscape is transformed from natural to cultural. The state's spiritual aspect evolves with functional role differentiation in human society, and sentimental ties to the homeland represent an important element of continuity for the society. While Schaffle's discussion on societal development progressed from the family up to the nation, Ratzel's reached from the individual farmstead which was for him the most primitive state, up to the nation-state.

Ratzel's Laws

Based on the concepts of the organic state, Ratzel developed seven laws[1] of the expansion of states:

1. *The size of the state grows with its culture*: "The rationale of the first law contained Ratzel's interpretation of the political history of the world. He said: "States show a gradation of size in accordance with their historical age." He saw a close relationship between political expansion and economic and religious expansion. Ratzel stressed that organic states go through periods of youth, maturity and old age—the theme Ritter had promised for cultures. The cultural dispersals become the forerunners of the growth of the state which then utilizes the same routes and fills (i.e., occupies) the same areas."

2. *The growth of states follows other manifestations of the growth of peoples, which must necessarily precede the growth of states*: "We have referred to diffusions which advance faster than the state, which precede and prepare the ground for it. Without political purpose of their own they come into the closest relationship with the life of states and do not stop at national boundaries. It is the principle of the mutual interest of the human race which binds nations together and which dominates them, yet without being involved in them. This mutual interest in life lies in the ideas and goods which tend together toward trade between peoples."

"Commerce and communication far precede politics which follows in their path and can never be sharply separated from them. Peaceful intercourse is the preliminary condition of the growth of the state. A primitive network of routes must have previously been formed. The ideas of uniting neighbouring areas must be preceded by apolitical information. If the state has entered its growth period, then it shares, with commerce, an interest in route connections. Every commercial route paves the way for political influences, every network of rivers provides a natural organization for state development, every federal allots commercial policy to the central government. Colonization usually follows the flag of commerce."

"The clear relationship between geographic discovery and the growth of state has long been recognized and is exhibited in the accomplishments of those who did both, such as Alexander, Caesar, Vasco da Gama....To the present, the greatest success of expansive politics has been prepared under the guardianship of geography. The best contemporary example is that of the Russians in Central Asia."

3. *The growth of the state proceeds by the annexation of smaller members into the aggregate. At the same time, the relationship of the population to the land becomes continuously closer*: "From the mechanical integration of areas of the most varied sizes, populations and cultural levels, there arises, through proximity, communication and the intermixture of their inhabitants, an organic growth. The growth of states which does not transcend mere annexation makes only loose, easily sundered conglomerates which can only be temporarily held together by the will of one whose intellect realizes a larger conception of space."

The process of the amalgamation of regional districts similarly enjoins the closer relationship of the people with their land. The growth of the state over the surface of the earth can be compared to the down growth which leads to an attachment to the soil. It is more than a metaphor when one speaks of a people as taking root. The nation is an organic entity which, in the course of history, becomes increasingly attached to the land on which it exists. Just as an individual struggles with virgin land until he has forced it into cultivable fields, so too does a nation struggle with its land making it, through blood and sweat, increasingly its own until it is impossible to think of the two separately. Who can think of the French without France, or the Germans without Germany? Ceaser's greatness lay in the fact that he gave to the more stable body a definite, secure boundary as well as spatial expansion.

4. *The boundary is the peripheral organ of the state, the bearer of its growth as well as its fortification, and takes part in all of the transformations of the organism of the state*: "Spatial growth manifests itself as a peripheral phenomenon in pushing outward the frontier which must be crossed by the carriers of growth. The closer these carriers live to the boundary, the more intimately do they share an interest in this process; and the larger the frontier the more pronouncedly peripheral will the growth be. A state which stretches out

toward a desired district sends out at the same time growth nodes which exhibit more activity than does the rest of the periphery. This is desirable in the shape of the countries and in the distribution of their inhabitants and other power media. The outcrops of Peshawar and Little Tibet, and those from Merv and Kokand permit immediate recognition of that which even their history does not show; that in their direction British India and Russia grow together, determined to envelope all the benefits of the lands which lie between them, just as Rome through conquering Gaul grew counter to the advancing Tentons."

5. *In its growth the state strives toward the envelopment of politically viable positions* : "In its growth and evaluation the state practices selection of geographical benefits in that it occupies the good location of a district before the poor. If its growth is related to the dispossession of other states, it victoriously captures the good areas and dispossessed continue in the bad. Therefore, in the younger lands (colonies) whose entire history is known to us, the new political structures lie pronouncedly tiered along the sea, on the rivers and lakes, and in the fertile plains, while the older political forms are driven into the initially less accessible and less desired interior, into the steppes and deserts, the mountains and the swamps.... The envelopment of politically valuable locations is also expressed in the shape of the state...for since political growth consists of motion, or more the joining of countless movements, the state sees advantage in annexing those natural regions which favour movement. Thus, we see it striving to attain the coasts, moving along the rivers, and spreading out over the plains...the development of British dominion in India takes the form of an enclosing of the more powerful native states from the base of the more easily overpowered and weaker districts."

6. *The first stimuli to the spatial growth of states come to them from the outside*: Ratzel maintained that "as far as our knowledge of primitive states extends their growth has never advanced without foreign influence. The origin of such growth is colonization in the broader sense. Men from regions of larger spatial conceptions carry the idea of larger states into districts of lesser spatial concepts. The native who is aware only of his own state is always at a disadvantage to him...Geographic locations pointedly show how the larger states in areas of small statism have grown inward from the most accessible outer side, i.e., from the coasts or the edges of the deserts."

7. *The general tendency toward territorial annexation and amalgamation is transmitted from state to state and continually increases in intensity*: "With an increasing estimation of the political value, the land has become of increasingly greater influence as a measure of political power and as a spoil in the state struggles. As long as there is political competition, the weaker states attempt to equal the more powerful. Carried over to the land there arises from

this a struggle for spatial annexation and amalgamation...From the smallest beginnings of growth to the giant states of the present...then...the same tendency toward the emulation of the large on the part of the small and toward the largest by those which are already large and wish to equal with the largest. This tendency is vital and, like a balance wheel, operates above variations and reverses to hold aloof the individual growth exertions...Naturally such emulation is not restricted to spatial size...And thus the drive toward the building of continually larger states continues throughout the entirety of history."

Let us examine what Ratzel meant by the word 'law'.

"But it is...primary goal of all sciences to find only that which the scientist calls a law? Geography in that case is not a science in the usual sense. Does not statistics deal with the same incalculability, with the many-faceted disposition of man, and which is, in this case, more expressive than strictly true? But the high probabilities which statistics derive from the comparison of many cases, what are they other than laws—we almost wish to say oscillating laws—in which strongly outstanding disturbances disappear in the totality... We too may attain such probabilities though we must of course also deal with further difficulty that history does not often offer us the many examples wanted for the statistical method" (*Anthropogeographie*).

Ratzel's laws of spatial growth, therefore, are not laws of 'necessity' at all. In speaking of the state as an 'organism', he concentrated his comparison on the relation of man in the collective sense, i.e., the state and the land. His thinking here is difficult to follow, but it is apparent that his comparison was not of the strict dog-eat-dog nature, so often attributed to him. He was referring to the relationship which develops between a people and the land which nourishes them, and the reciprocity which develops between them. Here again we must keep in the mind what it was that Ratzel meant by the term 'law'. He referred to tendencies rather than absolutes, as is clear from the following passages of his book, *Anthropogeographie*:

"There arises a political organization of the land through which the state becomes an organism in that a fixed portion of the surface of the earth enters into such a degree that the properties of the states are a combination of those of the people and of the land." "The state is not an organism merely because it forms a connection between a living population and the fixed earth, but rather because this connection is so strengthened by reciprocity that the two become one and can no longer be thought of as separate. The state with highly developed organism among animals and plants in which the members must make the greatest sacrifices of individuality in the service of the whole, measured by this standard reflects that the 'state' of man is an exceptionally undeveloped organism, for its members preserve an independence which no longer occurs even in the lower plants and animals."

"The comparison of the state with highly developed organisms is unfruitful. And if so many scientific attempts to approach the state as an organism have borne so little fruit, it is primarily because of the limitation of such consideration to the analogy between an aggregate of men and the structure of an organic creature."

These are hardly the words of one who sees the biological necessity of growing by securing essential missing organs, if necessary, by force. Thus, it is obvious that Ratzel (a zoologist by training) was only too well aware of the limits of the scientific biological analogy. He, then, viewed the state as a living organism (an organic entity increasingly attached to the land on which it lives) with no rigid limits, the key to successful growth being in the development of its civilization, as he attempted to prove with an analysis of the growth of past empires. He carried forward Ritter's notion of evolution from youth to maturity with a correlation between growing old age and diminishing size.

Ratzel included the idea of 'community' as a prerequisite for political union and for the development of nationalism with the diffusion of ideas. The process of integration and disintegration, he felt, formed a major portion of historical movements, depicted geographically as an interchange between larger and smaller political regions. He also recognized the relationship between cultural levels and areal scale of territoriality.

Competition for Space

At the end of the nineteenth century, Ratzel was witnessing what has been termed as the "closure of the world". Men were coming to occupy all of the inhabitable world while revolutionary developments in transport and communications tied all regions of the world more closely. With population still increasing, Ratzel believed that each generation would feel more keenly a scarcity of land. Each nation needed room for expansion, which he termed 'lebensraum' (room to live). The term can be traced back to Goethe, but Ratzel's famous essay "Der Lebensraum" dedicated to Albert Schaffle, forever linked Ratzel's name most closely with this term. Much of what he had to say about 'lebensraum' is in fact vague, but his idea was frequently misconstrued and extrapolated by later researchers.

He saw space filled through the expansion of originally isolated settlements. Smaller political units at lower stages of development were naturally subsumed in ever larger political units with increasingly advanced concepts and capabilities of spatial organization. Individual farmsteads in the American West, for instance, were subsumed in the larger society and state. While Spencer had attributed this process to 'appetites' of the longer and more powerful units, Ratzel saw it as happening quite naturally, although not necessarily without conflict. Some small units might not want to be subsumed, and larger units might compete for space. The acquistion or reservation of land for future generation was an important responsibility of any state.

Conflicts among units competing for space was inevitable, but Ratzel never went on to say which states should triumph, or what a state should do to survive. At the time he was writing, the far-flung British Empire was envy of Germany; and Ratzel's writing is not free of 'Anglophobic rhetoric'. Aside from recommendation that Germany maintain naval parity with England and hold onto African colonies, however, Ratzel made no specific suggestions about how a state could or should win any eventual struggle for 'lebensraum'. He presented an explanation for aggression, but not a rationale or recommendation for aggression.

A Critical Evaluation of the Organic State

Pounds (1963: 1972) makes a critical evaluation of the concept of the organic state, especially in the light of the contemporary cold war. He maintains: " The organic view of the state has coloured and perhaps has also done much to create the fundamental hostility between the communist and the non-communist worlds, which has been the dominant feature of the past quarter of a century...The struggle between the Soviet Union and the United States in such countries as Turkey, Afghanistan, Pakistan or those of Southeast Asia does, in fact, bear a superficial resemblance to that which the Social Darwinists assume to exist between states."

"The organic view permits of prediction only if one can accept the view that all states must expand territorially if they are to survive as separate states. Any such policy as that of coexistence must be ruled out: biological species do not undertake to refrain from their struggle for survival, it is claimed; states should not do so either. Any government that accepted the organic theory of the state, as that of the Nazi Germany appears to have done, must necessarily pursue a policy of aggression. The glib assertion of Neville Chamberlain, after the Munich settlement had surrendered a major part of Czechoslovakia to Germany, that this meant 'peace in our time' should have been recognized for the foolishness that it was. There could be no lasting peace with a state which believed that expansion and aggression were a condition of existence...yet the organic theory of the state is fallacious. Geographical space and society that occupies it, necessarily attains some element of organization, but in no proper sense does it take on the character of organism. It has no life or will other than that of the aggregate of its citizens, and its future is what their descendants make it. The idea that a state must grow if it is to live and that there is virtue in mere size is not only erroneous but also dangerous."

Ratzel's concept of the organic state, and also, the concept of 'lebensraum' provided the material base for the development of geopolitik in the latter period. Ratzel had few immediate followers. Two of his closest disciples were (a) the American Ellen Semple who studied under him and returned to the United States to undertake anthropogeograpahical studies, and (b) the Swedish political scientist Rudolf Kjellen of the Universities of Goteberg and Uppasala, who is often identified as the first and major post-Ratzelian disciple to have carried forward the Ratzelian model of the organic state and the concept of 'lebensaum' further towards Social Drawinism and sought to make them more applied.

Rudolf Kjellan (1864-1922)

Rudolf Kjellan wrote most of his important works in Swedish and whose contribution to political geography has been judged principally on the basis of one major book translated into German by M. Langfeldt.[2]

Kjellen elaborated on the Ratzelian model of the organic state by adding the dimension of moral and intellectual capacities or by introducing aspects of quality of the population, and the nation whose aggregate constitutes the body of the state. In addition to moral capacities, there was, in Kjellen's view, the 'will', the cumulative psychological force of the state. In assessing power, he reasoned that "the great power (grossmacht) is a concept which is not mathematical but dynamic, not ethnic or cultural but psychological...The great power is above all, a will richly endowed with power means". Or, in other words, Kjellen was particularly interested in the process involved in the transformation of a territory from a natural area to a cultural-political region. He viewed this process as a perpetual interchange among 'country, people and government.' This process of human occupation of a region gave it, in causal sequence, continuity, solidarity, interaction, loyalty and nationality; that is, the creation of a nation with what he called a 'geopolitical instinct'.

He regarded states not so much as legal bodies but as competing powers. He saw the state in a condition of constant competition with other states, larger states would extend their power over smaller ones, and ultimately the world would have only a few very large and extremely powerful states. In his most important theoretical work, *The State as a Form of Life*, Kjellen argued: "Vitally strong states with a limited area of sovereignty are dominated by the categorical imperative to enlarge their areas by colonization, union with other states, or conquests of different types...it is not the raw instinct of conquest, but the natural and necessary trend towards expansion as a means of self-preservation." Kristof remarked that "Kjellen sanctioned as natural the instinct of men and nations to satisfy their desires at another's expense."

Kjellen believed that a state must fulfil three requirements to be a world power. First, states must have 'spaciousness', that is, they must be located within a large contiguous land area. Secondly, states must have 'internal cohesion' in order to be powerful. He said that Britain would have never become a world power because it lacked both spaciousness and, because of its Irish and Welsh dissidents. Thirdly, Kjellen said that great states must have 'freedom of movement'. Russia had spaciousness and internal cohesion but, he observed, it would never be a world power because it lacked access to warm-water ports. However, he wrote that the Germans had the right to natural growth because of their 'psychological will'. He, however, chided Germany for not being a great state because it lacked all the three of his requirements.

In analyzing the state, Kjellen made the following distinctions: *Geopolitik* or geography and the state; *Demopolitik* or population and the state; *Oekopolitik, or economic resources and the state; Sociopolitik,* or social structure of the state; and *Kratopolitik* or government of the state. It is noteworthy that he placed the study of geography and the state first and the study of government of the state last. He believed that the power of the maritime empires would pass to the command of the land empires (obvious reflection of the Geographical Pivot-Heartland model of Mackinder), who would control the seas. Kjellen foresaw the emergence of a few giant states in the world, with Germany as the great power in Europe, Africa and Western Asia.

Kjellen defined geopolitik as "the theory of the states as a geographic organism or phenomenon in space, i.e., as land, territory, area or most especially, as country", or "the study of the strategies of political organisms in space".

Geopolitik

After the death of Rudolf Kjellen in 1922, Karl Haushofer became the leading exponent of Geopolitik. In fact, Haushafer borrowed the word 'geopolitik' which Kjellen had introduced in his book *Der Staat als Lebensform*. It is not difficult to understand how the ideas of Kjellen, coupled with the Ratzelian tradition, caught the imagination of many geographers in inter-war Germany. The group under the leadership of Karl Haushofer, formed the Institut fur Geopolitik, attached to the University of Munich, which dominated German geography from 1922 to 1945. Haushofer started editing the journal *Zeitschrift fur Geopolitik* in 1924. This was, certainly, an epoch-making development, particularly in the contemporary heritage of political geography.

Basic to geopolitik's ideas were Ratzel's organic state concept, its refinements by Kjellen, and the Geographical Pivot-Heartland model of Mackinder which sought to illustrate that any political power that would effectively occupy and control the Heartland (Eurasian core) could by definition achieve a dominant world position.

"To Haushofer and his group the ideas of Ratzel and Kjellen on the one hand, and of Mackinder on the other, formed a symbiosis which seemed to have special relevance to Germany's post-World War I position vis-a-vis geopolitik. Ratzel-Kjellen tradition sought to justify the need of populous states for living space (lebensraum), and hence the growth of some states, such as Germany, at the expense of less viril neighbouring states—"Germany's expansion is a natural phenomenon. The country is overpopulated. It must expand." Mackinder's Heartland thesis seemed to indicate to the German geopoliticians the necessity for a detente or even an alliance between Germany and the chief occupant of the Heartland—Soviet Russia.

Development of Geopolitik

Geopolitik owed much of its development to the journal *Zeitschrift fur Geopolitik*, and the Institut fur Geopolitik. The 'Institut' eventually attached to itself able geographers and workers in cognate fields. These men developed a considerable amount of 'geopolitikal' theory and began the elaborate of a vast array of data to be filed in the 'Strategic Index' of the 'Institut'. "The basic, incontestable truth is that Haushofer, directly in some instances, indirectly in others, coordinated, integrated, and rationalized the whole field of comparative geography for the uses of the Fuhrer. As time went by, the 'Institut' became more and more an instrument for national policy and a tool of the state—for which purposes it received a government subsidy in funds and patronage. Geography, particularly war geography, became a national preoccupation which influenced and moulded public opinion in post-war Germany from elementary school to university seminar, from street corner and book-store to factory, club, beer hall and dinner table."

The geopoliticians of Munich started with an organismic concept of the state, as well as with the practiced techniques of cartography and geographic research. Added to these were their 'weltanschauung', or world perspective, and a motivation springing from the national pathology that characterized Germany between the world wars. They defined their subject as "the science of the earth relationship to political developments". Karl Haushofer asserted that the word 'politik' is not preceded by the prefix 'geo' by accident. The prefix relates politics to the earth (ge=earth in Greek). The geopoliticians of Munich also attempted to apply the principles and methods of geopolitics to 'branch' sciences such as psychology, medicine, and jurisprudence.

'Geopolitikal' concepts in Germany centered round a number of subjects. The idea of organic state, living space (lebensraum) and the organic frontier received considerable attention in the contemporary German literatures. Behind the idea of political power of the state was its location with reference to a specific concept of the distribution of land masses and ocean spaces. The expression of the power of the state in wartime involved the study of

Wehr-Geopolitik or war geopolitik, for the 'aim of power war'. At the Institut fur Geopolitik, the strength and weaknesses of a certain area (raum) were compared with the location (lage) of the region and the nature of the boundaries (grenzen).

Geopolitik, then, according to Zeitschrift fur Geopolitik, "...is the science which deals with the dependence of political events upon the soil (i.e., physical setting). It is based upon the broad foundations of geography, especially political geography. Geopolitik aims to furnish the weapons for political action, and the principles for guidance in political life...Geopolitik must become the geographical conscience of the state."

In other words, the study of geopolitik should suggest the future course of political action and, like the still, small voice of conscience, keep reminding politicians of what they should do in the best interests of their state. Yet geopolitik was something more than strategy because it helped to formulate the objective of policy as well as being the means by which that objective might ultimately be reached.

It is indeed a fact that the German geopolitik cannot be fully understood without assessing the career of Karl Haushofer, reference of whom has already been made above. Haushofer was a career officer in German army and in 1908 he was sent to Japan. It was during his stay in Japan, he learnt lot of things which had a deep impact on his perception, specially that which concerned the space-power relationship. He was very much impressed with the contemporary monolithic political system in Japan and wished if it could be established in Germany. It was in Japan itself, he understood/realized that space (raum) was also a factor in power. He shared the Japanese claim that their people required more space and that the mere fact that the population was growing fast in itself justified them in taking it. "Confronted by the more numerous Chinese, Russians and Americans, Japan could find security only in large population and, of course, in the possession of land to support this increase. Planned conquest in Korea and China was to satisfy at once the political, territorial and economic needs of Japan." We have seen above that Karl Haushofer read with much enthusiasm, the Geographical Pivot-Heartland thesis of Mackinder, and those of the writings of Ratzel and Kjellen. In fact, the contemporary literatures of Mackinder, Ratzel, and Kjellen helped him to build theoretical and conceptual frameworks, while his stay in Japan helped him to acquire "empirically experience of the reality of the 'lebensraum' which gave observation statements on peculiar privilege over theoretical ones which guaranteed their generality" through Kjellen-introduced word 'geopolitik'.

Haushofer's *Die Geopolitik des Pazifischen Ozeans: Studien uber die Wechselbeziehunger Zwischen geographie and Geschichte* (Geopolitics of the

Pacific Ocean: Studies on Relationship between Geography and History), first published in 1924, was his monumental work. His other important works were: (i) *Geographische Grundzuge Auswartiger Politik*, published in Suddeutsche Monatshefte, in 1926-27; and (ii) *Weltpolitik von Heute*, published in 1936. He prepared a world model of three pan-regions based upon Germany, Japan and the USA. This was an interesting geographical organization in that it involved functional regions around each core state cross-cutting environmental resource regions which straddle the earth latitudinally. As political economy concepts they involved three regions with potential for economic self-sufficiency or autarky. If fully developed such a model would have consisted of three separate world systems each with its own core—Europe, Japan and Anglo-America—and periphery—Africa and India, East and Southeast Asia and Latin America respectively. Such a world model of co-existence was no better or worse than other models and may not be too far from the mark with the current device of the USA dominance of the world economy.

Nature of Geopolitik

To Haushofer and his followers, the science of geopolitik was dynamic, that the political conditions could never long remain stable, if only because the 'laws' of the state organism prescribed growth and the growth of one such entity could be only at the expense of others. "Every nation is primarily concerned with the task of maintaining itself in a hostile environment, and since its very existence depends on the possession of an adequate space, the preservation and protection of that space must determine all its policies. If the space has grown too small, it has to be expanded." He spoke of the mathematical ratio of people to the land; presumably each state was the judge of its own needs.

Expansion, according to Haushofer, was a categorical imperative in the Kantian sense for all nations. It should be "the guiding principle of small and handicapped states which seek to attain or to regain a place in the world politics". He further said that "great powers, unencumbered in their movements, can set themselves important long range objectives—small states, on the other hand, find obstacles in their way wherever they turn".

Geopolitik had the power to satisfy the urge of great powers to expand at the expense of the weak. The power politics of the Grossmachte were thus held to derive their sanction from a kind of natural law. The concept of 'lebensraum' (living space), thus, became the *raison d'etre* of Haushofer's geopolitik, in particular the 'lebensraum' of Germany itself. This, Haushofer argued repeatedly, was inadequate for Germany's need, and it could be extended only at the expense of the Slav countries to the east. "Alliance with Russia would not only permit this ambition to be realized but would also establish German influence in that pivot area, in which, following Mackinder, he placed the fulcrum of world power." Haushofer made use of various cartographic representations to convey his desires to the high-ranking Nazi official, Rudolf Hess, who openly shared his (Haushofer's) views. The objectives of policy which led to the series of crises from 1934 to 1939 were fully in tune with Haushofer's views.

Perhaps the most concise explanation, with regard to the nature of geopolitik, came not from Karl Haushofer himself but from his disciple, Otto Maull, who elaborated it with a definition of Geopolitik as, "Geopolitik concerns itself with the state, not as a static concept, but as a living being. Geopolitik investigates the states primarily in relation to its environment—its space—and attempts to solve all problems resulting from spatial relationships. Geopolitik is concerned with the spatial requirements of a state while political geography examines only its space conditions. In putting geography at the service of space-conscious politics, geopolitik devotes itself to questions of the future. Are the space needs of a state met? If not, how can they be brought into accord with geographical conditions? In what direction should any change be made? The extent to which these questions are answered determines a state's national and economic structure and influences its foreign relations... Geopolitik is a discipline that weighs and evaluates a given situation and by its conclusion seeks to guide practical politics."

It can be said with certainty that the Haushofer-Otto Maull tradition of geopolitik justified the *raison d'etre* of Nazi Germany. It was the 'state idea' to which the whole Germanic nation enthusiastically adhered. There is no doubt that the rise to power of National Socialism gave geopolitik much more prestige than it had previously enjoyed in Germany. Geopolitik—the Ratzel-Mackinder-Kjellen-Haushofer-Otto Maull tradition—suffered a sudden premature death with the fall of the Third Reich at the end of the second world war in 1945. However, many of its associated nations, such as the application of political-geographical concepts, have survived in the general field of 'geopolitics' or applied political geography. As Ladis Kristof has put it: "Geopolitics should cover all the fields parallel to and intermediate between political science and political geography. It should embrace the investigation of the objective impact of natural environment...on politics. Real geopolitics resembles political geography."

Kristof has sought to distinguish between them: "The only difference between political geography and geopolitics is in emphasis—in the focus of attention. Political geography tends to focus...on the geographical phenomena; it gives a political interpretation and studies the political aspects of geographic phenomena. Geopolitics tends to focus on the political phenomena and attempts to give a geographical interpretation and study the geographical aspects of these phenomena."

Geopolitics

Revival of geopolitics in the post-world war period may be attributed to a number of factors, such as those of the cold war, break-up of the colonial empires, followed by the emergence of large number of nation-states, and the more complex world than before. These were the post-war developments which provided the necessary impetus to the revival of geopolitics, notwithstanding the demise of the German geopolitik with the collapse of the Nazi Germany. However,the post-war geopolitics has increasingly come to be synonymous with the word 'imperialism'. Here a distinction must be made betwen geopolitics and imperialism: while the former is concerned with rivalry between major powers (core and rising semi-periphery states) and the later as domination by strong states (in the core) of weak states (in the periphery). Politically, geopolitics describes a rivalry relation whereas imperialism describes a dominance relation. Spatially, they are currently reflected in 'east-west' and 'north-south' spatial patterns respectively. The interesting question for political geography is the relation between the two concepts in their politics and spatial structure. In world-systems analysis geopolitics is about rivalry (currently East vs. West) in the core for domination of the periphery by imperialism (currently North over South).

However, with the collapse of the Soviet Union, the *raison d'etre* of the cold war has disappeared, but with the unification of Germany and the economic supremacy of Japan at the expense of the USA and Western Europe, geopolitics received fresh impetus. In the search for an explanation of the global geopolitical order, three complementary approaches may be identified from a myriad of essentially empirical researches.

Approaches to Modern Geopolitics

(1) The power relations perspective focuses on the regionalization and hierarchical character of states within the global order by examining a polity's ability to influence or change the behaviour of others in a desired direction. Political scientists have considered such power relations in terms of global equilibrium, by formulating post-war international relations as a model of bipolarity in the late 1940s and 1950s, loose bipolarity in the late 1950s and 1960s, and the multipolar world of 1970s, 1980s and 1990s. The recent emergence of additional global powers, such as Japan, China, Western Europe and Germany to that of the USA, and the fall of the Soviet system, together with the rise of primarily Third World regional powers, appeared to have led the world system as moving from its previous integrative stage to one of unfolding, hierarchical integration.

Yet, the second order or regional powers cannot be assumed to be moving towards a neatly ordered global hierarchy, in which location and power determine their scope and influence, although Cohen sees this as desirable from the vantage of the US foreign policy. Besides the thorny issue of whether the balance of power has prevented global catastrophe, it would seem that geopolitical equilibrium has preserved a hierarchy of powerful states at the expense of the small and weak. These issues apart, Cohen's model of regional shelterbelts is useful. Based on geography's traditional concern with the cultural realm, regions such as Southeast Asia and the Middle East are considered as inherently unstable, both as a consequence of their global geostrategic importance and as a result of their regional characteristics.

(2) The second approach examines the legitimizing ideology of the state, or, in other words, the basis upon which the state is founded and organized and through which it justifies its territorial actions, both domestically and globally. This philosophical and moral conception of the state's destiny or mission can be traced back to the internal developement of both superpowers, diametrically opposite to each other: USA and the erstwhile USSR, and host of other countries (late 1980s and early 1990s have witnessed the fall of communism in East Europe, followed by the collapse of the Soviet Union. Nevertheless, China has now emerged as the forerunner of the global communist movement).

For the USA, the expanding frontier was based on a continental mission of a society of democratic pathfinders destined to conquer and civilize the wilderness. Similar arguments were used in the nineteenth century to justify the US expansion and influence throughout its hemisphere—the Monroe doctrine. With its emergence as superpower, geopolitical and economic interests became inseparable from its moral mission as a leader of liberty and freedom; and thus as the container of communism.

The sense of uniqueness also legitimized the continental spread of Tsarist Russia, on the pretext that the Empire had a mission to spread the Russian orthodox religion. With the 1917 Russian Revolution, this mission changed but in seeing itself as the prototype of the new society of the future, the sense of uniqueness remained. The success of Soviet Socialism was premised on the truth of Marxism-Leninism and in the belief of a society moving forward with the forces of history. Besides legitimizing intervention in the Third World, the erstwhile USSR's view of itself and also as 'primus inter paves' within the post-war socialist camp meant it could justify military intervention whenever socialism was found to be threatened, for example, intervention in Hungary and Czechoslovakia, respectively. However, Gorbachav's Soviet Union refrained itself from intervening in its East European satellite states when peoples there revolted against socialism, and pulled down the socialist regimes in their respective countries, making the communist ideology irrelevant to the state.

(3) The political economy approach focuses on who gets what, where and how. Here, the underlying assumption is that geopolitics cannot be understood fully without considering the dynamics of the global economy, be it in terms of East-West or North-South relations. Wallerstein (1984) has taken this proposition further by considering the links between the processes of capital accumulation, resource competition and foreign policy as a part of a singular and interdependent global system in which capitalism determines the character and hierarchical configuration of states. Such a world system has thrust the USA in particular into a pivotal geostrategic and economic role, while the former Soviet Union played a less significant part in world affairs because of its limited economic capabilities, in spite of being a superpower. Japan is now challenging the global economic role of the USA largely because of its 'sustained' capacities and abilities.

By focusing at the international scale and by taking economic forces as determining realtions betwen states, there is, however, a tendency to relegate politics and cultural processes at the state level as causally related to economic forces, when in fact they can play an important and independent part in influencing the nature of international relations.

We shall now discuss two important geopolitical models which have especial relevance to the understanding of the global political systems, and the'rivalry-doninance relation' in historical perspectives.

Modelski's Long Cycles of Global Politics (1978)

Modelski is concerned with the global political system in which the extra-European arena is central to the argument and the emphasis is upon a system of states rather than the ordering of individual states. Modelski's model is also of greater interest because it was developed specifically to counter Wallerstein's approach. To him, Wallerstein has undervalued the importance of political process in the original statement of his world economy framework. Modelski's global system begins about 1500 A.D. and then proceeds to develop in a cyclical manner. He sought to create a new type of cycle of just over a hundred years in length—and we are now experiencing the fifth such cycles. Each cycle is associated with a world power which is defined as a state and engages in over half the 'order-keeping' function of the global political systems. Four such world powers have existed, viz., Portugal, Netherlands, Britain and the USA. These have dominated 'their centuries'—Portugal the sixteenth, Netherlands the seventeenth, Britain the eighteenth and the nineteenth, and currently the USA in the twentieth. Britain is unique in dominating two global cycles.

Table 2.1
Long cycles of global politics

Cycles	*World powers*	*World wars*	*Legitimating treaties*	*Key institutions*	*Landmarks of decline*
I	Portugal	Italian wars (1494-1517)	Treaty of Tordessillas	Global Network of Bases	Spanish Annexation (1580)
II	Netherlands	Spanish wars (1579-1609)	Twelve year truce with Spain (1609)	'Mare librum'	The English Revolution
III	Britain	French wars (1688-1713)	Treaty of Utrecht (1713)	Command of the Sea	Independence of USA
IV	Britain	French wars (1792-1815)	Paris and Vienna (1814-1815)	Free Trade	Imperialism
V	USA	German wars (1914-45)	Versailles and Potsdam (1919, 1945)	United Nations	Vietnam War

The details of the model/global cycles is given in Table 2.1. In each case the rise and fall of the world power is indicated through definite steps. A cycle starts with a weak global organizational structure of political competition which degenerates into global war. Such wars have wide geographical range and have global pay offs—the winner is able to order the resulting political systems. This phase ends with a legitimizing treaty which formally sets up the new world order centered on the new world power. No world power can maintain its control for ever and so a decline phase sets in. Initially, the world order becomes bi-polar and then multi-polar before the system becomes weakly organized again, is ripe for the rise of a new world power, and the cycle starts again.

Modelski's international political system is global from its inception. This is not just a matter of geographical definition: it relates to how the role of Portugal is interpreted. For Modelski, by taking over the trading network in the Indian Ocean, the Portuguese became the centre of a global system and hence a world power. In contrast, Wallerstein places most of the Portuguese activity in the external arena outside the world economy; Spanish American colonization is far more important in that it creates a new periphery. For Modelski, Spain only operated on the fringes of his system and never developed a 'world outlook'. Here is the crux of difference between the two approaches since the notion of a world outlook in the global sense is totally unnecessary for Wallerstein. His world system was originally a European world economy and only became global in scope around 1900 A.D.

The mechanism for change in his long cycles of global politics is twofold. First, there is what is called "the urge to make global order". Once the possibilities of a global order became known, an innate will for power has become expressed as an urge to shape world order. Only a few people may have such a world outlook but they respond to the inarticulated needs of the many. Second, the nature of international politics as a system means that structures run down and have to be reconstructed. All systems suffer a loss of order and survive by cyclical development. Table 2.1 describes a particular expression of this general process. It is on the basis of these two mechanisms that change has occurred in Modelski's global system.

Modelski, in the beginning of his model, has sought to point out that the global political system must be functionally distinguished from the world economy, particularly in terms of the mechanisms for change. However, his assertion does not reflect that he sought to under estimate the importance of economic processes—his politics is about who gets what in the world systems. In the world systems approach, it is a classic example of the poverty of disciplines. The state system and the economic system are integral part of a single process of development incorporated in the concept of the world economy. There are not two logics but one. The world economy could not operate except within the political framework provided by a competitive state system. It is a necessary definition of a capitalist world economy. The implication of this is that mechanisms of change are not economic but both. Instead of Modeleski's model, there is the need of a political economy model for bringing history into 'geopolitics'.

A Dynamic Model of Hegemony and Rivalry (1979)

In the world systems approach, there is a system of cycles which represents a far superior mechanism of change than in Modelski's politics. Political mechanisms are an integral part of the overall process of restructuring the world economy that occurs within these cycles. In the following model this political element has been sought to be illustrated.

Political activity has always been an integral part of the world economy. State policies are important processes in the changes observed in the world economy. Since they are neither independent processes nor mere reflections of economic necessities (economism), it follows that there is some choice available. If there were no choices, there would be no need for public institutions such as the state. Public agencies have the role of distorting market forces in favour of those private groups controlling the agency. There has never been a 'pure' world economy even in periods when free trade has dominated. The power of a public agency and hence its ability to organize the market depends upon the strength of its backers and their material resources. Strong states may promote a 'free market' while less strong states may favour explicit distortion of the market through protectionism, for instance. In this way states can act as a medium through which a first set of production processes, upon which the world economy operates, are translated into a second set of distribution processes and patterns. Since these intermediate processes tend to favour the already strong, it follows that political activity will often increase the economic polarization of the market (i.e., helping the core at the expense of the periphery).

The power of a state to organize the market to its own ends is not just a property of that state's resources. The fact that we are dealing with a world economy and not a world empire (that there is a multiplicity of states) means relative positions are more important than measures of absolute power. These state positions are relative not only to other states, however, but also to the gross availability of material resources within the world economy. The cyclical nature of material growth means that opportunities for operating various state policies vary systematically over time. This is not just a matter of different economic environments being suited to alternative state strategies. At any particular conjunction specially successful policies can only work for a limited number of agencies. Quite simply every successful state eliminates opportunities for other states. There will always be constraints in terms of the total world resources available for redistribution via state activities. Given the 'correct' policies, it is not possible for all semi-periphery states and the periphery to become core-like. Although this is not a zero-sum game in a static sense since the available production is always changing in a cyclical fashion, nevertheless, we do have here a sort of 'dynamic zero-sum game'.

If the state activity is an integral part of the operation of the world economy we should be able to model it within the temporal and spatial frameworks. Just such a model has been proposed by Wallerstein and his associates (Research Working Group 1979). They postulate political activity centers occurring over a time-period covering two Kondratieff waves.[3] This activity centres round brief hegemonic interludes when one state dominates the world economy. Hegemony builds up in three stages. Initially, the state gains primacy in production efficiency over its rivals. This enables its merchants to develop a commercial supremacy which finally leads into financial dominance. When productive commercial and financial activities of one state are more efficient than all rivals, that state's hegemony occurs. This favoured situation is brief, however, as rivals emulate the technical achievements and the hegemonic state's lead over its rivals declines first in production, then commerce and finally finance.

The rise and fall of hegemonic power relates to 'paired-Kondratieffs' as follows. If we start with a first growth phase, A-1, we find 'geopolitical rivalry' as core states complete for succession to leadership. On hindsight, however, we can see new technological advances are concentrated in one country so that increased productive efficiency gives this state a long term advantage. A-1 is associated with the stage of 'ascending hegemony'. In B-1 overall decline of the world economy leaves less opportunities for expansion but the ascending power now derives commercial supremacy and is able to protect its interests relative to its rivals. By this stage it is clear which state is to be new hegemonic power. B-1 is associated with stage of 'hegemonic victory'. With renewed growth of the world economy, we reach A-2—the stage of 'hegemonic maturity'. By this time the financial centre of the world-economy has moved to the hegemonic state which is now supreme in production, commerce and finance (i.e., 'true' hegemony). Since the hegemonic power can successfully compete with all its rivals, it now favours 'opening' the world economy. These are periods of free trade. Finally, 'declining hegemony' occurs during B-2 when productive efficiency is no longer sufficient to dominate rivals.This is a period of acute competition and new powers try to obtain a larger share of a declining market. There are periods of protectionism and formal imperialism as each rival attempts to preserve its own portion of the periphery.

According to Wallerstein's research group, the four Kondratieff cycles from the industrial revolution can be interpreted as two 'paired Kondiatieff' (Table 2.2). The first pair covering the nineteenth century, corresponds to the rise and fall of British hegemony and the second pair describes a similar sequence of events for USA in the twentieth century. There is no need to consider this table in great detail except to note how several episodes neatly fit the model.

In terms of our discussion of state involvement in the operation of the world economy, phase A-2 and B-2 are particularly important. In the A-2 the hegemonic power imposes open trade on the system to reap the rewards of its own efficiency. In the mid-nineteenth century, Britain proclaimed 'free trade' backed up by gunboats and a century later a new world policeman, this time with aircraft carriers, was going through the whole process of liberalizing trade once again. These policies certainly contributed to the massive growth of the world economy in the A-2 phase and were imposed through a mixture of negotiation, bargaining and bullying. Options for non-hegemonic power were highly constrained and they largely went along with hegemonic leadership.

Table 2.2
A dynamic model of hegemony and rivalry

	Great Britain	*U.S.A.*
	1790/8	1890/6
A-1 Ascending hegemony	Rivalry with France (Nepoleonic wars) productive efficiency, industrial revolution.	Rivalry with Germany, productive efficiency, mass production techniques.
	1815/25	1913/20
B-1 Hegemonic victory	Commercial victory in Latin America and control of India, workshop of the world.	Commercial victory in the final collapse of British free trade system and decisive military defeat of Germany.
	1844/51	1940/5
A-2 Hegemonic maturity	Era of free trade. London becomes financial centre of the world economy.	Liberal economic system of Breton, goods based upon the dollar; New York new financial centre of the world.
	1870/75	1967/73
B-2 Declining hegemony	Classical age of imperialism as European powers and USA rival Britain, New industrial revolution emerging outside Britain.	Reversal to protectionist practices to counteract Japan and European rivals.

After Wallerstein and his Research Working Group, 1979.

All these changes with the onset of the B-2 phase, however, as productive efficiency spread, economic leadership deserts the hegemonic power. These are the key periods because of the opportunities available for other core and semi-periphery states that declining hegemony provides. The imposition of free trade is no longer taken for granted as various states workout new strategies for the new circumstances. In the late nineteenth century, Britain entered the depression as hegemonic power and came out behind Germany and USA in terms of productive efficiency. The B-2 phases are clearly fundamental periods of restructuring in the world economy in which geopolitical processes play an important role. We are currently living through just such a phase.

What about the period before 1790? Wallerstein and his associates extend their model back to the very beginning of the world economy. This involves identifying paired-Kondratieffs in the sixteenth, seventeenth and eighteenth centuries. The first two coincide with Hapsburg and Dutch hegemony respectively but the third pair covers a period of English-French rivalry with no clear hegemonic victory. However, the use of Kondratieff cycles for this early period must remain highly tentative. As we have previously indicated we prefer to stay on much firmer ground by employing the early world economy logistic curve. The A-phase involved the establishment of the world economy and the geopolitical rivalry was largely concerned with preventing it being transformed into a world empire. With the consolidation in the B-phase we come to hegemonic episode based upon Dutch efficiencies in production, commerce and finance. At this time (C.1650) we find mercantilist policies being devised by England and France to upset the liberal trade regime imposed by the Dutch. This seventeenth century sequence of events has many similarities with those for the paired Kondratieffs in the nineteenth and twentieth centuries. This account for the attempt by Wallerstein and associates to apply their model to this period. However, the Dutch hegemony is very short and much less decisive than the later British and American versions.

The whole of the long B-phase is probably best interpreted generally as a competitive period finally centered upon English-French rivalry but with important contributions from Holland, Prussia, Sweden and Northeast America. The rivalry was finally settled by the advantage adhering to England in the wake of the industrial revolution. In all meantime, the general lack of hegemonic control meant that groups in Sweden and Prussia and even Northeast America could carve out important niches for themselves in the world economy. The first two cases illustrate early examples of the use of powerful state machineries to control part of the world economy for private ends. In the American, case semi-peripheral status was achieved without control of a state machinery although the eventual need for such a machinery led to the war of independence and subsequently the Federal Constitution.

Geopolitics: Present and Future

The similarities, betwen the American position in the twentieth century and in Britain in the nineteenth century, are very real in the dynamic model of hegemony and rivalry, and that of Modelski's emphasis. But there are important differences as well. So far the British hegemony went relatively unchallenged in the mid-nineteenth century but the US hegemony, particularly, since the end of the Second World War remained challenged politically and militarily by the Soviet Union, till the collapse of its system in 1992. But, for the remaining part of the decade, the US hegemony appears to go unchallenged particularly in the political and military arenas, and there is no equivalent rivalry to its hegemony. But, there is every likelihood of the fall in the US hegemony by the turn of the century. The declining US hegemony by the turn of the present century may be attributed to its fast increasing trade deficits. The declining hegemony of USA in the coming years is ushering in a new era of rivalry which can be termed 'west versus west'.

The replacement of the American hegemony by a new era of rivalry is now generaly acknowledged; and that can be referred to a 'multi-polarity' Five 'poles' are usually identified, viz., the USA, Western Europe, Germany (unified Germany has replaced USSR since the later's disintegration), Japan and China. But the really interesting question is what follows. In the paired-Kondratieff model, one of these rivals should emerge to form a new hegemony. This will be based not on military prowess but on economic efficiency, initially in production. The USSR has already ceased to exist. Germany and China are yet to achieve economic efficiency to the extent of global dimension, so they are ruled out to become potential rivals to the US hegemony. However, a historical reversal in the direction of uneven development has occurred with the massive penetration of the American market by Western European and especially Japanese manufactured products. As Japanese economic supremacy moves from production to commerce and finally to finance, we should be looking for changes in Japanese trade policy from their special branch of 'inscrutable' mercantilism to a new liberalism. In this scenario, the twenty-first century will be the 'Japanese century'.

Global geopolitics in the late 1980s and early 1990s witnessed abrupt fall of the socialism, or what Wallerstein terms 'anti-systemic regimes' in East Europe and the Soviet Union, which had significant impact on the revolutionary movement elsewhere. Anti-systemic regimes in East European states collapsed first, but it is important to observe that the Soviet Union did not intervene to protect the socialist regimes there, as it had done earlier in Hungary and Czechoslovakia. Gorbachav's Soviet Union adopted the policy of 'openness' and 'non-intervention'. The fall of the anti-systemic regimes in East Europe was followed by the fall of the Berlin Wall by the enthusiastic Germans on either sides and which finally led to the unification of Germany. The unification of Germany was followed by the breakup/collapse of the Soviet system, which brought down its status as a 'superpower' making it unmatchable to the US hegemony. Yugoslavia and Czechosolvakia also suffered territorial splits. The fall of the anti-systemic regimes in the Soviet Union and the other East European countries may be attributed to their failure to achieve economic susceptibility at par with the world economy. However, it is only in China (one of the five rising poles) that the anti-systemic regime still continues to exist but in no way the Chinese regime poses a serious challenge to the US hegemony—politically, militarily and economically.

The fall of the anti-systemic Soviet Union and its satellite states has wider ramifications on the contemporary geopolitics: (i) disappearance of 'the armageddon scenario', which, since the end of the second world war, had developed as a result of the stockpiling of nuclear weapons by the superpowers—USA and USSR; (ii) anti-systemic organizations like the Warsaw Pact and COMECON have been abandoned; (iii) the former Soviet Republics have formed the Commonwealth of Independent States, which is negotiating with West European states and the US, for their membership in the European Union and the NATO; (iv) the fall of the anti-systemic regimes and the subsequent emergence of Germany seem to have changed the balance of power in the continent; (v) emerging European Union is destined to play a key role in the world economy that is to challenge the US/Japanese hegemony in the near future, and also to contain the rise of Germany; and (iv) the fall of the anti-systemic regime has made the non-alignment movement among the peripheral states highly irrelevant to the contemporary global geopolitics.

In the current rivalry phase, it is only the traditional inter-state competition which is therefore important, but the great amount of internal unrest in the wake of social security cut-backs in the core and direct wage reduction elsewhere. Urban riots in the core, economic and political crises in the semi-periphery, for instance, in Poland, Iran, Nigeria, Brazil to mention one country from each of the four continents, and impoverishment within peripheral countries are equally important as the rise of Japan. It is not only the economies of the world economy that is being restructured, the polities are also being gradually transformed. The scenario constitutes the world systems approach to the traditional crisis of capitalism and the fall of the anti-systemic regimes. For Wallerstein the process will take another 100-150 years to complete but one cannnot simply envisage what the new system will look into any more than the European upper class of 1450 A.D. could predict the capitalist world economy. We can, however, suggest that any attainment of a more equalitarian system will depend on geopolitics giving way to imperialism as the key relation in the future dynamics of the world economy on the locus of change moves 'south'.

Global Change and Geopolitics: Differnt Versions, Diverse Relations: A New Dimension

Global change and geopolitics are both concepts that mean different things to different people. The enlightenment that scientific discourse is supposed to bring suffers from such ambiguities and misunderstandings. They should be, therefore, spelled out, versions of concepts should be compared and their implications clarified.

Some people are convinced that comprehensive shifts are taking place in the natural geosphere and the biosphere of the globe. Man's role has catastrophically changed the face of the earth. The debate concerning these global changes is about their social and economic impacts in different parts of the globe and remedial actions. The sustainability of the natural environment and thereby of human development is the issue. Global changes, to others, refer primarily to the radical increases in human mobility; the mobility of human themselves, their goods and bads (e.g., weaponry). Their symbols (e.g., money) and the impact of these increased volatilities for social life and the major formal tenets of social order; the units of territorially organized state system. This global change has implication of human development in various corners of the globe. Global change is, therefore, either change in overall physical nature of the world or change in the capacity and realization of human movement.

Geopolitics has also divergent meanings. In the older definitions of the term, states are assumed to be dependent on their physical features as far as their foreign policy and international relations are concerned. Their site and situation account, in fact, for their position in international affairs or leave them at best with a very limited number of options. This knowledge is in the possession of a limited set of professional students. They apply these views to concrete cares. In more recent years this notion of physical features as a determining factor for the conduct of the foreign policy has been increasingly challenged by academic geographers. At the same time, the meaning of geopolitics has shifted in academic discourse. Henceforth, it is not so much considered as a theory of inhibiting factors known by professionals, but as an object of study : the geographical perceptions of foreign policy makers. They are no longer supposed to be driven by external forces, but they are supposed to share geographically specific worldviews, political maps of the world that indicate friends and foes, strengths and weaknesses, and that supply, thereby, arguments for and against certain foreign policy options. Geopolitics should be concerned with the study of the ways in which such maps are constructed and how they function.

Two versions each of global change and geopolitics require to be dealt with here. The versions (1) and (2) of each concept can be mutually related. The four ensuing combinations demonstrate four different ways to discuss issues of international and foreign policy in the context of worldwide changes that are now taking place. In this way, the differential vulnerabilities of the state system come to the fore as well as its indispensibility to deal with the various challenges that 'global change' imply. Finally, the question how global change (1) and (2) and geopolitics (1) and (2) are internally related will be discussed.

How does global change (1) affect geopolitics (1)? This question deals with the changes in the natural environment and their impact on the natural factors that according to this viewpoint conditions foreign policy. We have to look at this in a longer time perspective. If several of the scenarios concerned with the changes in the geosphere/biosphere came to pass, this would seriously affect the resource bases of states and their rankings. Even fairly small upward changes in the general sea level will seriously threaten urban life, major infrastructure and important agricultural areas in many coastal lands. Changing climatic conditions dramatically alter agricultural potential in many places possibly in different directions. The ensuing changes in the rankings of composite power indices of countries and the changes in mutual trade potentials result in changes in situations of countries vis-a-vis each other. Reorderings of site qualities and situation characteristics would imply shifts in the patterns of harmony and conflict in international relations. If foreign policy is set by physical conditions, as geopolitics (1) holds, global change (2) will seriously change parameters of international relations in the long run.

How does global change (1) affect geopolitics (2)? How does the possibly impending degradation of the natural/physical environment at the global scale affect the mindset of foreign policy makers? Global change (1) is relatively new problem. It has in its last two decades seriously entered the domain of public policy. Through international organizations as UNEP, an interpretive framework has quickly been disseminated to policy makers. At the same time an important 'green lobby' has kept the global problem and its local specifications before the public eye.

Nevertheless, global change (1) is still driven by debate among professionals who still dispute some of the basic issues (e.g., is global warming really taking place?). As a consequence, it looks as if the issue of global change has entered the perception of foreign policy makers. Its salience is very much dependent upon the rest of the foreign policy agenda in a specific country as well as the connectedness of foreign policy makers to the professional world of scientists who conduct the debate on these issues. The relative power of the local emanation of the 'green lobby' is also important in this connection to the extent that global change (1) plays a role in the setting of foreign policy, it will affect perceptions of who are friends and foes in the world and accordingly may transform existing coalitions.

How does global change (2) conditions geopolitics (1)? In other words, how does the increasing mobility of humans and their tangible exchanges have an impact on the physical attributes of countries that provide the setting of foreign policy? First of all, the built environment and thus the resource base of countries change as a result of increased mobility. This mobility needs an important physical infrastructure. Its parts are assets that greatly affect the qualities of a country's site and situation. Ports and airports, motor roads and rail roads that are connected with international networks deeply influence the internal quality and international position of a country. Austria's and Switzerland's natural landscapes are now as important as their international connections. The competition between airports concerning their relative centrality in the networks of international corrections is nervously watched by governments who consider this to be major determining factor of their country's international position.

The question in this instance is to what extent such factors do indeed directly affect a country's international position. Secondly, as humans move across international borders and the international exchange patterns of tangible goods shift relentlessly and become more dense, two facts follow : resource bases that include a population and the capital goods encompassed by their built environments become more dependent on international movement and they may consequently change more rapidly. To the extent that physical characteristics indeed determine foreign policy, there is ample reason to expect incisive consequences of heightened international mobility. Ranks change more rapidly, interdependence grows.

How does global change (2) relate to geopolitics (2)? International human mobility increases and trade goods grow, but the exchange of intangibles (money, images) has caught up and surpassed these trends. World financial markets interconnect virtually all places on the globe; much economic activity is thus regulated from the few foremost financial centres that set the tone for the pattern of money flows in the world at large. An extensive set of symbols and images is shared or at least understood by large proportions of the world population. A large part of that repertoire is manufactured in a few places that have a large impact on perception. The vicinity of the rest of the world is, although intangible, deeply felt by large proportions of the world population. Foreign policy makers are confronted with a multitude of foreign signs and exchange of symbols that result in more tangible consequences, e.g., of money flows. These come across international borders and have an immediate impact on domestic politics. Thus, the traditional divide between foreign and domestic policy making has largely disappeared. Foreign policy makers are also far more immediately and more often confronted with foreign events than was the case in earlier periods. The construction of the geopolitical world maps that underlie the making of foreign policy has in consequence become more contested by the continuous flow of new information and by the wider domestic arena in which foreign policy has to be debated.

So far we have considered the different versions of global change and of geopolitics as if they were unconnected. In fact, they are not. The processes that affect the biosphere and the geosphere and that threaten to undermine existing equilibria in those two spheres, are driven by the ever expanding human use of the globe's natural assets. Population growth, non-renewable resource, intensive socio-economic development account for these processes. Mobility, particularly of persons and of goods, is a very important part of that kind of development.

Thus, global changes (1) and (2) emanate partly from the same source and are thus related. The theory of geopolitics that assumes an immediate effect of the physical environment on a country's international position, i.e., geopolitics (1), has for a long time been discredited for the conduct of foreign policy as it seems to underestimate the room for political manoeuvre and has a tendency to overestimate the military security arguments in the setting of foreign policy.

Geopolitics (2) has so far remained a suggestive research programme that is in danger of over-interpretation on the basis of a shortage of empirical data. It is evident that the construction of geopolitical world maps is an important and inevitable part of foreign policy making, the more so as the signals that result from global change (2) increase in number and become more difficult to interpret. It looks, though, as if a new emphasis on global change (1) (a deteriorating natural environment) necessitates a new look at the physical environment in which states operate. Thus, maps constructed as part of geopolitics (2) will take more of their contents from modernized versions of geopolitics (1). The resource bases of the different fragments of the territorial state system have as a consequence of global change (1) won a new sense of urgency. In addition, the resource bases of those different fragments turn out to be partially shared.

Notes

1. Translated by Ronald Bolin.
2. Rudolf Kjellen, Der Staat als Lebensform. M. Langfeldt trans. (Leipzig: S. Hirzel Verlag, 1917).
3. Kondratieff waves are long waves of economic development with a wave length of about 40-60 years. Shorter oscillations in the level of business activity may be superimposed upon such long waves but the latter imply fundamental transformation of economic systems rather than mere quantitative fluctuations. Kondratieff waves are named after the Soviet economist N.D. Kondratieff who worked during 1920s on long-term fluctuation in economic activity.

Chapter 3

Approaches to the Study of Political Geography

Carl Sauer in 1927 defined political geography as "the wayward child of the geographic family where method and material are free at the choice of the student". Sauer's statement was time-tested in the sense that the contemporary political geography lacked concrete methodological approaches, and whatever little was available that too concerned itself with geopolitik which stood in contrast to political geography. The reason for the lack of methodological approaches to the contemporary political geography may be attributed to the lack of professionalism. The organismic paradigm of the Ritter-Ratzel heritage did not make any deep insight into the problem of approaches in the contemporary politico-geographical scholarship.

It was not until 1935 that Derwent S. Whittlesey came out with an approach to the study of political geography. This could be said as the first attempt towards an approach to this subfield of geography which sought to reply Sauer's statement on the credibility of political geography in 1927. Whittlesey's approach to the study of political geography was contained in an article entitled, "The Impress of Effective Central Authority upon the Landscape", published in the *Annals of the Association of American Geographers* in 1935.

Whittlesey's Law-Landscape Approach

"By 'central authority' is meant sovereignty over an area of marked diversity. To be effective, the central government must exert more than nominal control over its area. Today effective central authority is a function of the nation-state", says Whittlesey.

In this article, Whittlesey examines various ways by which politics can modify the landscape He divides his treatment into four major sections—expressions of security, special features of boundaries, expressions of government activity, and the effects of the legal system. His subsequent discussion suggests the wide scope of political impress on the environment.

In the case of political security, he rates effects upon the distribution of settlement, the form of cities, and even the architecture of buildings. He envisions political boundaries as providing special features (such as military garrisons), special economic functions (here he anticipates Loesch), and even levels of personal risk. He further delineates the broad range of governmental impact upon the landscape—post office architecture, land and street patterns, migrations, regional development, and the lavish development of capital cities. Finally, in his particularly stimulating discussion of laws and the landscape, Whittlesey analyzes the role that tariffs, embargoes, and land laws play in various geographical distributions.

To begin with, although the political impress may be conceived in man-land terms, we are dealing with a variety of spatial distributions, some of which are visible in the landscape and others which may be illuminated only very indirectly. It may be useful, therefore, to structure political impress on the environment into four major components—political goals, agents of impress, processes and effects.

Political goals include such objectives as security, autarchy, spatial integration, status and economic growth. Nearly all governments seek security, although its rank among other goals may vary in relation to perceived threat or hostility in the environment. The Cuban government of Fidel Castro has lived with a high degree of both perceived and actual hostility, and security has been a prime objective of the regime. Autarchy, an objective perhaps more prized at earlier periods of history than now, is still a strong consideration among nation-states. The Soviet Union, especially in the years following 1928, made autarchy a keystone of its economic and foreign policy. The United States has sought to reduce its reliance upon external strategic minerals through stockpiling and technological innovations. A country's position along the autarchy-interdependence continuum may greatly affect its willingness to engage in inefficient resource exploitation.

The degree of spatial integration or segregation sought by a political system may vary widely. Urban political leaders may seek to segregate ghettos from other residential areas or they may genuinely attempt at integration. Nation-states such as Canada, the Congo, India and the Soviet Union have taken strong measures to foster the spatial integration of culturally diverse and often widely separated areas. Status, often an important objective, takes such diverse forms as citation as an 'all-American city', the presence of a national airline, the erection of a steel plant, or ordinances requiring one-acre minimum lot size. Rapid economic growth often provides an index of the efficacy of political leadership, and a government can rise or fall on this issue. The military regime in Greece, for example, justified its coup on this basis. In regard to the environment, such a goal may entail a particular stance concerning the degree of public intervention into the harnessing of natural resources for the national 'good'.

Agents of political impress are the vehicles or means by which political processes manifest themselves in the environment. The legal system, legislation, interest groups and voluntary associations, political partitions and degrees of political security are all examples of such agents. The political partitioning of space, particularly that separating national political systems, is critical. Discussions of boundary impact really centre upon the differential impact of divergent policies and degrees of centralized power.

The legal system, along with prevailing customs and mores, may regulate extensively the use and development of the physical environment. Regulations concerning property are basic to spatial patterns in any political unit. Alternative systems of land survey and tenure, inheritance and dowry arrangements may produce such contrasting landscapes as the seigneurial land patterns in French Canada, communal landholdings in Africa or pre-European North America, chekerboard land patterns in the contemporary Midwest, or the fragmented lands of Mediterranean Europe.

Legislation, one of the most direct means available for regulation or development of the physical environment, offers a wide range of ordinance types. At the community level in the United States property and income taxation, building codes, subdivision ordinances, zoning, and planning all exemplify these measures. At higher levels in the political hierarchy, tariffs, embargoes, pricing systems, national domains, government quotas on production and developmental projects can be utilized in political impress.

Finally, the degree of political security prevalent in a particular area can leave its mark in a variety of ways. Settlement patterns and architectural types reflect this variable. Mediterranean settlements often perch on hilltops in the protective shadow of churches, castles, or monasteries. As political security increased over time, maritime or land trade precipitated a downslope growth of settlement. The wide streets of Paris constructed to ensure security against possible uprisings, present another example. The threat of nuclear war at present has given rise to efforts, not all of them successful, to disperse key industrial firms and military bases.

Only several *processes of political impress* will be noted here. *Symbolization* refers to political activities which create on the landscape symbols designed to signify certain values to indigenous inhabitants or to others. In occupied territories and along hostile boundary lines, especially those separating competing ideological and political systems, 'showcases' sometimes appear to symbolize the success of a particular path. Landscape symbols may also have a calculated function, such as the political integration, independence from foreign powers and developmental potentialities of the interior which the new capital cities of Brasilia and Islamabad proudly proclaim.

Political symbolism in the landscape may assume a variety of styles. Chicago's lakefront is a homage to the city of the 'master plan'. Every community expresses its values and aspirations in its monuments, restorations, public buildings and architecture. Some national governments maintain boundary makers and supporting patterns to indicate past glories or disputed areas, whereas others go to great lengths to eradicate any suggestion of prior political sovereignty. The changing of names on gravestones in the South Tyrol represents an extreme measure of the latter type.

Redistribution constitutes another very basic process of political impress on the environment. Utilization of the environment often involves the collection of funds from diverse areas of a political systems to finance projects in spatially-concentrated locales. The process, often a purposeful one, may have its roots in political goals, such as providing incentives in Canada or Australia for settlement and resources exploitation or supporting the Appalachia programme in the United States. The spatial distribution of funds for developmental projects has always been a serious bone of contention between different segments of a state.

Spatial competition and conflict is a process closely related to and by no means mutually exclusive from redistribution. Within any political unit local interests vie for the rewards of redistribution and developmental schemes. Success in competition not only brings tangible benefits for the local citizenry but strengthens the reservoir of support for politicians among their constituents. Again, the issues are multifarious—government contracts, shipyard closings, hospitals, libraries, school sites, highways, etc. This process illustrates the useful perspective provided by the spatial structure of a political economy. Actually, the analysis of the entire process can take the form of a game in which players representing various geographical sections of the political system compete for the spatial allocation of public funds.

Effects are the last analytical component of political impress on the environment. Some of these effects (e.g., land and street patterns) would be visible in the landscape, whereas others (e.g., prices, land values) would not. Geographers have at their disposal various techniques and concepts for analyzing these effects. Thus, the analysis can focus on geometry movement, networks, nodes, hierarchies and surfaces. On the other hand, it is possible to discuss effects in terms of their structural-functional attributes. In that sense any kind of barrier takes on a divergent function in regard to spatial-political integration.

"Examples of cultural impress of effective central authority upon the landscape can be multiplied indefinitely. The cases cited suffice, however, to point to a group of geographic phenomena often overlooked. Each deserves more detailed study, particularly in its regional setting. Phenomena engendered by political forces should have a recognized place as elements in the geographic structure of every region."

This approach which was first of its kind in political geography seems to have been drawn from the contemporary American possibilist paradigm. The law-landscape approach of Whittlesey could not make any immediate breakthrough in the contemporary politico-geographical studies but in the latter decades it did inspire a lot of people to think in terms of law-landscape change in the political areas. A few years later, in 1939 Whittlesey attempted to define the subject matter of political geography: "The kernel of political geography is the political area. Every political unit describes an areal pattern of nuclear core, constituent or administrative regions, problem areas, vulnerable zones, capitals, strategic spots and boundaries—all affecting its success even if not vital to its persistence. These features take form with respect to specific conditions of the natural environment. Commonly they harmonize with the earth conditions and the peopling of the place at the time of their origin. Once established, they tend strongly to perpetuate themselves...The political areas which endure longest are noted for making frequent alteration by law in order to keep their institutions abreast of changing times."

He continues to say: "A factor in the persistence of those political areas which retain their identity is the pertinacity of the past in the realm of government. Political feeling is one of the strongest of all human imitations. Political attachments are correspondingly tenacious, and some part of the heritage of environmental conditions long vanished remains in the political order of every period.The political geography of few, if any, areas can be understood without recourse to their past. Study of the present-day political landscape must be supplemented by a review in their original setting if such relics of past landscapes as survive in the patterns of today. The present can be set in its perspective only by reconstruction of the fragmentary records of history, and in some places the still more meagre remains of archaeology."

On the *relationship between law and region*, Whittlesey points out: "The agent whereby the political structure of any area is constructed is the law. Like any other human concept, the law freely flits from one region to another. Laws are frequently enacted which are so at variance with nature in the political area affected that they have to be rescinded...Others, while somewhat inharmonious, manage to operate; to some extent they modify utilization of earth resources. In time, the fundamental law in each political area becomes roughly suited to the few compulsive conditions laid down by nature...Variations in culture patterns in uniform environments on opposite sides of a political boundary are common, and prove the possibility of modifying the landscape by political means. The operations of law can be traced only through patient study of the incidence of individual laws...Even in the region of its origin every legal system is subject to continuous alteration to conform changes... in the character of human occupance itself. The interplay of law and region is incessant. Each affects the other and in the process is itself modified. As in every other aspect of geography, earth conditions permit a wide range of laws in most regions, and at the same time, set limits that nullify laws which stand outside the permitted range."

Whittlesey seems to have drawn this conceptual framework in political geography from his concept of 'sequent occupance' which sought to bind together morphological-historical and legal approaches, current in his time, within the purview of the contemporary American possibilist paradigm. In fact, the morphological approach and historical or genetic approach stood in contrast to each other. The former concentrated on the study and analysis of features such as location, size and shape, boundaries, capitals and core areas and the regional breakdown of the states' area into natural or cultural and other types of regions while the latter sought to study the objective of explaining how a state had come into being in the area within its present boundaries. It was Whittlesey who sought to combine the approaches together but Richard Hartshorne was, to some extent, averse to these approaches, because to him, the morphological approach was 'dull and static', while to that of the historical/genetic approach, he remarked, "it is not clear to me...that such historical studies of genesis are essential for every study in political geography...or a necessary preliminary section, in the study of the political geography of any state."

In view of the persistent weaknesses in the morphological and historical approaches, Richard Hartshorne offered yet another alternative approach which sought to study/analyze the functions of politically organized areas, i.e., the sovereign state—the intrinsic fundamental function of the state is " to establish itself as an effective unit, rather than merely in international law". In an article entitled, "The Functional Approach in Political Geography", published in the *Annals of the Association of American Geographers* in 1950 Richard Hartshorne attempts to present his approach. Here, in the approach, he attempts to bring forward the regional paradigm in political geography.

Hartshorne's Functional Approach

"The fundamental purpose of any state, as an organization of a section of land and section of people, as Ratzel first put it, is to bring all the varied territorial parts, the diverse regions of the State-area, into a single organized unit."

Analysis of the Political Geography of a State: Internal Functions

"What does the state attempt to organize in all regions of the state-area?" In all cases, it attempts to establish complete and exclusive control over internal political relations—in simplest terms, the creation and maintenance of law and order. Local political institutions must conform with the concepts and institutions of the central, over all, political organization.

In many social aspects—class structure, family organization, religion and education—a state may tolerate considerable variation in its different regions. But because of the significance of these factors to political life, there is a tendency—in some states a very marked effort—to exert unifying control even over these institutions. In the economic field, every modern state tends to develop some degree of unity of economic organization. Every state must strive to secure the supreme loyalty of the people in all its regions, in competition with any local or provincial loyalties, and in definite opposition to loyalty to any outside state unit.

Throughout this statement of the organization of the state-area as a unit, the geographer is primarily concerned with emphasis on regional differences. The state, of course, is no less concerned to establish unity of control over all classes of population at a single place. In political geography, the interest is in the problem of unification of diverse regions into single whole; the degree of vertical unification within any horizontal segment concerns not only as a factor aiding or handicapping regional unification.

Our analysis of the primary functions of any state leads directly to the primary problem of political geography. For no state-area constitutes by the nature of its land and people, a natural unit for a state, in which one merely needs to create a government which shall proceed to operate it as a unit. The primary and continuing problem of every state is how to bind together more or less separate and diverse areas into an effective whole.

For the political geographer, this presents a wide range of specific problems for analysis. In every state-area, larger than such anomalies as Andorra or Liechtensteir, the geographer finds: (1) regions that are more or less separated from each other by physical or human barriers; (2) regions that in greater or lesser degree diverge in their relations with outside states; and (3) regions that differ among themselves in character of population, economic interests, and political attitudes. Let us look briefly at each of these types of problems.

*Centrifugal Forces**

Geographers are familiar with the effect of particular types of physical features in handicapping communication between regions...In most modern

* **Centrifugal forces are those which lead toward division and may even threaten the breakup of the state.**

states, however, these problems have largely been overcome by the development of the telegraph and the railroad. They continue to be of importance, however, in parts of the Balkans, in the highland states of Latin America and in China.

Since state organization requires communication not only from one region to the next, but also from a central point to each peripheral region, distance itself is a centrifugal factor. Obviously distance within a state depends on its size and shape. Size and shape are significant to the state in other, quite different respects, but...suggest...wait until...have determined that in...analysis, rather than attempt to proceed deductively from size and shape to consequences.

Of human barriers, the most common is the absence of humans. Uninhabited or sparsely inhabited areas were, until recently, difficult and dangerous to cross. It was primarily on this account that relatively low mountains, in Central Europe or the Appalachians, long functioned as dividing zones. Further, the presence of such relatively empty areas created, and still create, a feeling of separation in the regions on either side. Both on this account and because of distance, oceans continue to function as the strongest separating factor, other than the Arctic ice, even those which have long been crossed with relative ease.

Perhaps, the most difficult barrier to overcome is separation by a zone populated by a different people, especially an unfriendly people. The Germans have apparently convinced the world that the separation of East Prussia by the Polish Corridor was an experiment that is never to be repeated.

Serious difficulties may arise for a state if any of its regions have closer relations with regions of outside states than with those within the state. This is commonly the case where a boundary has been changed so that it now cuts across an area formerly within a single state. The partition of Upper Silesia in 1922 presented a particularly intense case. But there are many cases, not dependent on boundary changes, in which a region has closer connections, particularly economic connections, with regions of other countries than with other regions of its own state. We are familiar with the political importance of this factor in each of the major regions of Canada, each more closely related in certain respects with the adjacent areas of the United States than with the other regions within the dominion. In some cases mutual interdependence among the regions of the state-area is less than the dependence of individual regions in remote, overseas country. This is a major problem of the Australian Commonwealth in which each state unit is primarily dependent on separate trade with Great Britain.

Separation of regions by barriers or by divergence of outside connections is commonly less important than the centrifugal forces that result from diversity of character of the population. To secure voluntary acceptance of a single common organization requires some degree of mutual understanding; obviously this is easier in a population homogeneous in character. Further, where regions differ in social character, the tendency of the state to force some degree of uniformity of social life meets with resistance. Thus, the very attempt to produce unity may intensify disunity. Hungary, before 1918, was the classic example, since then Yugoslavia has been perhaps the leading, among several successors.

What particular social characteristics may be important depends on the particular state. Everyone thinks of language and religion...education and standards of living, types of economic attitudes and institutions, attitudes towards class and racial distinctions, and, especially, political philosophy.

Racial differences, as studied by the physical anthropologist, may be of no relevance to our problem. The distribution, percentagewise, in the different countries of Europe, of blondes and brunettes, dolichocephalic versus brachycephalic—what does it matter? These facts have no reflection in social or political attitudes in those countries. Though standard material in most geographies of Europe...have no significance to political geography, or for that matter, to geography in general.

In contrast, the United States is a country in which regional differences in attitudes of people toward the racial components of the regional groups—as indicated by skin colour—are of tremendous importance in social, economic and political life. We have mapped and studied the underlying differences in racial composition but we have not studied the phenomenon itself, namely, the differences in attitudes. We need a map, a series of maps, portraying different kinds and degrees of Jim Crowism in the United States. These...would rate as a first requirement for an understanding of the internal political geography of the United States, for in no other factor do we find such marked regional cleavages, such disruption to the national unity of our state. For geography, in general, in one quarter of our country, these attitudes are fundamental factors in every aspects of the human geography, and are significantly related to its physical geography.

Geographers are more familiar with differences in economic interests since these are more closely bound to the land. But these seldom seriously disrupt national unity. It is true that almost every modern state has experienced marked political tension between the divergent interests of highly industrial regions and those of still primarily agricultural areas. But these differences tend to lead to interlocking rather than competing interests. Even when competing, economic differences..., are easier to compromise than differences in social and political attitudes.

Furthermore, the state is only in partial degree an economic unit. Since it is basically a political unit, the state necessarily imposes the greatest degree of uniformity in political life. Political attitudes are peculiarly inflexible. If a region is accustomed to one set of political concepts, ideals and institutions—most people especially if its people feel that they have fought in the past to establish those political values—it may be extremely difficult to bring them under the common cloak of a quite different system. Even when regions, formerly in separate states, have voluntarily joined together to form a state, on the basis of common ethnic character—for example, the three Polish areas in 1918, or the Czech and Slovak areas—the marked difference in past political education led to difficult problems.

In times and areas of relatively primitive political development such factors were no doubt of minor importance. In long-settled areas of relatively mature political development, these may be of first importance. The classic example is, again, Alsace. Thanks particularly to the French Revolution, the people of that province had become strong supporters of political concepts, ideals and institutions that could not be harmonized within the semifeudal, authoritian monarchy of Hohenzollern Germany.

Conversely, one may understand, on this basis, the negative reaction of the Swiss in 1919 to the proposal that the adjacent Austrian province of Vorarlberg should be added to their state.

*Centripetal Forces**

The preceding discussion of political attitudes points to an essential ingredient that has been lacking in the discussion up to this point. We have been considering a variety of centrifugal factors in the regional geography of a state-area which make it difficult to bind those regions together into an effective unit. In considering how such difficulties may be overcome, we have not asked whether there was any force working to overcome the difficulties, anything tending to pull these regions into a state.

The omission...has been the single greatest weakness in our thinking in political geography. If we see an area marked clearly on both physical and ethnic maps as suitable for a state, but which for many centuries was not integrated as a state—as in the Spanish peninsula, the Italian peninsula, or the German area—we cudgel our heads to find factors in the internal geography that will explain the failure. We forget that before we speak of failure, we must ask what was attempted.

One of the concepts that prevented integration in Italy is likewise the key to the failure of medieval Germany to develop a unified state, at the time when

---

* Centripetal forces are those which lead to unity and coherence of the state.

kingdoms of France and England were being effectively established. For centuries the personal holding of the title of King of Germany, and whatever opportunity that might give, were far more affected by the higher title of Emperor. Inspired by the grander idea of reincarnating the empire of Rome, they fought to build a state, straddling the Alps, uniting many different peoples. The sacrifices made in the vain attempt to accomplish the greater idea destroyed the possibility of achieving the lesser when later emperors finally were reduced to, considering German unity.

The fact that a country has a name and a government, that an international treaty recognizes its existence as a state and defines its territorial limits—all that does not produce a state. To accomplish that, it is necessary to establish centripetal forces that will bind together the regions of the state, in spite of centrifugal forces that are always present.

The State-Idea

The basic centripetal force must be some concept or idea justifying the existence of this particular state incorporating these particular regions, the state must have a *raison d'etre* or reason for existing.

Although ignored in much of the literature of political geography, this is not a new thought. Ratzel defined the state as a section of land and a section of humanity organized as a single unit in terms of a particular, distinctive idea...At the primitive level, Ratzel explained that this idea may be no more than the will of a ruler to which, for whatever reasons, all the regional parts through their local leaders grant their loyalty. In such a case, as in the empire of Charlemagne or that of Ghengis Khan, the state may endure hardly longer than the lifetime of the individual ruler. In the attempt to perpetuate the binding idea of loyalty to a personal ruler, there evolved the concept of hereditary monarchy. Where that succeeded, however, we find there was always something more—politically-minded people in the various parts of the kingdom came to regard the state, for reasons independent of the monarch, as representing something of value to them.

To be sure, a state in which the original idea has lost its validity will not fall apart at once.The forces of inertia, vested interests, and fear of the consequences of change may help it going more or less effectively for some time. But inevitably a structure that has lost its original *raison d'etre*, without

* State-idea is a complex of traditions, experiences and objectives. It is made up of written history, folklores, stories of national heroes, religious beliefs, and the language and art forms in which these things are communicated. It is the body of the literature, the painting, the architecture, the music which are distinctively national. And it is the characteristic economic, social and political institution.

evolving a new one, cannot hope to stand the storms of external strife or internal revolt that sooner or later will attack it. For when that day comes, the state to survive, must be able to count upon the loyalty, even to the death of the population of all its regions. "Those states are strongest", Ratzel had concluded, "in which the political idea of the state fills the entire body of the state and extends to all its parts."

What does this mean for the study of the political geography of a state? It means...we must discover the motivating centripetal force, the basic idea of the state. Under what concept, for what purposes, are these particular regions to be bound together into one political unit, absolutely separated from every other political territory. We must discover and establish the unique distinctive idea under which a particular section of area and of humanity is organized into a unit state...until we can determine for any particular state the idea under which it is organized, we shall have no basis on which to analyze its political geography, we shall not have started on the significant contribution that geography can make to the study of states.

The idea of an Iraqi state sprang from two factors: (i) the recognition by the 'great powers' of the special strategic and economic significance of the Mesopotamian region, and (ii) the need to provide 'a pied a terre' for Arab nationalism banished from Syria. On the basis of these two considerations, there was established a territory embracing the settled Arab region of the Tigris-Euphrates plain, together with adjacent but dissimilar regions of mountain and desert tribes, the whole to be developed as a separate Arab state.

To determine the distinctive idea of such a state, therefore, we must study the current situation rather than the remote past. In the well-developed modern state, politically-minded people in all regions of the state-area are conscious of their loyalty to the state and have some common understanding, even though not clearly phrased, of what that state means to them. In such a case, we may recognize, the existence of a nation—as something distinct from the state itself.

The Concept of Nation

...in the most primitive level, the concept of nation represents simply a feeling of kinship, of belonging together, an extension of the concept of family, more properly an extension of the concept of the in-group versus outsiders. While usually expressed in terms derived from the language of the family—terms like 'blood', 'bread', 'race', etc., it is in reality less of kin and more of kind—similarity of cultural rather than of biological characteristics.

The direct significance of this elementary concept of nationality to the state lies first in the fact that all peoples tend to prefer government by those of their own kind, even if inefficient or unjust rather than any government over them by foreigners, however, beneficent. The second reason is that the individual seeks to identify himself with his state, nationality, someone said, is 'pooled self-esteem'. Indeed, the state is sure of the loyalty of the people only if there is such identification. Each citizen must feel that the state is 'his' state, its leaders, 'his' leaders. For this to be possible, he must feel that those who operate his state, who govern him, are people like himself.

The main purpose of a state, however, is not the furtherance of a particular language or culture. Its main purpose is political. The values over which it has complete control are political ones. As the people in a state mature in positive political experience, their feeling of belonging together becomes less dependent on common adherence to particular political concepts, ideals, and institutions. It is for the sake of these that they are ready to devote their ultimate loyalty to their state.

It is difficult to summarize the analysis of the concept of nation into a single statement but for those readers who wish a definition: "a nation may be defined as a group of people occupying a particular area who feel themselves held together in terms of common acceptance of particular values that are of such prime importance to them that they demand that their area and people should be organized in a distinct state, as the political agency by which those values may be preserved and furthered."

The relations between the state and the nation are mutual and manifold. In the older nation-states of Western Europe, the nation was in no small part the product of the state. William of Normandy...established the kingdom of England, later expanded to include Wales. In the process, however, whatever degree of Anglo-Saxon nation had developed was destroyed in the conflict with the Norman French conquerors. But, in the course of centuries, the state created a new nation—the English.

Likewise, there was no French nation—not even a common language of what we think of as the single to French people—until centuries after the kings of France had established more or less effective unity over the state area...call by that name. In Norway and Eire, the relation of state and nation was reversed; the nation antedated and demanded the state. The Polish nation also antedated the Polish state. The Hapsburg monarchy did not disintegrate directly because of the large number of different ethnic regions of which it was formed, but rather because that state never evolved political concepts or institutions that could gain acceptance...

The United States...presents still a different type. The nation antedated the state but was itself originally only a part of an older British nation that had been developed by the United Kingdom. One further ramification may be briefly suggested. Once the concept of a nation has been well established within an area, its spread outward is not necessarily limited by the frontier of the state-area.

The Concept of the Core-Area

A core-area is neither sufficient nor essential to the evolution of a nation or state. What is essential is a common idea that convinces the people in all the regions that they belong together. Historically, in certain states, a core may have played a major role in spreading that idea to other regions and it may continue today as in France, Argentina or Mexico to focus the interest of the regions on itself as the centre of what has become a functioning unit but the common idea for a state may develop where no core-area exists.

The Application of the State-Idea in Political Geography

Whatever is found to be the *raison d'etre*, the underlying idea of the state, it is with this concept...that the geographer should start his analysis of the state-area. What use is he then to make of it?

His first concern is to determine the area to which the idea applies; then, the degree to which it operates in the different regions; and finally, the extent of correspondence of those regions to the territory actually included within the state.

On this basis we may approach the most elementary problem in political geography, namely, that of distinguishing within the legal confines of its territory, those regions that form an integral part of the state-area in terms of its basic idea, and those parts that must be recognized as held under control in the face of either indifference or opposition on the part of the regional population.

If the idea of the State is based on the recognition of the existence of a nation, then the major geographic question to consider is whether there is close correspondence between the area of the nation and that of the state. Are there regions within the state whose populations do not feel themselves parts of the nation? Are there regions of the nation that are not included within the state—the issue of irridentism?

"The entire area over which the nation extends, but in a varying degrees of intensity, may then be compared with the area presently included in the state. We have thus determined not only the areal correspondence of state and nation, but also the regions in which the national character is partial rather than complete. We shall thereby have presented, in part in map form, the basic factors and relationships involved in the primary problem of political geography—the analysis of the degree to which the diverse regions of the state constitute a unity."

Internal Organization

...one other problem for analysis—the relation of the internal territorial organization of the state-area to the regional diversities...though all the regions of a state are closely included under the state-idea, have complete loyalty to the overall concepts of the national unit, regional differences inevitably cause some differences in interpretation and implementation of those concepts.

If these differences are relatively minor, as in most of France or in Uruguay, the regions may accept unitary government from a single central authority. If the differences are great, the attempt to impose such a uniform system may provoke opposition endangering the national unity. Since such regional differences are important in most countries, most states attempt to operate under a uniform, centralized government, the number of examples of this type of problem is very large. Spain at the moment provides one of the most striking example.

Certain states recognize openly the need to permit diverging interpretations of the overall concepts of that state and hence significant differences in the institutions and laws thereunder. This is the system of a federal state, of which Switzerland provides the oldest example and the United States the largest. In both cases, a notable degree of regional heterogeneity is guaranteed by the constitutional division of power.

The possible ways of organizing the state-area are not limited to the unitary and the federal systems. The United Kingdom...has evolved in the course of its long history a most complicated system under which Wales, Scotland, Northern Ireland, the Isle of Man and the Channel Islands—each has a different degree of autonomy adjusted to its particular linguistic, religious, economic and political geography.

Analysis of External Functions

In a functional approach to the analysis of the political geography of a state, the first half was concerned with the internal problems of the state-area. The second half is concerned with the external relations of the state-area to the other areas of the world, whether those are also recognized as states, controlled by outside states, or unorganized. For convenience we may group these relations as territorial, economic, political and strategic.

Territorial Relations

Under the territorial relations we are...concerned in the first instance with the degree to which adjacent states are in agreement concerning the extent of territory which each includes. Whether the area in question is large or small, agreement ultimately requires the determination of a precise boundary. The first thing to know about an international boundary therefore, is the degree to which it is accepted by all the parties concerned-i.e., the adjacent states and the population whose statehood is determined by the location of the boundary. The second question concerning any international boundary (whether or not it is fully accepted) is the degree to which its boundary function is maintained by the bordering states, the degree, that is, to which all movements of goods and persons across the line are effectively controlled by the boundary officials. In examining that, the geographer will, of course, observe the ways in which the control is made easier or more difficult by the character of the zone through which the boundary line is drawn.

The use of territorial waters by merchant ships of a foreign state, commonly for the purpose of entering the ports of the country concerned, represents the most common occurrence of use of territory of one state for the purpose of another state. In this case, the purpose is mutual. In other more special cases problems arise from the desire or need of the people of one state to utilize the territory of a foreign country to have access to still other countries or in some cases to a different part of their own state....

Nearly all states recognize the need to providing transit service for trade across their territories between states on either side.... Most important are provisions for transit from an inland state to the sea-coast in order to have access to the countries of the world accessible by sea routes.

Economic Relations

In the analysis of a state-area, the need to consider its economic relations with outside areas arises from the fact that in many respects a state operates, must operate, as a unit economy in relation with other unit economies in the world. The difficulties arise because while it must operate completely as a political unit, a state-area operates only partially as an economic unit. ...The first problem is to determine to what extent the economy of one state-area is dependent on that of others, though the mere analysis of self-sufficiency is only a beginning. In general, the geographer will analyze the economic dependence of one state-area on others in terms of the specific countries concerned and their location and political association in relation to the state....

Since all sound trading is of mutual advantage to both parties, to say that one state is economically dependent on any other necessarily implies also the converse. But the degree to which any particular commodity trade shipping service or investment is critically important, varies in terms of the total economy of each of the two states concerned. It is only in this sense that the common question "is a particular state economically viable?" has any validity, since every state above the most primitive level is in some respects critically dependent on others.

The problem is far from simple but perhaps we can suggest two generalizations. As between two countries that differ greatly in the size of their total national economy, the economic relationships between them are more critically important for the lesser countries. This is true because these economic relationships...will form a larger proportion of the total national economy of the lesser state.

The second generalization rests on the fact that the critical significance of the trade depends on the possibility of alternatives, of finding other sources for needed supplies or other markets for products which must be sold to maintain the national economy.

In the nineteenth century, international economic relations, though both supported and retarded by state action, were generally operated as the private business of individuals and corporations. With the depression of the 1930s, the rise of totalitarian states, and the last war, there has been an increasing tendency for the state itself to direct the operations of international trade and investment. In these respects states function increasingly as economic units so that the economic relations among them become increasingly important in the politico-geographic analysis of the state.

Political Relations

The most obvious form of political relation of a state to any outside territory is that of effective political control—as a colony, possession, dependency or 'protectorate'. Commonly we recognize only a small number of states as colonial or imperial powers...The legal forms of colonial relationship vary widely—even within a single empire, such as that of Great Britain. Further, these legal forms may or may not express the reality of the relationship, the degree to which political organization is imposed and operated by the outside state. It is the latter...that is our concern in political geography.

One characteristic of colonial areas that is of particular concern from our present point of view is the degree to which the governmental system of the home state is extended over the colonial territory...Many imperial powers have always extended their legal systems into colonial areas...so that within any colonial area, there may be an overlapping of two authorities—one having jurisdiction over citizens of the home state, the other over native people.

Many countries recognized by treaty as independent states, and functioning in large degree as such, are nonetheless under some particular degree of political control by an outside power...The clearest case of political domination of supposedly independent states by an outside state today is found in the obvious control by the Soviet Union over the internal policies as well as foreign policy of the 'satellite' states on its west, from Poland to Bulgaria, even though this relationship is expressed in no formal treaties. Nearly all the states of the world have accepted certain political commitments in joining the United Nations, insofar as this applies to all states, such commitments are universal rather than geographically distinctive.

Strategic Relations

In this analysis of the external relations with other state-areas, we must certainly recognize that the state-area as a unit, has virtually important strategic relations with the other areas of the world. Every state-area in the world lives in a strategic situation with other states, a situation that may be in part created by its own actions and policies but in major part is determined for it by those other states.

...Switzerland in modern times... is situated in the midst of a group of larger neighbours, each fearful of expansion of power by the others. In this situation Switzerland has found its best hope for security in a policy of armed neutrality because such a neutralized area was in the mutual interest defensively, of the neighbouring powers. In a much earlier period, in the sixteenth and seventeenth centuries, when Austria was the only major power bordering Switzerland, and many of its neighbours were small states, the Swiss Confederation followed a very different policy of strategic relations, frequently allying itself with any of these various neighbours in conflict with the others. The strategic relations of a state, in other words, must be adjusted to the particular strategic situation in which it finds itself at any time.

...In studying the relations which such an area operating as a unit, enters into with other areas, we are concerned with engagements which it has, or has not, made with other units, whether for defensive or offensive purposes. Interpretation of these associations necessarily involves an appraisal of the space relationships of all the strategic areas involved, whether as power units or as territories of passage. The problem is logically inherent in the political geography of states and its geographic quality seems clear.

Thus, to summarize, the state-area...is an organized unit of land and people, organized by man according to a particular idea or purpose. The state-area is an organization that has genesis, structure and function. Logically, therefore, the analysis of a state-area may be approached from any or all of these three viewpoints.

The fundamental internal function of the state-area is to establish itself as an effective unit...This requires the conception and establishment of an idea of the state, a purpose or set of purposes...to overcome the centrifugal tendencies. Externally, the state-area functions as a unit area in friendly or unfriendly relations with other state-areas, relations that may be classified as territorial, economic, political and strategic. Its specific relations with any outside area may involve a complex of all these and further they are interrelated to its similar relations with all other outside areas in a world system which forms a single whole. The study of these interrelations among state-areas is primarily a study in space relationships among unit-areas, a system that must be sufficiently flexible....

In his 'functional approach' Hartshorne appears to have combined 'processual inferences' from structural elements, with that of some behavioural elements, notably the 'state-idea'. Undoubtedly, the functional approach heralded a new era in the politico-geographical scholarship, and for years to come it dominated the subfield. It tended to strengthen the idiographic tradition in political geography, drawing much from what is called 'neo-Kantianism.'

However, Hartshorne's functional approach simply considers the sovereign state only for its application whereas the approach could not be successfully applied to the analysis of 'dependent' or 'protectorate territory', or to any other types of political territories/ regions, other than the 'state'. Hartshorne could not specify what really constitutes the state-idea? What are its ingredients and variables, and how to map and measure its spatial dimension? Hartshorne does not clearly distinguish between the state-idea and the national-idea? Are they same or different? Is the national-idea necessary for the state-idea or vice versa or not at all? There are some states where the state-idea stands in contrast to the national-idea, e.g., South Africa; the former Soviet Union, India and others. Similarly, it is not necessary that the *raison d'etre* should reflect the state-idea or vice versa.

Large number of states which have appeared in the post-1945 period do not seem to have developed the state-idea, but they continue to hold the same *raison d'etre* which their colonial masters had cultivated. India is the best example where no state-idea, unique to its state-area has developed but its *raison d'etre* reflects the colonial legacy. The Republic of South Africa is another example, which has a *raison d'etre* without a state-idea. It is not necessary that all States should have the state-idea and *raison d'etre*. There cannot be any universal validity to the state-idea-*raison d'etre* model. At best, the model can be applied only to the core states of the world economy.

However, the Hartshorne's model seems to have provided an alternative approach to Jean Gottmann who developed a particular theory of political integration in an article entitled, "The Political Partitioning of Our World: An Attempt at Analysis", published in *World Politics* in 1952. The theory of the political partitioning seems to have been based on the philosophy of exceptionalism, as it is particularly based on the analysis of the unique and the particular.

Gottmann's Political Partitioning Model

...Political world is a limited one; it extends only over the space accessible to men. Accessibility is the determining factor; areas to which men have no access do not have any political standing or problem. ...Partitioning thus results from accessibility; all the vast globe was partitioned as it was discovered and mapped. The political units or territories, as they emerged, acquire a position in space which became and remained a major characteristic of each unit. A position is not a simple thing, easily describable....

...Every position in our partitioned space can be termed unique.... The uniqueness of its territory's position provides each country with a unique historical background. The uniqueness of a geographical position is indeed essentially a political product, which means a work of man—all the more so as it is the accessibility of space to man which causes its political partitioning and makes of it organized, differentiated space.

...Relations between one compartment of this space and the others cannot exist unless there is movement across the limits of the territory considered.... The extent of accessibility is determined by an analysis of the existing status of traffic, communications, transportation and trade. The French language describes this set of movement across space by the very useful word 'circulation'. It encompasses all the variety, the complexity and the fluidity of the exchanges developing throughout the world. Movement seems...to cover the flow of people, armies, material goods, capital, messages, and ideas across the space open to men's activities, in all directions and for all purposes. Let us use the expression 'movement factor' to describe all these processes.

...Analysis of the movement factor as it applies to a position, whether point or area, helps us to understand easily the motives and imperatives of the policies and political problems focused on or emanating from that position. Movement, however, makes for fluidity and change...briefest glance at history demonstrates how migration, travel, trade relations, evaluation of transportation techniques, cultural relations, and so forth, have constantly brought about changes inside the countries participating in them. These changes inevitably create fluidity and instability. If the movement factor has made for change and instability, it has always encountered an established order as well, favouring a certain pattern of flow and resisting change....

The abstract strength of an existing order is rooted in the spirit of the nations involved. Spirit is another difficult notion, the use of which may appear rather unscientific. What it signifies here is a psychological attitude resulting from a combination of actual events with beliefs deeply rooted in the people's mind...the word 'iconography' to describe the whole system of symbols in which people believe. These symbols are many and varied. A national iconography...encompasses the national flag, the proud memories of past history as well as the principles of prevailing religion, the generally accepted rules of economics, the established social hierarchy, the heroes quoted in the schools, the classic authors. ...A national iconography usually stops at a boundary: the frontier line is in grave danger.... For any group of people, the iconography is the common cherished heritage. It is a powerful factor and it fights for stability and resist change...two main factors or groups of factors—'movement' and 'iconography'—which oppose one another in the play of forces constantly shaping and reshaping the political map.

...We find an unbroken thread woven through the history of practically every region of the world which shows how the movement factor and the local iconography combined to support the establishment of political authority over a certain area. The fluidity of the political map shaped with the help of such complicated and varied forces may be easier to understand once a method of analysis is applied which follows these two dominant leads: what...called the movement factor and the iconography. ...An understanding of how iconography and movement combine to shape political authority and limit it in space may perhaps help in the further analysis of the world's partitioning.

Like Hartshorne, Gottmann also hypothesizes two dominant sets of forces—circulation and iconography—which act upon the coherence of the political unit. He identifies iconography as a force for stability and coherence, whereas circulation (or the movement factor) leads to political change. He argues that circulation and iconography are not always in spatial conflict, rather they focus at crossroads, though it would seem that circulation usually comes first, creating crossroads, and the iconography fixes itself at the point so established. In fact, the political integration is the interplay of these two forces.

There are similarities and differences between the ideas of Hartshorne and Gottmann. While Hartshorne recognizes circulation as a means of overcoming the physical barriers to political integration, to Gottmann it creates instability and leads to change. Similarly, iconography can be recognized in Hartshorne's theory as one of the centrifugal forces and it does not always make for the stability but to Gottmann iconography leads to coherence and unity, and above all it resists movement and change.

However, Gottmann has identified the basic ingredients and variables of iconography, and it is clear from his identification of iconography, that it is nothing but the 'national-idea' which may be one of the ingredients of the state-idea. However, iconography is not necessarily the state-idea. Gottmann's approach, somehow appears to be applicable to West European countries or the countries which form the core of the world economy. Some of the larger states of the world always have the problem of conflict between the national-idea which is historical and tradition-bound and draws inward and the state-idea which is politics-bound and looks outward. The Soviet Union disintegrated because of the sustained conflict between the Russian national-idea and the Soviet state-idea. There can be conflicts of lesser and greater iconographies, of sectionalism and nationalism, of national and international iconographies. Another of Hartshorne's ideas, that of the Naturity of states, expresses a state-area coextensive with the national iconography".

While Hartshorne was making an appeal for a more functional approach, he also recognized that many answers to the questions he raised were to be found in the past, hence, many aspects in the evolution of a political region could not be ignored. The main problem was to find an approach that assured relevance of material in tracing past events and processes. Stephen B. Jones was to fill this need, and he came out with a paper entitled, "A Unified Field Theory of Political Geography", published in the *Annals of the Association of American Geographers*, 1954. This theory (or 'mental gadget' as Jones called it) is concerned with the evolution of politically organized space and is built upon the ideas of Whittlesey, Hartshorne, on several interesting conceptual statements of Gottmann concerning the evolution of political partitioning based on accessibility, and by Karl Deutsch.

Jones' Unified Field Theory: Idea-area Chain

The theory simply states that 'idea' and 'state' are two ends of a chain. The hyphen with which Hartshorne connects them represents the other links of the chain. One of the links is Gottmann's circulation which...shall call movement.

The chain is as follows: political idea-decision-movement-field-political area. This 'chain' should be visualized as a chain of lakes or basins and not an iron chain of separate links. The basins interconnect at one level, so that whatever enters, one will spread to all the others.

Political idea, in this sequence, means more than just the state-idea. It means any political idea, it might be the idea of the state or it might be the idea of a speed limit on a country road. It might merely be a gregarious instinct, not consciously expressed. War begins in the minds of men, and so do all other politics...A favourable decision is a necessary prerequisite to action. A formal parliamentary decision is not necessarily meant...Though most of the fishermen in the basins of idea and decision are political scientists, Gottmann and Hartshorne, both geographers, enter them when they speak of iconography and the idea of state.

Both political scientists and geographers have studied the phenomena at the other end of the chain—political area. This term is used very inclusively to mean any politically organized area, whether a national state, a dependent area, a subdivision of a state, or an administrative region or district. It includes all three categories of areas listed by Fesler—general governmental areas, special or limited purpose governmental areas, and field service areas. The one common characteristic of all political areas is that they have recognized limits, though not necessarily linear or permanent. An administrative centre within the area is common, but not universal.

Movement...is essentially Gottmann's circulation. What new twist is given comes from placing it in a chain of concepts relating it to decisions. Every political decision involves movement in one way or another. There may be exceptions...Some decisions create movement, some change it, some restrict it. Some create a new kind of movement to replace or to control the old. The movement may not involve great numbers of men or great quantities of matter—it may consist only of radio waves—but usually persons and things move as a result of political decisions. These politically-induced movements may be thought of as 'circulation fields'. The movement of state highway patrolmen produce a field, shipments of military-aid materials produce a field, the despatch and delivery of farm-subsidy checks produce a field.

The existence of a political area, field, movement, or decision conditions what may take place in the basin lying idea-ward... Benjamin Thomas has shown how the political area of Idaho, created upon a flimsy and essentially negative idea in the first place, conditioned further political thoughts and decisions until the present Idaho-idea is as firm as any.

The essential characteristic of a field in physics, is not movement but spatial variation in force. The gravitational field exists even when no apples fall. Since we are not bound to a physical analogy, this distinction need not greatly concern us. However, it may sometimes be important to keep in mind that movements and fields are not necessarily identical...Movement to polls creates a field but it is not identical with the field of the party powers. A field exists in time as well as in space. Applying the ideas of Whittlesey, we may say it has a time dimension as well as a spaee dimension....

Application to Political Areas

Application of this theory to a case of one new national state is fairly simple. Zionism is the idea, the Balfour Declaration the conspicuous decision, permitting migration and other movements. A field of settlement, governmental activity, and war leads to the State of Israel. Such telegraphic brevity oversimplifies history, but the theory seems to fit. For a state with a longer and more complicated evolution, history could not be so readily compressed. The theory provides a path between geographical and political study...It does not reduce political geography to five easy steps. It does not permit world politics to be shown on a chart in five column captioned as 'idea', 'decision' and so forth. It may, however, provide some intellectual clarification and it may prove a handy way of working back and forth among historical, political and geographical ideas and date.

...the process of national integration whether looked at by geographers... can be interpreted as a process of changing field. Conceivably, the outlines of the political area may not change. The former colony of Burma is perhaps enroute to becoming a true nation-state without change of boundaries or capital, but a study of the political fields would show changes.

One virtue of the field theory is that it is not confined to politically organized areas. It is applicable without difficulty to an unorganized area like the Mediterranean; which is undoubtedly a political field...decisions may affect the Mediterranean as a whole and may create or control movement over the entire sea. The ideas may vary: Mussolini's dream of a new Roman empire, Britain's concern with sea command, the American strategy of the containment of communism...The accumulation of decisions created a field, the sea conditioned it.

In the case of administrative areas, a political area may arise from a decision with little or possibly no intervening movement. A new government agency may lay out its field service areas before it actually engages in any actions. In some cases, analysis will show that these field service areas reflect pre-existing fields, such as the areas used by other branches of government or known fields of economic activity and in many cases existing boundaries will be followed. It is possible, however, that an administrative area might spring directly from a decision, and reflect no exiting field. TVA may be an example.

There is nothing deterministic about the idea-area chain. A given idea might lead to a variety of areas, a given area might condition a variety of ideas...study of Micronesia under four rulers demonstrates this point. Although the area ruled was not identical in all four eras, it was basically the same. The number of possible uses for these small islands was limited. Nevertheless, the four rulers—Spain, Germany, Japan and the United Sates—made different choices. Then fields were different in kind and intensity. If one insists...that a theory must be able to predict specific behaviour, then the field theory may not deserve its name. With no theory whatsoever, a well-informed person with some map-sense could have predicted many American problems and decisions in Micronesia. As a guide to study, however, the field theory is applicable to such cases.

Studies of National Power

Studies of national power may also be fitted into the field theory... Lasswell and Kaplan define power as "participation in the making of decisions". If power is participation in the making of decisions, if power is necessary before an idea can produce movement, then we can easily fit power into our theory. Hartshorne distinguished between political geography and the study of power...a geographer might sometimes tackle the question of "how strong is a state"? If no one else had done so, but that in so doing he was "migrating into a field whose core and purpose is not geography, but military and political strategy". That power is linked with decision supports Hartshorne, to the extent that geography has been more closely associated with the other end of the chain, but our aim is to pull political science and geographer together, not to separate them. If power is more concentrated in the basin of decision, it is by no means absent in the others.

Boundaries, and Capital Cities

The unified field theory fits boundary studies into the general pattern of political geography. A boundary is, of course, a line between two political areas but it is also a line in a region....The boundary region is truly a field in which the line between the political areas conditions much of the circulation. A boundary field may even be or become a political area as in the case of buffer states and frontier provinces.

Studies of capital cities may be expressed in a field-theory terms.... The idea of, or need for central administration leads to a decision on the site of the capital. The choice is conditioned by the field and in turn distorts or recreates the field. Once the capital is chosen and the field about it established, many further decisions and movements are conditioned, leading in most cases to the creation of a primate city much larger than any other in the country.

Not only capitals but other cities may also be brought into the scope of the theory...many of the problems of a growing city arise from the fact that its circulation expands faster than its iconography. The metropolitan district outgrows the political limits and vested local interests and loyalties make political expansion difficult. A sort of 'metropolitan-idea' may develop leading usually to functional authorities rather than to political integration. In a few words, the urban problem is to make the political area fit the field.

Kinetic and Dynamic Fields

Since politics consists of conflicts and the resolution of conflicts...these fundamental activities must be expressible in field terms. There are conflicts of ideas but they do not amount to much until they are embodied in decisions that create or obstruct movement. (It may be wise to re-emphasize that 'movement' includes such things of little bulk as messages and money. A restriction on foreign exchange is restriction on movement). Fields may be in contact, but not in conflict if the movement is merely kinetic. But if there is a dynamic aspect, conflict often will arise. For example, New York city's growing need for water forces its activity in this respect to be dynamic, bringing conflict with other claimants to Deleware River supplies. The international oil industry is inherently dynamic since new sources must be discovered. The result is potential conflict, sometimes anticipated and resolved at least pro tempore. The relations of political dynamics to such fundamentals as resource needs and population pressures have of course been repeatedly studied, and the present theory does little more than incorporate them into the concept of the field.

There are no upper or lower limits on the magnitude of an idea. Man thinks easily of the world government and can dream of spaceships and planetary empires. There are upper limits on decisions, movements, fields and political areas though these limits change with events...such ideas as the great religions, nationalism, liberalism, and communism have, insofar as they could produce decisions and movements, created fields. Whittlesey has shown how man's ideas of space have changed through primal and regional to worldwide conceptions, ideas, fields of exploration, in some cases political areas have expanded, reached above and below the earth's surface, and made better use of time....Toynbee holds that every culture tends to evolve its 'universal state', a domain roughly co-extensive with the culture. If this is true, then we have another example of the chain from idea through a vast number of decisions...and movements, creating a field and tending towards a political area which would be the universal state of that culture.

Utility of the Theory

The unified field theory according to S.B. Jones, satisfies the first requirement of a successful theory, i.e., a compact description. It may reduce the apparent diversity of aims and methods in political geography...it may help to unify not only the theories of political geography but political theories in general. It may help complete the tie between morphology and function, between region and process. It may show a relationship between grand ideas and the earth's surface.

This unified field theory can provide no more than a clue to explanation, if it even attains that success. It can hardly provide an ultimate answer to any question. But to relate several disciplines, to show connections, may give hints. The user of this theory is at least sure to be warned against single-factor explanations and be led to seek contributions from sister sciences.

It is as a tool for better work that...the chain of words in which theory is expressed constitutes a sort of check list.. by means of which one can orient oneself and tell when one should explore further. To return to the analogy of a chain of basins, one knows through which basin one has entered and where one can travel back and forth. If one begins with the study of a political area, ideas lie at the other end. If a study begins with movement, the scholar knows he should explore in both directions. For some of the basins one may need pilots from other disciplines but at least one has a map of the chain. The theory tells students of geography and politics what...they need to learn from each other, what each has to add, but not how each fences himself off.

Another possible effect of this theory upon geographical work is that it may inspire the making of new types of studies and the compiling of new kinds of maps. Many maps either show or imply a field, but with the idea-chain in mind...The theory is 'geographical' in that it makes mappable through the concept of field, the results of ideas and decisions that are...not mappable.

The idea-area chain may unite in one concept two main parts of geographical theory, the possibilist and regionalist views. Possibilism focuses on main choices among environmental possibilities. Choices are decisions. They imply ideas and must lead to movements. The regional or chronological approach, beginning with the study of areas, can lead through movement to decisions and ideas.

Finally, the unified field theory may have utility outside academic circles. It seems possible that the concept can be used as an aid in evaluating diplomatic and strategic ideas and plans...diplomacy and strategy begin with ideas, lead to decisions, result in movement and therefore, produce fields. In reverse, diplomacy and strategy are conditioned by the political areas and fields of the earth which limit the possible decisions and practical ideas.

However, the literature of contemporary political geography is wanting in methodological approaches by which general theory and hypotheses can be developed and tested. The four traditional approaches in political geography discussed above, have offered conceptual frameworks for looking at problems rather than specific methodological directions that can be used in theory building. What is needed is a methodology to link effectively political process and its spatial attributes—methodology that, having identified a specific political process, can pinpoint spatially significant phenomena which relate to this process, can observe the impact of these phenomena within some control context, and can correct one process or parts thereof to another...to suggest a model that, though presented as descriptive, may with further research be developed into a normative one.

Works of political geographers as Whittlesey, Hartshorne, Gottmann and Jones are contained in the conceptual building blocks for advancing theory. Whittlesey's emphasis on the law-landscape impress, Hartshorne's linking of functionalism to geographical space, Gottmann's recognition of the disconfirmity between political ideas and political area, and Jones' attempt to develop a unified field theory for linking political ideas and political area are the underpinnings of modern political geographical thought. However, with the exception of Jones, none attempted to suggest a holistic approach, applicable to all levels of the political hierarchy. Moreover, the limited concern with the methodological design may have inhibited the development of useful expository models based on these contributions which could, in turn, have led to normative model.Thus, Saul B. Cohen and Lewis D. Rosenthal have provided an alternative approach to the study of political geography, in an article entitled, "A Geographical Model for Political System Analysis", published in the *Geographical Review* in 1971.

Political Systems Model

They contend that political geographers turn more directly to political processes and to the spatial consequences than has heretofore been the case, and that their efforts be cast within a political geographical systems framework. Process is the key to the spatial arrangements and relationships with which the geographer is uniquely concerned. This is not to say that the political geographer should be less geographical or spatial, but that without more attention to the political...Explanation of areal arrangements and landscape is the object of the geographical study of political processes. Whatever predictive value the model developed here may have applied not to the political process, but to the geographical consequences of political process, Political geography is concerned with the spatial attributes of political process.

Political Process

A major point of departure for analysis of political process is the 'political system' within which process operates. Indeed, the concepts of process and system are inseparable. The bases for political systems are the societal forces that shape political institutions and the transactions through which the institutions operate, together with the pertinent environment. In such a context, the political system can be viewed as the end product of the processes by which man organizes himself politically in his particular social and physical environment and in response to outside political systems with their unique environments.

Other elements of the framework of analysis are the 'locational perspective' and the 'open/closed political system'. The locational perspectives in which the political system is viewed by those both within and outside it, is essential to the understanding and the analysis of political process. Where the system is assumed to be (on the local, regional, or global scale) has a great deal to do with the strategy for shaping the system, both by those who guide it and by those who would try to change or otherwise affect it.

Locational perspective is related to perceived needs for external links or connectivity—that is, the degree to which the system is open or closed. Although no system, be it physical, economic or political, ever achieves a completely open or completely closed state, political systems can be classified according to their position along a spectrum, ranging from most nearly open to most nearly closed.

The relationship of the political system to the landscape is direct and far-reaching which may hypothesize that the open system molds landscapes that are the products of interdependence. Patterns of agglomeration, features of specialized resource use (intensivity and fast rates of change), port-of-entry build-ups, internationally diffused features and symbols—these are some of the landscape consequences of the open system. The closed system molds landscapes that are the products of self-containment. Patterns of uniform spread, features of diversified resource use (extensivity and slower, more even rates of change), large numbers of interior central-place facilities, nationally diffused features and symbols—these are consequences of the closed system. Viewing a system within its open or closed context, then provides a benchmark from which to interpret and forecast landscape change.

Since open/closed systems are produced by the movement of men, goods and ideas, the system can be measured through indexes such as visa and immigration policies, diplomatic and other political ties, tariff and trade practices and the use of communications media.

Time scale is implicit in any discussion of process, not just with reference to the open/closed system of locational perspective. In considering relationships between the process and spatial attributes, there are several different time dimensions. The introduction of the transaction and its diffusion from place to place may be short term. The resulting area formation and area interaction, and the attendant changes in basic political structure, take considerably longer. Finally, the relationship of changing political structure, as a process in effecting change in their societal forces, and attendant fundamental landscape change, would take still longer.

...Political processes are inseparable from the overriding societal forces by which man orders his political life. Formal political institutions and social structures such as kinship, class, status, authority, communication, elitism, and bureaucracy are mechanisms (aided by symbols and myths) by which man makes operational such forces as nationalism, internationalism, federalism, capitalism, socialism, democracy, totalitarianism, imperialism, colonization, tribalism, religion and racism. These are examples of societal forces; when such forces, or the ideas and beliefs behind them; relate directly to the political system they become appropriately defined as ideology. Although some of the forces are primarily political (nationalism, democracy, totalitarianism), others that are commonly thought of as economic or cultural are implemented through the political structures of a society and are therefore, included.

By casting political process within the context of societal forces, it becomes operationally feasible to view individual transactions as interconnected episodes. Thus, the transactions dealing with the prevention of land fragmentation may be viewed within the principal forces of feudalism and democracy. Legal systems of premogeniture and land consolidation are interlinked with kinship and class structure, reflecting such human drives as self-preservation, authority, security and territorial affinity, and are instruments that have preserved or changed the social order. In the case of premogeniture, this law of undivided inheritance by one principal heir maintained class structure in feudalism by warding off dilution of wealth and power. The same law when applied to small farmers and peasants, fulfilled a secondary function of guarding against uneconomical farm plots.

Land consolidation laws, such as those promulgated in north-western Europe since the mid-eighteenth century, helped to change kinship and class structure by altering relationships of individuals to the village, and to the family. Most consolidation laws served to change the social order, encouraging democracy directly by aiding the emergence of an independent farm class, or indirectly by encouraging economic progress in the hope of maintaining political stability.

Concern with overriding societal forces, then...can find a focus in the study of acts of governing that flow from these forces, the act of governing, whereby man applies power, usually through law, to shape the institutions by which the governing process operates, is the key to law-landscape analysis. Significant subsets of governance are elections and other form of leadership legitimation and succession, the degree of compliance with rules of law and tradition, and the perpetuation of military, social-class and trade-union elites. These acts are made operational by specific political transactions, legal, quasi-legal, and extra-legal, the spatial characteristics of which form the analysis thread.

Spatial Attributes

A basic objective of analyzing process in a spatial context is to examine man's behaviour in space. The law-landscape theme is viewed, therefore, as a reflection of the broader political process-spatial attributes theme. We may be concerned with man's activity in space...or with man's impact on space, which eventually may lead to landscapes with changed or different characteristics whose aggregation will shape or reshape political areas.

'Spatial' is defined as the distributional patterns of political processes and the spatial relations of these patterns with pertinently related phenomena, using space in its sense as a boundless medium. Such patterns and relations form unique 'political action areas' or fields of action. In the political context such action may or may not be synonymous with 'political area'. Indeed, though the action area may not often be identical with the political area at the outset, the interaction of political process and landscape impact comes to a close when action field and political areas are identical. In the usual sequence, it is a major objective for the central authority to establish eventually a state of conformity between political action area and the original political area, if for no other reason than that lack of conformity is commonly accepted as a challenge to the effectiveness and legitimacy of the government.

Jones made no specific reference to the issue of area interaction in his unified field theory but at a later date he did consider area interaction or repercussion as an element worthy of treatment. In the present discussion, area interaction arising out of the spatial impact of political decision is a major element in the analysis—an output of area change. The dialectic in the process of action and reaction (either internally or externally) applies both to a political action area and to a political area. Thus, in connection with the development of a political action area, one can anticipate the development of a 'counteraction area'. A counteraction area reflects the political efforts of any counter force—individual or group, formal or informal, centralized or dispersed—to limit the extent of an emergent political action area or to counter it.

The force and extent of political action areas and counteraction areas are expressed...by various measures of political socialization, i.e., attitudes toward and participation in, political institutions and other expressions of political system. What creates an action area is the acceptance of political policy by groups that count politically and the attendant social and economic consequences. In the medium run specific landscape amendment, and in the long run general landscape, change become the output of the political process input. One can hope to forecast the landscape changes attendant on specific political transactions, given either a deductive theory or an empirical-inductive base. The accumulation of a number of landscape changes, stemming from one or a series of reinforcing processes, may even create the basis for converting a political action area into a new political area by becoming a part of political myth and eventually, by influencing ideology to include territorial annexation (e.g., 'Germanization' of the Sudetenland, which, after annexation in 1938, became a Reich District, Sudetengau).

The Model

Figures 3.1 and 3.2 attempt to show man in his political role in society and the relation of that role (as expressed in political ideology, political structure, and political transaction) to the land (places, areas and the general landscape) and to indicate the consequences of that relation in the formation of political system.

Figure 3.1 illustrates the interactions between the several facets of main political role and the multidimensional aspects of the land. For example, the interaction between political transaction and place (defined as a locational attribute) is a building block in the formation of political area, and the relationship between political structure and political area (defined as having

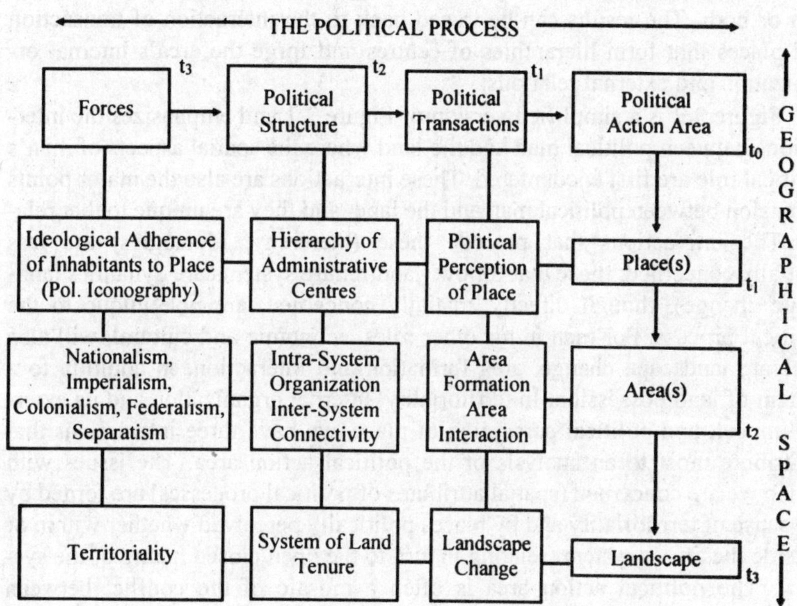

Figure 3.1: The Political System with Time-scale (After S.B. Cohen and L.D. Rosenthal, 1971)

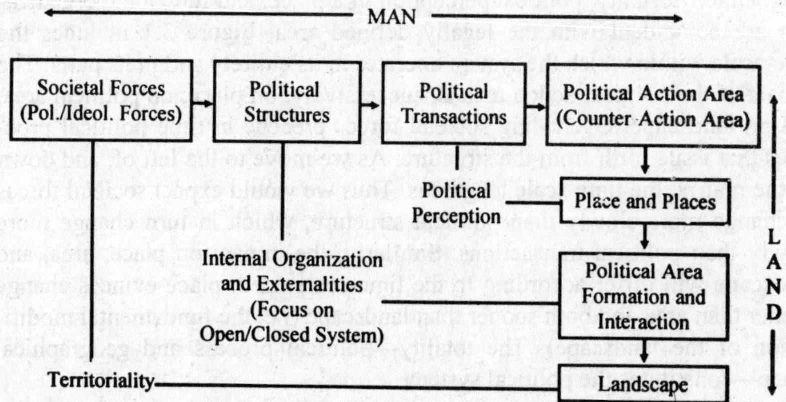

Figure 3.2: The Political System (After S.B. Cohen and L.D. Rosenthal, 1971)

content and organization) is expressed through area formation or area interaction or both. The results can be traced back to the interaction of transaction and places that form hierarchies of centres and forge the area's internal organization and external relations.

Figure 3.2 is a simplified version of Figure 3.1 and emphasizes the interactions between political man and the land where the spatial aspects of man's political role are first encountered. These interactions are also the major points of tension between political man and the land, and they are unique to that relation.The interactions that precede these (hierarchy, ideologies) are less spatially concerned; those that follow (land-tenure systems are dynamics landscape change), though directly spatially concerned, are not unique to the political process. For man in his other roles, economic and cultural, will also generate landscape change, area formation and interaction, in addition to a system of land possession. In territoriality, internal organization and its external impact, and political perception of place, we have three interactions that contribute most to an analysis of the political action area. The issues with which we are concerned (spatial attributes of political processes) are forged by the sense of territoriality and by places politically perceived whether within or outside the area's system (relating in turn to the open/closed nature of the system). The political action area is often a mosaic of the conflict between territoriality and political place perception, and the action area may be confined to, or may go beyond, the original political area and the system or systems under which that area is organized.

Dissolution of the political area or resolution of the conflict occurs when the area (or counteraction area) coincides with the original political area, that is, when territoriality, political perception of a place, and functional organization are coincident with the legally defined area. Figure 3.1 includes the time-scale within which the system operates in its entirety and in its parts. The impact of the political action area is, successively, on place, on political area, and on landscape. Overriding societal forces precede in time political processes that issue forth from the structure. As we move to the left of, and down on the matrix, the time-scale lengthens. Thus we would expect societal forces to change more slowly than political structure, which in turn change more slowly than political transactions. Similarly, the impact on place, area, and landscape will differ according to the time-scale used: place evinces change sooner than area and both sooner than landscape (i.e. the fundamental modification of the landscape). The totality—political process and geographical space—constitutes the political system.

Although it is true that each aspect of the total system or matrix, interacts with every other so that political transactions amend political structures, and that these in turn alter the value system of a society, our concern here is man or society perceiving and acting on the land that he or it occupies or covets. Figure 3.2 emphasizes the concern with the political action area and its components: the long-term impact of man on the land is subordinated to a short-term analysis—the transitional relation between man and the land.

A major problem in measuring interaction between process and geographical space in the context of political systems is that within a political system landscape and area changes may take place as a result of population growth, economies of scale, and so on, regardless of political inputs. The political input that we trace must, then, affect the 'rate' of change in landscape, whether this rate formerly was zero (a static equilibrium state) or a steady rate of growth or decline (a dynamic equilibrium state).

Cohen and Rosenthal conclude their model with a case study of Venezuela, where two dominant forces—nationalism and social democracy—provide vantage points for the study of the impact of process on geographical space. In the context of laws relating to petroleum exploitation and immigration various aspects of Venezuela's spatial organization are examined. The conclusion is that the Venezuelan case confirms the law-landscape thread as the key to the analysis of the political system. For example, "the hierarchical role of administrative centres and the political significance of place are essential characteristics in the understanding of place. Political conflict, as expressed through rivalry between state capitals (Ciudad Boliver) and new development centres (Ciudad Guayana) over where to build bridges, to locate factories, or to build up the strength of local political parties, exemplifies the operation of the political process in space" (Fig. 3.3).

The political system model suggests that the law-landscape association remains to be added on the focus for the analysis of the effect of political process on the organization of territorial space.

Contemporary Relevance to these Approaches

There is no doubt that the theses of Hartshorne, Gottmann and Jones on political integration dominated political geography for over a generation, being faithfully reproduced in many books and literatures. Hence, they cannot be merely dismissed as inconsequential, they must be reviewed and evaluated to produce a critical understanding of their strengths and weaknesses.

As Taylor in1985 puts it: There are two basic criticisms of the integration theory. First, it focuses attention on the individual state. Analysis is directed towards separate treatment of each state presented with some relatively abstract concept to be applied to case studies. Such a state-by-state process under-values the existence of the inter-state system and concentrates explanation at the state level. Hence, the political geographers have been enthusiastic purveyors of the error of developmentalism. The second criticism relates to

Figure 3.3 The Venezuelan Case: The Model Illustrated (Cohen & Rosenthal, 1971)

← THE POLITICAL PROCESS →

Forces	*Political Structures*	*Political Transactions*	*Political Action Area*
1. Independent political and economic development—freedom from foreign controls	1. Centralized federal system	1. Immigration law, exit tax, expropriation law	1. Limiting the impact of foreigners within the national borders
2. Orderly political succession	2. National political parties	2. Petroleum law	2. Extending the impact of petroleum beyond the national borders
3. Freedom of the individual	3. Quasi-political institutions: Pro-Venezuela, CVP, Petroleum Workers Union		
Ideological Adherence Of Inhabitants To Place	*Hierarchy Of Administrative Centers*	*Political Perception*	*Places*
a. Love of the land, prounion bias of Accion Democratica Party	a. Strong central government with increased delegated authority to state governments	a. Limitation of Caracas primacy by Acción Democratica Party	a. Caracas
b. "Sowing the petroleum"—investing in refineries and petrochemicals, restricting size of foreign concessions	b. Polycentric controls over oil industry (competition between Maracaibo and Morón)	b. Desire for national refining center	b. Morón, Curaçao
c. The "New Frontier"—appeal of new planned city, centralized planning of regions	c. Corporación Venezolana de Guayana planning headquarters in Caracas and operational headquarters in Guayana	c. Appeal and patronage of frontier dynamic	c. Ciudad Guayana
d. Pro-Venezuelan economic nationalism, Venezuelan democracy as political answer to Cuban totalitarianism	d. Reduction of influence of regional garrisons	d. Pride in local resort facilities and fear of Cuba	d. Macuto resort strip, Puerto Cabello naval base
Ideology	*System Organization and Connectivity*	*Area Formation—Area Interaction*	*Areas*

↑ GEOGRAPHICAL SPACE ↓

1. Social democracy	a. Acción Democratica political concentration on rural areas to offset rightist and leftist strength in Caracas	a. Urbanization of outlying rural villages, establishing factory compounds outside Caracas	a. Greater Caracas (spillover from Federal District into adjoining states)
2. Nationalism	b. CVP and Petroleum Workers Union	b. Maracaibo-Barinas-Morón triangle of oil industry activities	b. Caribbean coast, , offshore islands, and disputed area of Guyana
	c. CORDIPLAN and regional corporations	c. Competitive interaction with state of Boliver prods establishment of Corporación Venezolana de los Andes	c. Regional authority-urban planning region (Corporación Venezolana de Guayana)
	d. Governmental hotel corporation, democratization of navy elite	d. Centralized control of armed forces, links to Caracas through weekend and longer term vacations	d. Macuto and extended Caribben coastal strip
Territoriality	***System Of Land Tenure***	***Landscape Change***	***Landscape***
a. Lure of the big city	a. Mixed private and public investment	a. Large-scale public housing, retailing and industrial expansion, highway extension	a. Reduction of European influence—Modernization
b. Desire to regain former territories	b. Public ownership of mineral lands	b. Oil and gas pipelines, refineries, domestic marketing facilities	b. "Americanization"—modernization
c. Pioneering myth	c. Replacement of *latifundia* with cooperative system	c. Irrigation and power works, highways, steel plant	c. Instituto Agrario Nacional farm colonies, new city
d. Nationalizing the coast	d. Public ownership of beaches, surveillance of territorial waters	d. Tourist hotels, naval installations	d. "Riviera"flavour, ports, harbor and land installations

↑ GEOGRAPHICAL SPACE ↓

The System: Toward the median of the spectrum, moving from more open to more closed
The Perspective: Caribbean and Hemispheric

Hartshorne's assertion that integration—the organization of a territory—is the fundamental purpose of the state. It is treated as self-evident that the state operates for itself. But the balance of forces that are provided to explain the success or failure of a state in its prime purpose are abstracted out of the social formation in which the states exist. At this point of the argument it is useful to repeat that 'all organization is bias'. The establishment and disestablishment of states represent victories for some social groups and defeat for others. This is what it tried to convey of federalism but it is equally true of all enterprises at state building. It is for this reason that one cannot banish vertical integration of social groups from our political geography as Hartshorne proposes. The state can only be understood as a response to the needs of certain groups at the expense of other groups. Integration is a process that can be looked back at with pride by the winners but we should not forget the losers in such conflict.

However, Jones' unified field theory appears to be more relevant to the understanding of the evolution of political areas/regions in the periphery rather than those in the core areas in the world economy.

The political system analysis model, developed by Cohen and Rosenthal, seems to be intrinsically based on the philosophy of exceptionalism within the purview of the possibilistic paradigm. Since the model suggests for the political processes and to the spatial consequences, which in itself reveals (i) the uniqueness of the spatial consequences and arrangements as a result of the political process, which in turn, manifests (ii) possible human responses, that people have considerable discretion to choose between them. Political process may be variable, depending on the level of human responses. Spatial attributes of political process also reveal exceptionalism/uniqueness which are man's creation (political). So the model is possibilistic with a regionalistic approach.

However, Jackson and Samuels observe: "The very concept of system in modern social science militates against the ideas of viewing phenomena in terms of their separate attributes for the thought process involved in the study of attributes distracts the student's mind from the essence, that is, the system in the organization or phenomenon involved. This naturally inhibits the development of general theories of organization, and in the case of geography tends to mould investigation either in terms of the geographical determinants of given processes or alternatively in terms of the spatial impress of the processes involved/concerned. This, however, is not to deny the methodological sophistication of the model presented, and the author's emphasis on interconnectivity and feedback." In the words of Muir, "the model is sufficiently broad to encompass the overall political man-environment relationship and to embrace existing political geographical concepts such as Whittlesey's law-landscapes thread, territoriality, political space perception and decision making".

From idiographic characteristics of Cohen and Rosenthal's model for political systems analysis, we move to another model, developed by E.W. Soja in 1974, in an article entitled, "A Paradigm for the Geographical Analysis of Political System", published in K.R. Cox, D.R. Reynolds and S. Rokhan edited book, *Locational Approaches to Power and Conflict*.

Soja's Analysis of Political Systems

Soja pointed out that the proposed paradigm can best be viewed as a temporary basin for introducing some compatibility to the diverse research of political geographers. Central to the organizational structure of this paradigm is the integrating concept of a 'spatial system' as set out in the systems approach of Berry. A spatial system consists of places, the attributes of these places and the interactions both between places and between their attributes. Soja has developed his model on the Berry's framework. The essential characteristics of his model are as follows:

(i) The central focus of geography as a social science is upon the spatial organization of human society. Geography is distinguished from the other social sciences by its characteristically spatial perspective and the sets of themes and concepts this perspective generates. At the same time, however, it is closely associated with the other social sciences in sharing a common focus upon man and society.

(ii) The major inputs to geographical analysis consist of the attributes of locations in space (either points, lines or areas) and the interactions between these locations. Each of these two kinds of inputs gives rise to distinctive modes of geographical inquiry. Areal analysis stresses the attributes of locations, the association between these attributes, and their influence on the formal organization of space. Spatial analysis on the other hand, focuses upon the interaction between location, the relationships between various kinds of spatial interactions, and their impact on the functional organization of space. Although it is conceptually valuable to recognize these distinctions between these two modes of analysis, most geographers combine them in their research, drawing upon the attributes of location to explain patterns of interaction and vice versa.

(iii) Areal and spatial analyses are tightly woven together in the concept of a spatial system—a segment of space (real or hypothetical) which is formally and functionally organized through a patterning of attributes and structuring of interaction. A system of settlements or central places, e.g., would consist of location tied together by certain shared or complementary attributes (e.g., size proximate location, types of services performed, socio-cultural features) and the structuring of interactions between them(e.g., flow of money, influence, people, goods and information). A spatial political system could similarly be viewed as a cluster of location or unit areas integrated through the areal association of key attributes (including cultural and attitudinal variables) and the intervening of interactional patterns.

(iv) Spatia! systems and their components can be studied over time to ascertain their dynamic properties. Such a developemental or evolutionary perspective, closely associated in geography with the study of spatial diffusion, adds an emphasis on process to the predominantly morphological focus inherent in the earlier discussion. A stress on either form or process, therefore, can exist within both areal and spatial analyses (Fig. 3.3).

Soja further concludes that the contemporary geography has developed a more theoretical orientation. Much of it rests on the assumption that there is an inherent geogprahical order in human society, a spatial anatomy of human behaviour, and societal organization which has regular and discoverable characteristics. Rather than emphasizing the unique character of specific areas, modern geographic research has centred round the search for order and regularity in spatial systems—a search that has spawned an increased interest in the behavioural basis of spatial interaction and organization.

Fundamental to this approach of Soja is the philosophy of positivism, giving an emphasis on model and laws of spatial arrangement, hence a close link with the quantitative revolution. The model, however, suffers from the lack of holism; hence it cannot be applicable in its entirety to the variable character of the earth's political units/regions.

None of the approaches seem to deal with the contemporary worldwide problems and global issues which have become much complicated and complex, particularly after the rise of modern nation-states in the erstwhile colonial areas. Such an approach is desirable which can provide a much longer temporal perspective. "This involves a framework centred upon the capitalist world economy which emerged in Europe in the period after 1450 and expanded to encompass the whole world by 1900. Both Pope Alexander VI in 1492 and President Reagon at Cancun in 1982 are part of this single story." To this P.J. Taylor suggests, for Wallerstein's world-systems approach... This involves both substantive and theoretical addition to the original ideas and criticisms from a range of alternative perspectives. In simplest terms...choice of Wallerstein's framework is based on the fact...most useful for ordering and understanding the subject-matter of political geography.

Wallerstein's World-Systems Approach

The second half of the present century has seen a massive growth in the social sciences. Although firmly based upon European roots, this growth has been largely American-led. The world-systems approach is first and foremost challenge to this modern social science...The challenge is a fundamental one because it questions the whole system of concepts and categories employed by modern social science. This is most clearly seen in their alternative treatment of social change...

Wallerstein, in his world-systems approach*, attempts to combine selectively critical elements of Brandel's materialist history with Frank's neo-Marxist development studies as well as adding several new features to develop a comprehensive 'historical social science'. Here, in this approach, Wallerstein explicitly brings 'history back in' to social science and also with the incorporation of Frank's ideas he attempts to bring geography back in to social science. Quite simply there is more to understanding the world we live in than can be derived from study of the advanced countries of the world in the late twentieth century, however, rigorous or scholarly the conduct of such study is.

Wallerstein challenges modern social science on the following three basic grounds:

1. *The myth of universal laws*: Modern social science is the culmination of a tradition that attempts to develop general laws for all times and places. A well-known example of this is the attempt to equate the decline of the British Empire with the decline of the Roman Empire nearly two millenia earlier. Similarly, assumptions are often made that 'human nature' is universal so that motives identified today in advanced countries can be transferred to other periods and cultures. To this Wallerstein does not retreat into idiographic position emphasizing the uniqueness of events, and he does identify order which is not universal. The important point is to specify the scope of generalization.
2. *The poverty of disciplines*: In the increasing complexity of the modern world with massive growth of state activity, it is becoming increasingly difficult to identify problems as distinctively economic, social or political. By studying events separately in disciplines the type of solutions to problems that can by found is severely curtailed. There is, therefore, increasing awareness that the disciplines are more a hindrance than a help to understanding our world. One reflection of this feeling is the return of the pre-social science concept of 'political economy' with its more holistic tradition. Wallerstein's approach is part of this new synthesis with perhaps more emphasis on overcoming the most basic division in the study of human society that exists between all the social sciences and history.
3. *The error of developmentalism*: Wallerstein's basic point in this regard is

---

* Wallerstein develops this approach which can be found in several of his works, published in 1976, 1977, 1979, 1980 and 1982. The approach, therefore, spreads over all these works and needs to be conceptualized into one.

that states or countries are inappropriate units for studying change. They are not self-contained systems developing separately from one another but are all part of a larger whole. To treat them separately and to model change accordingly is to make the fundamental 'error of developmentalism'. More than anything else the world-systems approach is a challenge to developmentalism.

Systems of Change

If modern social science is studying the wrong unit of change by concentrating on states or countries, what is the correct unit? Wallerstein argues that change can only be adequately understood if the object of analysis is a self-contained system which he terms as entity. Such entities are defined by their mode of production. To him the mode of production is broadly conceived as the organization of the material basis of a society. This is a much broader concept than the orthodox Marxist definition in that it includes not only the way in which productive tasks are divided up but also decisions concerning the quantities of goods to be produced, their consumption and/or accumulation along with the resulting distribution of goods. Wallerstein identifies just three basic ways in which the material base of societies have been organized. These three modes of production are associated with a type of entity or system of change:

1. "The mini-systems and the reciprocal-lineage mode of production" which describes a society in which production is largely differentiated by age and gender and exchange is simply reciprocal.
2. "World-empires and the redistributive-tributary mode of production" occurs when a society is class-based, with production carried on by a large majority of agriculturists who pay tribute to a small ruling class.
3. "The world economy and the capitalist mode of production" is also class-based but the distinguishing characteristic is ceaseless capital accumulation operating through a marked logic.

However, the later two modes of production describe societies whose divisions of labour are larger than any one local grouping and so are designated 'world-systems'. There have been countless mini-systems in the evolution of mankind, numerous world empires since the Neolithic Revolution but only one successful capital-expanding world economy, which originated in Europe in 1450 and spread to cover the whole world by about 1900. Hence, a world-systems analysis of the current situation treats our world as a single entity, the capitalist world economy., The primary message of this approach cannot treat single countries but must incorporate the whole world-systems.

Types of Change

The error of developmentalism can be avoided by choosing the correct object of analysis. For the study of contemporary social change there is one such entity—the world economy. The current world-wide recession is evidence of this reality. But the world-systems approach allows us to specify much more than the study of contemporary social change. Three types of change can be identified:

1. 'transformation' that occurs between different modes of production;
2. 'discontinuities' that occur between different entities at approximately the same location where both entities share the same mode of production; and
3. 'continuities' which occur within systems.

The Basic Elements of the World Economy

The capitalist world economy has the following three fundamental structural features:

1. 'A single world market' whose logic permeates economic decisions throughout the system.
2. 'A multiple state system' in which no one state is able to dominate totally. It is this political competition which gives economic decision makers a room for manoeuvre which is not available in unitary world economy.
3. 'The three-tier structure stratification' in systems which prevents polarization by the existence of middle groupings between the extremes. One representation of this structure is to be found in the spatial organization of the world economy where Wallerstein adds a 'semi-periphery' category between the commonly recognized core and periphery.

A space-time matrix is not an arbitrary, artificial creation. Here, we are trying to describe the concrete historical entity of the world economy. Both dimensions of the matrix are calibrated in terms of system properties of the world economy. Neither space nor time is treated as in any sense separate from the world economy. They are not space-time containers through which the world economy travels. Rather they are both interpreted on the product of social relations. The time dimension is described on a social product of the 'dynamics' of the world economy. The space dimension is described as a social product of the 'structure' of the world economy. The space-matrix is a simple model which combines the dynamics and structure to provide a framework for political geography.

With regard to the dynamics of the world economy, Wallerstein recognizes that the goal of ceaseless accumulation produces consecutive periods of stagnation and growth. Long Waves (Kondratief Cycles* and Logistic

* Kondrateiff was a Russian economist. He proposed cycles for the dynamics of world economy which consists of two phases, one of growth (A) and one of stagnation (B). He has identified four cycles which have occurred since 1780.

Waves)* are interpreted as the basic rhythm of the world-system, with the stagnation providing the necessary conditions for restructuring the world economy, heavily involving the semi-periphery.

The Spatial Structure of World Economy

Spatial structure usually conjures up a static picture of an unchanging pattern. The spatial structure is a part and parcel of the same processes that generate the cycles described above. Spatial structure and temporal cycles are two sides of the same mechanisms which produce a single space-time framework. The spatial structures are essentially dynamic.

The Concept of Core and Periphery

The concept of peripheralization implies that these new areas did not join the world economy as equal partners with existing members but they were joining on unfavourable terms. They were, in fact, joining a particular part of the world economy which we term the periphery. It is now common place to define the modern world in terms of core (meaning the rich countries of North America, Western Europe and Japan). This core-periphery pattern is often treated as a static, almost natural phenomena. The world economy uses the terms core and periphery in entirely different meanings. Both refer to complex processes and not directly to areas, regions or states. The latter only become core-like because of a predominance of core processes operating in that particular area, region or state. Similarly, peripheral areas, regions or states are defined as those where peripheral processes dominate. Since these processes do not act randomly but generate uneven economic development, broad zones of 'core' and 'periphery' are found. Such zones exhibit some stability—parts of Europe have always been the core—but also show dramatic changes over the lifetime of the world economy notably the rise of non-European areas—first the USA and then Japan.

Core and periphery processes are opposite types of complex production relations. The core exploits and the periphery is exploited. In the simplest terms, core processes consist of relations that incorporate relatively high wages, advanced technology and a diversified production mix whereas periphery processes involve low wages, more rudimentary technology and a simple production mix. These are general characteristics, the exact nature of which changes constantly with the evolution of the world economy. It is important to understand that these processes are not determined by the particular product being produced.

* Logistic waves are longer waves of up to two hundred to three hundred years of duration.

The Semi-periphery Category

One of the most original elements of Wallerstein's approach is his concept of the semi-periphery. This is neither core nor periphery but combines particular mixture of both processes. Notice there are 'no' semi-peripheral processes. Rather the term 'semi-periphery' can be directly applied to zones, areas or states when they exhibit neither a predominance of core nor peripheral processes. This means that the overall social relations operating in such zones involve exploiting peripheral areas while the semi-periphery itself suffers exploitation by the core.

The semi-periphery is interesting because it is the dynamic category within the world economy. The restructuring of space during recessions involves zones rising and sinking through the semi-periphery. Opportunities for change occur during recessions but these are not only limited opportunities—not all the semi-periphery can evolve to become core. Political processes are very important here in the selection of success and failure in the world economy. Wallerstein actually considers the semi-periphery's role to be more political than economic. It is the crucial middle zone in the spatial manifestation of his three-tiered characterization of the world economy. The semi-periphery is political in nature as a stabilizing force between the economic-geographical extremes. It plays a key role in the dynamics of the world economy since it is in the semi-periphery where most acute class struggle occurs, particularly when it becomes the focus of periodic restructuring.

A Space-Time Matrix for Political Geography

The above discussion produces a 10 × 3 matrix involving ten phases of growth and stagnation and three types of spatial zones. In Table 3.1 this framework is used to portray those features of the evolving world economy that are necessary for understanding political geography.

The establishment of the world economy as a system operating from Eastern Europe to the New World involved the development in both the Atlantic trade and the Baltic trade. The former initiated from Iberia but gradually came to be financially controlled from the incipient core of Northwest Europe on which the Baltic trade was based. Once this core becomes established, Iberia is relegated to a 'conveyer belt' for the transfer of surplus from its colonies to the core. It is during the logistic B-phase that the basic elements of the world economy identified above become consolidated:

1. There is a single world market organized and controlled from Northwest Europe.
2. A multiple state system emerges epitomized by the initiation of international law to regulate relations between states.

Table 3.1

A space-time information matrix

		Core	Semi-periphery	Periphery
Logistic Curve	A.	Initial geographical expansion based on Iberia but economicadvances based on north-west Europe	Relative decline of cities of Central and Mediterrarean Europe	Iberian empires in 'New World', second feudalism in eastern Europe,
	B.	Consolidation of north-west European dominance, first Dutch and then French-English rivalry	Declining areas now include Iberia and joined by rising groups in Sweden, Prussia and North-east USA	Retrenchment in Latin America and East Europe, Rise of Caribbean sugar, Frnech defeat in India and Canada
Kondra-tieff Wave I	A.	Industrial revolutionin Britain, 'National' revolution in France. Defeat of France	Relative decline of whole semi-periphery. Establishment of USA	Decolonization and expansion -formal control in India but informal controls in Latin America.
	B.	Consolidation of British economic leadership. Origins of socialism in Britain and France	Beginning of selective rise in North America and Central Europe	Expansion of British influence in Latin America. Initial opening up of East Asia.
Kondra-tieff Wave II	A.	Britain as the 'workshop of the world' in an era of Free trade	Reorganization of semi-periphery, civil war in USA, Unification of Germany and Italy, entry of Russia	The classic era of 'informal imperialism' with growth of Latin America.
	B.	Decline of Britain relative to USA and Germany. Emergence of the Socialist Second International	Decline of Russia and Mediterranean Europe	Expansion-scramble for Africa. The classical age of imperialism.
Kondra-tieff Wave III	A.	Consolidation of German and USA economic leadership Arms race.	Entry of Japan and Dominion states	Consolidation of new colonies (Africa) plus growth in trade elsewhere (especially China)
	B.	Defeat of Germany; British Empire saved. USA economic leadership confirmed.	Socialist victory in Russia, establishment of USSR. Entry of Argentina.	Neglect of periphery. Beginning of peripheral redly. Import substitution in Latin America.
Kondra-tieff Wave IV	A.	USA as the greatest power in the world both military and economically. New era of free trade.	Rise of Eastern Europe and 'Cold-War'. Entry of OPEC.	Socialist victory in China. Decoolonization leading this time to 'neo-colonialism'.
	B.	Decline of USA relative to Europe and Japan. Nuclear arms race.	Entry of 'Little Japan' in East Asia and new regional powers-China, Brazil, Mexico, India. Rise of debt to core	Severe economic crisis and conflict. Expansion of poverty.

After P.J. Taylor, 1985.

3. A three-tiered spatial structure clearly emerges that can be identified in the new division of labour for agricultural production: 'free' wage labour developing in the Northwest European core, partialy free 'share cropping' arrangements in the Mediterranean semi-periphery, and in the periphery, two different forms of coerced labour-slavery in the New World and the so-called 'second feudalism' in Eastern Europe. Despite massive changes in the world economy since this time these three essential features have remained and are just as important today as they were in the seventeenth century.

Following the consolidation of the world economy, it has grown economically and geographically in fits and starts as described by the four Kondratieff waves. Some degree of symmetry in these changes can be identified from Figure 3.4 by designating British and American 'centuries'. These related to the rise of these two states, defeat of their rivals (France and Germany respectively), their dominance of the world economy (including their promotion of free trade) and finally their decline with new rivalries emerging (including the rise of protectionism and/or imperialism).

In order to illustrate the rest of the matrix, let us highlight the route of today's major states through this matrix. Britain became part of the core by the time of the logistic B-phase when it restructured its state in the civil war. It has

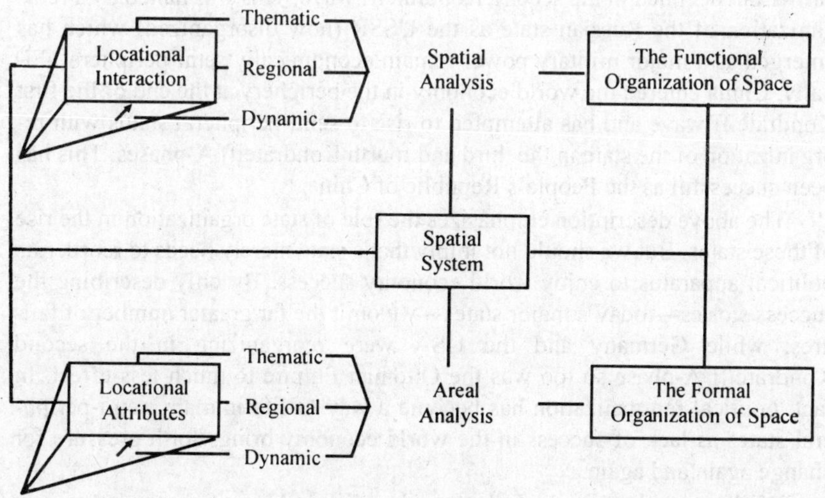

Figure 3.4: A Paradigm for Locational Analysis of Spatial System (After E.W. Soja, 1974)

maintained that position despite relative decline since the second Kondrateiff B-phase. France's early position is similar to Britain's but defeat in the periphery and relative decline in the logistic B-phase led to a restructuring of the French state in the revolution.

However, subsequent defeat in the core of the first Kondrateiff wave led to a second relative decline but within the core. The USA and Germany (Prussia) have had much more volatile histories. Both carved out semi-peripheral positions in the logistic B-phase but their positions were unstable.

In the USA peripheralization was prevented by the war of independence. This victory was consolidated by the civil war in the second Kondrateiff A-phase when southern cotton became part of an American periphery (rather than part of a British periphery) in a restructured American state. From this onwards the USA prospered to become the major power of the twentieth century. Initially, its major rival was Germany which also restructured its state in the second Kondrafteiff A-phase under Prussian leadership but subsequent prowess was set back in the third Kondrateiff wave by military defeat.

Today, Germany is again a major economic challenger of the USA in the core. But the major economic challenger is Japan which only entered the world economy in the second Kondrafteiff wave. It has also restructured its state, suffered military setbacks but has now finally come through towards economic leadership. Russia, on the other hand, entered the world economy earlier but declined in the second Kondrateiff wave. This was halted by a reorganization of the Russian state as the USSR (now disorganized) which has emerged as a major military power remain economically semi-peripheral. Finally, China entered the world economy in the periphery at the end of the first Kondrateiff wave and has attempted to rise to semi-peripheral status with reorganization of the state in the third and fourth Kondrateiff A-phases. This has been successful as the People's Republic of China.

The above description emphasizes the role of state organization in the rise of these states. But we should not imply that a state merely needs to reorder its political apparatus to enjoy world economy success. By only describing the success stories—today's major states—we omit the far greater number of failures; while Germany and the USA were reorganizing in the second Kondrateiff A-phase so too was the Ottoman Empire to much less effect. In fact, political reorganization has become a way of life in many semi-peripheral states as lack of success in the world economy brings forth pressure for change again and again.

Wallerstein claims to be following the spirit of Marx if not the letter, so it is important to identify his differences with orthodox Marxism. As well as the error of developmentalism, there are two other key differences. First, in terms of mode of production, Wallerstein uses a broader definition, resulting in his identification of capitalism not being reliant on the existence of 'free labour'. Hence, both 'feudal-like' social relation in parts of the 'third world', and 'socialist-like' social relations in the 'second world' are all parts of a single division of labour which is the capitalist world economy. Secondly, Wallerstein proposes an alternative 'meta-history' which is also related to his indentification of fewer modes of production. Orthodox Marxists share with liberals a progressive theory of history, so that, for instance, the transition from feudalism to capitalism is interpreted by both on a victory of 'advanced' bourgeois forces over 'traditional' feudal forces. Wallerstein identifies this transition as a regression in that capitalism was the European, feudal ruling classes' solution to the crisis of their world-system-feudal Europe. The ruling class remained largely intact as the mode of production changed to provide new means of exploitation.

This interpretation is important for understanding the current situation. The rhythm of the system is accompanied by secular trends which are asymptotic and, as these run their course, so the world economy enters its crisis phase. The next trasnsition will be towards either a more egalitarian system which we may term socialism or a new mode of production will again be invented to perpetuate inequalities. World-systems approach is a contribution towards making the former more likely but the future remains to be won.

.One of the advantages of adopting the world-systems approach is that it enables us to be much more explicit in the theory behind our history. Weallerstein's world-systems model clearly indicates that it attempts to combine together both idiographic and nomothetic approaches so as to make it more holistic, and applicable to the changing scenario of the world-state systems.

However, the collapse of communism in East Europe, followed by the disintegration of the Soviet Union, and unification of Germany, and the rise of some states in the periphery, particularly India and South Korea, etc., and their subsequent attempt to enter the world economy, and a number of areas rapidly becoming semi-peripheral, the relevance of the world-systems approach, therefore, appears to be at stake, and requires suitable modifications in the light of the changed scenario.

The above approaches to the study of political geography make it clear that it is no longer "a wayward child of geographic family". It has established itself as a distinct subfield of the discipline, since Carl Sauer's remark. Nevertheless, political geography is still in the 'pre-paradigm' period, in the light of the Kuhn's terminology. This is because of the fact that there are conflicts between several distinct approaches, and models rallying behind individuals like those of Whittlesey's law-landscape approach. Hartshorne's functional approach, Gottmann's political partitioning model, Jones' unified field theory, Cohen-Rosenthal's political systems model, and Soja's geographical analysis of political systems, but none of them appeared to have dominated over the others. In the 1950s there were approaches to that of Hartshorne, Gottmann and Jones, and which held considerable command on political geographers but none could dominate over the others. Systems analysis was incorporated into the politico-geographical studies, largely because of the fact that geography by that time underwent theoretical and quantitative revolutions, and this subfield could not remain unaffected, and people like Cohen and Rosenthal, and Soja attempted to provide alternative models, based on the contemporary methodological and theoretical changes in geography, which sought to reveal the growing concern for the topical specialism in political geography as a result of the growing disillusionment with the regional-paradigm in geography as a whole. These models were shortlived and could not dominate the other; therefore, 'professionalism' has not taken place in political geography.

So far as Wallerstein's world-systems approach is concerned, it has been borrowed from economics, and, therefore, is not politico-geographically experessive. It can be used as an alternative approach, and at the same time, the adoption of it in the contemporary politico-geographical study does not mean that the subfield has attained the phase of professionalism. What is required is that political geographers should attempt to take political geography from the pre-paradigm phase to the phase of professionalism.

Chapter 4

Concepts of Territoriality, State and Nation

Territoriality

Territoriality is an attempt by an individual or group to influence or establish control over a clearly demarcated territory which is made distinctive and considered at least partially exclusive by its inhabitants or those who define its bounds. Most works emphasize territoriality as a fundamental human need, based on identity, defence and stimulation.

The concept of territoriality owes much of its origin to Robert Andrey's book, *The Territorial Imperative* (1966). "A territory", Andrey writes, "is an area of space, whether of water or earth or air, which an animal or group of animals defends as an exclusive preserve. The word is also used to describe the inward compulsion in animate beings to possess and defend such a space. A territorial species of animals, therefore, is one in which all males, and sometimes females too, bear an inherent drive to gain and defend an exclusive property. We may be permitted to wonder if in all territorial species there does not exist, more profound than simple learning, some universal recognition of territorial rights." With regard to man whether he is such a territorial species, Andrey remarks: "Man...is as much a territorial animal as is a mocking bird singing in the clear California night." The implications of such a statement, obviously, are enormously far-reaching. If it is essentially correct, then man's sense of territoriality as an instinctive drive is a greater determinant of his politico-territorial adjustment and organization than what he has learned through social and cultural evolution.

deBlij (1972) remarks that " if we define the concept of territoriality as a pattern of behaviour whereby living space is fragmented into more or less well-defined territories whose limits are viewed as inviolable by their occupants, it becomes clear that political geographers have for some time recognized this phenomenon. Any such territories, after all, will acquire certain particular characteristics—Gottmann called it iconography. The

Ratzel-Kjellen-Haushofer school of geopoliticians were in the process of defining a form of territoriality when they conceptualized the state as an organic being. Hartshorne and Jones argued that the state be viewed as an entity whose characteristics could be linked, ultimately, to the behaviour of the individuals constituting it."

"Combining the concepts of territoriality and dominance behaviour, perhaps we may extrapolate to the superimposed boundaries that evolved from truce lines or colonial imposition, to the racial compartmentalization of South Africa (surely an especially good example of dominance behaviour), to the competition for Northern Ireland (where the social order that arose out of dominance behaviour is being challenged) and to the ghettoization of US cities. In so doing we assume that territoriality in man does exist more or less. Andrey proposed and that dominance behaviour prevails—a sort of generally accepted superior-inferior, dominant-subordinate hierarchy that operates vertically and is expressed spatially."

One idea about which there is still much uncertainty lies in the roots of territoriality. If indeed, territoriality is a phenomenon of human behaviour, is it instinctive or has it been acquired and modified by learning—through cultural revolution? In other words, is it less an 'imperative' than Andrey suggested? And the concomitant, human aggression—is it similarly universal and is it genetic in its origins or is it neither? E.W. Soja, reacting to the views of Andrey and others, points out in 1971 that "only when human society began to increase significantly in scale and complexity did territoriality reassert itself as a powerful behavioural and organizational phenomenon. But this was a cultural and symbolic territoriality, not the primitive territoriality of the primates and other animals...Thus, although cultural territoriality fundamentally begins with the origins of the cultured primate man, it achieves a central prominence in society only with the emergence of the state. And it probably attains its fullelst flowering as an organizational basis for society in the formally structured, rigidly compartmentalized, and fiercely defended nation-state of the present day."

What Soja sought to spell out was that territoriality as it was expressed by our complex societies was not the same phenomenon as that which commanded our distant ancestors—or our animal contemporaries. Nor, according to some anthropologists, is man the 'naked ape' driven by savagery and killer instincts.

A. Alland in 1972 argues forcefully that aggressiveness and territoriality are not universal human imperatives at all, in fact, he goes so far as to say that territoriality is born with and nurtured by culture. Viewing some primitive peoples like those still living a hunting-and-gathering existence, Alland observes that these have the weakest of territorial imperatives; supposedly they are the ones that should have the strongest instinct of this sort, if territoriality is indeed a biological urge. He seems to have not been so convinced either about the vigour with which nation-states are inevitably created and defended, he views draft-laws, anthem-singing, sledge-reciting, and flag-waving an evidence that states do not find defenders so easy to come by.

R.D. Sack is credited with having brought the concept of territoriality within the purview of political geography. He has conceptualized the theory of territoriality which seeks to emphasize territorial behaviour in human beings as a conscious decision-making strategy. Whereas Robert Andrey insists that the universal requirements of identity, security and stimulation are met by instinctive territorial behaviour in species as different as robins and human beings, .

Territorial Behaviour

Sack, in his papers, entitled, "Territorial Bones of Power" (1981), and "Human Territoriality" (1983), seeks to identify two basic forms of spatial relations: (a) action by contact; and (b) territoriality. Most of geographical analysis has been concerned with action by contact, both direct and indirect, as in all spatial interaction theories dealing with flows of people, commodities and ideas. The key concept of this spatial relation is distance decay. In contrast, there is a spatial relation of territoriality based on the key concept of territory. This is the attempt to affect, influence or control actions by enforcing control over a specific geographical area.This behaviour is territoriality and the area is the territory.

Territorial Symbols

However, it cannot be proved that group values toward the shared space are instinctual. There is abundant evidence that territorial attitudes may be cultural. It is usually emphasized that individual perception of space varies cross-culturally; similar variation might be observed among culture groups.

Territorial attitudes are often fostered in what might be called 'territorial indoctrination', the use of specially territorial iconography to reinforce integration. This introduction may take place through the schools or in the folk culture. The school system of each state concentrates on national geography and each child receives a distinct map image of the state. Geography in the history class can affect a national territorial image. "American children, for example, hear the phrase Manifest Destiny, and see a map of continual territorial expansion." Such geography lessons carry important political overtones, and may foster a political climate for territorial claims or boundary disputes. National anthem often sing of the land as a sacred trust.

Territorial symbols in iconography are not restricted to nation-states, but are common among subunits of sovereign states. Most of the states in the Indian Union have their own distinctive cultural-linguistic symbols expressing a common territorial past and destiny. The same is true in case of all the fifty states in the United States. The importance of territorial iconography stems largely from the territory's assumed durability, for men long to be a part of something stable and permanent. Men, institutions, beliefs, and laws change but the land undergoes transformation perceptible only to geologists studying millenia of evolution. Abraham Lincoln listed people, laws and territory as the three ingredients of a nation, and then added, "the territory is the only part which is of certain durability." The land may, of course, be invaded and lost, divided, or even possibly reduced to a pile of radioactive dust, but still it seems less perishable than anything else.

Functions and Strategies of Territoriality

Sack identifies four distinct functions of territoriality and their different combinations produce nine different strategies (Table 4.1).

A. The most important function of territoriality, as implied in its definition, is the enforcing control over access to the territory. Territory explicitly involves an 'in-group'; and an 'out-group'. In inter-state relations this is termed as citizenship. All states control flows across their territorial boundaries on the basis of distinguishing their own 'citizens' and 'foreigners'.

B. A much more subtle function of territoriality is its role in reifying power. Unlike physical features such as rivers and roads, power is an intangible concept until it impinges on behaviour. In the modern world one way in which power is made explicit and real is through its direct link to the territory of the modern state. It is for this reason that much political action from defining boundaries to siting capital cities has been considered 'neutrals'.

C. Territoriality has a vital function in displacing attention from the social relation of dominance. Dominance becomes transformed into neutral enforcement of the law of the land, so that the social relation is displaced to a territorial rule. All modern states rely upon most citizens obeying their laws as a member of a territorial community, the nation-state.

D. Territoriality acts as a container of events. The territory becomes an object to which other attributes are assigned. In peace this will involve all the territory being subject to particular outside pressures such an International Monetary Fund's demands for welfare cuts to pay all debts. The IMF will assess a country as a container of a set of potential resources. In wartime the territory is a container of enemy personnel. In the twentieth century this has led to civilian populations being targets of air-raids. The application of this concept in the nuclear age leads to genocide or even speciecide as we have seen.

Table 4.1

Functions and Strategies of Territoriality

Types of Strategy	*Functions of Territoriality*			
	A. Enforcing Control	*B. Reifying Power*	*C. Dis-placing social relations*	*D. Containin g Events*
1. Territorial definition of social relation	x	x		x
2. Efficient span of control	x			x
3. Mismatch of territory and process	x	x	x	x
4. Territoriality as an end not means		x	xx	
5. Inequality by different access	x			
6. Divide and rule	xx	x		x
7. Social conflict obscured	x		x	
8. Obscuration by geographical scale	x		x	
9. Territorial succession	x	xx	x	x

x = important function; xx = very important function.
After R.D. Sack:1981/83.

Table 4.1 shows how different combinations of these four functions can be used to produce nine types of strategies:

1. The territorial definition of social relations is a combination of A, B, and C. The state's territory is the container for defining citizenship which may be used to provide preferential access to resources in the territory. This is reified through mystical justification by nationalism. The ultimate losers of this strategy are stateless refugees.
2. An efficient span of control relates to enforcing the containment of events. As a state increases in size its boundary extends and control may become more difficult. One of the explanations for the 'fall' of all world empires is that they over-extended their span of control. In the world economy, the Spanish and Portuguese empires seem to have become classic examples of this process when both states declined to semi-peripheral status and became little more than conveyer belts for wealth from 'their' periphery to the core in Northwest Europe.
3. Mismatch of territory and process will occur in some of the boundary drawing exercises described earlier. This combines all four functions and is perhaps best illustrated in the definitions of African colonial boundaries and their continued use by the independent states. Territory is the basis of a new control attempting to reify power with a new nationalism

by displacing traditional ethnic social relations.

4. Territory appears as an end rather than a means in the modern state system through nationalism. The territorial function of displacing social relations is vital here as 'class differences' are overwhelmed by national consensus.
5. Territoriality in involving control of access can become a stragtegy of generating inequality. The best example of this is the process of social imperialism whereby welfare provisions for all citizens of a core state have multiplied the inequalities between core and periphery.
6. Divide and rule is in many ways the basic strategy underlying the world economy's need for an inter-state system. By dividing up opposition into separate territories in which power is reified, capital interests have been able to contain revolts to specific territories and avoid a worldwide revolution.
7. Social conflict is obscured where enforcing control and displacing social conflict are combined. The result is a situation where conflict occurs between territories in place of the original generating social conflict. An example of this is the classical Marxist interpretation of the First World War where conflict between industrial and banking groups culminated in a war of nations.
8. Obscuration by geographical scale again involves A and C but this time is concerned with a double use of territory. This is the allocation of political power to a scale of operation at which it is relatively powerless. Political power is limited to the scale of ideology, sovereign territories, while the scale of reality, of basic change, is the world economy.
9. Territorial secession is, in many ways, the reverse of the functions described. They are turned and used to generate partition of the territory. In this sense it is related to strategy 3 but concentrates more on the breaking of the reification of power of territorial state. Palestine, Cyprus, Northern Ireland, Lebanon, Korea, Vietnam, and of course, Germany, are or have been examples of such successful strategies on one side or the other.

Commenting on Sack's theory, Taylor (1985) observes that "the first importance of...is that it is a beginning in defining new theories of conscious decision-making which exercise once and for all dangerous natural analogies in political geography. Second, and more important, is the fact that we are provided with a framework that allows us to go beyond Herz's simple security definition of the territorial state and expand on Gottmann's addition of opportunity. Using just Herz's concept we are led to argue that technological developments have made the territorial state obsolete, with this more sophisticated theory we can see that there is much more to the state than a shell. Other uses of territoriality will ensure the survival of this phenomenon as long as the world economy survives."

To conclude, we can say that it is important to envisage human territoriality as conditioned primarily by cultural norms and values which vary in structure and function from society to society, from one time period to another, and in accordance with the scale of social activity. At the lowest and most personalized level, there is the bubble of personal space immediately surrounding the individual which in many cultural contexts is considered by the individual as inviolable space. At the societal level, territoriality becomes a means of regulating social interaction and a focus and symbol for group membership and identity, ranging from the scale of urban gangs and their turfs, through patterns of territorial regionalism, to the compartmentalization of the world into a system of states.

The State

A state is traditionally defined as an area of land (or land and water) with relatively well-defined, internationally recognized boundaries. Within this territory resides a people with an independent political identity and loyalty which is usually referred to as nationalism and territoriality. In other words, a state is an area organized politically in an effective manner by an indigenous, or resident, people with a government in effective control of the area.

The word 'state' comes from the Latin 'status' and its medieval usage related to either the 'state' or condition of a ruler or the 'state' of the realm. The idea of a public power separate from ruler and ruled which is the supreme political authority in a given territory does not occur at this medieval period or earlier periods. The modern concept develops from this medieval usage in the sixteenth century first in France and then in England. It is argued that these two countries provided early examples of the properties that make up the modern state—a centralized regime based on a bureaucracy operating within well-established boundaries. By the end of the sixteenth century the modern concept of the state was well established in these two countries and modern political analysis focusing on the nature of the state can be said to begin from this time onwards.

The notion of sovereignty* assumes the existence of the state. The territoriality only operates through the medium of the state. This is a two-way relationship. At the simplest level the state is defined by its possession of sovereignty. This tends to distinguish it from all other forms of human organization. Sovereignty amounts to nothing less than supreme coercive

* Sovereignty is the ultimate authority exerted by the government of a state over its territory and people against which there is no appeal.

power within a territory—the state "gives order to all and receives orders from none" inside its recognized boundaries. Invasion by a foreign power or internal insurgency aiming at creating a new state are both violations of a state's sovereignty. If not defeated the state no longer has a monopoly of coercion in its territory and faces extinction. The disintegration of the Soviet Union, the division of Yugoslavia and the division of Czechoslovakia are examples of exinction by internal violation of sovereignty.

Idea of the State

As regards the idea of the state, Bergman (1975) observes: "Throughout much of Western Europe the institutional framework of the Christian Church survived the collapse of the Western Roman Empire. Church organization had been based on the empire system with the Pope in Rome and with the bishops in major cities holding exclusive territorial responsibility. The Church pattern survived the retreat of the imperial authority because bishops cannot abandon their dioceses; the diocesan pattern remained intact under the barbarians. Thus, the Church administration remained to teach the barbarian tribes two important legal principles. One was territoriality, the principle of 'dominum'. Many of the tribes had wandered in 'regnum' political association for hundred of years, united only in allegiance to powerful leaders. Under the influence of the Church they gradually evolved territorial rule. The Merovingians (5th-8th centuries), for example, called themselves Kings of the Franks but the later Capetians (10th-14th centuries) were already Kings of Franks."

The second principle taught by the Church was 'entail', succession through only one inheritor of the king's lands and wealth. Barbarian custom had divided rights and possessions among sons, splitting up realms, and often causing civil wars. The Church sought to insure kingdoms' integrity upon the deaths of individual kings. The barbarian tribes' assimilation of the principles of dominum and entail stabilized political organization and laid the foundation for the development of principalities and territorial states.

During the centuries the barbarians were converted to Christianity, the hope remained that either the pope or else a purely secular ruler could reestablish one universal Christian empire. The Church allied with the powerful Frankish kingdom, and on Christmas Day in 800 A.D. Pope Leo III proclaimed the Frankish king Charlemagne protector and, it was hoped, restorer of Christendom in a new Holy Roman Empire. This art defined a new relationship between Church and State power. The emperor ruled over earthly matters by divine right and Church sanction. As the sole repository of earthly sovereignty, he 'was' the State. The Church remained sovereign and protector over men's souls; its concerns were of eternal life, and it retained exclusive authority to interpret Christian practice. There was no salvation outside the

Church. The Church monopolized religious authority just as sovereign monopolized political authority.

"This separation of function and responsibility between Church and State lent each stability. The Church legitimized the sovereign, and the sovereign protected the Church. With the development of the numerous independent European kingdoms outside the Holy Roman Empire, the Church reached similar philosophical accommodation with each of them."

"The sovereign exercised political power, but the Church was a far more implicative institution than was political authority. The sovereign (i.e., the State) demanded only obedience, neither claiming nor seeking additional adherence or allegiance. The Church, on the other hand, claimed belief and personal commitment. In earthly matters men were variously ranked and previleged, but they were all equal in the Church. The people did not have a stake in political affairs, there was no political community. The only community was the Church, the 'community of Christ'. European sovereigns could play musical chair with Europe's thrones and redraw the political map at will. Louis XIV quite correctly remarked, "I am the State". So, the earlier idea of the state was necessarily linked up with the religion, more specifically with the Christianity. But the idea of the State changed over time."

However, the basic idea of the modern state seems to have first appeared at the same time as the emergence of the world economy itself. Foregoing discussion is a testimony of it.

To deBlij (1972), "The emergence of modern Europe may be said to date from the second half of the fifteenth century. Western Europe's monarchies began to represent something more than mere authority, increasingly they became centres of an emerging national consciousness, pride and trade. At the same time, the trend toward fragmentation, which had dominated the feudal period, was reversed as various monarchies, through marriages, alliance or both, combined to promote territorial unity. Feudal privileges were being recaptured by the central authority, and there was progress in the parliamentary representation of the general population. Renewed interest was shown in Greek and Roman philosophies of government and administration. Europe was ready for change."

Change did come to Europe, and in many forms. The emerging states engaged in intense commercial competition and mercantilism was viewed as the correct kind of economic policy to serve the general interest of all. The search for precious metals, the standard of wealth, sent the ships of several countries traversing the oceans to lands that lay open for discovery and appropriation. Kings and noblemen sent many of those ships on their way, but in the growing cities a new class of influential men was on the rise—the merchants. Their capital strength increased by leaps and bounds, and before long the merchants and businessmen in the Western European states were demanding a greater voice in the politics of their countries.

A.E. Moodie (1957) observes: "The political history of the Modern Age is largely the study of the successful struggle to wrest...omnipotence from an individual or from a privileged few and, through the growth of parliamentary government and the extension of the franchise, to bestow self-government." Europe's revolutions in industry, commerce, and agriculture were paralleled by a socio-political revolution as well. During the second half of the eighteenth century and much of the nineteenth century. Europe witnessed the rise of nationalism as an all-pervading political force. People transferred their prime allegiance to their territory, their state—a state that they helped create through participation in a revolution that swept away the old order. The prime example of this process undoubtedly is the French Revolution, the revolution that eroded the Czarist era in Russia is also considered a case.

Idea of the state in the post-French Revolution period in the nineteenth century underwent a further change with liberty, freedom, democracy, and fraternity, having formed the basic ingredients of it. The geographical consequences of this change in the idea of the state in the post-Revolution period, and particularly in the post-Napoleonic period, were the realignment and redrawing of territories, based on ethnic criteria followed by the emergence of some more states in Central Europe.

However, the Russian Revolution in the present century added equality and fraternity to the idea of the state, while the technological developments have made the idea of the territorial state obsolete, and a large number of states with ethnic-cultural distinctiveness came into being. If we attempt to trace out the root of the idea of the change in the concept of the state, then we have to look back to the Protestant Reformation Movement which destroyed the Church-State relationship and redefined sovereignty in its spatial context.

The Protestant Reformation introduced a new idea of individuality and individual autonomy into European thinking. Martin Luther denied the church's position as mediator between God and man; he preached individual responsibility for one's soul. If each man is responsible for his own soul, why not for his own politics? The doctrine of individual responsibility for the afterlife bears the seed of the doctrine of individual responsibility in this life. How then could the church any longer sanction king's divine right to rule? Political philosophers struggled to develop a new theory of the nation and the state, and in the eighteenth century, the Reformation and the ideas of the Enlightenment finally combined to break up the church-state nexus reached in 800. The Swiss philosopher Jean Jacques Rousseau replaced the notion that sovereignty resides in the king with the idea that sovereignty resides in the people themselves, and he laid the foundation for allegiance to the state as the people. Man was thought to be capable of perfectibility, however, through social action. Politics was the instrument not only of physical protection, but of moral redemption. Perfectibility and virtue became attainable only through absolute identification with a majority will expressed in the government. The theory demanded a new level of individual dedication to the state which became the most implicative social institution. "To be a citizen was the greatest pride...".

Bergman (1975) observes: "The French Revolution sought to introduce the reign of national liberty, and it gave birth to the French nation. The Declaration of the Rights of Man stated that 'the principle of all sovereignty resides essentially in the nation; no body nor individual may exercise any authority which does not proceed directly from the nation'. The nation is the political community; it feels that it belongs together and that it ought to enjoy self-government. A state is a political authority, and ideally, it is representative of a nation, hence a nation-state. As the means of achieving community and virtue, the nation-state usurped the role of the Church, and as the sole repository of sovereignty it usurped the role of the monarch. The revolutionary slogan of liberty, equality and fraternity inverted the older religious tradition, conceiving fraternity as the goal of political action, rather than the starting point. While pressing for immediate liberty and equality, however, the revolutionaries sacrified many imperfect fraternities while awaiting the establishment of a political utopia."

The evolution of the nation-state may be traced through four broad phases: pre-agrarian, agrarian, industrial, and post-industrial. In pre-agrarian societies, tribal loyalties and patriotism predominated. Hunting and gathering bands were typically too small and isolated to allow for, or require, the existence of an independent political institution. Agrarian societies, in contrast, were mostly state endowed. The emergence of literacy and a specialized clerical class made possible the centralized organization and storage of records, rules and culture. However, communities remained isolated, and the clerisy could not dominate beyond localized territories.

Industrial society, however, permitted a specialized division of labour and the emergence of a high culture. In such a complex society, a centralized state agency takes over the role of socialization, education and authority. In the post-industrial society, the state has grown to play a dominant role in social relations. "A new world organization is evidenced in the development of supranation-states, based on such things as trade and defense agreements."

Innovation Diffusion

The modern idea of the state, particularly that of the nation-state, was the major innovation of the Revolutionary Europe in the nineteenth century that the people with the cultural distinctiveness based on political *raison d'etre* and iconography must have the freedom to decide their destiny through the political organization of their territory. This idea first spread across Europe and gradually over different parts of the world. Therefore, the idea of the modern state, particularly that of the nation-state, has spatial-temporal dimension and must be studied in this perspective.

During the nineteenth century nationalistic ideas matured in Europe, most often based on cultural-linguistic distinctiveness, but maturation brought a change through the century. The struggle for new national political systems and states to emerge from old empires and feudal states produced a new competitive nationalism. The concept's original liberal humanitarianism became aggressive exclusivism. Emphasis on the dignity of the individual yielded to emphasis on the power of the nation, and national politics, born in efforts to reduce the absolutism of the sovereign, were transformed into exaltation of the government.The seeds of these developments can be seen in Rousseau's original ideas, and their fruits has seen many a nineteenth and twentieth century wars.

The nation-state concept emerged triumphant in Europe after World War I when the European map was redrawn to achieve self-determination for nations in nation-states. Nationalistic ideas spread throughout European colonies during the twentieth century and today the concept of the independent nation-state covers the entire globe. The power of the church in human affairs is considerably declined, and most surviving monarchies are not sources of power, but only icons of the national unity.

Thus, while the modern nation-state is theoretically the political expression of a nation, state and nation can be differentiated. In most European cases nations antedated and demanded political expression in states. Throughout most of the rest of the world, however, the territorial pattern of states is largely the remanent of patterns of colonial administration. As these areas have gained independence, state structures have struggled to evolve political values and institutions commanding the loyalty of the state populations. As the people in a state mature politically, it is hoped that the feeling of nationality, of belonging together in a political community comes to be based less in obvious cultural indices such as language/religion and more in common adherence to certain political concepts and ideas associated with the state.

"Each state must win the allegiance of its population. Most of the African states are artificial units, geographical expressions carved on the map by European imperialists. These are the units which have to be tried to turn into nations.Many Asian states force the same difficulty and even many Latin American states, which had been independent for over one hundred years, still have not welded the state populations into nations."

State-Idea and Raison d'etre

It is the innovation diffusion of the modern idea of the state, and particularly of the idea of the nation-state, that the question of the internal functions of the state arises and the state is created to develop the state-idea and to defend it. "The fundamental internal function of the state-area", writes Hartshorne (1950), "is to establish itself as an effective unit in fact, rather than merely in international law. This requires the conception and establishment of an idea of the state, a purpose or set of purposes, sufficiently strong to overcome the centrifugal tendencies resulting inevitably from the separate and divergent interests of the diverse regions that are included, in a particular pattern, in the structure of the state-area."

"The basic centripetal force must be some concept or idea justifying the existence of this particular state incorporating these particular regions, the state must have a *raison d'etre*—reason for existing."

What really constitutes the state-idea? Preston E. James (1968) answers it: " The state-idea is a complex of traditions, experiences and objectives. It is made up of written history, folklore, stories of national heroes, religious beliefs, and the language and art forms in which these things are communicated. It is the body of literature, the painting, the architecture, the music which are distinctively national. And it is the characteristic economic, social and political institutions. The state is created to defend and develop the state-idea...".

However, "the state-idea is not always easy to identify.... Although the identification of the state-idea requires direct contacts and close observation within the state itself. It is not easily quantified; yet these attitudes and objectives can be measured, and certainly they can be mapped...Of course, a state with a positive state-idea to which the great majority of the citizens adhere with enthusiasm is a relatively viable state... and viability is a measure of the effectiveness with which a state can be administered to fulfil the purposes (state-ideas) for which it was created."

Some geographers claim that the state-idea and *raison d'etre* are not necessarily the same; that a state may have a *raison d'etre* without a developed state-idea (which generally comes later) and that conversely the state-idea may develop in a state without a strong *raison d'etre*.

With regard to the *raison d'etre* of the state, Hartshorne (1940) observes: "Any state, to become well established, must present to the population of its areal parts a distinct *raison d'etre*, its justification for existence as an areal unit separate from the neighbouring state-area. This *raison d'etre* must be based upon desires or values of first importance to the population of the regions included in the state...These include, notably, religion, language, and literature, historic memories and the form of government...Since few states are homogeneous in all these respects, the problem is to construct a *raison d'etre* that will enlist the loyalty of the regional groups having different associations and ideals."

The concept of the modern state is necessarily linked up with the concept of the state-idea and *raison d'etre* and the relevance of the concept is readily manifested in the world economy itself, where each state with a distinct state-idea-*raison d'etre* is intensely involved/engaged in commercial competition and mercantilism, for its development and benefits and with a view to fulfilling the purposes or a set of purposes it has presented to its citizens.

The following discussion concentrates on the theories of the state. However, some political geographers have criticized traditional political geography for its dearth of theory and in particular its failure to consider the issue of how to theorize the state. Taylor (1985) observes that "the problem is not that political geography has had no theory of the state—it is impossible to study any phenomena without an implicit theory of its nature—but rather that the theory being used has not been adequately presented so that the full implications are not expressed." Here we shall discuss the Marxist theories of the state, and the state in the world economy.

Marxist Theories of the State

"It is well known that Marx himself never developed a theory of the state. It was a project that he set himself but never completed. Hence, Marxist theories of the state are products of his many followers and this has inevitably led to alternative interpretation of what such a theory should say: there is not a Marxist theory of the state but many Marxist theories of the state."

Two ideas have dominated Marxist political thinking. The first, from the Communist Manifesto of 1848, dismissed the state as nothing more than "a committee for organizing the affairs of the bourgeoise", and the second, manifesting the state as consisting of a 'base-super-structure model' of society where this engineering analogy is used to depict a foundation of economic relations upon which the ideological and political superstructure is constructed. These two simple ideas are difficult to accommodate to the complexities of the modern state. If they are taken into consideration they will lead to reduction of all politics and the state to a mere reflection of economic forces. Such crude reductionism is called 'economism'. The theory of the state which Lenin proposed reflected economism. He found a deep relationship between stages of economic development and types of state. "Hence parliamentary democracy gives rise to the form of state of competitive capitalism, the bureaucratic-military state comes up with monopoly capitalism, and socialism replaces these with the dictatorship of the proletariat." In modern orthodox Marxist theory, economics and politics are fused in another stage known as state monopoly capitalism. However, Lenin provided the model of economism which was every much as developmentalist as the cycle theory of states or even Rostow's stages of economic growth. However, the modern Marxist theorists have sought to avoid the model of economism in their theories of the state.

Pluralist Theory

The pluralist theory conceptualized the state as a set of institutions which manages the public needs of society. These institutions are neutral bodies to which different groups in society can appeal and so formulate policies that favour their members. The state is in effect an umpire adjudicating between competing interests. Since modern society consists of very many overlapping interests—labour, farmers, business, home owners, consumers and so on—no one group is ever able to dominate the state. The balance of interests served will vary as governments change but the state will remain pluralist in nature and able to respond to a wide range of interests. "This is quite obviously the opposite of the Marxist class theory which in these terms is strictly a non-pluralist account of the state."

There are two fundamental properties of pluralist and related non-Marxist theories of the state. The first is that the state is treated as neutral, it is a body above the day-to-day politics of its constituent institutions. The second property of such theories is that they treat the political sphere as separate from the economic sphere. This is the basis of the whole notion of a 'political science', of course, so that no problem is envisaged in the relations of politics and economics. They are separate, though as autonomous systems. However, the pluralist theories of the state represent an important example of the poverty of disciplines.

Economism and pluralist theory can be seen as opposite ends of a scale measuring the autonomy of the political from the economic. At the economism end there is no autonomy. At the political science end there is absolute autonomy. In between them there are different degrees of 'relative autonomy', where politics is not determined by economic processes but is not independent of them either. However, most modern Marxist analysis have located themselves in the relative autonomy sector of this scale and it is from such a position that Ralph Miliband launched his attack on the pluralist theory in his book, *State in Capitalist Society*, published in 1969.

The bulwark of the pluralist theory is the existence of elections. "In 1848 the state may have looked very much like a one-class institution but with franchise reforms the modern liberal-democratic state looks very much like the pluralist model." However, Miliband sought to uncover the class nature of the apparently pluralist state. His method is to marshal data on the social, political and economic elites of the modern state and to show that they all come from the same class background. By showing the many interlinkages in terms of family, education and general economic interests, Miliband is able to paint a picture of a single dominant class in which pluralist competition is a myth. This dominant class is able to manipulate the state apparatus irrespective of which party is in government. This is known as the 'instrumentalist' theory of the state. It restates the class basis of the state and completely contradicts the neutral pluralist view.

However, N. Paulantzas, in his book, *The Problem of the Capitalist State* (1969), argued that Miliband's empirical approach, in his instrumentalist theory of the state, was seriously flawed because it involved analyzing the state on terms laid down by non-Marxist Theory. It is not that empirical analysis is wrong in itself but the way in which it is integrated with the theory is important. He goes on to say that Miliband's study reduces to a description of particular roles within the state apparatus* and investigation of links between people carrying out these different roles. The inevitable result is an emphasis on interpersonal relations which is reminiscent of the original pluralist thinking. To Paulantzas, the class nature of the state is not a matter of empirical verification or falsification. A state is not capitalist in nature because a dominant class with capitalist links manipulates the state for capitalist ends. The state is capitalist because it operates within a capitalist mode of production. This puts constraints on the range of action that is possible so that the state has no option but to conform to the needs of capital. The introduction of liberal democracy does not change this fundamental characteristic. It seems to be a logical argument for which empirical proof appears to be unnecessary. Such a 'structuralist' position need not reduce to economism. However, he shares Miliband's relative autonomy assumption with the state dependent on the economic only in the last instance.

Derivationists versus Relative Autonomy

M. Dear and G. Clerk, in their work, *The State and Geographic Process: a Critical Review* (1978), attempted to introduce into geography the Miliband-Paulantzas dichotomy at the same time when the works of the erstwhile West German Marxists also appeared in J. Holloway and S. Picciotto edited book *State and Capital* (1978) and this completely cut across the arguments that sought to separate Miliband and Paulantzas.

This 'derivation' school rejected the notion of relative autonomy and so

* State apparatus refers to the set of institutions and organizations through which state power is exercised.

undermined the arguments of both protagonists. By assuming relative autonomy any theory implicitly accepts the separation of the economic from the political. By doing this the proponents of such theories cut politics off from the main motor of change in capitalist society—the accumulation process. For the derivationists, therefore, the key question is not about the 'degree' of separation between the political and economic, but why does it 'appear' this way in capitalist society. Both Miliband and Paulantzas cannot answer this question because they have forsaken the "holism of political economy".

"A Marxist theory of the state must be derived from the mechanisms and concepts described by Karl Marx in his basic theoretical work, *Capital*. To the need for competition in the economic sphere they add the need for cooperation in the political sphere. The state becomes necessary to counter the self-destructive processes of unbridled economic competition. This may even involve political processes that appear to be anti-capitalist. The evolution of the welfare state, for instance, involves ensuring the reproduction of a skilled and healthy labour force for the long term interests of capital. In this role of coordinating capital and reproducing labour the state may appear neutral and above the political conflict between capital and labour. This is why non-Marxist theories of the state appear so reasonable and are so widely and easily accepted."

Concept of Hegemony

All Marxist theories incorporate some notion of ideology in their formulation but it is referred to in this context to theories that specifically emphasize the state as a form of mystification whereby class conflicts are hidden behind a national consensus. This is very close to the conception of the state as the scale of ideology. It is the work of Gramsci and his followers which is most closely associated with scale of ideology in the Marxist literature. Gramsci is most well known today for his concept of hegemony. This derives from Marx's original argument that the ruling ideas in a society are the ideas of the ruling class. In Gramsci's work hegemony is the political, intellectual and moral leadership of the dominant class which results in the dominant class actively consenting to their own domination. Hence, alongside the coercive state apparatus (police, army, judiciary, and so on), there is the ideological state apparatus (education, mass media, popular entertainment and so on) through which consent is generated. Notice that these ideological functions need not be carried out by public agencies—in this theory the state is much more than just the public sector.

Historically, the vital battle for state sovereignty involved subjugation of other authority within the state's territory, both local magnates and the universal ideas of the church. In the latter case, the issue centered on education and the state's attempts to 'nationalize' its population by converting religious education into a state ideological apparatus. The successful combination of coercion and hegemony will produce an integral state. Here one can get a parallel with the Hartshorne-Gottmann tradition of the territorial integration theory and the concept of state-idea and iconography. The notion of hegemony, however, is much more pervasive and directly derives from the class-basis of the state. In this argument, Marx's original 'committee' assertion of 1848 remains broadly true: the difference between then and now merely relates to the changing relative balance between coercive and ideological means of control.

However, these Marxist theories have attempted to approach Lenin's economism in different ways but they have not tackled the problem of Lenin's developmentalism. Although we have brought the argument a long way forward from simple economism, all the analyses described above remain rooted at the state level.

The State in World Economy

"The political sphere that we deal with in this study is not the single state but the whole inter-state system. Hence, we need a theory of states where the multiplicity of states is a fundamental property of the theory. Clearly none of the above offer this type of theory. Nevertheless, the various themes highlighted above do provide pointers toward provision of four need and our approach does clarify some of the contentious issues"(Taylor, 1985). In the following discussion, an attempt has been made to bring together all theories of the state and the world-systems approach.

Relative Autonomy and Multiplicity of States

The basic empirical problem confronting the Marxist theories was that the same economic system—capitalism—was producing different state forms. Although the USA and Italy were both capitalist states, for instance, they showed altogether different politics. It is this variety of politics which was to be the subject matter of Marxist analysis. The break with economism was obviously necessary and relative autonomy was a very attractive concept upon which to base these new analyses. We have seen earlier that the derivationists have serious doubts on the validity of this position but they have not replaced it with another means for accounting for the variety of politics under capitalism. The world economy approach does provide a simple explanation of this variety which makes the concept of relative autonomy unnecessary.

The notion of relative autonomy is implicitly based upon the idea that both state and economy cover the same territory. The issue of the relation between economics and politics is treated on a state-by-state basis for Western

Europe. When viewed in this manner it is easy to see how the problems of relating one national economy to one state polity emerges. But this whole issue disappears with the world economy perspective and its multi-state system. Instead of a one-to-one problem there is a one-to-many situation—one world market and many states. Hence, we do not have to appeal to a relative autonomy argument to explain the variety of political forms that states take under capitalism. Instead there are numerous fragments of the world economy each with their particular sovereign states. Since these 'fragments of capitalism' differ from one another, there is no reason to suppose that the forms that the states take should not differ from one another. Quite simply, different fragments of capitalism are associated with different state forms. The variety of politics remains to be understood but there is no need to resort to relative autonomy for explanation.

Derivation of World Government

Dismissal of relative autonomy brings us into line with the state derivation position. But we soon find that there are problems in applying this theory to the world-systems framework. In its initial form the state is derived to overcome the anarchic consequences of a free capitalism. If we translate this to a world economy then this theory predicts a world government to compensate for global anarchy. This is, of course, quite the opposite to the capitalist world economy as conceived by Wallerstein. Multiple states are necessary for manoeuvre by economic actors on the world stage. Production of a world government would, therefore, signal the end of capitalism as mode of production. In the world economy framework, the state does operate to maintain reproduction of labour and facilitate accumulation but not at the system level where states provide platforms for their capitals to operate in the world market.

Within the state derivation school, there have been debates that have raised the issue of the world market. Some people have insisted that state derivation must start from the existence of capital at the world level and not at the state level. As will be apparent by now the world-systems approach to the state is closest to the derivationist school due to its insistence on analyzing the economic and political as complementary aspects of one overall process. However, the inter-state system and world market as two sets of relations underlying the same process of appropriation and accumulation. We did not so much drive the inter-state system from the world economy as to define it as an integral part of the overall system—it is after all one of the three fundamental characteristics of the world economy identified by Wallerstein. But we need to go further and attempt to understand the variety of states within the inter-state system. No rigorous theory for this exists but enough material is available for us to draw the outline of such a theory.

The Variety of State Forms: A Space-Time Introduction

The form that states take depends upon the particular conjuncture of economic, social and political forces in its territory in the past and at the present time. Hence, strictly speaking, every state form will be unique, and can be generalized in terms of the space-time structures. Particular conjunctures can be aggregated into a simple 3x2 matrix with time represented by A and B phases of growth and stagnation and space apportioned between core, semi-periphery and periphery. We should be able to discuss the form that states take within each of these six positions. In all cases the states will have to carry out two basic tasks: (i) provide the conditions for accumulation of capital, and (ii) maintain legitimation of the system. In the following discussion, we will extend the ideas of O' Connor (1973), based as they are on German derivationists, that states generally lie within the space-time categories of the world economy. In particular, we will consider the legitimation function as a varying balance between forces of coercion and consensus.

Core states are the most stable and consensus has been far more important than coercion in maintaining control. This is because the capitals of core states are strongly placed in the world market and can pass on some of their surplus to core labour. This is the process of social imperialism. It is much more than simple bribery, however, and involves the incorporation of labour into the system. These are the truly 'hegemonized' states. But the strength of this hegemony varies between A and B phases. In periods of growth, more resources are available to keep the system stable. These are the periods of building hegemony in the wake of union successes, social security and advances and finally the welfare state. With the onset of stagnation, pressures to maintain conditions for accumulation lead to cut-backs in public expenditure with resulting dangers in the loss of legitimacy. In core states, however, the hegemony has coped remarkably well with the current B phase.

The opposite situation obtains in peripheral states where instability dominates. Here there is no surplus to buy off labour which is largely left to fend for itself while being coerced into submission. The result is an 'overdeveloped structure' relative to the economic base. But this does not represent strength, it reflects the weakness of peripheral states in the world economy. As before in our arguments overtly 'strong' states deceive by their appearance. It may be argued that in post-colonial societies, a military bureaucratic group emerges to oversee the interests of three exploiting classes: (i) the metropolitan core interest, (ii) the local urban industrial interest, and (iii) the land owning interest.

These three 'capitals' have a common interest in maintaining order as the basic condition for accumulation. But they compete in terms of relation of the state to the world economy. Generally speaking, metropolitan core interests and local landowners favour an open economy whereas local industrial interests favour protection. This is the peripheral/semi-peripheral strategy dichotomy. To the extent that urban-industrial groups are able to leave their interests promoted by the military-bureaucratic regime, the state becomes more like a semi-periphery state. But such promotion can fail, of course, and the state will sink even lower into the periphery. The case of Ghana and the failure of Nksumah's 'African socialism' is an example of this. It is a matter of the pattern of opportunity existing for advance in the world economy which varies with A and B phases, of course.

Lastly, we come to the most interesting examples, those of the semi-periphery state which are the most dynamic sectors of the world economy where political actions by states can affect the future structure of the system.This is where class struggle is greatest and where the balance between coercion and consensus is most critical. State governments in this zone specialize in strategies which emphasize accumulation as mentioned earlier. Semi-peripheral economic policy is all about 'catching up', it is the zone of protection in particular and mercantilism in general. This will make legitimation difficult so that much of the semi-periphery is associated with dictatorial regimes. But coercion itself is a very expensive form of control and will stretch resources to the extent of hindering the 'catching up'. Hence, the semi-periphery is also associated with powerful consensus forces, specially fascism and communism and generally nationalism. These are strategies for mobilizing the state's population behind the dominant classes without the greater material expenses of social imperialism of the core. Putting nation before the self, has become the most important form of consensus, the basis of state hegemony, and the major centripetal force in the twentieth century.

Finally, we come to the point that the analysts have examined the theory of the state, through consideration of its functions. These include the view of the state on: (a) supplier of public goods and services; (b) regulator and facilator of the economy; (c) social engineer with an agenda of its own; and (d) arbiter between the many groups which compose the society. A more complex debate has been initiated in the neo-Marxist literature which begin with the question: why is it necessary to constitute an agency called the state in the society? The search for an answer to the question has prompted a very wide debate. The two most common answers have focused on the instrumentalist and the structuralist viewpoints. The former seeks to link the state elite and the ruling classes. The latter examines how and why the state operates with respect to class conflict and contradictions inherent in the social system.

Later debates have examined the state as an input-output mechanism. Its outputs consists of administrative decision taken in the interests of diverse social groups; its inputs are constituent demands and mass loyalty. If the outputs do not satisfy the various constituencies a 'nationality crisis' results, in which the viability of the state is brought into question. This may lead to a 'legitimation crisis' if mass loyalty to the state is withdrawn.

A very common view of the state is, therefore, as a 'crisis-manager'. The state acts to contain the political repercussion of the socio-economic system. The local state is a key instrument of crisis management, as is the recent trend toward 'corporation'. Corporation refers to an institutionalized form of group or class conflict, in which formal avenues of conflict and compromise are established and maintained in order to minimize the risk of unpredictable crisis. The expansion of the state apparatus is an important manifestation of contemporary corporatist relations.

The question of the state is of vital importance in the rebirth of political geography. Some analysts question whether or not, we need a theory of the state. Others claim that a theory of the state is of fundamental, central significance to a proper theory of modern political geography.

The Nation

The words 'nation' and 'nationalism' come from the Latin word 'nasci' meaning 'to be born' and imply 'common ancestry' and 'place of origin'. 'Nation' is intended to describe an historic entity whereas 'nationalism' is the ideology associated with this concept. To Hartshorne (1950), a nation represents "a feeling of kinship, of belonging together, an extension of the concept of family, more properly an extension of the concept of the in-groups versus outsiders. While usually expressed in terms derived from the language of the family—terms like 'blood, breed, race, etc.—it is in reality less of kin and more of kind—similarity of cultural rather than of biological characteristics."

However, John Stuart Mill, writing as early as in 1861, defined a nation as "a portion of mankind united among themselves by common sympathies which do not exist between them and any others—which make them cooperate with each other more willingly than with other people, desire under the same government and desire that it should be government by themselves exclusively." As Bertrand Russell (1938) put it: "A creed or sentiment of some kind is essential to social cohesion, but if it is to be a source of strength it must be genuinely and deeply felt by the great majority of populations."

A nation is, therefore, " a group of people, occupying a particular area, who feel themselves held together in terms of common acceptance of particular values that are of such prime importance to them that they demand that their areas and people should be organized in a distinct state, as the political agency by which those values may be preserved and furthered" (Hartshorne, 1950). However, Hartshorne's definition is in a sense more confined to the nation-state. The definition of Graham Smith (1986) is more expressive when he defines the nation as " a community of people whose members are bound together by a sense of solidarity rooted in a historic attachment to territory and a common culture and by a consciousness of being different from other nations". It is this definition which makes the concept of nation as necessarily spatial or geographically the most expressive.

However, if a nation is defined to be a historic community sharing a common culture then such entities (communities) can be identified throughout history. The people of ancient Egypt, or the people the Indus Valley would constitute a nation on this criterion. Amin, however, in 1980, attempted to propose just such an approach to the concept of nation as part of his wider attempt to rid the theories of their Euro-centric bias. P.J. Taylor (1985), in his analysis, observes that "however much we might sympathize with Amin's motives, most studies now agree that the concept is much more useful if its use is restricted to the modern world economy. The best way of satisfying these differences is to adopt Smith's (1982) approach where the nation is interpreted as the modern version of the older category 'ethnic community'. Hence world empires of the past may have incorporated ethnic communities but only in the modern world-system have such communities sriven for recognition as nations."

Anderson (1983) considers the nation to be above all else an 'imagined community' for four reasons: (a) despite the limited bounds of an individual's activities, the nation is associated with a larger sense of communion to that of his or her local environment; (b)) it is imagined as limited in geographic reach by finite, if elastic, boundaries beyond which lie other nations; (c) it is imagined as sovereign and thus the ideal is freedom in a sovereign state; and (d) it is imagined as community based on a territorial relationship which subsumes other community cleavages.

Karl W. Deutsch (1953) attempts to make some distinctions between some terms which, though, appear common, but, are essentially different. He makes a distinction between a 'society' which is defined as a group of persons who have learned to work together, and a 'community' which is defined as a group of persons who are able to communicate information to each other effectively over a wide range of topics. Similarly, a 'country' can be distinguished, which is a geographic area of greater economic interdependence and thus a multiple market for goods and services, from a 'people', which is a group of persons with complementary communications habits. A 'nation' is then a people which has gained control over some institutions of social coercion leading eventually to a full-fledged 'nation-state' and 'nationalism' is the preference for the competitive interest of this nation and its members over those of all outsiders in a world of social mobility and economic competition, dominated by the values of wealth, power and prestige, so that the goals of personal security and group identification appear bound up with the group's attainment of these values.

"While peoples are found at almost any period in history, nationalism and nation have occurred during only a few periods. A nation is the result of the transformation of a people, or of several ethnic elements, in the process of social mobilization."

The Growth of Nations

"The processes of partial social mobilization and of nation-building", says Deutsch (1953), "have been recurrent phenomena in history, at least, in certain general characteristics. What uniformities can we find in this growth of nations in the past? And in what ways is our own age different in respect to the growth of nations from any age that has gone before?"

Uniformities which have been found in the growth of nations include the following:

1. "The shift from subsistence agriculture to exchange economies" seems to have characterized all classes of wider national integration. Where the exchange economy came to embrace the bulk of the population and to bring many of them into direct contact with each other in the interchange of a wider variety of goods and services, there we find a tendency to national character, or least, regional, linguistic and cultural awakening...where these shifts take place, the ethnic and in part the linguistic situation becomes, as it were, loosened or softened and capable of setting again into new and different molds.

2. "The social mobilization of rural populations in core areas of denser settlement and more intensive exchange": The shift to an economy and culture based on wider interchange takes place at different times and different rates of speed in different regions.The result is often the existence of more 'advanced' regions side by side with more 'undeveloped' ones. The former are then often in a position to function as centres of cultural and economic attraction for some of the population of the latter and thus to become nuclei of further integration...Political geographers have sought to identify core areas around which larger states were organized successfully in the course of history.

3. "The growth of towns, and the growth of social mobility within them, and between town and country": There is no developed nation, it appears, without towns which have or have had a period of considerable growth, of mobility within the towns, and of increasing ties of social mobility, communication, and multiple economic exchange between town and country.

There have been towns, of course, where one or more of these conditions did not exist, and to that extent national development has been incomplete, absent, halted or retarded. On the other hand, to the extent that there was such growing mobility and communication within towns and between town and country, national development was accelerated.

4. "The growth of basic communication grids, linking important rivers, towns and trade routes in a flow of transport, travel and migration": Most nations do not seem to have grown from single centres. Many nations have had several capitals and have shifted their central regions several times in the course of their history. Even the classical example of growth around one centre, France, for long had two capital cities—Paris and Orleans; and some significant phases of the unification of the French language took place at the Champagne fairs and along the trade routes leading through that region—not to mention the role of the North-South routes and connections in helping the North to consolidate its victory over separatist and Albigensian elements in the Midi during the religious wars of the thirteenth century. A more extreme case, Germany, has no single core that could easily be identified and it seems more helpful to think of Germany as essentially a grid of routes of traffic, communication and migration.

The same notion of a basic grid seems to be applicable to the unification of China, Russia, Switzerland, Canada and United States. It would be interesting to investigate the relationship of such a grid to the incomplete unification and more recent separation of the areas that now comprise India and Pakistan.

5. "The differential accumulation and concentration of capital and skills, and sometimes of social institutions, and their 'lift-pump' effect on other areas and populations, with the successive entry of different social strata into nationalistic phase". A major factor in national differences and national pride today are the differences in the general standards of living. To some extent such differences tend to cut across the differences between social classes; there is a social, moral or traditional component in what is considered 'bare subsistence' in a given community, or in what counts as 'luxury' in another, and significant of what is considered the poor population in a relatively wealthy community may be appreciably better off in terms of physical goods and services than even many of the relatively well-off members of a poor or economically backward people. This difference between the generally prevailing standards of wealth, comfort and opportunity among different regions or peoples has sometimes been called the 'Kulturegefalle' by German writers who have employed this concept to bolster claims to German supremacy or exclusiveness vis-a-vis the populations of Eastern Europe and the Balkans.

It should be clear that, as technology progresses, the relative importance of the man-made factors of production, such as capital and skills, has tended to increase relative to the importance of the few natural facilities which were the only ones that more primitive technologies could exploit. There is a reason to believe that present-day differences in living standards are due far less to differences in natural factors of production and far more to differences in the supply of skilled labour, schools, housing and machinery.

Particular peoples and nations may then tend to crystallize, as it were, around particular concentrations of capital and technology, or of particular social institutions which offer individuals greater opportunities for the pursuit of goods or factors which they have learned to desire. Thus, in different parts of the world, we find growth of peoples around specific social institutions or specific concentrations of economic opportunity.

Where large economic or industrial developments have taken place, they have had a 'lift-pump' effect on the underlying populations.They have induced migration of populations to the regions of settlement, employment and opportunity, and put these newcomers into intensive economic and political contact with the locally predominant peoples, and with each other. The physical, political and economic contact had one of the two cultural and linguistic consequences: either it led to national assimilation, or, if national assimilation to the dominant group could not keep pace with the growing need for some wider group membership for the newcomer, then the 'lift-pump' effect would tend to lead eventually to a new growth of nationalism among the newly mobilized populations. Eventually, it might result in the assimilation of some previously separate groups, not to the still-dominant minority, but to the 'awakening' bulk of the population.

The intensity and appeal of nationalism in a world of sharply differentiated income and living standards perhaps may tend to be inversely proportional to the barriers to mobility between regions and classes, and directly proportional to the barriers against cultural assimilation, and to the extent of economic and prestige differences between classes, cultures and regions.

6. "The rise of the concept of 'interest' for both individuals and groups in unequal but fluid situations, and the growth of individual self-awareness and awareness of one's predispositions to join a particular group united by language and communication habits": The concept of a nation is bound up with that of a national interest. Already the non-national or proto-national institutions of the city state and the princely state imply the notion of group interests and interest of state, and all these notions of national, state, or city interests imply in turn the interests of individuals. But this concept of individuals with interests has itself gained its present importance only gradually in the course of certain developments of history. Even today different regions and civilization ascribe to it different degrees of significance, and it may loose again in the future much of its present importance.

At the bottom the notion of interest perhaps implies a situation in which men are pitted against each other in a competitive situation in which some of them can improve or even maintain their positions only at the expense of others.

Nationalism is one peculiar response to this double challenge of opportunity and insecurity, of loneliness and power. Men discover sooner or later that they can advance their interests in the competitive game of politics and economics by forging coalitions, and that they stand to gain, the firmer these coalitions can be made, provided only that they have been made with individuals and groups who have to offer in this game the largest amount of assets and least amount of liabilities. To form the firmest possible connections with the most promising group of competition would seem to be sound long-run strategy. With which group such firm connections can be formed is by no means arbitrary; in politics and economics such coalitions will depend on the cultural patterns, personality structures and communication habits of the participants. Their chances of success will thus depend to some degree on the links that make a people, the ties of nationality.

Organization along ethnic or national lines is by no means the only type of alignment which may be tried in the competitive game. Yet, of all these problems, patterns of organization, ethnic or national alignments often combine with the greatest adaptability to a competitive world. So long as competitive institutions continue to prevail, nationalism can mobilize more people and organize them more firmly than can many competing types of organizations. The potential rewards of nationalism then grow in proportion to the potential resources of wealth and power to which members of a particular people have, or can gain, access on preferred terms.

When men seek for themselves, they thus may come to find their nationality; and when they seek the community of their fellows, they may discover once again the connection between ethnic nationality and the capacity for fellowship. In any case, the phase of self-doubt and self-appraisal tends to be followed by a phase of decision and of conscious or even deliberate identification with a group; and with the loosening of the ties of religion or status that group is likely to be a group delimited at least in part along with national lines, in terms of habits of language and communication.

Many emotionally, culturally and politically sensitive individuals react to a sojourn abroad, i.e., away from their native region or culture, with a far stronger assertion of nationalism and of allegiance to their own language, culture and people.

7. "The awakening of ethnic awareness and the acceptance of national symbols, intentional or unintentional": Group awareness...seems clearly a matter of social institutions. Some secondary symbols are attached to some as-

pects of group life and are repeated and disseminated over and over again by an organization or institution, often for a purpose that has nothing to do with nationality, or which might even be opposed to it. After a time, the institution may change or disappear, the organized repetition of the symbols may cease—but if there were enough of a primary reality capable of being symbolized, and if there had been going on that basic process of social mobilization...then the results of the dissemination of those symbols may well prove irreversible...that is partly self-regenerating, and so long as the foundations for ethnic group exist and social mobilisation and communication continue to weld its members together, national group awareness may be there to stay.

A process of social mobilization may even transform the function of existing symbols or institutions so as to turn them into agencies of group awareness, regardless of their original purposes. Thus, nationalism was promoted sometimes by a supra-national church.

Once the process of group consciousness has started, there appear also the deliberate pioneers and leaders of national awakening...side by side with the awakeners of national pride and fashioners of symbols as the first organizers...Together with all this activity, we find the gradual acceptance...of national symbols of national colors, flags, animals, and flowers, of anthems, marches and patriotic songs....

8. "The merging of ethnic awareness with attempts at political compulsion, and in some cases the attempt to transform one's own people into a privileged class to which members of other peoples are subordinated": What does this process accomplish and what does it aim at? When a nation has been built up and when it has been reinforced finally by the full compulsive power of the state, then four things have been accomplished:

(a) A relatively large community of human beings has been brought into existence who can communicate effectively with each other, and who have command over sufficient economic resources to maintain themselves and to transmit this ability for mutual communication to their children as well. In other words, there has been brought into being a large, comprehensive and very stable, human network of communication, capable of maintaining, reproducing and further developing its channels.

(b) There has been both an effective accumulation of economic resources and a sufficient social mobilization of manpower to permit the social division of labour necessary for this process and to permit its continuation.

(c) There has been a social accumulation and integration of memories and symbols and of individuals and social facilities for their preservation, transmission and recombination, corresponding to the level of mobilization and integration of material and human resources, or even pointing beyond it.

(d) There has been at least some development of the capacity to redirect or reallocate, or form a new combination of economic, social and human resources as well as of symbols and items of knowledge, habit or thought—that is to say, of the capacity to learn. Some of the social learning capacity is developed invisibly in the minds of individuals; some of it can be observed in the habits and patterns of culture prevailing among them; some of it finally is embodied in tangible facilities and specific institutions. Together, all these constitute the community's capacity to produce and accept the new knowledge or new goals, and to take the corresponding action.

"On all four counts, it should be evident, the nation represents a more effective organization than supra-national but largely passive layer-cake society or the feudal or tribal localism that preceded it...On all these counts, there may be considerable contrasts between different nations. The social models accepted for imitation, the established institutions, the economic practices, and the methods of compulsion within each nation are all intimately connected with the cultural traditions and leading social classes prevailing there...yet...the worst-led nation represents, relative to its numbers of population, a greater amount of social communication facilities, of economic resources, and of social learning capacity than any pattern of ethnic or social organization preceding it."

Thus, Deutsch develops his model, illustrating eight stages of development from initial economic exchange processes to the final national stage, but his model provides an example of the error of developmentalism because nations do not simply evolve in a linear sequence. They are made and in their making they encompass contradictory expressions. The rationalism of modernity is combined with irrationality of ethnic traditionalism. The following discussion, therefore, concentrates on the elements and characteristics of the nation.

Elements and Characteristics of the Nation

The analysis of a nation always reveals it to be composed of a territorial and a human element, and to be moved in its evolution by an historical/political force, a dynamism which manifests itself in voluntary and collective action, i.e., the state. The foregoing analyses have disclosed historical territories fairly well defined (but not politically stable): Ireland, which is an island, as well as Bohemia, a plateau, rimmed by mountains which separate it from the Germanic world, and link to the rest of the Slav world by the Moravian isthmus. Poland, on the contrary, has been built in the eastern part of the European plain around a river basin lacking natural frontiers. France has grown up in a region of passage from the Rhine to the Mediterranean, and in the main, its best lands are composed of a series of river basins, between which there are no natural obstacles to intercommunication. In France, as in Ireland, the process of unification of the heterogeneous elements has been continuous right up to the present day, but in Bohemia, the unification of the groups of Slav invaders was followed, from the Middle Ages onwards, by the establishment of inassimilable foreign groups both in the valuable peripheral regions and in the towns throughout the lands.

Nations with the greatest degree of unification, and with the most distinctive personalities, are those having no 'natural frontiers' and whose territories are in no way sketched out by nature; they have developed in regions of intense life and traffic where contact with their neighbours has often been characterized by severe friction. The flexibility of geographical framework and environment, and a position which demands the energetic undertaking of relations with the external world, together with heterogeneity of the human elements, provide peculiarly suitable conditions for the formation and development of a national spirit within the state.

The common pursuance of a political/social and economic life, moulded by the relationships between the people and the territory, exerts a unifying influence upon the heterogeneous elements of the state, and stresses certain of their psychological and physiological traits at the expense of others. These modifications are mirrored in each individual, and so spread throughout the whole group; becoming firmly established therein, they endow it with a distinctive personality, and the people are held together from within by the communicative efficiency, the complementarity of the communicative facilities/habits, and slowly make them a nation. The community which permits a common history to be experienced as common, is a community of complementarity habits and facilities of communication in which the territoriality is deeply rooted.

The communicative facilities of a society necessarily include a socially standardized system of symbols which is a language and which acts as a binding/cementing force in the making of a nation. Complementarity is greater if it permits individuals to communicate efficiently no matter how often the people of the society change their residence or occupation.

However, "it is difficult to enumerate and impossible to measure the intangible that make a nation. Nationalities come into being only when certain objective bonds delimit a social group. A nationality generally has several of these attributes; very few have all of them. The most usual of them are common descent, language, territory, political entity, customs and traditions and religion", says H. Kohn (1945). Identifying the basic elements and characteristics of a nation, particularly those of the forces of cohesion for the integral community, Reinhold Niebuhr (1959) observes: "...common language and a sense of ethnic kinship, geographic unity and continuity, a common historical experience and frame of political thought, a common area of economic mutuality, and sometimes, the fear of a common foe. Any of these forces may be defective, but they cannot all be defective if the unity of the nation is to be preserved. A common religion was usually regarded as an equally prerequisite until modern religiously pluralistic nations...refuted the theory. It is worth noting, however, that only solid communities bound by other ties of mutuality can afford the luxury of religious pluralism."

A common language is the most frequent and obvious sign of social cohesion. Customs, traditions, folkways, feasts and festivals, costumes and decorations can all be evidence of national cohesion. "We think of the people of France as being French. Their Frenchness is demonstrated primarily by their common use of the French language, though this is spoken also by a significant part of the population of both Belgium and Switzerland. But within the whole body of French speakers, the French themselves are distinguished by a complex social ideas and attitudes. These have, in turn, been shaped through centuries and are known to us 'French tradition' or 'French culture'. This is the cement which binds the people together and make them cohere into a nation." However, customs, traditions, folkways and festivals etc. can also be evidence of regionalism powerful enough to threaten the integrity of the state. Some of the national movements in the nineteenth century Europe began with the assiduous cultivation of everything pertaining to customs and folklore of the national groups of which it was comprised of.

The language, culture, custom, tradition, political, social and economic influences—as well as working and struggling for a common ideal—all these go to form psychological character of the unified nation. To this unity the nation owes that vitality which is expressed in the dynamism needed to combat in the external field, the dangers which beset the state, to preserve in internal affairs, its national cohesion, and to facilitate the assimilation of alien elements. Action in the external field occurs in periods of over-stimulation, under the spur of recurrent crises from which even weak organisms derive sufficient energy for violent reaction. On the contrary, the will to common action, and the ability to absorb alien elements are manifested quietly, peacefully and uninterruptedly in the day-to-day business of normal life. The power of assimilation might almost be taken as a measure of the vitality of a nation, but this power is quite different from the coercive measures which are enforced by some governments to assimilate their allogeneous subjects.

Religion has ceased to be an important force or factor in national cohesion over much of the world. The more developed states have neither a state church nor a state religion. But in some states, observes Pounds (1972) that, "religion still provides either a cohesive or a dividing force. In (former) Yugoslavia the division between Orthodox and Catholics is, in effect a national division. The former British India split along religious lines into Hindu India and Muslim Pakistan when British rule was withdrawn. Despite the assertion in the Indian Constitution that the state has no official religion, it is difficult to deny that in fact, it has been established around the Hindu faith. It cannot be doubted that religion is a powerful political force in the Arab world nor that the Catholic Church constitutes a significant part of the cement of the Polish and Irish nations...Indeed, the identity of a religion with an ethnic group can have very significant political consequences. The fact that Catholic Ireland was ruled by Protestant England, that Catholic Poland was partitioned between Lutheran Prussia and Orthodox Russia—in addition, of course, to Catholic Austria—gave the priesthood in both instances a unique role, both political and religious. In Poland, during the years of partition, it was the priesthood which played a dominant role in preserving a national identity."

Pounds (1972) further observes that "there is a presumption that those peoples who, through the accident of birth, inhabit a single state area will acquire the marks of the corresponding nation." "Political frontiers", says Kohn (1945), "tend to establish nationalities." The pressures brought to bear on such peoples by the society amid which they find themselves are so strong that it requires a conscious and purposeful effort to resist them. Minority and dissident groups perhaps tend, more often than not, to be absorbed or assimilated ultimately by their enveloping societies. Thus, the Bretons have, on the whole, been absorbed by the French nation, the Welsh by the British, the Slavic Lusatians by the Germans. This process of absorption or assimilation of minority groups or national minorities by the dominant society amid which they live may be either hastened or resisted. The Prussian campaign against the Poles in the nineteenth century; the Polish campaign against the Ukrarians after 1919; the Hungarian against the Slovak, Romanian and other minorities before 1914; the Spanish against the Calalans; and the Russian against the Baltic peoples, and numerous other groups. Such efforts may occasionally be successful; usually they leave a legacy of lasting hate. But such groups may resist the slow, quiet assertion of its superiority by the dominant group. Such resistance is rarely violent and rarely successful.

"On the other hand", Pounds (1972) rates, "if a dominant group is active in forcing its culture upon a reluctant subnation and the later is vigorous in resisting such pressure, the scene is set for a struggle for national preservation and independence. Such struggles acquire heroic proportions; they are the raw material of legend and a source of inspiration to later generations. They may provide the cement which welds a nation together, and if successful, they may create a state to match the nation. The Polish struggle against the Russian in the nineteenth century, that of the Czechs against the Austrians...of the Serbs,

Bulgars and Greeks against the Turks...these are examples of the strivings of national groups to resist absorption into a larger and more powerful groups... Such experiences normally intensify the feeling of cohesion, of belonging to the group. The most articulate nations today have in some measure been molded by pressures. The pressure may not always be an attempt by an outside power to thwart or destroy the nation; it may be merely an experience through which its members have passed. For example, in the mid-sixteenth century, the territory which now forms the Netherlands was made up of several small, separate and quarrelsome states; yet the Dutch nation was born, coherent and distinct from other national units...The birth of other nations can rarely be dated with such precision, but many have passed through an intense emotional experience which have matured them quickly."

"The French nationality was born of the enthusiastic manifestation of the will in 1789, while the English nation took the shape under Queen Elizabeth I in the second half of the sixteenth century when the kingdom was threatened by the Spanish armada."

The Indian nation was to have born in 1857 when the native feudals rose against the foreign domination but it failed to come up, not because of religious cleavages, but because of sectarian interests of the native feudals. However, the Indian peoples experienced a common historical habitation, and association during the British *raj* and also acquired complementarity of habits and communicative efficiency, but nevertheless, they failed to develop into a nation. This was largely because of the fact that territorial communal cleavages, which hitherto remained dormant, gradually became expressive and active and hardened also, and stood in the way of the dynamism which sought for the social cohesion for an 'Indian nation'. Partition along the communal lines was a great blow to the process of "the making of an Indian nation".

However, "every nation has its peculiar symbols, customs and practices, and the best word for them is iconography. The feeling of being a nation is compounded of any or all of these elements, and no two nations feel the same way for the same reasons. Many of these new states of the mid-twentieth century are arbitrary creation, whose people are engaged today in this same task of establishing a sense of unity and creating a body of national legend of which they can be proud. Each nation has a view of itself, and at the same time a concept of other nation. It knows what it perceives to be its national space, and this space it is probably prepared to defend. It may, on the other hand, embrace territory to which it has little emotional attachment and which it be prepared to abandon without too much soul searching in an emergency. The nation's concept of itself, like its attributes to other peoples, is a product of its history and tradition. It is not always a rational attitude and it is rarely devoid of a kind of self-congratulatory egotism. The folklore which helps to give a nation a sense of unity also tends to represent it as more noble, more just, more democratic than others... Perhaps no nationality has a more clearly expressed self-concept than the Chinese."

Nationalism

It is a feeling of belonging to a nation. Or it is the desire of cultural-linguistic and religious groups to achieve a political status that would give them a limited measure of self-government, sufficient at least to allow them to project and deepen their cultural individuality. It is a doctrine based on the idea that every nation should have its own state. This idea emerged in the eighteenth century, became a major force in the world politics in the nineteenth century and has come to dominate the politics of the twentieth century. It was originally associated with the rationalism of the eighteenth century, especially the rejection of the personal authority of the monarch as the source of a state's sovereignty. Instead sovereignty lay with the people. This notion is given political expression in the famous opening sentence of the American Constitution of 1887: "We the people...". The specific idea that 'the people' constitute a 'nation' appears in the French Revolution with the setting up of a National Assembly in 1789 and the French proclaiming themselves 'le grande nation' in 1790. By 1815, at the Congress of Vienna, the novel idea that state should coincide with 'nation' was first expressed and the Greek independence in 1821 represents the first direct result of this idea, i.e., nationalism. Revolution between 1830 and 1848 became 'national' revolution and the concept finally triumphed at the Peace Conference in Versailles in 1919 when national self-determination was recognized as the prime criterion of the new European political order. Much of the crisis in the present-day world may be attributed to the "diffusion of the idea of nationalism"—disintegration of the Soviet Union and Yogoslavia, reunion of Germany, division of Czechoslovakia and the collapse of the socialist system in East Europe necessarily manifest the areal/spatial expression of it, i.e., nationalism.

Theory of Nationalism

Karl Deutsch is credited with having developed the geographical theory of nationalism in 1953. His 'communication' theory of nation and nationalism builds upon Whittlesey's nuclear area and extends it to the consideration of the communication grid of a country. A community based upon a common language and/or memories is termed a people which is separated from other peoples by a communication gap. When such a people seek power to control their own destinies through the process of nationalism, a nationality comes into existence.When power is achieved, a nationality becomes a nation which on acquiring its own sovereign state becomes a nation-state. For Deutsch this communication involves two procedures: assimilation, by which he means additions to the community, and mobilisation, by which he means the rise of a political public within the community.The later is defined by the media etc. Finally, he combines these various concepts into a model of the growth of nations (mentioned earlier) in which he sought to analyze the stages of development, this time 'national development.' However, Deutsch's model of the growth of nation suffers from the error of developmentalism.

Nationalism, according to Nairn(1977), is the result of the tidal wave of modernization that swept Europe in the nineteenth century as a result of industrialization and urbanization which brought about many economic and social changes, particularly in western Europe. It was more advanced than in the Central and Eastern Europe. Nationalism is then a compensatory reaction to this uneven development. Beginning in the area bordering the advanced zone, the new rising urban-industrial interests were unable to compete with the more efficient core producers. They have to evolve strategies to survive, to prevent peripheralization. The only resource available to the local capitalist interests, other than the material resources, not available to the metropolitan interests, was their cultural affinity to their 'people'. By emphasizing differences between ethnic communities, local interests could form broad national alliances with which to challenge the core. Hence regions where nationalism grew up as a major new force on the European stage were Central Europe and the unification nationalisms of Germany and Italy. From this beginning nationalism spread like a wildfire, following the uneven development unleashed on the world by modernization.

Next came the separation nationalisms of Central Europe to be followed by the nationalisms outside Europe in the twentieth century. But nationalism became more than a reaction of semiperiphery and periphery. With the demise of British hegemony, the new vigorous nationalism spread to the core as a major force in the subsequent political competition resulting in the second phase of formal imperialism. By the twentieth century, it was to become the dominant ideology throughout all zones of the world economy.

Where do the two sides of nationalism fit into this theory? So far the use of 'tradition' has been made clear but of the 'progress' side of the ideology? Although the urban industrial interests of the semiperiphery and periphery used images of an idyllic past to mobilize the people, they could not be true conservatives and present progress. The whole purpose of the strategy was to close ranks with a view to catching up the core. This could only be done by borrowing the salient features of advancement and modernization against which the movement was reacting. A medieval Germany or Italy would be no match for a modern Britain or France. Hence, the rhetoric of nationalism with its glorifications of the past was ultimately only a cover for rapid modernization. The classic case is, of course, late nineteenth century Germany where massive industrial growth went hand in hand with a popular German cultural revival.

Nationalism gives the people back their tradition and provides an identity in an alien world. It is for this reason that nationalism is particularly associated with periods of radical disruption such as wars, etc., and with strong charismatic leadership, as has been the case with the Indian nationalism under the charismatic leadership of Mahatma Gandhi. Nationalism, however, acts as compensation for the alienation of mass society.

The intellectuals played a dominant role in the rise of nationalism. The new class of intellectuals of the nineteenth century Europe, often from lower-middle class backgrounds were able to provide the historical, philosophical, ethnographic and even geographical basis of the new nationalisms. The intelligentsia were the agents of refraction, the most advanced part of the new national middle class. Nairn (1977) postulates a social diffusion process beginning with a small intelligentsia, initially reacting to the French Revolution, which he terms phase A. This is followed by phase B from 1815 to 1848 in Europe where the ideology spreads through the middle classes. But it is still a minority movement and this accounts for its ultimate failure in the 1848 revolution. Phase C occurs in the second half of the nineteenth century in Europe when it diffuses to the lower classes and modern popular nationalism is born. The intelligentsia were, therefore, the initial purveyors of ideas to be used for the general interests of their class.

Blaut (1980) takes strong exception to Nairn's 'relegation'of class struggle to below nationalism, the association of nationalism to fascism in the Janus model and more specifically to the Euro-centric 'diffusionalism' of Nairn's model which underrates the contribution of the non-European periphery to nationalism and national liberation in particular. Blaut provides an alternative space-time identification of nationalism with the source in USA (1776) and Haiti (1804). Blaut's critique raises several important questions involving definitions and whether identification of nationalism as a false consciousness relegates or enhances the fundamental importance of class struggle. Nevertheless, Nairn's model provides a major attempt at explaining nationalism that transcends the ideology itself.

Typology of Nationalisms

Orridge (1981) presents a typology of nationalism, in which, he identifies five basic types:

(a) State Nationalism

This is the nationalism of the core states. This nationalism is the source of much dispute over the timing of the emergence of nation and nationalism. Earlier patriotism was nothing but loyalty to monarch or state or even country but not to the collective idea of a people as a nation incorporating all sections and classes. Nevertheless, the centralizing tendencies of these states within relatively stable boundaries did lead to a degree of cultural uniformity and cohesion by 1800 which was not found in other areas of comparable size. England and France are the key examples but similar nation-states were emerging in Portugal, Sweden, the Netherlands and, to a lesser extent, Spain. In all of these cases "state preceded nation and it can be said that state produced nation". The result was proto-nation-states. The 'people' were entering politics but nationalism as an ideology was not fully developed until later in the nineteenth century. Hence, the nation preceded nationalism.

(b) Unification Nationalism

This type of nationalism was characteristic to Central Europe where medium-sized states were prevented from evolving under the contradictory pressures of small (city-scale) states and large multi-ethnic empires. There were a mosaic of small independent states mixed with provinces of larger empires, such as Germany and Italy. This type of territorial-political pattern came into being in Central Europe largely as a result of the Treaty of Westphalia in 1649 but the French Revolution, followed by the Napoleonic wars after 1800, disrupted the pattern in Central Europe. Although, the Congress of Vienna in 1815 attempted to reconstitute the old territorial political pattern in Central Europe, but by the time new forces had been unleashed to dominate the rest of the century. Nationalism was the justification for uniting most of the German culture area under Prussian leadership into a new German nation-state and transforming Italy from a mere geographical expression to an Italian nation-state. These are the examples of unification nationalism and in these two cases "nation preceded state". The re-union of Germany in the post-Cold War period seems to be a natural manifestation of unification nationalism.

(c) Separation Nationalism

Most successful nationalisms have involved the disintegration of existing sovereigning states. In the nineteenth and early twentieth century this nationalism lay behind the creation of a large number of new states out of the Austro-Hungarian, Ottoman and Russian empires. Beginning with Greece in 1821, a whole tier of new states was created in Eastern Europe from Bulgaria, through the Balkans to Scandinavia. Emergence of a large number of nation-states in the post-Cold War period, following the disintegration of the Soviet Union and Yugoslavia, may be attributed to separation nationalism. This type of nationalism was, until recently considered to be a phenomenon of the past at least in core countries.

'Autonomous' nationalism of this type is appearing in Punjab, Jammu & Kashmir and all north-eastern states of the Indian Union but none of these has, at present been successful in establishing their own nation-state, but the Indian Union is contemplating to grant more political autonomy to them, even at the cost of amending the constitution. Here, in the separation nationalism, it is the nation which preceded the state, and it can even be said that nation produced the state.

(d) Liberation Nationalism

The break-up of European overseas empires may be attributed to the national liberation movements. The earliest was the American war of independence in 1776 which finally led to the creation of USA, independent of British control. The Latin American revolutions after the Napoleonic wars were more explicitly 'nationalist' in character. These can be considered liberal nationalist movements. In the twentieth century such movements have invariably been socialist nationalist movements varying in their socialism from India's mild version to Vietnam's revolutionary version. "Another way of dividing up liberation nationalism is between those based upon European settler groups and those based upon indigenous peoples. In the former case, we have the USA and Latin American republics, and the orignial white Commonwealth states of South Africa, Canada, Australia and New Zealand who negotiated independence without liberation movement. In the latter case, most of the Afro-Asian states come which have become independent since 1945." Here in this category, the state concept preceded both nation and nationalism.

(e) Renewal Nationalism

In some parts of the periphery 'ancient' cultures withstood European political capture for a variety of reasons and were able to emulate the state nationalism of the core, often using polities similar to unification nationalism. These states had a long history as ethnic communities upon which they could easily build their new nationalism. National renewal for former greatness became the basic cry. Hence, Iran could rediscover its Persian heritage. Turkey after losing its Ottoman empire could concentrate on its Turkish enthnicity. The classic cases of this type of natioalism are to be found in Japan and China. "This form of nationalism can also occur as part of a process of creating a new state identity which attempts to redefine the relations of the state to the world economy. As such, this renewal is associated with the modern revolutions. Stalin's socialism in one country had many of the trappings of a renewal of the Russian nation. Other renewals have occurred in Mexico, Egypt, China and most recently in Iran."

Taylor (1985) observes: "Political leaders in a wide range of contexts have been able to appeal to the nationalist doctrine to justify their actions...On the one hand, it is a good thing, a positive force in world history as when it is associated with weak states freeing themselves from foreign oppression. But it also has a dark side, the negative force associated with Nazism and Facism in Europe, and militarism, throughout the semi-periphery and periphery. It is, as it were, both good and bad. This is most clearly seen in attitudes to nationalism after the two world wars in the twentieth century. In 1919, the First World War was blamed on the suppression of nationalism, in 1945 the Second World War was blamed on the expression of nationalism." To Nairn(1977) nationalism is like 'the modern Janus' after the famous Greek statue which looked in two directions at once, both backwards and forwards. To him, it is the essence of the ideology, a simultaneous appeal to both progress and tradition.

There is no denying that nationalism is recognized as a legitimate force in international geopolitics. The creation of the League of Nations and then of the United Nations Organization was largely based on the doctrine of nationalism that each nation-state, represented in the international organization, must have global expression of its national character. However, nationalism is easier to define as a doctrine than it is to define on the ground, and the difficulty was realized when the new nation-states had to be carved out of the territories of the defeated states of Germany and Austro-Hungary as per the guidelines of the Treaty of Versailles after the First World War. No doubt, national self-determination provided a simple guide to this process—states should be formed around nations as determined by the people. In fact, people were allowed to decide to which nation-state they belong or should they have a separate state-area for them, or how to determine their nationality?

It is through plebiscite that the nationality of the people was determined. Plebiscite was not a new method to ascertain the territorial character of a nationality. It was used immediately after the French Revolution to legitimize the extension of the French State, and as a tool in the unification of Italy and Germany.

In some of the cases, a different criterion other than the plebiscite, was followed to determine the territorial character of the nationality, and that was to follow the linguistic pattern of the people. The language criterion was accepted as a legitimate indication of national preference, but still there remained the problems of defining national languages and mapping their distribution.

Linguistic reorganization of the Indian Union in the 1950s, and the process which is still continuing, has implicitly recognized the principle of 'national self-determination' of the major linguistic groups, with a consequence of mutually exclusive sub-national movements.

Taylor (1985) observes that "Nations do not exist as neatly packaged bundles of peoples waiting for a state to be drawn around them. No less than states, nations are man-made and reflect the politics in which they are created. Any theory of nationalism cannot, therefore, be merely a theory of ethnic distribution, rather it must be a theory of political construction of nation.

Nation-building

The concept of nation-building is more relevant to polyethnic states, particularly to the 'mutually exclusive' multinational states. Though "nation-building may be viewed as the process and the devices through which the sentiment of loyalty for the nation-state is fostered and fissiparous and divisive tendencies are pacified and eliminated", but in reality, "it refers essentially to the process", says Dikshit (1982), "of bringing together culturally and socially discrete groups into an organic (i.e., fully functional) spatial system and the establishment of a strong national identity inseparably bound with the territory of this system. There are four important aspects of this process: First, progressive development among the constituent political communities of a deep and unambiguous sense of identity with the state and its ideals. Secondly, the broadening and intensification of social communication among the constituent communities and regions. Thirdly, social, economic and psychological commitments are eroded and the people become available for new patterns of socialization and behaviour. Lastly, improvement of transport facilities by minimizing physical distances and thereby facilitating a greater flow of goods and services between the different regions of the state. This and the development of mass media and growth of urban centres by bringing the different components of the state's population together, give rise to common norms of behaviour that reinforce a sense of unity and national identity."

Hartshorne's concept of state-idea is more appropriate to the nation-building process, whereby the diverse/mutually exclusive regions can be brought together under a common organization, so that the state may achieve an integrated personality. To Weiner (1965), nation building refers "specifically to the problem of creating a sense of territorial nationality which overshadows—or eliminates subordinate parochial loyalties."

The study of territoriality, state, nation, nationalism and nation-building has assumed special significance, especially in the light of the major politico-geographical changes in Eurasia in the post-Cold War period and in Africa as a result of ethnic violence, ethnic cleansing and xenophobia, etc.

Chapter 5

Spatial Factors of the State

"Regardless of the kaleidoscopic change of contemporary events, both in and around the country, the foreign policy of India has shown a natural tendency to return again and again to the same Nehruvian paradigm of non-alignment." "By allowing the 'defense in depth', the Russian soldiers (erstwhile Soviet Union) successfully fought the battle against the German invaders during the Second World War", or "the Indian troops achieved a major strategic success over the Pakistani troops, when the latter invaded Kashmir in 1971. Here, in the Kashmir sector, the Indian troops switched over to the same strategic operation, which the Russians did in the early 1940s." "The French State is one of the longest surviving states in the world, ever since the proclamation of the 'le grande nation' in 1790, by the French people." "Pakistan suffered disintegration in 1971, when its eastern wing declared secession, and became independent."

The above statements/international events merely reflect/manifest the intrinsic deterministic political role of the three primary spatial factors—'location', 'size' and 'shape'—in the survival or demise of the state. Where is the state? What is its spatial extent or how large is it? What shape does its spatial extent create or possess of? All this information about a state seems to be intrinsically vital before any indepth evaluation of its internal and external political space relationship is done. In fact, each of these factors is important for its own sake, and each plays a significant role in association with various other factors in the politico-geographical drama of specific political areas and of the world as a whole. The political destiny of the state seems to be very much dependent on the combined role of these factors. However, sometimes, the location becomes more important rather than the shape and vice versa. Sometimes, it is of paramount importance, sometimes of only minor concern, depending upon the region and its place in world history—both in the past and at the present time. The interplay of these three factors may tend to determine the relative importance of the political area with respect to other political areas, and may account for the ease of expansion or vulnerability to attack.

Freedom of action versus restriction because of 'encirclement' in foreign relations may likewise be indicated by the spatial association of these factors—location, shape and size. The internal space relationship of the political area depends to a certain extent on the pattern of the areal association of these factors, which intrinsically and explicitly harp on the pattern of population distribution and mobility, health and energy of the population, development of economic strength, utilization and mobilization of resources, infrastructural development, and the degree of cohesiveness vis-a-vis secessionism. On the other hand, the areal association of these factors tends to determine the alignment and type of internal and international boundaries.

Here, in this chapter, each of these factors is dealt with separately so as to assess and evaluate their political relevance in the spatial/territorial perspective.

Location

The German diplomat, Richard von Kuhlmann, once remarked: "Geographical position (location) and historical development are so largely determining factors of foreign policy that regardless of the kaleidoscopic change of contemporary events, and no matter what form of government has been instituted or what political party may be in power, the foreign policy of a country has a natural tendency to return again and again to the same general and fundamental alignment." Similarly, the French diplomat, Jules Cambon, said: "The geographical position of a nation...is the cardinal factor conditioning its foreign policy—the principal reason why it must have a foreign policy at all..."

The above statements tend to conform the legitimate political importance of location in the external space relationship. It is, therefore, rightly observed that location provides the geographic setting in which a specified political area must largely depend for existence/survival, and for the success in competition with other political areas.

The geographical location of a state or a political area is significant in two ways: (i) its absolute location in relation to the terrestrial globe, which influences in particular its climate, and that is expressed in terms of degrees of latitude and longitude; and (ii) its location relative to water bodies and land masses, and also to other states/neighbours. The former is known as the astronomical or absolute location while the latter is called the relative location.

Astronomical Location

The astronomical location refers to 'the latitudinal extent' of the state or the political area on the globe rather than the longitudinal extent. It precisely tells where the state is situated or what is its precise location. Thus, astronomical or geometrical location is mathematically determined/drawn/calculated. The latitudinal extent of India (7°30'N to 37°10'N, including the areas under illegal occupation of Pakistan and China) is its astronomical location, which is very precisely drawn upon the world grid.

The astronomical location has special relevance in the life of any given political area or the state, as it largely determines the climatic characteristics of it. Climate, in a large measure, sets forth the broad limit of resources, such as: agricultural resources, forest resources, water resources, etc., and also of human resources, like physical traits, capacity to work, capacity to fight, quality of perception, and level of thinking, group feeling, community behaviour and character, and a host of other human characteristics. Precisely speaking, the 'genre de vie' (way of living) of the people of any given state or political area, is largely conditioned by the climatic phenomena of it. It is the cardinal factor conditioning the complementary habits and facilities of communication for a people—the principal reason why the people must be brave at all and why it must have developed a 'genre de vie' at all.

It is, therefore, rightly observed that astronomical location, acting implicitly through climate, exerts a powerful influence on the economic and human structure of a given political area, which often plays a dominant but fundamental role in its relationship with other political areas of the international system. It has long been felt that the climatic conditions are of marked importance to the activities of states, and therefore, to the formation of their political structures and attitudes.

In the contemporary global pattern, all the core states (developed and powerful states in the world) are located entirely in the temperate zone, while the peripheral states (underdeveloped/developing poor and fragile states) are situated in the warm tropical zones. In the global power politics, and its economic systems, it is the core states which exploit in peripheral states.

The people of the temperate zone enjoy the stimulation of pronounced seasonality of climate, and marked cyclonic variety of weather. These climatic characteristics greatly enhance the human quality and perception and the sustenance of human capacity. Whereas, the people of the warm tropical zones are always at great disadvantage owing to persistent heat which greatly reduces the sustenance of human resources. Jean Bodin, writing toward the end of the sixteenth century, remarked that "northern peoples excel in bodily physical strength, southern peoples in craft and genius. Climate being most favourable between these extremes, the middle (temperate) peoples are best adapted to control politics...". Montesquieu, in the eighteenth century, remarked: "One should not be astonished that the weakness of the inhabitants of warm climates should make them slaves, and the courage of those in the cold climate should keep them free. This is a result of natural conditions.

It has long been felt that people of the temperate states are more conscious of their duties and rights rather than the people of the warm tropical states. Democracy has successfully survived in the temperate states, whereas in most of the Afro-Asian and the Latin American tropical states, democracy has either perished or become too fragile to survive. One of the distinguishing features of the temperate states is their political stability which is practically absent in the tropical states. Some of the ancient cultural/political realms, which flourished in the warm areas, could not survive long because the inhabitants therein lacked bodily physical strength, and perceptual sustaining capacity, nevertheless, they developed superior art and culture.

Regardless of their rich material resource base, the people of the tropical states greatly lack in, what may be called, the accumulative technical skill to utilize and mobilize it. As a result, they cannot dominate the world. Contemporary global politics is very much dependent on science and technology which appear to be the monopoly of the temperate people, and they alone seem to condition the destiny of the international scenario. Political power, by this argument, seems to be clearly related to climate.

Relative Location

If the astronomical location of the state is a determinant of its political health, energy and vigour, strength and genius, the relative location of it, then, decides the state's external space relationship. Or, in other words, it can be said that the relative location is the cardinal factor conditioning the foreign policy of the state—"the principal reason why it must have a foreign policy at all."

Relative location of the state is a multifaceted issue. It is expressed in terms of (i) accessibility, whether it has access to the oceans, or lies far or near the world's major trade routes, (ii) whether it extends from one ethnic-cultural area into another, and (iii) how many neighbours it has, or with how many neighbours it shares common boundaries, and who among them are, its friends and foes.

Probably the most obvious feature of the state, in terms of its external space relationship, is whether it has access to the sea or not. Accessibility to the open sea seems to have pushed the English people and the Japanese out upon the oceans, making them the greatest seafaring peoples in the world, providing them with the greatest opportunity to command the seas. Control over the sea routes inevitably led them to decide the destiny of the world, particularly of the old world. Germans, on the other hand, could not develop themselves as the seafaring people simply because they lacked that much of direct accessibility to the sea as the English and the Japanese. Accessibility to the sea has long been the cardinal factor in the British and Japanese foreign policies, whereas, the Russian and German foreign policies reflect a strong inclination towards 'continentality'. While the British and the Japanese think in terms of the global perspective, the Russians and the Germans think in terms of the regional perspective, mostly confined to Europe, and the neighbouring Mediterranean region.

Accessibility to the sea provides opportunity for the control of the strategic locations such as the straits, canals and bays, and also of important ports. However, accessibility to the warm seas is more strategic and meaningful with regard to the control of the maritime traffic rather than the accessibility to the cold frozen sea.

However, states which are deprived of the access to the sea, or do not have access to the sea, are referred to as 'landlocked' (Fig. 5.1). Large number of African and European states are landlocked. Similarly, in Asia, states like Nepal, Bhutan, Laos, Mongolia and Afghanistan are landlocked which had been created as a result of "sustained campaign for secured frontier" by the European colonial powers. However, the collapse of the Soviet Union, and subsequent proclamation of independence by a number of erstwhile Soviet republics, led to the emergence of few more landlocked states in Central Asia, such as Uzbekistan, Kazakhstan, Turkmenia, Tajikistan, Kirgizia, etc.

Landlocked states have often been involved in campaign seeking to terminate their isolation, and thus this characteristic is of great politico-geographical interest and importance, so far as the "politics of access to the sea" is concerned. The political destiny of landlocked states is determined by the three probable possibilities: (i) To form political federation/confederation with coastal states. Such federations existed in the recent past in Africa but collapsed due to contradictory interests between the federating units. (ii) To secure territorial corridor. Bolivia and Paraguay in Latin America have been provided territorial corridor, through Chile and Brazil. Moreover, they have secured right to use the tributaries of the Amazon and the Paraguay rivers to gain access to the sea. The Polish corridor once became famous, as it carried Poland to the Baltic Sea. (iii) To secure the right of transit across neighbouring states. Nepal and Bhutan have the right to import commodities through the port of Calcutta in India. Most of the African and European landlocked states have acquired the right of transit across the territories of their neighbours.

It is the 'landlocked location' that tends to make such states potentially weak. They always remain at a greater strategic disadvantage, as their survival depends, to a large extent, on their neighbours. Sikkim, a landlocked Himalayan state, suffered a forced merger with India. Afghanistan, a landlocked state in the trans-Hindukush region, witnessed, for more than a decade, forced occupation by the erstwhile Soviet army. If any landlocked state happens to lie

Figure 5.1: Landlocked States

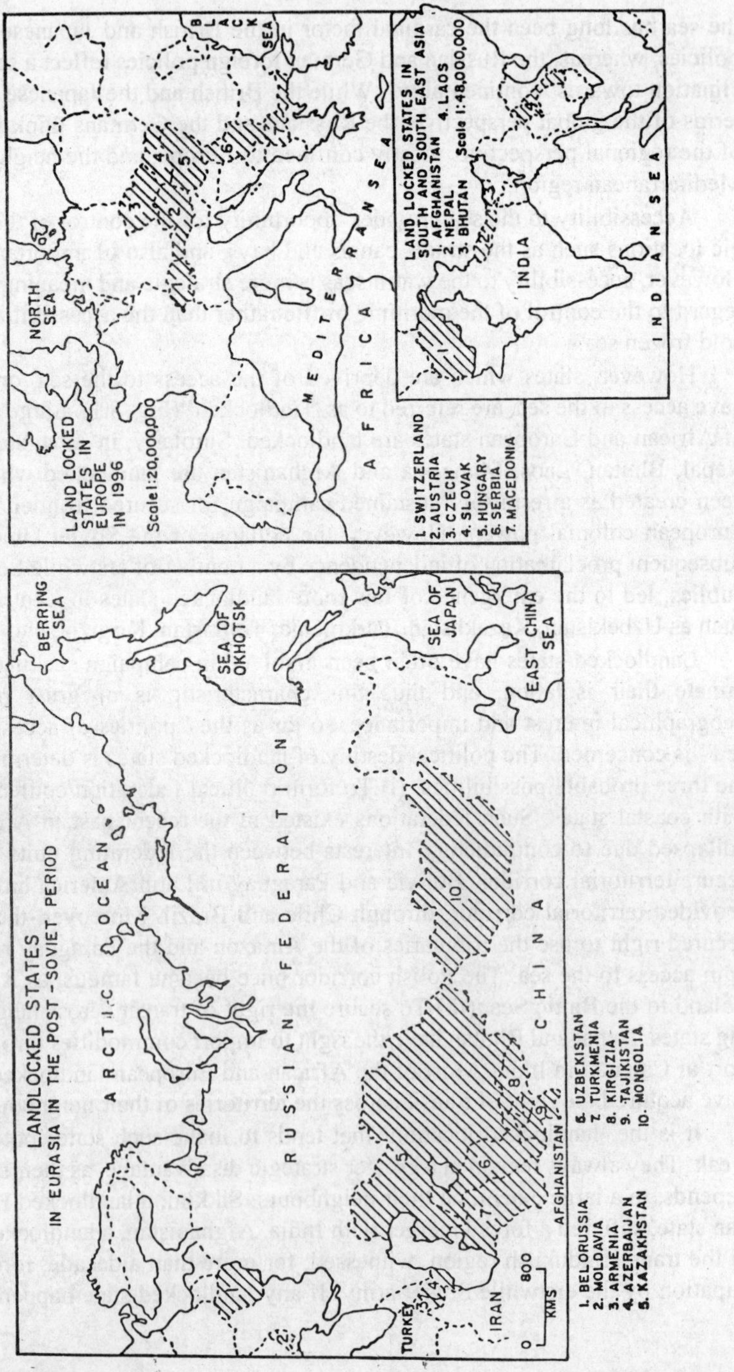

between two hostile neighbours, then its position becomes potentially dangerous as its people are caught in between contradictory interests of the hostile neighbours, leading to unprecedented crisis in its internal space relationship. Afghanistan, again, provides the best example of it.

However, a landlocked state with a relatively larger spatial dimension may not be always at a greater strategic risk, rather it can provide it in times of war with the advantage of the 'inner line'. "Given a system of good communication, a well-developed system of intelligence, and good armies under able leadership, a country can use its interior landlocked location to shift troops from one front to another, and thus win victories by local superiority. Frederick of Prussia, Napoleon, and also Bolsheviks during the civil war of the Revolution made the best use of interior location factors which, except for the advantages they offered in war strategy, were highly disadvantageous."

A larger landlocked state with a developed land transport and railways is a potential force to reckon with. Even in the pre-railway phase (if chronology is to be believed) the vast interior space provided the "horse and camel mobility" to the Asiatic tribes to carry out successful strategic operations against the coastal people of Europe, driving them out, and establishing vast empires across Eurasia. When such vast interior space comes under railway networks, it becomes a potential threat to the coastal states or to the fringe areas. The reason is obvious that such large interior state would always try to force upon the peripheral areas to gain access to the sea. History is full of conflicts between interior continental states pushing to the sea, and the maritime/coastal ones trying to block their access to the sea. The Anglo-Russian conflicts, and the Anglo-German conflicts in the late nineteenth century as well as in the early twentieth century are examples of how maritime Britain attempted to block the Russian operations to gain access to the Mediterranean Sea and the Arabian Sea. In such a process of the continental (Russian)-maritime (Great Britain) conflict, Afghanistan was created. The purpose of such territorial creation was to contain Russia gaining access to the sea.

Regardless of strategic advantage for a large interior continental location, there is much to be believed that 'an accessible' location of the sea or for that matter the maritime location offers greater 'feasibility', 'fluidity', and 'mobility' across the vast oceanic space on the globe.

Spykman has used the word 'rimland' for the region which in Mackinder's conception is the inter-crescent, i.e. the enclosing area on the west, south and east of the 'pivot' or the 'heartland'. Spykman's rimland has an 'amphibious' location, or it consists of amphibian states, whose maritime location goes side by side with the continental location. Evaluating its locational importance, Spykman writes: "The rimland of the Eurasian land mass must be viewed as an intermediate region, situated as it is between the heartland and the marginal seas. It functions as a vast buffer zone of conflict between sea power and land power. Looking in both directions, it must function amphibiously and defend itself on land and sea. In the past, it has had to fight against the land power of the heartland, and against the sea power of the off-shore islands of Great Britain and Japan. Its amphibious nature lies at the basis of its security problems." India is an amphibian state. In the past, it witnessed a series of invasions from across its land borders by the Central Asiatic peoples, and the Mughals, who were the descendants of the Turanian nomadic people—the Mongols—who founded the vast Mughal empire in India, which lasted for few centuries (1526-1857).

The Mughal continental power crumbled before the British maritime power which moved on to India across the oceans, making inroads into the coastal areas, inflicting defeats on the local rulers before approaching the Delhi sultanate.

The politico-geographical importance of relative locations of the state can also be expressed in the light of its territory extending from one ethnic-cultural area to another. Such an extension of territory is often known as 'panhandle', if it is too narrow and protudes down between the territories of other states. The Afghan 'panhandle' protudes down between the territories of Tazakistan (erstwhile republic of the former Soviet Union)and Pakistan. In a way the Afghan panhandle protudes down into these three different ethnic-cultural areas. It has long functioned as a 'separating force'. Similarly, the Namibian panhandle in Africa, south of the Equator, protudes down between Zambia, Zimbawe-Rhodesia, Angola and Botswana. It also juxtaposes the three different ethnic-cultural areas in Africa south of the Equator.

A panhandle or a prolongation of a territory, may be a source of weakness for the state to which it belongs, if the political heartland of the state is eccentric or marginal. In that case the state cannot properly integrate it, which ultimately leads to the centrifugalism. On the other hand, it may cut a particular state off from the sea or from access to a navigable river, or to a source of some much needed raw material. A state with a panhandle extending down between neighbouring states may create trouble for those states if its political core is close to the panhandle. Past history is full of such examples, particularly in Europe.

When an international boundary is so aligned that it cuts across the same group of people/community/nationality, then the 'split' nationality, lying on either side of the boundary, demands for its own sovereign state for the true expression of its culture. In that case, either of the 'involving' states confront with the problem of the 'irredentist claim'. India faces this problem in its north-eastern region where the Nagas on either side of the international boundary have long demanded a separate/sovereign homeland for them. Pakistan too, faces the problem of 'irredentist claim' in its North-West Frontier province, as the inhabitants of it have closer cultural affinity with the people on either side of the Durand Line.

Large number of African states, which were created to suit the colonial aspirations in the late nineteenth century, have their boundaries not responding to the regional cultural patterns, and now most of such states are confronting the internal political problem, arising out of the 'irredentist claim' which places the location of a state at a greater strategic disadvantage and security risk.

The location of a state, in terms of its neighbours, often called the 'vicinal location', appears to be very crucial, as it shapes the inter-state relations in the region to which the state belongs. "The number of neighbours is purely a physical matter, but their various characters involve human elements. The boundary lines which separate each state from its neighbours are of immediate and vital concern whenever any aspect of the vicinal location of a state is concerned." India has so many neighbours on its border, and with each of them it has territorial problems/disputes. The Sino-Pakistani collusion on Kashmir against India, has always remained a cardinal factor in its foreign policy or in its approach to China and Pakistan.

When in a region, there happens to be a number of smaller states, with a larger powerful state by the side, then the smaller states, in order to maintain the balance of power, come together to form an alliance. Most of the smaller neighbours of Germany, during the inter-war period, had come together to forge an alliance to combat Germany. Pakistan's entry into the CENTO and SEATO in the early fifties might be attributed to such a balance of power in the Indian subcontinent.

On account of its pre-conceived notion against India, Pakistan had never looked to South Asia. It had been more inclined to West Asia or Middle East, and as a result its foreign policy witnessed a series of setbacks. Proclamation of independence by its eastern wing, and its subsequent emergence as a sovereign independent state in South Asia, clearly manifests the contradictory approaches that Pakistan had adopted with regard to its locational suitability vis-a-vis India.

The vicinal location in the contemporary world is a changing phenomenon with the creation of more and more states. The creation of Bangladesh in 1971, for example, brought about a significant change in India's vicinal location. Decolonization in Africa and subsequent emergence of a number of states has revolutionized the vicinal location of the majority of states in the continent.

During the past few years, a large number of states have come up in Europe, following the collapse of the Soviet Union, Yugoslavia, and Czechoslovakia, and as a result the vicinal location of western democratic states in Europe has changed considerably. Unification of Germany in the early 1990s has changed its vicinal location to an extent that it now holds the balance of power of the continent in its favour.

Although the location of a place on the earth is fixed, the political values and implications of this location are continuously changing. It is this interaction of stable and changing conditions which is at the basis of political geography. People have been fascinated by the apparent stability of the 'well-grounded earth'...They are apt to look at geographic locations and their relations without taking account of changes in time.

Strategic Location

The importance of location varies with the political situation. States or parts of states may, under certain circumstances, acquire a strategic importance. This means that they are bases from which the sea, land or air could be patrolled, routes protected or an attack launched. The possession of strategic bases may protect a state or threaten its enemies. In either case, it adds to the state's power. The value of strategic location varies with the balance of political forces and also with changes in technology.

In the early seventies, the USA got possession of Diego Garcia island in the Indian Ocean from Great Britain. With its possession, the USA acquired the strategic command in the Indian ocean region. It patrolled the sea routes across the ocean, and looked after the strategic straits, linking the Indian Ocean with other oceans; and provided safe passage to the west-bound vessels. The possession of Diego Garcia by the USA was a major blow to the military potentials of the erstwhile Soviet Union, particularly during the Cold War period. It brought the Socialist Bloc well in time its missile (IBM) reach. The possession of the island created a 'balance of terror' in the Indian Ocean region.

However, the cessation of the Cold War and subsequent disintegration of the Soviet Union has considerably reduced the strategic importance of Diego Garcia for the United States. But, for the littoral states, it still has some importance, particularly for the oil-rich West Asia states which recently witnessed a war. The United States had directly got involved in the war and got Iraq defeated.

Possession of the Laccadive and Amindive islands in the Arabian Sea and the Andaman and Nicobar islands in the Bay of Bengal provides India a strategic command in the region. The 'implied' control of the Karakoram highway across Gilgit in the occupied part of Kashmir has brought China to the shore of the Arabian Sea or has provided China a direct access to the Indian Ocean which has long been denied to Russia.

The Turkish straits of Dardenelles and Bosphorous, connecting the Black Sea with the Mediterranean via the Sea of Marmara, have always remained crucial for the security of Russia. It is through these straits that the combined army of the English, French and Turkey once invaded Russia, and defeated it in the Crimean War in 1854-56. Russia had always tried to gain access to the Mediterranean Sea through these straits which Great Britain had consistently opposed. Because of the immense strategic importance of these straits, the European powers have always tried to make them international so that it could not go into the hands of one particular power, i.e., Russia. They even made the Black Sea an international sea, and Turkey becoming a member of the NATO during the Cold War period, was aimed at counter-balancing the Soviet menace in the region.

In the post-breakup scenario, it is the turn of Ukraine to see that the Turkish straits should not fall in the hands of the NATO powers, otherwise the security of the region would be under great stress. It is this reason that Ukraine has opposed the US move to disband its nuclear war heads stationed in the Black Sea. Similarly, Russia has entered into an agreement with Ukraine with regard to the stationing of the former Soviet fleets in the Black Sea with a view to securing its military access to the Turkish straits.

Regardless of the contemporary 'satellite geopolitics', the location of the states continues to play the most decisive role in its internal and external space relationships. It has been rightly remarked that "the essence of location approach to the explanation of state behaviour lies in the fact that the geographical location of a state bequeaths upon it certain set of spatial relationships vis-a-vis other states. So many of the potential activities and potential characteristics of a state may be largely attributed to the state's location, that location may become a useful focus for explaining the state's general pattern of behaviour."

The Buffer Zone

A buffer zone may be defined as a distinct political realm of a relatively smaller spatial dimension that tends to create new areal patterns as it happens to lie between more powerful and potential rival neighbours, and consists of smaller political units without any commitment, for there exists a set of interrelated political issues, like those of helping to allay potential friction between the powerful, potential rival neighbours, and of containing their expansionist policies, in a general setting of politico-geographical uniformity. Others have defined it as "small political units located between large nations. They survive because they are separate states that would otherwise be powerful neighbours and because the attempt to conquer them would be met, not by the relatively weak resistance of the buffer, but by much stronger opposition of the other neighbours." The Netherlands, Belgium and Luxembourg have served as a buffer between Germany and France. Poland, erstwhile Czechoslovakia and Romania, were also developed into a buffer zone between Central Europe and the erstwhile Soviet Union. Mackinder's 'inner crescent' or Spykman's 'rimland' must be conceived as an intermediate region between the heartland and the marginal sea. It seems to have functioned as a vast buffer zone between sea power and land power. It must have functioned amphibiously and defended itself on land and sea.

The concept of buffer zone is not a brain-child of the nineteenth century European territorial politics. It is an old concept. The Treaty of Verdun in 843 tended to divide the great empire of Charlemagne into three parts. The western portion of the empire, chiefly Latin in culture, went to Charles the Bold, while its eastern portion, chiefly Germanic in culture, fell to Louis the German. The middle or the central portion, an area of transition between the Latin and the Germanic culture went to Lothair I. After his death, the area was partitioned by Charles and Louis in 870 by the Treaty of Mersen. But it stood throughout history as a physical and cultural buffer between the states of Latin culture on the west and the states of Germanic culture in the east. The modern political units in this buffer portion are the Netherlands, Belgium, Luxembourg, Alsace-Lorraine, and western Switzerland; all of these states, with the exception of Switzerland, have been the scenes of many wars. Except for Alsace-Lorraine, which is a part of France, all of them are still independent. It seems to have long functioned as a potential "buffer zone of conflict" between the continental powers.

Similarly, in South America also, states and territories exist today which had their origin in part in buffer roles. The Treaty of Tordesillas (approximately, the 50th meridian west) was designed to separate the rival Spanish and Portuguese spheres. In the north, where contact was not effective, three European Guianas were set up/established, separating sections of (Spanish) Venezuela and (Portuguese) Brazil. But, in the south, toward the Plata estuary, direct competition between Spanish and Portuguese did develop. However, it did not develop into a potential buffer zone of conflict between the competing powers.

European territorial politics in the nineteenth century, and the subsequent competition between the European powers for more and more territories in Africa and Asia, felt 'geographical need' or realized the 'geographical necessity' of transitional areas, which could separate their political realms. Therefore, the zone of buffer states was more a geographical necessity for the colonial states. It is not always necessary that the buffer zone should be a zone of conflict. It may also function as 'zone of contact'. Thailand, one of the largest buffer areas, separating the British empire in Asia from that of the French realm in Indo-China-Pacific region, in the nineteenth and the early twentieth centuries, had functioned as buffer zone of contact between the two European cultures for decades (Fig.5.2).

A string of small Saharan states, now in Africa, tend to form a cultural-political buffer zone between the Semitic Mediterranean African states in the north and the Black African states in the south, i.e., north of the Equator. The Saharan buffer zone has primarily been a 'zone of contact' rather than a 'zone of conflict'. During the Cold War period, a large number of smaller states in East-Central Europe, West Asia and South-East Asia were driven to become buffer zones of communist-non-communist/nationalist-imperialist, ideological conflicts and which led them into becoming, what Cohen has termed 'Shatter' belts (zones). "It is a strategically located region which is occupied by a number of conflicting states and is caught between the conflicting interests of adjoining great powers." States in a buffer zone need not necessarily have common interests. They may have conflicting interests, but they exist/survive because the great powers require them. It is their *raison d'etre*. The West Asian states, which were a cultural buffer, developed into a potential zone of ideological buffer between the socialist-sponsored nationalist forces and the capitalist-sponsored totalitarian/imperialist forces. The newly emergent states therein were caught in between the divergent and conflicting interests. The position of these newly emergent states in West Asia became very tenuous and tempestuous.

Origin and development of the buffer zone results from:

(i) absorbing adjacent entities/territories and integrating them;

(ii) precipitating boundary disputes that lead to shift in boundary delimitation; and

(iii) emergence of large number of nation-states following the breakup of the traditional territorial systems/structures, or, reemergence of erstwhile smaller political units.

The former/erstwhile Soviet Union, during the inter-war period, caused a 'forced integration' of some Baltic states, such as Estonia, Lithuania, and Latvia, which hitherto remained independent, thus extended its boundary further west. But soon after the World War II, especially with the beginning of the Cold War in the post-war period, the erstwhile Soviet Union brought in a large number of East European states under its political influence, including that of the truncated East Germany. In fact, these East European states, such as Poland, Czechoslovakia, Bulgaria, Hungary, and Romania, were allowed to retain their national/territorial identities. These states were gradually developed into what is better called the 'satellite states', lying on the western frontier of the Soviet Union. Regardless of their political affiliation to the communist territorial ideology, and being members of the erstwhile Warsaw

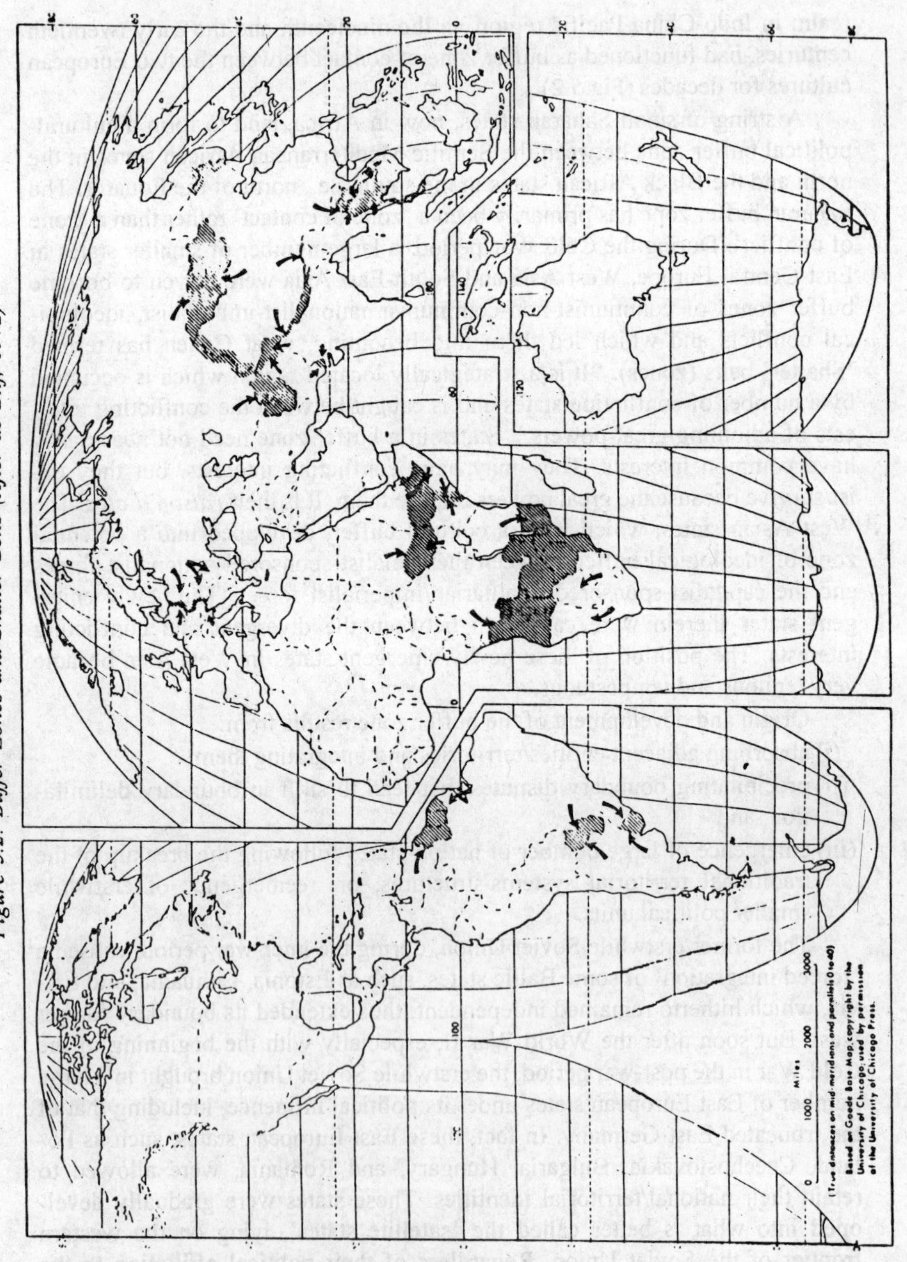

Figure 5.2: Buffer Zones and Shatter Belts (After de Blij, 1972)

Pact, they tended to form together a broad 'European buffer zone' between the erstwhile Soviet Union and the powerful NATO countries.

The creation of these satellite states was more of a Soviet necessity rather than of the West European necessity. Though there *raison d'etre* was tied up with the Soviet Union, they functioned as the most volatile buffer zone, providing immense security to the West European states on the one hand, and also to the Soviet Union on the other. This volatile European buffer zone lay on the major threshold of the territorial ideological conflict of the contemporary world. Later, Austria and former Yugoslavia also became part of this buffer zone. Austria was a neutral state but Yugoslavia started as a satellite state but soon distanced itself from the Soviet Union.

Another potential buffer zone that developed as a result of the annexation, and absorption of adjacent territories, lay extended along the Sino-Russian boundary in Mongolia, and possibly Manchuria in Asia. It was during the Soviet period that the Soviet Union forced a population migration eastward into East Siberia. This involved the most effective integration of the eastern territories which hitherto remained under a loose federal control. However, the objective behind this population migration, coupled with more effective integration of territories in the east, was to render the occupation of this eastern 'frontier' more effective. China's claims to ethnic and historical affinities with the peoples of this frontier region of the contemporary Soviet Union, and Soviet aid and propaganda programmes in Manchuria, in the contemporary situation, might be viewed as a prelude to competition for a buffer zone.

Laos in South-East Asia was artificially created to act as a buffer between the Eurasian continental communist powers in the north and the non-communist maritime powers in the south. Earlier, it was a part of the French Indo-Chinese realm. Here again, evidences of attempt at annexation and absorption can be identified. China supported the communist elements while the SEATO powers provided military help to the non-communist pro-western elements. But these two power organizations, on either side of Laosian frontier, did not make any open aggression/invasion to the country. However, China continued to encourage infiltrations while the SEATO powers maintained their arms shipments. Though there was a crisis in the late 1950s and early 1960s, it did not escalate into a full scale war between the land power and sea power. And Laos functioned as a buffer till the early 1970s when a permanent political solution for it was achieved.

Again in South-East Asia itself, another example of attempt at absorption can be found in case of Campuchia which does fulfil the functions of a buffer between Vietnam, a communist country, independent of Chinese influence, rather a potential rival of China, and China itself, as well as pro-West Thailand. Thailand has long been a 'distant US satellite' in South-east Asia. Thus,

Campuchia lay at the crossroads of Vietnam, China and Thailand. Soon after the US defeat in the Indo-China War, followed by the unification of Vietnam, and the subsequent withdrawal of the United States, placed Vietnam in an unchallangeable position in Indo-China vis-a-vis the South China Sea. The United States implicitly precipitated a political crisis in Campuchia which led to a serious political crisis there. As a result, Campuchia suffered a worst political instability and crisis leading to large scale exodus of Campuchian people to Vietnam. This gave an opportunity to Vietnam to absorb adjacent Campuchian territories, and integrating them to it. The legitimate monarch was overthrown, and a political vacuum or void was thus created in Campuchia. China, there, helped to instal a puppet regime of the Khmer Rouge which was opposed to Vietnam. The United States had tacit support to this regime. In the meantime, it escalated the Sino-Vietnam conflict on territorial aspects, which ultimately led them into potential rivals.

Vietnam stepped up its military operations inside Campuchia against the Khmer Rouge regime, rather it invaded Campuchia leading to a serious civil war. While supporting the Khmer Rouge regime, China did not openly intervene or invade it. Sustained military campaigns against the Khmer Rouge ultimately led to its overthrow and a new government was installed there, but the political crisis continued for decades as China continued to support armed infiltrations. China could not directly oppose Vietnam in Campuchia, while Campuchia appeared to be a 'geopolitically-required buffer area' for Vietnam, against China and the United States (through Thailand).

Though the overthrown monarch has been brought back from exile, and an election was held under the UN supervision recently, and a popular coalition government has been installed with the concurrence of the neighbours, yet Campuchia continues to be a potential buffer zone more between the two erstwhile communist allies (now potential powerful rivals, i.e., China and Vietnam).

After the defeat in the Crimean War, Russia abandoned its expansionist policy in the Mediterranean region but involved itself in the territorial process of expansion and absorption in Central Asia, and in the process, it integrated large territories to the Czarist State. The main objective behind this territorial expansion in Central Asia was to (i) threaten the British realm in South Asia, and disintegrate it, and (ii) to approach the sea.

The rapidity with which Czarist Russia was absorbing territories and expanding to Central Asia, simply endangered the British realm in South Asia. Alarmed by the growing power of Czarist Russia to the north, the British India felt the need of a buffer zone so that the integrity of its realm in South Asia could be maintained. The British gained success in the diplomacy when they got Czarist Russia, agreeing on an Anglo-Russian Convention in 1897, which stipulated for a buffer zone consisting of Persia and Afghanistan between British realm in South Asia, and the Russian realm to the north (Fig.5.2). The convention further stipulated the inviolability of this buffer zone.

For long this buffer zone existed. In the post-war/cold war period, the Afghan buffer area played a very decisive role in maintaining the integrity of Pakistan when it simply stood against the Soviet expansion into South Asia. Since there was no powerful neighbour to the south of Afghanistan, after the British withdrawal in 1947, much of its buffer functions were vitiated by the Soviet Union, which attempted to absorb it in the 1980s, and there was no strong opposition to it.

The Simla Agreement between British India and Tibet in 1914 was aimed at (i) defining the Indian-Tibetan boundary through the alignment of the McMohan Line along the high crest-cum-watershed of the Assam Himalayas; and (ii) developing outer Tibet into a buffer zone between China and British India. In fact, Tibet started functioning as a buffer since 1905 when its independence was recognized by China. However, the Simla Agreement divided Tibet into inner zone and the outer zone, the former was placed under the Chinese suzerainty while the later was left free to decide its destiny, and the southern boundary of the outer zone was defined as the McMohan Line. In fact, the whole Tibet functioned as a buffer between British India and China till the British withdrawal in 1947, and the subsequent Chinese move in the early 1950s into Tibet, integrating it with the mainland, and securing India's unequivocal assurance on Tibet, being a region of China, that it lost its buffer character. Though Tibet put up a resistance to the Chinese attempted move to absorb it, but in vain. It was too weak to match the might of the communist monster, while its southern neighbour, India, explicitly approved of the Chinese move.

Soon after its complete absorption, Tibet witnessed rapid influx of Chinese people in a planned manner or in other words, China forced a population migration southward into Tibet, so as to effect a change in the demographic character. This drive has objectives other than just demographic and economic, for China has long desired to render the occupation of Tibet more effective.

India's acceptance to China's claim on Tibet being a region of the later (Sino-Indian Agreement, 1954) undoubtedly raised question on the legality of the entire Sino-Indian boundary. China took up this opportunity to precipitate boundary disputes in the Himalayas, disapproving the McMohan Line between South-Eastern Tibet and North-Eastern India, and the boundary between Ladakh and Tibet (as established according to 1842 treaty between the ruler of Jammu, the emperor of China and the Lamaguru of Lhasa; and the 1846 Amritsar Treaty), it sought for the shifts in boundary delimitation with a view to create a high order frontier which could perform the function of a buffer.

Ever since China went communist, and Pakistan became a member of the multinational military organizations, such as CENTO and SEATO, and India rapidly becoming a pro-western neutral state, the continental part of the Indian subcontinent gradually developed into a volatile zone, particularly with respect to Tibet vis-a-vis China. China precipitated the McMohan line crisis, saying that it was never demarcated and defined in the most impressive terms, and in all probability established to function as an administrative convenience within a colonial empire. The McMohan Line, rather than running along the foothills of the Assam Himalayas, lies well inside these ranges, separating people of Tibetan ties and traditions from one another. On linguistic, ethnic, historic and other cultural bases, the border certainly would seem to be ill-positioned.

Pakistan becoming a member of the SEATO (South East Asia Treaty Organization, now abandoned), brought it close to the Chumbi Valley of the Tibetan frontier, between former Sikkim and Bhutan, within the striking zone of the SEATO. As China could not gain adequate supporters in the Assam region or in the north eastern frontier area, or for that matter, could not collect infiltrators in its Tibetan region, it did openly invade North-East India in 1962, and occupied a substantial part south of the foothills of the Assam Himalayas, across the McMohan Line.

China precipitated the boundary dispute, and sought for shifts in boundary delimitation, further south of the McMohan Line across Assam, simply because it required a buffer area for the survival of Tibet as a Chinese region so that its sovereignty over it could remain unchallenged (Fig. 5.2). A buffer separating Tibet from India would be helpful in the sense that large number of the Tibetan refugees who had taken shelter in the Dooras and Assam, could not be used as infiltrators by India against China. China was equally alarmed by the presence of the Anglo-American sea power in the erstwhile East Pakistan for being a member of the SEATO.

However, China soon withdrew its troops well north of the McMohan Line, and abandoned its policy for a limited buffer area. Since then much has changed in the area that East Pakistan emerged as a sovereign state, as Bangladesh, and the US defeat in the Vietnam War led to the abandoning of the SEATO, and more important is India, becoming a regional power of the first order.

China had long desired that Kashmir-Ladakh should be a buffer zone between it and Russia, particularly when the Czrist Russia in the nineteenth century was engaged in expanding in Central Asia after the Crimean War. China also sought for a similar type of agreement with Russia over Kashmir-

Ladakh region, as Russia and Great Britain did over Afghanistan, which sought to secure its neutral position, making its territories inviolable. Russia disapproved China's plea on the region because it had a desire over it. Since then much water had flowed down the Indus. India became independent and Jammu and Kashmir along with Ladakh acceded to India which was followed by the Pakistani invasion in 1949, resulting into the occupation of a substantial part of it. Pakistan in the early 1950s became a member of the CENTO (Central Treaty Organization, now abandoned), thus it brought, of course, implicitly the Anglo-American maritime power on the Kashmir. Thus, Kashmir became a secondary vortex of international rivalry, with the USSR (now disintegrated), China, India, Afghanistan and Pakistan, on its threshold. Or in other words, the CENTO maritime power was brought face to face to the continental communist power in Kashmir.

However, Kashmir could not develop into another 'Laos', because of the fact, that regardless of being a member of the CENTO, Pakistan maintained cordial relations with China which helped neutralize the western pressure against China in the region. This was enough for China to question the legal validity of the Ladakh-Tibet boundary which runs along the most inhospitable inaccessible region of the Himalayas. Taking the opportunity of the inaccessibility of Ladakh, and also of the persistent Indo-Pakistani rivalry over Kashmir, China in the early 1950s clandestinely occupied a substantial part of Ladakh, and built a road across it, linking its Sinkiang province with western Tibet. In one stroke, China secured a buffer zone across Ladakh, without any knowledge to India. In a way it kept Tibet secured, not only from a possible Indian onslaught but also from the CENTO powers. More so, it also kept the USSR much away from the scene. In fact, the Sino-Russian rivalry over Kashmir-Ladakh has historic reasons.

When China's clandestine design of attempted incorporation of the Ladakhi territory became known, India strongly protested, but Pakistan maintained acquiescence. After a few small-scale border clashes, China openly invaded Ladakh in 1962, and extended its control much beyond the line of its earlier control. However, China withdrew its troops to that line of its control across Ladakh which it held in 1959. In unequivocal terms, China made it clear that it would not give up Ladakh.

Pakistan has also ruled out vacating the occupied territories of Kashmir. In 1963 Pakistan and China agreed on certain terms and conditions, regarding the delimitation of boundary between China's Sinkiang and the contiguous parts of Pakistan-occupied Kashmir. India protested to this agreement but without any positive reaction.

Kashmir now appears to be more a buffer zone than a state of the Indian Union. It is a 'complex buffer zone' of conflict. Occupied part of Ladakh is a buffer area between India and Tibet. Pak-occupied Kashmir is a buffer area between India and Pakistan. Development in Afghanistan in the 1980s enhanced the buffer character of Kashmir for China. In the present fast changing political scenario, particularly in Central Asia, the buffer character of Kashmir has become a geopolitical necessity for China again, as its Muslim-dominated Sinkiang province rapidly showing the sign of political instability, and any truck with the Afghan rebellions would have disastrous effect on China's integrity. Hence, a buffer between Sinkiang and Afghanistan, across Kashmir is vital and a geographical compulsion for China (Fig. 5.3).

The Himalayan buffer zone (consisting of Nepal, erstwhile Sikkim, and Bhutan) was unilaterally created by British India, which was a part of its expanding frontier philosophy into the Himalayan region, as against the continental power. The Himalayan buffer zone could be seen as a 'split' continuation of the Afghan buffer zone which British India had successfully carved out to neutralize the land power threat.

The post-Cold War period, particularly in Europe, witnesses rapid and significant territorial changes as large number of nation-states have emerged in East-Central Europe, following the collapse of the Soviet Union, defederation of Yugoslavia, and peaceful disunion of Czechoslovakia, and above all, the reunification of Germany. In a changed politico-geographical scenario in Europe, the united Germany has emerged as the most powerful state in Central Europe. A string of nation-states which have recently come up, now tend to perform the function of a broad buffer zone between Germany and Russia particularly.

This newly-emerged buffer zone in East-Central Europe is nothing but the old 'Cordon Sanitaire', as it includes in it Finland, Lativia, Lithuania, Estonia, Poland, Czech Republic, Slovak Republic, Austria and Hungary etc. These states now tend to form the physical and cultural as well as political buffer between the states of the Germanic culture, and the great area of Slavic cultural background of Russia. They are partly Germanic and partly Slavic in their culture and traditions, and this implies that they do not necessarily concur either with Germany or Russia. In the wars between the western and eastern states, these buffer nations have also been the areas of intense fighting. During the inter-war period, except for the Baltic nations, the entire area was under the Germany's political influence, and after the war or particularly during the Cold War period, this entire area, developed into a Soviet satellite zone that also performed the buffer function. Cessation of cold-war, followed by the reappearance of erstwhile Baltic states, and the collapse of the communist system in East Europe seemed to have revived the age-old buffer zone in East-Central Europe between the two erstwhile continental powers.

Traditionally, the buffer zone used to come up as a result of the 'territorial

Figure 5.3

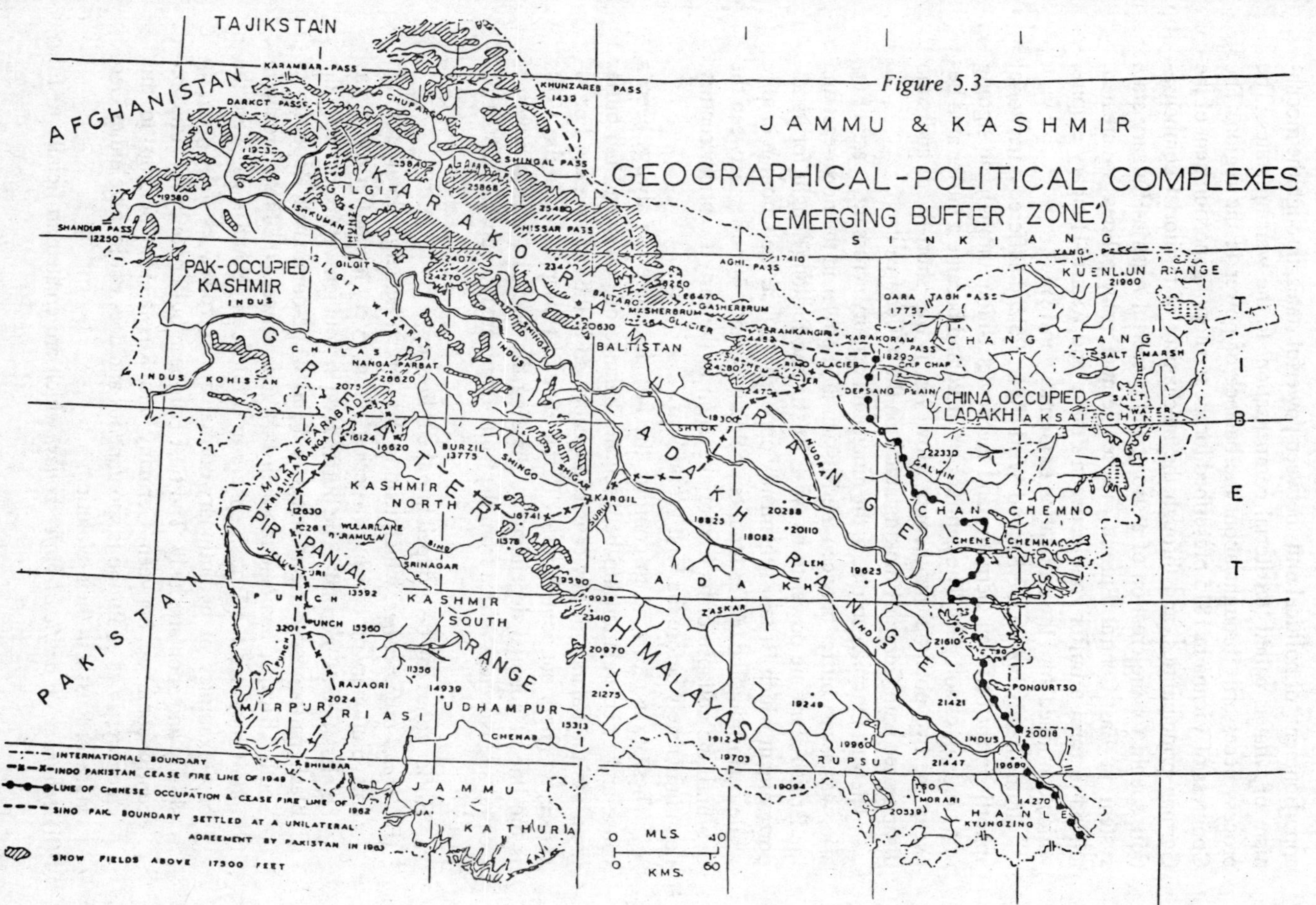
JAMMU & KASHMIR
GEOGRAPHICAL-POLITICAL COMPLEXES
(EMERGING BUFFER ZONE')
TAJIKSTAN
AFGHANISTAN
PAK-OCCUPIED KASHMIR
SINKIANG
TIBET
PAKISTAN
CHINA OCCUPIED LADAKH
AKSAI CHIN
CHANG TANG
KUENLUN RANGE
KARAKORAM
LADAKH RANGE
LADAKH
BALTISTAN
GILGIT
GREAT HIMALAYAS
PIR PANJAL
KASHMIR NORTH
KASHMIR SOUTH
RANGE
HIMALAYAS
CHAN CHEMNO
RUPSU
HANLE
JAMMU
KATHURIA
UDHAMPUR
RIASI
MIRPUR
PUNCH
SRINAGAR
LEH
KARGIL
INDUS
ZASKAR
SHYOK
NUBRA
CHENAB
KARAKORAM PASS
SHANDUR PASS 12250
KARAMBAR PASS
KHUNZARES PASS
SHINGAL PASS
HISSAR PASS
AGHIL PASS
QARA TAGH PASS
MLS. 0 40
KMS. 0 60
INTERNATIONAL BOUNDARY
INDO PAKISTAN CEASE FIRE LINE OF 1949
LINE OF CHINESE OCCUPATION & CEASE FIRE LINE OF 1962
SINO PAK. BOUNDARY SETTLED AT A UNILATERAL AGREEMENT BY PAKISTAN IN 1963
SNOW FIELDS ABOVE 17500 FEET

apportionment' of political units between powerful states, through the mechanism of what is called 'territorial compensation' to the warring states. The process necessarily brought about the balance of power in the region. The Congress of Vienna in 1815 prescribed for the territorial apportionment of the German principalities, and through the mechanism of territorial compensation, sought for the creation of a strong and powerful Austria-Hungary state system in East-Central Europe. These German principalities so created, tended to form a buffer zone between France and Austria-Hungary empire, which continued until the unification of Germany in 1871.

Immediately before the Second World War, Poland suffered a territorial apportionment between Germany and the Soviet Union, through the signing of a non-aggression pact. The central part of Poland became a buffer area between the two potential neighbours. However, it was short-lived, and soon disappeared with Germany making attack on the buffer area itself.

The vast Ottoman empire in the nineteenth century across the coastal Eurasia, was a vast buffer between the Russian land power in the north-east and the British maritime power to its west. Russia had for long sought for its apportionment which Britain vehemently opposed. In fact, the Ottoman empire while performing the buffer function, held the balance of power between the two until the collapse of its territorial system in the early twentieth century, i.e., immediately before the First World War.

These examples tend to conform the fact that there has always been a cause and effect relationship between the balance of power and the buffer zone. As the balance of power is changeable, so is the buffer zone. For instance, an important contemporary buffer zone that disappeared in the 1970s is the line of colonial dependencies dividing the black nationalist states of Central and Northern Africa from the white-dominated Republic of South Africa.

Buffer zones can be grouped into the following:

(i) *Normal buffer zones*, which tend to develop and emerge slowly through an evolutionary process over a period of time. Very few buffer zones may be classified as 'normal'. The buffer zone in Southern Africa between the black nationalist African states and the white-dominated Republic of South Africa, or Thailand in South-East Asia between the French realm in Indo-China and the British sphere of influence in South Asia, were the best examples of evolutionary/normal buffer zones, as they grew up slowly and spontaneously. The East European buffer zone which has recently come up between Germany and Russia, also belongs to this category, as its evolution is spontaneous and does not involve either Germany or Russia in their evolution.

(ii) *Arbitrary or artificial buffer zones*, which are created artificially to fill some preconceived geographical frames according to the regional suitability of the states involved. Majority of the buffer zones were arbitrarily created by powerful states themselves to perpetuate their regional security and integrity. Nepal, Bhutan and erstwhile Sikkim, and Afghanistan are examples of buffer areas created either 'unilaterally', or bilaterally' by the state(s) concerned. Some artificial buffer areas have been created 'multilaterally', involving more than two states in their creation. Kashmir is rapidly developing into a buffer zone by China, Russia, Afghanistan and Pakistan because all of them feel it to be a 'geopolitical necessity' for them. The Palestine State is coming up in the West Bank, and the Gaza Strip, through the active US mediation between Israel and the Palestine Liberation Organization (PLO). The Palestine State would be finally developed into a buffer by the USA between Israel on the one hand, and Jordon and Syria on the other. The state is coming on a preconceived geographical frame.

It has been rightly observed: "...Buffer states were a purely mechanical device of international politics; they separated physically two potential warriors, making it more difficult for them to exchange blows. The grey-areas of the ideological frontiers of today are capable of a more sophisticated intellectual political role. In contact with and willing to internationalize currents from both poles, they are not merely transitive but also transformative: like an electrical transformer they adjust the tensions of the two political voltages to permit at least some flow of current without danger that flying sparks will fire the whole house."

Decay of Buffer Zones

Buffer zones in the post-Cold War scenario have lost much of their '*raison d'etre*' mostly as a result of :

(1) growing detente between the potential rivals/neighbours;
(2) demise of socialism vis-a-vis totalitarian system, followed by the collapse of the Soviet system and its territorial disintegration;
(3) emergence of a large member of nation-states/federations/confederations;
(4) emergence of regional political/economic cooperation, and development of the world systems (GATT and WTO etc.);
(5) cessation of Cold War; and
(6) declining *raison d'etre* of the concept of the balance of power in the age of 'satellite geopolitics'.

The territorial widening of the European Union in the post-Soviet period has, to a greater extent, caused the decay of the erstwhile East European buffer zone, as most of the former Soviet satellite states, now seek for the member-

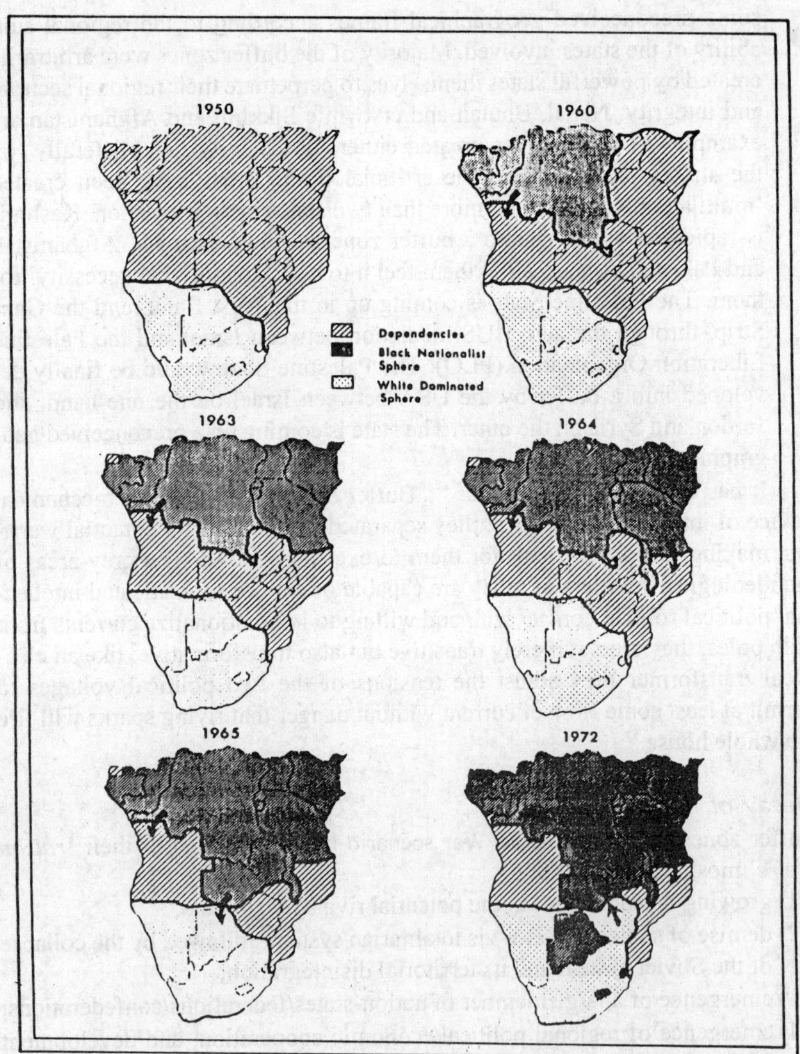

Figure 5.4: Buffer Zones in Africa: Development and Decay (After de Blij, 1972)

ship. Even Russia has drawn itself much closer to the European Union.

Growing detente between Russia and China has reduced the buffer character of Mongolia. Similarly, the growing Sino-Indian ties in recent years have substantially reduced the buffer *raison d'etre* of Nepal and Bhutan. Sikkim has long acceded to India.

The territorial widening of the ASEAN (Association of South-East Asian Nations) in recent years and the growing Sino-US cooperation in the Asia-Pacific have already led to the decay of South-East Asian buffer zone, which once existed between the Chinese power core and the South-East Asia Treaty Organization (SEATO). In fact, the SEATO disappeared in 1971 when the United States lost the Indo-China War.

Afghanistan, created as a buffer zone in the 1890s between the Czarist Russia and British India, continued to be so in the post-war period between the Soviet power core and the Central Treaty Organization (CENTO). In the 1980s, its buffer character remained at stake largely because of the Soviet intervention and occupation. In the 1990s, however, its buffer character was restored as the Soviet army withdraw from it, but the disintegration of the Soviet Union in 1992, followed by the emergence of Islamic republics, once again brought down the buffer character of it. Now it cannot be a buffer between Pakistan on the one hand and Iran, Turkmenia, Uzbekistan and Tajikistan on the other hand because of the Islamic solidarity between the states involved. However, Pakistan during the 1980s did function as a 'buffer' between the Soviet occupied Afghanistan and Indian Union.

The buffer zone between the black nationalist states of Central and Northern Africa and the white dominated Republic of South Africa also shows the sign of rapid decay, as the state is now being ruled by the indigenous black people and the white minority rule has ceased to exist. Independence to Namibia and its liberalization from the white-dominated South Africa a few years back has also contributed to the gradual decay of the African buffer zone in the south (Fig. 5.4).

It is now an established fact the *raison d'etre* of some of the states, largely depended on their buffer function, is at stake mainly because of the declining importance of the buffer zone in the global geopolitics, as well as of the increasing tendency of the satellite geopolitics.

The Size

The size of a state, 'the amount of earth space it incorporates', is directly related in many ways to problems of effective national control and organization. It is a fundamental element in the political geography of states—for 'space is power'. It is evident that geographical space is directly related to political viability. Much of the internal political strength and weakness of the state depends on its size. There is a 'cause and effect' relationship between the territorial size of the state and its political structure. Much of the states' external political space relationship, in terms of power potentials and diplomatic initiatives, to a large extent, depends on their territorial size. A glance at a map of the contemporary world political situation reveals that powerful states tend to accompany large territorial size, while the smaller states are not viable in terms of the military power potentials. History is full of examples of 'struggle for space' between states, because states, in the past, tended to increase their territorial size through direct military confrontation with other political units. An increase in their territorial size meant a qualitative and quantitative increase in their political strength and military potentials. Even today, states are 'implicitly' involved in the struggle for space, i.e., to bring as much political units as possible under their political and economic /military sphere of influence, so that they can determine the political destiny of the world.

Problem of Terminology

Given an enormous range in the territorial size of states, it is useful to have some terms to identify states within certain size categories. However, some attempts in the past, have been made for size categories of states. One of the earliest attempts was made by Volkenburg and Stotz in 1954, when they grouped the territorial size of states into giant size, very large size, large size, medium size, small size, very small size, and miniature size.

Pounds has worked out the average size of states of the world to about 1,040,000 sq km or about 390,000 sq miles—about the size of Bolivia, Colombia or Egypt—and nearly half are within the range of 25,000 to 250,000 sq km. However, the number of independent/sovereign states has increased during the past few years; and Pounds model requires some changes, specially those with regard to the number of states falling within the categories of average size and micro states. However, he attempted to classify states of world (as of 1971) into the following categories on the basis of their areal size.

Table 5.1
Area of States

Categary	*Area (in sq km)*	*Number*	*Approximate total area (in sq kms)*
Giant states	Over 6,000,000	6	67,500,000
Outsize states	2,500,000-6,000,000	3	8,550,000
Very large states	1,250,000-2,500,000	11	19,143,000
Large states	650,000-1,250,000	15	14,635,000
Medium states	250,000-650,000	29	12,123,000
Small states	125000-250000	21	4,075,000
Very small states	25000-125000	35	2,459,000
Micro states	Under 25000	25	162,000
Total		145	

deBlij, in 1972, has also proposed a classification of states, in terms of their territorial size, as shown below:

Table 5.2

Category	*Area (in '000 sq km)*	*Examples*
Very small states	Under 160	Liberia, Sri Lanka, Panama, Netherlands
Small states	160-960	Nigeria, Pakistan, France, Ecuador
Medium states	960-2,240	Mexico, Libya, Saudi Arabia, Mangolia
Large states	2,240-16,000	Canada, U.S.A., China, Brazil
Very large states	Over 16,000	Russia

Some time back in 1965, Haggett, Chorley and Stoddard attempted to measure the size of states through a scale of value which they called the G-scale, based on G—the area of the earth's surface. The G-scale expresses the logarithmic ratio of the area of any country or continent to that of the earth's surface. It is obtained from the following formula:

$$GX = \log \frac{Ga}{Rx}$$

where Ga is the area of the earth and Rx is the area of country. Table 5.3 shows the G-scale values for some of the largest and the smallest states of the world.

Table 5.3

G-Scale for Some Selected States

(Ga=Earth's surface Area =5, 10, 000, 000 km.^{2}, log Ga =8.70765)

States	*Area (in km^2)*	*G-scale*
Erstwhile USSR	22,402,000	1.35736
Canada	9,976,000	1.70869
China	9,561,000	1.72714
USA	9,363,000	1.73623
Brazil	8,511,000	1.77817
San Marino	61	6.92232
Nauru	21	7.38543
Monaco	1.5	8.53056
Vatican City	0.4	9.10534

"However, the practical value of the G-scale is extremely limited, for it is based on the ratio of the geographical size of a state to the total area of the earth's surface as if area by itself provides any index to the development or power potentials of the sovereign political areas...the G-scale values would have been useful if these gave us a ratio between the real and the ideal territorial extent. Today, however, a few states subscribe to the imperial ideology of a worldwide empire."

For practical purposes, and for evaluating the role of 'territorial size' of states, in their political geography, they are classified here into three broad categories: large states, medium states, and small states.

Large States

Large states are, inevitably rich both in natural and human resources. While the former tend to strengthen the material conditions of the sovereign political areas, the latter provide the human power to their sustenance. Other things being equal, "the larger a state is in area, the greater are the chances of its supporting a large population and a diversified natural resource base—the two most important elements in the politico-military potentials of the state". Large states, such as the USA, Russia, and China, are inevitably, the powerful states of the world. While the USA dominates the Atlantic basin, and Russia dominates Eurasia, China in the Asia-Pacific region. These states have in their territorial possession, a vast diversified resource base with a vast human resource base to utilize and mobilize the resources to their global political/military sustenance. These large states are almost self-sufficient. These states have achieved high degree of industrialization based on their variety of natural resources. The vast human reserve, besides providing huge manpower both in times of war and peace, constitutes a vast internal market for indigenous industries, and also a working force. A well-diversified natural resource base, that a large state inevitably possesses of, tends to minimize dependence of it on outside areas. Hence, it is free of any outside control. There are certain industries or groups of industries which are normally developed in larger countries. It has been rightly observed that "large countries normally possess an automobile industry, an aircraft industry, locomotive building, heavy machinery, both mechanical and electrical, for here are found, most of the strategic resources, while smaller countries rarely possess any of these industries".

Large states do have empty spaces within their bounds, though sometimes, such empty spaces/territories are not as useful as developed territories. However, empty space that may appear valueless does add strength to the state. Empty territory may have unrealized resources which may become valuable following discovery or technological advance that makes their utilization possible. The purchase of Alaska in 1867 from Russia was vehemently opposed as it involved some $7, 200, 000 and at that time the expenditure on the purchase was thought to be a wasteful expenditure as the region looked unproductive. Now, with the discovery of vast resources of petroleum, and its commercial exploitation has changed the face of it, and more so, it has substantially minimized the United States' dependence on the Middle East and the Caribbean oil supply.

A second value of empty territory is that it offers an expanding population or potential home territory of its own. Such a value is psychological and material as well. The knowledge that the land is there to be occupied and utilized is a stimulus that releases physical and mental energy. Expanding Chinese population in the 1960s found a potential homeland in the hitherto, unexplored empty territory in the west, beyond the 'Loess Line'. Similarly, the erstwhile Soviet Union, in the 1950s and early 1960s, forced population migration to the east into Siberia which provided considerable material strength to it. The Homestead Act (1862) allowed President Lincoln of the USA to promise every farmer his own farm, and American families could hope for a place that was solely theirs. Thus national dissatisfaction with the stress and rigours of the time was averted, and the land was utilized quickly and efficiently. While revolution and unrest took place in Europe, the United States consolidated and expanded its national base. Even in India such an example can be found. The Government of India offered empty Terai territory at the Himalayan foothills in Uttar Pradesh to the Sikh refugees who came in quite large number from across the border in the 1950s, and thus minimized the chances of the Sikh unrest in contemporary India. Similarly, West Bengal was saved from political unrest when the Bengali refugees were offered settlement in the unoccupied Dandakaranya territory in Orissa and Madhya Pradesh.

When a state's population is clustered in such a manner that large distance separates them, the land between the clusters is necessary as a connecting bridge. The usefulness and desirability of connecting land is illustrated in the history of both the United States and Russia, although it is by no means restricted to those two states. In Russia, it is 9,216 kilometres from Moscow to Vladivostok by the Trans-Siberian railway. Most of this distance is empty land between isolated communities. Railway maintenance and operation on such a distance with so little traffic contributes to the low transport efficiency rating in the Russian rail system. Politically, however, this railway is the lifeline connecting the Pacific East to the Russian ecumene; without it, one might anticipate the emergence of a separate state facing the Pacific Ocean.

Large states always maintain strategic superiority over the others. They also remain at a greater advantage as their large size counterbalances the deficiency of soldiers, equipment, or preparedness during war—in short, a trading of space for time, soldiers or equipment. Large size can nullify an otherwise successful strategy. It affords time to move factories and population away from the fighting zone. It allows armies to fall back toward their source of supply, thus, shortening supply lines and earning logistical strain. Likewise, every step an invader advances away from its supply base, logistic stress is increased and efficiency weakened and lessened. When one considers the psychological advantage of fighting on home territory and the advantage of simplified logistics, it is no surprise that nation can successfully balance an inherent weakness by sufficient space. Twice, the Russian army demonstrated this strategic tactics of 'defense in depth' or 'space for time', first, against Napoleon-led French invasion in the early nineteenth century, and second, the most successful one, at the time of the German invasion during the Second World War. Regardless of their superior war materials and vast armies, the German suffered heavy losses. China was able to maintain her independent status in the west even after the Japanese had overrun all of the coastal sections of the country and most of the lower river valleys.

In an age of nuclear explosives, a large area allows a state to disperse its vital segments of production and population clusters. Technology may shrink space but cannot completely eliminate it. The few minutes of warning afforded by the Dew-Line that once existed across Alaska and Canada was thought to be enough both to save millions of lives in case of attack and to launch retaliatory missiles. Notwithstanding the satellite geopolitics and warfare, large states still have some strategic advantages and cannot be totally eliminated. All large states, like the USA, Russia and China, have already dispersed their vital industrial units and segments of production and population clusters to escape nuclear holocaust.

However, large states do have some problems with respect to their internal space relationship. A large state does contain well-diversified human resource base. Large number of cultural-religious groups which normally exist in large states, tend to make the regionally grouped diversities, mutually exclusive and each group in a large state seeks to perpetuate its claims of political status and position, and that usually tends to create socio-cultural cleavages which inevitably, produces great stress and strain often leading to the disintegration of the state. It is very difficult to maintain cohesion in a large state with mutually exclusive regional diversities. A great majority of large states are suffering from political instability and crisis. Such large states with diverse cultural groups find the federal system beneficial for it "recognizes territorial cores for divergent nationals while maintaining a central administration to hold the national loyalty of all the people".

Empty territory in large states as mentioned earlier, sometimes adds strength to them, also becomes the source of centrifugal tendencies, if it diagonally intervenes between population clusters. Each population cluster, separated from others by an intervening empty territory, such as deserts and mountains, inevitably develops a separate identity for it, and a separate feeling also which normally leads to secessionism. China is facing this problem in its southwestern province of Sinkiang while India is having acute political crisis in its north-eastern states, and in north-western areas where subnational movements now greatly threaten the integrity of its federal system.

The former Soviet Union which extended its frontier too far outward to be sufficiently integrated with the central area of it, during the inter-war period and also during the post-war period, ultimately broke into fifteen sovereign political regions in the early 1990s, because it could not hold together various diversified regions any further. One of the greatest disadvantages that a large state usually faces, is with regard to its long frontier both maritime and land frontier, which becomes very difficult to maintain and protect. India provides the best example of it that in the past, on several occasions, its Himalayan boundary had been crossed over by enemies.

Political ecumene of larger states is normally eccentric in nature, and as a result the contact between it and the outlying areas becomes too difficult because transport networks cannot be developed on account of the 'distance factor' within, leading to serious political crisis. Chinese political ecumene lies marginally along the Yellow Sea coastal plains, east of the great eastern scarp, and is, therefore, thousand kilometres away from its Muslim-dominated Sinkiang province which shares common boundaries with recently emerged Muslim republics in Central Asia, and as such, it now precipitates serious political crisis for China. Similarly, the political core of the erstwhile Soviet Union was marginally placed along its western frontier around Moscow, and therefore, was not truly expressive of the federating republics. The result was obvious that the system collapsed leading to its disintegration.

Political ecumenes of large states like the USA and Australia are nevertheless eccentric/marginal along the coasts, but these two states do not have strong centrifugal forces operating within, just because the regionally grouped diversities there are mutually inclusive which have neutralizing effects on the cleavages.

Notwithstanding the demerits, inherent in the internal space relationship in large states, they still have more strategic advantages over disadvantages. Brazil in Latin America and India in Asia are rapidly emerging as regional powers in their respective zones.

Medium States

More than half of the states in the world, at present, are of medium size, which are often called as 'intermediate-sized states'. As the size approaches either extreme, a state profits from the advantages and suffers from the disadvantages of largeness or smallness. Medium-sized states share the partial advantages of both social cohesion, and economic-military efficiency.

With the possible exception of the United States, all the 'core states' are of medium size, and they are the most developed, and politically more stable political entities in the world. Even the powerful semi-peripheral states are medium-sized, which have come up recently, following the disintegration of the Soviet Union. It is rightly observed that "while these states are not capable of policing various disturbed areas around the world, they are prosperous political entities".

Britain, France, Germany and Japan are the most prosperous medium-sized states. While the first three are the leading super powers, the last one is the leading economic power in the world, which has taken on the United States in terms of the global economic system. Most of the medium-sized states maintain favourable trade balances and prosperous economies than some of the larger states like Russia and China. They dominate in the world economy and determine the destiny of the world economic order.

Medium-sized states are politically more viable than the larger states because in medium states centripetal forces are much stronger than the centrifugal forces, and they have a strong *raison d'etre* which is reflective of the effective control by the administration.

Medium-sized states are mostly nation-states. They do not have plural societies like those of the larger states. Nations coincide the states in most of the cases, and as a result, a strong sense of feeling of oneness abounds in such states. Social cohesion is tradition-bound that leads to the blending of "national idea with state idea", which tends to eliminate the effect 'cleavages' of whatever kind that may exist. Medium states have survived several onslaughts on them. Germany which suffered several attempted disintegrations and truncations still survived. France witnessed several invasions to its land during 1871-1945, but it survived. Japan survived atom bombs. There are so many examples to reveal that larger states have consistently failed to subdue medium states simply because of strong national loyalty that the people exhibit. Medium states have to defend a relatively smaller boundary line, and each point on the boundary is accessible from the political ecumene and each territory is well-integrated with the political ecumene, through a good transport network. This tends to strengthen the complementary habits and communication efficiency among the people of states.

Medium states do not have much regionally grouped diversities, and that is the reason why 'unitary political structure' is geographically suitable to them. There is high degree of political stability in intermediate-sized states.

Medium states perform the function of the balancer in the regional as well as global system of balance of power. Such states are more stable—politically, economically and socially—than the larger states.

Small States

Large number of small ctates are coming up each day with the disbanding of the former totalitarian territorial states, mostly as a result of collapse of the colonial system, and secessionist and liberation nationalisms. Geopolitically, small states are very precious because of strong social cohesion they possess. They have a uniform socially standardized symbol of language—a strong sense of national identity. Such states usually have cultural-religious uniformity, more so, they exhibit one basic means of earning a living, for example, the people of most of the small states in Central America earn a living by the specialized banana plantation.

Except for few small states, like Israel and Netherlands which have specialized economies of their own, most of such states are yet to recover from their primitive subsistence phase.

Politically, small states are not viable. A large number of them are suffering from internal dissension and rebellions. However, Israel and Netherlands are the small states which have survived despite several attempts on them. During the seventeenth century, "Netherlands emerged as a world power". Israel, at present, is the leading power in the Middle East and all attempts to eliminate it by the Arab states in 1948, 1956, 1967, 1973 and 1991 met with great failure. Israel has developed a strong *raison d'etre*. Netherlands, for centuries, has been a stable political entity. But, for majority of the smail states, the following statement seems to be more apt: "The disadvantages of smallness are the reverse of the advantages of largeness. Small nations cannot support armies of sufficient size to protect their boundaries or their internal autonomy; consequently, they exist at the tolerance of stronger neighbours. The economies of small nations are of necessity dependent on neighbours; and the advantage of specialization becomes a weakness if others refuse to purchase the speciality. Furthermore, small markets make it impossible to generate an efficient size."

It is the medium size which really adds political strength, while the large or larger size has inherent inner contradictions, often leading to political crisis or instability, and small size is politically enviable. Medium states, therefore, do not suffer from disadvantages of largeness and smallness.

The Shape

A glance at the world map reveals that each and every political entity, with its spatial extent across the earth's surface, tends to assume a significant geometrical shape, or the earth's political surface is criss-crossed by variable geometrical shapes that the political entities assume. Some people are sceptical about the role of 'shape' in the political geography of the state, as one of them is quoted as saying that "geometrical shape of a state presents problems only a degree less acute than those raised by its geographical extent". Still, others feel that the shape of a state in many respects is a haphazard characteristic without much significance. It is also held that "shape in itself has little meaning, but that it has to be taken into consideration as one factor which together with other factors constitutes an important element in the political geography of a country".

Notwithstanding the scepticism that many people have expressed with regard to the political desirability of the shape of a state, it can be said with much confidence that the shape of a state has considerable importance in the internal administration and social cohesiveness of its people. It is also a significant factor in international politics/relations in that it affects the length of the state's boundary, the number and variety of its neighbour countries, and the locational situation of the people who live in its various parts.

Typology of Shape

As mentioned earlier, the political surface of the earth is criss-crossed by variable shapes that the geographical/spatial extent of the sovereign political entities assume. Accordingly, a typology of shape is presented below.

Compact Shape

Ideally, the compact shape is preferable and the most sought after of the shapes. Many states on the map appear to lie spread about their central area and are nearly circular or rectangular in shape. Theoretically, since all points of the boundary of such a compact state lie at about the same distance from the geographical centre of the state, there are many political advantages:

(i) The boundary is the shortest possible in view of the area enclosed.

(ii) Since a compact state does not necessarily have peninsulas, islands, and other protruding parts, the development of effective communication to all parts of the state does not have to face difficulties and problems. The state is completely integrated which results in effective administrative control of the entire state which adds to the strengthening of the centripetal forces so much so that its *raison d'etre* does not fall at stake.

(iii) Since the political ecumene of a compact state is equidistant from the fringe areas, and as the entire territory is well integrated through the effective network of communication, there is very high degree of political stability because of the strongest possible internal social cohesion in the state. Even if the state has a variety of social groups and physical environments consequent of its geographical size, such diversities are easily

Figure 5.5: Shapes of States

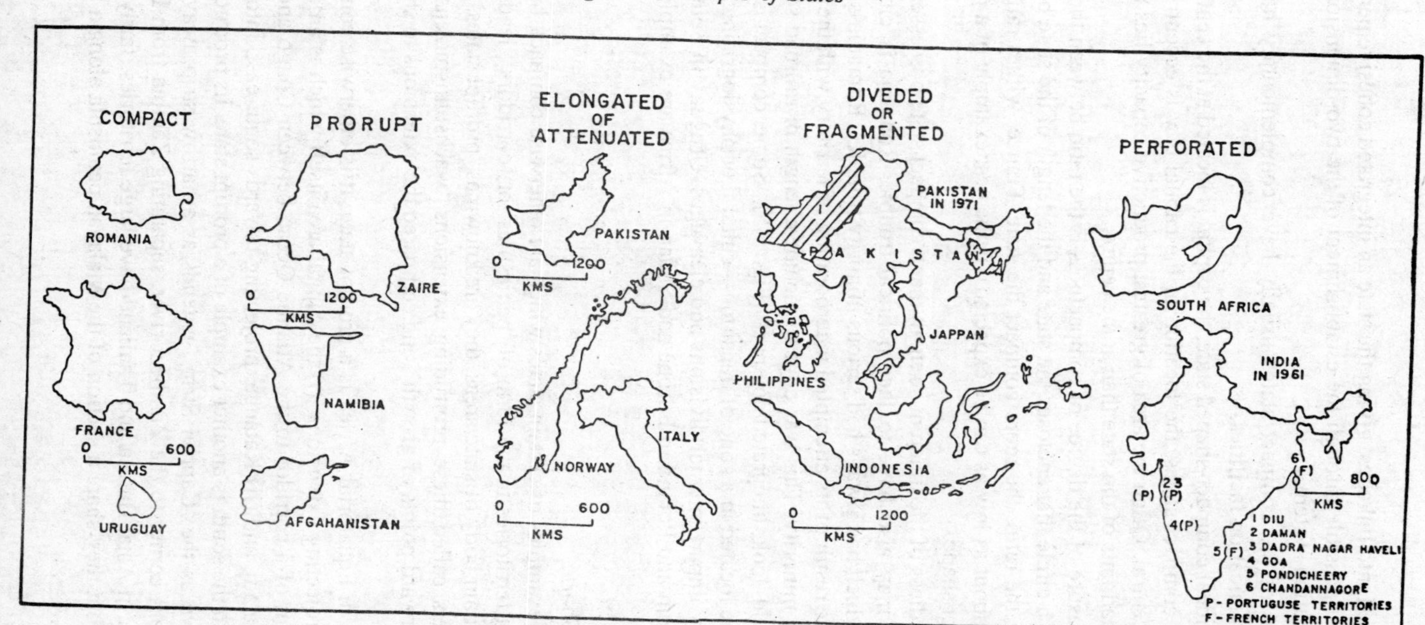

changed into linkages, giving the state an integrated cohesive personality. It is all possible through the establishment of the two-dimensional communication system.

(iv) People of the compact states usually have complementary habits and communication facilities.

(v) In an ideal compact-shaped state, the capital is located at the centre, but in many compact states, the location of the capital city is eccentric, rather than central. Often the area of greatest productive capacity lies in one of the quadrants of the state than at the centre.

A measure of the degree of compactness is the ratio between the circumference of a circle that encloses the state and the length of the state boundary. The lower the ratio, the more compact the state. France, with a ratio of two (which is about as low as can be expected), is the best example of a rectangular compact shape.

Regardless of the inherent strength that a compact state possesses, a compact state may also have to face political trouble. Romania is cited as an example which has always had serious minority troubles. Romania's compact shape is the result of its attempted incorporation of territory with the dissident Hungarian minority. This was done to include a length of railroad so that the state should look integrated/compact (Fig. 5.5). Some compact states are found to be located in a zone of transition—cultural or physiographic, or both, which may impart internal divisions and cleavages. Uruguay in South America, Belgium and Poland in Europe and Sudan in Africa are examples of this category.

Prorupt Shape

There are examples of certain states which are otherwise compact, but for the protruding territories in the form of 'peninsulas' or 'corridors', leading away from the main body of state areas, they are known as 'prorupt states'. German geographers called these protruding extensions 'wachstumspitzens', which meant 'forward points of growth', and compared the extensions to shoots of a plant.

Zaire in Equatorial Africa is a prorupt state. It is otherwise compact but for two projecting extensions: (i) the capital area itself which is an extension in the form of a corridor to the Atlantic Ocean between Congo and Angola port of Matadi, and (ii) Katanga, projecting towards south-east, into Zambia. Namibia in the south is another example of a prorupt state. Its protruding territory known as the 'Caprivi Strip', extends as a narrow strip away from its northeastern corner to the Zambezi river, separating Zambia from Botswana (Fig. 5.5). In Asia, Burma and Thailand have large territories, fairly compact in shape, but they share a section of the Malayan peninsula along a boundary which was almost down the middle of this narrow strip of land.

Prorupt states or territories often face serious problems of administration, for proruption itself is a source of centrifugal tendencies because the inhabitants of the territory remain more inclined to the neighbouring nations than to the main political ecumene of the state. The Afghan panhandle or the Wakhan territory has remained a potential source of trouble for the state throughout its history. A prorupt state is always faced with the problem extending communication to the protruding territory.

Many proruptions result from the creation of buffer zones. The Afghan panhandle or the proruption is the creation of the Anglo-Russian Convention of 1890s. The Netherlands' Leinburg district between Germany and Belgium is a buffer and has the added element of connecting the Netherlands to the strong fortress at Maastricht. Columbia, in Latin America, has a proruption connecting it to the Amazon port of Leticia through Brazilian territory. A similar extension in Bolivia provides a connecting link to the Paraguay river which leads to the port of Buenos Aires. Bolivia lost her corridor to the Pacific Ocean as a result of Chilean and Peruvian conquests.

Elongated or Attenuated Shape

An elongated or attenuated state may be defined as one that is at least six times as long as its average width. The state extends along an axis so as to appear elongated. Such a shape commonly results from surrounding physical barriers which the state could not cross during the period of its expansion. Chile is an elongated state. It lies between the Pacific and the Andes. Pakistan is hemmed in between the rugged Hindukush and the Thar desert. Italy is on a peninsula between the Adriatic and Tyrrhenian seas, while the Scandinavian peninsula is shared by the elongated states divided by the Kjolen mountain range, Norway and Sweden (Fig. 5.5). Elongation or attenuation tends to increase social groups and physical environment, and adds to the difficulties of travel and communication, and also increases the length of boundary to be protected. Chile and Norway do not possess railroads to the administrative efficacy for their integral/cohesive political personality. Chile has at least three distinct environmental realms—the Northern desert, Central Mediterranean, and the Marine west coast in the south. As a consequence, the regionally grouped diversities are mutually exclusive to harden the socio-political cleavages in the state.

The north-south division of Italy is one that permeates life in that country, and is related to the different exposures of the two regions to European mainstreams of change. The north-south extension of Pakistan has given rise to problems of travel and communication, resulting in the emergence of there distinct potential sources of centrifugal tendencies: one each in North-West

Frontier Province where the Paktoon people demand secession; in Sind, which is in the south where the people, culturally distinct from the Punjabi, have a different set of political ideas; and in Baluchistan, which is more outer-oriented.

One of the recent examples of an attenuated state, going in for disintegration, is Czechoslovakia. Its west to east elongation, coupled with the existence of mountain barrier, had long greatly contributed to the separatist feeling of Slovakia, which ultimately broke apart into a sovereign political entity in the name of Republic of Slovakia. Nepal which is confined between the mighty Himalayas and the Siwalik mountains, in a west-to-east elongation, has a lengthy boundary to be protected from China and India as well, and at the same time, its elongation across mountains and valleys has added difficulties of travel and communication, resulting in variable social character, which is not complementary to one another. Competitive political ideas reflect the east-west internal division. The most westerly and most isolated province of Austria—Voralberg—once attempted to secede and join the Swiss Confederation. An elongated or attenuated state, therefore, seldom emerges as a viable political entity, and always has a high degree of instability in its political geography.

Divided or Fragmented Shape

A large number of independent sovereign political entities do not have territorial contiguities, rather they consist of two or more individual parts, separated by intervening land, or by international water/sea, and are, therefore, divided or fragmented states. Former Pakistan consisted of two political units—West Pakistan and East Pakistan—which were more than 1300 kilometres apart from each other, and separated by Indian territory. Indonesia is another example. It comprises more than 1,300 islands stretching from the Indian Ocean to the Pacific Ocean, and covers a distance of more than 4,800 kilometres. Erstwhile Pakistan was an example of 'continental type' a divided state, and Indonesia is an example of 'insular type' divided state.

Japan, Greece, Philippines, New Zealand, Papua New Guinea and Great Britain are some of the examples of insular type 'fragmented states'. Divided states always have to face problem of travel and communication. Individual parts/islands of such state usually have people of different ethnic backgrounds, and interests also, which put considerable strain on the smooth functioning of the state as a whole. And as consequence such states find it quite difficult to develop an integrated national personality. Centrifugal forces always maintain an edge over the centripetal forces, thus making them politically enviable. Territorial political problems of fragmented states normally develop when the question of locating a new capital city arises. Each unit wants to perpetuate its claim, as a result, the federation collapses. The West Indies Federation came up in the Caribbean, comprising Jamaica, Trinidad and Barbados, and a host of other islands, failed on the question of choosing a site for the capital city and collapsed, because each major unit staked its claim.

Nevertheless, the 'insular type' divided states are politically more stable than those of the 'continental type' divided states, for intervening water and circumventing water provide greater contactual mobility between the units rather than the intervening territory of another state. Pakistan could not hold together its eastern wing, which had all along developed its separate identity, and with the help of the intervening state, it emerged as an independent sovereign political entity—Bangladesh—in 1971.

A third type of divided state is that which lies partly on a continental landmass, and partly on one or more lands. The Malaysian Federation consists of a mainland section on the Malay peninsula, and a host of smaller intervening islands, including the northern part of Borneo. Italy, with its island territories of Sicily and Sardinia, also come under the category of fragmented state.

Perforated Shape

States that fully contain the territory or territories of one or more sovereign political entities, or completely enclose other political entities, are said to possess a perforated shape. The perforating states also face the problem of travel and communication. Perforating states are nothing but landlocked states. A perforated state always lies in a strong position (Fig. 5.5).

The dominion of India, immediately after its independence in 1947, became a perforated state for a very short period because it contained within its political bounds, as many as 554 perforating princely states, which became 'quasi-sovereign political entities', following the lapse of the paramountcy, through the Indian Independence Act, which further stipulated that, "Princely States, irrespective of their geographical sizes, will continue to enjoy the right of transit to perform their economic and other functions, across the Dominion Territory, under the Standstill Agreement...so agreed upon between the Dominion and them". However, with the peaceful accession of these quasi-sovereign princely states, the perforated character of the Indian State disappeared.

In most of the cases, the perforating entities are forced to merge with the perforated states. Italy is a perforated state as it fully contains within it the Republic of San-Marino and the Vatican City State. Though Italy does not face any political problem, do the perforating territories have any such troubles with Italy. The Republic of South Africa had always faced political troubles from the perforating Lesotho State, in the form of fomenting 'xenophobia' among the black nationals against the white-dominated regime in South Africa. It is a substantial impediment to the territorial integrity of the Republic of

South Africa.

Some states, when analyzed on the basis of the preceding criteria will be found to have more than one shape characteristics. Italy provides the best example. It is an elongated state, and as much as a fragmented state, and also a perforated state. Chile is an attenuated state, and at the same time it possesses a fragmented shape. Now, it has to be ascertained which of the shape characteristics determine the political geography of the state? It is not the fragmented shape or perforated shape of Italy that determines its internal division. It is its elongated shape that creates politico-territorial contrasts within the state. A state, therefore, may have several shape characteristics, but that which affects its political geography is its shape in the true sense of the term. The rising tide of nationalism, followed by changes in the political-territorial structure/alignment, particularly during the cold war period and after the cessation of the US-Soviet rivalry, has brought about significant changes in the shape characteristics of a number of states.

Exclave and Enclave

Relevant to shape characteristics are 'exclave' and 'enclave'. An 'exclave' is a small part of a sovereign political entity, separated from the main territorial unit and surrounded by the land of a neighbour, such as Seutikursha, a small part of few square metres of Indian territory surrounded by Bangladesh and tiny area of Bangladesh, Tinbigha, on the Indian side. There are some 130 Indian exclaves, locally called 'Chhittmahal' in Bangladesh, and some 95 exclaves of Bangladesh on the Indian side.

Exclaves are not always small, and nor are they always unimportant in terms of area and population. For example, in the pre-unification days, West Berlin happened to be an exclave of the Federal Republic of Germany on the side of German Democratic Republic. It played a vital role in the contemporary European politics, being an important Euro-urban political centre in Central Europe. Similarly, the area of Spain around Llivia on the French side of the Pyrenees is another example of an exclave.

On the basis of the degree of separation from the main territorial unit, the exclaves have been grouped into several categories:

(i) *Normal exclaves* are small parts of territories of certain states which are completely and effectively surrounded by the territory of their neighbours. Large number of normal exclaves of India are on the side of Bangladesh and of Bangladesh on the Indian side.

(ii) *Pene-exclave* are part of a state, which, although not physically separate, can only be reached conveniently via another country.

(iii) *Quasi-exclaves* are areas that for all practical purposes have ceased to be treated as exclaves.

(iv) *Virtual exclaves* are areas treated as the exclaves of a country of which they are not legally an integral part.

(v) *Temporary exclaves* result from inclusive territorial arrangements being made after an armistice; occupation zones or demilitarized areas may create temporary exclaves. With the unification of Germany, West Berlin, which was created after an armistice, ceased to be an exclave.

An 'enclave' is a small piece of territory on the side of the neighbour but which does not fall under its jurisdiction. The micro-states of San-Marino and the Vatican City in Italy and Andorra in Spain are classic examples. Tinbigha is an enclave in India. The former French oversea possessions of Pondycherry and Chandannagor, and the former Portuguese overseas possessions of Goa, Daman, Diu, Dadra and Nagar Haveli, were all enclaves in India. Rather differently, West Berlin was an enclave, if seen from the point of view of the former German Democratic Republic and its allies in the former Soviet bloc.

It is observed that exclaves and enclaves are not an important phenomenon in the political geography of a state; they are rare and mostly small. "But their special status is of value in illustrating the relations of states in difficult geographical circumstances and in illuminating the importance of uninterrupted territory to present-day states."

Relevant to 'shape characteristics' of sovereign political entities are 'projection', 'bridgehead', and 'glacis'. A projection is a long narrow extension of the territory of one state separating any set of two neighbouring states from each other. The Afghan panhandle or the Wakhan territory separating Tajikistan and occupied Kashmir in Asia, is an example of projection. A bridgehead, on the other hand, represents an extension of territorial control by one state across an international river in side the territory of the neighbour. Dutch bridgehead across the river Meuse at Maastricht is an example of it. A glacis is an extension of territorial control of a country across a mountain divide. The best example was that of the Austrians in South Tyrol across the main crest of the Alps before the First World War. However, after war, Italy annexed South Tyrol.

It is the location that makes why a state should have a foreign policy at all and for that it is the *raison d'etre* of international relations and politics. The geographical size of the state is, inevitably, expressive of its economic and military potentials. The geographical/geometrical shape with all its other spatial characteristics of the state is of particular concern with regard to its internal political space relationship. Notwithstanding, the first changing global political scenario, subsequent to satellite geopolitics, these three primary spatial factors still remain to be highly relevant in the political geography of political entities.

Chapter 6

Frontiers and Boundaries

Frontiers and boundaries as spatial expressions of main social and political organizations and territorial partitioning have always been recognized and identified to be of prime importance as structural elements in the political geography of the state. Both frontiers and boundaries are, by definition, the peripheral elements/features of politically organized space, and in most of the non-geographical literatures they are often used as synonym. But in geography particularly, they are not synonymous, and have different meanings and connotations, notwithstanding, both being the peripheral elements or features of the politically organized space. There is a fundamental difference between the two. A frontier zone is an area between two social systems or entities. It is that geographical position at which opposite forces of expansion or resistance neutralize each other and become steady. A boundary, on the other hand, is a necessary component of the sovereignty. Sovereignty must be bounded: a world of sovereign states is a world divided by boundaries. Boundaries are, therefore, an essential element of the modern world economy.

With the rapid fall of territorial states in the past, and the rise of political entities of variable size, there was a rapid disappearance of frontiers and the appearance of boundaries, which replaced them, for "without them (boundaries) the present system of states might well be reduced to a chaotic condition, since it would be impossible to know where the sovereignty of one state ended and that of another began".

Concept of Frontiers

The word 'frontier' has been derived from the Latin 'frons' (and more directly from the French 'front') meaning 'forehead', which is etymologically suggestive of "that which is in front...designated an area which was part of a whole, specifically that part which was ahead of the hinterland. Hence, it is often called the foreland or borderland, or march". The Russian equivalent of the English 'march' is 'ukraina', and that of French is 'marche', and that of German is 'mark', all meaning literally 'borderland' or 'margin'. Intrinsically, the word 'frontier' is indicative of the "spearhead of civilization."

The frontier is neither a legal nor a political or intellectual concept; it is essentially a natural/social concept as it involves in it the growth of ecumene or spearhead of civilization. The Russian 'ukraina' was an example of an advancing frontier, a spearhead directed against the 'dark' and unchristian Tartary, and the Cossacks were not a nation or ethnic group but a social group, pioneer settlers and conquerors of the advancing borderlands, men not unlike the American frontiermen. Thus, in the historical origin, the frontier was rather a phenomenon of "the facts of life—a manifestation of the spontaneous tendency for growth of the ecumene. In antiquity, and later too, the frontier was on the margin of the inhabited world, but each particular ecumene, for instance, that of the agricultural society as opposed to the nomad society, also had a frontier. The 'limes' of the Roman Empire were those of the ecumene of western civilization".

With the development of patterns of civilization above the level of mere subsistence strictly adapted to particular environmental conditions, the frontiers between ecumenes became meeting places not merely of different ways of physical survival, but also of different concepts of the good life, and hence increasingly political in character. To Kristof, "the frontier was not the end (tail) but rather the beginning (forehead) of the state; it was the spearhead of light and knowledge expanding into the realm of darkness and of the unknown."

Since there were few ecumenes in the world which were separated by wide inaccessible-intervening areas that tended to function as frontiers, as they had no relations with the ecumenes. Therefore, their orientation was independent of them (ecumenes). So was the outlook of the inhabitants of the frontiers who were very few in numbers and had different ways of life (*genres de vie*), much inferior to that of the people of the ecumene. They were always looked upon as barbarians. However, the part played by the human element in the shaping of frontiers was revealed in the definition of their double role/function which was to mark the maximum range of a people's dynamism and to delimit the one in which two opposing dynamisms neutralize each other. Therefore, the frontiers had always remained a region of contact between two different sets of ways of life (*genres de vie*),.and in some instances, intermingling had occurred. Wide expanse of marches between the European, the Chinese and the Indian ecumenes had always been zone of overlapping of cultural realms.

From the Frontier Zone to the Boundary

In their geographical evolution, the frontiers seemed to have passed through the three distinguishing periods/phases. In the earliest phase, the frontier was no more than the limit of the state, and beyond it lay the void like an unknown ocean beyond the shore—as those of the vast expanses of territories beyond the colonies in America and Asia, particularly when the European settlements were confined to the seaboards, e.g., the vast American expanse beyond the mid-Atlantic seaboard, across the Appalachian mountains, or beyond the embryonic British colony, being crystallized on the Atlantic seaboard, was a frontier whose territorial extent was still unimportant—a geographical void that required the least organization of all. If viewed from the western perception, the entire Indian subcontinent constituted a geographical void on the eve of the European arrivals.

The second phase began with the organization of frontier marches, which lay transitional between the territory of the state and the empty regions, still in existence. The extensive territory surrounding the intensive core/ecumene of many modern states originated in this way. The marchlands can be deserts, forests, mountains or marshes, and are physically a region of natural obstacles, and demographically a region of very thin population than the ecumenes.

The empires of antiquity, however much they differed from each other, were all surrounded by frontier marches. The Egypt of the Pharaohs, China, India, Persia, the Roman Empire and the Arab world were all isolated by semi-desert zones crossed only by a thin stream of traders : these zones were the primeval protective void. But most states organized these zones in a rudimentary fashion by stationing troops in them, by placing them in charge of an administrator, or by making them into vassal states. For this reason frontier marches varied in their political character.

The entire north-eastern region of the Indian subcontinent was organized into a frontier marchlands after 1826 by the British colonialists, when its inhabitants who were racially and demographically inferior to the people of the ecumene, were organized/annexed in such a way as to have been placed under direct colonial administration. Moreover, the British State in India was strong enough to impose its authority throughout the north-eastern marchlands. Nepal, Bhutan and Sikkim emerged as frontier dependencies of British India in the Himalayan marches, which ultimately became its vassals.

In its final phase of evolution, the frontier changed into a frontier line. This simply happened when the ecumene/civilization advanced and the marchland around it receded gradually. Some observable changes took place in the marchlands, in the meantime, which included the clearing of the forest and extension of cultivation which tended to increase its economic importance. Its demographic character also underwent changes and it was no longer a no man's land. Its physical makeup was rapidly adapted to form part of a more and more organized defence; it changed into a fortified frontier, more effective than the former isolating zone. The frontier became a line. It became necessary in the light of the hostile and aggressive attitude of the opposing state that the frontier defence was pushed closer to that state. Expansion of civilization on either side of the frontier, particularly the marchlands, brought them closer to each other, creating a potential military situation, which necessitated the alignment of a line so as to prevent open hostilities and war. The McMohan Line was a geopolitical necessity, as the Indian marchlands in the Assam-Himalayan region was necessarily threatened by recurrent Chinese hostilities in the early part of the present century. In order to prevent China's open hostilities along the frontier, the McMohan Line was aligned along the high-crest-cum-watershed of the Eastern Himalayas.

Such, in broad outline, was the demographic, economic, political and military evolution which changed the marches and frontier zones into frontier lines.

"With the rise of the world economy, a frontier emerged between the system and the systems it was supplanting. The history of imperialism was associated with pushing forward the frontiers of this new world systems. It produced classic frontier in American West, but also other similar frontiers in Australia, South Africa, North Africa, North-West India and Asiatic Russia. The frontier ended with the closing of the world system at the beginning of this century...there are no longer any frontiers—they are now phenomena of history."

The North-West Frontier of India: Its Evolution

The western frontier of British India provided a glaring example of how the frontier could come up, end the phases through which it passed in course of its evolution. "The political frontier of British India lay far to the west of those hot and humid regions which, to the western perception, constituted the real India. The heights of Kashmir in the north, with an almost temperate climate, are succeeded on the south by the Punjab (the land of the five rivers), and the valley of the Indus with its gentle slope to the sea between the sanddunes of Rajputana and the Thar desert on the east, and the mountainous border of Iran on the west. The Hindukush and the Sulaiman and Brahuis mountains form a good protective system where it was only necessary to organize the control of the passes between the mountains. But it took many years to reach this mountainous region. In the first part of the nineteenth century, the western frontier zone of British India consisted of the mountains of Kashmir in the north, the open valley of the Punjab in the centre, and the Thar desert in the south. Later, when the theory of river frontiers prevailed, the possession of Sind was desired at all cost...The mountain barrier of the north-west was reached when Dalhousie annexed the Punjab. In 1876, Baluchistan became a British frontier dependency. Afghanistan remained neutral as the buffer-state between India and Russia. The defence of the mountain passes was organized. Finally, in 1901, the North-West Frontier Province was founded—a veritable frontier march, the guardian of the most dangerous passes of the northwest, and in 1937 this province became autonomous."

Thus, the north-west frontier region was gradually built up. Firstly, it included a mountain state in the north, a river basin in the centre, and a desert region in the south. It then became necessary to extend it to the mountains bordering the opposite plateau, to complete the occupation of the mountain and the desert region to the south, and to organize the supervision of the passes and the cols. All the possibilities offered by the terrian have been recognized, tried and made use of to develop a thorough-going technical, military and administrative organization. From the plateau of Iran to India, the frontier march extends over an area equal to that of a large European state. However, with the spread of the Anglo-Indian ecumene across the western marchland, much of its function receded in the late nineteenth century which necessitated the frontier defence being pushed closer to the incoming Czarist sphere of influence towards the Hindukush, and the Durand Line was laid across it in 1895 as a part of the Anglo-Russian convention. Thus, the wide mountainous-riverine-desert frontier tract, lying west to the ecumene, was rapidly developed into marchland whose limit was geographically aligned along the Durand Line.The State of Pakistan was created across this frontier marchland after it was fully integrated with the territorial-administrative system of the British *raj*.

Types of Frontiers

In the past, there were four distinguishable types of frontiers, viz., natural or physical frontier, ethnic or anthropogeographical frontier, geometrical or astronomical frontier, and political frontier.

Large and wide, inaccessible/inhospitable regions with absolutely no human concentrations, lying between the ecumenes, tended to constitute 'natural frontiers'. Even wide expanse of deserts/mountainous regions/river basins with inextricate features/marshes and forests within the limit of the territorial states, which were not geogprahically integrated with the political ecumenes but were no-man's territories, and the states had simple de facto control over them, such regions or areas were intrinsically classified as 'natural or physical frontiers' in the past. All frontiers in the past had emerged as natural frontiers. There existed a vast natural or physical frontier in Central Asia, between the advancing Russia and the Great Chinese Wall in the antiquity. The vast stretch of the Eurasian steppe also functioned as a physical frontier between the Asiatic people and the Germanic people for several centuries. Before the advent of the Europeans, the vast Sahara was essentially a physical frontier between the Semitic and the Negroid people in Africa, as their authority or sphere of influence did not coincide with each other, but simply passed across the wide expanse of the no-man's land. The Himalayan and the trans-Himalayan regions together constituted a broad physical frontier between China and the British *raj* as their authoritative limits were not known to each other. The great but inaccesssisble Amazon basin is still a wide physical frontier in Latin America. In the nineteenth century, the Congo basin also acted as a physical frontier between the black African people and the white European settlers. Natural frontiers had always remained in 'a state of flux'. This type of frontier had come into being mostly through the force of the geographical determinism. However, most of the buffer zones/states, during the period of colonial competitions in the nineteenth century, were created across the physical frontier zones.

Ethnic or anthropogeographical frontiers were those which lay between the two or more political ecumenes, and were thinly or sparsely inhabited by the people of different racial stocks who might be culturally backward and inferior to those of the inhabitants of the ecumenes. The vast Balkan region with its Slav population in South-East Europe, was an excellent example of an ethnic frontier in the contemporary world that lay between the Turkish ecumene and the Germanic ecumene. The large tract of South-East Asia emerged as an ethnic or anthropogeographical frontier in the nineteenth century, particularly during the period of colonial rivalry between the British Empire in South Asia and the French realm in Indo-China. West Asia was another such frontier in the contemporary world. The ethnic or the anthropogeographic frontier was indicative of the fact that in "the making of the frontier, human elements also played operative roles in its organization regardless of it being the gift of nature. Large number of nation-states have come up in these erstwhile/traditional anthropogeographic frontier regions of the Balkan peninsula, South-East Asia, and West Asia in the early part of the present century. These frontiers had always remained zones of contact between differing, and often opposed human elements.

The period of colonial expansion in the nineteenth century saw the rise of a large number of 'geometrical or astronomical frontiers' drawn on almost empty areas of partly unexplored continents; the frontiers consisted of straightlines and were drawn across the unknown interior territories, regardless of the territorial features or ignoring all geographical reality. These frontiers were the result of colonial rivalries between European powers over extending their spheres of influence across the unknown/unexplored interior territories of Africa. They began from a point on the African coast where they first settled, and from there they decided among themselves, on the empty map of Africa, the political realms of their colonial control, with the help of meridians and parallels, ignoring the geographical reality of the partly explored continent. The limit of their sphere of influence landward, passed through unknown territories which were intrinsically discernible zones with varied spatial characteristics. The westward expansion of the American State from the Atlantic coast against the retreating Indians, and the invasion of the British descendants who pushed the Australian aborigines into obscurity and the frontier expanded regardless of the territorial features, because the interior was still unexplored.

Be it the American west or the Australian interior, or European territories in Africa, they were all under the 'de facto' control of their territorial masters. The development of the marches was confined to the coastal ecumenes and landward; they were either ephemeral or intermittent in nature.

There was a vast 'political frontier' from the mountainous border of Iran in the west to the Hindukush mountains in the east, between the British empire in South Asia, the Turkish empire across South-East Europe and West Asia, and the Russian empire on the northern periphery of the frontier. This vast mountainous-cum-desert frontier was the result of a spontaneous tendency of growth of the British State in South Asia, Turkish State and the Russian State on the Eurasian periphery. It was more a part of the British frontier philosophy to keep this frontier alive with a view to perpetuating its political authority in South Asia, in response to expanding the Russian frontier into the Slav-held territory of the Turkish empire. The Assam and trans-Himalayan Tibetan frontier was a political frontier which sought to distinguish between two different political systems—the British and the Chinese. Political frontiers were more rapidly organized into marchlands because of their 'fluid' political character.

Apart from the above types of frontiers (which are now the phenomena of the past) there are two more types of frontiers, viz., 'ideological' and 'settlement'. Ideological frontier existed till recently over a wide area in Central Europe between the Soviet realm in East Europe and the Atlantic-Mediterranean Europe. This ideological frontier was the genuine manifestation of the cold war between the two power axes—Washington and Moscow—which soon began after the Second World War. This frontier was a zone that sought to distinguish between the two different economic systems, or it attempted to distinguish between the Atlantic core and the Eurasian semi-periphery system. However, with the fall of socialism in East Europe, reunification of Germany, collapse of the Soviet system, followed by its territorial disintegration, and the disunion of Czechoslovakia and Yugoslavia, the ideological frontier has disappeared. 'Settlement' frontier tends to manifest the expansion of ecumene into the empty lands within the territorial jurisdiction of the state, or, in other words, it is indicative of the extension of the national territory into the area, which hitherto, remained not occupied owing to its inhopsitable character. Settlement frontier is a dynamic phenomenon, indicative of the social mobility within the territorial limit of the state.

"Though frontier conditions may sometimes be deliberately created by governments, the state tends to view frontiers and frontiermen as a temporary expedient, as appropriate to a period of transition. The ultimate goal is a boundary, not a frontier. This is what the Chinese frontier policy of keeping the Chinese in and barbarians out aimed at. Since frontier conditions affect and unsettle, the internal order and quiet, the state must, ultimately, either make an effort to integrate the frontier lands within its socio-economic-political system—to enclose them within the state boundary—or, if it cannot be done economically or at all, to exclude them from its realm: put them beyond the pale of its community."

Frontier, therefore, was an area at the margins of the integrated territory of the state, or any political unit, into which expansion might take place. The concept was essentially outward-looking and implied the existence of an unknown that was yet to be conquered, understood and assimilated. It was that zone in which at a given moment the forces of expansion of two neighbouring states tended to mutually neutralize each other. On the contemporary world, map boundaries are the norms. The earth has been more or less accurately surveyed and precise lines delimit the territories of states. This is a recent development: prior to the twentieth century maps of the most parts of the world showed huge tracts of unclaimed land. Indeed such land on the frontier was generally regarded as a necessary 'safety valve' for accommodating the populations of fast growing states. These 'safety valves' were mostly represented by marchlands, neutral territories, and buffer states. However, the very necessity for a boundary automatically implied that the safety valve or for that matter the frontier was under pressure from both sides and might not, therefore, be claimed as the legitimate future territory of either one or the other of the states in contact with the boundary line.

Boundaries

In terms of national politics, boundaries are important because they mark the limits of a states' sovereignty. They are drawn either where the territory of a sovereign state abuts that of another or at the farthest extent of its territorial seas. In a few cases they extend even further when jurisdiction is extended over the surface of a continental shelf but not over its overlying waters. Boundaries also extend down to the centre of the earth, according to international agreement, thus allocating rights to subterranean resources. Similar agreement has not been reached over the upward extension of sovereignty into the air space, however, because of the difficulty of agreeing on an upper limit.

Concepts of Boundaries

The nature of boundaries has changed through historical time because their function—the separation of sovereignties—has also changed. As population became more and more dense and human settlements more numerous, and as the rights and obligations of government increased, so it became necessary to draw boundaries with ever greater precision. The modern boundary is, in most cases, a finite line along which two sovereignties meet. To Stephen B. Jones, "ideas about boundaries are related to their geographical and historical milieu". In fact, the boundary concept in antiquity was centered round "a no-man's land" which frequently separated the territory which was inhabited and used by one tribe to that of the other. In fact, the primitive tribe had a frontier perception of the boundary, which, in the true sense of the term, reflected unclaimed, unsettled and unused territory into which peoples from each side might at times intrude but over which neither side claimed or exercised an exclusive control. Even today, some of the African primitive people still hold the view of an unclaimed territory, defining the zone of an 'authority'. The Chinese and the Roman boundary concepts of antiquity also manifested an idea of a stable and exact frontier which ought to be secured through the erection of frontier wall. It was intrinsically sought to perpetuate a clear-cut limit between themselves (Chinese or Roman) and the barbarians. The Chinese and Romans were not the only wall builders. The early Anglo-Saxons built walls to defend their authority over the land they ruled.

The ruler of the medieval or feudal state did not know precisely how his state was made up, its boundaries were closely defined only here and there, where for some reason or the other, there had arisen a need for precision. It is a strange reversal of our present state of affairs to find that medieval rulers did not know the extent of the lands they ruled and, when they were in doubt, consulted the local people. A well known feature of feudalism was that it produced a patchwork political map. Discontinuous holdings were common and were tolerable because of the decentralized nature of feudal rule and warfare. Some of this discontinuity persisted into the period of monarchies but with increasing dissatisfaction. The discontinuous nature of Brandessburg-Prussia was a well known case. The two principal parts of this domain were separated by a band of Polish territory for a century and half. This was slowly whittled away. One of the tasks of subsequent centuries has been to smoothen and strengthen boundaries and to clear up the confused pattern of sovereignty in Europe. However, the process of boundary making is very different in the various sections of the world economy. Stephen B. Jones (1959) had identified six distinguishable types of boundary concepts, viz., 'natural', 'national', 'imperialism', 'contractual', 'geometrical' and 'power political'. These categories are not exclusive to one another : from one perspective, for instance, we would identify all boundaries as reflecting the power politics of their respective producers. Nevertheless these are useful concepts that tend to reflect the different ideas of the state in the evolving world economy.

The concept of natural boundaries was a product of the Age of Reason and of nationalism chafing at old restraints. Its origin was largely the product of the French Revolution of the late eighteenth century. When the revolution swept away the remnants of French feudalism, the concept of natural boundaries took predominance over historical claims.

In contrast to the French expansionist idea, implicit in their doctrine of natural boundaries, the German developed the concept of boundaries based on folk or nationality. "It was understandable that the Germans of the early nineteenth century, not having attained a national state, should idealise it and needing a criterion for German nationality..." Although nationality is basically a 'we-feeling' in a group of people, it embodies a strong territorial bond. The desire for territorial contiguity seems to be intensified by nationalism.

The French doctrine of natural boundary, and to that of the German concept of national boundary, were the realizations of particular power-political positions in the core and semi-periphery of the contemporary world economy which gave birth to the boundary doctrine of 'imperialism' in the nineteenth century itself. European imperialism provided a worldwide sense of space and opened up an immense exploitable world. Friedrich Ratzel is credited with having laid the foundation of the tradition of the boundary doctrine of imperialism. In one of his seven laws of state expansion, he observed: "The frontier is, as a peripheric organ of the state, the bearer of its growth and its security, conforming to all changes of the state organism." It was the character of the state as an organism which appeared to be the very basis of the doctrine. The organismic concept came out with an analogy between such biological frontiers as timber-line and the frontiers between human groups. The German geopoliticians later made use of the concept. Ratzel's tradition was carried forward by Lord Curzon who later developed the concept of scientific frontier, i.e., a frontier that sought to unite natural and strategical strength, "by placing both the entrance and the exist of the passes in the hands of the defending power". It is only in the periphery that the European imperial powers made use of this doctrine of boundary when they moved into it.

In fact, in the periphery itself that these types of boundaries emerged. In the non-competitive arenas in the nineteenth century, such as India and Indo-China, the boundaries reflect the one core state at the expense of weak pre-capitalist social formation. This is where frontiers were extended and then converted to boundaries. The limits were finally achieved when two powers began to approach one another's peripheral territory. The process led to the formation of a buffer state in the periphery as in the cases of Afghanistan between Imperial Russia and British India, and Thailand between French Indo-China and British India.

The contractual concept of boundary and the concept of geometrical boundaries appeared to have developed simultaneously. The contractual concept of boundary was largely a product of the American State, the essence of which was that "two states should agree on a line and stick to it, as individuals agrees on property lines". Whereas the doctrine of geometrical boundaries had European origin which envisaged the use of long geometrical lines as boundaries with some geodetic sophistication.

In competitive arenas, the boundaries are usually far more arbitrary since they reflect 'contractual' and 'geometrical' arrangements between the competitors. These were done to prevent disputes between them. Boundaries in such competitive areas either follow physical features or simply geometrical lines of longitude or latitudes. Examples of contractual-geometrical boundaries are, of course, the USA's western boundaries to north and south along the 49th Parallel and the Rio-Grande, respectively. Contractual-geometrical boundaries largely occur in Africa which had been the most competitive peripheral arena in the nineteenth century. Here, the concepts of 'natural' or 'national' boundaries had no relevance as ethnic groups and river basins were divided up in complete contrast to the boundary then evolving in the core.

The power-political boundary concept had its origin both in America and in Germany also, but in a different perspective and situation. The westward expansion of the American State, at the expense of the weak natives, was basically power-political, as it reflected one of advances of the strong and retreats of the weak. The German perspective on power-political boundary was the product of inter-war geopolitics, which looked upon boundaries "as the biological battlefields in the life of people". The essence of this concept was that boundary was not only a line demarcating legal systems but also a line of contact of territorial power structures. Specific boundaries at any given historical period become then merely the politico-geographic expression of the existing balances of forces at that period. Power-political boundaries not only emerged in the periphery only but also in the continent where the Franco-German boundary and the German-Austro-Hungarian boundary in the late nineteenth century reflected the contemporary territorial contact of power structure. Similarly, the pre-war German boundaries in the twentieth century also reflected its power-political expression, thrust upon its neighbours. The McMohan Line also manifested balance of forces between British India and China.

Boundaries in the post-war scenario have tended to coincide more with the features of nationalities. Boundaries in East Europe, in particular, reflected the territorial contact of the various nationalities. The post-Cold War scenario in Europe also reflect the same tendency that states are breaking up on nationality lines and their boundaries expressively coincide with the patterns of nationalities. In Asia-Pacific regions, the international boundaries reflect the same old tradition as one that thrust upon them by the core states during the period of the colonial competition, though China and others have expressed displeasure over such alignments. In Africa, the nineteenth century 'contractual-geometrical paradigm' still prevails, though independent African states are now opposing such territorial alignments imposed on them by the core states. Thus, modern international boundaries reflect contrasting processes in the core and periphery which are the hallmarks of the world-systems approach.

Evolution of Boundaries

Boundaries are one of the spatial expressions of the given legal order as they are supported by 'jural laws'. They are man-made politico-geographical occurrences. A boundary does not exist in nature or by itself. It always owes its existence to man. A survey of the global patterns of boundaries will reveal that they have evolved through (i) 'arbitrary process', (ii) 'evolutionary process', and (iii) 'arbitration process.'

Boundaries in the peripheral competitive and non-competitive arenas seemed to have evolved through the arbitrary actions of the core states, regardless of the local territorial and human elements. They were more of administrative convenience rather than of compromise, and expressive of 'colonial expediency'. The British Indian boundary along the Himalayas was expressive of what may be called a 'unilateral' action of arbitrariness, without taking into confidence the opposite party. Great majority of boundaries in the periphery had been arbitrarily aligned by the imperialist core states to their satisfaction and political sustenance. Imperialist boundaries and power-political boundaries, imposed on the peripheral territories also reflect arbitrariness. Even in Europe, boundaries in the past had evolved in an arbitrary manner. The post-feudal period in Europe had witnessed arbitrary alignment of territories and the boundaries evolved accordingly.

The American State and the Australian State, both have acquired their present territorial size through arbitrary process of territorial aggrandizement at the cost of the weak social formation of the original inhabitants/natives. Internal federal boundaries have been drawn up unilaterally, regardless of the territorial human elements. Geometrical boundaries in Africa had long been drawn up in an arbitrary manner, in a sense, that they did not conform to the geographical reality of the continent. Boundaries, drawn up arbitrarily without reference to the territories and peoples, are usually *de facto* in nature. Boundaries, which are the product of contract between the concerned territories and peoples, have developed/grown up through the evolutionary processes involving certain phases. The ideal sequence of events in the establishment of a boundary is as follows: The first stage involves 'negotiation' between the concerned states which leads to the 'description' of the boundary which involves the identification of location of the boundary and the terrain through which it has to be aligned. Reference may be made to conspicuous physical features, such as crestlines, watersheds, hilltops, passes/saddles, coastlines, rivers, and even to cultural features, such as buildings, farm fences, and roads. The more detailed the description, the less likely is there to be subsequent friction. This first stage, represented by the language found in many treaties, is referred to as the 'definition' of the boundary, which indicates that the involved states have agreed upon the geographical coordinates and features.

When the involved states have completed the formalities of the description and definition of geographical coordinates or features of the boundary in question, then the real job of the cartographers begins who, then, locate the coordinates and 'delimit' them on large scale maps by joining them through a line. This is the second stage of the boundary evolution. Delimitation is done with extra care and utmost caution, and cartographers of the concerned states, who delimit the boundary in the presence of their respective officials, are required to have detailed geographical knowledge of the area and the art of delimitation. Any deviation during the process of delimitation may give rise to serious disputes in the future.

The third and the final stage of the boundary making is that of the 'demarcation', i.e., the task of marking the boundary on the ground which is the job of the surveyors. Demarcation is done by various methods such as fences, pillars, stones, wires, and by mere lines of poles. Utmost caution is again maintained in the process of demarcation, so that in no way it should deviate from the 'delimited line'. Very few world boundaries are actually marked on the surface. It is an expensive process and when states do not face such problems along their boundaries as to absolutely require demarcation, they often delay this stage permanently. However, fences have been built in certain delicate areas where exact demarcation was required. Demarcation on the high crest-cum-watershed areas is extremely difficult because of inaccessibility, permanent snowfields and lack of suitable methods. Most of the mountain boundaries which pass along permanent snowfields have yet to be demarcated.

Most of the contractual boundaries appear to have evolved in this way. In the periphery itself, some boundaries have developed through the evolutionary processes, involving description, delimitation and demarcation. The Anglo-Russian convention of the nineteenth century sought to perpetuate the boundaries of Afghanistan. Boundaries which have come up this way may be grouped as *de jure* boundaries, because their alignment reflects bilateral or in some cases, multilateral agreements.

Some boundaries have come up neither through the arbitrary process nor through the evolutionary process, rather through 'arbitration', acceptable to the parties concerned. This was particularly true in the periphery. For example, the mountainous boundary across the Andes between Chile and Argentina in Latin America was the result of the arbitration of King Edward II. The award which he made in 1902 was binding on the concerned parties. When the concerned states failed to agree on the location of the boundary, they sought for arbitration. The arbitrator employs experts, cartographers and other officials so as to study the problems, to describe and delimit the boundary, and finally make the award. The demarcation of it is left with the concerned parties. The award is not always impartial. Indo-Pakistan boundary across the Runn of Kutch results from the arbitration and to Pakistan, the arbitrator has not been fair to it. The boundary has given additional strategic advantage to India as it is alleged by Pakistan.

The evolution of Indo-Pakistan boundary, other than that which runs across the Runn of Kutch, is somewhere between the arbitrary process. evolutionary process and arbitration. The arbitrator, Sir Cyril Radcliffe was appointed by the colonial master, not by the involved dominions, and the boundary award was thrust upon them in an arbitrary manner. In the majority of the former colonial areas, boundaries had been created in such a way. Particularly, in the non-competitive peripheral areas, international boundaries have come up this way, reflecting a core-periphery relation. Evolution of boundaries in the former Soviet realm in Eurasia simply reflected the semi-periphery processes of power politics.

Functions of Boundaries

One of the foremost functions of a modern boundary is to generate loyalties, and to impose duties over the people, and to constraint for the sake of internal harmony and compactness and of external separateness and individuality. It tends to serve as a dominant focus of political identification for the territory it binds, defines, and at the same time, persuades the people to shift their loyalties, expectations and political activities toward a new centre. Since it is a political creation, it must function as a centripetal force, reflecting the state idea vis-a-vis the *raison d'etre* of the state which it defines.

Boundaries function as separators of territorial sovereignty (regional limits). In this role, they can function in a limited sense, as 'attractors'. Crossing points become location factors on either side for border towns whose support comes directly and indirectly from administering and servicing the movement across the boundary. In this perspective, the concept of a border landscape or border land can be elaborated into a notion of a limited mirror image effect, i.e., a great similarity between the opposite border lands in the spatial arrangement and function of certain phenomena, reflecting the impact of the same regional focus, the boundary. Furthermore, the conscious creation of official border zones by a state on the one side or by agreement or coincidence of adjoining states on either side, will tend to emphasize this marked effect on the landscape.

National boundaries also function as filters or screens; they are seldom completely impenetrable barriers, nor are they normally passed with so much ease as to be no barrier at all, but rather have a filtering (quality) or screening (quantity) effect on movement. Problems arise in the measurement of this impact. One can equate the barrier function for any given movement to the friction of distance in terms of time, cost or some other index. The measuring in this manner of any two movements across the same boundary will serve to indicate the individuality in the boundary's function according to the particular movement measured. It might for instance, seem to be a very minor filter for a certain commodity while at the same time it could act as a major barrier to permanent immigration. Some kinds of movements such as air waves carrying television signals can in no way be effectively controlled at the boundary in respect to this flow (aside from the location and size of the transmitter) must be made at the points of reception of the information.

Since the boundary is the meeting place of two or more different economic entities, each having different economic structure and economies, it must have intrinsic commercial function. It acts as a tariff barrier/wall, providing protection to internal industries to prosper within. In fact, it provides tariff protection to internal commodities from outside competition. The price differential on either side of the boundary usually affects the location of outlets for the products of the various industries affected by tariff provisions while the industry may prosper, the area under the shadow of the boundary may not. In the most competitive but emerging arenas of the periphery, the states have erected strong tariff wall against the core states. The European states have together formed a greater tariff wall, providing protection to their industries against the inroads of the American and the Japanese goods. The tariff-wall functions of boundaries of the European states have much declined as they are drawn more and more closer to one another. However, the tariff-wall commercial function of the boundary in the coming century will gradually diminish because of the greater flexibility in the liberalization of the global trade.

To check smuggling is another commercial function of a political boundary of the present-day state system. If smuggling from across the national boundary continues unabated, it ruins completely the national economy, making the boundary itself meaningless and ineffective. Strict vigil is, therefore, maintained all along the boundary. Check points at regular intervals are errected, and custom officials are posted there.

The political boundary also performs legal functions. The state laws prevail at this line. Taxes must be paid to the government by anyone legally subject to taxation whether he resides one or one hundred kilometres from the boundary. Even though a resident living within sight of the border may have closer linguistic, historical and religious ties with the people on the other side, he is subject to regulation prevailing on his side of the boundary, including compulsory education to a certain age, selective service enlistment, and so forth. Furthermore, the national government is capable of controlling emigration and immigration at points along the border.

However, with the increasing satellite geopolitics vis-a-vis the political importance of the space, the traditional function of boundary as a line of defence has declined considerably. No doubt, political boundaries had long functioned as lines of defence. The ancient, medieval and even the modern boundary concepts, till recently rallied round its defensive character. To the major powers of the world possessing modern military equipments, however, the artificially or naturally fortified boundary is no longer an asset. But this is not to suggest that the defensive function of the boundary has completely been lost. India is erecting barbed wire all along its tension-ridden boundary with Pakistan and also with Bangladesh which is indicative of the defensive character of it. Political boundaries of the Muslim states in West Asia do perform defensive function intrinsically while those of West European states, have ceased to be defensive.

Political boundaries in the periphery are more defensive in character while in the core, they are more economic in nature, and in the semi-periphery they are somewhere between defensive and economic in character. Hence, the boundary functions require to be viewed more from the changing core-periphery relations rather than any other. There cannot be any universal generalization of the boundary function. Even in the periphery states with different 'core identification', notwithstanding being neighbours, have different perceptions of boundary functions. Boundary functions also tend to change between states with the same 'core identification' in the periphery, since they gained independence at substantially difficult times. Variable character of the boundary functions is a mere politico-geographical expression of varied types of states, variable character of their genesis/growth, outlook and perception, and place in the world economy.

Classification of Boundaries

The classification of boundaries can be carried out on the basis of two different types of criteria. They can be grouped or categorized from the point of view of their static characteristics; for example, their correspondence to physiographic or morphological features, their separation of ethnic regions, their straightness, and so forth. This is basically a descriptive classification. It tends to utilize the morphological approach in political geography. Boundaries have also been drawn to follow straightlines of latitude and longitude or arcs, and in some cases, they have been aligned in such a way as to separate ethnic communities of various backgrounds and identities. This classification is often known as the 'morphological' classification of boundaries.

Boundaries can also be classified according to their relationship with the cultural landscape. In fact, Richard Hartshorne in 1936, suggested a fundamental two-fold division, arising from the relationship between the boundary and the surrounding cultural landscape. Some boundaries were established prior to the permanent occupation of areas by the present inhabitants. In some cases patterns of settlement were already developing so that the boundary ultimately established has a different relationship to the cultural realities of the area involved. This classification is known as the 'functional' or 'genetic' classification of boundaries.

Recently, John Nystuen has suggested a new classification of boundaries in terms of their impact on activities. While not specifically formulated for political boundaries, nevertheless, this classification adds to our understanding of these phenomena.

Morphological Boundaries

It has been the tendency since long to make boundaries conform with some conspicuous natural features. Kautilya's *Arthasastra* makes an indepth reference to physical boundaries, and if chronology is to be believed, then it can be said that the political boundaries of Chandragupta Maurya's great empire in the fourth century BC passed along the Himalayas and the Hindukush mountains. Ancient Indian kings used to prefer river boundaries where mountains were absent. Even the boundaries of Mughal India conformed with natural features. British India carried forward the same heritage of natural boundaries. Although natural features were used for boundaries for millenia before but it was not until the French Revolution in the late eighteenth century that such boundaries emerged as a major boundary doctrine. Expressively, the French doctrine of natural boundaries reflected expansionist philosophy.

Natural features have certain basic characteristics: (i) they are the most conspicuous features on the earth's surface; (ii) hence, they are easily identifiable, recognizable, and measurable not only on the surface but also on the map; (iii) natural features are intrinsically stable features and no other observable phenomena on the surface can match them in this way; and (iv) they have immense strategic values than those of others. Because of these spatial characters they have often been preferred to others, particularly when the question of politico-territorial limit of the sovereignty has arisen between states.

"Naturally marked boundaries have been subject to almost endless classification. The relative merits of different natural features for the purpose have often been examined and one kind of boundary has been preferred to another kind. Such questions, however, have little point because when such boundaries were adopted, their advantage lay chiefly in the fact that they were obvious and unambiguous. In the first instance they are not chosen because they were difficult to cross or because they presented a military barrier to invasion. It is only in the modern times that actual course of a particular boundary has come to be a matter of military significance to the state that is enclosed by it."

Morphological boundaries have been grouped into those (i) which follow the course of a mountain or hill range; (ii) which follow the line of rivers, canals, and lakes; (iii) which run through a desert, a forest or a swamp; and (iv) which conform with some other physical feature that may once have been conspicuous in the landscape.

Mountain Boundaries

Mountains have always been preferred to other natural features for boundary making, for "a definite line of watershed carried by a conspicuous mountain crest, ridge or range, is undoubtedly the most lasting, the most reliable, identifiable, the most unmistakable and the most efficient as a barrier". Boundaries drawn along mountains and hills are found to be unambiguous and obvious. Most of the traditional boundaries which emerged along the mountains and hills in the historical past, have still retained their function—both as a line of defence and a line of defining the territorial sovereignty (Fig. 6.1).

Mountains and hills are unmistakenly identified on the maps and hence, delimited accurately, making the demarcation on the ground much easier. However, in case of an inaccessible and very high altitude area, it is extremely difficult to carry on demarcation. Most of the high altitude mountain boundaries have been left over undemarcated. Notwithstanding their finest spatial characteristics, as the most stable, efficient, unambiguous and so forth, mountain barriers have quite often presented problems. Only in the rarest instances, there exists a clearly defined crest line, and the crest line rarely does continue far without being interrupted by a transverse valley. Normally mountains are made up of number of sub-parallel ranges separated by interconnected valleys.

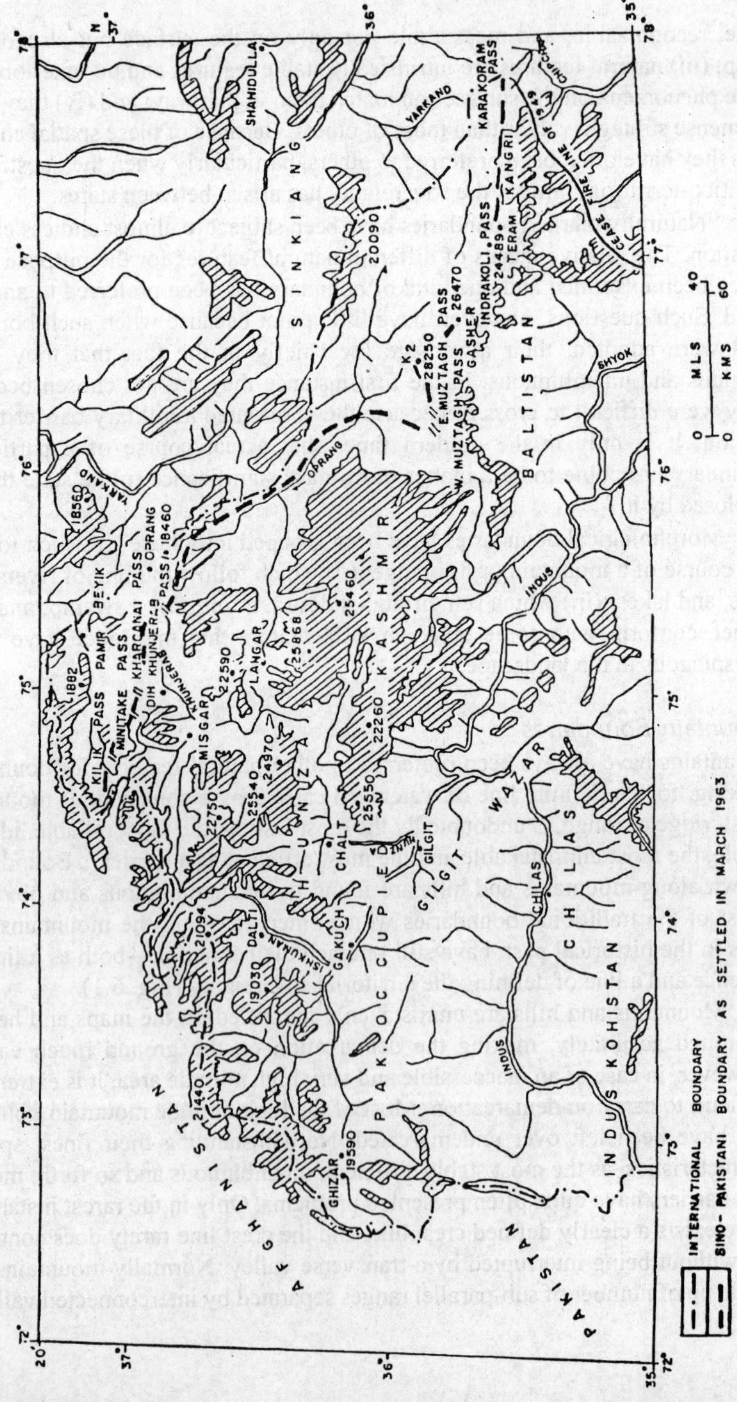

Figure 6.1: Mountain Boundary (China-Pakistan Boundary Agreement)

Rarely does the crest coincide with the water divide. "Both sides of the highest and most continuous mountain range in the world, the Himalayas, are drained ultimately to the same river system, the Ganga-Brahmaputra delta."

A conspicuous mountain range usually has breadth and length and in its valleys may occur human societies which have adapted themselves to the mountain environment, and developed their economies accordingly. Transhumance is the most expressive human activity across the mountain ranges for the simple reason that good pastures occur on the mountain slopes, and some pastures do occur on the crest sides. There are examples that with the alignment of inter-state boundaries in such areas, the mountain dwellers have to abandon their permanent transhumance activities, as it happened in case of the Polish-Czech boundary along the Tatra, and the Slovenia-Austria boundary along Karawanke. Most of the more formidable mountain ranges constitute minor cultural regions rather than cultural divide. Any boundary chosen to follow a chain of mountains must, unless the area is totally devoid of human clusters, break up human societies to some degree.

Most of the boundaries drawn along the mountain ridges and ranges are based on earlier maps with varying degree of errors. Seldom, features such as the crest and watershed etc. on the maps coincide with the realities on the surface/ground, causing serious disputes over the alignment. A serious dispute arose between Chile and Argentina over the alignment of boundary along the Patagonian Andes because the map which was used for the delimitation for the 1881 treaty was not truly expressive of the region. As a result both states had different interpretation. There was no crest line in the Andes, the water-divide did not conform with the higher ranges but the map showed the coincidence between the two. It was through an arbitration of Edward VII that Chile and Argentina finally agreed to comply with the Boundary Award made by His Highness in 1902. The *de facto* McMohan Line between India and China which was delimited on the maps, prepared by the British official to follow the high crest-cum-watershed of the Eastern Himalayas, may not conform with the ground realities of the region. The crest is not continuous and there are numerous interruptions by transverse valleys. Mountain boundaries which follow the crest-cum-watershed present serious problems to demarcation, nonetheless, they offer greater durability and desirability in the politico-geographical arena (Fig. 6.2).

River and Lake Boundaries

Rivers and lakes have the advantage of being more clearly marked on maps and more narrowly defined on the land than mountains and hills. Rarely are there any problems with the river boundaries as with the crest line and watershed as their continuity is often interrupted by transverse valleys, making the

Figure 6.2: Sino-Indian Boundary in Eastern Himalayas

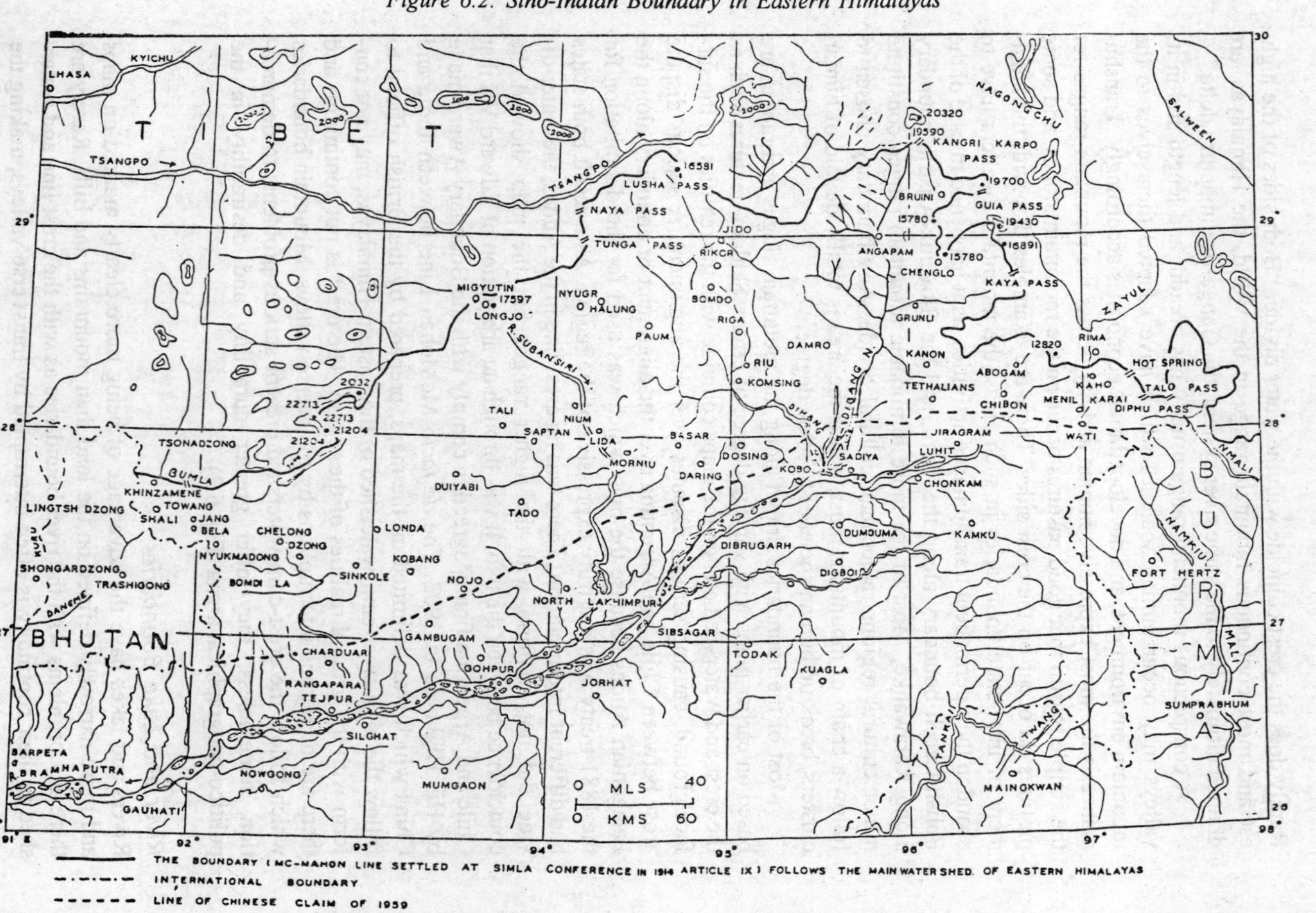

definition almost difficult. Another problem with the definition and demarcation of the mountain boundary is that seldom does the crest line conform with the watershed when majority of maps show a clearcut coincidence between the two. This cannot happen in case of a river. For this reason, rivers in particular have been used in boundary definition and delimitation. Rivers since long have acted as barriers to movement and performed their separating functions especially well if flood plains were wide, increasing the difficulty of crossing them. As obvious, continuous and permanent features in the landscape they were protective barriers.

Against the use of rivers as boundaries, it has often been said that they do not usually coincide with the divisions between human societies. There is a tendency for the whole valley of a river to emerge as a distinct region, and also to become a unit for purposes of water use and human settlement. The river valley possesses a regional functional unity of its own while a mountain range does not often possesses that quality. Ancient states flourished in river basins. Rivers have long functioned as important arteries of trade and transport. Large rivers usually have major basins, economic and cultural, and even political development on both sides is often similar but the alignment of political boundaries across them has undoubtedly disrupted settled communities, creating major problem in the utilization of water, and also in the flow of traffic. The alignment of the Indo-Pakistan boundary across the Indus and the Ganga basins in 1947 has created more human problems than before.

Any definition of a river boundary will have to be more specific than merely to state that it "runs along the river". The alignment of river boundary is done either (i) along the median line; or (ii) along the centre line of the navigable channel or the principal channel (thalweg); or (iii) along one of the banks.

The median line is a line equidistant from the river banks. The problems here are obvious. If the river is navigable, the navigable channel will swing from one side of the river to the other, and if the median line is the boundary this means that the navigable channel repeatedly crosses the international boundary thus established. In order to mark the median line, the exact location of the banks must be known or agreed upon, and this, in a river of changing volume and a wide flood plain, presents difficulties.

It was decided in 1920 that in navigable rivers the boundary should follow the principal channel or the thalweg. Since then, it has been the most frequently adopted method. Navigable channels are the deepest parts of the rivers but are rarely or never exactly in the middle of the stream. They are subject to constant modification. Thus, although the buoys marking the international boundary stay fixed at the surface, the navigable channel may undergo such significant shifts that is no longer possible to use it on both sides of the line of buoys. This requires frequent adjustment and maintenance by the concerned states.

No less confusing are boundaries which have been aligned to follow one bank of a river or the other. Such boundary lines have not always been deliberately chosen; they have arisen from the clumsy and ambiguous wording of treaties and agreements that were made at a time when such matters as the precise relationship of the boundary line to the river were not considered important. If the definition of the boundary states that "it will run along the contact between land and water on the right bank", then the boundary will shift with the changing volume of water of the river. This would be intolerable. If the boundary is fixed then part of the non-riparian state is flooded and this would mean that it had right to water, which by definition, cannot share. It is, therefore, observed that this criterion of river boundary is far from satisfaction. For nearly 64 kilometres, the boundary between Iraq and Iran follows the left or the northern bank of the Shatt-el-Arab, and is the potential source of disputes between the two Muslim states in West Asia.

It has been found that the course of a river may gradually change through erosion of one bank and accretion on the other. It is also liable to sudden change when the river abandons its old bed and flows on a new. This change in the course of a river also brings about an equally gradual shift of boundary while the avulsion or sudden shift of the stream does not, and in such a case or situation, the boundary shall continue to follow "the centre of normal channel" which has been fixed earlier. Even if the river abandons its channel and goes dry, no alteration of the earlier location of boundary is permissible. This principle has been followed between the USA and Mexico along the Rio-Grande which has been notorious for frequent changes in its course. Sometimes, the formation of outlines of a state's territory beyond the main stream of the river itself and which are not frequently accessible by a bridge poses serious politico-administrative problems for the concerned states. The common practice to deal with such problems is to eliminate the outliers of territory within purview of the negotiation, definition and delimitation, as has been done between the USA and Mexico along the Rio-Grande.

One of the potential problems resulting from the changes in the river courses is that of frequent occurrences of chaurs or islands in the valley, which in most cases, gives rise to serious boundary problems between the involved states. All great river boundaries normally suffer from this problem. These islands, sometimes become productive, and the farmers of one state may raise crops there while of the other state may harvest them. The state may collect revenue from the migrants who temporarily migrate to such islands for cultivation. If the chaurs or islands become permanent, then problems tend to become permanent. Some such islands in the river may have strategic importance, and in that case, the concerned states may attempt to occupy them, leading to potential war-like situation. The Amur and the Ussuri rivers are littered with such islands which have long given rise to serious river boundary disputes between China and Russia (former Soviet Union). An island in the Muhuri river between Tripura (India) and Bangladesh has created considerable tension between the two states.

Indo-Bangladesh river boundary along one of the dead channels of the Ganga (the Matabhanga) has always remained a source of tension between the two. The river boundary does not follow any particular bank or the midstream or the principal channel nor is there any median line drawn across it, but its course has changed considerably. Both the states have failed to evolve any compromise formula. Similarly, the shifting course of the Ganga between Murshidabad (India) and Rajshahi (Bangladesh) has always been a source of tension between the two. Here, the shifting is due to erosion along the right bank and accretion along the left bank. Since the boundary along it has neither been aligned along any particular bank nor along the principal thalweg, the dispute is of a perennial nature (Fig. 6.3).

Lake boundary usually follows the median line as in the case of the USA-Canada boundary across the Great Lakes (Fig.6.4). Lakes do not present such problems as the rivers do, hence lake boundaries are more stable. There are some pertinent questions with regard to the median line formula in determining the boundary across the lake. Does it divide the lake into two equal parts? Is it a line (at all points) equidistant from either shore? Or is it a line drawn through the middle points of a number of lines drawn from shore to shore across the lake? These questions require to be settled bilaterally between the involved states. However, the median-line formula has not been adopted in the division of Lake Victoria in Africa between Uganda, Kenya and Tanzania. The division is based on lines of latitude and longitude drawn from the points where international boundaries of these states reach the water. But the boundary between Zimbabwe-Rhodesia and Zambia across the man-made Kariba Lake follows the median line (Fig.6.4).

Forest, Swamps and Desert Boundaries

These features on the earth's surface had served as frontiers in the historical past because of the ambiguous extent and scanty population. In fact, they were no-man's tracts between the settled communities and functioned as cultural and defensive barriers. The forests of North-East Europe have been cultural barriers, separating Finn from Russian, Russian from Lithuanian, and Lithuanian from Pole. Some of these barriers have been changed into boundaries when they narrowed down with the gradual penetration of human communities.

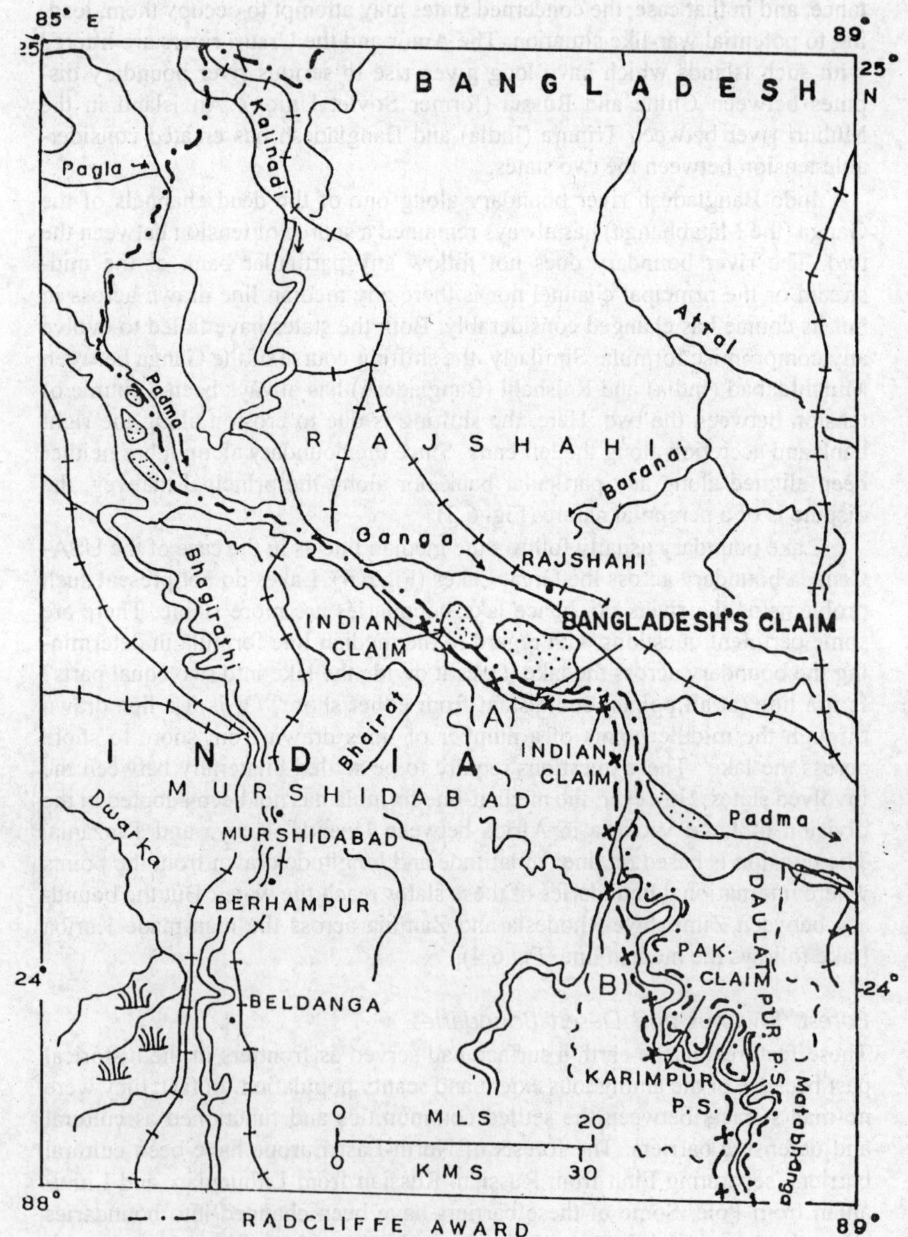

Figure 6.3: River Boundary

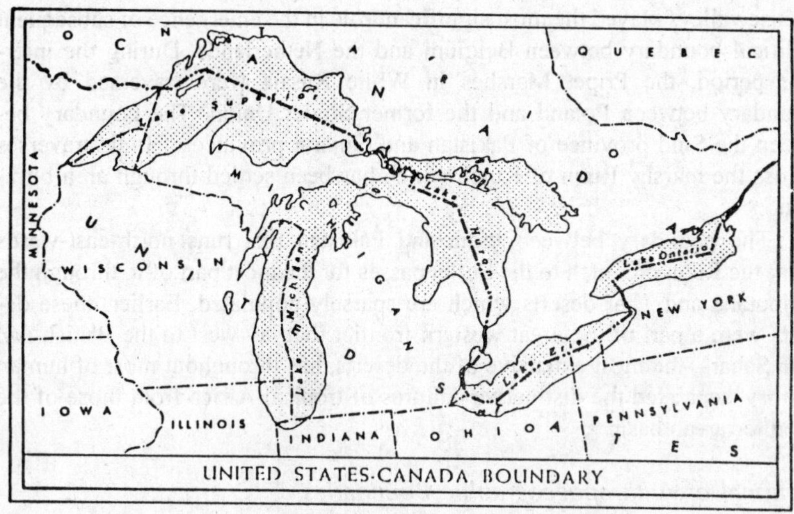

UNITED STATES-CANADA BOUNDARY

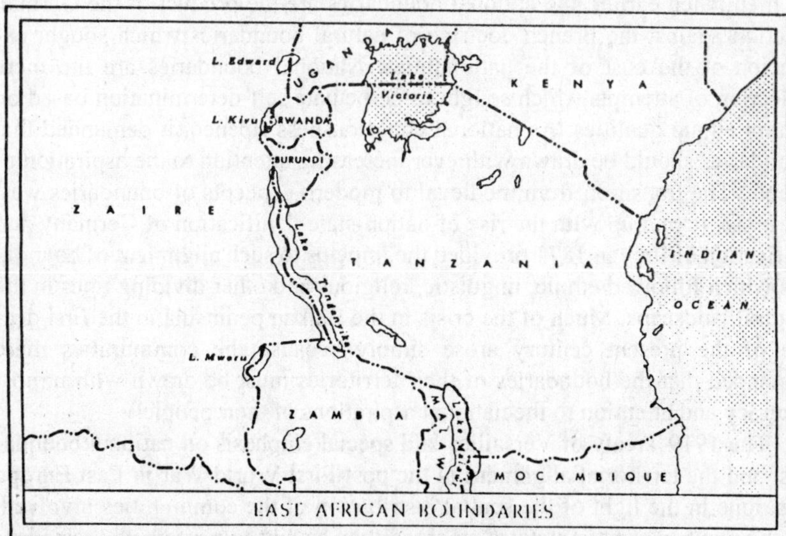

EAST AFRICAN BOUNDARIES

Figure 6.4: Lake Boundary (After de Blij, 1972)

Though swamps are less extensive and less effective as cultural barriers, they played decisive role in space politics. Marshes along the lower Rhine and Meuse valleys played the most significant role in the emergence of subsequent political boundary between Belgium and the Netherlands. During the inter-war period, the Pripet Marshes in White Russia were traversed by the boundary between Poland and the former Soviet Union. The boundary between the Sind province of Pakistan and Gujarat province of India traverses across the marshy Runn of Kutch which has been settled through an arbitration.

The boundary between India and Pakistan that runs north-east-wards from the Runn of Kutch to the Sutlej passes for the most part of it, through the Rajputana and Thar deserts which are sparsely populated. Earlier, these deserts were a part of the great western frontier that lay west to the British *raj*. The Sahara, the most extensive of the deserts, has throughout most of human history, separated the distinctive cultures of tropical Africa from those of the Mediterrarean basin.

National or Anthropogeographic Boundaries

As mentioned earlier, the national boundaries are the product of the German reaction against the French doctrine of natural boundaries which sought expansion at the cost of the nationalities. National boundaries are the mere reflection of attempts which sought to perpetuate self-determination based on certain ethnic qualities. As national consciousness ripened, it demanded that boundaries should be drawn with ever increasing attention to the aspiration of people. The transition from medieval to modern concepts of boundaries was, therefore, bound up with the rise of nation-state. Unification of Germany and unification of Italy in 1871 provided the impetus to such alignment of boundaries which followed ethnic, linguistic, religious and other dividing lines in the cultural landscape. Much of the crisis in the Balkan peninsula in the first decade of the present century arose simply because the communities there demanded that the boundaries of their territories must be drawn with utmost accuracy and attention to the national aspirations of their people.

The 1919 Treaty of Versailles laid special emphasis on national boundaries, and the territorial alignment in the post-First World War in East Europe was done in the light of the spatial distribution of the communities involved. As the number of nation-states emerged they sought to perpetuate their identity based on their cultural distinctiveness. The importance of physical boundaries declined substantially and those of national boundaries increased. States which emerged during the inter-war period and after the Second World War, as a result of the nationalist movement, have their boundaries drawn along ethnic and cultural features. The Indo-Pak boundary which was thrust upon the dominions follows the religious cleavage. Most boundaries, w exception of some of those in Latin America and new states of Africa, tional boundaries.

The alignment of national boundaries has, in most cases, led to the ...ns- fer of population and the creation of minority problem. No state can be said to be inhabited solely by the community for which it has been created; there may be people, though in small numbers, belonging to other communities also, which may have religious/cultural ties or affinity with the people of the state on the other side of the boundary. The division of British India on the religious pattern in 1947 left millions of Muslims in India and millions of Hindus in Pakistan. The division was followed by large-scale transfer of peoples but still peoples in substantial number remained in these two states as minorities, creating intense communal problems. Alignment of national boundary also leads to 'forced' influx of people who move to neighbouring states as the refugees. Post-war history is full of examples of 'forced migration' of one ethnic community by the other. Even people who have developed territoriality for generations are uprooted and driven out of their territory (Fig. 6.5).

Internal federal boundaries of the Indian Union have been made to follow the regional linguistic pattern which have given rise to intense regional rivalries within the Indian State.

National or anthropogeographic boundaries are not as sharply defined on those of the physical boundaries and because of their ambiguous character, they can create political disputes within and outside. National boundaries have created more problems than physical boundaries; nonetheless, they are most preferred.

Geometrical Boundaries

Boundaries which have been made to follow lines of latitude or longitude or in some cases, as drawn from fixed points, are known as geometrical or astronomical or mathematical boundaries . They are the product of the Age of Imperialism and Colonialism. The earliest example of such a boundary can be traced back to the late fifteenth century when the Pope divided the still undiscovered parts of the world between Spain and Portugal. It was in the Treaty of Tordesillas in 1495 that the earlier alignment made in 1481 was amended and the boundary was defined to have passed along the meridian running 370 leagues west of Cape Verde Islands. Several centuries after, the delimiation of the northern boundary of Florida was agreed upon between the USA and Spain, using the 'straight line' method in 1795. In 1818, the 49th degree of latitude was recognized as boundary between the USA and Canada.

It was at the Berlin Conference in 1884-85, attended by the European colonial powers that geometrical boundaries were preferred to other boundaries

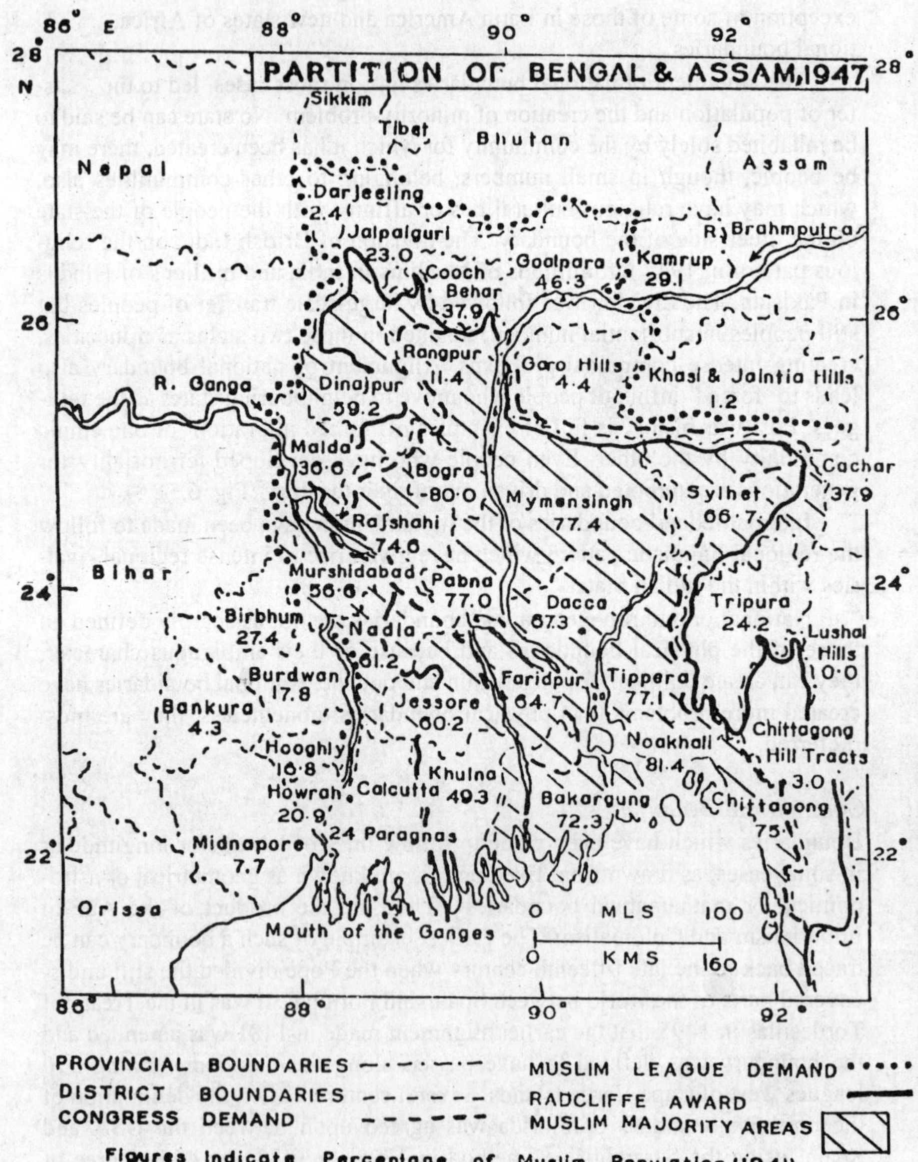

Figure 6.5: Anthropogeographical Boundary

for such areas as in Africa which were still partly undiscovered and unclaimed. Preference to these boundaries sought to establish the limits of their hitherto ill-defined sphere of influence across Africa.

Geometrical boundaries reflected only the relative power of the states concerned, paying no attention to local conditions and desire of the indigenous people. These are all arbitrary boundaries, imposed from above or thrust upon the people.

Geometrical boundaries are easy to define and delimit on the map and their demarcation on the ground with modern methods of survey presents no problems. There is a superficial similarity between meridians and parallels and other straight lines drawn between points, known as turning points. A number of boundaries are actually made up of a series of short, straight, oblique (i.e., neither north-south nor east-west) segments traced between turning points (Fig. 6.6).

Many boundaries in Africa, West Asia, Middle East, Russia and Australia are, in fact, oblique. A geometrical boundary may come up across a truce line or along a ceasefire line and that too, depends on the nature of compromise between the states—powers involved. The 38th parallel in Korea was established in 1945 as the boundary between North Korea and South Korea by negotiation between the USA and the former USSR. The 17th parallel was the boundary between North Vietnam and South Vietnam, separating the Chinese sphere of influence and the French realm in Indo-China. However, with the unification of Vietnam in the early 1970s, this boundary disappeared. If Korea becomes one, the 38th Parallel will automatically disappear.

A final category of geometrical boundary consists of an arc of a circle drawn with a prescribed centre and radius. The boundary of Gambia in Africa belongs to this category. It has been drawn with a series of arcs of circles with their centres and radii on the Gambia river itself as the boundary runs parallel to it. Examples of this category of geometrical boundaries are rare and unimportant also. The geometrical boundary is being used today as a possible solution to the division of the Antarctica continent where spheres of influence between the major powers have begun to develop recently.

Geometrical boundaries are politically successful only when they are defined/delimited/demarcated before the development of settlements. Regardless of errors in demarcation they pose no problems but if they are defined and demarcated after the development of settlements, problems and disputes are bound to occur because in that case, the alignment is done ignoring the ground realities and desire of the communities. A great majority of African native communities are now demanding reorganization of the territories which must conform with the national aspirations of the people if they lie across the boundaries.

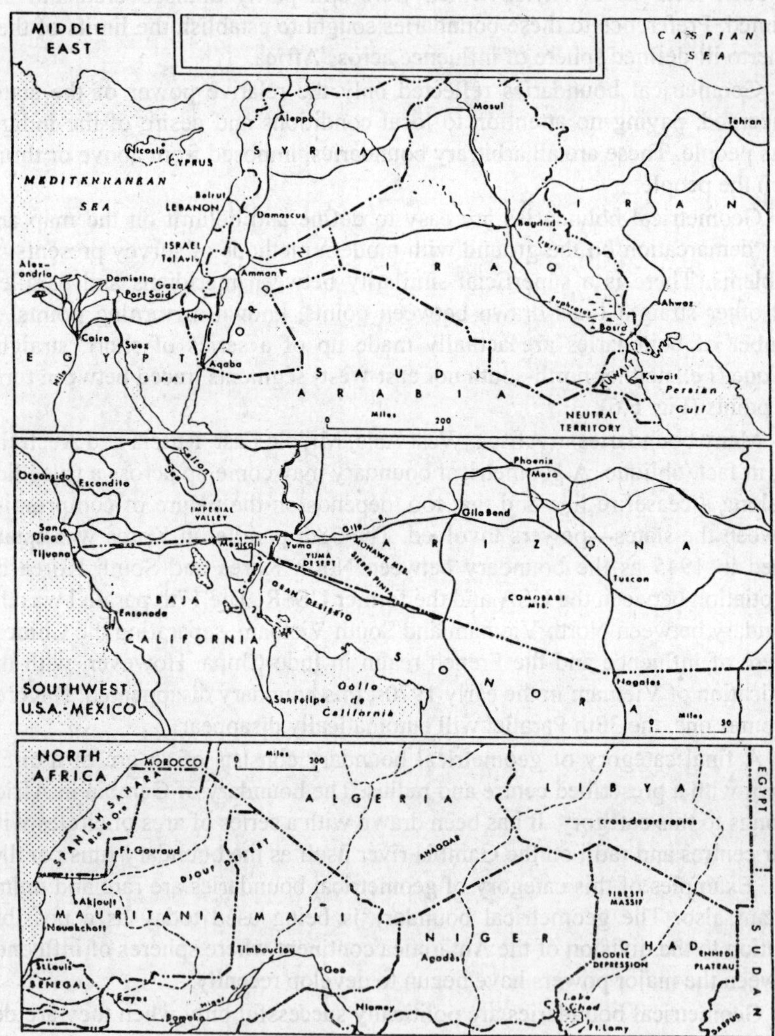

Figure 6.6: Geometrical Boundaries on Land

Sometimes the form of any one boundary can be classified equally well under two or more of the above types (i.e., a river can be a cultural divide or a geometrical divide), it is, therefore, necessary to have an open-ended type, known as 'complex'. Furthermore, any given boundary between two states, especially if it be a long one, will usually vary in its form from place to place, and hence becomes a mix of several of the above forms. This is known as a 'compound' boundary. Finally, if the boundary neither follows the physiographic feature nor any cultural features, and which is not a geometric one, it is then called as 'inderminate' boundary.

Functional or Genetic Classification of Boundaries

Functional or genetic classification of boundaries is based on the relationship between the boundary and the cultural landscape at "the time the boundary was established". Some boundaries have survived into the present from a period which antedates the rise of nationalism, while some have come to be established after nationalism has found its territorial expression. Richard Hartshorne is credited to have developed this idea in 1936. He has used the nomenclature which has been derived from physical geography.

1. *Antecedent boundaries* are those which were defined and delimited before the main elements of the present-day cultural landscapes began to develop as or those that preceded the development of most of the features of the cultural landscape. As societies developed, they adjusted themselves to the boundary which thus acquired a historical and pragmatic sanction. The boundary between the United States and Canada. established and modified by the treaty agreements between 1782 and 1846, may be said to have been aligned before the development of the cultural landscape on either sides. However, during the period of its definition and demarcation, there were few settlers and some hundreds of nomadic trappers and Indians in the region. It was not wholly unoccupied but the boundary that was established between Canada and Alaska at the time of the agreement in 1825, passed through unsettled/unoccupied and undeveloped territory, and hence, the word 'pioneer' is assigned to it (Fig. 6.7).

2. *Subsequent boundaries* are those which were established after the cultural patterns had been formed, and as a general rule, they conform with the cultural pattern. There is a greater degree of conformity with the main cultural features. Boundaries that developed as a part of the President Wilson's paradigm after the First World War in East Europe belonged to this category. Even the boundary across the Patagonian Andes between Chile and Argentina established as a result of the arbitration of King Edward VII in 1902 is a subsequent boundary. It is with the rise of nation-states that subsequent boundary is coming up. The religion-based boundary between India and Paki-

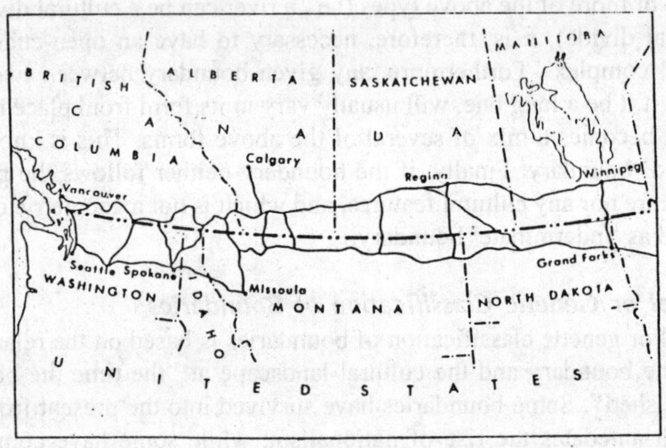

Figure 6.7: Antecedent Boundary

stan, and the federal linguistic boundaries within India, fall into this category (Fig. 6.8).

3. *Superimposed boundaries* were established like subsequent boundaries, after the territory to be divided had been settled and developed, but unlike the latter, they ignore completely the cultural and ethnic characteristics of the area divided. Most of the geometrical boundaries in Africa fall into this category. The boundaries of the Hapsburg empire in 1918 belonged to this category as it cut off Romanians from Romania, Poles from Poland, Serbs from Serbia, and the Italians from Italy.

Superimposed boundaries have come to be developed along truce lines or ceasefire lines. The boundary between the Netherlands and Belgium has been established along the truce line. The 38th parallel between North Korea and South Korea also falls into this category. There is much talk of recognizing the ceasefire line of 1949 between India and Pakistan across Kashmir. If it is really accepted and recognized, it will be a superimposed boundary. Similarly, the line of actual control across Ladakh between India and China also appears to be a superimposed boundary (Fig. 6.9).

Hartshorne used the term 'entrenched' for the long-existing boundary, arguing that whatever the initial and intended functions of a boundary, it begins to affect the cultural landscape associated with it and ultimately becomes an inextricable part of that landscape.

4. *Relict boundaries* are those which have been abandoned for political purposes but which, nevertheless, remain 'discernible' in the cultural maps.

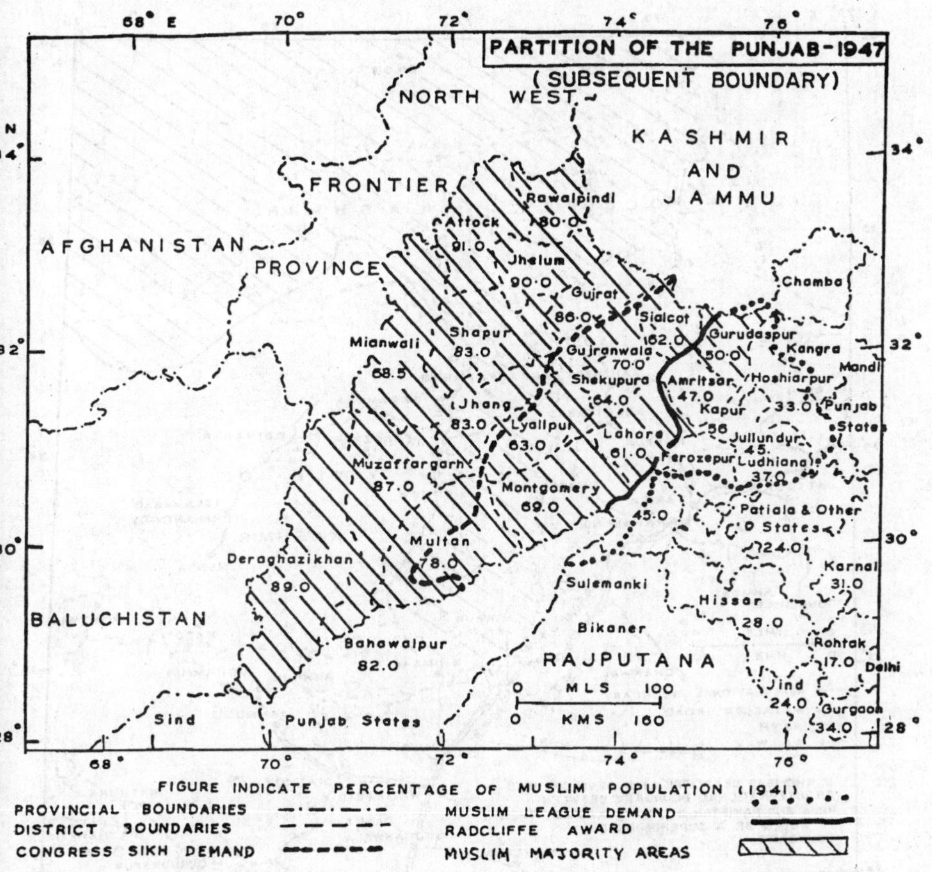

Figure 6.8: Subsequent Boundary

Relict boundaries can be determined with the help of the presence of the former architecture of buildings. The former Russo-German boundary in Upper Silesia can be identified with the help of the architecture of buildings which differed from one another in the two empires. A number of examples of relict boundaries can be found in Europe and Asia where the empires have disappeared but their iconographies still persist.

Apart from morphological classification and functional or genetic classification for boundaries, John Nystuen in 1966 has offered another classification for boundaries in terms of their impact on activities:

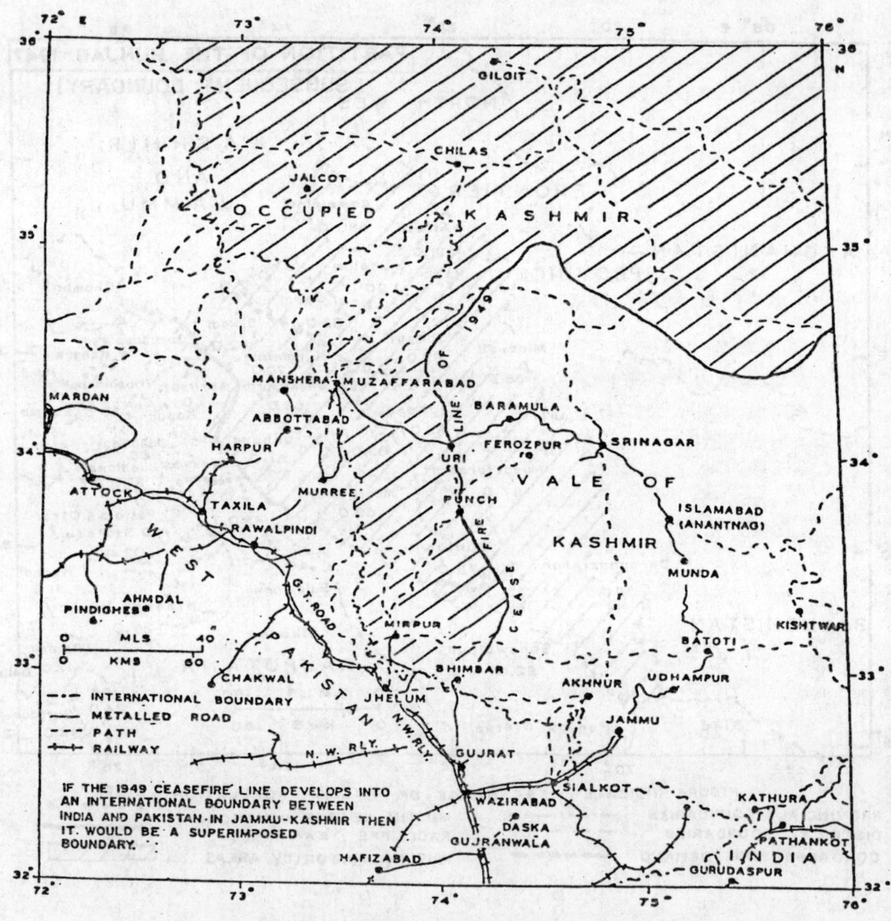

Figure 6.9: Superimposed Boundary

1. *Absorbing boundaries* are those which tend to absorb energy touching them and hence are characterized by a reduction in the density of activities they contain within the domain.
2. *Reflecting boundaries* are those which tend to contain activities by turning them back into the domain. The direction of movement is changed but the energy is not diminished.
3. *Permeable boundaries* are those which contrast with the impermeability of the first two types in that part of the energy reaching them passes through in some filtered and/or screened manner. The remainder is either

absorbed or reflected.

Though the classification does not seem to have been specifically formulated for political boundaries, nevertheless, the classification adds to our understanding of these phenomena. By this classification, John Nystuen was able to define three types of processes involved with boundary interaction: crossing, contained, and boundary-dwelling. Theoretically, he tried to discuss a boundary's 'transfer potential' and 'unit permeability'.

One of the pertinent questions "what boundary is best?" The answer to this question has changed over a period of time. In the nineteenth century and also in the early part of the present century when the international relations were governed by the dynamism of the balance of power, it was the strategic boundary along any of the conspicuous features such as mountains, crests and watersheds which was considered to be the best, as it afforded defence and tended to foil invasion. Attempts were usually made to acquire militarily defensive boundaries. However, the defensive nature of boundary declined/diminished to a greater extent on account of: (i) technological and scientific innovations, and (ii) collapse of the territorial states and the rise of nation-states. In a changed scenario from empire to nation-state, the national boundary that follows the ethnic patterns was conceived of as the best boundary as it was expressive of the national identity. But soon its inherent weaknesses became apparent as its alignment was found to have disrupted centuries' old economic and social tradition, and infrastructure, accompanied by mass exodus of population. The alignment of the Radcliffe Award on the basis of religious cleavage across the Indus basin and the Ganga basin, caused widespread disruption of infrastructure in the respective regions. That boundary now seems to be best boundary whose definition and delimitation, as well as demarcation is based more on technical and economic considerations, rather than on military and ethnic considerations.

Distinction Between Frontiers and Boundaries

On the basis of the above discussions, and what Kristof and Moodie have done, frontiers and boundaries can be distinguished as under :

1. Frontiers are 'outer-oriented', simply because they lie at a greater distance from the political ecumene, and have very little or practically no relation with the ecumene, hence its main attention is carried outward towards the peripheral areas. But the boundaries are 'inner-oriented' since they reflect the territorial limit of the sovereignty, which is done by the governments concerned.
2. On account of its peripheral orientation, and thinly inhabited by the people, who are from from every point of view, inferior to the people of the ecumene, the frontier becomes manifestation of centrifugal forces

whereas the boundary that of centripetal one, because it reflects the state idea vis-a-vis the *raison d'etre* of the state.

3. A frontier is an integrating factor between states on either side as it offers excellent opportunity of movement of different communities across it, facilitating mutual understanding between them. The western frontier of the British *raj* had offered excellent opportunity of mutual contact between the Hindus and Muslim who settled down there. But the alignment of boundary separated and disrupted them. Hence, it is said that "a boundary...is a separating factor."
4. In their origin, the frontier is neither a manifestation of a legal concept or political concept, rather it is a reflection of the spontaneous tendency for the growth of the ecumene. But, the boundary is purely a legal concept, and expressive of the jural law.
5. Frontiers are transitional between geographical regions rather than between states. Hence, they are natural and geographical, whereas boundaries, separating the limit of sovereignties between states, are purely political in origin and functions.
6. On account of being natural, the frontiers are areal, expressive of wide extent and transitional functions, whereas boundaries are linear in character, as they are artificially defined, delimited and demarcated by people.
7. With the growth of civilizations and ecumene, the frontiers have disappeared, and they have been replaced by boundaries. Therefore, the frontiers are a phenomenon of the past and boundaries are a phenomenon of the present, as more and more states are coming up.
8. Lastly, frontiers being expressive of spontaneous growth of ecumenes remain *in situ* regardless of their character and function. Boundaries are a changing phenomenon and highly movable. With every shift in the balance of power, subsequent to the creation of states, the location of boundary lines continues to change and move.

On the contemporary world map boundaries are the norm. The earth has been, more or less, accurately surveyed and precise lines delimit the territories of states. This is a recent development; prior to the twentieth century maps of most parts of the world showed huge tracts of unclaimed land. Indeed such land on the frontier was generally regarded as a necessary 'safety valve' for accommodating the populations of fast growing states. The role of frontier as a safety valve for future growth is still a widely held view.

However, in practice, boundaries are much less premanent than they appear on a map; they are temporal—the outer line of a state as it exists today constantly changing and constantly adjusting. Frequently, some place beyond the legal limits of the state there exists a line of some type that the state feels is the extreme limit of its national concern.

Chapter 7

Territorial Sea and Maritime Boundaries

Rapidity with which the frontiers have been replaced by boundary lines, in the same rate the vast, and unoccupied oceanic frontier has now become subject to various claims and divisions. The concept of boundary is no longer confined to the land surface itself, rather it has also been extended to the sea. And the interesting aspect is that the land boundary simply affects only two states it separates but a maritime boundary unlike its counterpart on the land, marks the limits of the spatial encroachment of a state's sovereignty into the area of the high seas, and affects many states. There has been little agreement as to the width of the state's political jurisdiction/extent over the sea. Studies in this category consequently, have been largely legalistic in approach, and little attempt has been made to treat offshore boundaries as part of the general complex of political boundaries.

However, very few geographers have done pioneering works in the field of the law of the sea, concerning the extent of the territorial sovereignty over the adjacent sea. Their works may be grouped into the following categories:

(i) those which are concerned with the delimitation of maritime boundaries. In fact, these studies made their greatest single advance at the time of the Hague Conference on the Law of the Sea (1930), and more and more works have been done after the 1958 Conference on the Law of the Sea, and also after subsequent conferences; and

(ii) those which are concerned with the exploitation of economic resources such as fish or mineral deposits on the continental shelf and the passage of commercial traffic through international straits. This interest came sharply into focus after 1945 when first the USA and then other countries began to lay claim to exclusive rights on the continental shelf, and when Latin American states began to claim wide areas of the oceans as exclusive fishing zones.

The regional variation which is found on the oceans is not as obvious as the regional variation on land. In one sense, this simplifies the drawing of boundaries because there is no significant debate about 'natural boundaries', although President Jefferson once suggested that the 'Gulf Stream' was the natural boundary of the United States. Boundaries are generally fixed at uniform distances from the coast or some selected baseline. It is also important to note that maritime boundaries are not demarcated, they are marked on charts and it is the responsibility of the navigator to ensure that they are not violated.

Larger part of the oceans unlike the land, is not claimed by individual states, which is parcelled out amongst states. This means that states can actively compete with each other for the resources of the high seas without the involvement of any overriding authority, which is always present on land. This has led to strenuous effort on the part of many countries to formulate a code of international law to govern states' activities on the high seas.

The world's oceans and coastal seas are not permanently occupied as are land areas, and parts of the sea may have a greater variety of use than an equivalent area of land at different but closely related times. States are generally finding it harder to enforce prescribed regulations concerning the activities of individuals in territorial waters than it is on land. The majority of the oceanic resources are more mobile than the corresponding resources on land. Even petroleum and natural gas could be defined to be mobile resources in the sense that where a field straddles an international boundary, the reserves may be almost completely extracted from the other side of the line. Such a situation has necessitated bilateral agreements on continental shelf boundary. Another important difference between the land areas of a state and its territorial waters is that the same state allows innocent passage of an alien vessel through its territorial water but it does not/cannot allow the same on its land. The law of the sea has taken special care regarding landlocked and geographically disadvantaged states, so that they may have access to the continuous seas.

Let us first discuss the histogenesis of the concept of territorial sea-as the spatial expression of the extent of man's political organization over the adjacent sea.

Territorial Sea

The concept of territorial sea appears to have its origin with the opening up of new frontiers in the periphery by the European core states as a result of their rivalries which were followed by the Italian wars and the Treaty of Tordesillas in 1494, which tended to divide the yet unexplored world into a Spanish and a Portuguese realm, and the boundary passed through the meridian 370 league west of the Cape Verde Island. But the following centuries witnessed more intense rivalries between the core states over more possessions in the periphery.

The Hollanders successfully challenged the Portuguese, and the English challenged the Dutch, and so on. Notwithstanding their rivalries in the periphery, the European states were also involved in disputes over fishing rights in the North Sea. The Norwegians, Danes, English and Dutch used to exercise control over various parts of the North Sea and North Atlantic but the limit of the control was vague and not precise. The limit of their control, to a great extent, depended on the capacity of their fleet and fishing vessels. However, it was the Dutch who were among the first to "recognize the need for a zone of water which was to belong to the state, and over which it would possess sovereignty as though it were a piece of its land territory". It was not until the end of the sixteenth century that the question of states' rights to adjacent water developed into a full-scale legal battle.

Early in the seventeenth century the famous Dutch lawyer Hugo Grotius, in his famous *Mare Liberum* argued that no state could control and rule the open sea. Grotius's reaction simply reflected the fact that the Dutch had no large coastal bays and identations which the English possessed. In response to Grotius' assertion, the English jurist John Seldon in his *Mare Clausum*, published in 1635, put forward the British standpoint, arguing that England owned the seas which surrounded the British Isles and separated them from Europe. Throughout the century, the Dutch stuck to the principle of a narrow belt of territorial sea and their counter part, the English stood firm on the principle of extensive closed seas. But this dichotomy gradually narrowed down with the rapid expansion of merchant fleet, and the English particularly realized the need that the limit of the territorial sea must be properly determined. Still there developed another dichotomy between the principle of effective occupation versus the principle of contiguous belt of territorial sea along all coasts.

It was in the midst of such a dichotomy that the Dutch jurist Cornelius Van Bynkershoek published his famous treatise *De Dominio Maris* in 1702. The essence of his philosophy as contained in the treatise, that states could indeed claim sovereignty over water just as they had over land, seemed to have been stemmed from two basic principles: (i) an unguarded coast should not have territorial waters adjacent to it but if a state desired to have claim of sovereignty over the adjacent waters of its coast, it must get its coast fortified; and (ii) the principle of intended and continuous occupation—a state had the right to claim, for permanent possession, any part of the sea over which it exercised such effective control, whether adjacent to its coast or not. It could be achieved through domination from shore or through the deployment of naval fleet.

Bynkershoek's shore-domination principle in the early eighteenth century tended to reflect "a conception of sea-sovereignty much more modern than anything that had been suggested in the previous century". Since the sea was common to all, he explained that "dominion of adjacent seas, as far as a cannon could throw a shot, was reasonable and could be conceded to those who owned the shore". His proposal that a coastal state should exercise sovereignty over that part of the adjacent sea which it could command by means of guns mounted on the shore came to be generally accepted. Nevertheless, the English preferred the principle of a contiguous belt of equal width, which was subsequently favoured by the Danes, French, and Italians which sought to perpetuate the equal width zone of territorial waters, and the problem, then, was one of determining the exact width of such a belt.

Though the Danes in 1745, claimed a width of one league, which was equal to four nautical miles. The Dutch, while agreeing to a belt of equal width, insisted on using the cannon-shot as their determinant of territorial sea over the adjacent waters. Galiani, an Italian writer, is credited with the proposal of a three-mile limit for the territorial sea from the coast. It was believed, then, that his proposal was based on the maximum range of the cannon-shot/artillery of his days. It is still a matter of controversy whether the maximum range of the eighteenth century artillery was three mile or less than that ! Nonetheless, it came to be accepted that a line of three nautical miles from the shore represented the limit of the sovereignty of the coastal states, and outside of it lay the high seas.

Though a three-nautical-mile limit was earlier accepted as the maximum limit of the states' sovereignty over the adjacent seas, and the major power in the contemporary world strictly adhered to it. The three-nautical-mile limit of the territorial water with nineteenth century and early twentieth century was more of a political compromise rather than an administrative convenience.

Variable Claims to Territorial Waters

With the collapse of the colonial system, followed by the rise of nation-states in the periphery, the national claims to adjacent waters became numerous and variable. It has been rightly observed that "never have national claims in adjacent seas been so numerous, so varied or so inconsistent". The three-nautical-mile limit was never universally accepted though the major powers or the contemporary core states strictly adhered to it.

Variable claims to territorial waters in the post-Second World War scenario appear to be the result of the core-periphery conflict. As more and more nation-states are coming up in the periphery with varied national interests, the claim to their adjacent seas is also changing at the expense of the three-nautical-mile limit.

The leading core states of the present world maintain a three-nautical mile limit for their territorial waters but they strongly denounce the variable and wider claims to adjacent seas by other states. The core states which handle roughly 80 per cent of the world's merchant shipping have always favoured the freedom of the seas over a large part of the water surface of the earth as possible. Variable claims to territorial seas other than the three-nautical-mile limit, would lead to a reduction of the area of the high seas to a greater extent and which would subsequently affect the freedom of the mobility across the seas. The core states normally feel that wider belt of territorial waters would greatly jeopardize their trade and commerce and also the mobility across the straits would be closed down. While the newly emerged coastal nation-states in the periphery feel that narrow belt of territorial water, as claimed by the leading, developed maritime states would greatly hamper their national interests and hence they are no longer bound to adhere to their former colonial masters/rulers. The conflict between the states adhering to a three-nautical-mile limit, and those to wider variable claims has widened much and spread throughout the world.

It was in 1952 that three prominent Pacific coastal states of Latin America—Chile, Peru and Ecuador—issued the Declaration of Santiago, claiming exclusive fishing rights to a line some 200 nautical miles from their coasts. The basis for such a wider claim was that the west coast of Latin America off these states does not possess a potentially rich continental shelf, so these states saw nothing wrong in their wider claims to the world's richest fishing water. The Santiago Declaration in 1952 was in response to the Truman Declaration of 1945 by which the United States extended its claim to the wealth of the continental shelf. Later, Peru and Ecuador laid claim over the entire 200 nautical mile belt not just as a contiguous zone but as territorial waters. However, Chile stuck to a three-nautical-mile limit for its territorial waters.

The United Nations Conference on the Law of the Sea (UNCLOS I) was first held in Geneva in 1958 to discuss the problems arising out of unilateral claims by a great number of newly independent nation-states which tended to threaten: (a) freedom of navigation in high seas, and (b) freedom of innocent passage across the international straits. The UNCLOS I codified most of what had developed in the field since its earliest days, and also the developments which had taken place since the Hague Conference in 1930. The conference used as the basis for deliberations from draft conventions prepared by the International Law Commission—an organ of the UN General Assembly. There was no agreement, however, on several important issues, notably special fisheries zones under coastal state jurisdiction and the breadth of the territorial sea. In 1960, the number of states claiming three-nautical-mile limit declined though not very sharply but the number of states claiming a 12-mile limit increased. Included in this category of states were China and the erstwhile Soviet Union. A 12-mile limit tended to close down the entrances to the Gulf of Bothnia, the Gulf of Finland, and also to the Straits of Malacca.

The UNCLOS II, also held in Geneva in 1960 could not come up to the expectation and it also failed to solve the pertinent problems. The four Geneva conventions of 1958, then remained with all their imperfections, as the core of the law of the sea. There were several conventions on the territorial sea and the contiguous zone on the continental shelf, on the high seas and on the conservation of the living resources of the high seas. The continental Shelf Commission codified a new concept in international law deriving from the Truman Declaration that "coastal states had jurisdiction not only over an adjacent belt of the sea abut also over the resources of the continental shelf, extending outward on indeterminate distance".

The signing of the United Nations Convention on the Transit Trade of Landlocked States in 1965 at New York was a significant development in the sense that the geographically disadvantaged states acquired for themselves the right to approach the sea through their neighbours' territories.

By 1971 a number of Latin American states (which included Argentina, Uruguay, Brazil, Panama, Nicaragua and El Salvador) claimed the 200-mile limit either as territorial sea or for the exclusive fishing rights. In Africa, Guinea and Senegal claimed a 130-mile limit while Sierra Leone announced a claim of 200-mile limit. India sought for a 100-mile limit for fishing. It was interesting to observe that the states which strictly adhered to the principle of the three-mile limit were nevertheless, extending their privileged fishing areas to the 12-mile limit including the United States.

With the increase in science and technology on the one hand and more and more wider claim over the adjacent waters, both as contiguous zone and territorial seas on the other there was an intense scramble between the states. However, it was largely felt that the "seabed and ocean floor beyond the limits of present national jurisdiction be reserved exclusively for peaceful purposes and that their resources be used in the interests of mankind, and these resources be declared the common heritage of mankind that they be used primarily for the benefits of the poorest countries and an international agency be created to assume jurisdiction over the area". This was the feeling of most of the nation-states which emerged in the periphery. This initiative on the part of the newly independent nation-states set off a chain of events which led to the UNCLOS III.

The UNCLOS III which opened with a brief organizing session in New York in December 1973, had its first working session in Caracas for 10 weeks in 1974, and numerous other sessions in New York and Geneva, concluded in December 1982 with the signing of the convention. Till 1984 some 159 states and other entities (not including the United States) had signed the convention and ratified by 14. The United States' non-participation may be attributed to some control which the UNCLOS III placed on the indiscriminate use of the seabed resources, and the attempted creation of the international seabed area. In the UNCLOS III itself, an attempt was made to universalize the adoption of the 12-mile limit, but it was opposed . on the ground that a 12-mile limit would close off all maritime passages less than 24 miles wide. Indonesia and Malaysia both have opted for a 12-mile limit which had once closed off the Straits of Malacca to the foreign vessels. The United States and former Soviet Union threatened military action against Indonesia and Malaysia. Though these two South-East Asian states adhere to the 12-mile limit, they provide safe passage to the foreign merchantships. All coastal states with straits between them have agreed to provide safe passage to commercial vessels, nevertheless, the limit of their territorial waters exceed the width of the straits.

As the 200-mile claim is fast becoming a common practice, there is every apprehension that if the limit is given universal recognition, then at least one-third of all the earth's water surface would cease to be high seas, all passages and channels between islands and between continents and islands would fall under national jurisdiction.

Distribution of Offshore Claims

Since there is no universal limit to territorial waters, there are variable distribution of claims, ranging from the three-mile limit to the 200-mile limit. Till January 1984, some 26 states adhered to the three-nautical-mile limit. Prominent states to this catgegory were Denmark, the Netherlands, erstwhile German Democratic Republic, erstwhile German Federal Republic, United Kingdom, United States, Belgium, Ireland, Australia, Chile, Singapore, United Arab Emirates, Jordan, and Bahrain. Most of the states in Europe which had earlier developed the 3-nautical-mile concept belonged to this category. There were only two states—Finland and Norway—to have a four-nautical-mile limit. The six-nautical-mile limit was claimed by Dominion Republic, Greece, Israel, Lebanon and Turkey. However, Turkey lays a 12-nautical-mile limit over the Black Sea.

By the mid-1980s, the number of states, claiming a 12-nautical-mile limit increased substantially. Nearly a half of the total independent sovereign states of the present world exercise their sovereign jurisdiction over a 12-nautical-mile limit. Some of the important states to this groups are France, Iceland, Poland, Portugal, Romania, Sweden, Italy, China, former Soviet Union and Ukrainian SSR, India, Bangladesh, Pakistan, Indonesia, Malayasia, Sri Lanka, Thailand, Myanmar Japan, Iran, Iraq, Saudi Arabia, Canada, Columbia, Venezuela, Mexico, South Africa, Morocco, Algeria, Egypt, Sudan, Ethiopia, Libya, etc.

Ivory Coast, Kenya and New Zeland had earlier claimed a 3-nautical-mile limit, but in the 1980s they have extended claims over a 12-nautical-mile limit. Similarly, Cambodia, now Kampuchia, had, in the 1970s, a 5-nautical-mile limit of its territorial water but in the mid-1980s, it extended its claim to a 12-nautical-mile limit. A 12-nautical-mile limit, as claimed by a substantial number of states, in the late 1980s, has undoubtedly put a great strain on the freedom of seas. There is no denying that more and more states in the coming days would lay claim to a 12-nautical-mile limit. Most of the states in this category are those which have come up in the periphery/semi-periphery of world economy. These states felt that by widening their territorial seas, they would gain more access to the marine resources, particularly fishing, and would secure a 'security belt' along their coast.

Albania in the mid-1980s, claimed a 15-nautical-mile limit, while Angola to a 20-nautical mile limit. Nigeria and Togo exercised a claim over a 30-nautical-mile limit, while Syria laid a claim to a 35-nautical-mile limit. Madagaskar, Cameroon, and Tanzania claimed a 50-nautical mile limit, while Gabon to a 100-nautical-mile, and Senegal to a 150-nautical-mile limit. Some fifteen states, mostly African and Latin American, such as Argentina, Brazil, Peru, Ecuador, Ghana, Liberia, Somalia, Congo, etc., have laid claims to 200-nautical-mile limit.

Since there is no universally accepted limit to territorial sea, and no unanimity among the nations of the world with regard to a common width to the territorial seas, individual states are making unilateral claims dividing the oceanic surface into hapazard ways, much to the detriment of the freedom of seas.

Need for Territorial Sea

It was the conflict between the core countries with regard to the opening of the new frontiers in the periphery on the one hand and conflict between them over the fishing in the regional seas on the other hand, and more recently the core-periphery relationship/conflict in rapidly changing world economy, which seemed to have necessitated the extension of sovereignty over the adjacent seas or waters, i.e., the territorial sea.

Development of naval fleet in the late seventeenth century, followed by the scramble for the oceans among the European states, particularly between The Dutch and English, quite often led to several naval wars between them in the following centuries. Threatened by the invasion from the seas, the European states, particularly those of the Norwegians, Danes, English and the Dutch, felt the need for a protective zone along the adjacent seas of their territory. It was in this context probably, Van Bynkershoek developed his shore-domination principle, followed by Galiani's 3-mile width suggestion for the extension of the states' sovereignty over the adjacent seas/waters. Naval wars, therefore, seemed to have demonstrated the need for the territorial water repeatedly. All earlier treaties, concerning the maritime boundaries between the European maritime states, were aimed at maintaining the security zones. Even a state which sought to remain neutral also felt the necessity of a protective territorial sea. Defence, therefore, has always remained the most important requirement/function of the territorial sea. The state has every right to exclude or to search suspicious vessels within its limit, to erect defensive works in the sea, and to lay mines. The state can torpedo any ships of the alien state, if it ventures to enter within the limits of its territorial waters. There are examples of coastal states having torpedoed the enemy ships in the recent past.

In the earlier phase of the concept, it was the defence of the maritime states which was more important than anything else. Notwithstanding the military significance and defensive function of the territorial sea, the principle that sovereignty extended over the territorial sea obviously conferred upon the state an exclusive right to fish in this area. The North Sea has long remained a zone of potential conflict between the Norwegian, Danes, Dutch and the English, for fishing which quite often led to frictions between themselves.

The right to fish was disputed and the fishing vessels of stronger states used to fish in the adjacent waters of the alien states. The Dutch fishing vessels used to fish in the adjacent waters of Iceland, which was then under the possession of Denmark. Similarly, the British fishing fleets also used to fish in the waters of Iceland. It was not until the end of the sixteenth century that these states felt the necessity of their right on adjacent/neighbouring waters. However, it was in the mid-seventeenth century that the states exercised fishing rights over a belt of 24 miles in their neighbouring waters. But soon this 24-mile limit for fishing rights was contradicted as a result of the Dutch-English rivalry, which sustained for decades, finally led to some multilateral arrangements with regard to the fishing rights, and also saw the rise of the concept of territorial sea.

These arrangements were: (i) coastal states to have exclusive fishing rights in their territorial seas; (ii) fishing rights in the territorial waters would be indisputable; (iii) coastal states to have the right to arrest and fine fishermen of other coastal states in their territorial waters, and the laws of the coastal states' to be applied in case of illegal fishing by other coastal states; and (iv) coastal states might allow foreign fishermen to operate within their territorial waters but such permission required to be done under international norms and agreements.

Iceland is that island-state whose national economy, to a greater extent, depends on fishing. Its waters had been much frequented by the United Kingdom and Germany, which particularly had a serious impact on Iceland's national economy. In 1958, the parliament of Iceland authorized the state to extend control to a distance of 12 miles. As a result, the foreign fishing vessels lost the right to fish in about 10,560 square kilometres of water. The United kingdom in particular, ridiculed the move of Iceland and continued to fish under naval protection. At one stage naval war between the two seemed inevitable on this issue. At last, the United Kingdom accepted Iceland's claim in view of the importance of fishing in the state's national economy.

In recent years number of claims have been made by coastal states to fish beyond the limit of their territorial waters for two reasons: (i) to protect the fishing industry of the state in question, and (ii) to prevent the depletion of certain fish species. There is a kind of unanimity in this regard that a state may legitimately claim to exercise some kind of control, outside the limit of its territorial sea, short of complete sovereignty, and that this control may in certain cases extend to the fisheries. All those states which have laid claims to a 12-nautical-mile limit of their territorial waters, must have done it keeping in view their exclusive fishing rights.

The Permanent Court of International Justice has settled a number of fishing disputes between the states, one of such settlement was between the United Kingdom and Norway in the 1950s. A number of bilateral agreements have been achieved between states with regard to the fishing of certain types of species, e.g., the United States and Canada have agreed to limit salmon fisheries in certain areas of the high seas off the coast of the Pacific North West. Recently Russia and Japan have signed an agreement, in which Japan has been allowed fishing to a limited extent in the Sea of Okhotsk to which it has, hitherto, remained excluded.

The importance of the territorial sea has been further enhanced by the discovery of the mineral potential of the continental shelf. But the discovery of oil from the continental shelf has, in fact, demonstrated better than any other factor for the political division of both the surface of the sea and the underlying rock. The UNCLOS III has given specific recognition to this importance of the territorial sea that the state within its limit in its territorial water, has exclusive right to the seabed resources, particularly its mineral resources. These resources are inviolable and protected under international seabed area. Had there been no territorial water limit, the powerful maritime states would have made these seabed mineral resources violable. With the growth in science and technology on the one hand, and rapid depletion of the land-based resources on the other, there has been increasing effort to tap the seabed resources. Territorial sea has offered manifold flexibility in this regard. The powerful core states dare not exploit seabed resources within the limit of territorial waters of the peripheral states. However, this can be done only with the permission to do so.

Maritime boundaries provide protection to coastal states against smuggling. Smuggling has always been a corrupt practice aiming at destroying the internal economic order of the state, creating chaotic conditions. Some of the most expansive claims to jurisdiction over the sea from time to time, have been made by coastal states, irrespective of being core or peripheral states, which were aimed at checking the practice of smuggling. The states may intercept and search any vessels not only within its territorial waters but also beyond the limit of its jurisdiction.

Most of the maritime states in the eighteenth and nineteenth centuries felt the need to search and intercept foreign vessels which were found to be involved in unlawful trade/activities in their adjacent waters. Great Britain in the eighteenth century, extended its 'fiscal jurisdiction' on several occasions. It started with a 6-nautical-mile limit to 300-nautical-mile limit for that jurisdiction. By doing so it sought to perpetuate the right to protect the revenue by suppressing smuggling. In 1876, notwithstanding the British claim, most of the North Sea littoral states agreed on a 27-nautical-mile limit for their fiscal jurisdiction to curb smuggling and unlawful trade in their adjacent water. However, the USA laid claim only to 12-nautical-mile limit and Spain in 1874-75 claimed a zone of 18-nautical-mile limit for fiscal jurisdiction to intercept and search foreign vessels, engaged in unlawful trade and smuggling.

Practically all states, irrespective of being core or peripheral nations, are unanimous that jurisdiction should be taken beyond the limit of the territorial waters for the purpose of securing the fiscal interests and certain other interests. However, states are yet to agree on a common and universal limit for the fiscal jurisdiction. It now depends on the might of the coast guard to intercept and search such vessels which are engaged in unlawful/illegal trade practices, detrimental to the national economy.

The defensive role of the territorial sea which had declined to a greater extent, following the development in the military technology, particularly after the Second World War, has again reappeared. This time it is not the military threat from the neighbouring states or threat from any other maritime nation, but it is from terrorism. With the globalization of terrorism in the 1980s and early 1990s, the 'potential' states (which are prone to terrorist attacks) now feel greater necessity of the right to intercept vessels of suspicious character, much beyond the limit of their territorial water. India is contemplating to extend its right to intercept and search all those vessels which it feels to be involved in supporting terrorist activities on the land, much beyond the limit of its territorial sea.

One of the distinguishable roles of the territorial sea is to function as a tariff wall against foreign goods, and outside competition for its markets so that indigenous products should not suffer and internal market should not be flooded with foreign goods. Thus, the territorial sea provides fiscal protection to the prosperity of local industries and indigeneously-built commodities. It is only under treaties and agreements (bilateral or multilateral) that foreign goods are allowed entry through the territorial sea. Custom duties must be paid to the government before taking the foreign goods to the land. The economic law of the state prevails in the territorial sea.

Problems of sanitation and pollution also make it intrinsic that maritime states have jurisdiction of bays and estuaries of great width and territorial seas as well. Of increasing importance today is the need to control the behaviour of ships, particularly those of the oil tankers which normally discharge harmful oily waste into the sea, killing birds and other marine life. Such pollution in the sea may occur either due to accident or some technical defects in the tankers, or in case of war. In the recent Gulf War a big oil slick struck the shore of the Gulf states, causing extensive damage to marine birds and marine life, and also endangered human life on the shore. Some-times pollution results from seepage from offshore drilling rigs within the territorial water. In that case the oil company is prosecuted under the environment protection law. ONGC has been fined to pay the compensation by the Government of India for the extensive damage of marine life it has caused off the Bombay coast by its negligence.

When a foreign vessel or tanker deliberately or accidentally discharges wastes into the territorial water of a state, the state then has the right to punish the captain of the vessel and seek compensation from the state to which the vessel belongs. There are numerous examples of states having fined and punished foreign vessels for causing pollution and sanitary problems within their territorial waters. Though there is no international agreement in case of an accident of an oil tanker in the high seas, leading to a big oil slick, yet if the oil slick flows down to the territorial sea of any state, the state may seek for compensation from the state to which the tanker belongs. Some states have proposed a zone of 100 miles from their coasts within which their government would have the authority to check pollution and to take legal proceedings against the vessels (and the states to which they belong also) which would be found guilty of polluting the sea.

It is the manifold function of the modern state system that the politico-geographical necessity of the territorial sea, in the light of the core-periphery relation in the world economy, seems to be highly justified. However, the role of territorial sea has been changing over the years as more and more states are coming up in the periphery and their needs and requirements are charging, and with core states having turned more and more towards the use/exploitation of seabed resources.

Maritime Jurisdiction Zones

The sovereignty of a state, technically or legally, ends at the limit of its territo-

rial sea but some measure of control, as we have seen above, extends beyond the limit of the territorial sea further into the ocean. However, there is no clearcut outer limit to such control . On the shoreward side of the baseline which is regarded not even as part of the territorial sea but the inland waters, enclosed by the base line, which are regarded not even as parts of the territorial sea but as internal waters of the state. UNCLOS I, II and III have recognized seven jurisdictional zones stretching horizontally from internal waters out to the high seas. In some cases, the status of the seabed and subsoil differs from that of the superjacent waters of the zone concerned. The more fundamental rule governing the status and delimitation of the zones will be outlined here (Fig. 7.1).

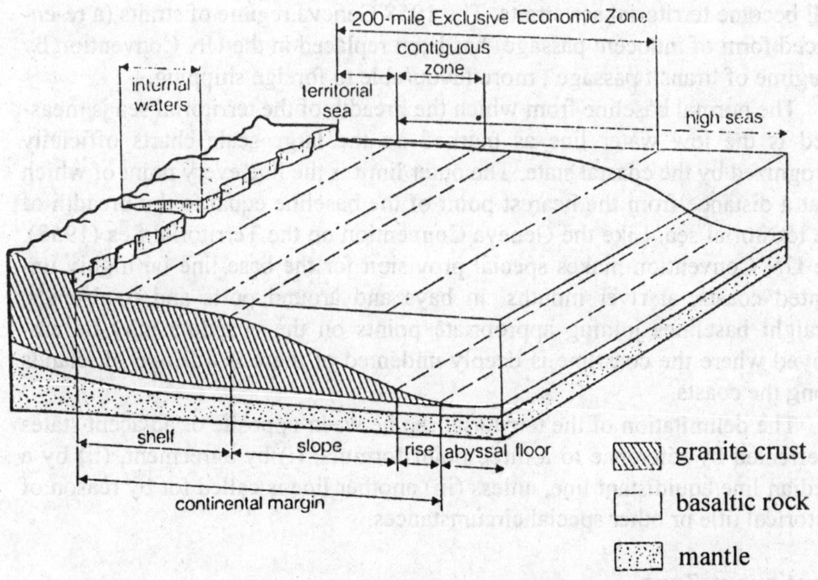

Figure 7.1: Three-Dimensional Nature of Sea Divisions (After A. Couper, Geography and Law of the Sea, London: Macmillan, 1978)

Internal Waters

Internal waters comprise all waters lying landward of the base line from which the breadth of the territorial sea is measured.They include rivers, lakes, bays, ports and the waters landward of the low tide line. The principal distinguishing feature of the internal waters, as compared to territorial sea, is that the sovereignty of the coastal state in these waters is not limited by a right of innocent passage in favour of foreign shipping. Though the question is not free from doubt, there is probably no right of entry into a foreign port except in distress, unless provided by treaty.

The Territorial Sea

The breadth of the territorial sea has been a matter of controversy for over half a century with claims varying all the way from 3 to 200 miles. Fortunately, it is now likely that the breadth of 12 miles will be generally recognized following Article III of the UN Convention. The coastal states' sovereignty over the territorial sea is limited by its obligation to accord a right of innocent passage to foreign shipping. The increase to 12 miles in breadth of the territorial sea means that many straits through which there was previously a belt of high seas will become territorial sea straits. The 1958 Geneva regime of straits (a re-enforced form of innocent passage) has been replaced in the UN Convention by a regime of 'transit passage', more favourable to foreign shipping.

The normal baseline from which the breadth of the territorial sea is measured is the low water line as marked on the large scale charts officially recognized by the coastal state. The outer limit is the line every point of which is at a distance from the nearest point of the baseline equal to the breadth of the territorial sea. Like the Geneva Convention on the Territorial Sea (1958), the UN Convention makes special provision for the base line on highly undented coasts, at river mouths, in bays and around ports and roadsteads. Straight baselines joining appropriate points on the coastline may be employed where the coastline is deeply undented or there is a fringe of islands along the coasts.

The delimitation of the territorial sea between opposite or adjacent states is effected by reference to a three point formula: (i) by agreement, (ii) by a median line/equidistant line, unless (iii) another line is called for by reason of historical title or other special circumstances.

Contiguous Zone

Under the 1954 Geneva Convention on the Territorial Sea and the Contiguous Zone, the coastal state was entitled (but not obliged) to claim a contiguous zone extending out to 12 miles from territorial sea baselines. The residual status of this zone remained high seas and accordingly, the various freedoms of the high seas continued to be enjoyed by other states. By way of exception(to be restrictively interpreted), however, the coastal state was entitled to exercise the control necessary to (i) prevent infringement of its custom, fiscal immigration regulations within its territory or territorial sea; and (ii) punish infringement of those regulations committed within its territory or territorial sea. Under the UN Convention, this zone has been extended to 24 miles and the residual status is now that of exclusive economic zone but otherwise the main features of the zone have been retained.

Continental Shelf

Pending its replacement by the new UN Convention, the 1958 Geneva Convention on the Continental Shelf will continue to govern the status of it. Under the convention, the coastal state enjoys certain sovereign rights over the shelf but subject to these exceptions: the residual status of the waters above remain that of the high seas. In principle, therefore, freedom of navigation for foreign vessels continues to exist in those waters. Ships of all nationalities must, however, respect the 500-metre safety zones which the coastal states is entitled to establish around continental shelf installations and neither the installation nor their safety zone may be established where interference may be caused to the use of recognized sea lanes essential to international navigation.

If and when the new convention enters into force, the waters of the continental shelf up to 200 miles will overlap those of the exclusive economic zone. So far as the continental shelf is concerned, the Article 78 of the UN Convention simply provides that the rights of the coastal states over the continental shelf do not affect the legal status of the superjacent waters (which will be that of exclusive economic zone up to 200 miles and that of continental shelf beyond 300 miles, if the legal continental shelf extends that far). Article 78 goes on to say that the exercise of the coastal state's rights in the continental shelf must not infringe or result in any unjustifiable interference with navigation.

Exclusive Fishing Zone

Prior to UNCLOS I and II in 1958 and 1960, no differentiation was generally recognized between the territorial sea and exclusive fishing zones. Following failure to agree upon more extensive breadth for the territorial sea in 1954 and 1960, however, a new trend developed in state practice towards recognition of exclusive fishing zones beyond territorial sea limits. The trend can be traced through a series of bilateral fishery agreements, culminating in the multilateral European Fisheries Convention (1964) and the subsequent series of more extensive unilateral claims such as those made by Iceland. In the beginning, such extensive claims were strongly resisted but, by the 1970s, influenced by the growing support for the concept of a 200-mile exclusive economic zone, the major fishing states increasingly joined the rank of states claiming 200-mile exclusive fishing zones. The trend in this direction was certainly helped by the decision of the International Court of Justice in the Fishery Jurisdiction Case (1974 United Kingdom vs Iceland) to the effect that, although Iceland's 50-

mile fishery limits were not 'opposable' to the United Kingdom, there was an obligation upon the parties to undertake navigation and to take into account, among other things, Iceland's entitlement for a preferential share of the fisheries within these limits.

It is likely that the more comprehensive exclusive economic zone provided for in the UN Convention will eventually be recognized generally. In the meantime, there can be no doubt that the concept of the exclusive fishing zone is already established.

Exclusive Economic Zone

Reference is made in a later section to the substance of the coastal state's rights in the exclusive economic zone (EEZ). Here it will suffice to note that the zone extends to 200 miles from territorial sea baselines that the problem of delimitation between neighbouring states is similar to that considered above in relation to the continental shelf, and that the EEZ has a naval jurisdiction status as compared with other offshore zones.

Prior to the introduction of the new EEZ concept, a common pattern had been followed in relation to the states of specialized functional zones beyond the territorial sea. The outer limit of the territorial sea has been as marking dividing line between a more landward area in which the fundamental principle of sovereignty had predominated, and exceptions to it were restrictively interpreted, and the more seaward functional zones in which the fundamental principle of the freedom of the high seas predominated but the coastal states enjoyed limited rights by way of exception. For example, the continental shelf and exclusive fishing zone were of this nature. In case of any doubt with regard to the outerlimit of the territorial sea, there would always be a presumption in favour of sovereignty of the coastal state. Seaward of this line, however, the presumption was in favour of the high seas. The concept of EEZ departs from this pattern. It is a zone *sui generis* in which there are no presumptions one way or other, the rights of the coastal state and of other states being those actually specified in the UN Convention. This has, of course, been a matter of concern to the shipping community which feels that it has lost the pre-existing safeguards favouring freedom of navigation.

The High Seas

The Geneva Convention on the High Seas defined the high seas as "all parts of the sea that are not included in the territorial sea or in the internal waters of a state". Given the introduction of the EEZ and of 'archipelagic waters', it was necessary to amend the definition in Article 86 of the UN Convention to "all parts of the sea that are not included in the exclusive economic zone, in the territorial sea or in the internal waters of a state, or in the archipelagic waters of an archipelagic state".

The principal jurisdictional feature of the high seas is the freedom of the high seas, which in reality comprise a bundle of freedoms. It includes the freedom of navigation, fishing, the laying of submarine cables and pipelines, overflight and others which are recognized by the general principles of international laws. Under the UN Convention, two of these others have been identified: freedom to construct artificial islands and other installations permitted under international law, and freedom of scientific research. Such freedoms have to be exercised with due consideration for the interests of other states in their exercise of the freedom of the high seas and (a new element in the UN Convention) with due consideration for the rights under convention with respect to activities in the 'area'.

The 'area' in question is the seabed and ocean floor and subsoil thereof beyond the limits of the national jurisdiction, for which a new and highly complex deep sea mining regime is being established.

However, the UN Convention has made no special provisions for the mid-ocean archipelagos, despite the fact that states like Philippines and Indonesia had been pressing for recognition of their rights to adopt a baseline system enclosing the archipelago within a series of straightlines joining the outermost islands and reefs of the archipelago. In the UN Convention, however, there is a separate part on 'archipelagic states' which allows such enclosure within 'archipelagic baselines' and creates a new category of 'archipelagic waters' for enclosed sea (though there may also be internal waters within the archipelagic waters). The territorial sea, a contiguous zone, EEZ and continental shelf of an archipelagic state are measured in the usual way, but from the archipalegic baselines.

The UN Convention recognizes the rights of ships of all states to enjoy a right of innocent passage through the archipelagic waters similar to that enjoyed in the territorial sea. It also recognizes, however, the right of the archipelagic state to designate sea lanes and prescribe traffic separation schemes within archipelagic waters. The right of 'archipelagic sea lanes passage' enjoyed by foreign shipping through such lanes is similar to the re-enforced right of innocent passage through territorial water.

Delimitation of Maritime Boundaries

Maritime boundary delimitation is a complicated issue because of both the number of real and permanent boundary situations throughout the world, and the complexities of the delimitation process. There are approximately more than 200 national political units bordering on or located on the oceans. A majority of them are independent and some dependent territories. Virtually all these are entitled to an exclusive economic or fisheries zone, extending to a maximum distance of 200 nautical miles from the coastline, in addition to their territorial waters which are contiguous to the shore and most exclusive zones border on one or more adjacent or opposite zones of other states. In many cases territorial seas and continental shelves of the adjacent/neighbouring states also abut on one another. The result is an almost bewildering array of some 400 or more international maritime boundary statistics throughout the world. In time, all these should be formally delimited.

The delimitation process itself involves several types of issues but the most important being (i) the sources of authority, and (ii) principal methods by which the delimitation is carried—equidistance, modified equidistance or the line based on 'relevant circumstances'.

To date, there are more than 60 states which have claimed an EEZ and more than 30 states claim an exclusive fisheries zone whose geographical dimension are the same as an EEZ. A question here is whether or not a boundary separating the continental shelves of two states need necessarily be the same as the boundary separating their exclusive economic or fisheries zones. In the Mediterranean Sea there are 16 cases of territorial seas of adjacent states abutting on one another. A number of these EEZs face one another across the narrow sea.

Sources of Authority

For the territorial sea boundaries, both the 1958 Geneva Convention on the Territorial Sea and the Contiguous Zone, and the 1982 Law of the Sea Convention stipulate that, failing agreement between them to the contrary, states with opposite or adjacent coasts are not entitled to extend their territorial seas beyond the median line. But a caveat is then included to the effect that these provisions shall not apply where it is necessary by reason of historic title or other special circumstances to delimit the territorial sea boundaries in a way which is at variance with the median line provisions. In absence of agreement, it is incumbent on the state favouring a territorial sea boundary other than median line to prove that this variant is necessary.

So far as continental shelf boundaries are concerned, the International Court of Justice (ICJ) made a rule that delimitation should be effected by agreement, in accordance with equitable principles, taking account of all relevant circumstances. This phraseology formed the basis for the early texts of the Convention at UNCLOS III, and only towards the end was there a change in Article 74 (dealing with the boundaries of EEZ) and Article 83 (boundaries of the continental shelf). The texts now read: "delimitation...shall be effected by agreement on the basis of international law as referred to in Article 38 of the Statute of International Court of Justice, in order to achieve an equitable solution."

Article 38 of the Statute states that in its decisions, the Court shall apply (i) international conventions, establishing rules expressly recognized by the contracting states; (ii) international customs as evidence of general practice accepted as law; (iii) the general principles of law recognized by civilized nations; and (iv) judicial decisions and the teaching of the most highly qualified publicists as subsidiary means for the determination of rules of law.

In the absence of an agreement on boundary delimitation, states can go to third party settlement, particularly the International Court of Justice. This procedure has been expanded under Article 27 of the Law of the Sea Convention to the effect that where no settlement of a dispute over maritime boundaries has been reached, states may choose any one of four procedures for settling the dispute: the International Tribunal for the Law of the Sea, the ICJ, an arbitral tribunal established under the provisions of Annex VII of the Convention, or a special arbitral tribunal constituted under Annex VII of the Convention. However, it has been made clear that this procedure would be applied only to those states which have signed or ratified the Convention or acceded to it . Of the nearly 400 potential maritime boundaries, about 75 have been agreed upon with the agreements having come into force.

A third source of authority is the judicial decisions, particularly of the International Court of Justice. There have been four major court cases: The North Sea Continental Shelf Cases of 1969, involving the Netherlands, Denmark and the former Federal Republic of Germany; the United Kingdom-France Continental Shelf Arbitration of 1977; the Libya-Tunisia Continental Shelf Case of 1982; and the US-Canada Maritime Boundary Case of 1984. All four have stressed the need for an equitable solution to the boundary dispute, i.e., a solution based on equitable principles.

Methods of Delimitation

There are three methods or systems of delimitation. One is the equidistance method which depends on the baselines along the coasts of the respective countries whose offshore areas are to be separated by the boundary. There may be difficulties here if one state utilizes 'normal' baselines, following the sinusities of the coasts, and the other employs a straight baseline system connecting the outermost islands, promontories and rocks. There is nothing magic about an equidistance limit. It does not lead necessarily to a condition of equity, in which either the total area or the living and non-living marine resources are divided equally between the parties. But it is a technique to be used when other techniques are inappropriate and inadequate. The US-Mexico boundary in the Gulf of Mexico, which has been agreed upon but not yet ratified, is an equidistance line, as in the PuertoRico-Venezuela boundary and the boundary between American Samoa and the Tokelau and Cook islands.

The second method is that of modified equidistance in which there are one or more variations in the line to account for particular conditions. There may, e.g., be islands or rocks located some distance off one state's coast. If such features were given full effect in the equidistance boundary delimitation, they would have a disproportionate effect on the location of the line. So the parties agree to ignore the feature completely in the delimitation; to give it partial effect, as occurred with respect to the Scilly Isles in the UK-France arbitration or to describe an arc about a part of the feature.

Rather than rely on baselines which follow the sinusities of the coast, states may by agreement, define artificial baselines for the purpose of measuring their equidistance-type boundaries, as in the case of the French-Spanish maritime boundary in the Bay of Biscay. The location of specific turning points on the equidistant line may be shifted in order to smooth out the boundary. Small areas on each side of the maritime boundary may be exchanged. But the basic premise remains for a boundary on the equidistance method.

The third category of methods is what might be called 'relevant circumstance' boundaries. These are maritime boundaries whose delimitation was based on criteria other than equidistance. The choice of alternative methods was apparently necessary in order to achieve an equitable solution. There are many forms of relevant circumstances which might be used as a basis for such a boundary but a few of them are to be mentioned here.

One form of relevant circumstance is natural prolongation. The argument is that a state's adjacent continental shelf is a natural extension of the land territory into and under the sea. Particularly in cases where the shelf adjacent to a coastal state extends beyond the median line out towards a structural depression in the seafloor, it is argued that the state should have control over the whole undersea area. An example here is the Chinese claim to the floor of the East China Sea beyond the median line with Japan in the Okinawa Trough.

Another circumstance involves the coastal front theory. A country should have jurisdiction over the seabed and water column immediately in front of its coast. Still another is the proportionality criterion. The International Court of Justice in its decision in1969, referred to a "reasonable degree of proportionality which a delimitation...ought to bring about between the extent of the continental shelf areas appertaining to the coastal state and the length of its coast measured in the general direction of the coastline". The 1969 decision also noted the general relief of the coasts of the parties as a factor to be taken into account of in a delimitation carried out in accordance with equitable principle.

Lastly, there are a number of 'socio-economic elements' which break down into three main parts. First, in a dispute over ownership of a marine area, there is the question of who got these first. Which country first learned to utilize the area, which first surveyed and charted it and harvested the resource? Second, what country now is the predominant researching state in the area? Which one carries out law enforcement and defence activities? Which maintains the aids to navigation? Third, which country is most dependent for its economic well-being on exploiting the resources of the coastal areas in question? These situations/circumstances have on occasion been used in supporting national position. Whether or not they are persuasive in a particular court of law is another matter.

There are, of course, other 'relative circumstances.' A major oil spill in a disputed area might be shown to have far greater negative effects on the coasts of one country than of another. A state, through its actions, may have inadvertently acquiesced in the other country's claim to the area in question. There may be old treaties relating to the allocation of marine territories which would be relevant to the controversy.

A final parameter of the delimitation process concerns technical questions about the exact positioning of a boundary line. Are parties to a delimitation process utilizing comparable charts? Are the low-water lines along the coasts compatible? And are the scales the same? More important are the map projections. A geodesic line, or a great circle route which approximates it, appears as a curved line on a Mercator's projection, when what is shown as a straightline is, in reality, a rhumb line, not the shortest distance between two points. In the 1867 US-Russia Treaty defining the boundary between Alaska and Siberia, there is mention of straight lines joining fixed points. But the map the negotiators used has been lost. If the negotiators were thinking of a straight line as it appears on a Mercator's projection, the boundary would follow the rhumb line as shown on the map. If they were using a polyconic projection, a straight line on the map would be a great circle, and appear as a curved line on Mercator's projection. In the case of the Berring Sea, the difference between the rhumb and great circle lines is an area of nearly 15, 000 square nautical miles.

Measurement of the Territorial Sea

It had been decided at the Law of the Sea (LOS) conferences at Monaco in 1929 and at the Hague in 1930 that the territorial sea must be measured from low watermark at spring tide. But the 1958 Geneva Conference, later adopted the 'mean low water' as the baseline for the measurement of the territorial sea. On a simple, straight coast without any island or shoal, the delimitation of the territorial sea presents no problem. But most coasts are neither simple nor straight. They may be irregular in the extreme with offshore islands and submerged rocks. The latter may be submerged only at high tide (drying rocks) or so low that waves break over them at all stages of the tide (awash). There may be offshore sandbanks called 'low-tide elevation', which are exposed at low tide but covered by water at high tide. These low-tide elevations slowly but continuously keep changing their shape and position. These low-tide elevation present the most difficult problem as to how the baseline or datum line is to be delimited/measured from the coast? The 1958 Geneva Convention had decided that such low-tide elevations might only be used to extend the territorial sea if they fell within the territorial sea as measured from the coast. It was agreed upon that a state, with a claim of three-nautical-mile territorial sea, and a low-tide elevation two miles from its coast, might extend the territorial sea three miles from the low-tide elevation—a total of five miles. But, on the other hand, a state with a claim of three miles but a low-tide elevation at four miles from the coast, could not extend its territorial sea from the low-tide elevation simply because of the fact that the measurement from the low-tide elevation would have increased the breadth of the territorial sea to seven miles.

Bays and estuaries involve more problems in the measurement of the territorial sea. They are the most complex features occurring on the coast. If either is less than six miles across, assuming that the territorial seas have a width of three miles, then the whole is the part of the territorial sea. It also proposed that no bay wider than 10 miles should be claimed as inland water. In fact, a closing line drawn across the entrance to the bay or estuary would be taken as the baseline for the measurement of the territorial seas. This closing line is referred to as the 'line of closure'.

It now becomes necessary to distinguish between a bay and a mere coastal indentation. For this, the semicircle rule is applied. A straightline is drawn between the natural entrance points of the indentation. "The water thus closed off forms a bay if its area is as large as, or longer than, that of a semicircle the diameter of which is equal in length to the closing line." If smaller, it is regarded merely as a coastal indentation, and the limit of the territorial sea is drawn parallel to the curvature of the coast. However, there are many bays which are much wider and, therefore, require much caution in the determination of the baseline vis-a-vis the territorial sea. It is stipulated in the LOS that the length of the baseline between the natural entrance points of the bay, particularly should not exceed 24 miles, which is twice the maximum claim to territorial waters.

When the mouth of the bay is more than 24 miles wider, its waters can be claimed only through the application of accepted methods of territorial waters delimitation. If the mouth of the bay is less than 24 miles in width, a semicircle is drawn with the closure line as its diametre. The area of the semicircle is now compared to the water of the bay behind the line of closure. If the bay has an area smaller than that of the semicircle based on its closure line, it cannot be cut off by such a line. If the water area of the bay is larger than that of the

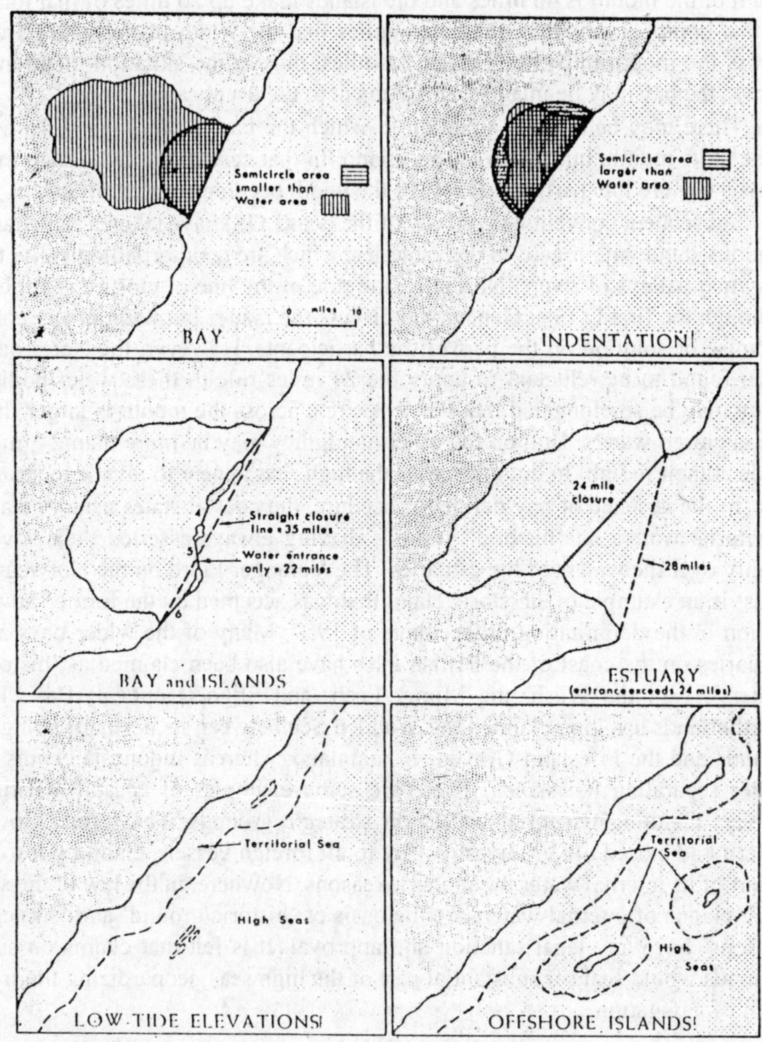

Figure 7.2: Measurement of the Territorial Sea

semicircle, it is indeed a part of the inland waters of the state in question (Fig. 7.2).

There may be a complex situation when one or more islands are located in the mouth of the bay—then what procedure requires to be followed, if the width of the mouth is 40 miles and the islands make up 20 miles of that total? In that complex situation, the rule applies that the width of the water areas across the mouth must not exceed 24 miles, thus in the situation mentioned above, the bay may be inland water, subject to the usual calculation.

There may be another situation in which the bay is more than 24 miles wide at its mouth, but which tapers inland. In that case, the coastal state may draw a closure line particularly where the width becomes just 24 miles.

Subsequent conventions of Law of the Sea (LOS) have taken a rather ambiguous stand with regard to the estuaries, which are geomorphologically, the drowned valleys of rivers. Normally, the rule of the line of closure is applied although the first LOS at Geneva did discuss the matter but without any compromise or solution on the part of the participants. However, the states have been found to be reluctant to apply the 24 miles rule to these water bodies. They may be so elongated that the semicircle across the mouth is larger than the enclosed waters. But, on the other hand, they may be more than 24 miles wide at their mouth. In both the cases the high seas appear to invade them.

In the absence of any defined procedure, the coastal states usually claim territorial waters on 'historic' grounds, having always asserted their sovereignty over the waters of the estuaries. The Varanger Fiord on the Norwegian coast is an example of a historic claim that was accepted by the former Soviet Union in the delimitation proceedings of 1957 Many of the wider bays and estuaries on the coast of the British Isles have also been claimed as 'historic waters', e.g., the Wash, the Moray Firth, and Sligo (Donegal) Bay. The Nertherlands has long claimed the Wadden Sea between its northern string of islands and the Friesland-Grovengen mainland, whereas Indonesia claims all water separating its islands. There are some examples of coastal maritime powers claiming territorial waters on strategic grounds. The former Soviet Union had closed off Vladivastok Bay to all foreign vessels, claiming it to be a part of its internal water for strategic reasons. Nowhere, in the law of the sea, such claims of internal waters are the basis of 'historic ground' and 'strategic reasons' have any legal sanction and approval. It is felt that claims on such grounds would seal off substantial part of the high seas, jeopardizing the freedom of navigation.

The Median-line Boundary

The median-line rule is applied under certain exceptional conditions. Though the subsequent conferences on the law of the sea remained silent about the application of the median-line rule, nevertheless, the rule is applied under the bilateral agreement between the coastal states involved. The median-line, in case of the maritime boundary, is defined as a line every point of which is equidistant from the nearest points on the baselines from which the breadth of the territorial sea is measured.

A median-line is required under the following conditions: (i) when two adjacent coastal states, claiming the same width of territorial seas, still require a maritime boundary to connect their land boundary to their high-seas boundary; (ii) when two coastal states share a common estuary or a wide bay; (iii) when two coastal states may lie along a relatively straight coast, with their boundary reaching the coastline at right angles; and (iv) when adjacent coastal states feel interested in the territorial seas and the continental shelf beyond. In some other cases the maritime boundary may be oblique.

A number of examples of such situations occur in the (i) Swedish-Finnish boundary at the head of the Gulf of Bothnia; (ii) Israel-Jordan border on the Gulf of Aqaba; (iii) India-Bangladesh boundary at the head of the Bay of Bengal, at the mouth of the Ganga; (iv) Uruguay-Argentina boundary in the estuary of the Rio de la Plata, and (vi) India-Pakistan boundary in the estuary of the Indus. And there are some few hundred cases of such complex situations in the present world. Sometimes the islands lie so close together that the delimitation of their territorial seas shows an overlap/abut; at other situations coastal states face each other across a narrow channel. The Caribbean Sea is full of actual and potential situation of this kind.

The presence of smaller and longer islands in the bay or in the estuary often makes the median-line delimitation complicated, as is the case in the median-line delimitation of the Indo-Bangladesh maritime boundary at the head of the Bay of Bengal at the mouth of the Ganga as there are a number of offshore islands. The median-line delimitation can ward-off a long series of discussion and negotiation, particularly in cases related to the exploitable resources in the territorial seas and also on the continental shelf (Fig. 7.3).

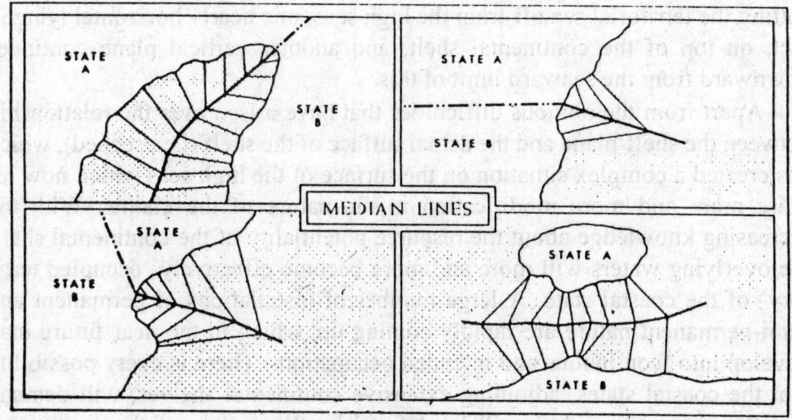

Figure 7.3: Median Lines

As opposed to the median-line delimitation is the rule of the 'thalweg'. This resembles the navigable-channel method determining river boundaries but the thalweg of the river boundary often passes through the narrow channel, and the traffic, across it, has to pass through the international boundary. The thalweg in the estuary or in the bay is usually sufficiently wide so that the adjacent coastal states find no problem in the accommodation within their own section both incoming and outgoing ocean traffic.

The Continental Shelf

Of all complexities with regard to the maritime boundary is that of the continental shelf which is geologically a part of the continent. It is composed of the same kinds of rocks and is likely to contain the same minerals as those of the continents. On an average, the continental shelf is about 100 miles wide but there is considerable regional variation from 5 to over 600 miles. The angle of slope of the shelf is so gentle that it is imperceptible. At a depth of about 100 fathoms (600 feet), the angle of slope increases, and the continental slope gives way to more steep continental slope. The continental shelf of the world covers about 7.6 per cent of the total area of the sea. It is with the Truman's declaration in 1945, extending the US jurisdiction over the natural resources of the subsoil and seabed of the continental shelf that it acquired political-legal significance in the international politics. Large number of Latin American coastal states followed suit. Conventions on the Law of the Sea (LOS) dealt with in detail, the problems arising out of the claims to the continental shelf.

Claims to the continental shelf undoubtedly, have produced unprecedented situations, whereby the boundaries of states represented by planes do not run vertically but nearly horizontal and parallel to the surface of a landform. Thus, the maritime boundary consists of three planes: one vertical cutting the territorial sea off from the high seas; one nearly horizontal lying in fact, on top of the continental shelf; and another vertical plane continues downward from the seaward limit of this.

Apart from the obvious difficulties that have arisen over the relationship between the shelf-plane and the actual surface of the shelf (i.e., seabed), which has created a complex situation on the surface of the high seas which now require more and more modification in the nature of the claims. With the increasing knowledge about the resource potentiality of the continental shelf, the overlying waters will more and more become effectively 'occupied territory' of the coastal state. A large number of installations of permanent and semi-permanent nature are rapidly coming up, which in the near future may develop into 'continuous and intended occupation.' There is every possibility that the coastal states, adjoining extensive continental shelves, will demand that their entire boundary will be defined by the margin of the continental shelf.

Such a demand by the coastal state may lead to at least six major consequences:

(i) the concept of a standard-width territorial sea requires to be abandoned;
(ii) there would be conflicts over the allocation of 'shared' continental shelf;
(iii) states without continental shelves may seek redress by claims to vast reaches of the oceans;
(iv) coastal states may seek to establish, what is called 'conservation zones';
(v) poor and weak coastal states may grant authority to multinational corporations to search for resources and petroleum; and
(vi) the core-periphery conflict may be widened further.

The Pacific coastal Latin American states have already claimed sovereignty over the continental shelf for a distance of 200 miles. Argentina claims sovereignty over a wide extent of the South Atlantic Ocean, including the British territories of Falklands. The Persian Gulf states claim sovereignty over the adjacent area of the continental shelf. India claims that its boundary should coincide with the outer margin of the continental shelf, both in the Arabian Sea and the Bay of Bengal. Sri Lanka has claimed conservation zone as far as 100 miles from its coast. Pakistan has proclaimed its intention of controlling all exploitative activity on the continental shelf adjoining its territory. Conflicts have arisen between India and Bangladesh over claims to the adjacent continental shelf. China claims substantial part of the South China Sea because the shelf below it is potentially rich in petroleum and natural gas.

The continental shelf of the North Sea has long remained a bone of contention between the adjoining states over the allocation of resources. A potential zone of conflict is that of the adjoining shelf of South-East Asia. It has developed into a zone of intense regional competition for the allocation of 'shared' continental shelf. Notwithstanding the creation of the Association of South-East Asian Nations (ASEAN), coastal states were involved in conflicts. Some of the sea nations of the ASEAN have allowed the US companies to carry out search for oil exploration.

A large number of states without potential continental shelves off their coasts claim hundreds of miles of territorial waters invading the high seas. There are certain pertinent questions with regard to the claims over the continental shelf.

1. Should a state be allowed to claim for itself all resources found below a depth of zero to 600 feet of water—just because the water ends there—for hundreds of miles of its coast, while another state cannot claim more than 12 miles of water or subsoil because that subsoil drops away precipitously?

2. How can the USA claim continental shelf resources 100 miles from the coastline while Ecuador and Peru cannot claim marine resources a similar distance away?

It is the technical ability of the coastal states to exploit the resources of the continental shelf rather than any uniquely defined boundary. As a result, the Continental Shelf Convention is now gradually being replaced by the 322-kilometre (200 miles) Exclusive Economic Zone which includes fisheries as well as the resources of the seabed. This new concept was agreed by the third UN Convention on the Law of the Sea in 1982.

The Exclusive Economic Zone

The Exclusive Economic Zone (EEZ) has its genesis in the 1945 Truman proclamation on the continental shelf. However, even before that, at the beginning of the twentieth century, there had emerged the idea of extending a coastal states' jurisdiction to encompass the resources lying in its adjacent waters. In fact, prior to UNCLOS III (1982), many states including the United States, exercised various rights, many of which are now encompassed by the concept of the EEZ in waters of the territorial sea. This change is so widespread that it is recognized by the American Law Institute as customary law, dictated that the concept of an EEZ be redefined at UNCLOS III.

Article 57 of the UN Convention on the LOS limits the EEZ to be further than 200 nautical miles from the baseline of the coastal states. This agreed upon limit has enormous implications in the vast amount of the ocean's surface of the world may be enclosed in such zones. It is conservatively estimated that 32 per cent of the ocean's surface, covering 28 million square miles, will be enclosed beyond coastal states' territorial waters.

It is obvious that the benefits of such enclosure will not be shared equally by the countries of the world. Some anomalous results will follow, including allowing some states to claim jurisdiction over areas of the ocean 10 to 100 times larger than their landmass. Micronesia, for instance, can close an area of about two million square nautical miles, which could produce an estimated revenue of three million dollars annually. Another disproportionate impact involves the unequal distribution of natural resources throughout the zones. Typically, the greater living and mineral resources within 200 miles are disproportionately located within the zones of the economically developed states. It, therefore, seems logical that the treaty allows for a balancing of interests of the coastal states and other states in the EEZ. The coastal states, according to Article 56 of the Convention, have 'sovereign rights' for the purposes of exploring and exploiting, conserving and managing the natural resources, living and non-living within the zone, including the seabed and the subsoil. Also, coastal states have jurisdiction over artificial islands, marine scientific research and the protection and preservation of the marine environment within the EEZ. However, the coastal states shall have 'due regard' for the rights and duties of other states and these states must comply with the coastal states' rules and regulations in the zones.

Variable claims and counterclaims to the EEZ have created four distinct categories of States:

(i) The territorialist group, consisting of Latin American states including Brazil, Ecuador, El Salvador, Nicaragua, Peru, Uruguay and Argentina, and four African states, viz., Dahomey, Guinea, Somalia and Sierra Leone.

(ii) The heterogeneous coalition comprising of (a) coastal African states of the Organization of African Unity; (b) moderate Latin American states with Venezuela, Mexico, Colombia; (c) Asian states, viz., India and Sri Lanka; (d) coalition of industrially advanced coastal states, viz., Canada, Iceland, Norway, Australia and New Zealand; and (e) the Archipelagic states, viz., Indonesia, the Philippines, Fiji and Mauritius.

(iii) The coalition of the landlocked and geographically disadvantaged states.

(iv) The coalition of the major maritime countries (core states).

Notwithstanding the above categories, the potential winners of the claims to the EEZ are those states with (a) long coastline and significant resources off their coasts; (b) with wide continental margins but the potential loser states are those (i) with short coastlines and narrow coastal margins; (ii) self-locked states without major oil deposits relatively near-shore; and (iii) landlocked states.

Considerable number of maritime boundary disputes will arise in the next few years, particularly with regard to continental shelf and the EEZ.

The problem of defining the extent of territorial seas is not limited to the outer margins. Agreeing a landward baseline is often extremely difficult. Inland waters like Hudson Bay are normally counted as part of the land area, but not always; countries like Norway with strongly indented coastlines are usually deemed to have a baseline that joins the major promontories; in the case of island states such as Indonesia and the Philippines, straight boundaries are often adopted encompassing the whole of the archipelago.

In the majority of cases the solution has been to agree a median-line equidistant from the nearest point of the baseline of the coasts of the countries concerned, but such a simple solution has not always proved acceptable. An attempt at a comprehensive solution to such problems is proposed in the UNCLOS III Convention on the Law of the Sea. The UNCLOS III proposed to establish a contiguous zone extending for 24 nautical miles beyond the limit of the territorial seas. The new concept of the 322 kilometre (200 mile) Exclusive Economic Zone which includes fisheries as well as the resources of the seabed, was first agreed by the United Nations Conference on the Law of the Sea in 1977, and the UNCLOS III in 1982-83 proposed to give it an international expression and recognition. However, 22 states, including former Federal Republic of Germany, Italy, Japan, the UK and the US (mostly core states of the world systems/economy) decided against signing, mainly because they were dissatisfied with the proposed conditions governing seabed mining under the high seas. Nevertheless, it is expected that the Convention will be ratified by all parties eventually, providing a comprehensive framework for administering the oceans.

Chapter 8

Population and the State

"A state only begins to exist when it has attained a population sufficient for a good life in the political community", said Aristotle (1921). In fact, population constitutes one of the basic elements for the state, for no state can exist without a population. Antarctica and Greenland cannot be brought under the category of the state simply because they do not contain population, sufficient enough to make them states in the true sense of the term. However, the idea of state cannot be applied to the migratory people or the nomads who do not have definite and well-bounded territories for them. To them, boundaries have no meaning. They keep on moving from one place to another across international boundaries. Thus, there are two extreme cases: (i) territory without population, and (ii) population without territory. In both the cases, territoriality, i.e., the fundamental human need based on identity, defence and stimulation cannot grow or develop. It is the sense of attachment to land or more broadly to geographical area that makes a population intrinsically tied up with the territory vis-a-vis state.

There are various ways of evaluating the structure and function of state components but from any point of view people are most important. The people are paramount in determining the type and effectiveness of government, and it is the people who develop the potential of the territory. The human variable includes both the 'quality' and the 'quantity' of the people.

Since population and the state are closely interwoven, and the state is the subject matter for political geography, hence it cannot studied without the population. Hence, population studies constitute an important element in political geography. Population has long been considered as the most important resource basic to the power-potential for the state.

In assessing the role of population numbers in any state's power or economic potential requires a much more sophisticated calculus. Great numbers of people can provide a power base but they can also be an insupportable burden to a state's economy or polity. A state must count its population, feed it, clothe it, house it, educate it, organize it, and put it to the most productive possible work. Any state's ability to achieve these tasks depends upon many more characteristics of the population than its sheer numbers. Numbers may not be so important as the physical resources available to the population; how well organized is the population? Or the attributes of the population? Thus, in examining any state's population as a resource, we must start with its number, but then look beyond that statistics into a variety of additional characteristics of the population.

The Census

Census is the total process of collecting, compiling and publishing demographic, economic and social data pertaining to all persons in a defined territory at a special time. Census thus provides the primary source of information about the population of a state/country; given its government backing, its legal status, its coverage and the scale of the operation and resources devoted to it, it permits a far greater content and depth of analysis than can normally be produced by other methods.

Enumerations of population were carried out in ancient times, but the earliest modern censuses took place in Scandinavia and some Germanic and Italian states in the eighteenth century. The first census of Iceland, for example, was conducted in 1703, of Sweden in 1748, of Norway in 1760 and of Denmark in 1769. The first general census of the USA took place in 1790, although there had been earlier state censuses. Both in Britain and France, the first census was held in 1801, and in India in 1881. During the nineteenth century all European countries initiated periodic population censuses. During the present century, and especially since 1945, most countries of the world have begun to conduct censuses, although with widely varying frequency and reliability.

Two qualities in a census are particularly important: periodicity and universality, i.e., the need to hold regular censuses and to include every individual in a given area. Britain and India, for example, have held regular censuses at ten-year intervals. Sampling is also used in many countries to establish certain categories of information within a full census or to replace that census. There is also a general distinction in census method between a *de facto* approach as in Britain, where individuals are recorded at the place where they were found at the time of the census, and a *de jure* approach, as in the USA, where people are recorded according to their usual place of residence.

Types of data collected by censuses vary enormously from country to country. The United Nations, in an attempt to foster comparability, has suggested that the census should include total population, sex, age and marital status, mother tongue, literacy and educational qualifications, economic status, urban or rural domicile, household or family structure, and fertility.

Apart from the census, population data are also obtained from the surveys, registrations, migration reports, estimates and projections. In fact, the surveys are conducted for supplementing the census data for investigating the determinants of a particular demographic attribute. In recent years, surveys have been done for collecting a variety of information such as fertility, morality, morbidity, mobility, employment, underemployment, health, education, welfare, etc. In India, a National Sample Survey Organization was set up in 1950 immediately after independence, with an objective of obtaining comprehensive and continuing information relating to demographic and socio-economic statistics through sample surveys.

The registration system is not a new one. It is an old system of collecting population data, and in China it was very common in the ancient days. Gradually, the system of registration spread to Korea and Japan. In recent times, registration system has been adopted by different countries to record births and deaths, marriages, divorces, adoptions, entry into the country, attaining the military age, entry into gainful employment, etc. The major purpose of the system is to collect data pertaining to vital statistics. In India, the registration of births and deaths has been made mandatory for each family.

Most of the developed countries maintain migration reports and publish such reports from time to time. These countries mostly experience immigration from the peripheral areas of the Third World. There are various ways to obtain the estimates of population but one that is obtained by carrying the population from the previous census either by mathematical extrapolation of the past trends or by a component method using birth and death registration and symptomatic data reflecting migration. Such estimates are usually published in national reports such as *National Statistical Yearbook*. Both post-censal and inter-censal estimates are found in such yearbooks. Population projections may be prepared for a total population or by age, sex, marital status, manpower required, school management, etc. Population projections usually relate to the estimates for population for future. The United Nations has at times compiled projections made by national governments and has modified these so as to conform to a global set of assumptions of its own.

Thus, there are a variety of sources to population which the states or countries use to measure their relative power-potentials from time to time.

Let us see what impact can the growth of population produce on the power-potentials of states, and also on the political space relationships.

Population Growth

It is probable that the population of the world has been continuously growing since the earliest periods of human history. It is certain, however, that this growth has been regular neither through time nor even in spatial distribution. It is evident from Table 8.1 that the rate of increase of the world population has been so rapid since the prehistoric period to the present time that the period required for the doubling of the size of the world population has constantly decreased. The estimated world population doubled on an average after every 1500 years. Between 8000 BC (when the population was estimated to have been about 5 million) and 1650 AD (estimated being about 500 million), the world population increased by hundred fold. It required 200 years for the world population to double in size from about 500 million (470 million) in the year 1650 to about 1000 million (1091 million) in 1850. The next doubling of the size of the world population was accomplished in still lesser time as the world population doubled its size from 1000 million in 1850 to 2000 million in the year 1930, i.e., only in a period of 80 years. Again, the size of the world population was doubled from 2000 million in 1930 to 4000 million in 1975, which took just 45 years to reach this number. It is estimated that the world population would require just only 36 years to double from 4000 million to 8000 million (around 2015 AD), if the population of the world continues to grow by a rate prevalent in 1970.

Table 8.1

Estimates of world population

Years	*World population (in millions)*	*Years*	*World population (in millions)*
8000 BC	5	1921	1811
14 AD	266	1930	2070
350	254	1940	2295
600	237	1950	2513
800	267	1955	2745
1000	280	1960	3027
1200	384	1965	3344
1340	378	1970	3678
1500	427	1975	4033
1650	470	1980	4415
1750	694	1985	4830
1800	919	1990	5275
1850	1091	1995	5733
1900	1571	2000	6199

Source: World Population Trends and Prospects by County, 1950-2000: Summer Report of the 1978 Assessment (UN Publications).

The manifold increase in the world population may be attributed to several factors which include better medical facilities, as a result of the scientific and technological development, control over certain diseases which used to spread in the form of epidemics, manifold increase in various kinds of social services, partial control over natural calamities, and more and more remote areas have been made accessible so that facilities have been made available to such areas.

The manifold increase in the world population has its obvious spatial-political consequences such as those of imperialism/colonialism, regionalism, communalism and nationalism. These spatial-political phenomena can be best illustrated in the light of the regional differences in the world population growth.

Table 8.2

Medium estimates of world population 1750-2000

(in millions)

	1750	*1800*	*1850*	*1900*	*1950*	*1970*	*2000*
World	791	978	1262	1650	2515	3635	6130
Developing Countries			919	1088	1682	2580	4742
Asia (ex. Japan and USSR)	468	600	770	881	1298	1953	3336
Africa	106	107	115	133	222	344	763
Latin America	16	24	34	74	162	283	638
Developed Countries			343	562	834	1055	1388
Europe (ex.USSR)	125	152	208	296	392	462	527
USSR	42	56	76	134	180	243	353
North America	02	07	26	82	166	228	354
Japan	30	30	31	44	83	103	122
Oceania	02	02	02	09	13	19	32

Source: J.D. Durand (1967), The Modern Expansion of World Population. *Proceedings.* American Philosophical Society, III, 137.

Population growth by continent is extremely varied. The greatest influence on world population growth has certainly been the increase in the number of Asians who even without the Asian population of Russia, have long constituted the majority of mankind. Their proportion is now increasing. The numerical significance of Europe has also been great but its rate of increase has declined considerably during this century. The America and Africa both have an absolute increase far in excess of Europe (including the erstwhile USSR) and their combined populations have recently overtaken that of

Europe. Although growing rapidly, the population of Oceania contributes little to world population growth.

Even in the continent itself, the regional variations in the population growth significantly affect the spatial pattern of the power structure and potentials. Pounds (1972) has critically analyzed this phenomenon with examples from the late eighteenth and early nineteenth centuries. To him, France was the dominant political power in Europe during the late eighteenth and early nineteenth centuries. "French armies under Napoleon fought from Spain to Moscow. The triumph of French armies is not wholly explicable in terms of either of the political weakness and internal divisions of France's enemies or of the enthusiasm which the French soldiers derived from the new social order created by the French Revolution. In large part it was a victory of numbers...The rate of increase of the French population in the nineteenth century was one of the lowest in Europe. Germany overtook France about 1870, and Great Britain also overtook her thirty years latter. It would be far too naive to explain the rise of German power in the second half of the nineteenth century and the German defeat and displacement of France from her position of pre-eminence in the war of 1870-71 merely in terms of a changed balance of population. But the efficiency of the German army as a fighting machine was not unrelated, to its size, and without the changed population ratio, the success of Germany might not have been so clearcut as in fact it was. The Soviet Union's numerical superiority was certainly a factor in the defeat of the Germans at Stalingrad (Volgagard) and elsewhere... As long as there is at least the possibility that the hydrogen bomb will not be used in any future war, weight of numbers must remain one of the more important considerations in assessing the power-potential of a state. In any calculus of power, the 800 millions of China must weigh heavily and offset the lower educational levels and the less developed manufacturing sector of the economy."

It is very important to note that in Europe itself, the growth of German nationalism during the second half of the nineteenth century was partially an outcome of the growth of the Germanic population. Most of the communities in Southeastern Europe, particularly the Slavs which experienced higher growth rate during the late nineteenth century and early twentieth centuries than the non-Slavs communities, jealously sought to perpetuate their self-determination and regional identification. This precipitated a serious politico-military crisis which ultimately led to the outbreak of the World War I. If the World War I was an outcome of the 'separation nationalism', then the separation nationalism itself was a natural fallout of the manifold increase of the population growth, particularly in the European periphery. Modern nationalism in the Afro-Asian periphery is largely the outcome of differential growth rate of population.

If a large population resource is a political necessity for the politico-geographical sustenance for the state, it is also at the same time a potential factor for political weakness, crisis and miseries for the state. There are two basic reasons for such political situations: (a) the population growth outruns/exceeds economic growth, leading low per capita welfare; and (b) differential rates of population growth within the countries that particular communities experience higher growth rate than the others. In both the cases, the population will increase to the detriment of the national power. Table 8.3 provides a list of some selected states of the peripheral areas which have experienced relatively higher growth rate but there is a very high degree of political uncertainty and instability in these states.

Table 8.3

Population growth in some selected states in the peripheral regions of the world economy

States	Average annual growth of population (per cent)		
	1965-80	*1980-87*	*1987-2000 (projected)*
Bangladesh	2.8	2.8	2.4
Chad	2.0	2.3	2.6
Zaire	2.8	3.1	3.1
Burundi	1.9	2.8	3.2
Ethiopia	2.7	2.4	3.1
Niger	2.7	3.0	3.2
Somalia	2.7	2.9	3.1
Rwanda	3.3	3.3	3.8
Central African Republic	1.8	2.5	2.6
Nigeria	2.5	3.4	3.0
Liberia	3.0	3.3	3.0
Senegal	2.5	2.9	3.1
Yemen Arab Republic	2.8	2.6	3.1
Iran	3.2	3.0	3.0
Iraq	3.4	3.6	3.4

Source: World Development Report, 1989

On the contrary, most of the states in the core area of the world economy have registered a relatively lower growth rate (Table 8.4); as a result, there is marked political stability and economic progress.

In these states, the rate of economic growth exceeds the rate of population growth; as a consequence, per capita supplies of goods has increased to an extent that political uncertainties could not develop there. Some of the states in this category are powerful nations in the world.

Table 8.4

Population growth in some selected states in the core areas of the world economy

States	Average annual growth of population (per cent)		
	1965-80	*1980-87*	*1987-2000 (projected)*
United Kingdom	0.2	0.1	0.1
Belgium	0.3	0.0	0.0
Netherlands	0.9	0.5	0.3
Federal Republic of Germany	0.3	-0.1	-0.2
Sweden	0.5	0.1	0.0
Denmark	0.5	0.0	-0.1
France	0.7	0.5	0.4
Switzerland	0.5	0.3	-0.1
United States of America	1.0	1.0	0.8
Japan	1.2	0.6	0.4

Source: World Development Report, 1989.

There was a time when the national power was equated with the higher growth rate of population vis-a-vis the large population size. Now the situation has changed considerably. "Of more importance than numbers of people may be the ratio of the population to the physical resources at its command. Calculation of a state's development potential must include in the equation per capita inventories of agricultural land, of minerals, and of energy supplies as well as some analysis of a state's ability to produce the necessary variety of each of these material resources. Compare Australia and Sri Lanka: their population each number about thirteen millions, and yet Australia's per capita gross domestic product is some sixteen times higher to that of Sri Lanka ! Certainly, the population to resource ratio is a factor in this great difference. Even after we have analyzed population as a ratio to resources, we cannot fully explain state development. The per capita gross domestic product of Japan is five times than that of Brazil, and yet Japan lacks resources while Brazil is a land of vast resources. Japan's population is slightly higher than Brazil. Clearly still more variables must be introduced into our calculus."

Arable land or a mineral is a resource only if the state population possesses technological sophistication adequate enough to develop it for consumption or for exchange in international trade. The technological development of mankind as a whole has progressed steadily, translating more and more 'materials' into 'resources'. The metallic content of mineral ores which can be mined, for instance, drops with advanced technology, vastly increasing world supplies of mineral resources. Also new uses are found for minerals. Two hundred years ago who would have thought that black sticky material called petroleum would ever prove so valuable? It cannot be said with certainty what resources the future may discover in the seas, among minerals today of little value; or even in the air itself (as Germany developed a process for removing nitrates from the air during World War I).

Individual states' capacities to utilize the material endowment of their territories vary greatly. Many underdeveloped states must import technology either by letting foreign interests exploit their resources or else through outright foreign aid. Often tapping states' potential resources may require the innovation of new techniques. Most of the techniques of the modern agriculture, for example, have been developed and applied in the mid-latitude states which have long registered/achieved lower population growth rates. Tropical states, mostly with relatively higher growth rates, cannot borrow much of this technology but must discover ways of enhancing tropical agriculture out of their own experiences and efforts to achieve sustenance. This necessitates investment in technological research which can only be achieved where the living conditions are very high. Obviously, it is in the temperate states which have caused major innovation diffusions across their territories. On account of lower growth rates, the standards of living in these states are relatively very high. This is the reason that they make heavy investment in technological and scientific research.

Whether states are technology-exporting or technology-importing and whether they have their own technology creating and developing apparatus, is another factor in analyzing a state's power-potential. Still another important factor in a population's productivity is per capita capital investment, and it is again much higher in the temperate states rather than in the tropical states, where it is too low to make any substantial change in their power structure. A state's power-potential does not wholly rest upon its sheer population number. It can just be a factor but what is more important is the capacity of its people to cause major innovation diffusions in the field of science and technology. Japan which is too small a nation in terms of population and area, and without a military, has virtually achieved commercial victory over most of the core states including the USA. The twenty-first century would be better known as the 'Japanese century'.

Notwithstanding the arguments against the higher growth rate vis-a-vis the large size of population, it is assumed that the numerical size of the population is important in other respects besides a military sense. On the extent of the domestic population and on its purchasing power depends the size of the domestic market. The state with a small population is likely to have difficulty in supporting those industries which are strategically desirable. Furthermore, only a country of considerable population could operate some of the larger scale industrial undertakings economically and effectively. Robinson argues: "it is not going too far, perhaps, to say that..most of the major industrial economies of scale could be achieved by a relatively higher income nation of 50 million; that nations of 110-115 million (are) probably too small to get all the technical economies available."

"How then do we explain the obvious success, both political and economic, of some small states—the Scandinavian countries and Switzerland for example? These states are necessarily less diversified than larger states, they have a smaller variety of resources and industries and they contain a relatively important agricultural sector." "Despite intense nationalism and strong security feelings that are perhaps warranted, there are compelling economic factors that make it impossible for a small nation to have even a single basic plant for a number of industries that are feasible for a larger country at the same level of economic development." However, "there exists a strong feeling of community and solidarity, a product of a long-shared historical past, and..in these states social decisions, necessary for the adjustments to the potentials of economic growth, may be far easier to reach than elsewhere. Among the larger nations this task is far more difficult since the ties among the various sectors of their populations are looser, and regional and other cleavages can more readily develop." Most temperate states, have registered lower growth rates for the past few decades, and experienced higher gross national product/per capita welfare, usually demonstrate strong internal cohesion because the population there is homogeneous. It has been rightly observed that owing to "closer internal ties (the state) find it easier to make the social adjustments need to take advantage of the potentialities of modern technology and economic growth.

Demographic Transition

It is a general model describing the evolution of levels of fertility and mortality over time. It has been devised with particular reference to the experience of developed countries which have passed through the process of industrialization and urbanization and have corresponding effect on their birth rates and death rates. The model suggests four highly stylized phases in the process:

1. In the first phase, both birth and death rates are high. Deaths due to famines, diseases or wars are the most important influence on population growth which tends to be at a low level. This is called the high stationary phase.
2. In the second or early expanding phase, the population begins to grow as a result of a stable birth rate and a rapidly declining death rate. The latter

falls as a result of improved nutrition, sanitation and medicines.

3. The third or late expanding phase is characterized by a slowing in the growth rate as the death rate stabilizes at a low level and the birth rate declines. This decline is associated with the growth of an urban/industrial society.
4. In the fourth or low stationary phase, birth and death rates have stabilized at a low level, population growth is very slow and the birth rate is more likely to fluctuate than the death rate.

Core states of the world economy such as the USA, Britain, France, Germany and Japan, holding the bulk of the power-potentials of the world, and which normally decide the political destiny of the world, are entering the fourth phase. But most of the states of Latin America, Africa, South Asia, South-West Asia and South-East Asia, belonging to the periphery of the world economy are in the second phase. These states have very low standards of living and levels of education, and are much behind the core states and the developed states as well in terms of military and economic power-potentials. On the contrary, there is a marked political instability in their political systems.

Optimum Population

The concept of optimum population has been defined in various ways by different people. To Dalton, it is the population which gives the maximum income per head. According to Robbins, the population which just makes the maximum returns possible is the optimum or best population whereas Carr-Saunders defines it as that population which provides maximum economic welfare.

The optimum population is that ideal size of population which provides the maximum income per head. Any increase or decrease in the size of the population above or below the optimum level will decrease the per capita income. Given the stock of natural resources production technique and the stock of capital, there is a definite size of population corresponding to highest per capita income. Other things remaining the same, any deviation from this optimum-sized population will lead to a reduction in income per capita head. If the increase in population is followed by the increase in per capita income, the country is underpopulated. And it can afford to increase its population till it reaches the optimum level. But if the increase in population tends to decrease in per capita income, the country is said to be overpopulated, and it requires a decline in population till per capita income is maximized.

Optimum population is a major source of political strength, internal cohesion and unity, as it brings in a state of political equilibrium within the political system, making the political process to intrinsically coexist with the system. Underpopulation and overpopulation both are a potential source of the weakness, particularly in terms of socio-economic and political developments.

Underpopulation

The weaknesses in terms of national power that arise from too small population are equally significant and equally obvious. In such a state there is presumably an abundance of arable land, so that the diseconomies of minute holdings and hidden unemployment should be absent. On the other hand, the state as a whole may provide only a small market, so that the advantages of large scale production cannot be realized and some strategically important industries cannot be profitably established. It must be remembered, however, that the same is true of all small countries. The very thinness of the population is often itself a source of weakness. Society approximates more nearly the conditions of a frontier, public order is more difficult to maintain, and the problem of defending a large area with a military force recruited from only a small population has always been a difficult one. The examples of Australia, New Zealand and Canada, with 16 million, 3 million and 8 million people and the very low overall densities of two or ten per square kilometre come to mind. Despite efforts to encourage immigration which is in itself very restricted, and to develop industry at home, their population remain too small for their areas.

Underpopulation occurs among people with high living standards farming extensively; we find it in the Prairies and parts of Australia, New Zealand, Canada and Brazil, partly as a result of the mode of settlement of near-virgin territory. Underpopulation may also occur at low technical levels, as among many pastoral nomads of arid regions and 'Chitemene' bush followers of the State of Zambia. In areas of advanced economy, it is difficult to rectify regional underpopulation, especially of rural areas, without government encouragement or colonization schemes. The breakup of 'latifundia' in Italy and the agrarian reform measures in Egypt are both examples of government attempts to reduce local underpopulation. It was one of the claims of the erstwhile socialist economies that regional inequalities were overcome. In backward societies, the problem of underpopulation may be contained by improved medical facilities and diet with a declining mortality rate.

Overpopulation

Overpopulation is said to occur when there is an excess of population over utilized or potential resources. It may result from an increase in population, a decline in resources, a decline in the demand for labour, or a combination of these factors. In other words, overpopulation may take place where resource development does not go hand in hand with population growth, and where growth of tertiary services lag behind technical progress.

Absolute overpopulation may be distinguished from relative overpopulation, the former occurring when the absolute limit of production has been attained though living standards remain low, while the latter indicates that present production is inadequate for the population although greater production is feasible. Relative overpopulation is more common than absolute overpopulation.

Overpopulation may be found at various levels: rural, industrial, regional, and national. Rural overpopulation is common but is more striking in populous underdeveloped areas. In South-East Asia, where there is high fertility and declining mortality, intensive agriculture, land fragmentation and minimal mechanization, natural checks to overpopulation have expressed greater control in the past. The demographic evolution of China has been frequently interrupted by famines, floods, droughts and epidemics. The 'minifundic' of Malta and southern Italy, the crowding 'fellaheen' in the Nile delta and the conquested districts of western Ireland are similar in cause if not in character. Rural overpopulation may also result from (a) uneven distribution of lands between farmers, (b) increased mechanization and reduced demand for agricultural labourers, (c) a change from cultivation to livestock farming and again reduced demand for labour, and (d) rapid rural population growth. Many of these features can be seen in old countries of Europe. Famine, hunger, prolonged unemployment, and increase in number of landless labourers, beggars, social tension, riots and political instability are the basic symptoms of rural overpopulation. Extremism in rural India, particularly in Bihar, Andhra Pradesh, and West Bengal is the natural outcome of the rural overpopulation. Unfortunately, solution other than emigration is slow and difficult but in the long run social and cultural revolutions will be more effective.

Industrial overpopulation is less obvious because of the greater flexibility and mobility of labour in manufacturing compared with agriculture. It results either from technical progress causing redundancy of labour or of a product from the decline of a whole industry or group of industries. In Britain, the textile industry offers many examples of the former, while ship-building is representative of the latter. Temporary or periodic declines, associated with trade recessions or cycles, cause temporary overpopulation; the world crisis of 1930 is a notorious example.

Where there is excessive reliance on a few basic industries, the whole region may be considered overpopulated; the 'depressed areas' of inter-war Britain became great sources of internal and international migrants. In Belgium, Italy and Japan, regional overpopulation is so common that it is a national problem. Even underpopulated countries like Australia, New Zealand, Canada and Brazil have their 'islands' of overpopulation. Nowhere are discrepancies so marked in Indonesia, where massive overpopulation in Java, and some parts of Sumatra and Sulawesi contrasts vividly with underpopulation in Kalimantan (Borneo), the Lesser Sunda islands, the Moluccas and west Irian. Overpopulated islands, especially those with national status, are often faced with more serious problems than mainland countries, as in Malta, Mauritius, Reunion islands, Hong Kong, Puerto Rico, Bermuda, Barbados, and other West Indies islands.

Invariably overpopulation expresses itself only at the lowest levels of society; rural overpopulation affects the landless and smallholders—the Naxalite movement in rural India has been a geographical manifestation of it. Industrial overpopulation usually hits the unskilled and semiskilled workers, creating economic cleavages and social tension in the society, whereas regional/national overpopulation tends to make the society aggressive.

It is the overpopulation which made Japan aggressive in the present century, and its army overran substantial parts of China, including Manchuria, and brought them under its military-administrative control. Germany became aggressive during the late nineteenth and early twentieth centuries simply because it had a population much higher than the available 'space' and 'resource'. Overpopulation might have been a motivating force in the growth of the Nazism and Fasicism in Europe. All great revolutions, such as the French Revolution in 1789, the Russian Revolution in 1917, and the Chinese Revolution in 1949, seemed to have occurred as a result of 'overpopulation'. The 'resources' available in France, Russia and China were far below the minimum requirement for the sustenance of the rapidly growing population, resulting into 'crises' of unspecified dimension.

Maximum Population

Overpopulation is linked with the older concept of maximum population above which the land cannot nourish any more without a decline in living standards and an increase in mortality. An absolute or true maximum population would seem unattainable in a modern economy but may well be achieved in a primitive subsistence economy, especially where birth rates and death rates are equal. No sound estimate of the absolute maximum world population is possible. In view of man's changing techniques and requirements, a relative or realized maximum is a more useful concept than an absolute maximum, as for instance, in Italy and Ireland where it was relieved by massive emigration.

Distribution and Density

The concepts of distribution and density of population, though not identical, yet are so intimately interwoven that there is genuine reason to discuss them simultaneously. The analysis of population distribution and density holds immense significance for political geographers as its meaningful interpretation holds the key to the analysis of entire demographic character of the state in terms of internal and external political space relationships. It is important here to make a distinction between population distribution and density. The distribution of population is more locational while the density is more proportional. The former refers to the spatial pattern in which population finds its location such as linear, dispersed, nucleated, agglomerated, etc., and the latter is concerned with the ratio between the size of population and the area.

Certain states have populations that are concentrated heavily in one area; it may be the zone of greatest productive capacity, it may be the most heavily industrialized, or it may be the contemporary core area, and may focus upon the largest city (primate city). Other states, whose population totals and average densities may almost be same, may have more than one such area of population agglomeration; in other words, such states possess more than one focal point. These areas of population concentration are separated by zones which may form barriers to contact, perhaps there are deserts between them or mountain ranges. And perhaps people of one such area speak a language that differs from that spoken in the other. If such is the case, these are obviously divisive elements present in the state which to a greater extent create internal dissension/disunity/restricts the spread of the state idea, and weakens the *raison d'etre* of the state.

Peoples with distinct characteristics seek to perpetuate their regional identity at the cost of the national identity. In fact, they feel more strongly about their area of concentration than they do about the state of which they form a part, as a result the political space relationship does not develop to the extent as required for the desirability of the national power. A potential but dangerous situation arises for the state if any of its population clusters occurs close to the international boundary away from the political heartland; in that case, the society may develop its own identity with a political action area carved out across the territory. Such a situation often leads to centrifugalism, and if the population of the cluster is racially and ethnically same with that of the population of on either side of the boundary, then it may certainly be subjected to the 'irridentist' claim by the neighbouring state.

However, if the distribution of population in the state is homogeneous or if there is only one 'heart' of distribution, and other things being equal, then the state is said to possess a greater degree of internal unity with a state idea having engulfed the people as a whole.

"Since there is no ideal population density, it cannot be said that density *per se* is a factor in national power. Population density is important only when it is high or low in relation both to local resources and to the technological stage of their development and utilization. Political implication of density must be analyzed in terms of underpopulation and overpopulation than the density of population itself."

Pattern of Population Composition

The composition of the population or the population structure, refers to those aspects of population which may be measured, however, inadequately. But we must restrict ourselves to aspects for which data are usually obtained from censuses: age structure, sex ratio, educational and technical attainments, economic composition, nations and national minorities, language, and religion. These are all factors in the power-potential of the state.

Age Structure

On the age structure depends the 'effective' population of the state, i.e., the population which intrinsically concerns the power-potential or the national power of the state. The age structure of the population is directly influenced by three variables: mortality, fertility, and migration. These variables are not entirely independent, and any change in one may eventually influence the other two, but social and economic conditions only influence age structure through them.

It is through the construction of the pyramidal diagram that the age structure is analyzed. The vertical axis of it is graduated in years or groups of years from 0 onwards, and the horizontal axes show either the numbers or the percentages of males and females within these groups.

Certain basic types of pyramid may be distinguished. First, if a population has unchanging fertility and mortality, it is a stationary population, and each step in the pyramid will differ from the one below only by the number of deaths at the age or age group. If, however, the number of the births increases from year to year, the population type will become 'progressive', and the pyramid will widen at the base; decline in the number of births will produce a 'regressive' population with a pyramid which is narrow at the base and has a shape of a bell. Figure 8.1 presents six examples of contrasting age pyramids at mid-century, ranging from that of Brazil which is very progressive to that of France which is regressive. The former is typical of a host of countries with high fertility and high or diminishing mortality, and the latter is typical of Western Europe, where both fertility and mortality are low. Of course, in the nineteenth century, most West European countries had progressive pyramids. Even in the age pyramid there is a core-periphery dichotomy with the core states having a regressive population and the peripheral states a progressive population.

The effect of war and migration on the age structure is vivid. If one constructs the age pyramids for Iran and Iraq for the decade 1980s when the two

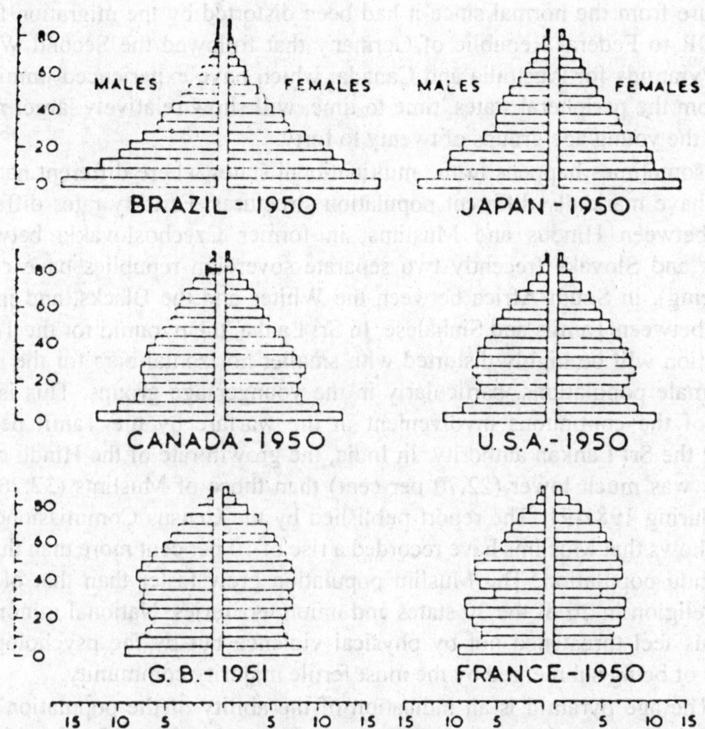

Figure 8.1: Six Age-Pyramids of the Mid-Century, Contrasting Young and Old Populations (After Clarke, 1972)

states were involved in war and mutual destruction, then one can find that the male totals for both the states for the years twenty to thirty-nine have been drastically reduced, and those for the years twenty-five to twenty-nine have been reduced almost by half. These are the basic age groups for the males for the battle fronts. Pyramids for all those states which were actively involved in the Second World War had shown similar pattern for their population immediately after the war. States like Afghanistan involved in internal strife and civil war for decades, will have a distorted bell-shaped pyramid as much of its younger population (both male and female) has been eliminated/killed in the strife and civil wars.

The pyramid for erstwhile German Democratic Republic (GDR) reveals a departure from the normal since it had been distorted by the migration from the GDR to Federal Republic of Germany that followed the Second World War. Pyramids for Australia and Canada, which have experienced immigration from the peripheral states, time to time, will show relatively larger male bars in the young age groups of twenty to forty.

It sometimes happens in the multinational states where different nationalities have markedly different population structures. Fertility rates differ in India between Hindus and Muslims; in former Czechoslovakia between Czechs and Slovaks (recently two separate sovereign republics have come into being), in South Africa between the Whites and the Blacks, and in Sri Lanka between Tamils and Sinhalese. In Sri Lanka, the pyramid for the Tamil population will be highly distorted with smaller horizontal bars for the male and female populations, particularly in the younger age groups. This is because of the continuous involvement in the warfare by the Tamil people against the Sri Lankan authority. In India, the growth rate of the Hindu community was much lower (22.70 per cent) than those of Muslims (32.76 per cent) during 1981-91. The report published by the Census Commissioner of India shows that Muslims have recorded a rise of 10 per cent more than that of the Hindu population. The Muslim population grew faster than that of any other religion in 26 of the 30 states and union territories. National minorities can thus feel threatened not by physical violence but by the psychological danger of being submerged by the most fertile majority community.

"The age pyramid is an indication of the ability of the population of a state to perform work, either at the time represented or in the foreseeable future. The length of the working life varies with the degree of economic development of a country. In the more developed countries it begins in the teens and goes on into the sixties and even later. In the peripheral underdeveloped and developing (semi-periphery) states in which work is mainly hard manual labour in the fields or forests, it begins earlier and ends earlier. Here, in the underdeveloped and developing states, people age more quickly and die much earlier because of the shorter life expectancy as compared to the developed states."

Since the life expectancy in the developed states is much higher and greater, there is a relatively large proportion of the population in the higher age groups. However, these higher age groups require to be supported by the active and effective part of the population. Similarly, the lower age groups have to be supported by the rest of the community for a period which varies with the degree of economic development. In some states children are economically useful at ten years of age; in others, not until they are almost twice that age. It has been observed that the peripheral states usually have high proportion of the population of the younger age groups in which child labour is of greater economic importance.

The analysis makes it clear that the percentage of population that is (a) below fifteen years of age, and (b) over sixty-five and above, is not economically and politically useful in any large measure. However, there is wide regional variation in it as in the peripheral states wherein people grow quickly and die earlier. It is now evident that the power-potential of the state does not rest on the total population alone but it is the total effective population, in terms of the age groups, which is important in the estimate of national power at a given point of time.

Sex Structure

Although the number of the two sexes are not widely divergent, their disparity is of interest to geographers because of the contrasting roles of the two sexes in economy and society. In fact, it is through the sex structure that the 'effective population' of the state is estimated and measured. The sex structure or the sex ratio may be recorded in three different ways:

(a) the number of females per 100 or 1000 males or vice versa;
(b) males (or females) as a percentage of the total population; and
(c) the proportion of males (or females) as a decimal of unity.

Nearly all developed countries have higher male mortality than female mortality, and the disparity in the deaths of the two sexes is much greater than in the births. At birth, males are, therefore, destined to a shorter life-span than are females. The difference between male and female mortality is greater in USA, Canada, Argentina, Australia and the European population of New Zealand follows quite closely behind, but it is difficult to discern a significant worldwide pattern.

The more rapid decline of female mortality, influenced by environmental causes, seem largely due to biological factors. It appears that the gentler sex is also the stronger sex. Evidence of the relative weakness of males is their higher infant mortality, which rapidly reduces initial numerical superiority. In most advanced countries mortality among males generally exceeds female mortality throughout life, so that women are particularly preponderant in the older age-groups. On the other hand, in several countries of Asia, Africa and Latin America, high maternal mortality and sometimes the neglect of females raises young adult female mortality above that for males, and partly accounts for the overall excess of males.

Under normal conditions adult women outnumber men by a very minute percentage. In addition, war, internal strife and civil war, and migration have been found to be responsible for sharp decline in the number of males than of women, as in the case of Iran, Iraq, or Afghanistan, or most of the European states, and Japan which were involved in the World War II. "The much higher fraction of the total population made up of women may reduce somewhat the effectiveness, particularly militarily, of the population in these and similar countries." However, it is equally important to note that in most of the technologically advanced states in the temperate world, women now stand on a par with men, or (in some cases, the sex ratio is higher) in technical and military efficiency in most spheres, but still they are powerful states. Nevertheless, the sex structure is an important indicator of effective population, which in itself, is an important factor to the power-potential of the state.

Table 8.5

Sex structure

	Population: females per 100 males				Life expectancy at birth (years)			
	Total		Age 0-4		Female		Male	
Regions	1965	1985	1965	1985	1965	1987	1965	1987
1. Low Income Economies	96	96	96	94	49	62	47	60
2. China and India	94	94	94	94	51	65	48	64
3. Other Low Income	100	100	99	97	45	55	43	53
4. Middle Income Economies	100	100	97	96	59	67	55	62
5. Lower-Middle Income States	100	100	97	96	57	66	53	61
6. Upper-Middle Income States	101	100	96	96	61	69	58	64
7. Low and Middle Income	97	97	96	95	52	63	49	61
8. Sub-Saharan Africa	103	102	100	99	44	52	41	49
9. East Asia	96	96	95	94	54	69	50	66
10. South Asia	94	94	95	94	45	57	46	57
11. Europe, Middle East & North Africa	101	99	96	95	59	66	56	62
12. Latin America & Caribbean	100	100	97	97	60	69	56	63
13. Highly Indebted States	100	100	98	97	57	65	53	60
14. High Income Economies	104	104	96	95	74	79	67	73
15. OECD Members	104	105	96	95	74	79	68	73
16. Others	95	87	96	95	63	72	59	65

Source: World Development Report, 1989.

Education and Technical Development

We have already discussed that the technological capacity of society is the prime indicator of its power-potential. But the technological capacity itself depends on the level of education. It has been rightly observed that the "size of the labour force gives no indication of its quality. This depends on the level of education and the volume of mechanical equipment and other tools available." These are the primary and secondary levels of education which concern most in terms of the technological capacity and technological development of the society. Table 8.6 reveals the level of primary and secondary education of the major regions of the world (based on the income economies).

Table 8.6

Percentage of the age group enrolled in education

Regions	*Primary*		*Secondary*		*Tertiary Total*	
	1965	*1986*	*1965*	*1986*	*1965*	*1986*
1. Low Income Economies	73	103	20	35	2	3
2. China and India	83	113	25	39	2	2
3. Other Low Income	49	76	9	25	1	4
4. Middle Income Economies	93	104	26	54	6	18
5. Lower-Middle Income	89	104	24	51	6	17
6. Upper-Middle Income	97	104	28	59	6	20
7. Low & Middle Income	78	103	22	40	3	7
8. Sub-Sahara Africa	41	66	4	16	0	2
9. East Asia	88	123	23	45	1	5
10. South Asia	68	84	22	32	4	5
11. Europe, M. East & N. Africa	83	97	32	56	7	13
12. Latin America	98	108	19	48	4	20
13. Highly Indebted	85	106	21	52	5	18
14. High Income Economies	105	102	62	92	21	39
15. OECD Member	107	102	63	93	21	39
16. Others	74	90	27	61	7	17

Source: World Development Report, 1989.

The data on primary school enrolments are estimates of children of all ages enrolled in primary schools. Figures are expressed as the ratio of pupils to the population of school-aged children. The primary school age differs among countries. The data on the secondary enrolments are calculated in the same manner, but again the definition of secondary school age differs among countries. It is most commonly considered 12 to 17 years. The tertiary enrolment ratio is calculated by dividing the number of pupils in all post-secondary schools, technical and vocational institutions and universities by the population in the 20-24 years age group.

The table shows that the low income and lower-middle income countries of the peripheral region have comparatively lower education levels, and the rate of increase during the twenty years has not been much appreciable. While the level of education of some upper-middle income countries of the periphery has experienced some 'concrete' progress during the period. It is high income/higher income and OECD (excluding Greece, Portugal and Turkey) have achieved highest educational level during the period—an index of their power-potential.

However, the youth population, that is, 20 to 24 years, is used as the denominator for the tertiary institutions, since it represents an average tertiary level cohort. In higher income countries, youths of 18 to 19 years may be enrolled in a tertiary institution but in low income and middle income peripheral regions, many people older than 25 years are usually enrolled in such institutions, which tend to reduce the technical efficiency of the countries. It has an obvious impact on the 'efffective population' of the countries.

"The lack of trained personnel in public administration and industrial management and in science and technology must necessarily weaken the total power-potential of a country. It is a policy objective of some low income and middle-low income countries to improve their levels of education and technical competence but even with technical aid from the developed countries, progress is very low."

Economic Composition

Economic composition is an important variable in estimating the national power of the state. An analysis of a population's economic composition unfolds the diverse economic, demographic and cultural attributes of an area which forms the basis for the state's social and economic development.

Economic composition is the manifestation of the ratio between the economically-active population and the economically-non-active population. Economically-active population is that part of 'manpower' which is actually engaged in the production of goods and services. Economically-non-active population comprises that part of manpower which is engaged in activities like household duties in their own houses, retired personnel, inmates of institutions, students and those living on rents, pensions, royalties, and dividends. It also includes children below working age.

The activity rate of a population is the proportion which is economically active, and may be expressed age-specifically. Comparison of activity rates for different countries can be accepted only with reservations of varied definitions and age limits used. Non-comparability of data is particularly applicable to the economic activity of women, and therefore, activity rates are generally given for males only. There are also great regional variations in the economic activity of youths and aged persons; there is no uniformity in the length of active life, and although the active population is sometimes equated with the 15-64 age group, however, we must not forget the arbitrariness of these age limits.

The size of the active population depends on demographic, social and economic factors. There is no doubt, of course, that is fairly closely related to the size of the total population, but the demographic regime and age structure are also important determinants. In young rapidly growing populations of underdeveloped countries, the active population tends to be small and there is 'heavy youth dependency' because of the high proportion of children; but, nevertheless, boys and old men play a great role in the economic activity of such countries. At the other extreme, advanced ageing at the apex and the base creates a state of 'heavy old age dependency'. Other things being equal, the activity rate is highest when there is only ageing at the base, an intermediate stage of 'light dependency' which prevails at the moment in most highly developed countries, but not for long. In developed/higher income countries, there is counterbalancing effect of the limited economic activity of the young and the old due to social and economic changes in recent decades.

The evolutionary stages as mentioned above are helpful but not clearcut; for instance, although ageing at the apex is the main cause of the present reduction in the activity rates of Western Europe, post-war bulges have accentuated the process. Wars and migrations also play havoc with prognosticaties of future activity rates which are based on trends in age structure.

Numerous other factors also influence activity rates. Economic changes are obviously instrumental, and so is the urban-rural ratio. The activity rates of women, children and old living in agricultural communities clearly differ from those in towns. On the whole, they are higher in the country, but it cannot be empirically generalized. At the initial phase, urbanization had tended to reduce/restrict the activity rate among women because of the fewer economic opportunities in the towns. But now with more varied economic opportunities available in the urban centres, the women economic activity rate has registered phenomenal growth in the developed countries. However, at the same time, longer education and improvements in social conditions have diminished the activity of children in the urban areas.

The levels of income and employment also affect activity rates but there are many conflicting assessments of their importance. On the other hand, it is easier perhaps to assess the influence of the state of health of the population on activity rates; it is certainly true that physical disability is higher (in poverty-stricken, economically backward countries of the periphery than in highly developed ones), and efficiency lower. Nevertheless, such countries have a young labour force contrasting with the ageing labour forces of developed countries in which there are reductions in the proportion of active young adults and increase of older adults.

Sometimes a distinction is made between employed and unemployed active population. The employed active population consists of all those persons who are at work during the reference period of the census including those who are temporarily absent from work due to illness, industrial disputes, etc. The unemployed active population, on the other hand, consists of those who were not at work during the reference period of the census but are seeking some work. The incidence of employment in any area is often measured in terms of employment rates, proportion of fully employed, underemployed, tables of working life, etc. The employment rate is expressed in terms of number of employed persons in total economically-active population. Underemployment refers to the difference between the amount of work performed by persons in employment and the amount of work they would normally be able to and willing to perform (International Labour Organization, 1957).

Unemployment occurs in number of forms, and may be (a) persistent and general, (b) cyclical, (c) of short duration, (d) structural, i.e., within a particular industry or occupation, (e) technical, caused by improved production techniques, or (f) concealed, i.e., where workers' productive powers are not fully utilized. The incidence of unemployment is much higher in the peripheral countries of Africa, Asia, Central America, and to some extent, Latin America. In these areas, the growth of population is higher, and the society is predominantly agricultural. The level of education and technological efficiencies are so poor that these areas witness/register very low or practically no resource mobilization, and employment generation as well.

On the other hand, these areas are experiencing townward movement of impoverished peasants and active population incapable of improving their lot in the rural areas has engendered a state of chronic unemployment or underemployment. Employment can be an index of estimating the power-potential of the state, especially in terms of resource mobilization and employment generation, while incidence of unemployment is an indication of declining power-potential. Nevertheless, unemployment is a global phenomenon, even the higher income countries like the USA is not completely free of it. The higher income countries with their superior technological efficiencies have consistently sought to find out ways and devices for resource mobilization and employment generation which expressively manifest in their power-potentials.

Occupational composition is another variable in the analysis of the power-potential of the state. More varied the occupational composition, the greater is the possibility of power-potential. The occupational structure of a society is the product of a variety of intimately related factor. Earlier, the occupational composition was largely based on agriculture. Advancement in science and technology, followed by industrialization and urbanization, sought to create an element of specialization in the occupational composition by creating highly specialized types of jobs. All these developments together breed a new urban culture which is more service-oriented. This has modified the occupational structure considerably.

Colin Clark has attempted to categorize occupational activities into the following three categories/groups/sectors:

1. Primary activities including agriculture, forestry, hunting and fishing.
2. Secondary activities including mining, quarrying, manufacturing, production of electric power and gas, and construction.
3. Tertiary activities including commerce, transportation and communication, and service of all kinds.

Countries with more than 60 per cent of their male workers deriving their livelihood from primary activities are considered underdeveloped such as those of the African countries, and a number of Asian countries also. Those countries of the temperate West Europe and North America, and Japan where agricultural workers form less than 35 per cent of the total workforce, and are involved in secondary and tertiary activities are considered developed. The countries with 35 to 60 per cent male workers involved in primary activities are considered semi-developed.

Most of the powerful countries of the world have long switched over to secondary and tertiary sectors, primarily as a result of sustained technological development. It has an obvious impact on the pattern of occupational composition which is necessarily varied and diverse, making a 'desirable' impact on the power-potential of the countries.

International comparisons of occupational data are only feasible with a simpler classification. The UN Demographic Yearbook, 1964 notes ten groups, and provides an International Standard Classification of Occupations with an eleventh group for members of the armed forces:

1. Professional, technical and related workers
2. Managerial, executive and administrative workers
3. Clerical workers
4. Sales workers
5. Farmers, fishermen, hunters, lumbermen and related workers
6. Workers in mine, quarry and related occupations
7. Workers in transport and communication
8. Craftsmen, production process workers and labourers not elsewhere classified
9. Service, sport and recreation workers
10. Workers not classified by occupation

Derruau has earlier proposed a classification of societies in broad terms according to their social structure and occupation composition:

1. Primitive rural society with a tribal structure as in Negro Africa.
2. Rural society with contrasting classes of landlords and peasants as in Iran and southern Iraq.
3. Traditional western rural societies with a high proportion of rural non-farm people exemplified by West Germany.
4. Rural societies with numerous agricultural labourers as found in Languedoc.
5. Colonial societies with peoples of contrasting traditions, techniques and living standards found in the northern and southern parts of Africa.
6. Societies with small rural populations at high living standards and large numbers employed in trade and commerce as in Australia.
7. Industrial societies with marked urbanization and marked segregation of classes.
8. Communist societies with little differentiation in living standards like in former Yugoslavia and China.
9. Communist societies with marked differentiations in living standards like in the former USSR.

The rates of evolution of these various societies differ considerably bringing increasing contrasts in social structures that tend to threaten the social cohesion and unity.

The industrial composition of active population refers to branches of activity, and it is based on the type of establishment, product made or service rendered. The United Nations Statistical Commission has adopted a nine-division classification which is sufficiently restricted to be of great value for international comparisons and trends:

1. Agriculture, forestry, hunting and fishing
2. Mining and quarrying
3. Manufacturing industries
4. Construction
5. Electricity, gas, water and sanitary services
6. Commerce
7. Transport, storage and communication
8. Services
9. Not classifiable elsewhere

The proportions employed in these nine industry groups vary markedly from country to country and from region to region with decisive impact on the power potential of the society.

Nation, Nationality and National Minorities

Nation and nationality are difficult concepts and their definitions have been varied and confusing. The reason for this confusion is that the terms may include racial, linguistic, cultural, psychological or administrative considerations, or a combination of these. "A nation is a group of people, occupying a particular area who feel themselves held together in terms of common acceptance of particular values that are of such prime importance to them that they demand that their area and people should be organized in a distinct state, as the political agency by which those values may be preserved and furthered." A common language is often a feature of nationality, and a common religion may help, but homogeneous racial stock is rare, and long historical tradition not indispensable. Indeed, none of these qualities is vital, save the sentiment of nationality and desire for common government, peculiar or exclusive to the nation. Nationality depends upon sentiments which can easily be swayed by propaganda. At times nationality rouses profound passions, but passions are ephemeral, and nationality impermanent. It may have no deep roots, and may die when its purpose is achieved. Nevertheless, some national minorities preserve remarkable unity despite strong pressure, perhaps because they are minorities. Nation and nationality are, therefore, intangible terms, the criteria for which may vary widely. In one country race may be considered the best basis for definitions, in another language, in a third culture, in a fourth historical habitation and so on.

The most important aspect of the nation from the political point of view is that it is not necessarily the same as the body of citizens of a particular state. There is hardly a state in the modern world in which every community completely accepts the cultural tradition (including language and religions) of the majority.

The concepts of nation and state are not easily distinguished because nations evolve within states, sometimes coincide with them (nation-states) and sometimes overlap them. However, the dominant nation is represented as extending over a large geographical area than the state, so that the "state is largely contained within the nation". Nation-states are much rarer than multinational states (there are, at present, some 2000 'nations' but only 20 nation-states), or the state may contain national minorities which may be—and often are—fragments of another nations. In Europe, there are few examples of the nation-states, same in the north-west, and often the complexity of nationalities has been a cause of strife, and which has a diabolic impact on the power-potential of the states concerned. However, some of the countries where Europeans have settled have moulded themselves into nation-states despite the diverse origins of immigrants because the latter have soon acquired a new allegiance.

However, Pounds (1972) has identified three types of relationships between state and nation:

1. The state embraces one nation or a part of one, without significant national minorities such as Sweden, Hungary, and former German Federal Republic and German Democratic Republic, now United Germany.
2. The state embraces most of its dominant nation, and a small part of which forms national minorities in neighbouring countries, such as Denmark, Bulgaria, Greece, Spain, Italy, France, India, Japan, Mexico, Norway, Turkey, and Finland.
3. The state contains almost the whole of the nation which it represents, together with large and significant national minorities, for example, Ethiopia, Myanmar, Brazil and Romania.

However, there are states, on the other hand, which can be fitted into such a scheme only with difficulty, such as:

1. Multinational states, like Canada, Yugoslavia (now stands disintegrated) and Malaysia, which are partnerships of two or more national groups on more or less equal terms.
2. The states newly created in Africa, which do not reflect the national, that is, cultural-linguistic groupings of the Africans but a former power balance of the European imperial powers.
3. The group of Spanish-speaking Latin American countries in which, as far as social cohesion is concerned, there is more in common between all Europeans of whatever origin than between the European and the Indian groups within, such as in Ecuador, Columbia and Brazil.

The social cohesion of the peoples of any particular state is a dominant factor in the political-power of the state. Here, in the social cohesion of the peoples of the state, what is more important is the 'national minority' which refers to national groups which constitute individually only a minority within the state, such as the Muslims and Sikhs in the Hindu-dominated India, or the Hindus in the Muslim-dominated Pakistan and Bangladesh. Pounds (1972) has analyzed various patterns of relationships between nation and national minority, or between the state and the several cultural-linguistic groups of which it is composed, and identified the following categories:

1. The culturally unified states, in which there may be said to be complete unity and cohesion from the cultural linguistic point of view. This does not, however, presuppose that there are no differences deriving from social class or economic position. Examples are Netherlands, Hungary, Sweden and New Zealand.
2. States in which national minorities are drawn so intimately into the cultural life of the state that, whether they continue to use their own language and practise their own culture or not, they cease to be regarded as a dis-

ruptive element. The Scottish and Welsh have long been drawn so closely into the cultural life of the United Kingdom to such an extent as to have made the *raison d'etre* of it geographically more expressive.

3. States in whcih ethnic minorities are not integrated with their dominant nation in which they jealously preserve all aspects of their own culture and in which they aim at autonomy within, or even an independence of the state within which they live. The Muslims and the Sikhs are examples of such national communities in India, and/or, linguistic minorities in the linguistic states of the Indian Union, are not fully integrated with the 'majority' or 'dominant' linguistic groups of the states concerned. They preserve all aspects of their cultural-linguistic identities.
4. States in which the population belongs mainly to two or more balanced national groups. Numerically considered, one group at least is clearly a minority—but so strong a minority that it can establish its own conditions of coexistence in a multinational state. These conditions are sometimes embodied in a federal structure such as those of Czechoslovakia, Yugoslavia and Canada. However, Czechoslovakia and Yugoslavia have already got disintegrated and ceased to exist as unified political entities. Two nation-states have come into being—the Republic of Czech and the Slovak Republic, following the disintegration of Czechoslovakia. In fact, the Czechs and the Slovaks sought for peaceful secession while the Serbs, Croats and the Muslims, particularly who brought about the fall of Yugoslavia, secured secession through violence and war. However, in Lebanon the polity is balanced between the Muslims and the Christians. In Canada, the federal polity is being threatened as a result of the uncompromising attitude between the English and the French people, both the 'nations' seek to perpetuate their identity in such a way as to create tension which may ultimately lead to disintegration. However, Canada narrowly survived a territorial split in a recently concluded referendum in which the French Qubec sought for secession.
5. States, a part of whose territory is subjected of irredentist aims on the part of a neighbouring state. This is an extension of the third category. The best example is the German claims to recovery of the Sudetenland from Czechoslovakia before the outbreak of the World War II, and which led to the famous Munich Pact which recognized the German claims. Pakistan's claims to Kashmir, a Muslim-dominated Indian state, is another best example of irredentist claim which it has furthered by encouraging terrorism.

A peculiar situation arises when a particular nation or a people has its concentration spread over two states across the international boundary. It is a source of considerable concern for both the states. The Nagas are such a 'nation' whose concentration is contiguous across the international boundary between India and Myanmar (Burma). Now the Nagas demand that their area and people should be organized into a 'distinct state' so that they can preserve their identity and cultural values.

6. Plural societies. This term is used to cover those statewide groups in which cultural-linguistic divisions, sometimes of a minor order, get expressed through social and economic barriers and cleavages, leading to 'locational conflicts.' Or, in other words, most underdeveloped states suffer from horizontal cleavages among numerous traditional societies. Each modern state in the periphery incorporates a *melange* of traditional communal groups and political cultures which by accident came to be included within the boundaries of one state.

This multiplicity of communal groups defines the states' problem of pluralism. Though pluralism is not a serious problem in the developed economy but it is certainly a serious problem for the developing and underdeveloped economies where racially and culturally weak communities are discriminated and segregated economically and socially. In India, it is a very common phenomenon. However, in India, the national minorities like the Sikhs, have a fairly high sustainable economy than the dominant Hindu nation but the Muslim, the principal national minority, is substantially below the general economic level.

The racial policy adopted in 1948 by the White regime in South Africa was popularly known as 'apartheid'. It sought to segregate and discriminate the non-White Black peoples economically and socially as a natural outcome of the pluralistic nature of the South African society, furthered by the philosophy of the White peoples' racial superiority. However, only recently, the South African government has abandoned it. Other examples of plural societies are Sri Lanka, Malaysia, Indonesia, and all those parts of Africa where the native Africans live side by side with Europeans and Asiatic immigrants.

Many areas in the periphery of the world economy, i.e., Latin America, Africa and Asia exhibit, superimposed upon their traditional societies, a modern society and economy. The superimposition of this modern society and economy upon the traditional societies and economies in many peripheral underdeveloped states has created vertical dualistic cleavages, and has led to the problem of 'dualism' in these countries.

"Both the problems of pluralism and that of dualism can be defined geographically. The traditional societies in the periphery are invariably regional because of the colloidal nature of traditional spatial organization and the modern society is a lattice superimposed upon a mosaic of traditional cultures and economies. The integration of the plurastic and dualistic societies, and of the state space into one functioning political and economic unit, is the great challenge facing the underdeveloped (peripheral) states."

National Unity

It is the national unity on which depends, to a considerable extent, the power-potential of the state. National unity itself rests on the social cohesion of the peoples with varied backgrounds, i.e., the response of the national minorities to the 'national iconography' whether or not they enthusiastically subscribe to it. Do they respect the national anthem, national flag or any other national symbol? Disrespect to national iconography is an offence under the rule of law of the state, and it explicitly amounts to erode the "very fabric of national unity" weakening the basic foundation of national 'will' and 'interest'. National minorities may sometimes constitute a focus of active opposition to what the majority regards as the national interest. This mostly occurs in time of emergency/war. It may even risk the *raison d'etre* of the state.

Pounds has observed that no problem of national unity arises in (i) the culturally unified state, and (ii) states in which national minorities are drawn so intimately into the cultural realm/life of the state. But national unity is a serious problem for (a) states in which ethnic minorities are not integrated with the dominant nation, and (b) states in which the population belongs mainly to two or more evenly balanced national groups. In situations like these, it is extremely difficult to secure national unity, and thus national power. There are many examples of the use of dissident or hostile minorities, or even of major national groups within a state by a hostile power as a political lever. Pakistan's continuous abetment to terrorism in North-West India by using the Sikhs and Kashmiri Muslims against the Indian State and Constitution is aimed at dividing the Country. In fact, these communities have not been fully integrated with the cultural whole of the traditional Indian systems of belief, and Pakistan is making all efforts to use the opportunity against India.

It is unlikely that a state likes to grant autonomy or independence to one of its provinces/constituent units unless the local demand becomes so strong or a strong sense of territoriality has risen that it is less embarrassing to yield than to resist. No state likes to make any breach in the legal or juridical unity because a breach in monolithic structure of the unitary state looks much like a confession of weakness. Occasionally, a government has in this way held out too long against the rising pressure of national feeling in one of its minority groups: Yugoslavia against that of the Croats before the World War II, the Hindus against the Muslims in British India, the Iraqis against the Khurds, the English against the Irish, and the Austro-Hungarian empire against that of all their Slavic and other subject peoples before World War I. What happened in each of these examples shows that it is a mark of the wisest statesmanship to recognize such national pressures before the breaking point is reached. The most recent example is that of the Soviet Union succumbing to the pressure of the major ethnic groups which led to the emergence of a number of nation-states which once formed the parts of the former Soviet system. It was the satesmanship of the former Soviet President Gorbachov to have yielded to the pressures of the national minorities before a catastrophe of unspecified dimension could occur. A great majority of Afro-Asian states which came up in the post-war period appeared to be the outcome of the recognition of their national aspirations by their colonial mentors who preferred to yield rather than to resist the uprisings.

"A state government has at its side, if not always at its command, a number of social subsystems other than the political. Any social organization which unites large numbers of the population in collective association, voluntarily or involuntarily, expands the population's level of cognitive and, it is hoped, affective integration. Alexis de Tocqueville observed that one of the distinguishing features of American democracy was wide range of voluntary associations, widespread participation which effectively politicized the population while alleviating some political tensions."

The Minorities Problem

One of the basic ways to solve the minorities problem is to yield to their pressures, allowing them to have their own politico-territorial expressions, provided their concentrations are contiguous and they have developed territoriality over generations. Political expression can be achieved either through autonomy or independence. In the tenth of his fourteen points, President Woodrow Wilson declared that "the peoples of Austria-Hungary...should be accorded the freest opportunity of autonomous development. Throughout the nineteenth century, especially after the battle of Waterloo in 1815, there was a wave of national uprising in Europe, and the smaller cultural-linguistic groups with contiguous concentration sought to perpetuate their individual territorial character through political expression. One of the main purposes of the Congress of Vienna in 1815 after the battle of Waterloo was to have territorial realignments intrinsically conformed with the political aspirations of the linguistic-cultural groups living in the territorial states".

In 1919-20, the new boundaries laid down in Eastern Europe were made to conform, as far as possible, with the linguistic-cultural divisions. But, at the same time, the peace conference had dealt kindly with the territorial claims of certain countries, especially Romania, Czechoslovakia and Poland, and correspondingly harshly with those of the neighbouring countries of Hungary and Bulgaria. More national minorities were included within the boundaries of some of these East European countries than Woodrow Wilson had in fact approved. To safeguard their national interests, Romania, Turkey, former

Yugoslavia and Baltic states were obliged to accept minorities treaties, by which they undertook to protect the rights of the national minorities.

In fact, it is in the secular polity that the national minorities are assured of their fuller cultural-linguistic and religious development/expression that they are forced to integrate with the dominant nation. India's secular polity has allowed the major national minorities to perpetuate their cultural-religious identities and systems of beliefs. The Constitution of India guarantees and assures full and complete protection of life and liberty to all citizens, irrespective of birth, nationality, religion, or race and language, and provides equal opportunity to all in matters of employment, etc.

However, in a theocracy, minorities are not allowed to perpetuate their cultural distinctiveness. They are forcefully drawn into the cultural life of the majority nation. In Nepal, non-Hindu minorities are deprived of certain constitutional rights. Similarly, the non-Muslim peoples in the most of the Islamic states, except Malaysia and Indonesia, are denied the basic constitutional rights. In fact, Pakistan and Bangladesh have solved their minorities' problem by 'forced migration' to India. The Soviet Union collapsed because it failed to solve the minorities problems, i.e., it yielded to the pressures of the minorities. Sri Lanka is yet to come out with a clearcut policy with regard to the problem of the Tamil people (principal national minority). As a result, it is witnessing the worst period of its existence because of the prolonged civil war between the minority Tamil nation and the majority Sinhalese nation. Multinational states must come out with a definite minority policy if they do not want to risk their *raison d'etre*.

Exchange of Population

One of the possible devices to solve the problems raised by the continued existence of pockets of national minorities lies in the exchange of population. The best example of the exchange of population was that of between Greece and Turkey in 1923, "when they agreed for a compulsory exchange of Turkish nationals of the Greek orthodox religion established in Turkish territory, and of Greek nationals of the Moslam region established in Greek territory". Most of the European states have voluntarily sought for this method. However, the exchange of population could not take place in the Indian subcontinent under any rule of law, though the division of British India was done on the communal pattern. There was every scope for the exchange of Muslim population from India to Pakistan, and Hindu population from Pakistan to India. Since the exchange of population was not encouraged, millions of Hindus continued to stay in Pakistan and millions of Muslims remained in India, creating minorities problem of unspecified dimension. However, Pakistan sought for the forced migration of the Hindus to India.

Exchange of population does not appear to offer a means of solving minority problem, except perhaps on a local scale, owing to logistic and administrative difficulties. If neighbouring countries are able to organize a peaceful and orderly exchange of population, they are usually adept enough to a tolerant policy that would make exchange unnecessary. However, exchange of population in underdeveloped region, particularly in Africa and Asia, has in most of the cases, accompanied by violence in the 'involved' states.

Plebiscites

It follows logically from one nationalist tradition that if sovereignty does indeed lie with the 'people', then people should be consulted in any proposed changes in sovereignty. This is the principle of national self-determination which requires the use of plebiscites (voting to decide the political destiny) for changing state boundaries. Three distinct periods are normally identified when plebiscites were used to decide such matters: (i) in the aftermath of the French Revolution in Savoy, Nice, Geneva, and Belgium to legitimize the extension of the French State; (ii) between 1848 and 1870 notably as a tool in the unification of Italy which involved a total of nine plebiscites in the conversion of the kingdom Sardania into the kingdom of Italy; and (iii) resulting from the Paris Peace Conference of 1919. However, use of this method was surprisingly infrequent given the allies' war aims: only six plebiscites were carried out, four to define the parts of the new Germany's border and two to define the parts of the new Austria's border.

The object of the plebiscites was to do as little injustice as possible by ensuring that at least the majority in a given area is satisfied. It did not try to eliminate minorities, given the mixture of nation in some parts of Europe, that would have been impossible. But it was hoped that the minority treaties would give adequate protection to the group caught on the wrong side of a new political boundary.

Holding plebiscite has always been a difficult task. This had been the reason for the infrequent use of plebiscites in 1919. "Which areas are polled and how the vote is aggregated and interpreted will affect the result." The simplest method which is often used for plebiscite is the majority method whereby a province is polled and the whole area is allocated on the basis of which rival state obtains most votes. It was on this basis in 1921 Sopron was allocated to Hungary despite many localities voting to join Austria. The creation of such 'national minorities' can be lessened by defining different zones in a province and allowing majorities in the different zones to opt for different state membership. This was applied in Schlesurg where one zone opted to join Germany and the other to join Denmark.

A more sensitive method is to allow minor border adjustments on the basis of the polling returns. This was done in Allenstein and Marienwerder in locating the boundary between Germany and Poland.

Clearly nationalism in practice was not as simple as the theory of nation self-determination applies. If the rulers for Sapron had been applied to Upper Silesia, for instance, the whole province would have gone to Germany. But there were many more problems which we can only begin to appreciate this far away in time and space. Perhaps, the most basic question is that who is entitled to vote in such plebiscites? This problem is yet to be solved because no standard and acceptable criterion has been found out. In any case can a plebiscite ever be entirely fair when one of the two competing states has recently had sovereignty over the province/territory being polled? Plebiscite which was to be held in Kashmir as per the 1949 UN Resolution to decide the political destiny of the Kashmiris, could not be held as substantial part of it went under Pakistan's occupation and the remaining was under Indian control. Pakistan was to have left the occupied part followed by Indian pullout as per the Resolution. But, neither India nor Pakistan complied with the UN Resolution, as a result plebiscite could not be held there.

The Refugee Problem

"Since the end of the World War II, migratory movements on a quite unprecedented scale have occurred throughout the world. Millions of people have been driven from their houses and the population structure of the entire countries radically changed. Political upheavals involving the redrawing of frontiers, transfer of sovereignty and changes of regime have forced entire populations into exile and caused mass movements far in excess of those normally resulting from supply and demand on the world employment market."

Each year, since the end of the World War II, millions of people are forced for political and cultural reasons, to leave their homelands and try luck either in the neighbouring states or elsewhere. These people, displaced from their homelands, and taking shelter in the neighbouring states or elsewhere, are known as the 'refugees' who tend to constitute the 'stateless' people in the states where they have been granted asylum. The refugee problem is the worst type of problem for the mankind.

There is a clearcut contrast/difference between free migration in which groups seek opportunity not available in their homeland and forced migration, in which groups may be fleeing active persecution or escaping an environment so difficult that they must relocate in order to find an acceptable existence. It is this forced migration which leads to the refugee problem for the neighbouring areas.

There are two German terms, being used for the displaced/uprooted people:

(a) 'Vertriebenen' are those people who have been forced to flee, usually by government action. The most recent example is that of the Chakma people, a Buddhist community in Bangladesh who have been forced by the Bangladesh government to flee to the neighbouring Tripura state of India. The Chakma refugees have put a great strain on the economy of the state government. It is on the humanitarian ground that no government decides on pushing back the refugees to their homeland. It is the national minorities which are the worst victims of forced migration. The Tutsi people of Rwanda who constitute the principal national minority in the country have been forced by the government of the Hutu people who are the majority community in the state. Forced migration of the Tutsi people has created the refugee problem of unspecified dimension for the neighbouring Zaire that the UNO has been obliged to be involved in the massive relief and rescue operation.

'Vertriebenen' can also be found within the country, particularly in the multiethnic/multiracial states where the demographically superior people forcefully displace the numerically inferior people from their homeland; for instance, the Nagas are forcing the Kukis fleeing their home area in Nagaland; the Khasi people are displacing by force the non-Khasi people from Meghalaya and the best example is that of the Kashmiri Hindus, who have been forced by the majority Muslim people to flee to neighbouring areas of Himachal Pradesh, Haryana and Delhi.

(b) 'Fluchtlinge' are the people who fled. They might have been forcibly expelled had they remained long enough; on the other hand, they might have been subject to political and other disabilities had they stayed. Large number of Tibetans fled to India before the Chinese authorities started their operation in the early 1950s. Even, the Sikhs and the Bengali Hindus migrated to India before the Pakistan authorities initiated action against them. Each day, a large number of Cubans are fleeing to the USA by small boats, just to escape the persecution by the communist regime there.

The Palestinian Arabs were a 'Vertriebenen' as they were forced to flee to the neighbouring Arab states of Jordan and Syria by the Jewish state of Israel. Now, with the self-rule being granted to them as a result of 'Peace Accord' between the PLO and Israel, the Palestinian Arab refugees have started coming back to the West Bank and the Gaza Strip.

It has been found that to some extent the refugees have been able to join their own people, or least, to become part of groups whose language and culture they shared. Thus, the Sikh and Bengali refugees from Pakistan were able to join their own people, at least in terms of religion, culture and language, and, tradition in India. This 'assimilation', in due course of time, grew into what may be called the 'fellow-feeling' particularly in the Punjab area, which ultimately led to the birth of the Sikh nationalism, and that sought to perpetuate 'Khalistan' in the 1980s. So, it can be said that much of the crisis in Punjab was a natural outcome of the relocation and resettlement of the Sikh refugees there and which have till recently, a diabolic impact on the nation-building process in the country, and thus on the power-potential of the Indian State.

People who are forced to migrate on political grounds/reasons are called political refugees, i.e., the people who do not share the political ideology or political creed, or renounce to subscribe to the political philosophy. Large number of Chinese fled to Taiwan because they renounced the communist regime in the mainland, notwithstanding, their cultural affinity with the people of the mainland. Cubans and Vietnamese are fleeing to the USA in large number because they do not accept the dominant political creed of the communist regimes of their respective states.

People who are forced to flee on religious/linguistic/racial/cultural/ethnic grounds are called the 'national' refugees, because it is the dominant 'nation' which forces the national minorities to flee or migrate elsewhere. The Hindu who fled from Pakistan to India, and the Muslims who migrated to Pakistan from India in 1947 were national refugees because religion was the foremost expression of both Hindu and Muslim cultures. The Tutsi refugees in Zaire and Uganda are national refugees as they have been forced to flee from their homeland in Rwanda by the majority Hutu people. The Palestinian Arabs displaced by the Jewish from the Palestinian region tended to constitute the national refugees in the neighbouring Arab states of Jordan and Syria.

The total influence of such movements of people on the power-potential of states, both those from which the refugees come and those to which they go, is difficult to measure. The refugees are a heavy and almost insupportable burden on the states that receive them. It is impossible for Zaire to cope with the Tutsi refugee problem without the UN help. India is yet to recover from the economic 'injury' which it suffered as a result of the massive influx of the refugees from East Pakistan (now Bangladesh) during the liberation movement there; followed by the war in 1971. Continuous flow of refugees, putting unprecedented strain on the economy and the people as well, that gradually reduces the power-potential of the state. The power-potential of the state also suffers when a skilled community of a state, whether constituting the national minority or not, is forced to migrate/flee to another country. The influx of skilled workers from former German Democratic Republic, under threat and duress to the erstwhile Federal Republic of Germany, certainly added to its power-potential while it caused a loss to the power-potential of the former German Democratic Republic.

Language

Language is probably the single most important cultural index. Each language has its unique way of dealing with facts, ideas and concepts, so that exact translation from one language to another is virtually impossible. Language expresses culture, and it affects thought and action. Many linguistics and psychologists argue that as language structures logic and perception, it conditions a people's view of reality. A community of language defines a group within which basic communication is eased.

With the decline of emotional religion, language has become the chief determinant of nation. It is a source of common tradition and sentiment, a source of cultural unity far more powerful than race, with which it may have no close affinity. The creation of political frontiers and the national or official languages, diffused by the press, radio, television, literature and schools, has affected the linguistic pattern of the world; linguistic uniformity has increased behind national frontiers, and languages of important powers have become international.

The languages of the world are extremely diverse; today they number over 3000 and often contain numerous dialects. Many languages belong to the same stock or family, they have common descent; the Indo-European, Semities Dravidian and Malayo-Polynesian families are well known examples. Some language families are spoken by hundreds of millions of people but others by only a few thousand. In the New World there are more than 1000 different languages belonging to over 125 families. They contrast immensely with the Indo-European family which is probably spoken by more than 1000 million people, and has nine sub-groups as under:

1. Germanic, including English, German, Dutch, Flemish and Scandinavian languages.
2. Romanic or Latin, including French, Spanish, Portuguese, Galicians, Catalan, Italian and Rumanian.
3. Celtic including Gaelic, Erse, Welsh and Breton.
4. Slovanic including Russian, Polish, Czech, Slovak, Slovene, Serbo-Croat and Bulgarian.
5. Baltic including Lithuanian and Lettish.
6. Greek.
7. Albanian.
8. Armenian.
9. Indo-Iranian, including Persian, Kurdish, and many modern languages of India.

It is indeed a reality that languages have changed over generations. Many of these changes are due to inventions, and many are due to changing modes of life. Languages are intimately related to the environment and to man's activities.

Linguistic homogeneity is more a factor for national unity, and thus, an intrinsic element for power-potential. A state with a common language that engulfs the entire territory, usually develops an extraordinarily durable *raison d'etre*, and a sustainable state idea. But multilingualism presents great difficulties to unifying any state's population, and each state must devise a way of dealing with linguistic diversity among its population. In a multilingual state, each linguistic group seeks to perpetuate its distinctiveness over other linguistic groups which normally leads to 'hardened' linguistic 'cleavages', risking the *raison d'etre* of the state. It is generally difficult for a multilingual state to develop a state idea unique to its linguistic-territorial pattern. The resultant effect is that of political disaster.

Many states grant equal status to two or even more national languages. If the languages are distinctively regional, a federal system of government can recognize this linguistic pattern. Such polyglot states often select one language, however, as official for the federal centre and in communications among the state components. The predominance of Hindi in India is a self-evident extra constitutional fact despite the constitutional guarantee of equality for each of the fourteen other official languages. The Swiss Constitution recognizes four national languages (German, French, Italian, and Romanch) but only three official languages (German, French, and Italian). The Canadian Constitution recognizes two national languages, English and French, which are mutually so exclusive as to have consistently threatened the *raison d'etre* of the country.

India's linguistic problems are the most complex in the world, and the problem of communication among the Indian population is staggering. There are more than 845 census recorded languages of which fourteen are constitutionally recognized official languages, which are mutually unintelligible, unrecognizable, and exclusive. Each language is distinctively regional and tradition-bound, and speaks of a *genre de vie* (way of life). Therefore, each has its own literature, periodicals and broadcasts.

The 1950 Indian Constitution proclaimed Hindi as the Official language to be used in federal administration and publications. And within a stipulated period of fifteen years from the proclamation, English would be replaced by Hindi as a medium of expression for all elements of the composite culture of India. But, when the time came to replace English with Hindi, it simply could not be done because the non-Hindi speaking people of the major regions resisted it. Linguistic riots broke out particularly in the South where the people saw Hindi as rooted only in the North and they suspected Hindi supporters of promoting their language only to achieve linguistic-political-economic domination over the South, while the people of the Hindi belt felt that the retention of English would give the southerners an edge over them in matters of politics, employment and business. A subsequent compromise solution, the official Language Bill of 1967, provided for the continued use of English as an associate language of the federal government. The discontinuance of English must be approved by the legislature of each state in which Hindi is not the official language because otherwise these states would feel that they had lost their position vis-a-vis the federal government. However, the non-Hindi linguistic states have not approved the discontinuance of English yet. Each linguistic state now jealously cultivates its own language to such an extent that it has yielded to subnational movements, much to the detrimental of the *raison d'etre* of the Indian Union. It is the English language which cuts across the linguistic cleavages, bringing them together under a common system.

The issue of official language in a plural society is both highly practical and highly emotional. Controversy on this point has in many states aroused more passion than any other aspect of nation-building. Whatever solution is chosen, some resentment remains. If the native language of one group is chosen, whether that group constitutes a majority or minority of the population, all other groups suffer some disadvantages. The most obvious disadvantage is the need to learn a second language to compete for access to the state political, administrative and economic power structure. Any individual's career opportunity depends on the language(s) in which he is competent. In Canada, for instance, both English and French are official languages, but English is so prevalent that French-speakers feel discriminated against. Nearly two-thirds of Canadians are native English speakers.

A language which dominates in a national political and economic structure may slowly diffuse throughout the national space and eventually come to be accepted by all. The many regional dialects spoken in what is today's France all succumbed to the language of Paris as Paris rose to political and economic pre-eminence and supremacy throughout the seventeenth and eighteenth centuries.

If a foreign language is chosen as official language, which perhaps the modern minority segment of the population prefers, psychological problems arise. Nationalists in former colonial territories find themselves having to express their new nationalism in the language of their former masters. Majority of the African states do still use English or French as an official language. Arabic is official of the other remaining states. Most Latin American states retained Spanish when they achieved independence and Brazil retained Portuguese.

Differences in language contributed significantly to the political differences between West Pakistan and East Pakistan, and the latter ultimately emerged as a sovereign independent state. Language differences have caused political disorder in Sri Lanka, where the Tamils have bitterly resisted the imposition of the Sinhalese over them, resulting into a fierce civil war between the Tamil and the Sinhalese peoples which now largely threatens the integrity of the state. In Indonesia, there are at least 30 main languages belonging to the Malayo-Polynesian, Melanesian and Paupau groups and where Malay is the *lingua franca.* As a result, there is considerable tension in the society. Language is, therefore, the most important factor in measuring the effectiveness of national unity, and, thus the power-potential of the state. High degree of uncertainty in the geography of Indian federalism may be attributed to the territorially-grouped linguistic diversities.

Religion

Zelinsky has once noted that "among the multiple definitions of religion we must include: a mental complex..., a highly diversified body of customs...; a formal institution, i.e., Church, or denomination; and a group of persons sharing some degree of religious identity by virtue of tradition or common observance." There is no denying that religion once formed the basis for the growth of 'nation', or, in other words, the birth of 'nation' in the eighteenth and nineteenth centuries was centered round the religion because it provided the most frequent and obvious sign of social cohesion. Religion is expressed through custom, tradition and iconography which set for the attitude and perception and the *genre de vie* of the people.

However, religion has ceased to be an important factor in national unity over much of the world. The more developed states have neither a state church nor a state religion. But in some under-developed and developing regions, religion still provides either a cohesive force or a divisive force. Several countries of the Middle East have governments that are so closely related to the state church/religion that it is unclear where the rule of one ends and the other begins. Such states are called 'theocracies'. These states are extremely resistant to social change, and some of their local laws and customs are reminiscent of medieval behaviour.

Although it does not match linguistic diversity, the diversity of religion is considerable. The four great world religions—Christianity, Islam, Hinduism and Buddhism—certainly incorporate a large proportion of mankind (Fig. 8.2). It is true that Islam, Hinduism and Buddhism (often combined with Tooism, Shintoism and Confucianism) have more or less compact spheres, on which Christianity has failed to make any deep penetration despite its spread to most other parts of the world; but in certain localities the pattern of religion is so complex that cartographic representations are extremely difficult and problematical. The Middle East is one such locality/region which has been a seat of four different but mutually inclusive religions (Zoroastranism, Judaism, Christianity and Islam) as well as a scene of religious conflicts and of sectarian divisions. Another is Kashmir which is spatially divided between Is-

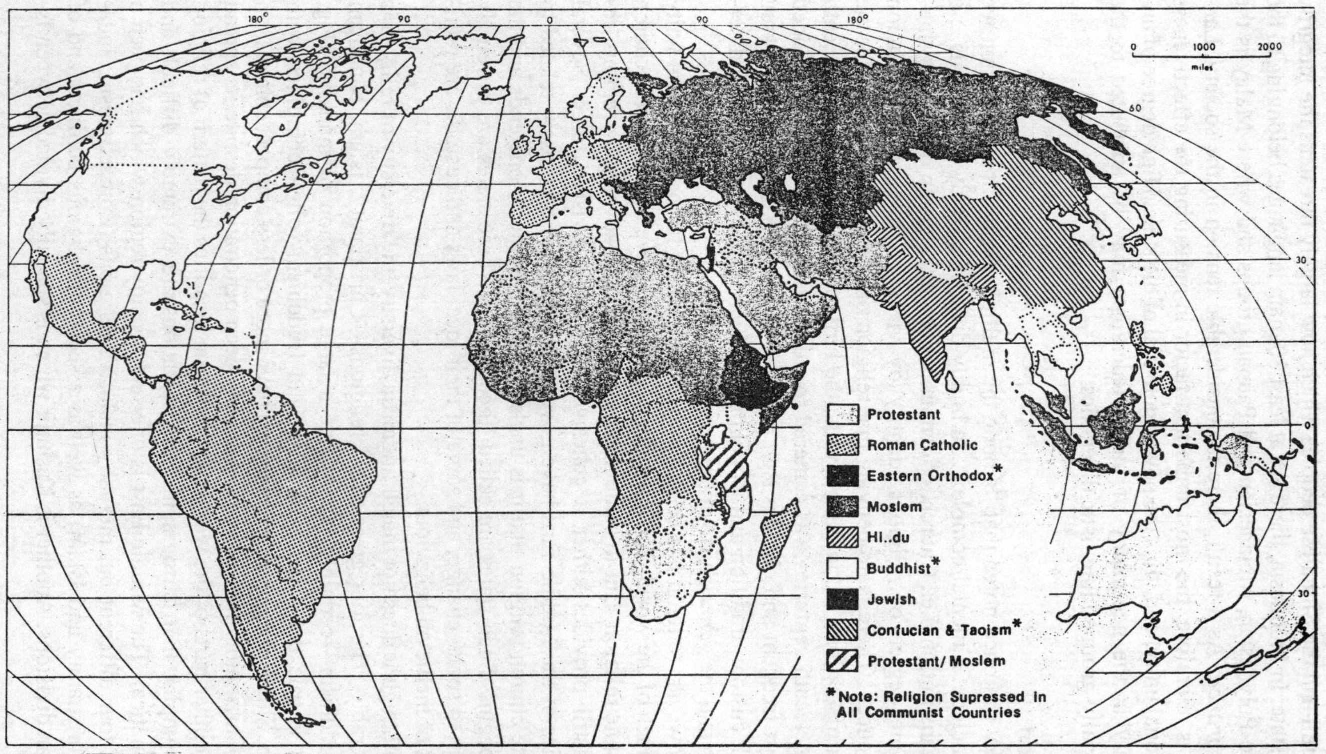

Figure 8.2: Religions of the World. In many areas of the world, religion is not a strong political influence, and thus this map is somewhat misleading. For example, the most prominent religion is shown on the map for each country even though it may not include a majority of the people of the country. In addition, religion is suppressed in all Communist countries. (Source: UNESCO)

lam, Hinduism and Buddhism. A third region is South India and Sri Lanka, where Buddhists, Hindus, Christians and Muslims are all found in large numbers. It should be stressed that although the broad pattern of the main religions has appeared to remain fairly stable during this century, it is far from static; most religions are, on the one hand gaining converts but also losing agnostics, atheists, humanists, rationalists, etc. The southward spread of Islam in Africa is remarkably swift, particularly since decolonization and political independence.

Each major religion is subdivided: Christianity is divided into the Roman Catholic, Orthodox, Coptic and Protestant; Islam is primarily split between Sunni and Shia; Hinduism is divided into caste structure; Buddhism is similarly shattered. But sectarianism goes much deeper.

Indeed the identity of a religion with an ethnic group can have very significant political-territorial implications. The fact that Catholic Ireland was ruled by Protestant England: that Catholic Poland was partitioned between Lutheran Prussia and Orthodox Russia, and a number of such examples can be found in the past to reveal that religion had always been a major cause of regional tension and internal strife. It is indeed a reality that religion had caused more wars than another single factor except hunger. Religion has always remained a motivating factor for population migrations. Most of the large population migrations in the past were engineered by religious passion that people were persecuted on religious grounds.

Divisions within the main religions are a separatist force, help in the formation of distinct cultural nuclei, and may become a source of national weakness. Few states are fortunate enough to possess religious uniformity: the Scandinavian countries are amongst the most homogeneously Protestant and the Iberian and Latin American countries the most homogeneously Catholic. These states, therefore, have evolved 'state-ideas' unique to their territorial-religious structure, and strong *raison d'etre* for them. In contrast, the Catholic-Protestant splits are strong in Canada and the United States and significant in the United Kingdom, Australia and New Zealand, and Hindu-Muslim rifts in India.

Multireligious structure presents great difficulties in unifying any state's population, and each state must devise a way of dealing with religious diversity among its population. If the religious diversity is regional and religions are mutually exclusive and unintelligible, then the situation is potentially dangerous for the survival of the state. Each religion in the state seeks to perpetuate its distinctiveness and that hardens the 'cleavage' which resists the dynamism of religious tolerance.

Most of the multireligious states, therefore, have switched over to the federal polity with a view to recognize the territorial pattern, arising out of the religious diversity. Such polyglot states offer equal opportunity to all religious communities irrespective of their numerical strength. This is the way that the multireligious states have developed their *raison d'etre* vis-a-vis the state idea. The predominance of Hinduism in India does not mean that the Indian state seeks to perpetuate Hinduism at the cost of religious minorities. The Indian Constitution undertakes to assure full and complete protection to all inhabitants without distinction of religion. Nevertheless, the Hindu-Muslim strife in India has added a new dimension to the political geography of India, which has caused a major risk to its *raison d'etre*, and thus to its power-potential.

Migration

Migration, like fertility and mortality, holds a place of prominence in a geographical analysis of population change in any area. It cannot be considered a mere shift of people from one place of residence to another as it is most fundamental to the understanding of continuously changing space-content and space-relationships of an area. Migration of people may be considered as an instrument of cultural diffusion and social integration that results into more meaningful distribution of population.

Human history has been marked by migrations from densely population areas to sparse, from regions of low resources to regions more plentifully endowed, from persecution and oppression to supposed freedom and peace. In the past, before the system of states had crystallized, whole ethnic communities or nations migrated, whereas in modern times, it has been only a minority of any nation that moves.

It was during the Reformation Movement in Europe, a substantial number of European people migrated to North America. They migrated there in search of freedom and peace and where they permanently settled. Since they brought with them the heritage of craftsmanship, they used it there and set forth a new social order. It has been estimated that in a little over a century, from 1821 to 1932, almost 60 million persons migrated. Most, perhaps about 98 per cent of the total, were of European origin and the bulk of the remainder were from India and Japan. And most, about 90 per cent, went to the Americas—the majority of those to the United States. An examination of the countries from which these migrants came and of the dates of their emigration reveals that the 'political' factor was not the most important one causing for their migration. It seemed that the most migration during the period took place because the migrants own countries were too 'crowded' to offer them sustenance, and they migrated with the consent of their respective governments.

Overcrowding, accompanied by food shortages and natural calamities, seemed to have caused large scale migration to under-populated area in the eighteenth and nineteenth centuries. However, migration for political reasons was important after the suppression of the European risings in 1848 but did not again become the dominant motive until the period of the World War II.

Indians during the British period, in large numbers migrated to sparsely populated British-held East African territories where they started plantations and were involved in petty local trade. The migration was economically motivated and 'state sponsored'. Once Indian immigrants in East African seaboard states did constitute major communities. Chinese who spread through Southeastern Asia and today constitute the majority of the population in Singapore and large minorities elsewhere. Migration in the preceding centuries was a means of relieving population pressure in crowded countries and of increasing the population in the underpopulated countries.

It is indeed a reality that migrations from overcrowded states to underpopulated states have greatly helped the latter, particularly in the resource mobilization, provided the migrants get mixed up with the peoples of the states. Indian migrants have largely helped the East African seaboard states in their resource mobilization efforts and economic development. However, the Indians were expelled from these East African states on the alleged charges of having persistently exploited the local people. Similarly, Chinese migrants helped built the economy of Malaysia and Singapore. Migration is age selective and mostly the younger people do migrate. If the migrants, mostly consisting of younger population, and the states where they migrate, have ageing population, then the immigrants can prove to be an asset for the states particularly in terms of resource generation vis-a-vis economic development.

However, there are also social and economic obstacles to migration. In general states with a higher standard of living do not welcome immigrants from countries with a lower standard because the immigrants would be a burden on the economy and society. Australia excluded people with a relatively low standard of living and still tends to do so in spite of its very real need for greater population. Latin America is the only continent which has space and the rather tolerant political and social attitude toward certain migrants that makes possible a large scale movement of people. But here too, immigration from Asia and Africa is severely discouraged because of the low standard of living of the immigrants who are of no use in the economic development, rather they would be a burden on the society and economy. Immigration is now strictly controlled in the USA, Canada and also in the United kingdom. They have devised a quota system which would permit only a handful of immigrants per year from those countries of the periphery which are most overcrowded and economically underdeveloped.

Since the Second World War, major migrations were of political nature and had intrinsic impact on the power-potential of both the emigrating and immigrating countries. If the emigrating population is of 'high quality', it reduces the power-potential of the state which it leaves, but adds to the power-potential of the state where it goes. The Jewish migration to the United States is an example that it has enhanced the technological capacity of the United States. Similarly, if the migrants are able to join their own people or become part of groups whose religion and culture they share, then it also adds strength to the state, and particularly to the nation. The Jewish State—Israel—was born in this way. Similarly, the Sikh migrants in the Punjab following the partition in 1947, helped built the economy of the state, and the country as well.

Migration is a factor of population growth. It has been observed that if the immigrating people belong to different 'nations' other than the 'nation' of the immigrating state, and at the same time have higher growth rate, then soon the immigrants would outnumber the original inhabitants/nation, making them minority or forcing them to flee. Migration tends to create complex demographic pattern which makes profound impact on the unity/integrity of the immigrating state; for instance, continuous influx of population from neighbouring states into India has put a diabolic impact on the nation-building process, thus on its national power. Internal migration has considerable impact on the power-potential of the state. Government-controlled westward migration in China has largely enhanced its power-potential because more resources have been discovered and mobilized which have their impact on balanced economic development. But, in India internal migration has widened regional imbalances. People from Bihar and other backward states are migrating to the developed states like Punjab, Haryana, etc., where they have made the economy sustainable by their 'labour' but the immigrants own states are suffering mostly, thus intensifying the core-periphery conflict in the Indian economy/system.

The most frequently coined phrase for environmentally induced population migration is 'environmental refugees'. It has been noted that throughout the Third World land degradation has been the main factor within migration of subsistence farmers into the slums and shanty towns of major cities, producing desperate populations vulnerable to disease and natural disasters and prove to participate in crime and civil strife. Such exodus exacerbates the already dire urban problems. There is the copious evidence that carrying capacity of many life-supporting systems is being overloaded to a breaking point and where such systems have collapsed, the option for the poor are either to flee or stay and starve. The term 'environmental refugees' can also be used to people who are evacuated from their homes due to large development projects or because of industrial accidents and disasters.

Thus, the category of 'environmental refugees' was expanded to include a variety of forced migrants, including internal or international migrants, temporary or permanent migrants. Some migrants are economic more than political refugees, namely, people who are motivated more by the 'pull' forces of their destination as opposed to the 'push' forces which drive genuine refugees out of their houses. The three most frequent types of 'environmental refugees' can be identified as under:

(a) those temporarily displaced as a result of sudden environmental change such as natural or industrial disaster;
(b) those permanently displaced through long-term or irreversible environment change, such as those forced to move by dam construction or desertification; and
(c) those who leave in search of a better quality of life, an environmental degradation has eroded their resources base.

However, in many cases, a non-sustainable use of renewable resources eventually led to conflict over scarce resources and to the migration of those who could no longer live off the land, forests or fish stocks. Another question

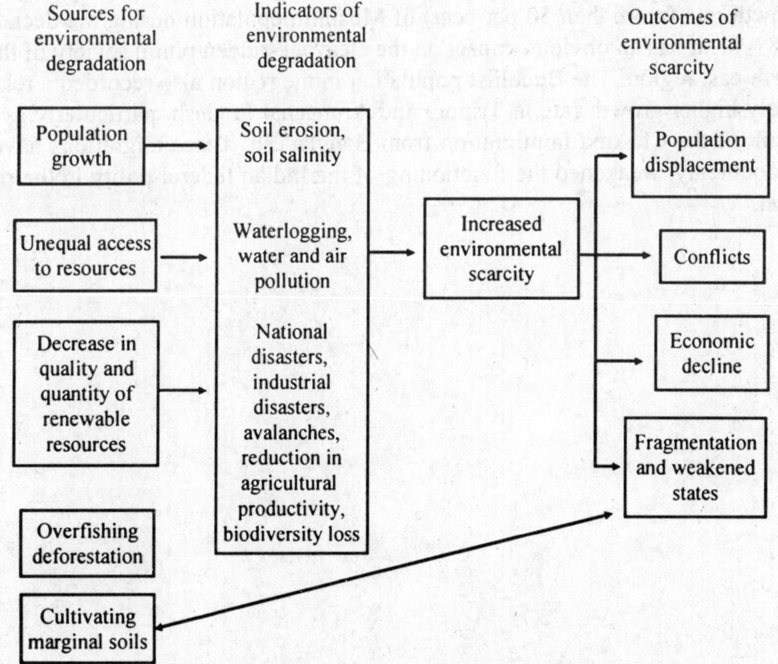

Figure 8.3: Linkages between Environmental Degradation, Migration and Conflict

to debate is the issue of possible linkage between the levels of impoverishment of the peripheral countries and their involvement in conflict—inside and outside their borders.

Kliat (1955) attempts to explore the three-fold linkage among migration, environmental degradation and intense security and stability through a model (Fig.8.3). The model can be explained in term of 'strained' India-Bangladesh relations because of enormous Bangladeshi migration to the nearby Indian states of north-eastern region. Population growth and density in Bangladesh is amongst the highest in the world and recurrent natural disasters such as floods and cyclones and resource scarcity push out hundreds of thousands people to nearby and better off Indian State. Some 12-17 million Bangladeshi migrants have already moved to India and caused shift in the ethnic balance within the seven states of the north-eastern region and repeatedly led to violent insurgency and ethnic strife between 1980 and 1990.

The continuous inflow of Bangladeshi migrants into the north-eastern region has substantially changed the demographic pattern; for example, Assam, Aurnachal Pradesh, Mizoram and Nagaland registered a relatively higher growth rate (more than 50 per cent) of Muslim population during the decade 1981-91. It has an obvious impact on the cleavage-ridden plural society of the north-east region. The Buddhist population in the region also recorded a relatively higher growth rate in Tripura and Arunachal Pradesh, particularly as a result of the Chakma immigration from Bangladesh. These migrations have, undoubtedly, weakened the functioning of the Indian federal-polity in the region.

Chapter 9

Resources, Development and Power

"It is important to consider the population of a state, its efficiency and effectiveness, without, at the same time, discussing the natural resources which are available for its use. People must have land on which to live and to grow their food. Almost all human food is derived directly from the soil, and its volume and quality depend directly on the extent and nature of the soil. The cultivable soil must then be regarded as a primary resource in the estimate of national power... Beneath the soil are minerals minerals...and some of these minerals are important for human welfare and essential in national defence... A state which lacks the more important minerals or which has only small reserves may feel especially vulnerable... So, in order to be considered in the military power-potential of the state, the resources must be developed..." (Pounds, 1972).

Thus, we find a 'cause and effect' relationship between the resources, their development and the power-potential, and a state, with a higher degree of desirability of resource mobilization and development, acquires a greater amount of economic strength. "Economic strength has always been an instrument of political power, if only through its association with the military."

Before examining the relationship between the resources, their development, and the power-potential of a state, we must first define 'resource', 'development' and 'power' in general and then attempt to seek a definition of resources within the context of political geography.

"A resource is a concept employed to denote sources of human satisfaction, wealth or strength. Labour, entrepreneurial skills, investment funds, fixed capital assets, technology and the cultural and physical attributes of an area may all be referred to as resources of a nation." The word 'development' here means, "a process of becoming and a potential state of being." The achievement of a state development would enable individuals to discover, identify and mobilize resources and to make their own histories and geographies under conditions of their choosing. The process of development is the means by which conditions of human existence may be achieved. They, in turn, would necessarily involve people in a productive, crisis-free and non-exploitative set of relations with nature and in the struggle to remove oppression and exploitation from the relations between themselves."

The term 'power' is the ability to achieve certain ends, often used as a synonym for such characteristics as capacity, skills, and talent. But, in political term, the power of a state is that "which permits participation in the making of decision". Political power is of two kinds. It consists first in the ability to make and enforce decision inside the boundaries of the state, and second, power consists in the ability to make decision and implement them in fields which either be geographically outside the boundaries of the state or impinge on the interests of other states.

However, power of the former kind is dependent on the political structure of the state. It has nothing to do with the state's intrinsic wealth and resources. But, in international politics, power is basically related to the area, population resources, their development and industrial potential of the state as modified by geographical location and level of technology. The basis of political power in this context is fundamentally 'geographical'.

As we have general definitions for resources, development, and power, it is now almost clear that any definition of resources, within the purview of political geography, must be done in the context of the power-potential of the state, particularly that power which enables the state to make decisions and implement them in fields, lying geographically outside the boundaries of it, or the ability/capacity of the state to impose its will on its neighbours, or the capacity to interfere in the decision-making process of its neighbours. The power, which enables the state to make its decisions felt on the neighbouring states or states lying outside its geographical boundaries, requires some form of strategy. "The strategy is the art of using power for the attainment of goals in competition." National strategy has been adopted in preference to 'grand strategy' or 'global strategy', for a nation's strategy may be neither grand nor global. To speak of national strategy does not imply a genre of strategy peculiar to a state, though to be sure, no two nation-states can have identical national strategies, if for no other reason than that they are geographically distinct. The national strategy is not necessarily wrought with logic. "It may contain as much prejudice as plan. If a plan exists, rarely will it be consistently followed."

Stephen B. Jones (1954), therefore, defines resources, within the context of political geography, as "anything a nation has, can obtain, or can conjure up to support its strategy...for resources are as tangible as soil, as intangible as leadership, as measurable as population, as difficult to measure as patriotism.

There is no common unit, and no statistical summation is possible".

Classification of Resources

Stephen B. Jones (1954) has provided a five-fold classification of degrees of availability of resources, within a temporal framework, i.e., the time aspect of availability. The classification is as follows:

1. *Power resources available immediately*. These include active mines and factories which are already producing objects with immediate power-potential, such as steel sheet and chemical fertilizer.
2. *Resources available only after activation*. Among such resources would be standby equipment and any plant not currently in production. In a sense, these resources also include the mothball fleet. The time required for activation varies from a few hours to several weeks according to the need for 'warming up'. An integrated steel works might require two or three weeks before full production could be reached.
3. *Resources available only after conversion*. An automobile factory could turn from the production of cars to that of light trucks after retooling which might take many months unless jigs and other equipment had been prepared in advance. Similarly, most factories producing consumer goods could convert to the manufacture of goods having power-potential only after considerable time lag.
4. *Resources available only after development*. These include fuel resources or ore deposits known to exist but awaiting the opening of a mine or the construction of a processing plant. Such development may well take several years, it is not uncommon, for example, for the opening of a new coal mine—particularly a deep one—to cover a period of four or five years. It is unlikely, therefore, that such undeveloped resources would be taken into consideration in making political decisions. The decision to resort to war, for example, is likely to be made only in the light of resources that are already in some phase of development. On the other hand, if a war should last longer than the protagonists at first expected it to, it is likely that resources, undeveloped at the start, would be exploited before the conclusion. The construction of such highways as the Burma Road or the Alaskan Highway are, in effect, wartime resource developments which were not wholly anticipated when the war began, as also was the development of the atomic bomb. Germany's development of domestic iron ores and her use of coal for making petroleum are further examples of the wartime development of resources.
5. *Hypothetical resources*. Coal, petroleum, ore bodies and other resources whose existence is only presumed but not proved cannot be said to have any power value. No political authority is likely to count on them unless

careful investigation has at least raised them to the level of category 4 above. To this category must also belong the future development of cheap nuclear power, the harnessing of the tide, and the use of other such potential resources.

No state ever completely utilizes every potential resource available to it. There is always a person, material, or machine that could be better employed. Sherman Kent has applied three distinct terms of these, underutilized resources as 'fat', 'slack' and 'flexibility'. Other factors being equal, an advantage lies with a state that has the most underemployed resources. The wealthier, more highly developed industrial nations are usually better positioned in this respect. Britain had, at the start of World War II, extensive external assets, a large merchant marine, access to necessary raw material and the credits to buy them without going into current production, a large and up-to-date supply of capital equipment, a large inventory of finished goods, a national diet of three to four thousand calories per day etc. Important elements of German 'fat' may be said to have existed in the excess capacity of machine tools, a large amount of brand new plant and new housing. The Italians had practically no 'fat', indeed little enough lean. The United States, for instance, has a great reservoir of fat in the form of educated, skilled, and capable retirees who can quickly re-enter the workforce if needed. Unused factory space, and capital in the form of machines and money, also are present in quantity. Each of these items may be called upon immediately to strengthen the political power of the state.

'Slack' is a term applied to resources that are not fully utilized. While full utilization of resources is never possible for an extended period of time, it can be a crucial factor in time of national need. The larger the educated and trained manpower base, the greater the potential slack that exists. Industrial plants operating at less than full capacity, such as those using one shift instead of three, represent slack. States employing their total productive capacity may find themselves unable to meet additional challenges.

'Flexibility' is a quality closely related to fat, slack and the national attitude toward adjustment. To Kent, "flexibility means the ability to make typewriter factories over into machine gun factories...ability to make synthetics from scratch where natural resources have dried up". Since no state can remain constantly on a war footing, the ability to rapid convert from place to military readiness is imperative to state survival. Such a flexibility may take the form of substituting one material item for another, or substituting one behavioural form for another. If society is incapable of responding except in traditional patterns, the outlook can be bleak. In World War II, air power suddenly forced people to change their entire perspective of time and place. As national leaders invent and classify the resources of a state, particular weight must be given to the amount of fat, slack and flexibility available.

Sherman Kent's 'fat' and 'slack' correspond to S.B. Jones' 'resources available after activation'. Steel production, for example, is expansible in several ways. Plants may be operating below capacity. To activate this unused capacity would be taking up slack. Or they may be operated temporarily above capacity by postponing repairs. This would be using up fat. 'Flexibility' covers the two concepts of 'conversion' and 'development'. The quotation from Kent illustrates both. Making war goods in typewriter and cereal factories is conversion. Making synthetics from scratch(if the basic processes are known and not hypothetical) is development. The difference is significant because the lead-time (lead-time is a phase of the problem of potential power) of change is likely to be greater for development than for conversion and investment of money, manpower and materials larger. The expansion of steel production by building new mills is development, and involves the temporary diversion of steel from other uses.

Jones' five-fold classification of degrees of availability of resources seems to have special relevance to the core states. It is in the core states of the world economy only that resource identification, activation, conversion and development are possible because of the core processes that "consist of relations that incorporate relatively high wages, advanced technology and a diversified production mix". However, the degrees of availability of resources in the peripheral countries of the world economy normally remain very low because of the peripheral processes which "involve more rudimentary technology, low wages and simple production mix". Similarly, terms like 'fat', 'slack' and 'flexibility' are necessarily applicable to the core states of the world economy, in particular the hegemonic core powers.

Resources and National Strategy

S.B. Jones (1954) makes the following discussion under four heads in the light of the power inventory and strategic needs of the state and within the purview of the availability of resources: (i) the harmony of resources and national strategy; (ii) the augmentation or reduction of resources by national strategy; (iii) the allocation of resources in relation to national strategy; and (iv) the relativity of power in the light of national strategies. The discussion is necessarily based on the philosophy that "so long there is politics among sovereign states, there will be estimation of power in the light of the required national strategy and the availability of resources".

Harmony of Inventory Strategy

That national strategy must be in harmony with national resources may seem like a truism, but the statement is true only in general sense. It can be very misleading doctrine if resources are considered to be a fixed sum and if national strategy is conceived in strictly military terms and only in isolation. The doctrine has been used by some isolationists who argue that the United States cannot isolate itself (by means of some wonder-weapons, perhaps), but that it must isolate itself because it cannot afford a broader strategy. One possible answer of course, is to say that the broader strategy may be the cheaper in the long run. However, there may be different versions that a state must balance its commitments and its power. In other words, if two strategies appear equally good, then one must choose the cheaper.

Harmony of resources and needs may be all very well but what if a state cannot muster the force to cover its vitally necessary commitments? One answer is to recalculate the risks and cut the commitments, and the other answer is to turn to science to augment natural resources, which requires research, capital, labour and time, all of which must be comprehended in the long term national strategy.

Import and stockpiling programmes are of course, another way of augmenting a state's resources or of conserving domestic supplies. Since the United States has traditionally discouraged imports and since large stockpiles are uneconomic in a business sense, such programmes require a consciously strategic viewpoint. A state may augment its resources through the acquisition of colonies or formation of alliances. An alliance may be the only resort of a small state. In estimating the power of an alliance, due consideration must be given to strategic aspects. The power of an alliance is never the simple sum of power inventories of its members.

A state may augment its power by building up the power of its allies or, without an alliance, of its presumptive friends. This, of course, is an objective of American foreign aid programmes. The motivation of foreign aid programmes ranges from pure humanitarianism through the belief that sound independent nations are safe to the strictly military desire to build up foreign facilities and sources of supply.

Power resources can be reduced instead of augmented if the national strategy is unsound or obsolete. Clumsy diplomacy or a speech or act that is stupid in relation to foreign policy may cut national power, or looked at another way, may require an increased use of resources to achieve a given end. Wishful thinking plays a role in national strategy. A state's resources may be as effectively reduced by it as by the drainage of an oil field or a drop in the birth rate. Two ingrained American habits of mind are faith in machinery and a desire to pull back from overseas commitments. Any strategic theory that embodies or seems to embody these ideas is sure to find advocates.

The Problem of Allocation

One of the knottiest problems of national strategy is the allocation of resources between private and governmental demands and among the various branches of the government. In a democratic state, such allocations are strongly influenced by habits, moods and political pressures, held or generated by the public. Certain cliches crop up, for example, it is said that the civilian economy can bear only so much military or foreign aid expense. Pushed to the test, a state must pay the price of victory or lose.

The division of resources among the armed forces may bring up the cliches of balance which usually means that increases and cuts in the budget shall be equally shared. The argument is heard that air power has the greatest inherent capabilities of any arm because of the velocity of its vehicles and their global, three dimensional mediums of operation; the air arm should therefore receive the lion's share of appropriations. Even within an armed service we find arguments of allocation of resources. Hitler's navy was torn between the submariners and the advocates of a balanced fleet, with each side claiming that war would be lost if its counsels were not honoured.

Allocation of resources requires to be discussed only in the light of given national strategies. National strategy is to the power inventory as management is to the material inventory of a factory. Generally speaking, there are two philosophies of resource allocation. One holds that a country should cleave to the strategy that seems best in terms of its own resources. The other holds that the best strategy is always relative to opposing strategies and calls for more flexibility, or for less complete commitment to one programme. Strategic air power provides an illustration.

National power must constantly be re-evaluated in terms of the methods and instruments available to national strategy. The hegemonic core countries in the post-war period have constantly approached the problems of the allocation of resources in a more balanced and rational way so as to maintain their national strategy on a grand scale.

Allocation in Space and Time

Power resources exist in space and time. In the language of physics there are space and time dimensions of the field of power. Strategy is the art of movement in such a field. In a sense, space and time are resources. The nation having these resources can adopt strategies that would be suicidal without them. Space consumes more than time; it consumes fuel, supplies and manpower. Yet trading space for all of these is generally a sign of unpreparedness rather than of wisdom. But space and time are more than resources. They are conditions of resource allocation and use. Hence, again, the strategic ray of the power triangle is valuable. Space and time aspects may be left of an inventory. They are integral parts of national strategy.

Harold Sprout and Margaret Sprout made use of space as a strategic condition when they compared British sea power, based on an island close to the continent where the main rivals lay, with American sea power facing two broad oceans. There are three derivatives of time: velocity, pace, and timing. Velocity and space have been discussed under operational quality. Timing was implicit in the discussion of the degrees of availability of resources. Availability is strategically meaningful only in terms of how long it takes to bring a given item to the state of 'immediately available'. Locational availability also can be translated into terms of time and timing. In the Battle of Britain, radar helped the British get their planes to the right place at the right moment. One might say that radar gave the Royal Air Force (RAF) a complete picture of the space-time field which helped offset the fact that the Luftwaffe was the larger force and held the strategic initiative.

The Problem of Relative Power

That national power is always relative is almost axiomatic. A superficial approach to the relativity of power has been to compare the power inventories of the state or alliances under discussion, with emphasis upon actual or potential power according to the purpose or leanings of the writer. Such a simple method has of course, long been rejected by those more deeply concerned with the problems. No substitute formula, simple or complex, will come out. This emphasis on the interplay and strategic beams leads to greater uncertainties when two or more states are involved and considered.

Emphasis upon the strategic aspect of relative power does not render the power inventory useless. Basic data on such fundamentals as manpower, steel production and the like are indispensable, and it is generally true in world politics. ...If strategic considerations make the estimation of relative power more complex, they may compensate by making it less fatalistic. It is less necessary to kneel before statistical superiority unless the margin is great. The Free World had had no reason to fear the (erstwhile) Soviet Union-statistically. But generally the former Soviet Union had held the initiative in world affairs. If the statistically weaker state has often called the tune for the statistically stronger, a reversal of roles is at least theoretically possible.

The simplest statement about relative power is that the margin of power between A and B is more significant than the absolute power of A and B. However, one cannot express a margin of power statistically any more accurately than one can measure absolute power. Relative power is sometimes discussed as if a state had only its own resources. But tight blockade is rare. Alliances, trade with neutrals, conquests of territory, scientific substitution, all may increase relative power. On the other hand, we cannot assume that a state necessarily commands all its own resources. Some may be highly vulnerable (like the French coal fields in both the world wars); some may be withheld by public unwillingness to sacrifice; administrative clumsiness may prevent full employment of resources.

Power relations are never simple between A and B. They occur in the configuration of international politics. The gradual change from the bipolar world to the multipolar world has brought about many changes in the relative power of a large number of states. The unification of Germany has profoundly affected the relative power of France and Great Britain in the European continent but without changing the absolute power of either of these states by itself. Collapse of the Soviet bloc has largely affected the relative power of Russia in relation to the United States. The relative power of the Arab states and Israel is profoundly affected by the mere presence of the United States and its allies in the Middle East. Even weak states affect relative power if they influence when or where competitive crises arise. The weakness of the states of the Eurasian rimland is the despair of the American strategist.

If it is a margin of power that really counts, one must ask for how long a period the margin must be maintained and what for competition is taking place. In a short war, margins of skill and readiness may count far more than relative potentials. In long wars, relative potentials obviously become more significant, if the disparity in skills is not too great. In short crises not leading to war, relative diplomatic skill may be decisive.

Relative power considered item by item, must be evaluated differently if the given item is scarce or abundant. If some element is scarce, the margin between just enough and not enough may be very significant. If both parties to a competition have some item in plenty, some derivative factor may be significant. However, much more important are such derivatives as the rate of production, how much it could be increased, the manpower requirements of coal mining in the two countries, and the speed with which a hydrogeneration industry might be developed if liquid fuels run short.

However, the power inventory must be triangulated by national strategy. To extend the philosophy of relative power, not only a state's own inventory and strategy must be considered but also the inventories and strategies of the other state or states involved in the international political configuration. Theoretically in this age of global competition, this would mean sixty or more strategic beams sweeping the international skies—with an effect more dazzling than illuminating.

The complicated interrelationships of national strategies and relative power may be some what simplified if we consider national strategy to have two aspects, one of which we may call 'autonomous', the other 'responsive'. There is not a dichotomy between these but, rather, a gradation. For example, England was forced to adopt sea power as its principal weapon. In fact, there was little attempt to employ sea power independently until the reign of Henry

III. Insularity permitted the British to rely on sea power but did not command it. Similarly, the decision of Britain to maintain a fleet equal to the two closest rivals was an autonomous decision, for Britain was free to adopt a smaller or greater ratio, limited only by the willingness to risk and the willingness to sacrifice. The location of the principal British naval bases was less autonomous, it depended on the probable enemy of the period and that enemy's resources and possible strategy. The distribution of British ships among the fleets and bases was also not fully autonomous; it was responsive to the political changes and the moves of the opponents.

The autonomous aspects of national strategy are extremely important. They are the main aspects about which decisions are made in advance of conflict. These decisions are likely to be swayed by factors extraneous to the true problem. The decision of the Truman administration to take a stand on the immigration to Palestine was autonomous. Extraneous factors of domestic politics played an important part. The effect of this and subsequent decisions on American power in the Middle East was significant.

The last aspect of relative power may be called 'historical peristalsis'. In both politics and technology, change is endless but not continuous. Nor is the phase always the same from one country to another. The peristaltic changes in naval technology, the political response to such changes, and relative power relations resulting from both are necessarily significant to the power inventory and national strategy. Similar processes take place in diplomacy, propaganda and all the other implements and methods of national strategy. To use a more refined but less apt analogy, the light of the strategic beam fluctuates. Hence, the evaluation of the power inventory must change. Though a sound national strategy should reduce the wastage, strategy is not a substitute for resources but is the art of using them. Let us discuss different categories of natural resources and their relative importance in the power-potentials of states. Natural resources are commonly categorized into following:

(a) Flow (or renewable) resources, which naturally regenerate, or which can be recurrently produced to provide new supply units within a human time-span.
(b) Stock resources (minerals and land) which have taken millions of years to form and from a human perspective are fixed in supply.

"The distinction between them is blurred, however, and it is more appropriate to think of a use-renewability continuum (Fig. 9.1). At one extreme, potential supplies are naturally determined, infinitely renewable and unrelated to current usage levels. At the other, utilization massively exceeds regeneration and use is consumptive, producing unusable forms of matters and energy. Between these extremes, renewability is dependent on human decisions, future supply availabilities being determined by usage rates and investment in

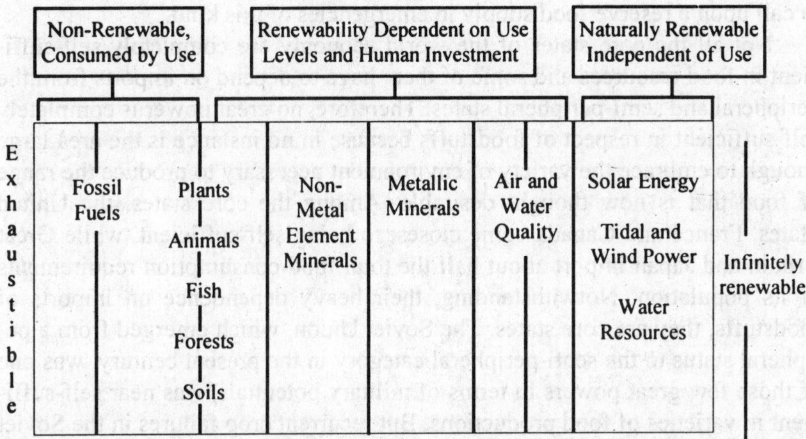

Figure 9.1: (Resource) Continum of Natural Resources (J. Rees, 1986)

artificial regeneration. All resources which reproduce biologically (including the capacity of the environment to biodegrade pollutants) can be mixed to exhaustion; soils only remain renewable if managed, and since none of the minerals are consumed by use, regeneration could theoretically occur through recycling. Infinite recycling may, however, be impossible given the laws of entropy."*

Food Resources

"Food is probably the most important of the economic elements and has become a powerful political weapon in a world torn by conflicting philosophies and doctrines. Lack of an adequate food supply, resulting in undernourishment and finally in starvation, has been one of the chief causes of unrest throughout history" (Valkenburg and Stotz, 1963). "An adequate supply of foodstuffs", says Pounds (1972), "is a condition of human welfare, and its assurance is necessarily a primary preoccupation of government. If a food supply is not assured in time of peace, it certainly would be precarious in wartime, when movement and transportation are usually more restricted and the labour force available to produce it is reduced. A state usually needs to be able

* 'Entropy' refers to a measure of the amount of uncertainty in a probability distribution or a system subject to constraints. The term originated in thermodynamics but has been used in a wide variety of contexts.

to call upon a reserve food supply in emergencies of this kind."

Not all the core states of the world economy are completely self-sufficient in food resources and some of them have to depend on imports from the peripheral and semi-peripheral states. Therefore, no great power is completely self-sufficient in respect of foodstuffs because in no instance is the area large enough to embrace the variety of environment necessary to produce the range of food that is now thought desirable. Among the core states, the United States, France and Canada come closest to being self-sufficient, while Great Britain and Japan import about half the total food consumption requirements of its population. Notwithstanding, their heavy dependence on imports of foodstuffs, they are core states. The Soviet Union, which emerged from a peripheral status to the semi-peripheral category in the present century, was one of those few great powers in terms of military potentials, was near self-sufficient in varieties of food productions. But recurrent crop failures in the Soviet Union, particularly in the 1980s, led to irregular food supplies to its people which caused heavily to it that it had to depend on imports of foodstuffs, mainly from the United States and Canada. However, the paucity of food supply, particularly in the past decade, seems to be one of the prime reasons for the collapse of the Soviet system leading to the territorial disintegration of the federation.

China and Brazil, in the semi-peripheral realm of the world economy, have made some significant progress in the production of foodgrains and other crops within their respective territories. An increase in the production of foodgrains and other crops in these two countries in the past few years has offered greater flexibility to a well balanced diet to maintain health and energy, which, in turn, has made their power-potentials more desirable in the regional power structure. India, an emergent semi-peripheral state, has achieved some 'notable' successes in its agriculture sector, particularly in the field of foodgrains production that a substantial part of Indian people now have access to a well balanced good diet to maintain their good health. It has an important bearing on the nation's image not only at the regional level but also at the global level.

It is probably true, however, that the United States, Canada, France, China, Brazil, and to some extent India, can survive without importing foodstuffs for a considerable period of time if necessary, though diets may become somewhat monotonous and some form of rationing will be unquestionably necessary. These countries have good reserve stocks of foodgrains which they have built up over years, mostly as a result of the sustained agricultural growth, followed by good harvests.

However, a large number of European countries, notably, Britain, Germany, Belgium, Switzerland, Sweden, Holland, Austria, Hungary, Poland,

Bulgaria, and some other central and eastern European countries are mostly dependent on imported foodstuffs. Under normal conditions Britain imports about half the total food consumption requirements of its population. Most of the erstwhile East European countries used to import substantial amount of foodstuffs from the former Soviet Union, particularly when the later had good harvests for successive periods. But in the 1980s when the Soviet Union faced recurrent crop failures, these states looked for the US support.

"It is not easy to quantify and compare the degree of dependence of different countries on the import of food. Statistics are, as a general rule, available on the volume and value of food imports. But food importers are all too often also food exporters. Some countries export a quality foodstuff while importing larger quantities of a similar commodity that is cheaper and of lower quality. France thus exports vintage wines, but it imports, mainly from North Africa, very much larger quantities of vin ordinaire. Again each country in general attempts to extract the maximum value from its land." Some countries have brought about significant changes in their cropping patterns, giving more of their lands to relatively valuable industrial crops. These countries now import substantial quantities of the less valuable bread crops like wheat and rice. Most of the west and central European countries fall in this category.

On the basis of the gross and the net value of agricultural imports, together with the per capita net import, Pounds (1972) attempts a classification of states into:

1. The territorially very large states have a high degree of self-sufficiency in food resources. This is because of the fact that they are large enough to embrace the variety of environment necessary to produce the range of food and that is why the net import in these states is very small or even negative.
2. The industrially developed and densely populated states of West Europe and Japan are heavily dependent on the import of food stuffs. Therefore, the net import in these states is very large.
3. Finally, the developing countries or the peripheral states, most of them are not large states and their net import of agricultural products is small and negative, are in the first category states. There is an apparent correlation between low agricultural imports per head and a low per capita national income.

However, for some large scale exporters of agricultural goods, the per capita index is, of course, negative. Some large states are making desperate attempts to increase their agricultural production through extension of farming, rehabilitation, and reclamation of marginal areas. The Chinese experiment in this regard is worth mentioning. India and Brazil are also making efforts to bring their marginal areas under cultivation. Some peripheral and semiperipheral states have witnessed agricultural revolution in their respective areas in the past decade and as a result, the agricultural production has substantially increased in these states. This phenomenal development in the agricultural sector in these states may be attributed to the increase in the infrastructural facilities in the agricultural sector. Notwithstanding the development in the agricultural sector, some of these states still depend, to a large extent on the imports which is clear from the Table 9.1.

Table 9.1
Agriculture and food

Countries	*Cereal imports (thousands of metric tons)*		*Food aid in cereals (thousands of metric tons)*		*Average index of food production per capita (1978-81=100)*
	1974	*1987*	*1974-75*	*1986-87*	*1985-87*
China	6033	15897	0	583	124
India	5261	846	1582	208	109
Brazil	2485	3871	31	07	107
Bangladesh	1866	1781	2076	1589	95
Zaire	343	415	01	56	99
Nigeria	383	677	07	0	105
Kenya	15	274	02	107	93
Pakistan	1274	378	584	456	105
Egypt	3877	9326	610	1977	106
Thailand	97	255	0	18	107
Ecuador	152	347	11	53	101
Chile	1737	249	223	18	104
Colombia	503	863	28	0	97
South Africa	127	266	-	-	84
Peru	637	1894	37	237	98

Source: World Development Report, 1989.

As is revealed from the Table 9.1 that a few peripheral and semi-peripheral states registered a fall in the import of cereals during the period mentioned while a great many of them witnessed an increase in the imports of cereals. Similarly, some states of the peripheral/semi-peripheral regions registered a rise in the food-aid imports of cereals during the period mentioned. This scenario in the food sector of these states had adverse impacts on their political situation where a degree of uncertainty prevailed in their political geography.

Table 9.2

Agriculture and food

Core states	Cereal imports (thousands of metric tons)		Food aid in cereals (thousands of metric tons)		Average index of food production per capita (1971-81 =100)
	1974	*1987*	*1974-75*	*1986-87*	*1985-87*
USA	460	1306	-	-	97
Canada	1513	447	-	-	110
France	654	1130	-	-	106
FRG	7164	4462	-	-	112
UK	7540	3722	-	-	108
Japan	19557	27795	-	-	109

Source: World Development Report, 1989.

It is clear from the Table 9.2 that while the United States, France and Japan registered an increase in cereal imports over 1974, but the remaining core states witnessed a fall in cereal imports over 1974.The increase and decrease in the cereal imports of these states may be attributed to the changing nature of the cropping pattern over the period. However, all the states in this category experienced no food-aid in cereals. This was an important factor in their power-potentials. Notwithstanding their dependence on imports, these states still hold the key to the destiny of the world.

The average annual agricultural growth rate in all the core states has registered an appreciable increase during 1980-81.This was largely as a result of the development of infrastructural facilities in the agricultural sector. However, the average annual agricultural growth rate in peripheral/semi-peripheral states during the period was not encouraging during this period which is clear from the Table 9.3.

Table 9.3 depicts that the financial involvement in the agricultural sector had been substantially increased during 1970-87 and the period also witnessed a substantial increase in the fertilizer consumption in all the states. But surprisingly, the annual average agricultural growth rate for some peripheral/ semi-peripheral states was not encouraging, notwithstanding their best efforts. The food productions in these states were intrinsically fluctuating in nature, often leading to heavy imports putting strain on the foreign exchequer. Such a situation in the 1980s witnessed the rise of 'neo-colonialism', i.e., political independence of the periphery tempered by (economic) dependence on the core for survival.

Table 9.3
Agricultural growth

States	*Value added in agriculture (millions of Current dollars)*		*Fertilizer consumption (hundreds of grams per hectare of arable land)*		*Average annual growth rate (per cent)*	
	1970	*1987*	*1970*	*1986*	*1965-80*	*1980-87*
			Core States			
USA	27829	87482	816	918	1.0	3.5
Canada	3280	10449	191	474	0.7	2.6
UK	2995	8567	2631	3798	1.6	3.2
France	9366	26979	2435	3091	1.0	2.6
FRG	5951	16541	4263	4279	1.4	1.9
Japan	12467	65384	3882	4271	0.8	0.8
			Peripheral/Semi-peripheral States			
China	31818	90102	410	1740	3.0	7.4
India	23227	65254	110	571	2.8	0.8
Brazil	4392	27965	186	514	3.8	2.6
Argentina	2250	9053	26	43	1.4	1.6
Chile	558	-	313	400	1.6	3.6
South Africa	1362	4194	422	621	–	0.3
Zaire	585	1857	08	15	–	3.2
Malawi	119	411	52	131	–	2.5
Tanzania	473	1882	31	77	1.6	3.8
Zambia	191	222	73	148	2.2	3.2
Kenya	484	2139	238	518	4.9	3.4
Sudan	757	3044	28	67	2.9	0.8
Indonesia	4340	17760	133	980	4.3	3.0
Malaysia	1198	–	489	1570	3.2	1.4
Sri Lanka	545	1628	531	1015	2.7	3.1
Thailand	1837	7745	59	236	4.6	3.7
Burma	819	4707	21	206	–	–
Rep. of Korea	2311	13817	2450	2853	3.0	4.4

Source: World Development Report, 1989.

However, it may be noted, as Pounds (1972) remarks: "The fact that every developed country is dependent to some extent on important foodstuffs must be counted as a negative element in its power inventory. A successful land or water blockade can cut off the supply of imported food, and during re-

cent years, a significant object of strategy has been to do just this. In the First World War, the German submarine warfare so reduced the movement of foodstuffs into Great Britain that the possibility of starvation became very real. During the Second World War, the same strategy was less successful than during the first, largely because convoys could be protected more effectively by means of aircraft. It became policy of the allied powers in both wars to cut off the supply of goods to Germany. The oldest successful use of the blockade as a strategic weapon was probably that of Athens by her Peloponnesian rivals toward the end of the fifth century BC. Another was the successful blockade of Napolean's Europe by the British fleet. At this time, however, continental Europe was so nearly self-sufficient in regard to foodstuffs that the blockade had little effect on the food supply. It did, however, encourage the cultivation of sugar beets to replace the cane sugar that could no longer be imported."

Pounds continues: "The United Kingdom and Japan are two countries very vulnerable to a blockade, partly because of their heavy dependence on imported food, partly also because, surrounded as they are by the sea, the danger of a blockade is all the greater. The Soviet Union (now Russia) is probably the least vulnerable, in part owing to the great range of physical environment, in part to the somewhat lower living standards of the mass of the people and in consequence, the narrower range of demand. The value of imported foodstuffs per head of population is a rough guide to the vulnerability of a state to a blockade."

Agriculture is probably more susceptible to government supervision and control than other sectors of the economy. Pounds (1972) attempts to group governmental policies towards agriculture, the farmer, and, the land into four categories which are not however, completely distinct from one another.

1. We have first the traditional view that farming is a way of life which should be protected. Though lipservice is often paid to this ideal, it is doubtful that it does more in any country than provide a rather emotional justification for policies which are founded on other considerations.
2. In most countries today, the government, through its appropriate ministries, takes steps to improve the quality and efficiency of agriculture. The consolidation of the scattered strips of land which made up each farm in many parts of France and Germany has been a very profitable direction for state aid to agriculture. The setting up of cooperatives; the provision of technical help, the resting of soils, and the organization of marketing are some of the many ways in which government controls and assists farming.
3. Related to the last category of government activity is the encouragement, sometimes by subsidy, sometimes by quotas requirement of specific crops whose cultivation is judged to be in the national interest, i.e., cotton

in the United States and sugar beets in Great Britain.

4. Lastly, we have the most thorough going government control of the agricultural sector in the institution of collective and state farms. These correspond with nationalized industry. The state farm is owned and operated by the government. It is always larger than a private farm would have been under similar physical conditions, and theoretically at least it is highly mechanized and is run on advanced scientific lines. It combines the advantages of (2) and (3) above, and it adds to these the immediate asset of a high production-labour ratio.

However, the system of collective and state farms collapsed with the fall of socialism in East Europe, and with the disintegration of the Soviet Union. The 'commune' system is still at work in China though the Chinese State is gradually moving towards the market economy. The commune system in China seemed to be more successful than the Soviet system of the collective and state farms, especially in terms of the sustenance of food resources.

Every country is making determined effort to increase its food resources through the proper management of land and water resources so that it does not necessarily depend on the import of foodstuffs, and can feed its people even in period of extraordinary situations like famine, war and other natural disasters without much troubles. Intra-tribal rivalries and civil wars in most of the African states may be attributed to the lack of adequate supply of food to their people which has resulted in undernourishment and finally led to starvation in many of these states.

Most of the core and semi-peripheral states which produce surplus food resources, and export substantial part of their productions, normally play politics with the importing states whether they are core states or peripheral states. The United States for decades, especially after the Second World War sought to impose its decisions on Northwest European states which largely dependent on it for the imports of foodstuffs. The erstwhile Soviet Union, which used to supply the bulk of food requirement to East European states, had necessarily sought to interfere with the complete economic and political freedom of the states, making them its satellite states. Even today, the massive American food aids to Russia, particularly is aimed at imposing its (United States) decision on it (Russia) or at interfering with its (Russia) economic and political options in Europe and around. 'Neocolonialism' may not seem to be relevant in the European context or in the Japanese context but it is very much relevant in the context of the periphery. Most of the peripheral states which cannot feed their people usually experience/witness the US interference with their economic and political freedoms because they heavily rely on it for the bulk of their food requirements. A peripheral state which is deficient in food resources normally faces threats both from within in the form of political instability, and outside in the form of foreign interference and domination. The *raison d'etre* of such a state always remains at stake.

Food resources can be classified as flow resources and every effort must be made to maintain the flow of the resources. Every state irrespective of their position in the world economy must try to achieve self-sufficiency in the food production, so that the dependence on the import of foodstuffs is no longer required or needed. Once the dependence on the import is no longer required, there will be no problem of undernourishment, starvation, civil unrest, war and domination by other states. However, it seems to be a kind of hypothetical assertion. But still states can strive to achieve self-sufficiency in food resources by imparting knowledge of new technological and scientific innovations in the field of agriculture, particularly from the core states.

Stock Resources

Stock resources are those which are more narrowly localized and fixed in supply. They are readily exhaustible, and not renewable like the flow resources. Mineral resources are necessarily the stock resources. "No price can coax petroleum or copper from rocks in which these minerals do not exist. The extraction of mineral resources is thus more narrowly localized than the production of crops. There are few inhabitable parts of the earth's surface that are not capable of yielding some food. No state except some of the micro-states produce less than about half the food intake of its population, and all could produce more during an emergency. But mineral resources are distributed much less regularly than cultivable soil... Not a single developed state is self-sufficient. While iron ore is widely found, significant deposits of nickel and manganese each occur in only two countries, and tin is found only a little more widely. Under normal conditions there is then a large trade in minerals—both mineral fuels and the minerals from which metals are obtained."

However, mineral resources differ from that of agricultural resources in two major respects: Firstly, the soil given careful management and proper conservation will go on producing without significant variation, i.e., the flow is maintained to provide new supply units within a human time-span. Mineral resources, however, are exhaustible and every known deposits if worked continuously will fall short of. Hence, "mineral resources are, consequently an unstable factor in national power." Secondly, food resources are by and large perishable. It is true that wheat and other grains can be stored for many years but this usually necessitates a careful control of humidity and temperature as well as protection from insects and rodents. Most minerals on the other hand, can be stockpiled, and the majority do not deteriorate if left unexposed to the weather. These two considerations greatly modify the intrinsic power implications of mineral resources.

Sources of Energy

Energy, the stored ability to perform work or produce heat comes in many forms—electoral, mechanical, or nuclear among others. Energy is the most important factor in the power inventory of the state. In the 1970s, the European core states and Japan had to face an energy crisis of an unprecedented nature when the aggrieved Arab states stopped supplying oil to these countries. This could be cited as an example of the periphery's challenge to the core. This had an adverse impact on their power inventory for the whole decade. These states then showed more preference and inclination towards renewable sources of energy, and conservation of energy sources. Coal, petroleum, natural gas and uranium are the major non-renewable sources of energy, and a state's power-potentials to a greater extent depend on their uninterrupted availabilities and proper utilization.

Beginning with the industrial revolution, a trend emerged toward the greater consumption of higher quality fossil fuels and a relatively reduced use of renewable forms such as wood and water, as an energy source. These non-renewable energy forms produced more energy per unit of weight, needed less upgrading, and burned cleaner. The progression from the use of wood to coal, then oil and natural gas to uranium, illustrates the energy transition. The recent years witness the beginning of a conversion back to renewable forms. This transition which has just begun may take hundred years to complete. During this period many short term aberrations in the use of various energy forms will occur depending on prices, government policy, international trade relations, domestic supplies, and shortfalls, to name a few.

Whereas some areas including the United States, China and Russia, are largely self-sufficient in energy resources, many areas are notoriously deficient, including Japan and Western Europe. This situation has created considerable tension in recent years as energy consumption levels zoomed upward, prices increased and nations began rethinking their energy priorities. Among the changes occurring has been the 'second coming' of coal, in recognition of its relative abundance and flexible use both for generating electricity and as a source of steam power.

The present worldwide dependence on oil may or may not have reached a maximum but it certainly will crest by the turn of the century. The uncertainty that marked the energy picture in the latter 1970s and early 1980s made it difficult to know whether the peaking of petroleum production that occurred in 1970 reflected a watershed year or a temporary pause. In the early 1980s, for example, world petroleum demand decreased as consumption declined in response to earlier price jumps. Prices then fell through the mid-decade period but the long term trend in consumption was not clear.

What is known is that during the long term transition to renewable resources dependence on coal, the most abundant fossil fuel, will increase. The future of nuclear energy is not clear. Pressure from envrionmentalists and safety issues cloud its future following a period of growing use in the 1960s and 1970s.

With regard to energy interdependence, Hartshorne (1988) remarks: "The interrelatedness of the present world system is well illustrated in the case of energy. Dependency relationships cut across planned, developed and developing nations. Disparities in energy consumption are much pronounced between the developed and developing countries. Because developing countries depend more than the world as a whole on high-quality energy (petroleum), and because most do not have their own supplies or the means to pay for them, they are very vulnerable to world energy supply and price changes. The growing debt burden facing third world countries in the early 1980s occurred largely because of energy price increases and associated problems related to higher interest rates. Third world countries originally shifted from wood to oil and gas consumption rather than evolving through an intermediate stage of dependence on coal because petroleum was relatively inexpensive, transportation was easier and environmental problems could be avoided. But this shift became enormously expensive following the price jumps of the late 1970s, and foreign aid assistance could no longer be guaranteed to fill the gap."

"Developed countries re-evaluated their own priorities in this period in the face of rapidly increasing energy costs and often cut back on their assistance to third world nations. Developing countries actually suffer from energy malnutrition in two forms. Not only are high-quality energy sources in short supply, but so are traditional forms. Scarcities of traditional fuels pose as great a problem as access to higher-quality forms. In some countries wood fuel for home cooking is itself expensive and the food for which it will be used as heat for cooking. ...In essence, the more that price increases for higher-quality fuels force greater dependence on traditional fuels, the more trapped consumers face shortages...conservation offers one way to escape the trap but it is more appropriate option for highly developed areas than for developing regions. Developed countries can finance conservation measures and make adjustments more easily."

World energy production nearly quadrupled in the last forty years between 1950 and 1990. Roughly equal shares of production now occur in the developed, developing and centrally planned economies as groups, whereas two-thirds was claimed by the developed world alone in 1950. However, the Table 9.4 tends to show that the annual average energy production growth rate for most of the developed, developing and underdeveloped countries for the period 1980-87 was not encouraging. Although energy consumption during 1950-90 tripped on the world scale, developing countries started with such a low level in 1950 that they still lag behind the developed world dramatically. Developed areas consumed fifteen times as much energy on a per capita basis in the last decade than did the Third World. Planned economies operate at a consumption level one-third that of the developed world. However, the Table 9.4 reveals that all the countries except a few, experienced a gradual fall in the annual average energy consumption growth rate for the period 1980-87.

Table 9.4

Commercial energy: nature of production and consumption

	Average annual energy growth rate (per cent)			
Countries	*Energy production*		*Energy Consumption*	
	1965-80	*1980-87*	*1965-80*	*1980-87*
United States	1.1	0.4	2.3	0.1
Japan	-0.4	5.1	6.1	1.7
Norway	12.4	5.7	4.1	2.7
Sweden	4.9	6.6	2.5	2.3
France	-0.9	8.0	3.7	0.6
United Kingdom	3.6	2.6	0.9	1.1
FRG	-0.1	0.3	0.3	0.2
Netherlands	15.4	-1.2	5.0	1.3
Chile	1.8	3.2	3.0	1.5
Columbia	1.0	10.4	6.0	2.1
Venezuela	-3.1	-2.0	4.6	2.3
Brazil	8.6	10.4	9.9	4.0
South Africa	5.1	5.9	4.3	3.7
Zaire	9.4	3.6	3.6	1.2
Zambia	25.7	1.2	4.0	0.1
Nigeria	17.3	-3.3	12.9	5.9
Morocco	2.5	-1.1	7.9	2.9
Zimbabwe	-0.7	-0.4	5.2	0.4
Kenya	13.1	9.2	4.5	-0.2
India	5.6	8.1	5.8	6.0
China	10.0	5.5	9.8	4.4
Nepal	18.4	12.9	6.2	10.3
Pakistan	6.5	6.9	3.5	6.5
Indonesia	9.8	1.0	8.4	3.9
Burma	8.4	5.0	4.9	5.4
Iran	3.6	7.2	8.9	2.6
Iraq	6.2	3.0	7.4	4.9
Saudi Arabia	11.5	-14.4	7.2	5.0
Israel	-15.2	-16.3	4.4	1.3
Australia	10.5	6.6	5.0	0.6

Source: World Development Report, 1989.

In the relatively affluent nations of Europe, Australia, New Zealand and Japan, each person consumes the equivalent of 5 tons or more of coal a year. The per capita consumption in the United States and Canada is more than twice this amount, i.e., about 11 tons of coal equivalent annually. In most developing countries, however, consumption of conventional commercial fuels such as oil, natural gas, coal and electricity, is barely a quarter ton of coal equivalent annually with very roughly, unequal amount of energy obtained from fuel wood and other traditional non-commercial energy sources. With three-fourths of the world people, the Third World countries consume just one-fourth of the world's energy production.

Electricity production on the world scale clearly reveals the continuing disparity between developed and developing nations. In the last forty years, electricity production increases of four-fold occurred on the world scale, paced by the growth in the developed world. Ten-fold increases occurred in the developing and planned economies but their sparse output level in 1950 was so low that the gap actually widened between them and the developed world. However, the share of electricity produced by developed areas decreased from 90 per cent to 68 per cent during the period and to that of developing and planned economies, it increased from 10 per cent to 32 per cent.

The Third World energy production seems to be more complicated as it gives overwhelming emphasis on liquid (primarily petroleum) fuel. In 1990, a little more than three-fourths of energy production in developing nations occurred in this category. The problem with this one-sided output is that it is very expensive fuel and not evenly distributed. Most is found in the Middle East and is not readily available to other Third World countries, owing to financial constraints. Petroleum produced in the developing countries is primarily exported to the developed world. By comparison, the developed world consumes far more energy and has a more balanced production spread among solid, liquid and gas energy resources, with each type contributing nearly equal shares. Moreover, the developed world has excellent reserves of solid fuels, particularly coal, which will increasingly become important in the coming days. The planned economies are also better positioned for the future than are the developing areas but most of this power is used for mineral resource extraction in remote areas.

Possession of good reserves of high grade coal must be counted as a positive element in the power inventory. Occurrence of coal is, therefore, a stable factor in national power. It is on the domestic supplies of coal depends the establishment of the modern industry, which in itself, is an index of national power. All core states with developed economic-military potentials have good reserves of high grade coal, except that of France and Japan, whose coal reserves are not sustainable for a long period. China which is fast moving into the semi-periphery category at the expense of Russia (which goes to the periphery category, following the collapse of the Soviet system, followed by its territorial disintegration) has a vast workable coal reserves with its annual coal production having surpassed the production of the core states. Russia lost some of its best coal fields like the Donets basin and the Karaganda field as the Soviet Socialist Republics to which these field belong, have become separated and independent. The former belongs to Ukraine and the later to Khazakhstan. As a matter of fact, these two fields used to account for more than one-third of the total coal production in the Soviet Union.

The territorial loses as a result of disintegration and particularly, the loss of the Donets and Karaganda coal fields, have substantially reduced the power-potentials of Russia as it has caused a great setback to its industrial potential. Russia is no longer a super power rather it has relegated to a peripheral state in the world economy. It has now been left out with the Kuzbass field and the Pechora field which lie in the Arctic region. However, it has good reserves of high grade coal in the Tunguska, Lena and Zyryanka basins but these basins are yet to be made operative because of their occurrence in inaccessible regions.

Unification of Germany has added a new dimension to the coal industry of the unified modern Germany which has now access to East German coal fields which hitherto remained under German Democratic Republic. These East German coal fields have now been brought under transport networks, so that their utilization should add to Germany's power-potentials. In fact, this should be counted as a positive factor in Germany's power inventory. China is fast moving into a powerful country in the Pacific region, and challenging the US military presence in the region. It is the sustainable nature of the Chinese coal industry which offers a greater amount of flexibility in China's power inventory . China is, thus, becoming a semi-peripheral country in the world economy with its market-oriented economy based on its coal industry. The distinctive feature of recent coal policy in China involves the emergence of major industrial centres near the coal mines. In fact, the policy goal has emerged to create major coal bases in eight different provinces: Datong in Shansiui, Huolinhe in Inner Mongolia, Huainan-Huaibei in Anhui, Yanzhou in Shandong, Xuzhoo in Jiangsu, Liupanshui in Guizhou, Pingdingshan in Henan, and Kailuan in Hegei.

British coal industry has long remained a desirable factor in its power inventory. Industrial power of states must be measured in terms of their workable coal deposits and resources, their utilization and sustainable character, followed by management and conservation.

International trade in coal is very meagre. It is just about 5 per cent of the total coal production in the world. While Japan as a nation leads in coal imports, Western Europe is also an important importing region. Over one-third of coal imports flow to Western Europe. A portion of the flow occurs among Western European countries themselves now as the former trade barriers have been broken down by the 'common market'. Now, the European Union is coming up, with Germany in a new territorial size, much of the remaining restrictions on the flow of coal would be lifted gradually.

Australia is the leading coal exporter, followed by the United States. Both account for nearly one-half of the total coal export in the world. An interesting feature with regard to the international trade in coal is that hardly there is any politics involved in it. Coal has never been used as a political instrument/weapon in international politics. In fact, the flow of coal on the world scale is substantially confined to between the core countries, and also between the core and semi-periphery states, with practically no political/social/cultural contradictions in their outlook. Hence, there is no politics involved in its international flow.

No other fuel resources create so much of tension and politics on the world scale than does petroleum. The core-periphery conflict is largely an outcome of the petroleum politics in the present century. No part of the world economy identifies more closely with supply and demand uncertainties and political overtones than do the petroleum and natural gas industries. These products also have the distinction of being the most important commodities in international trade today. Major petroleum companies were the largest multinational firms and money transfers arising from oil payments, till recently, represented the largest block of transactions in the financial world. The industry has also acquired an oligopolitic structure due to the dominance of a few firms in the industry. Petroleum also provides one of the best examples of a truly global industry, wherein prices are reported almost exclusively in international terms.

Petroleum and natural gas supplies are very unevenly distributed, yet are in very strong demand to sustain high levels of economic activity in developed nations. Developing nations also seek greater access to petroleum, even though their fragile economies can scarcely afford the price when domestic sources are not available. Given the limited sources of supply and the widespread demand, it is not surprising to note that political considerations have gained prominence in the allocation process.

Among the major traditional oil-producing regions, Russia, the United States, the Middle East and Saudi Arabia, and the Caribbean are important. The (former) Soviet Union and the United States remained the leaders, notwithstanding the fact that the largest quantity of reserves occurred in the Middle East. The reserves in the United States and the Soviet Union in the

1980s simply accounted for 5 per cent and ll per cent of the world total respectively. However, both were surpassed by the Middle East which has one-half of the world reserves paced by Saudi Arabia which alone has one-fourth of the reserves capacity.

Though the United States' share of world production declined relatively in 1990 as production of oil grew elsewhere rapidly particularly in non-traditional areas and also in Russia and Middle East, but it still remains the world production leader, accounting for over one-fifth of total output. No new areas have been identified and brought under commercial production in the United States. Falling production in the decade has made the United States increasingly dependent on the non-Middle East areas for oil supply.

Despite the territorial disintegration, followed by loses of Caucasus, Ukraine and Central Asia oil fields to independent states which came up in the early 1990s, Russian share of world production remains stable in the decade, i.e., about 16 per cent. In fact, loses have been compensated by increasing commercial production from the Tyumen basin in West Siberia. Few more areas have been identified in East Siberia where commercial production is to begin shortly with the Japanese assistance. An agreement to this effect has been recently reached between Russia and Japan.

Russia's oil output even after its disintegration exceeds that of all Middle Eastern producers combined and matched that for all North American producers (USA, Canada and Mexico) as a group. Russian's gradual inclination towards the market economy, followed by its growing desire to firmly align with the members of the European community vis-a-vis the United States, has been a major political development in the post-Cold War period. Now, the members of the European community and the United States as well as Japan need not have to heavily rely on the Middle East oil. Under the changing political scenario, Russia will supply bulk of their requirements.

China's oil production has increased substantially particularly offshore oil production which has surpassed the production of Indonesia, Brunei and Myanmar combined in the Indo-Pacific region. Caribbean states account for 5 per cent and African states—Egypt, Libya, Algeria and Nigeria—account for 8 per cent of the world total respectively.

European dependence, particularly West European dependence on the Middle East oil seems to have reduced substantially in the late 1970s and early 1980s as North Sea production has accelerated. However, the economic boom of offshore oil on Western Europe which also benefited Norway, Denmark, West Germany and the Netherlands, is somewhat offset by political bickering. Disputes over taxes, who to sell to, and quotas have an uncanny resemblance to the problems with the Middle East.

Recent years have witnessed offshore oil production which in the 1980s accounted for nearly one-fourth of world total. Saudi Arabia leads in offshore drilling activity and accounts for over 20 per cent, and Abu Dhabi next to it, contributes roughly 10 per cent, giving one-third of the output of offshore oil to the Middle East. The second leading offshore producer is Britain, owing to the largeness of the North Sea producing area. Venezuela and the United States each contribute about 8 per cent of the world offshore output. Australia, China and India are emerging important offshore producers. Beginning of offshore production in the Bombay High has necessarily lessened India's dependence on the import of oil to some extent, thus saving substantial foreign exchange for the country. No doubt, an overall global increase in offshore oil prodution has necessarily lessened the importance of the Middle East in the oil politics.

No other energy sources as mentioned earlier, create so much of tension and politics as does petroleum in the post-war period. In the post-colonial period, it is the oil politics which keeps up the core-periphery dichotomy. The first such case of the dichotomy was the Suez crisis of October 1954 when Egypt sought to nationalize the Suez Canal, and closed it for the flow of oil to West European core states—Great Britain and France. Britain and France retaliated to the Egyptian move and resorted to military action against Egypt. In fact, both the European states sought to maintain their control on the Suez Canal, a main shipping route for petroleum which was "necessary for their industry and transportation, a steady and constant supply was a prerequisite of power...it was quite natural that they would use their power to secure the continued supply of so necessary a determinant of power".

It was in the backdrop of the Suez crisis and growing involvement of the multinational corporations of the core countries in oil production and distribution in the Middle East or the growing pressure of the American-West European core states on the oil producing Middle Eastern peripheral states that these peripheral states felt the need of an organization in 1960. At a conference in Baghdad, the Organization of Petroleum Exporting Countries (OPEC) was founded. Originally comprised of five nations, viz., iran, Iraq, Kuwait, Saudi Arabia and a Caribbean state (Venezuela), OPEC sought to provide a mechanism to deal with the multinational companies that controlled oil production and distribution in their countries.

Multinational petroleum firms successfully resisted reforms desired by host countries until 1960 by threatening to redirect oil purchases to other areas, leaving host countries largely impotent to deal with their problems. Over the years the multinationals established interlocking ownership and concession arrangements with the host countries which meant that they continued to control prices. They also established vertical integration in the industry, gaining complete control of all activity from well head to refinery and final consumption, including pipeline, barrage and ocean tanker transportation, providing a classic example of an oligopolistic system. The multinationals in effect controlled the resource, its processing and its distribution. Political and military tension in the Middle East, centered on the Arab-Israeli conflict, much as a part of an implicit core-periphery dichotomy in the region, tended to create an uneasy difficult working environment for multinationals in the 1950s and 1960s. The Suez crisis in 1956 was a direct and immediate manifestation of it. The situation created uncertainties in oil flows to West Europe. Newly discovered fields in Libya and Algeria provided an alternative source for Europe that helped overcome the problem of supply logistics created by the Suez Canal shutdown. By 1968 Libya outproduced Kuwait and became the fourth largest producer after Venezuela, Iran and Saudi Arabia. OPEC countries obtained more and more concessions from the multinational firms during this period.

OPEC's membership also increased. Mostly non-Arabian oil-producing states, this time joined it: Libya and Indonesia in 1962, Abu Dhabi in 1967, Algeria in 1969 and Nigeria in 1971 (Fig. 9.2). Eventually, the host countries of the Middle East negotiated three-fourths of the crude price for themselves. The Middle Eastern nations began nationalizing oil operations in the 1970s, much to the discomforts of the Atlantic core states, which further sharpened the core-periphery conflict in the region.

War broke out in the Middle East in 1973 between the Arab states and Israel. The Atlantic core states had tacit support to Israel and their pro-Israeli attitude forced the representatives of OPEC (oil producing Gulf states) who met in Kuwait, and took an unilateral action of oil embargo. It raised prices by 70 per cent and ordered a production cutback. By November 1973 an embargo was imposed on sales to the United States, Canada, Western European NATO allies including Netherlands and Japan. By December 1973, OPEC invoked a staggering 130 per cent price hike. However, Saudi Arabia was an exception to this nationalizing process and the US firms continued to play an integral role in its oil production.

It was the Arab oil embargo of 1973 which necessarily precipitated energy crisis, especially on West European countries and Japan as well. These nations had no other options but to switch over to energy resource management and conservation and to finding out alternative areas as well as energy sources. The energy crisis of 1973 started the turn around to coal which since then, has contributed a greater share of world energy forms, particularly in those nations which were badly affected by the oil embargo. In fact, the demand for 'steam coal' to power thermal electrical generating plants dramatically increased in the aftermath of the oil embargo.

Notwithstanding a conscious unanimity among the OPEC states of the

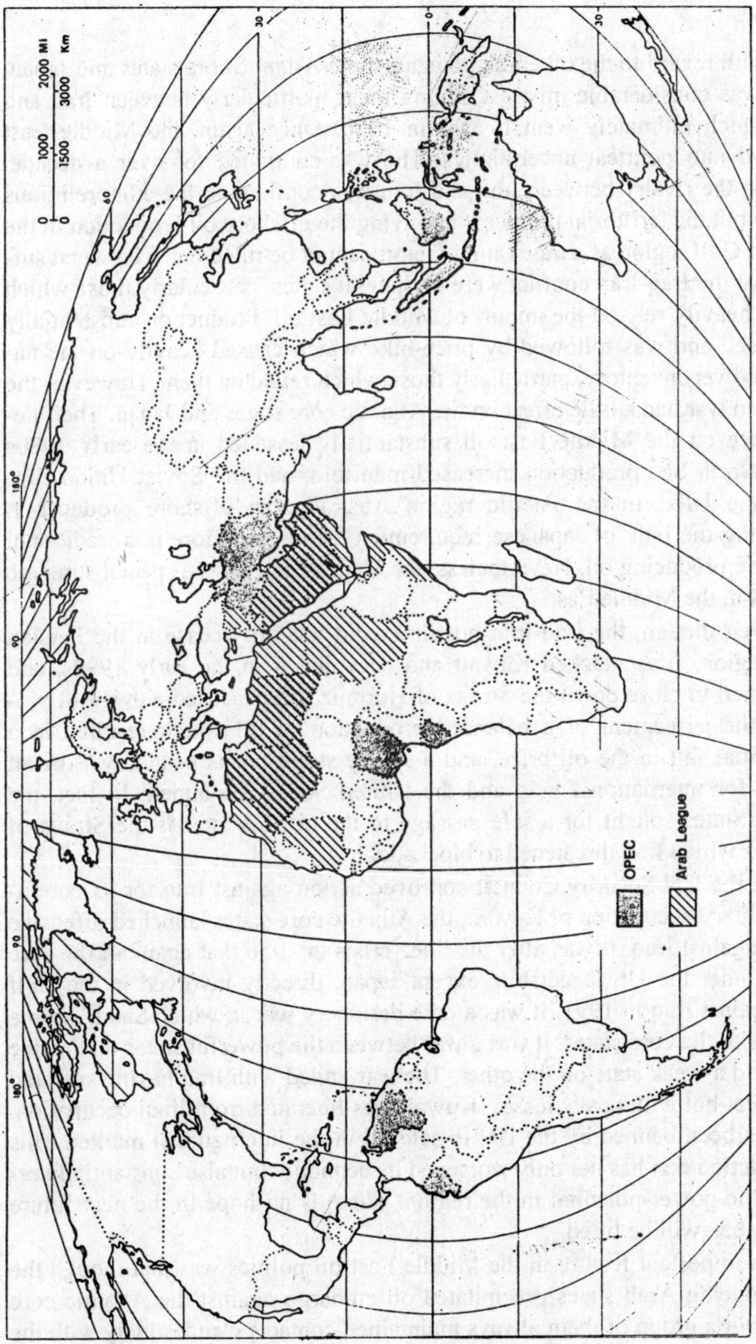

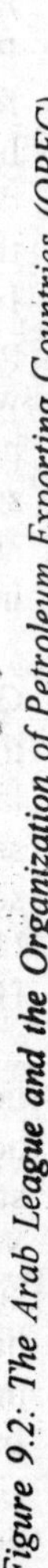

Figure 9.2: The Arab League and the Organization of Petroleum Exporting Countries (OPEC)

Gulf with regard to the oil embargo against the Atlantic core states and Japan, there was considerable mistrust among them, particularly between Iraq and Iran which ultimately went to war in 1980. Once again, the Middle East plunged into political uncertainties. The war continued for over a decade. Though the rivalry between Iraq and Iran was confined to the ethnoreligious factors but the territorial problems involving the offshore oil production in the Persian Gulf region as a motivating factor, cannot be ruled out. The worst sufferers of the Iraq-Iran conflict were peripheral states, particularly those which had to heavily rely on the import of Middle East oil. Production substantially decreased and was followed by price-hike which caused heavily on the nations' power-inventory, particularly those which relied on them. However, the Iraq-Iran war had a little effect on the Atlantic core states and Japan. Their dependence on the Middle East oil substantially lessened in the early 1980s when North Sea production increased manifold, and the Soviet Union supplied the bulk. In the Pacific region Australia, an offshore producer is supplying the bulk of Japanese requirement. More and more non-traditional areas are producing oil. Nevertheless, the United States has a special strategic interest in the Middle East.

Even though, the Iraq-Iran hostilities did not fully cease in the Persian Gulf region, Iraq attacked Kuwait and occupied it in the early 1990s, and threatened to close down the Straits of Hormuz. Iraq accused Kuwait of violating the agreement of a balanced production of oil which resulted in a substantial fall in the oil price, and a severe strain on its economy. Kuwait sought for international help and the United States responded. In fact, the United States sought for a safe passage to the oil flow across the Straits of Hormuz which Iraq threatened to blockade.

As the UN Security Council approved action against Iraq for its continued military occupation of Kuwait, the Atlantic core states launched offensive action against Iraq. It was after the Suez crisis in 1956 that again all the core states under the US leadership, except Japan, directly involved in the Gulf War against Iraq in 1991. It was a core periphery war in which Saudi Arabia sided with the core states. It was a war between the powerful states on the one hand and a weak state on the other. The war ended with Iraq having suffered the defeat but with heavy losses. Kuwait was liberated from Iraqi occupation. Iraq has been banned by the UN to sale oil in the international market. This UN sanction/ban has not only worsened its economy but also substantially reduced the power-potential in the region. There is no hope in the near future that the ban will be lifted.

An important feature in the Middle East oil politics was that though the oil-producing Arab states precipitated oil embargo against the Atlantic core states, but a group of them always maintained contacts clandestinely with the core states.

Disintegration of the Soviet Union, and Russia's growing orientation towards market economy and spontaneous desire for closer economic ties with the core states, have ushered in a new era in international oil situation. Most of the former republics of the Soviet Union which were important oil-producing regions earlier within the system, are also inclined towards market economy. Oil has been discovered in some more areas which are away from the traditional areas. In a changing scenario, therefore, the Middle East oil will not play a significant political role because dependence on it is fast reducing, and the Atlantic core states and Japan are gradually becoming more inclined towards the Russian and North Sea supplies. However, it has to be seen whether the oil-producing Central Asiatic Muslim republics of erstwhile Soviet Union decide on becoming OPEC members?

The fact, however, cannot be denied that the core-periphery dichotomy in oil production, supply and flow on world scale will continue even though the dependence on the Middle East is substantially reduced and new areas are coming up. It is important to note that none of the oil rich nations in the Middle East and the Caribbean region could develop itself into a powerful nation to challenge the hegemony of the Atlantic core states, even though the Atlantic core states are heavily dependent on the Middle East and the Caribbean oil for their power inventories.

Some countries have developed water power because they are either short of coal or petroleum. Switzerland, Austria, Italy, and Scandinavian countries are small countries to have developed water power because they are very poor in either of the energy resources but favourable conditions for the development of water power are there in these countries. They have tapped much of their water power-potentials. However, these countries are not militarily and politically strong enough to decide the destiny of even regional politics. Japan is exception to it because it has developed its water power-potentials to such an extent as to have emerged as the principal challenger to the United States's hegemony in the world. There is no doubt that the development of water power requires a very large capital investment and it is the core states which can make such investments. The United States, Canada, France and United Kingdom have developed substantial part of their water power-potentials. Peripheral countries are much behind the core countries in terms of water power development.

It is only the Atlantic core states which are technologically most advanced, and have developed nuclear and atomic power to sustain their industrial power. Although the United States retains the lead in the global production of nuclear power, France, United Kingdom, Japan and Russia are also large producers. West European nations have set up nuclear reactors on cooperative basis. Some peripheral states like India, Pakistan, China, Brazil, Israel and South Africa have also set up nuclear reactors for nuclear power generation on a very limited scale.

The outlook for nuclear power is now much more subdued than it was two decades ago. The high cost of construction due to inflation and the need for redundant safety systems is part of the reason for the growing pessimism about the future role of nuclear energy. Another part of the concern is focused on environmental and safety measures. The fear of meltdown, the potential for radiation leaks and for human or mechanical error, and problems associated with the disposal of radio-active waste have all contributed to growing public criticism of nuclear energy power reactors.

However, it is too early to say that the use of nuclear and atomic power has done more than underline the existing power ratios among the states of the world. The core-periphery dichotomy on the Non-Proliferation Treaty (NPT) is reflective of the peripheral states' reluctance to abide by the terms and conditions of the treaty.

Mineral Resources

Possession of mineral resources must be counted as a positive factor in the power inventory because the national strength of a nation to a greater extent, depends on its industrial development, and which necessarily depends on the internal supply of mineral resources. Such a situation intrinsically, makes the nation able to make decisions and implement them in fields which "either lie geographically outside the boundaries of the state or impinge on the interests of other states". Therefore, the possession of mineral wealth is an index of national power provided the nation is technologically advanced and capable to extract and utilize the wealth for its industrial potentials and development.

Mineral resources being stock resources are fixed in supply and concentrated in a relatively small number of places on the earth's surface and this gives each of these areas a certain importance. A handful of countries account for the greater part of the world's production of each of the important metallic and non-metallic ores. However, iron ore is widely distributed but its major reserves are contained in a few large ore deposits. It is the peripheral countries which now account for the bulk of iron ore production in the world. Russia's contribution has substantially declined, following the territorial loses as a result of its disintegration. Most of the core countries including the United States of America, now heavily depend on the import of iron ore, particularly from Brazil, Australia, Canada and India. Japan imports about half of the total iron ore that enters the international market. An irregular supply of iron ore to these core states may have serious consequences on their industrial-military power-potentials. China has good reserves of iron ore deposits and its production has increased manifold. Much of China's national strength lies in its proper and rational use of its vast reserves of iron ore deposits.

Much of China's iron ore-rich Manchuria province was under the control of Japan for a long period. Japan developed the resources of the province, utilized the fuel, iron ore and other resources of it to the extent that it set up a number of industrial plants for the production of pig iron and steel. These plants indeed enabled Japan to make decisions and implement them over vast areas of the Indo-Pacific region till it lost the battles against allied forces in 1945.

China has rebuilt all the industrial plants which Japan had set up during its occupancy period and their production capacities increased. It has given China an additional strategic advantage in the later periods. In fact, the development of iron and steel producing plants in Afro-Asian periphery necessarily reflected the regional necessities of the European core states which were then involved in rivalries and competition for dominant position.

Decolonization in the post-war period was a major setback to the European core states as they lost their overseas territories which used to provide them with necessary mineral resources required for their industrial-military power-potentials. Loss of Manchuria was a serious blow to Japan's war potentials.

Most of the core states except that of the United States, are poor in mineral resources, and loss of their erstwhile overseas territories necessarily placed them at strategic disadvantage. These core states are heavily dependent on the supply of mineral resources from the peripheral states of Latin America, Africa and Asia. The United States, Russia, Canada, South Africa, China and India are some of the countries which have relatively sound mineral resource base. The United States, Russia, Canada and South Africa are near self-sufficient in most of the major non-ferrous metals.

Copper, aluminum, lead, zinc, tin, manganese, nickel, and a number of other non-ferrous metals tend to form strategic metals/materials, along with steel. "These are required for essential uses in a war emergency, the procurement of which in adequate quantities, quality, and time is sufficiently uncertain for any reason to require prior provision for the supply thereof." Strategic minerals are even more necessary in time of war for the manufacture of large quantities of war materials. It is commonly believed that the loss of control over any such materials in war emergency is a matter of grave strategic concern for the states which lose them. No country can possibly be self-sufficient in this range of strategic minerals, though Russia and the United States more nearly approach self-sufficiency than others.

Though the United States is a leading copper ore producer in the world but it is equally a leading importer of refined copper. However, bulk of it comes from Chile across a strategically safe passage which ensures steady and constant supply. All the core states heavily depend on the import of refined copper. The United States is the leading aluminum producer, followed by Canada, Australia and Germany. However, the production in Russia has declined in the recent years. Russia, Australia, Canada and the United States are leading lead producers, while Canada, Russia, Peru, Australia and the United States are the leading zinc producers. The ASEAN countries, particularly Malaysia, Thailand and Indonesia, dominate the world in the production of tin. The Atlantic core states which heavily depend on these ASEAN countries for the supply of tin since long, had always sought to protect them against the communist pressure, particularly during the cold war period, and to maintain steady and constant supply of the metal, the SEATO was put on maximum alert during that period. Canada and Russia account for nearly one-half of world's nickel production. New Caledonia and Australia are other leading producers.

As a matter of fact, the European core countries and Japan get bulk of their requirements of strategic materials from the United States and Canada . But the supply pattern of these materials in the coming days will be different, once Russia is inducted in the European Union along with its former republics. The areal pattern of the supply of the strategic materials will then depend on the strategic needs of the core states. Cessation of cold war, unification of Germany, fall of socialism in East Europe, disintegration of the Soviet Union, Yugoslavia and Czechoslovakia, all have tended to change the strategic needs of the European core states and Japan as well.

There were many examples in the past when the central/axis powers attempted to cut off the supply of strategic metals to the allied states particularly during the World War II. "The loss of the tin mines of Malaya to the Japanese, the cutting off of the Swedish iron ore supply by the German, even the possession by the enemy of the mercury mines of Italy and Yugoslavia were thought to hold serious consequences to the allied powers during the Second World War." During the Cold War period, a balancesheet of mineral resources between the American and Soviet blocs were thought by some to be a key to the political future. That it was important, cannot be questioned but the "strategic needs, the capacity of expanding technology to use submarginal resources (such as the beneficiation and use of taconite), the reuse of scrap, and the exhaustion of existing resources gave such a balancesheet only temporary value".

While evaluating the importance of mineral resources in measuring the national power, Pounds (1972) says: "It is difficult to estimate the importance of the possession of metallic ores in assessing national power." This is partly because there is no formula by which the metals in question can be related to one another; nor can it be known with any degree of certainty what the technological level will be and what critical shortages would result if an emergency should arise or last what substitutes may become available in the future. It is easy to overestimate the importance of minerals in the power equation, and almost incorrect to claim that wars have been fought merely to gain possession of iron ore deposits. There is no reason whatever to suppose that Germany took part of Lorraine from France in 1871 only in order to gain possession of its iron ore; or to consider Great Britain's dispute with Venezuela in 1895-99 as being motivated entirely by a desire for minerals, or even to regard Chile's war with Bolivia as fought only for the control of the nitrate fields.. On the other hand, the Suez crisis of 1956 owed much to Great Britain's anxiety to retain control of the waterway through which much of her petroleum customarily passed. If wars are not fought for control of economic resources, this control is nevertheless an important weapon in war. The restriction by whatever means, of the enemy's access to scarce materials, is a legitimate policy of war. This may be affected by direct blockade in which the actual flow of materials is cut off. It may also be accomplished by diplomatic or commercial means if an actual blockade is geographically impossible. The struggle to prevent Germany and her allies from receiving an adequate supply of wolfrom, the ore of tungsten is one of many examples."

Manufacturing Industries

Possession of vast reserves of mineral deposits is not the only criterion for determination of power. There are larger number of countries in the periphery which have rich reserves of mineral deposits but are all of them powerful nations to challenge the USA, Great Britain, France and Germany in the global power politics; when most of these states are poor in mineral resources, except the United States? Peripheral states are no match to the core states in terms of power equation, notwithstanding the fact that they are rich in mineral resources, but they are lacking in highly developed manufacturing industry. Neither they have the technical skills and ability to identify, utilize and develop the mineral resources and processing them for industrial uses nor have they the capacity for huge capital investment in industrial sector. As a result, they continue to remain inferior to the core states in terms of power-potentials on the global scale. Mere possession of mineral resources, therefore, should not be counted as a positive factor in power inventory unless the deposits are extracted, utilized and developed for industrial uses and a huge complex of manufacturing industries comes into being there at. "A highly developed manufacturing industry is one of the most conspicuous determinants of power. Every great power of modern times has been an industrial base. No policy, however, blustering and aggressive, is likely to be effective unless supported by the ability to manufacture the machines of war." It has been long realized that a key to political power is industrialization.

The former Soviet Union could not compete the core states in the world economy simply because its industrial potentials were far behind than those of the core states. During the entire Cold War period, it remained as a semi-periphery industrial power in the world economy and after its disintegration, Russia has been relegated to a periphery industrial power. However, China is a rising semi-peripheral industrial state in East Asia. Unification of Germany has added further industrial strength to it. It is now a rising core state in the world economy, much to the discomfiture of other European core states.

Manufacturing industries offer two power advantages to a state: Firstly, they are conducive to a higher standards of living. If man with machine accomplishes significantly more than man without machine, the total productivity of a highly mechanized people will be greater than that of a people not so equipped. Much of this surplus will, of course, be abstracted by the government to maintain a large army or to invest in other countries or even in its own. But if neither of these happens, then the surplus will be distributed among those who help to create it. It will create a higher living standards. The extent to which this living standard rises above a hypothetical minimum is the 'slack' or 'fat' which can be drawn upon in an emergency. Secondly, the advantage is more direct. It lies in the actual possession of the plant and equipment necessary to turn out only the weapons of war but also the goods whose export will go to pay for necessary imports.

This advantage seems to correspond to S.B.Jones' third classification of resources, i.e., "resources available only after conversion". A steel industry may permit the manufacturing of tanks and guns in case of an emergency; it also allows an export of automobiles, machine tools, and all kinds of goods, if such demands arise. "The more varied and developed the range of industry, the less will be the degree of dependence on other countries. It is not necessary that industry should normally be engaged in making military items, though it is probable that their manufacture on a small scale would continue even under the most favourable international circumstances. What is important is that the industry as a whole could be converted to the manufacture of such equipment at short notice." It is the American manufacturing industries among the core states which offer the above mentioned power advantages to it. But next to it, is the Japanese manufacturing industries which are so varied and developed that they now challenge the US industrial hegemony not only in the Pacific region but also in the Atlantic region.

One of the emerging political phenomena in recent years is that of the growing 'industrial geopolitics', i.e., industrial rivalry between the United States and Japan for the domination of Eurasia.

"The strategic branches of industry may be said to be six in number. By general consent, the greatest importance attaches to the smelting and refining of metals. Next in importance are certainly the engineering, metal construction, and ship building industries. The production of chemicals including high explosives, fertilizers and cement along with manufacture of electrical and other instruments would rank next. The textile and clothing industries and the food and consumer goods industries would probably rank last. Most of the more advanced countries which have a balance between these industries and in some branches, the industries are larger than is warranted by normal, domestic, peace-time needs. These industries normally export a part of their total production, and this surplus capacity also constitutes a form of 'fat' to be drawn upon in an emergency."

An important question arises as to what criteria to be taken into consideration for assessing industrial capacity as an important measure of political power? Importance of this question lies in finding out some method of ranking states in terms of political power vis-a-vis industrial potentials and capacity. Several criteria, however, have been suggested for. One of such criteria is that of "the industrially employed population", i.e., employment in manufacturing. However, this criterion does not give a true picture of the industrial capacity of state because the absolute or relative data of industrial labour have little value, and the effectiveness of it, i.e., the man-tool ratio, is not known. On the other hand, merely to tabulate the actual industrial output gives no information on whether it was achieved with large or small expenditure on labour. Sometimes data on industrial labour force are misleading and it is difficult to come out with any precise conclusion, especially when the national power of a state is measured in terms of its industrial capacity. Industrial labour force of Belgium or Netherlands is quite higher than that of the United States, but can it be concluded that in the power equation, the United States is inferior to those states? Similarly, the figure for Great Britain is higher than that of Japan but in reality, the industrial capacity of Japan far exceeds than that of Great Britain.

Another possible criterion to measure the industrial capacity vis-a-vis political power is that of industrial production. "It is difficult if not impossible to equate steel with textiles or chemicals with consumer goods. How should Belgium's important iron and steel industry be weighted as against the electrical industry of the Netherlands? Furthermore, within each of the main branches of industry, how should one distinguish between the producer of low grade steel, such as France, and the producer of high grade and alloy steels, such as Sweden? Between the chemical industry which produces fertilizers and that which turns out high explosives or plastics or drugs? It is doubtful that a rating of states on any absolute basis is possible."

Another measure of economic and industrial development of a state is the amount of power which it consumes. There is a rough correlation between power consumption and gross national product. "A country rich in the use of energy is also a country whose people live well and long; and a country poor by one of these measures is poor by them all." It is difficult to arrive at even a reasonable approximation of energy consumption of most countries. Table 9.5 gives the per capita energy consumption of some selected countries.

Table 9.5

Gross national product (1987) and energy consumption of oil

Countries	*GNP (dollars per head)*	*Energy consumption (kg of oil per capita)*
Switzerland	21330	4105
United States	18530	7265
Norway	17190	8932
Japan	15760	3232
United Arab Emirates	15830	5094
Sweden	15550	6453
Canada	15160	9156
Kuwait	14610	4715
Finland	14470	5581
FRG	14400	4531
France	12790	3729
United Kingdom	10420	3805
Hong Kong	8070	1525
Saudi Arabia	6200	3292
Oman	5810	2130
Libya	5460	2674
Brazil	2020	825
Malaysia	1810	771
Chile	1310	822
Columbia	1240	757
Congo, Peoples' Republic	870	223
Egypt	680	588
Sri Lanka	400	160
Pakistan	350	207
India	300	208
China	290	525
Bangladesh	160	47

Source: World Development Report, 1989.

Again, it is very difficult to come out with a clearcut standpoint on the basis of the above table with regard to the economic development.

To Pounds (1972): "The production of cement can also be regarded as a very rough measure of economic and industrial growth. It is the essential raw material of which large buildings, including factories and high office buildings are built. It is also used in bridge and road construction. Its consumption, therefore, is a kind of index of current expansion in these fields."

Another possible measure of industrial capacity of a state is to assess the distribution of manufacturing value added to different important industries. It can be reasonably concluded that greater the value added, more is the power. A state that invests more in industrial sector, is sure to secure a place in global political power. It is very clear in the Table 9.6, which specifically deals with the G-7 countries, which are the industrialized nations in the world.

Thus, it is reasonable to infer that the United States of America, Japan and Federal Republic of Germany have made substantial investment in manufacturing sectors than the others. As a result, their industrial capacity far exceeds than those of older core states, except Italy and Canada which are emerging. While the United States and Japan weld considerable power in the world economy, Germany is a rising core state in Europe which may resist the American and Japanese economic pressures on the continent in the coming days.

F. Clifford German (1960) has come out with a model to express national power. Briefly, it starts with the area of the state, corrected for population density and the closeness of the railroad net. It then adds a factor for population, corrected for technical efficiency, employment in industry, 'morale' and the adequacy of the food supply. Allowance is made for the production of steel, solid and liquid fuels, and hydroelectric power; for the surplus or deficit in steel, petroleum, minerals and engineering; for the size of the armed forces and their possession of what is euphemistically called the nuclear deterrent.

However, German's model has been criticized on several points. Each of the factors included in the model to express national power, requires more qualification than it receives; many significant factors are ignored and omitted; and no room is made for 'fat' and 'slack'. Lastly, there exists no means other than the price mechanism, of comparing of one hydrogen bomb or one ton of steel with a few square miles of territory or kilowatts of industrial power.

"The volume of trade in manufactured products", says Pounds (1972), "provides a kind of index of the level of industrialization... The most developed industrial countries not only have a large export of manufactured goods but also a large import. As manufacturing industry becomes more sophisticated, it also becomes specialized, and this specialization arises not only

Table 9.6

Structure of manufacturing of group seven countries

Countries	*Value added in manufacturing (millions of current dollars)*		*Distribution of manufacturing value added (per cent: current price)*									
			Food and agriculture		*Textiles and clothing*		*Machinery and transport equipment*		*Chemicals*		*Others*	
	1970	*1986*	*1970*	*1986*	*1970*	*1986*	*1970*	*1986*	*1970*	*1986*	*1970*	*1986*
USA	253864	835793	12	12	8	5	31	35	10	10	39	38
Japan	73339	573536	8	10	8	6	35	38	11	10	40	37
Canada	17002	59617	16	15	8	7	23	25	7	9	46	44
FRG	70888	294808	13	12	8	5	32	38	9	10	38	36
France	38861	160556	14	18	10	7	29	33	8	9	39	33
United Kingdom	36044	118048	13	14	9	6	31	32	10	11	37	36
Italy	30942	140078	10	7	13	13	24	32	13	10	40	38

Source: World Development Report, 1989.

between factories and firms but also between countries. It can only be said that a negative index of import of manufactured goods characterizes the developing countries. There is fairly a high correlation between a large negative index, i.e., a large import of manufactured goods, and a low per capita GNP". It is clear in Table 9.7.

Table 9.7

Imports of manufactured goods (1987)

Countries	GNP (dollars per head)	Composition of 1987 imports of manufactured goods (per cent)				
		Textiles & clothing	Chemicals	Electrical machinery and electronics	Transport equipment	Others
USA	18530	2	13	13	21	51
Japan	15760	2	3	17	33	45
Canada	15160	1	7	6	40	45
FRG	14400	5	14	10	23	47
France	12790	7	18	9	21	45
United Kingdom	10420	6	18	10	12	55
Italy	10350	18	8	7	10	57
Brazil	2020	9	8	9	15	58
Columbia	1240	26	5	0	1	68
Senegal	520	9	24	7	28	32
Sri Lanka	400	76	1	0	4	20
Nigeria	370	9	20	5	2	64
Pakistan	350	79	0	0	0	21
Sudan	330	26	8	7	15	44
India	300	46	3	1	0	49
China	290	49	9	5	1	36
Zambia	250	22	0	4	0	74
Bangladesh	160	84	0	0	0	16

Source: World Development Report, 1989.

Thus, the Table 9.7 clearly reveals that the G-7 countries, in spite of their very high per capita GNP in 1987 had a fairly large import of manufactured goods which is in fact, expressive of a fairly high level of industrialization in the world economy. It is this reason that highly industrialized G-7 countries, particularly the core countries among them, weld considerable power in world politics, and control the world economy.

Over a large part of the world, the volume of foreign trade per head of the population is very small while to that of a handful of developed countries, particularly the G-7 countries, it is disproportionately very high. There are certain generalizations to account for them:

1. There is a direct association between the volume of trade per head and the level of economic development. There is a positive correlation between GNP per capita and foreign trade per capita. Higher the GNP per capita, greater is the foreign trade per capita. Most of the industrialized and developed countries of the West may be put in this category. It can be assumed to be an important measure of political power for the industrialized developed nations.
2. Not only do developed countries carry on more trade in the aggregate but they carry it on principally with each other. The developed and industrialized states are the most important trading partners of one another. These countries have very strong commercial linkages between themselves, and some of them have emerged as hegemonic core states to demonstrate their power-potentials in world politics. They have made the world economy 'bias' in their favour so as to maintain their hegemonic interests. The attempt of the less industrialized, under-industrialized countries of the periphery to resist the hegemonic interests of the core states in the world economy has failed to achieve any substantial success.
3. The idea that a large part of the world's trade consists of the exchange of manufactured products of the developed countries for the foodstuffs and raw materials of the less developed is not supported by the facts.
4. The less developed countries or the majority of the developing countries carry on very little trade between themselves. Most of their relatively small volume of trade is with the developed countries. It is expressive of the fact that the developed countries, particularly the hegemonic states with their exceptional industrial capacities, make the developing countries of the periphery necessarily dependent on them. It is, therefore, an expression of industrial capacity as an important measure of political power for the industrially developed hegemonic states.

Transport Infrastructure

A dense network of transport infrastructure is a necessary index of political power and an important measure of effective utilization of resources and their development that a state can obtain or can conjure up to support its strategy, i.e., the art of using power for the attainment of goals in competition. Therefore, "the means of transporting people and equipment are a necessary element of national power. Without them, raw materials cannot be assembled for manufacture nor when processed, can they be distributed to a market or consumer. Defence is impossible without the means of moving persons and equipment from one part of a country to another. The mere fact that there are strategic roads and strategic railways serve to underline their role in strengthening military".

Two important roles of transport infrastructure deserve consideration. One of its important role is the territorial-political considerations of state while the other is that of the economic integration of the state, so that the state can achieve a greater amount of accessibility across its allotted space.

Political Role of Transport Infrastructure

"A developed transport net, whether of air routes, roads or railways, is generally regarded as a prerequisite to national unity." It is a necessary element of centripetal force that tends to unify/integrate the nation. It is the most effective means to consolidate political authority. If any state government is to assert successfully its sovereignty throughout its territory, an adequate transport infrastructure is necessary. This is assuming, of course, that the central government does indeed have the preponderant military power in the state authority. Often the pattern of a transport network testifies to efforts its achieve political centralization.

Sources of both the Canadian and Australian federations explicitly manifest the role of the railway networks or to say, "the completion of both the Canadian and Australian federations was contingent upon the extension of the railroad system to the most westerly parts of the territories". High degree of political uncertainty in most of the post-war federations in the periphery may be attributed to the poor transport infrastructure. Much of India's northern periphery is not politically integrated with the rest of the country, particularly with the political core because transport infrastructure has not been adequately extended to the periphery. As a result, it is extremely difficult to patrol the borders.

China's internal transportation network exemplifies efforts to consolidate political control of the countryside. But still, China's western and southwestern periphery is very poor in transport infrastructure. However, in the United States the slow westward extension of the railroads was a kind of symbol, illustrating the growing unity of the territory of the United States.

Transport facilities and conditions thus evidence a state government's concern for the maintenance of internal authority. The ability to exert compelling force in all parts of the territory is fundamental to central political power; and the concern to guarantee sufficient internal accessibility to ensure this goal influence the pattern and extent of a transport net. Particularly in cases of colonial dromocracies (Greek word: dromos means running) or of dualistic states (federations) with tap-route transport nets, the transport network often reflects the *de facto* extent of central political control. Integration of the state polity necessitates completion of a more adequate internal network.

Economic Role of Transport Infrastructure

Mere possession of natural resources should not be taken as a measure to political power unless, there is sufficient transport infrastructure to allow the movement of resources to processing centres, to industrial centres, and then to consuming centres for distribution. An effective transport infrastructure is a geographical necessity for economic development and integration of a state, that it gives 'an economic *raison d'etre*' to it, besides a 'political *raison d'etre*'.

In the words of Edward F. Bergman (1975), "the internal transport facilities which contribute to the political consolidation of a state make a major contribution to any state's economic development." When transport facilities are poor and spatial organization is colloidal, regions are largely self-sufficient, and there is little trade. Whatever capital a society may have remains tied up in raw materials, in materials in transit, in stocks, and in inventories. Transport improvements and trade do cost money but movement and exchange make possible the specialization of location which yields benefits greater than the costs of transport. These benefits follow from variations in inherent natural productivity (such as inferior and superior locations on the transport network), and from realization of comparative advantages, economics of scale production, and agglomeration. All of these increase land and labour productivity and allow more efficient use of capital. Costs of increased trade over greater distances have consistently been lower than increases in productivity achieved through specialization. As regions abandon self-sufficiency and more completely exchange specialities, wealth, income and living standards rise rapidly with trade.

Men not only wish to minimize distance and the cost of movement but also to maximize the value of productivity of each location. Individual producers seek to minimize transport charges on their products but society as a whole wishes to maximize the total value of production and transport services, and a transport infrastructure once created is part of a society's total capital goods. Even if transport services themselves lose money, the external economies or diffused benefits of a transport infrastructure accrue to the economy as a whole. Therefore, in so far as it is responsibility or wish of the state to advance the economy, the state must assume responsibility for providing the transport infrastructure.

State governments will normally give priority to internal circulation both to create a common commercial market in the state and to discourage uncontrolled international movements. If the efficiency or pattern of the transport network suffers a marked discontinuity at the borders, this also alone favours specialization and trade within the state. The railroads of the continental members of the European Economic Community, for example, in the 1950s operated on four different and mutually incompatible electric power systems. These have since been standardized. The only time a state government will itself build tap-routes is when it believes that exports will earn capital needed for internal development.

Special Political-Economic Considerations

"In addition to the purely political and the purely economic criteria for planing a transport infrastructure, governments consider other criteria which we might call mixed political and economic... Internal transport policy may express the central government's regional development policy. The government may subsidize transport facilities in the state's poor regions as a way of bringing them into the national economy." The railroads in the regionally backward North-East India, for example, handle much less freight than in the more prosperous states like Punjab, Haryana, Gujarat, Maharashtra, etc., and their operating costs are much higher. However, the Indian Railways provide service at an economic loss nevertheless, as a regional subsidy. Some states manipulate freight rates on national railroads in order to direct traffic through national ports. The imposition of higher freight rates on improted goods than on national products often serves as a camouflaged import barriers just as effective as tariffs, and national exports can be subsidized by granting reduced freight rates on movement to the border or port of export. All of these devices are common on nationally-owned rail systems.

Lastly, governments may want to subsidize travel for certain population groups. Most countries' system grant reduced fares to students, the elderly, veterans, and civil servants (Bergman, 1975).

Comparative Advantages to Different Modes of Transport Infrastructure

Each of different modes of transport infrastructure has different relative advantages over the others, particularly in terms of states' economic consolidation and development. The role of railroads in giving a practical and functional unity to the states is supplemented by the role of roads, waterways, and airlines. Roads are more flexible than railroads; they can negotiate steeper gradients, can be constructed more easily and cheaply, and thus tend to be adopted where the volume of traffic would not justify or the nature of the terrain would not permit the building of railroads. It is commonly held that where railroads cannot be laid down, roads can be developed. Most of the developed countries with their reserves of mineral and fuel deposits spreeding over wider areas, have fairly developed networks of roads. Roads have some more relative advantages over railroads, particularly their speed and efficiency, and especially their advantage of door to door transport. The added mobility of road transport has allowed the decentralization of many industries. It should be added that in most parts of the world roads not only supplement but also parallel and duplicate railroads and canals.

Although roads have been found to be more flexible than railways but it is not to suggest that political and economic importance of railways is comparatively less. We have seen earlier that the successful functioning of both the Australian and Canadian federations has been made possible by transcontinental rail links. Similarly, political integration of Russia was an outcome of the Trans-Siberian Railways which link Moscow with Vladivostok on the Pacific Coast of East Siberia across the Ural Mountains. Railroads in the United States have helped the federation in its western expansion. Political unification of India is largely an outcome of railroads which the colonial power laid down during the period of its political occupancy.

If railroads have made tremendous contribution to the political unification of political regions, they have equally made significant contribution to economic consolidation of political regions, and added new dimension to industrial development of the regions. Railroads are more an index of industrialization than roads. Railroads offer greater desirability in the mobility of heavy and bulky materials at cheaper freight rates than do roads. This is the reason that greater concentrations of industrial clusters occur on the thresholds of railways in most of the developed countries. Rail links also offer greater speed and efficiency and this has been made possible by switching over to diesel and electricity, abandoning 'steam fuel'. It has added a new dimension to the economic development and consolidation of states. Railways have played a key role in the emergence of iron and steel industries in India, particularly in the 'coal and steel belt' spreading over parts of West Bengal, Bihar, Orissa and Madhya Pradesh which account for the bulk of India's pig-iron and steel requirements.

Communist China emphasized the need for more rail links in interior parts as a prerequisite to industrialization and accordingly, the first, second, and third five year plans underlined the need for more provisions for rail links not only for the areas rich in mineral resources and industrial potentials but also to countrysides. China's rail link network, therefore, exemplifies its determined efforts to accelerate industrial growth and capacity in the Pacific region. No modern industrial complex can come up without rail links.

Water transport by way of lakes, rivers and canals as well as sea is slow, relatively cheaper, especially for bulky goods such as coal, iron ore, timber, grains, heavy machinery and equipments. Rivers such as St. Lawrence, Mississippi-Missouri, Chang Jiang (Yangtze), Rhine, Ganga and Volga have contributed significantly to the industrial and economic development of their respective regions. The role of the great lakes deserves special mention as it has greatly contributed to the growth of industrial complex in the United States, particularly in the northeast. The Chang Jiang (Yangtze) offers greater desirability to the movement of coal and iron ore to Shanghai industrial complex. Some of the largest industrial centres in the world have come up at cross-points of major navigable rivers, rail links and roads in Europe and North America.

Canals have significantly contributed to the industrial development in West Europe. Canal-building began in Europe in the seventeenth century and continued up to the nineteenth century. Major navigable rivers in West Europe got joined together by canals which provided a united economic look for the region that ultimately led to the formation of the European Economic Community. Canals are now chiefly of importance when they supplement, extend and interconnect the navigable river systems. The St. Lawrence waterways, the New York State Barage Canal, the German Mittlelland Canal, and some of the canals in France, Britain and other countries are important chiefly because each forms a part of more extensive system of navigation. At present, some waterways, especially the Rhone, Rhine and Danube, are being made more easily navigable. Canals to link the Danube with the Oder and Vistula and the Vistula through the Pripet to the Dnepr are planned. Both these and also existing canals are likely to be successful only if they are able to handle a steady and continuous movement of bulky goods such as fuel, ores or timber. Germany and Netherlands make the greatest use of water-borne transport intrastructure, which in general contributes little to the transportation facilities of most countries. China has made some significant progress in water-borne infrastructure which has necessarily enhanced its industrial capacity to some extent.

The proposed Ganga-Cauvery link in India, if comes true, will definitely offer a greater flexibility and desirability to the movement of coal, iron ore, cement, grains and a host of other minerals at a relatively cheaper freight rate. However, the project is too ambitious, and the cost involved in the construction of it would be vastly in excess of that of constructing railroads. A large number of lakes have to be constructed as the terrian is not uniform. India, being a developing country, cannot simply invest such a huge capital in the construction of a trans-continental water link of such dimension. Water-borne transport infrastructure played a significant role in the economic recovery in the erstwhile Soviet Union in the post-war period, particularly in its European part. All the member-countries of the European Union, however, have emphasized the need for water-borne transport infrastructure, particularly for the movement of bulky materials so that the pressure on railways infrastructure can be minimized to save energy and higher freight rates.

However, the airlines cannot simply compete with the 'flexibility' and 'desirability' which the roads and railways necessarily offer to the economic consolidation and development of a country. All the great economic powers have dense networks of road and railway transport infrastructures. The airlines cannot transport heavy and bulky materials needed for industrial development. The air freight rate is far in excess to that of other modes of transport infrastructrues. Even in the developed countries, the economic role of the airlines is much limited. Internal airlines in all European countries are relatively very much less important. However, in the United States the airlines have largely replaced the railways in transporting passengers, and in intercontinental travel they have gone far too to take over the business formerly handled by passenger lines. The role of the airlines in the political and economic unity of a country is yet to be assessed, though a large number of developing countries have their own airlines operating within and outside but still the role of airlines in forging national unity requires to be analyzed and measured in terms of economic potentials vis-a-vis political unity. There is no doubt that the roads, railroads, and water-borne transport are much safe and reliable means of mobility than the airlines.

Resource Conservation and Management

The word 'conservation' means 'the saving of natural resources for later consumption'. All categories of stock resources are limited in supply, and these resources always remain under some sort of constant threat of extinction and exhaustion. As mentioned earlier, the occurrence of stock resources, particularly mineral and fuel resources is a positive factor in the power inventory of a state but most of the developed and powerful nations of today are faced with a serious crisis of resource exhaustion in their respective countries. Over more than two hundred years of constant exploitation of resources for industrial sectors have put them on to a point of 'resource crisis' of unspecified dimension which now put great strain on their welfare measures and power inventory. If the resource-input gradually slows down, the power-output will definitely decline, and the states have to heavily depend on the import of materials. If they depend heavily on the periphery, they will have to change their national strategies. This is what happened when the Arab nations put oil embargo against the West European countries in the 1970s, which notwithstanding their political inclination towards the USA, sought for the Soviet help for the supply of oil. This had an adverse effect on the national strategy of the United Kingdom, France, Federal Republic of Germany and Japan as well.

Power inventory now-a-days requires a high degree of conservation of stock resources and for that most of the developed and powerful nations are gradually switching over to alternative resources, so that whatever resources be left out may be kept for later consumption. Scientific and technological innovations in the core countries have made it possible to switch over to alternative resources. Most of the countries now stress the importance of soil conservation and quality conservation of water resources, and a war against environmental pollution. Developed countries in particular, stress the need for the management of natural resources-renewable and non-renewable, whether managed by private enterprises or public sector agencies. It seeks to:

(a) explain the processes (physical, socio-economic and political) involved in resource supply, exploitation and consumption;
(b) analyze the allocation of resource products and services over space and time; and
(c) develop alternative management strategies and evolutionary tools.

Resource management has been necessitated following the public concern over declining environmental standards, economic change, the equity of resource allocation and the capacity of the earth to sustain further increase in population and economic activity. It is a process or system of decision-making whereby resource use or conservation policies and practices are derived and resources are allocated over space and time. Developed nations, particularly the core nations, are now paying more attention to:

(a) evaluating the performance of mineral sector (public and private) according to alternative (i.e., non-economic efficiency) criteria, such as distribution equity, employment generation, supply security and the maintenance of environmental quality;
(b) assessing the role of government (at all spatial scales—local, regional, national and international) in affecting the development and allocation of mineral resources; and
(c) analyzing the structural limits inherent in the capitalist mode of exchange and their implications for public-policy making. A particularly important area of work concerns the unequal trade relations between mineral exporting LDCs (less developed countries) and advanced consumer nations.

Conservation and resource management have now become major concerns for the advanced countries, particularly for the core countries which though weld considerable power in world economy and politics but are now faced with resource crisis and problems of allocation that appear to have profound effect on the pattern of their power inventories and strategies. It is not only the advanced and developed countries alone which emphasize conservation and resource management but also all the countries of the periphery have recognized the importance of conservation and resource management as a prerequisite condition for economic development vis-a-vis power-potential.

However, there can be some simple generalizations on the role of natural resources in economic growth. These are:

(1) The possession of a sizeable and diversified natural resource endowment is a major advantage to any country embarking upon a period of rapid economic growth. Diversification may be less important than the dimensions of one or more resources, if their reserves are large enough and long run demand is steady and strong.
(2) Resources need not be situated within the confines of the country undergoing development but they must be accessible. Accessibility implies transportation and transportation in part implies imports, both of which demand accumulation of capital with which to obtain materials from extranational or discontinuous resource endowments.
(3) One of the major means for capital accumulation is an abundance of easily exploitable natural resources (Saudi Arabia, Ukraine, Russia, South Africa, Venezuela).
(4) In no sense, however, are natural resources responsible for development and economic growth; they possess no deterministic power. However, they possess talent, utility and are part of an overall regional capability.
(5) They also may set limits upon the approaches to natural resource planning and development. If a given raw material necessary for some phase of industrialization is not located *in situ* and is not available due to tariff barriers or high transportation costs, modification of that phase is likely. Or if rapid rises in agricultural, forest or mineral production are possible, they may strongly influence the system of priorities and scale of operations which will characterize a total developmental effort or history.
(6) Even if abundant natural resources will not determine the kinds of uses to which they will be put, their availability in agriculture particularly however, may influence critically the shift from agricultural to non-agricultural employments.
(7) The significance and functions of natural resources in economic development will differ markedly with the stages in the development process. Under normal circumstances, the role of the resource endowment is most important in the earlier stages of economic development when it acts as a means for capital accumulation and an accelerator for economic growth if abundant, and as a depressant upon that growth if niggardly.
(8) Similarly, the significance of indigenous resources is much less in the highly developed countries with their discontinuous world hinterlands, and larger supplies of capital, skilled labour, technology and entrepreneurial experience than to the relatively lesser developed regions frequently characterized by scarcities of all these factors.
(9) Any comprehensive programme for economic development demands the development of a sophisticated inventory of resource endowments, an ap-

praisal of present systems of resource utilization, an analysis of cultural and physical obstacles to resource potentials, taking into account conflicting uses and demands for given resources and the probable role of technological change over periods of time.

It is now almost true that in international politics power is basically related to the area, population, resources and industrial potential of the state as modified by geographical location and level of technology. A state, richly endowed with resources, with a technological capacity to develop them and utilize them, enhancing its industrial capacity, is sure to weld considerable power in world politics.

In the world economy approach, power is a direct reflection of the ability of the state to operate within the systems of its own material advantage. This depends on the efficiency of its production processes which requires to be measured by categories of core, semi-periphery and periphery. If power is overtly expressed then one can expect a core-semi-periphery-periphery sequence of success chances in a given conflict. But most expression of this power will be covert and structural. Although this is essentially an economic definition of power, it can be directly related to the notion of the 'strong state' as a complementary expression of power. The core states of today are the hegemonic states. In contrast, the semiperiphery tends to be occupied by authoritarian states which appear to be politically powerful but in terms of economic-military power-potentials, they are much below the core states. However, the semi-periphery is the most dynamic category in the world economy and the states have to employ political processes to restructure the system in their favour.

Finally, the peripheral states constitute the weakest element in the system. For much of the history of the world economy, this zone has not been in political control of its territory but has had colonial status. Even with political independence, however, economic dependence will remain, leading to concepts such as 'informal imperialism' and 'neocolonialism', whereby the destiny of the zone lies in the hands of the core states.

Chapter 10

Elements of Spatial Structure of the State

The state comprises of core area, capital city, boundaries and frontiers, as the main elements of its spatial structure. The core area refers to some central area within a state that acts as the mainspring for its subsequent territorial growth. The capital city is the control centre of the territory, the locus of political decision making, the symbolic centre of the states, and often very much more. The capital city's rational location is within the core area, which makes its role, as the locus of political decision making, geographically, the most expressive. The boundary is a necessary component of the territorial sovereignty of the political entity as it explicitly limits the political-territorial jurisdiction of the state, while the frontier is an area/zone between two social systems or entities. Here, in this chapter, the discussion will only concentrate on core area and capital city, as a separate chapter deals with the frontiers and boundaries.

The Core Area

There are examples to reveal that a great majority of states in the present-day world have not, in general, been created suddenly or abruptly, rather, they have developed slowly over a period of centuries, which might have involved territorial aggrandizement/acceretion, around some "territories which performed central function", and also voluntary accession of territories to them. Some states, such as Austria-Hungary, Bulgaria, Soviet Union, and perhaps Yugoslavia and Czechoslovakia look back nostalgically to a time when they were spread over a wider territorial area, than they now do. Some have even made the recovery of a former 'greater' state, a dominant objective of policy, such as the communists of the former Soviet Union attempted to revive the older territorial-political system, through a series of 'coups', but with disastrous effect on their relations with East European non-Slavik political entities.

Some states have been created for what is better termed 'geopolitical conveniences' of the major powers. Some states have resulted, on account of the great powers' rivalries, which ultimately culminated with their creation. Afghanistan is one such state whose birth, say hundred years back, was a result of the contemporary Anglo-Russian imperial rivalry. In fact, the buffer states, both in the nineteenth century and in the present century, have come up, largely as a result of great power rivalries, which ultimately aimed at the maintenance of the regional balance of power. Some states are the result of unilateral action of a particular state, which once commanded the destiny of the region. Nepal, Bhutan and also Sikkim (now a part of the Indian Union) were formerly created as 'frontier dependencies' by Great Britain, whose authority in the region was unchallengable, and which ultimately became sovereign political entities. Again, there are examples to reveal that some states, so created, now happen to coincide with 'nations', and also reflect the political aspirations of them. Most of the West Asian Muslim states may be said to belong to this category as they had been created by the European powers to suit their geopolitical needs and strategic conveniences. Israel, created in 1948, through a UN Resolution, to fill a pre conceived geographical area, now stands as one of the most important nation-states in West Asia, in the midst of the Muslim states.

Now, we have two categories of states: (1) those which gradually grew up around a central area/focus, and (ii) those which have been established without reference to a central focus/area, and their territory has subsequently been coherently organized.

Pounds and Bull (1964) have attempted to distinguish the sovereign political entities, i.e., states into two broad categories: (i) those which have been created arbitrarily to fill some preconceived geographical frame, as arbitrary states; and (2) those which grew slowly over a long period of time from some nuclear, or germinal, or core area as organic state. It is felt that the continued vitality of an organic state depends on whether its core area functions efficiently as a central focus, justifying its subsequent territorial growth.

Criteria and Characteristics of Core Area

The concept of core area dates back to the late nineteenth century, when Friedrich Ratzel in his *Politische Geographie* (1897) set forth a paradigm for the contemporary political-geographical thinking using the word 'territorial cells'. He stated that "states tended to begin as territorial cells, which would then become larger through the addition of land and people, and eventually evolved into states or even empires". Here, in this concept, Friedrich Ratzel is believed to have used one of basic themes of the contemporary Darwinian paradigm, which had considerable relevance to contemporary geographical scholarship: "change through time or evolution—a general concept of gradual or even transition from lower to simpler to higher or more complicated forms".

The American geographer, Derwent Whittlesey (1952) carried forward the Ratzellean tradition of 'territorial cell', along with the same Darwinian theme, replaced the word by 'core area'. To him, the "state tends to crystallize about a nuclear core that fostered integration, and in nearly all states the nuclear core is also the most populous part—its ecumene." He defined the core area as "the area in which or about which a state originates".

The Ratzel-Whittlesey genetic concept of the core area finds its recognized expression in Pounds and Bulls' viewpoint, when they contend that core growth states enjoy a greater degree of coherence and viability than the rest. The genetic idea of a core area is intrinsically helpful in understanding the origin and the process of early territorial growth of many states, either from a nuclear endowed with centrality or, as in the case of many colonial and new world states, from an area with access from the outside and with increasing primacy in its nodality internally.

In contrast to what Pounds and Bull have contended with regard to greater coherence and internal unity for a core-growth states, Richard Hartshorne (1950) pointed out that notwithstanding, the Magyar dominated Mid-Danube, appeared to provide the natural focus surrounding smaller lowlands and mountain highlands that facilitated greater territorial aggrandizement, and subsequent organization of the large area included in the Hungarian kingdom, that had hardly offered greater coherence and national unity for it. Again he pointed out that the United States emerged, largely because of the union of a greater number of regions, closely interrelated in an ever shifting balance, and that formed the basis for coherence and territorial unit. It is, therefore, not a core-growth state.

Therefore, what he concludes is that "a core area is neither sufficient nor essential to the evolution of a nation or state. What is essential is a common idea that convinces the people in all the regions is that they belong together. Historically, in certain states, a core area may have played a major role in spreading that idea to other regions and it may continue today as in France, Argentina, or Mexico, to focus the interest of the region on itself as the centre of what has become a functioning unit: but the common idea for a state may develop where no core area exists".

Andrew Burghardt (1969) developed a functional concept of the core area. He distinguished between historically-oriented core areas and contemporary core areas, especially in the light of the 'functions' that the core areas had performed within the framework of historical association and habitation, and also in the context of greatest political activities, confined to a particular region, within the state.

The concept of Ratzel and Whittlesey requires to be identified as the 'nuclear core' represented by the cases in which a small territory grows into a larger state, perhaps over a period of centuries, by intermittent absorption of land and people. "The nuclear core is the germinal area around which accretions of territory produced the modern territorial state." Besides the nuclear core, Burghardt recognized/identified the following two other distinct concepts of the core area:

1. Original core area as a germinal area which failed to obtain accretion of territory, and
2. Contemporary core as the current area of greatest political and economic importance in a state. This contemporary core may have superseded the nuclear core of a state; in other words, a state's core area can shift and relocate over long periods of time.

A state may have all these three distinct core areas, with different functional orientations, confined to a particular area. Such as the Moscow area of the Russian State, which had been, no doubt, the nuclear core of the state: the subsequent Russian territorial growth took place around it, and in the present century, particularly during the inter-war and the post-war periods, the Moscow area functioned as the original core area. The Moscow area has always remained an area of maximum political importance. Now with the industrial republics having seceded from the Soviet State, the Moscow area in Russia has acquired immense economic significance also.

In India, the nuclear core and the original core seem to be rooted in the Ganga plains, particularly, between Gaya and Mathura, being the seat of Hindu systems of belief or iconography but the contemporary core spreads in a split manner over a wide belt, across Delhi, Punjab, Haryana, Rajasthan, Gujarat, and Maharashtra. This belt has now acquired immense political and economic significance, expressive in India's national polity.

The contemporary core in the Republic of South Africa seems to be 'split' in nature, in the sense that the area around the port city of Durban, with its rich industrial-agricultural complex in the province of Natal, has considerable economic importance over other areas of the Republic, while the Cape Town area in the south welds considerable political significance over other areas in the state. Hence, the contemporary core is split in its spatial character.

While tracing the evolution of the modern states of the European continent, particularly in the light of their growth from nuclear and original cores, Pounds and Bull (1964) have also taken a functional view of it, and identified three categories: (i) fifteen states of the twenty-five states studied have had 'distinct' core areas; (ii) four states have 'peripheral' or 'external' core areas; and (iii) remaining six states have no 'distinct' core areas. The first category of states are those which have achieved their present limits by a process of accretion around a nuclear or core area, while the second category of states might have grown in the past, from core areas which are now peripheral or external, or even outside their present territorial limits. The third category of states are those which do not have distinct core areas, simply because they were established by certain creative act, either of external powers, or of internal forces suddenly mustered to resist external pressures.

de Blij (1972) has distinguished between states with 'central positioned' core areas, and states with 'marginally located' core areas, i.e., they lie on the margins, near the edges of states. These core areas are known as eccentric/external core areas, which once formed the 'nucleus' for subsequent territorial growth, have since been cut off by politico-geographical events. However, there are states which have quite distinct core areas, and 'incipient' core areas emerging elsewhere.

Kasperson and Minghi (1969) have remarked: "The concept of core area is less easily defined, as it lacks the concreteness and the universal applicability of the capital idea. It is an obstraction by no means widely accepted as a useful analytical tool, and it has been developed and tested as a working concept only at the nation-state level. Core area is not easily defined and in a real sense has two meanings which often become inextricably mixed and confused in any discussion. On the one hand, it can be seen in a contemporary context as that region within the political area where there is a concentration of population, transportation, resources, and so on. As such, a core area is often referred to as the 'heart' of the state. Another definition, more original but with less utility, is framed in historical terms and describes the core area on the nuclear areas in or about which the state has originated and from which the state idea spread. By this later definition its prerequisites for a success as a core are made up of some workable combinations including unusual fertility to support a non-agricultural development, physical features to facilitate defence and a nodal position in respect to the transportation and communication network...the essence of capital city and core area is their centrality within the political unit functionally if not necessarily geometrically. They form the central focus of a political region defined in terms of nodality. In many respects, there is a high degree of areal coincidence between the capital and the core by either definitions, although this is by no means the rule. Pounds, de Blij and Etzioni, all stress the function of core area for political integration, although only Etzioni demonstrates them."

To Deutsch (1953) political geographers have sought to identify core areas around which larger states were organized successfully in the course of history. Characteristic features of such core areas are unusual fertility of soil, permitting a dense agricultural population and providing a food surplus to maintain additional numbers in non-agricultural pursuits; geographic features facilitating military defence of the area, and a nodal position at an intersection of major transportation routes... It should be noted that the density that makes a core area is one of traffic and communication rather than mere number of passive villagers densely settled on the soil. Thus, the dense population of the Nile valley seems to have been less effective as a wider centre of integration than the sparse population of the Arab territories beyond Mecca and Medina, who more than compensated by the proportionately far greater mobility, activity and traffic...the theory of core areas, however, cannot account for the persistence of some states and the failure of others. What counts for more may well be what happens within each core areas, and perhaps particularly what happens in its towns.

Pounds and Bull (1964), who have recognized fifteen out of twenty-five states of modern Europe, to have grown around distinct core areas, through the accretion process over centuries, have also identified the factors responsible for it. To them, all such core areas date back to the early Middle Ages, and were regions of good soil with relatively high agricultural productivity. They were the 'regions of increment'. Archaeological evidences tend to show that they were relatively densely populated. All showed during their formative period in the early Middle Ages—roughly from the eighth to the twelth century—a very heavy investment in art and architecture, itself an indication of the surplus which these areas yielded, and most because of the seat, not only of civil administration, but also of ecclesiastical.

Most of the distinct core areas of the fifteen states lay also at the focus of routes, and as such they carried on trade during the ninth and tenth centuries vigorously. The wealth gained from trade must have contributed to the political power of the core areas which further intensified the territorial growth around them. Most of these core areas possessed in some degree a natural means of defence which gave them some protection during this early formative period. Physical barriers, such as, forests gave protection to the Paris and London regions; wide, marshy valleys enclosed the Polish core areas; mountains and waste provided protection to the core areas of Sweden and Switzerland. These seemed to have offered some degree of defence to most of these core areas in one way or other.

If chronology is to be believed, then it can be said that the core-growth states, irrespective of their central or eccentric location, have a higher degree of unity and cohesion than the others. But the cohesiveness tends to diminish from the core area toward the borders of the states. However, the actual degree of cohesiveness depends to a large degree on whether the actual boundaries have been cut back to eliminate areas and peoples not fully attuned to the ideals of the country, or expanded to embrace peoples who could not be expected fully to share these ideals within a measurable period of time.

Alternative Explanation for Core Area Concept

Hechter and Brustein, in 1980, offered an alternative explanation of the core area concept which has been the legacy of Ratzel-Whittlesey-Deutsch-Pounds-Bull tradition and heritage. In fact, the Hechter-Brustein model is an improvement on the traditional model and one which can be made compatible with the world systems approach.

The Hechter-Brustein model postulates a direct spatial correlation between the rise of the modern territorial state and pre-existing regional differences in economic organization. From at least the twelth century onwards there were three types of economic organizations in Western Europe with distinct geographical distributions:

(i) a sedentary pastoral zone largely located on Atlantic Seaboard from Scandinavia to northern Iberia;

(ii) a petty commodity zone in the western Mediterranean coasts, and up the 'dorsal spine' of Europe to the Rhine in southern Germany and Netherlands; and

(iii) a 'feudal' zone in four patches—central England, northern France, through to central Rhinelands, central Spain and central Portugal.

Each zone had a distinctive social organization with self-sufficient households linked by kinship ties in the sedentary pastoral zone contrasting with citizen merchants dominating the more advanced economic organization of the petty commodity zone. In between, the feudal zone was based on the unit of the manor with arable agriculture under landlord domination. From the eleventh century onward states in the feudal zone expanded at the cost of other zones. This zone had important political and economic advantages but the key criterion was the existence of the political divisions in their social organization which was the basis of the territorial state.

In the sedentary pastoral zone towns were small and unimportant and the social formation was dominated by the landed interests. In the petty commodity zone the urban merchants dominated the society. The towns became centres of consumption based on long-distance trade separated from the local agriculture except as a source of revenue.

In contrast, in the feudal zone, towns developed a central place function in inter-manorial trade leading to a rising autonomous urban merchant interest in competition with the landed interest. It is the potential conflict situation between fundamentally different interests which the territorial state evolved to contain. In the petty commodity zone and the sedentary pastoral zone the existing political monopolies did not require the existence of the new territorial state. Hence successful core areas, in the sense of nuclear cores, tended to occur in the feudal zone. In fact, four of the five initially strongest territorial states in the world economy, viz., Portugal, Spain, France and England, emerged from core areas in the feudal zone. This model can be referred to as an explanation of why it was the seaward countries—and these four in particular-that led the way in establishing the new inter-state system even though it was 'city state' Europe which seemed to be more economically advanced. But more important, these social conditions based upon conflict of interest produced the first modern states which would forge a world economy with themselves as part of a much larger core.

The Hechter-Brustein model, nevertheless, is an improvement over the traditional one, and offers an alternative explanation with regard to the specific social formation vis-a-vis territorial growth of European states at a particular time. The Pounds-Bull model, on the other hand, provides a general definition of core area which enables it to be used in other contexts in which different processes operate.

Examples of Nuclear Core (Ratzel-Whittlesey-Pounds-Bull Model)

Attempt has been made to identify and recognize the distribution of nuclear core in most of the states of modern Europe. France is often cited as a classic example of a distinct core-growth state in Europe. The nuclear core area of France, if chronology is to be believed, dates back to AD 987, and it lay around Paris along the river Seine, about 160 kilometres from the sea, and near the junction of important tributaries—the Oise and the Maine. The history of France is said to have been written in her rivers, the authority of the French kings, based on Paris, advanced, so it is claimed, up or down the rivers which converge on the city.

The core area, in and around the Paris basin in France, which germinated in the eleventh century and expanded subsequently, still remains the nuclear core area of France today. During the formative centuries, the provinces were made to depend so intimately on Paris that no fundamental change is now possible.

The nuclear core area of Great Britain seems to be much older than its French counterpart. It all started to germinate in AD 49, in the valley of the Thames, which widens eastward to the North Sea. It began during the Roman occupation. The city of Verulaminum was the capital of Roman Britain, which was near St. Albans, 32 kilometres northwest of London, and was in itself the largest city and the commercial centre. The boundary of Roman Britain lay along the Welsh and Scottish borders. Subsequent Anglo-Saxons invasions, and later by the Norsemen, destroyed the unity of Roman Britian, and the lower Thames valley, the nuclear core area was divided. It was not until the Norman conquest that the importance of the London area was restored. Here was built the king's chief castle; here was the church, Westminister Abbey, in which the kings were crowned; here the officers of the state, when they gradually ceased to be peripatetic, established their offices. A few kilometres south-east of London was Canterbury Carthedral, seat of the Archbishop and Primate of All England. Lastly, from London there still radiated that networks of roads constructed by the Romans, and up the Thames to the port of London came the ships of a growing commercial fleet. During its subsequent spatial growth, the London area first spread across northern England and along the Welsh border, but it was during the thirteenth century the territorial extent spread across Wales, and in the early seventeenth century, across Scotland. Thus, the present Great Britain seems to have grown around the London area through accretions.

The Polish State seems to have grown around the core area which was crystallized during the eighth and ninth centuries, and lay between the Oder and Vistula rivers. It was a region of considerable fertility and comfort. Throughout history it was protected by the flat, wide, and marshy valleys of the rivers which enclosed it on most sides. The Russian State grew up amid the mixed forest of the Muscovy region, around the headwaters of the Valga and Oka rivers, and here it enjoyed some degree of natural protection from the raiders of the Steppe. It also lay at a focus of routes which tended to follow the Russian rivers.

The core area of Switzerland seems to have crystallized, in the early thirteenth century across, the St. Gothhard Pass, which facilitated trade through the sparsely populated region of Central Alps. The rest of Switzerland grew around it, as it acquired greater political and economic monopolies in the subsequent days.

The core area of Sweden lay in the lowland region which encloses Lake Malaren, and dates back to the Middle and Late Iron Age; that of Denmark, on the islands near Copenhagen, that of Greece, in the plain of Attica, that of Italy, in the plains around Rome; that of Finland in the hinterlands of Helisinki, and Turku and dates back to early Middle Ages; that of Republic of Ireland in the hinterlands of Dublin. The Bulgarian State seems to have emerged in and around the fertile platform which slopes down from the Stara Planina to the Danube. The Hungarian core area lay in Transdanubia or Dunantul; and that of Romania in the plains of Walachia and Moldavia. The early German core area lay in the middle Rhinelands, but in the late nineteenth century Brodenburge-Prussia emerged as the political nucleus of it (Fig.10.1).

In Asia, the Chinese State appears to have grown in and around the valleys of Howang Ho and its tributaries. Here, the loess soil was highly suited to primitive agriculture, and the forests on its north-western outskirts provided some degree of defence to it. Here was located the earlier capital of China. As China became maritime oriented, the importance of the Yellow plains as the

Figure 10.1: European Core Areas (After Pounds and Bull, 1964)

political nucleus, diminished, and that of the lower Yanglze valley between Nanking and Hangchow, acquired political monopoly, and that witnessed subsequent territorial extent. During the Mongol rule, again, the earlier area in the valleys of the Howang Ho and its tributaries became the main political focus. During the Manchu period, the political decision-making focus lay down in the Yellow plains. Again, when the Manchu dynasty was overthrown, the lower Yangtze area became the political nucleus. No doubt, China is a core-growth state, but its core area had always remained 'oscillating' in character between the loessic Howang-Ho valleys and the extratropical lower Yanglze valley, throughout its history.

India is also a core-growth state. The Indian State, in the past, had grown up in and around the Ganga valley, particularly that part of the valley between Prayag (Sangam) and Pataliputra, which became the political nucleus in the fourth century BC that witnessed the subsequent territorial growth during the Mauryan period. Subsequent Hindu and Muslim empires grew around it. However, during the medieval period, particularly the Turk-Afghan-Mughal period, the political nucleus moved to the upper Ganga valley and it lay in the Ganga-Yamuna doab, mainly along the Ganga valley, between Prayag (Sangam) and Mathura. The environmental-strategic character of the Ganga plains, particularly above Pataliputra, provided fertile soil for agricultural production plus nodal position for water-borne trade in different materials. The Ganga valley also possessed in some degree a natural means of defence. It has been rightly observed, "that Hindu opinion always viewed it as such is seen from the fact that not only in Ganges the sacred river par excellence of India but the area from Gaya to Mathura, from Sangam to Hardwar, is recognized by every one to be the holy land of Hindus. Every dynasty...once it established its authority in its homeland dreamed of consolidating its rule by establishing itself in the area" (Fig.10.2).

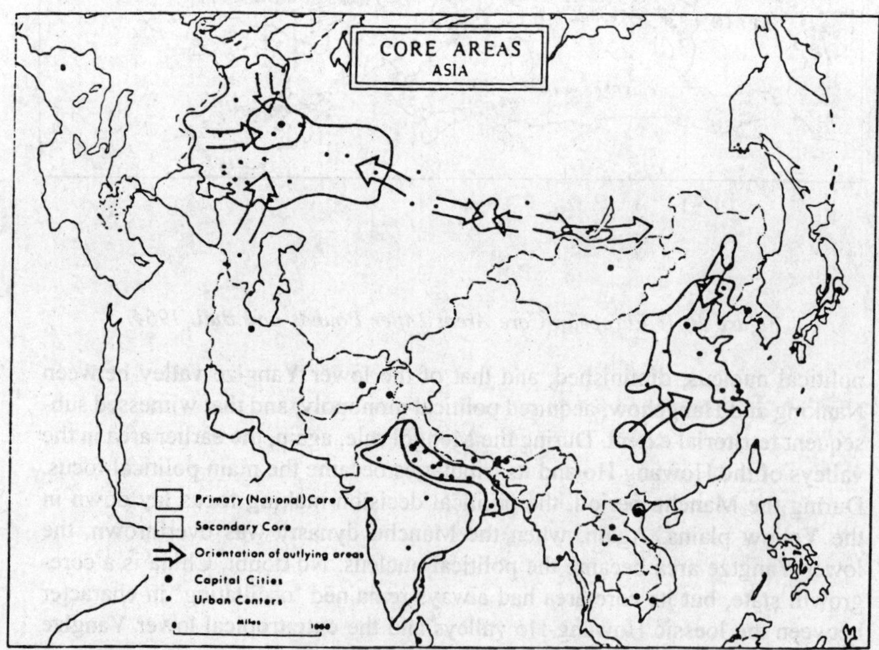

Figure 10.2: Core Areas in Asia

The core area of Campuchia lay in the alluvial plains around the vast and famous temple of Angkor Wat, which has always remained the Campuchian centre of national iconography, that of Thailand in the plains of the Chao Phrya river; that of Myanmar in the middle Irrawddy valley where Ava and Mandalay grew up as earlier political-cultural centres. The core areas of the archipelago states of the Philippines, Malayasia and Indonesia lie on the most productive and densely populated islands of each. In all the cases, the capital city also is situated there; Manila lies on Luzon, Kualalumpur on western Malaya, and Djakarta on Java.

The Persian State in West Asia had its origin in the valleys of the Euphrates and the Tigris in the early Middle Ages, while the Turkish State first nucleated around the Turkis straits, but in course of the subsequent development, maximum territorial growth occurred around Ankara on the Anatolia plateau, simply because of its strategic character.

Neither the USA nor Canada seems to have been a core-growth state. But Philbrick (1963) has recognized the North American core area. The north-eastern core area of the United States merges with the core area of Canada, located in the south-east of that state. The core areas of the USA and Canada are the primary manufacturing concentrations and they contain less than 10 per cent of the total areas of the USA-Canada, but they contain half the total population and nearly three-fourths of the industrial employment. This area is not only the contemporary core but also the historic or the original (indeed even nuclear) core of the USA-Canada. The state idea originated here, territorial expansion into the western frontier took place from here, and capital cities of the states that emerged are today situated here. Chronologically, the Mexican core area is much older than the USA-Canada core region. It lies on the southern central plateau which has (i) maximum population concentration, (ii) potential agricultural lands, and (iii) densest communication network and (iv) most of the major industrial units (Fig. 10.3).

The Australian core region is eccentrically confined to the south-eastern part of the state, with two ports of Melbourne and Sydney forming the central focii of the region. The salient features of this core area are good agricultural land, the vast majority of manufacturing units and the bulk of the Australian population.

Only Egypt, Sudan and Ethiopia, in Africa, may be said to possess nuclear core areas in the sense of regions around which subsequent territorial developments occurred, and states have coalesced together in which are embodied the traditions and iconographies. Egypt grew along the Nile valley, and the valley upstream from Cairo has been the focus of the earlier Egyptian State in historic times. Ethiopia (Abyssinia) crystallized around the mountain-gird basin of Addis Ababa. Sudan around the fertile, irrigable lands along the

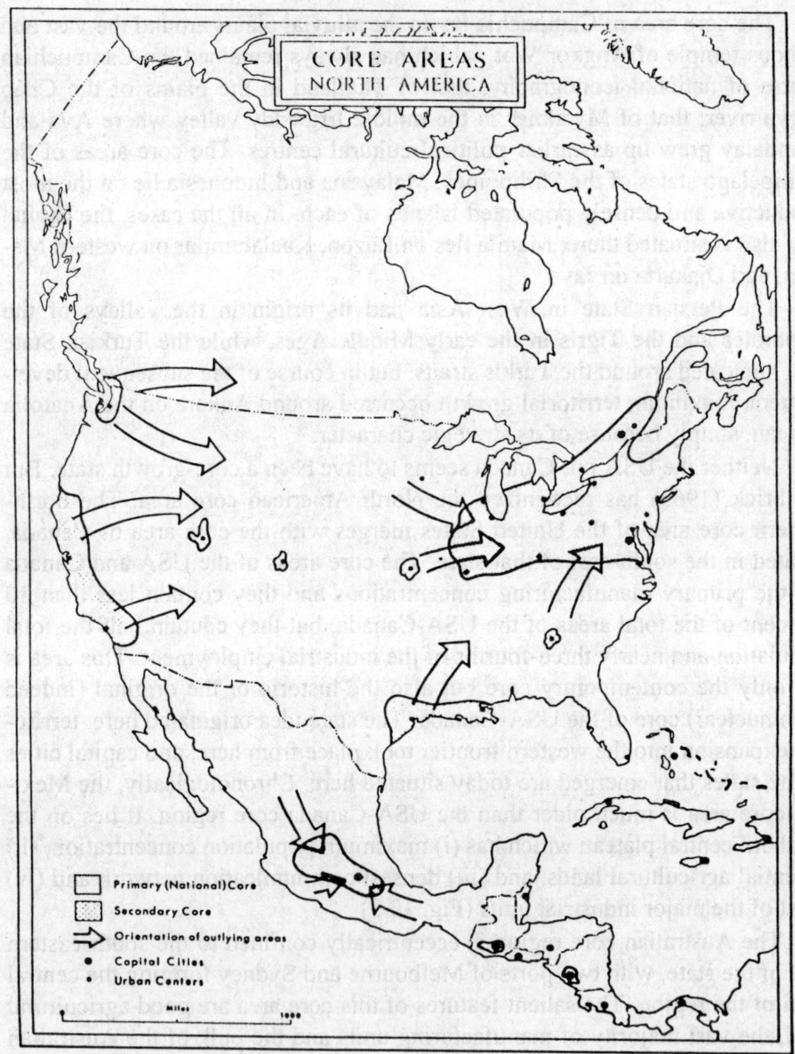

Figure 10.3: Core Areas in North America

White and Blue Niles where they join at Khartoum.

With the exception of Brazil, the states of Latin America grew from the administrative decisions of the Spanish empire. However, the Brazillian core area extends beyond Vitoria in the north, Curitiba in the south, and inland it includes Belo Horizonte, the steel producing centre, and most of the tierra templada of the east. Included in this core area are a number of urban centres, of which Rio de Janerio and Sao Paulo are the chief.

To sum up Taylor says (1985): "Pounds-Bull and deBlij not only attempted to confuse political processes over time in their core area concept but also tended to confuse political processes across the spatial structure of the world economy. Most of the core areas of modern non-European states consist of the original zones through which the territory was incorporated into the world economy. As such the vast majority are coastal or else are associated with raw materials which attracted European penetration. They are, therefore, the opposite of the initial European core area. Instead of a process generating a strong territorial state as unit of security and opportunity, in the non-European case core areas are vulnerable areas which provide opportunities for external interests. To equate European core areas with the development of territorial states in other parts of the world is a typical error of the developmentalism. Most peripheral states began their history as colonial appendices of imperial states... this constitutes another example of the neglect of imperaialism as a factor in the making of our world. Modern non-European territorial states are not repeating the political processes that generated the European State. In the world-systems approach, ... two sets of broad mechanisms are operative, one for the core and one for the periphery. The core area model as the germinal area of the modern state is a very early process that contributed to the development of core processes in the world economy and which have not been repeated in the periphery."

Capital Cities

One of the distinguishing features of core areas is that they usually have the capital city of the state located within them, so that the functions of government are generally performed within this region. Paris and London are obvious examples of it. A capital city is destined to become "an epitome of the national life, in which their history and traditions are enshrined, and its authority is buttressed by increasing size and wealth which accompany multiplication of trade and industry at the political centre. It embodies and exemplifies the nature of the core areas of states, and a reflection of the wealth, organization and power of the political entity" (Whittlesey, 1939). The capital is "a place wherein the political authority of a territorial limit is concentrated" (Spate, 1942). It is the control centre of the territory, the locus of political decision-making, the symbolic centre of the state and often very much more. It is one of the main distinguishing elements of the spatial structure of the state, for that no political entities should have their *raison d'etre* without it. It is the most politico-geographically expressive of the image of the state, particularly, in its spatial perspective.

Location of Capital Cities

As is reasonable to expect, the capital cities of most states tend to be situated in the core areas of their respective states. Here, in the core-growth states, it is the core area that preceded the development of the capital. As the core areas were the regions of increment or comfort, the capitals were suitably located, particularly on the thresholds of the lines of communication across the core areas, and also on sites which possessed in some degree a natural means of defence, which offered them some kind of protection during the early phase of their location/development. A strategic location was an obvious preference/choice within the core area so that the 'expanding space relationship' to it could be expressively/effectively achieved. For example, London was so strategically located in the Thames core area that it successfully spearheaded the subsequent territorial incorporation of Wales in the thirteenth century and of Scotland in the early seventeenth century, into the newly evolved territorial system.

Pataliputra, the ancient Hindu imperial capital, with its core location in the Ganga valley, particularly, along the river, and, on major contemporary trade route, in the early phase of the Hindu aggrandizement across the northern plains played the most decisive strategic role in integrating/organizing the territories under the imperial territorial system in the fourth century BC. In most of the core-growth states, the capitals are centrally located.

Particularly, during the late medieval period, when larger territorial states were in their formative stage, and their boundaries were expanding towards desired areas, there was a tendency for a frontier location for the capital cities so that they could successfully bring together and integrate the desired territories. During the formative period of the larger frontier, a peripheral location was always preferred for the capital, simply, because of the fact that the territorial organization of the marchland could be better achieved. Delhi, as a frontier capital, played the most decisive role in transforming the marches lying to the west of it, mainly during the formative phase of the British Indian Territorial State in the Indian subcontinent.

The frontier capital was later known as forward capital, and the credit goes to Vaughan Cornish who in his, *The Great Capitals* (1923), put forward the idea of the forward capital to which, O.H.K. Spate (1942) remarked as, "a great advance as it introduced dynamic and historical elements in the study of capitals". A forward position, that is, a position near the most active boundary, has been at all times in history a typical site for the location of a capital. A forward capital of yesterday may become a national capital today, or eccentric capital of the past, due to political-territorial growth, may develop into a central capital in a changed situation or circumstances. Delhi, which was a forward capital during the formative phase of the British India, is no longer a forward capital in a changed politico-geographical scenario.

The idea of frontier capital or forward capital thus appears to be increasingly concerned with the military-political reasons, rather than any other reasons. However, the choice of Brasilia, as the new capital of Brazil, much away from the contemporary Brazillian core region, but close to the interior Amazon region, does not reflect any obvious military reasons, but here, in choice of the site the economic reasons are more obvious, particularly in the light of their political implications. The vast interior Brazil had been gradually developing into a potential region of political configuration, on account of continued political negligence and ignorance, and of sustained economic discrimination for decades. This had given rise to the secessionist feelings among the inhabitants of the interior, which largely threatened the *raison d'etre* of Brazil. To overcome this, an interior or an interior eccentric site for the capital was felt to be a legitimate spatial necessity and Brasilia was chosen.

O.H.K. Spate (1942) has introduced a new idea of 'headlink' capital whereby it is viewed as the primary link in a chain representing the organizing direction of the state. "The capital is often the link through which the state in process of formation receives the vital external influences that impregnate its internal potentialities, for, ... no civilized state is the sole architect of its own civilization... it often guards a dangerous frontier, gathering behind it the not yet united components of the state, organizing them into a whole on the face of some external menace to their common culture, perhaps finally taking the offensive and becoming the forward capital of an advancing empire; such was the role...of Vienna before 1700...London as local centre, regional focus, border depot and fortress, but above all as the headlink that provides the organizing direction of the state, at the same time acting as a receiving chamber through which pass external influences, to be there translated into stimuli of the local culture." The headlink capital concept, therefore, seemed to be an 'implied' manifestation of the forward capital concept. The location of the capital in both the cases is at the extremity.

It is observed that most of the truly core-growth states, with their capitals in the core areas, have a long tradition of unitary political structure, but in a federal political structure, the location of the capital does not necessarily reflect the core. The capital is located on a 'mutually agreed neutral site'. Since the federation is a set of complex politico-territorial structure, with constituent territorial units, each having a central focus. It is extremely difficult to select any of the central focii as the possible site for the capital. It requires a lot of negotiations and compromise between the constituent/federating units, to agree on a 'neutral' or 'compromise-site' for the location of the capital. Washington, Ottawa and Canberra are located on 'mutually agreed neutral site' in an obvious reflection. Their choice has evenly balanced the conflicting interests of the federating units.

Apart from these, capitals tend to be located in the region of increment, i.e., in areas of climatic suitability. It has been rightly pointed out that in "states, possessed of extreme climates, capitals tend to seek the optimum margins that is the most temperate sectors of their areas". Most of the states, with wide latitudinal extent, tend to have their capitals, located on or near the sea coast, because of the greater climatic suitability that the maritime environment provides. While, most of the 'longitudinally' elongated states tend to seek a 'central' location, simply because it offers greater 'desirability and felxibility' to the capital particularly in its internal space relationship.

There have been several instances of change in the location of capitals, both in the past and present also. There are several geographical and political reasons for locational changes of capitals, which involve physical, political, economic or social, and military motivations. Rajagriha, the royal capital of the Magadhan republic during the period of Bimbisara in the sixth century BC, was surrouned by hills, and strategically situated. Notwithstanding its strategic significance, it had certain problems, such as those of water supply and not being on the routes. It was around 494 BC that Ajatashatru, the son of Bimbisara, abandoned the site of Rajagriha, and moved his capital to Pataliputra, in the vicinity of the Ganga. This locational shift of the royal capital provided more security, greater desirability and mobility, and assured water supply for centuries to the successive republics and empires.

In case of Thailand and Mayanmar (Burma) in South-east Asia, the location of the capital shifted thrice since 1700. Ayutthaya was the earlier capital for Thailand. It then shifted to Jhonburi in 1767, and finally shifted to Bangkok in 1782. Similarly, the capital of Mayanmar shifted from Ava to Mandalay in 1857 and to Rangoon in 1885. These locational shifts in Thailand and Burma were necessitated by the urge of the respective states to seek "vital external influences to impregnate their internal potentialities", and for that a sea-oriented eccentric location for the capital was a spatial compulsion. Turkey presents a complex pattern of locational change for the capital.Earlier, it all started with its territorial expansion across the Turkish Straits into the Balkan region. In the fourteenth century, the capital was moved to Adrianople, then in the fifteenth century, it was relocated to Constantinople because the site was well suited to serve as capital of an empire which stretched from the Danube to the Euphrates and the Nile. But the strategic importance of Constantirople as capital declined rapidly after the disunion and fall of the Turkish empire. The capital moved for a more 'ethnic location' to Ankara in 1923, in the midst of the plateau of Anatolia. Ankara is more expressive of the Turkish culture and tradition, rather than Constantinople which is more European in outlook and tradition. With Turkey being teritorially more confined to Asia it needed to have a capital with a central location on the plateau which was geographically more tenable.

The shift of capital of the United States from New York in 1787, to Philadelphia in 1790 and finally to Washington in 1800, was more for a federal requirement rather than to any other reasons. The relocation of the Brazillian capital to a new site at Brasilia in 1960 from Rio de Janeiro, which was founded in 1762, manifests the strong urge for economic rationalization and territorial organisation of the vast interior lands, which have, hitherto, remained neglected. Pakistan moved its capital from Karachi to Islamabad, close to the Kashmir frontier, for obvious political reasons.

The case of Russia, China and India is quite different; here also the capitals moved, and again relocated on the same sites, which were earlier abandoned. Moscow was the earlier capital of Russia, which then moved to St. Petersburg in 1712, and again moved to Moscow itself in 1918. Similarly, Peking was the earlier capital for China which was shifted to Nanking in 1927, and then relocated to Peking itself in 1949. Delhi was the capital of the Mughal India during the period of Shah Jahan. However, the capital moved to Calcutta in 1833, and again moved to Delhi in 1912.

"The shift of Russian capital from St. Petersburg back to Moscow may have been a mere measure of military precaution, but it symbolized a Russia turning back to its vital springs in the intermediate marches of Europe and Asia. Because Muscovy proper was geographically as well as historically the true heartland of Russia, the return, conditioned in part by the loss of the western fringes of the empire, has a geographical as well as a political singificance, ... the loss of Chinese power in Mangolia and Manchuria has as one of its offshoots the deposition of Peking...a typical link capital in the gate where the Manchus and earlier invaders had dominated their empire—in favour of Nanking, where tradition were Chinese, not Manchu. But here too the situation is complex; for to the new invasion of China, the coming of the Western sea powers and their pupils the Japanese, Nanking was both a link and a forward capital near the threatened sea frontier. Conversely, the Japanese occupation of Manchuria was soon reflected in increased importance for Peking." Calcutta functioned both as a forward and link capital during the formative period of British India but the shift of the capital to Delhi was more for a natural site for the capital of a continental empire, and also for a federal requirement in the subsequent decades.

The location of capital is not necessarily permanent. There are very few instances of capitals whose locations have remained permanent over centuries, like those of London and Paris. But, in most of the cases, 'locational shift' of capitals is a common political phenomenon, and it happens mostly because of changes in political and military, as well as social situations, when for obvious reasons the contemporary location/site becomes useless, and then it is abandoned, and a new site is chosen. Rio de Janeiro was capital for a little more than two hundred years but it was abandoned, and Brasilia was chosen. In some instances, the older but abandoned capitals have been relocated. Relocation of capitals on earlier sites is expressive of what is called 'historical imitation'.

Functions of Capitals

Capitals perform certain distinct functions. It is the seat for parliamentary and legislative, as well as executive and judiciary gathering. Here lies the residence of the Head of the State, and other executives, parliamentarians, ministers, and judges, who look after the administration of the states. The foremost function of capitals is, therefore, administrative, i.e., to bring the entire state area, regardless of its diverse geographical character, under a common politico-administrative and judicial system.

"In the capital also there gather the representatives or head officers of a large number of associations, institutions, and groups which find it necessary to have frequent and speedy contact with government agencies. These would include labour and commercial organizations, educational institutions, and great variety of bodies, official and unofficial, dedicated...to national prosperity or welfare."

It is also the seat of financial institutions, associations and planning commission and thus looks after the economy of the state area—a reflection of concentration of trade and industry, wealth and organization and power of the economic entity.

Here, in the capitals, are located the foreign embassies, and legation of other states, international organizations of trade and commerce, and some other inter-state establishments. It is, therefore, the meeting place of the representatives of the state with those of other states. It is through the capitals that the states perform their external functions and maintain internaional obligations. It is, therefore, the most cosmopolitan city of the states.

Capitals of the Islamic states in West Asia and Pakistan and Bangladesh in South Asia greatly perform certain distinct religious functions, because these are theocratic states, governed in the name of the Almighty. Religion is the *raison d'etre* of these states, and the capitals have to nourish it. In European states also, the capital is, in most instances, the seat of the State Church or of the dominant religious groups in the state. For example, Canterbury, seat of the Primate of All England, lies close to London, and the Catholic Church in Hungary is also close to Budapest. The Polish archiepiscopal has been moved to Warsaw from Gniezno. It also occurs in the areas where the Orthodox Church is dominant, with the Patriarch or enarch normally residing at the seat of the lay power in the state. However, the European states are not theocratic states, and the religious functions of their capitals are restricted.

Notwithstanding its function as the seat of the legislature and of the administration, it has also the role of focusing sentiment and strengthening the bonds which hold the nation together. In a federal structure, where each of the federating units seek to perpetuate their separate identity, it is the capital that balances their claims to an extent that the entire federation becomes integrated and united. The capital in a federation is located in such a way so as to create and defend the 'state idea' for it—the *raison d'etre* of the federation.

In a federal structure, there is a two-tier system for capital. One is the federal capital or the national capital, which intrinsically performs all the above functions, and the other is regional capital or the provincial capital, which is also the regional cultural centre and mainly looks after the regional administration. However, the erstwhile republics of the former Soviet Union were granted, under the Soviet Constitution, some measures of economic sovereignty allowing them to develop commercial ties with other states. The capital cities of these erstwhile republics were also the seat of foreign financial institutions.

The functions of capitals have changed much over time. Moscow, which once functioned as the 'legitimate' capital of the Soviet Bloc or the Socialist Empire in Eurasia, has now become the capital of Russia only. Belgrade has ceased to be the capital of Yugoslavia, as the state went disintegration, following the collapse of the system. The functions of Washington have increased manifold especially after the collapse of the socialist system. It has now more international obligations than before. London, which first emerged as a local centre, became a regional capital, then the capital of Great Britian, and now is the headquarters of the Commonwealth of Nations. The functions of capitals are ever changing because of the dynamic nature of the internal and external space relationships.

Classifications of Capitals

One of the earliest genetic classification of capitals seeks to classify them into (i) 'natural' capitals, and (ii) 'artificial' capitals. Natural capitals are those which have developed spontaneously over a long period of time, particularly in the core area, and succeeded in the course of time to make a very large part of the national territory its effective hinterland. Most of the core-growth states of the traditonal areas have natural capitals, for example, London and Paris are located in core areas of their respective states and their origin seems to have passed through an evolutionary process. Artificial capitals, on the other hand, are results of man-made decisons. They are created not as a result of evolutionary processes. It is said that they "were built all in one piece, as it were, to serve as the centre of the state". Such states, which have been created as a result of war and truce, or as a part of political convenience and adjustment between great powers, or have emerged as buffer states, are non-core-growth states, hence, they have artificial capitals. Federal capitals are all artificial capitals.

Natural capitals are tradition-bound as they reflect history and heritage of the core area, while artificial capitals are more politics-bound, since they manifest the political decision or political will of the parties involved.

However, Spate (1942) has come heavily on this distinction between natural and artificial capitals. He argued that this crude distinction between capitals completely begs the question for, "it may be more natural, more appropriate, to build a new city than to take over a going concern with its own nested interests... It is entirely natural for a federation to construct a new-hence so-called artificial—capital of the nested sectional interests that might attach to a city whose historic traditions or economic ties were with one of the components rather than with the country as a whole. Washington, is really more 'natural' capital than New York, Canberra than Sydney or Melbourne, Ottawa than Toronto or Montreal".

Rather, Spate has concluded that on the basis of historical inertia and historical imitation, capitals can be classified by functions into "those that are 'keystones' of a federation or complex state, those that are 'forward' as frontier organizers of victory and union, and those that are 'headlinks' through which the state receives nourishment during its formative phase and vivifying influences for indefinite or recurrent periods".

G. Hamdan (1964) has attempted a classification of capitals of those new states of Africa, which have inherited systems of extreme centralization from their colonial overlords, and now demonstrate the importance of the capital city to the viability of the state by its manipulation in function and location. On the basis of origin and historical evolution, he has distinguished such capitals into four categories, viz., 'historic', 'native', 'colonial', and 'post-colonial'.

'Historical' capitals are found only in Arab Africa because the political capital, like the nation-state, is a recent innovation in the rest of Africa. 'Native' capitals, such as Kano, are seen as transitional between the historical and colonial types. The 'colonial' capitals were created by the European administrations and dominate today over other types. The 'post-colonial' capitals reflect closely the colonial variety but in an increasing number of cases there are shifts to new locations for varied reasons—in response to changing patterns of centrality and accessibility, of necessity through the process of poilitical integration or disintegration, or simply as part of a policy to eradicate relics considered to be neo-colonialist. This model of Hamdan may have some relevance in the new states of the Indian subcontinent, which too have inherited a centralized bureaucratic system from the British colonial master; and the national capitals there now carry forward the *raison d'etre* of their respective states.

de Blij (1972) has offered a morphological classification of capitals, on the basis of their relation to their position with reference to the state territory and the core area of the state, and distinguished three categories, viz., 'permanent', 'introduced', and 'divided'.

(i) 'Permanent' capitals are also known as historical capitals (synonymous to Hamdan's historical capital). They may also be called 'natural' capitals because of their location in the 'distinct' core areas for centuries. These capitals have functioned as the leading political, cultural and economic centre for their states over a period of several centuries. They have retained their position, regardless of what happened to their states, or in other words, if the capitals have retained their position at least for two stages or the four stages of the lifecycle of states. London, Paris, Rome, and Athens are the examples of such capitals which retained their position, regardless of political turmoils, over centuries.

(ii) 'Introduced' capitals are those which intrinsically reflect new site or location, away from the traditional one; or a locational shift. This has especially happened when the older capital no longer functions, as normally expected of the seat of the government, and a new site is, therefore, desirable. When Kyoto failed to perform the expected normal function as the seat of the Japanese government, then the capital was moved to Tokyo in 1868. The new site was necessitated following revolutionary changes in the Japanese outlook. Capitals also move with the shift in the core areas, particularly when the core area suffers political division and looses its credibility.

Intra-regional or intra-territorial rivalries, within a state, also lead to the shift in the location of capital.This is particularly true in case of federal capitals when a compromise-site is chosen for it. Some introduced capitals result from ethnic demands, such as that of Ankara in Turkey. Loss of territories in Europe, coupled with the demand of a capital, which should be expressive of the true Turkish culture/tradition, led to the shift of the Turkish capital from Constantinople to Ankara.

To some extent, introduced capitals of de Blij seem to be synonymous with Hamdan's post-colonial capitals, particularly in ex-colonial regions of Africa and Asia. Pakistan's Islamabad is an obvious example of a post-colonial capital, which has been 'introduced' in response to changing spatial patterns of frontier politics vis-a-vis India-Pakistan rivalry, in the former British-colonial realm, in South Asia.

(iii) 'Divided' capitals are those which reflect some degree of dispersion of administrative funcions and offices in certain states, or in other words, the functions of government are not concentrated in one city, but dispersed over two or even more cities. Such a situation reveals compromise rather than convenience. The Republic of South Africa is an example where Pretoria is the administrative headquarters, CapeTown is the legislative headquarters, and Bloemfontein is the judicial centre. Pretoria reflects the Dutch traditon, while Cape Town manifests the English tradition, and Bloemfontein, a mixed tradition. Similarly, The Hague is the legislative capital of the Netherlands, and Amsterdam is the official capital. In Bolivia, intense rivalry between La Paz and Suere led to the arrangement existing today, whereby the two cities share the functions of government. La Paz is the official capital while Suere functions as the judicial capital.

Federal capitals may be added as the fourth cateogry to de Blij's morphological appraoch to the classification of capitals. Federal capitals are those which are situated on a 'neutral site', or on a mutually-agreed ground, which reflect compromise and not convenience, between the federating units of the system. Hence, federal capitals are not necessarilylocated in the core areas. The location of the capital in a federal structure has always been a matter of intense rivalry and dispute between the federating units, particularly at the time of the formulation of the constitution. The choice of a location for the capital in the USA, Canada and Australia has been quite difficult and in each case the conflicting interests of the parties have been balanced on 'agreed-site'. In the case of USA, the conflict rose between the north and the south but ultimately, it was decided on Washington, which is almost between the southern and northern boundaries of original states.

In case of Canada, it was quite difficult to arrive at a decision on a compromise-site because of an ethnic cleavage between the English-speaking people and the French-speaking people, who sought to perpetuate their claim on Toronto and Qubec respectively. However, after a long deliberation, both the ethnic communities agred on Ottawa in 1867 which was a neutral site on the river Ottawa. Similarly, Canberra was chosen as the federal capital of Australia in 1911, between the conflicting claims of Sydney and Melbourne. In fact, none of these federal capitals are significant centres of commerce and industry.

Federal capitals of ex-colonial territories, particularly of those states, which have inherited centralized bureaucratic administrative system and switched over to the federal system after independence, are located in the core area, or in other words, such federal capitals preceded the growth of federal structure. Delhi is such a federal capital which has long preceded the growth of the Indian federation. The choice of a location for the federal capital is such a vital and delicate issue that a slightest misunderstanding between the involved units may lead to the collapse of the federation as that has happened in the case of the West Indies Federation in the Caribbean, which collapsed immediately after its birth. The reason was obvious that Jamaica, Trinidad, Barbados and others could not agree on a possible site for the federal capital. Therefore, extra care is needed in the choice of a location for a federal capital so that in no way the sentiment of any of the federating units is hurt, and also in no way any of the federating units should perpetuate its claims over the other units. In both the situations, the federation is bound to collapse.

P.J. Taylor (1985) has attempted to present a new classification of capitals, based on the world economy processes, or on the world-systems approach. There are three types of capitals, according to the model—one is the result of core processes; second is the result of peripheral processes; and the third reflecting semi-peripheral political strategies.

"The capital cities resulting from core processes are what Henrikson terms the European concept.[1] The rise of the classic examples of this type are part of the initial economic processes that led to Europe becoming the core of the world economy.The merchantilist competition of the logistic wave[2] involved the development of vastly increased political involvement centred on the historical capital city. The new bureaucracies were located there, and these cities grew rapidly to dominate their territories. They became the political control centres that were attempting to steer the emerging world economy in direction beneficial to their particular territory... In contrast in the periphery new cities emerged or particular old cities grew where they were useful to the exploitative core-periphery relation. Most commonly these were ports directly linked to the core. They were the product of peripheral processes and have been often likened to 'plug holes' sucking out, as it were, the wealth of the periphery. In formal imperialism political control was directly associated with this process so that these 'parasitic cities' became 'colonial capitals'. Many of them retained their political status following independence and they remain the most extreme examples of Jefferson's primate cities."[3]

"But not all colonial administrative centres have remained as capital cities. Some governments have recognized the imperialist basis of their inherited capital city and have relocated their control centres elsewhere. This is a part of a conscious semi-periphery strategy to break the core-periphery links symbolized and practised through the old capital. Often it is expressed as a 'nationalist' reaction as capitals are moved from the coast inland to the old core of a pre-world economy racial formation. The shift of capital from St. Petersburg to Moscow again in 1918 was aimed at breaking with the peripheralizing processes of the past...other similar examples of relocations are from Istanbul to Ankara in the centre of Turkey's territory, from Karachi inland to Islamabad in Pakistan, inland from Rio de Janeiro to Brasilia and currently Nigeria is moving its capital from the colonial port of Logos inland to a new site at Abiya in central Nigeria. In all cases we can interpret the relocation on part of a semi-peripheral stratgegy which is attempting to lessen peripheral processes operating in the country."

"The semi-periphery strategy tends to produce what Henrikson terms the American concept[4] of a capital city, in effect a political company town. The case of Washington DC is also the result of an attempt to prevent peripheralization in the creation of the United States of America. It represents dominance of national politics over the needs of the world economy and has been the model for federal capitals... As a compromise between the sectional interests of North and South its closest parallels are the cases of Ottawa (between French (Qubec) and English (Ontario, Canada) and Canberra (between ...Sydney and Melbourne). Washington DC, Ottawa, and Canberra all represent part of a stragtegy for mobilizing a new territory for competition in the world economy...thus three types of capital city reflecting world economy processes: the initial core processes in Europe and the peripheral processes in Latin America, Africa, and Asia, both which generate 'primate cities', and capital cities which have developed as a part of a conscious semi-peripheral strategy which tend to be located in past and current semi-periphery states."

So far we have discussed the relevance and importance of core areas and capital cities in the political geography of states, being the two important elements of their spatial structure. Core-growth states of Europe have shown greater coherence and unity than the non-core-growth states. The concept of core area does not properly fit into the federal polity, because the 'involved' units in the polity may not have cores, instead, there is a common idea that holds together into a nation/state. There are examples of states, particularly, unitary states which have developed without a core but what they have done is to develop and defend the state idea—*raison d'etre*. However, there is need for some meaningful modification of the original core concept in the light of the world systems approach vis-a-vis world economy processes.

A well organized political entity cannot be imagined without a capital, for, it embodies and exemplifies the nature of the political entity. There is a greater amount of dynamism in the function and location of capitals because the present world is more 'process-oriented' than before. The study of capitals must be done in response to these 'processes'.

Notes

1. European concept of capital is the opinion forming centre of the state dominant in political, cultural and economic spheres.
2. Logistic waves refer to longer waves of up to three hundreds years in the world economy, particularly in the light of the growth of agricultural capitalism and industrial capitalism.
3. A primatie city is the country's leading city which is always disproportionately large and exceptionally expressive of national capacity and feeling.
4. The American concept of the cpaital is a responsive centre which specializes in politics.

Chapter 11

Federalism

"On the level of states, political geographers normally confront with the problem of system or subsystems dominant organization. The most popular scholarly typologies define system dominant states, in which separate territorial subdivisions are demarcated and their autonomy defined by the center as 'unitary' governments. States which strike a rough balance between a central government and a number of provincial governments are called 'federal'. The term 'confederation' is reserved for the loosest subsystems dominant category of federation. The simple dichotomy rooted in legal forms has its purposes, and we shall retain it here, but it must be regarded with considerable caution. Such scholarly typologies cannot be perfectly met for three reasons. For one, statesmen do not always agree with scholars. Scholars generally refer to Canada as a federation, and yet the Canadian government calls itself a confederation. Secondly, statesmen do not agree with other statesmen. In some states which proclaim themselves unitary, the subsystems (subunits) are constitutionally guaranteed greater autonomy than the subunits enjoy in other states which call themselves federal. Thirdly, the words of scholars, of statesmen, or even of constitutions do not always reflect the reality of political functioning. The (former) federal USSR was in fact a highly centralized state, while the unitary British government is one of the world's most democratic. Therefore, the categories used to define various governmental and territorial arrangements cannot be airtight; and each of the sovereign state is a unique system and framework reflecting a unique political tradition and culture." However, the discussion in this chapter will concentrate only on federalism because "it is the most geographically expressive of all political systems".

What is Federalism

Neumann (1955) writes: "Federalism is seen as one of the devices to curb the evil use of power by dividing among a number of competing power units... The common element is this: in each case, the citizen of the federal state is subject to two jurisdiction: that of the federal government and that of the states...Those who assert that federal state through the diffusion of constitutional power actually diffuses political power often overlook the fact that the real cause for the existence of liberty is the pluralist structure of society and the multi-party (or two-party) system. Federalism is not identical with social pluralism; and neither the two-party nor the multi-party system is the product of the federal state or the condition for its functioning.''

To Livingston (1952), ''Federalism, like most institutional forms, is a solution of, or an attempt to solve, a certain kind of political organization. It is true, on the whole, that federal governments and federal constitutions never grow simply and purely by accident. They arise in response to a definite set of stimuli: a federal system is consciously adopted as a means of solving the problem represented by these stimuli... The essence of federalism lies not in the institutional or constitutional structure but in the society itself. Federal government is a device by which the federal qualities are articulated and protected... No government has ever been called federal that has been organized on any but territorial basis; when organized on any other it has gone by another name... Federalism is a function not of constitutions but of societies. Viewed in this way, it will be seen that federalism is not an absolute but a relative term; there is no specific point at which a society ceases to be unified and becomes diversified. The differences are of degree rather than of kind.''

''A federation'', according to Robinson (1961), ''is the most geographically expressive of all political systems, based on the existence of regional differences, and recognizes the claims of the competent areas to perpetuate their individual characters. At the same time, it also recognizes their limitations as completely functioning units, it stresses the necessity for linking them with a common thread that draws them toward a common goal. This goal is national cohesion within the larger political framework. Federation does not create unity out of diversity: rather it enables the two to coexist.''

''A federation is born when a number of usually separate or autonomous political units mutually agree to merge to create a state with a single sovereign central government, but retain for themselves some degree of regional autonomy. The merger of the regional units in a federation is not absolute but partial, and its degree may vary with the circumstances of the particular groups of political communities involved. The legislative and executive powers in a federation is divided between the federal (i.e., central) and the unit governments, each of which acts directly on the people—the central or federal government has jurisdiction over all matters that bear on the development and the security of the nation as a whole and the unit governments have the rights to regulate matters of local and more immediate importance to their respective peoples'' (Dikshit, 1982).

''Federalism, therefore, has been a kind of universal answer to the question of overcoming problems of diversity and disparity in the interests of harmony and unity. Whenever events have seemed to demand cooperation and coordination, while interests and anxieties have held out for the preservation of difference and diversity, the answer has almost unfailingly been some form of federalism."

Federalism as a Geographical Phenomenon

Robinson, writing in 1961, noted that federalism is "the most geographically expressive of all political systems", i.e., it is purely a geographical phenomenon. Dikshit (1982) has attempted to identify the following two reasons for it to be considered as a geographical phenomenon or the most geographically expressive:

(i) It is based on the existence of the territorial-grouped diversities, that each component unit in it seeks for the perpetuation of its regional identity, and individual quality. Federalism is often described as the process by which a widening sense of social solidarity is reconciled with the attachment for local identity, through the provision of dual political organization.

(ii) Spatial interaction is a logical expression/manifestation of the federal polity or principle as it indicates the interdependence between the federal or the central government and the units or state governments as complementary to the "society-environment interdependence within a single area". In other words, "because of a 'dual' political organization and substantial regional autonomy, the regions in a federal state remain highly articulate, and spatial interactions in a federal state, unlike other forms of government, are clearly and easily recognized. Because federalism begins with a tacit recognition of regional personalities, and because spatial interactions in the political life of a federal state are clearly recognized, federalism becomes a suitable subject for geographical inquiry if geography is properly described as a science of spatial interaction." Federalism, therefore, is a logical expression of the spatial configuration of socio-political contacts within a single area.

The geographical expressiveness of federalism can be recognized more in the sense that every society, every nation is more or less closely integrated in accordance with its own peculiar historical, cultural, economic, political and other determinants. Each is composed of elements that feel themselves to be different from other elements in varying degrees and that demand in varying degrees a means of self-expression. These diversities may turn on all sorts of questions—economic, religious, racial, historical—and any of these can produce in a certain group within the population a demand for such self-expression. Furthermore, these diversities may be distributed among the members of a society in such a fashion that certain attitudes are found in particular territorial areas, or they may be scattered widely throughout the whole of the society. "If they are grouped territorially, that is, geographically, then the result may be a society that is federal. If they are not grouped territorially, then the society cannot be said to be federal. In either case coherence in the society may depend on the devolution upon these groups of the exercise of functions appropriate to the diversities that they represent. But in the first case only can this take the form of federalism or federal government... No government has ever been called federal that has been organized on any but the territorial basis, when organised on any other it has gone by another name" (Livingston, 1952).

It is true that the geographical diversities may not always follow the boundary lines of the component units. In many countries, and particularly in the United States, the operation of the federai system has displayed patterns of diversity that are more nearly associated with the regions or groups of states than with the individual states themselves. This is easily understood. Federalism embraces not merely a diversity of opinion on one issue but a whole pattern of diversities on a number of issues. It can scarcely be expected that state boundary lines will be adequate to mark off areas in which opinions differ on all possible questions. Indeed, on many, or even most, questions, the state boundaries will be of little significance in their limiting the areas of diversity. Federal organization is not perfect in every case.

Component states or units in a federation exist because of some great significant diversity of such importance that it is felt that only a federal organization can offer it sufficient protection. Day-to-day issues may easily and reasonably produce alignment that follow regional lines. "Regionalism in this sense is a valid manifestation of the federal principle." It conforms to the criterion suggested above, namely, that the diversities in the society be grouped territorially. It should be remembered that the regionalism in the politics of a federal country is made possible only by the federal allocation of functions to the states themselves. The fact that several states within a large region are dominated by similar opinions and hence unite in an effort to transform these views into policy does not detract from the importance of the states as the basic units of the federal system.

Federalism becomes nothing if it is held to embrace diversities that are not territorially grouped, for there are no territorial units that can serve as components of the federal system. It is indeed a reality that the federal society is usually organized on a functional basis which in itself expresses functional differences based on territorially grouped diversities. Therefore, territories differ in opinions, in composition, in interests, in function. If there were no functional differences, there might be no need for federalism. But the point that must be emphasized is that these functional differences are territorially grouped, and thus they provide a reason for and demand for a federal polity.

The social diversities that produce federalism may be of many kinds. Differences of economic interest, religion, race, nationality, language, variation in size, separation by great distances, differences in historical habitation and background, previous existence as separate colonies or states, dissimilarity of social and political institutions—all these may produce a situation in which the particular interests and qualities of the segments of the larger community must be given recognition. At the same time, these differences may not be too great, else the community may break up into independent groups. Federalism cannot make coherent a society in which the diversities are so great that there can be no basis for integration (Livingston, 1952). Federation does not create unity out of diversity, rather, it enables the two to coexist.

There is no way to estimate the relative weights of these factors except in results—they are largely incommensurable. But it seems clear that some are more significant than others, at least within a single society. For example, a society that enjoys a uniformity of social and political background can still hold together despite deep cleavages in other matters. The point is that the diversities and similarities are of many different kinds and when taken together they produce a total picture of the extent to which the society is integrated or diversified.

"The total pattern of these diversities produce a demand for some kind of federal recognition of the diversities. This demand in most cases meet a counter-demand (of inertia, which is equally a force) for increased unity or integration. These two demands or forces—the one impelling toward autonomy and independence for the component units, the other impelling toward centralization and suppression of diversity—meet each other head: the result of their conflict is the federal system. The federal system is thus an institutionalization of the compromise between these two demands, and the federal constitution draws the lines of this compromise. The constitution will be more or less federal in accordance with the relative strength of the two demands. Thus societies in which the demand for integration is stronger than the demand for decentralization will produce a set of institutions that is more nearly unitary: and a contrary situation will produce a contrary result. It is in this sense that federalism is a matter of degree and not of kind. The varying degrees of federalism are produced by societies in which the patterns of diversity vary and in which the demands for the protection and articulation of diversities have been urged with some or less strength."

The territorially-grouped diversities, which tend to constitute the *raison d'etre* for the federalism, intrinsically, engineer spatial interaction between the component units on the one hand and between them and the federal government on the other in terms of interdependence on complementary to the complex pattern of the society-environment interdependence within the political structure.

Each territorial/component unit in the federation is unique with regard to the pattern of its diversity which gets manifested in its orientation/inclination/interest/ and regional personality. So is the case with the other territorial/component units in the federation. Each of it seeks to perpetuate its interest and individuality in the political structure which requires some kind of cooperation/mutual understanding/mutual adjustment, and adaptability/compromise between the units involved in the federation. It is through the inter-unit mobility that the merging units in the federation are linked together to ensure interdependence between them that involves 'complementarity' (relating to the character of the units), 'transferability' (relating to the character and division of power and function between the federal government and the component units, and between them) and 'intervening opportunities' (relating to more closer social contacts, articulation, and dynamisms). It is this spatial interaction between the units involved in the federation that the regional character of the component units is allowed its expression and perpetuation in the federal constitution. More to say, the spatial interaction in a federation enables unity and diversity to coexist, making it "the most geographically expressive of all political systems".

Desirability to Federalism

Desirability/suitability/adaptability to federalism depends on certain geographical conditions which tend to form its 'basis'. Robinson points out in 1961 that "countries of large area and small population or even of rather large population, concentrated in widely scattered areas, are obviously suitable for this kind of system".

To de Blij (1972), "the federal framework is especially suitable for states in the large and very large size categories. Poor communications and ineffective occupation of large areas within state still affect, for example, of Brazil and Zaire. Such impediments to contact and control might disrupt unitary states, while a federal framework can withstand these centrifugal forces".

"In terms of shape (of the state), it is obvious that fragmented states and states with pronounced and important proruptions may be best served by a federal system. An elongated state possessing more than one core area also might turn into a federal arrangement."

de Blij (1972) further observes: "Federal states can adjust to the pressure of more than one core area(or a number of subsidiary cores) more easily than unitary states. A number of federal states in existence today are multi-core states, and in the case of Canada, Nigeria, ...and Australia it is probable that only a federal constitution could have bound the diverse regions together—in the case of (former) Pakistan, even temporarily. Thus, the federal state often has a number of individual population agglomerations, separated by large areas which are sparsely populated and relatively unproductive. These population clusters and their urban foci exist in some degree of isolation from each other. Canada and Australia, two of the largest federations in terms of area and two of the smallest in terms of population, illustrate this principle."

Parker, writing in 1949, observed: "All modern federations were, at their inception, political unions covering unprecedently huge areas scattered centres of population and comparatively underdeveloped communications...and federalism seemed the necessity form of government primarily for this reason." Cornell (1961) noted that "federalism may well have been suited to a particular phase of unification of large continental states with small populations and poor communications". "Even today", writes Sawer in 1969, "the size of a country and the efficiency of its communication are regarded as factors contributing to a choice between unification and federalism."

However, Dikshit (1982) points out that "what seems to have eluded these scholars is that the important fact about federalism is not the type or size of population and territories, but the fact that federalism is based on regional loyalties or a sense of locality. In new lands with vast open spaces, and a few cores of population widely set apart, this sense of locality may well be born because of physical distance. In older and densely populated countries, a sense of locality or regional identity may be, and often is, based on historical traditions, linguistic and religious and other ethnic diversities, or economic disparities and differences that are regionally grouped. The fallacy in establishing a causal relationship between the sheer area of states and the federal form of government is revealed if we remember that the thirteen colonies in 1787, or the four provinces of British North America in 1867, constituted only a very small portion of the areas now covered by these states. However, it should be remembered that over-centralization in (a large community)... leads to anaemia at the extremities and apoplexy at the centre. Large size in itself does, to a certain degree, favour the rise of federalism even though size and federation do not have a cause and affect relationship".

The federal framework offers a political solution for those territories held by "different competing and mutually exclusive political ideas" as such territories are occupied by peoples of widely varied ethnic origins, languages, religions or cultures. Each group of people is distinct in terms of its *genre de vie* (way of living) which is manifested in its ethno-cultural distinctiveness which it jealously preserves. It is the uniqueness of the people that leads to what is called the 'ethnic distance' among the various peoples which tend to sharpen the 'cleavages' between them. Each group of peoples, therefore, seeks to perpetuate their distinctiveness and individual characters, and it is through the federal polity that these cleavages are transformed into 'linkages' and the peoples with varied backgrounds, therefore, enthusiastically subscribe to the idea of federalism.

Notwithstanding the 'territorially-grouped ethnic diversity' being the prime *raison d'etre* for federalism, but the American example is a relatively simple illustration of the 'materialist basis' of federalism. "It is not a north-south sectionalism that emerges but a commercial versus frontier cleavages that dominates. In the urban areas and commercial farming areas which were firmly linked into the world economy, support for federation was very strong. In the more isolated areas with their more self-sufficient economy the advantages for federation were far less obvious. Suspicion of centralization prevailed and these areas tended to reject the federal constitution. The majority of world economy linked areas finally prevailed and the USA was formed on a constitutional basis for its economic groups to challenge the world economy order using mercantilist policies through the federal government... In the modern world most federal constitutions are devised to counter ethnic diversity. This does not mean there is no material basis to the federalism, however. Cultural features may be traced to economic causes in their emergence as modern political issues. When federal constitutions help bind territories containing different cultural groups they simultaneously help bind together territories with different links into the world economy. In every federal arrangement there are winners and there are losers and these can be defined materially with reference to the world economy."

Development of Federalism

Federalism has evolved and its nature has changed over time. It had contributed to the survival and rise of the state in the past and is now very much part of the '*raison d'etre*-state idea' of the states concerned. Federalism that emerged in the eighteenth-nineteenth century was one based on a dualistic polity in which the "federal and the state governments pursued virtually independent courses of action during a period when government was in any case minimal". So federalism began as a 'dual-polity or dual-federalism'. "The powers of the general government and the state, although both exist and are exercised within the same territorial limits, are yet separate and distinct sovereignties, acting separately and independently of each other, within their respective spheres." In fact, the eighteenth-nineteenth century federalism was intrinsically a federalism of powers between the general government and the state. However, the dualistic nature of the federal polity seemed to be a 'geographical necessity' of the time because the involved units in the federations were reluctant to abandon the rights and freedoms they enjoyed before the federation. It has been rightly observed that "this legal theory of divided sovereignty and the two distinct and separate spheres fitted the facts of the time well enough, for till long after the civil war in the United Sates the few activities of the national government could go along with the limited state activities without either impinging seriously on the other. The economic philosophy on which this dualistic federalism was based has today become outmoded. No modern state, whatever its economic and political philosophy, can avoid extensive state intervention.This is the era of active public-service state, not of the passive laissez-faire state. The performance of functions and services is the keynote of modern government, and in that performance cooperation, interdependence and interpretation of national and state agencies are inevitable" (Dikshit, 1982).

The dualistic federalism of the eighteenth-nineteenth century gave way to the 'cooperative federalism' in the mid-twentieth century as the involved units in the federation required more and more interdependence between them as complementary to the society-environment interdependence and social contacts of varied backgrounds. In the cooperative federalism states and national governments supplement each other and jointly perform a variety of functions. The national government, with its greatly enlarged powers and functions, has supplemented rather than supplanted the performance of functions by the states. The mid-twentieth century is one in which there is a division of powers betwen one general and several regional authorities, each of which, in its own sphere, is to coordinate with others, and each of which acts directly on the people through its own administrative agencies.

Regional and central governments in a federation should be coordinate as well as cooperative. Modern federalism is, therefore, a federalism of functions rather than of powers, more of politics than of laws. Dual federalism views the two sets of government primarily as equal rivals, whereas cooperative federalism views them as equal partners. The cooperative federalism or the twentieth century federalism is most geographically expressive rather than that of the eighteenth-nineteenth century dual federalism because there is more and more spatial interaction between the units involved on the one hand and between the federal government and unit governments on the other, leading to what is better defined as "spatial configuration of social contacts of territorially-varied backgrounds".

"Although states-rights sentiment exists in some form in almost every federal state, the nature and degree of the rivalry between the states and the central government that was supposed to exist in the dualistic phase of federalism has undergone a great change. Through a long process of adjustment the main areas of state and central functions are largely agreed (though disputes are by no means uncommon), and now the main rivalry is between the states themselves, where the centralized regulator (the federal government) plays the fundamental role as in any living organism, because different regions (or states in a federation) tend to regard themselves as rivals just as much as small nations are within a common market. The states are also rivals in their recourse to central government finance as a help to their development."

Organic federalism, or in a more refined term integrated federalism, appeared to have marked a new phase in the development of federalism. The concept is still ill-defined, however. In organic or integrated federalism, the centre has such extensive powers, and gives such a strong lead to the state governments in some of the most important areas of individual and cooperative activity that the political scientist may hesitate to call it federal at all. Here, in this kind of federalism, the "centre dominates every aspect of policy. Regional autonomy within the limits of the region competence is no sham, and the values inherent in such autonomy are protected by the constitutional structure and by the pattern of politics".

Origin of cooperative federation may lie either in 'mutual interest' of the political communities involved in the polity or in 'compromise' as a result of the willingness of the participating peoples to abandon some of their individual advantages in the interests of a greater state. However, a federalism established for one set of reasons may continue to exist for an entirely different set of reasons reflecting a substantial change in its nature. Indian federalism, which initially emerged as a result of a great deal of compromise and adjustment on the part of many peoples with various historical and ethnic backgrounds, now necessarily rests on the mutual interest of the political communities involved. Indian federalism must have involved a greater amount of spatial interdependence and interaction between the political communities involved since its inception which appears to have transformed the cleavages into linkages, thereby resisting the centrifugal tendencies.

"Some federations have been established against the wishes or without the consent of the majority of the peoples involved. These have been created by a powerful minority within the country, or by a colonial power, or through some other outside agency... Imposed federations usually have their origins in the desire of an interest group to perpetuate its privileged status or position...most imposed federations are shortlived...federations which have arisen and collapsed after the end of the Second World War(were): the Mali Federation, the Central African Federation, the West Indies Federation, and Pakistan..." (de Blij, 1972).

Imposed federations were not geographically expressive because of the fact that the regional claims of the component areas were not recognized and defined in the realms of the political functions. As a consequence, these federations lacked spatial interdependence and interaction between the political communities involved, leading to their collapse.

However, it is generally that the era of the true federalism, which flourished in the eighteenth-nineteenth and early twentieth centuries, is now at an end. Certainly experiments like the Central African Federation, the East African Federation, the West Indian Federation and the Pakistani Federation in the early 1960s and 1970s were shortlived and unhappy. The current trend is more toward 'confederation', such as the gradual emergence of the European Union, where there would be a central authority over all the member-states but which would be ultimately subject to control by the individual national (member) governments.

Pattern Flexibility

"The great variety of federal systems mocks efforts to arrive at a precise legal definition of federalism. The most famous definition of American federalism has it as 'an indestructible union of indestructible units'. This definition rules out both secession and the elimination of provincial autonomy, but...some self-proclaimed unitary states which would fit this definition as well. In no federal states are the subunits actually constitutionally 'indestructible' but any changes in the pattern must be approved by the affected units. The United States Constitution declares that no new State shall be formed or erected within the jurisdiction of any other State; nor any State be formed by the junction of two or more States, or parts of States, without the consent of the Legislatures of the States concerned as well as of the Congress.The former West German government had before it a plan for the restructuring of that country's state units, but, as in the United States, the affected units would have to approve any change, and so chances of change are slim."

Even if the component units in a federal state are guaranteed their integrity, the central government can subvert their power by superimposing upon them patterns of functional districts for its own purposes. In our era of increasing governmental centralization and planning for economic development, economic planning has been called 'the DDT of federalism'. Boundaries which are optimal for economic development are not necessarily optimal for policy making and representation.

The (former) USSR had tried a great number of economic planning on regional patterns since 1917, the newest of which divided the state into seven large regions. The granting of effective economic power to these new regions would have undoubtedly eroded the significance of the individual ethnic constitutional republics. The Soviet Constitution had granted the right to secession to the ethnic republics and the peaceful disintegration of the Soviet system, followed by the emergence of the fifteen nation-states in the early 1990s, may be attributed to it. The right to secede in the erstwhile Soviet Constitution, in a sense, reflected the pattern flexibility in a spatial political perspective.

Even in the United States the great number of federal government agencies, regionalization of the country, and the undeniable power of these federal agencies, often subvert the functional significance of the states as political regions.

"In all federal states the central government can, under certain conditions, intervene even in those powers reserved to the states. The Indian Constitution authorizes the central authority to take over any state's government across a wide range of circumstances, and India's ruling Congress Party has invoked this power frequently. Argentina, Mexico, Brazil and Venezuela have similar constitutional provisions. No State in the United States could elect a communist state government, for the United States Constitution requires the central government to guarantee to every state in this Union a Republican form of government." It is this pattern flexibility which tends to make the federalism the most dynamic political structure.

Concept of Symmetry and Asymmetry Models of Federalism

Tarlton (1965) is credited with having developed the symmetry and asymmetry model of federalism with a view to give the political structure a more realistic sense, based on its geographical characteristics. He observes: "Two concepts... can be introduced and their general content suggested. The first, the notion of symmetry refers to the extent to which component states share in the conditions and thereby the concern more or less common to the federal system as a whole. By the same token, the second term, the concept of asymmetry expresses the extent to which component states do not share in these common features. Whether the relationship of a state is symmetrical or asymmetrical is a question of its participation in the pattern of social, cultural, economic and political characteristics of the federal system of which it is part. This relation, in turn, is a significant factor in shaping its relations with other component states and with the national authority."

"An ideal symmetrical federal system would be one composed of political units comprised of equal territory and population, similar economic features, climatic conditions, cultural patterns, social groupings and political institutions. In the model symmetrical system each of the separate political units would be in effect be miniature reflections of the important aspects of the whole federal system. ... there would be no significant differences from one state to another in terms of the major issues about which the political organization of a state might be concerned. Nor would there be significant differences in terms of the political machinery and resources with which the state would approach those major issues... The division of power between central and state governments would be nearly the same in every case... In the symmetrical model no significant social, economic, or political peculiarities would exist which might demand special forms of representation or protection.

The basic justification for having a federal constitutional arrangement rather than a unitary one would be found in the completeness and integral character of the various political subsystems. Each member-state, while similar in most important features to every other member-state and to the overall character of the federal society, would be a separate unit possessing general problems of its own in the solution of which local authority would be thought to be best suited. The federal authority would, in the main, be limited to concerning itself with those problems either common to the federal system qua system (e.g., problems of international relations) or requiring systemwide attention and resources for solution."

"The ideal asymmetrical federal system would be one composed of political units corresponding to differences of interest, character, and makeup that exist within the whole society. The asymmetrical system would be one in which... the diversities in the larger society find political expression through local governments possessed of varying degrees of autonomy and power... An asymmetrical federal government is one in which political institutions correspond to the real social federalism... In the model asymmetrical federal system each component unit would have about it a unique feature or set of features which would separate in important ways, its interests from those of any other state or the system considered as a whole. Clear lines of division would be necessary and jealously guarded in so far as these unique interests were concerned.

In the asymmetrical system it would be difficult (if not impossible) to discern interests that could be clearly considered mutual or national in scope (short of those pertaining to national existence per se)."

"The higher the level of symmetry, that is, the more each particular section, state, or region partakes of a character general and common to the whole, the greater the likelihood that federalism would be a suitable form of governmental organization. On the other hand, if the system is highly asymmetrical in its components, then a harmonious federal system is unlikely to develop. If a formula were to be extracted from this, it would read: The elements of similarity among component units of a federal system must, if that system is to function at an optimum level of harmony, predominate over existing elements of diversity. Where diversity of elements is the rule, then it follows (presuming that sufficient political power and motivation exist to achieve unity at all) that a unitary and certralized system would be better. When diversity predominates, the 'secession-potential' of the system is high and unity would require controls to overcome disruptive, centrifugal tendencies and forces."

The degree of harmony or conflict within a federal system can be thought of as a function of the symmetrical or asymmetrical pattern prevailing within the system. Most real federal states, however, would be somewhere between the complete harmony of the symmetrical model and the complete conflict potential of the asymmetrical model.

Federalism and the State Idea

The concept of state idea has a special relevance to federalism for it is often said that federalism is created to defend and develop the state idea. "... it has been said of both the Central African federation and the Caribbean federation that they failed to hold together because each lacked a widely held state idea. ... although the nature and balance of American federalism has changed over time, it has contributed to the survival and rise of the state and is now very much part of the American state idea."

Variable political communities with territorial-regional identities and desiring a union enthusiastically subscribe/adhere to the idea of federalism. Federalism, as a centripetal force, overcomes problems of diversity and disparity in the interest of harmony and unity. Whenever events have seemed to demand cooperation and coordination, while interests and anxieties have held out for the preservation of differences and diversities, the answer has almost unfailingly been some form of federalism, for it leads to the 'nation-building'. Federalism is, in fact, fundamental to the process of nations-building, as it brings together diverse regions with different historical and ethnological experiences, associations and habitations under a single common political organization. It is through the process of nation-building that federalism is able to persuade peoples with varied backgrounds to shift their loyalties, expectations and political activities toward a new centre.

"Federalism is thus essentially a compromise between centrifugal and centripetal forces which are operative simultaneously. It is born only when a balance between these forces is reached, but because federation is essentially a bargain, the units merge only when the centripetal forces overwhelm the separatist ones, and the units see greater advantages in union than in separation. The basic problem of a federation has traditionally been to keep the centrifugal and centripetal forces in equilibrium so that neither the planet state shall fly off into space nor the sun of the central government draw them into its consuming fire. Erected essentially as a halfway house between unity and separation federalism clearly has a wide spectrum."

Whether it is a polyethnic/heterogeneous federation or monoethnic/homogeneous federation, it must evolve a state idea, based on the nature of federalism, which would justify the existence of the federation holding diverse regions together, that provides the federation with a *raison d'etre* reason for existing.

Nation-Building in Federal Societies

A federal society is one which is counterminously both polyethnic and multilingual in makeup and the society is, therefore, constituted of territorially-based communities which are clearly differentiated by language and ethnicity and cleavage defining such a federal society may be reinforced by other factors such as religion, geography and economics but the ethnic and linguistic factors are the determining ones.

Dikshit (1982) has come out with a model, dealing with some general patterns regarding nation-building in federal societies. The patterns are as follows:

1. "... one of the fundamental factors helping nation-building (and thereby the achievement of federal stability) is that the regional identities on which the constituent units of a federation are based should not be completely mutually exclusive even though they may largely be conflicting. When boundary lines of regionally identifying diversities in a federal state overlap, the cleavages have a tendency to be transformed into linkages, and the result is the canceling out of diverse tendencies and the emergence of an integrated nation, a stable federal partnership. The point is most clearly brought out by the example of Switzerland when the overlapping boundaries of language and religion have weakened their divisive force since each linguistic group contains representatives of both the faiths, and vice versa. This has meant that each block is divided against itself since a sizeable number of its own group possesses close affinity with a sizeable section on the opposing side owing to the ties of a common language of communication despite differences in faith. Thus, neither side has been able to fortify its camp and the fissiparous tendencies have cancelled out."

"When we compare Switzerland with Canada, the moral is easily drawn. Because both the French language and Roman Catholic faith have become very highly identified with the province of Quebec in Canada, here the religious and linguistic diversities, in contrast to the situation in Switzerland, had been plaguing the federal partnership right from the beginning. The point is obvious in the case of India also, where ever since the creation of linguistic states fissiparous tendencies have raised their ugly heads, since often times these states may be considered by their domiciles as linguistic homeland of some type."

2. "Multiethnic or otherwise heterogeneous federations having regionally grouped diversities, other things being favourable, the greater the factors of 'felt' diversities in the nation's life, the greater are the chances of a stable polity, for under these conditions the chances are great that the resultant spatial patterns of these diversities would not coincide, and their overlapping boundaries would neutralize the fissiparous tendencies."

   "...(in) India where, despite a large member of apparent diversities, language has become the only cleavage forming federal factor at the level of common man. As internal political boundaries have now coincided with the linguistic ones, the cleavages lines between the states have hardened, and language has begun to play the divisive mischief. Granted the sense of overall national unity and the recognition of a strong state idea unique to the nation itself, the chances of a more integrated polity would have increased if the country has possessed some inter-regional cleavages other than that of the language. For example, if, as some wrongly believe the universal systems of caste among the Hindus had run across the nation uniting all those of similar caste status together, rather than the caste lines being largely limited by linguistic boundaries, as in fact, is the case, the divisive influence of language would have been greatly neutralized."

   "... in the Malaysian example the process of nation-building would have been greatly facilitated if divisions in the Malaysian society were not based almost on communal consideration... . Malaysian...still lacks a well-defined state idea even though both the Chinese and the Malay recognize the common state idea. The historical memories of the sufferings and rejoicings of the two communities in Malaysia have been so highly dissimilar that the fundamental problem of nation-building in Malaysia is to develop potent symbols conducive to national unity-symbols which were not entirely Malay."

3. "Nation-building and state-formation, in the context of federal societies, implies that while some kind of regional consciousness and identity is retained, as time passes, national loyalties on the whole should get precedence over the regional ones... nothing works for nationalism as intercourse within the nation... A high degree of mobility is the greatest curb on

unhealthy provincialism...in Canada, where the French Canadians in Quebec were reluctant to leave their province because of the lack of educational facilities for their children in French, the process of all-Canada nationalism was greatly retarded. The lack of interstate mobility in the country, and despite more than a hundred years of political partnership, a strong all-Canadian nationality remains only an aspiration. The solubrius effect of such mobility of population in the growth of nationalism in Switzerland and Australia need hardly be emphasized...The lack of opportunities for such mobility has been the greatest stumbling block in the growth of nation-building in the so-called new federation... It was the lack of such mobility that had prevented the growth of any sense of shared identity between the two wings of former Pakistan. Retardation of the growth of nation-building in India over the past two decades is the direct result of the development of a high sense of linguistic patriotism among the states of the union ever since the reorganization of its states in 1956."

4. "From the examples of the failed federations it is proved that the essence of any political union (and thus of a continued strengthening of the sentiment for nationalism) is that the partners involved in the union should continue to feel that they are better within than without their union. For this it is necessary that the units in general benefit economically and politically from their political partnership and the impression is continuously reinforced that their political union, i.e., the nation-state, stands to their benefit in tiding over certain urgent economic problems that the constituents could not do in isolation. Secession of Bangladesh from the ill-fated Pakistani federation may be viewed as a direct result of this factor and so also the near secession of Biafra in Nigeria. As in all human affairs, in political organization too, the question of bread and butter remains of supreme importance."

   "This factor often assumes far greater importance in federal societies than in the non-federal ones. The reason is that owing to the existence of regionally grouped complexes of political, social and economic loyalties and interests these societies often possess well-formed subsidiary core areas may, under abnormal circumstances, aspire to, become centres for rival plans of political integration and/or concentrated disruption protest."

Federalism, being the most geographically expressive of all political systems, is essentially based on territorially-grouped diversities which intrinsically manifest a federal society that is both polyethnic and multilingual in makeup. However, federalism has also developed in a monoethnic society. It has been a panacea to the survival and rise of many states in the past and present as well which were confronted with the problems of diversity and disparity in the interest of harmony and unity.

The geographical expressiveness of federalism is further articulated by spatial interaction/interdependence between units (with varied backgrounds) involved as complementary to the (federal) society-environment interdependence. This spatial interdependence is achieved through a unifying idea which is preeminently political and goal-oriented and peoples with varied backgrounds enthusiastically subscribe to this idea. This is the state idea and federalism is deeply interwoven with it.When federalism becomes a part of the state idea, it greatly contributes to the survival of the federal polity/or the state itself, giving it a *raison d'etre* but, if, it is not, then the state collapses, as there are examples to it. Federalism is fundamental to the nation-building process.

Since federalism allows component units to retain their regional characteristics and individuality while subscribing to the federal principle, it has now become increasingly clear that regional loyalties or loyalties to the component units are getting precedence over the national ones, gradually making it redundant. A tendency is gradually building up towards confederation and there is every likelihood that large number of confederal unions will come up in the twenty-first century. The coming up of the European Union, consisting of fifteen nations, is the most recent example of it. Some more nations are likely to join it in the years to come.

Federalism in India

A large new state, such as India, faced with the problem of establishing a central authority strong enough to govern a vast area inhabited by millions of people with different historical and linguistic backgrounds and interests, almost inevitably has to establish some form of federal structure to sustain the pressure of divisive stresses. It was found immediately after independence that old historic centrifugal forces were getting the upper hand over temporary centripetal forces, created during the colonial period that tended to threaten the very *raison d'etre* of the new state in South Asia. Federalism was found to be an obvious choice to sustain such pressure of separation and centrifugalism. The Republic of India is a federation, although it has many distinctive features which seem to modify the essentially federal nature of the state.

Notwithstanding its geographical basis, the Indian federalism does not seem to be geographical expressive (Adhikari, 1992). "It must be remembered", says an expert, "that though India is a federation, her constitution departs from the ideal of a true federation in several vital and significant ways. She is not a genuine federation but a quasi-federation having several features of a unitary state." "India may be categorized as a unitary state with subsidiary federal principles rather than a federal state with subsidiary unitary principles", said Keaneth Wheare in 1951. Alexandrowiez (1954) points out that "the application of such a rigid definition of the federal principle to various types of existing federations may deprive of it of any practical meaning". To him, India is a true federation—although, like all other federations, it has distinctive characteristics—and that it is misleading even to refer to India as a quasi-federation. It is difficult to determine to what extent these differences are merely semantic over and to what extent they are based on fundamentally different interpretations of the nature of the Indian State.

However, the Republican Constitution contains a number of provisions which seem to give the Centre such extraordinary powers as to raise questions regarding the federal nature of the Indian State (Palmer, 1961): (i) Article 3 authorizes the Central Parliament, presumably by a simple majority, to form new states or to alter the boundaries of any state, without necessarily obtaining the consent of the state or states affected; (ii) Article 248 vests residuary powers in the Indian federation in the Centre, unlike the arrangement in most federations; (iii) Article 249 provides if two-thirds of the members of the Council of States approve, the Parliament may "make laws with respect to any matter enumerated in the State List" and specified in a resolution of the Council; (iv) Article 254 provides that if any law passed by a State Legislative Assembly is repugnant to a statute of the Federal Parliament, the latter shall prevail; and (v) Articles 352 to 360 contain the emergency provisions which empower the President in effect to suspend the Constitution and to take over the administration of a state or states of the Indian Union if he is satisfied that there is a threat to the security of the nation, or a breakdown of the constitutional machinery of a state or states, or a financial emergency. Many other provisions of the Constitution could be cited in support of the view that the central authority has in fact such extraordinary power as to support the view that India is no more than a quasi-federation, at best, or that if it is a federation at all, it has many unitary features (Palmer, 1961).

India, in fact, emerged as an administrative rather than a contractual federation—an imposed rather than a cooperative federation (Adhikari, 1986a; Adhikari, 1992). It was imposed from the above, not from below and that can be exemplified by the fact that the Congress Party that succeded the British Paramountcy sought to perpetuate its political culture and/or position without the consent of the vast majority of the peoples involved making it geographically inexpressive.

The territorial structure of the Indian Dominion was highly confused, as it contained some 545 princely states whose integration with the Dominion was a problem because these princely states used to enjoy some kind of autonomy during the colonial period which they were reluctant to abandon. After a sustained persuasion, and in some cases referendum/plebiscite, followed by the military intervention that the accession of these princely states was achieved except for Jammu & Kashmir. The accession of Jammu & Kashmir has raised many doubts. Pakistan invaded Kashmir soon after the Maharaja of it signed the Instrument of Accession, and India retaliated as a full scale war broke out between India and Pakistan in 1948. However, it was at the UN initative and/or intervention that a ceasefire was thrust on the waring Dominions but a substantial part of Jammu & Kashmir was left under Pakistan's occupation. However, the UN resolution which called for the ceasefire prescribed for a plebiscite in state to decide the destiny of the people, but it could be held only after Pakistan first abandoned/left the territory it occupied, followed by the Indian withdrawal. Neither Pakistan left the occupied part nor India withdrew and, therefore, plebiscite could not be held. However, India allowed Jammu & Kashmir to retain the amount of autonomy it enjoyed during the colonial period and Article 370 in Indian Constitution provides for a special status to it, words like, 'Sadar-e-Riyasat' and 'Wazir-e-Azam' were allowed to be retained.

The Republican Constitution for the federation was proclaimed on January 26, 1950, but the territorial structure continued to remain highly complex and confused. The former princely states, such as Hyderabad, Mysore, Jammu & Kashmir, Madhya Bharat, Patiala and East Punjab State Union (PEPSU), Rajasthan, Saurashtra and Travancore-Cochin, were put in the category of Part-B states in the new Republican Federation of India. However, the former three princely states were kept intact while the remaining were formed by joining together other former princely states—large and small. In addition to this eight Part-B states, the Constitution of 1950 provided for nine Part-A states, viz., Assam, Bihar, Bombay, Madhya Pradesh, Madras, Orissa, Punjab, United Provinces and West Bengal, corresponding to ten provinces of British India, and ten Part-C states, viz., Ajmer, Bhopal, Bilaspur, Cooch-Bihar, Coorg, Delhi, Himachal Pradesh, Kutch, Manipur and Tripura. The Andaman and Nicobar Islands were listed in Part-D category. Part-A and Part-B states were regarded roughly as of equal status (Jammu & Kashmir was in a rather different status because of the disagreement with Pakistan over this territory). Thus, the territorial system of the newly created Indian federation, in the early 1950s, seemed to be geographically inexpressive as it was neither based on the existence of regional differences nor it tended to recognize the claims of the component areas which sought to perpetuate their individual regional characters.

India is a land of vast continental size with internal distances between places within its political territorial bounds are so long as to have necessitated a federal polity. Size and long internal distances between places are two dominant centrifugal factors whose divisive actions were temporarily contained by a sustained centralized colonial administration. But soon after the withdrawal of the colonial administration, these divisive forces, once again, became active. Territorial vastness has created multiform topographical features that tend to make the territorial/regional pattern of diversities and disparities so intense as to have made them mutually exclusive. Multitudinous topographical/physical lineaments have their strongest manifestation in 'conflictual pluralism' of India's multicoloured-polyglot social structure. Each of the major ethnic communities (in the modern world system, ethnic communities are recognized as 'nations') with distinct territorial identification and *genre de vie* for long, have sought to perpetuate their regional/territorial distinctiveness, resulting into 'hardened' ethnic cleavages, notwithstanding, their strict adherece to Hinduism. Each of the major ethnic communities are tradition-bound and destined to preserve their national heritage and idea and distinguished from others by distinct historic habitation and experience, written history, folklores, stories of heroes, language, artform, iconography, body of literature, painting, architecture and music. The Bengali ethnic community, for example, is certainly distinguishable from the Assamese by the above indicators. Similarly, the Tamils are distinct from those of the Telegu and the Marathi ethnic communities. India is, therefore, a mosaic of ethnic communities and/or subethnic communities (nations and/or subnations in the modern world economy/system). Fissiparous tendencies of the conflictual pluralism in the age-old Indian society remained temporarily subdued during the peroid of the colonial administration. But once the colonial administration was withdrawn and replaced by indigenous administration, these age-old historical centrifugal forces became active (Adhikari, 1983; Adhikari, 1986b).

The territorial pattern of the early 1950s (with various kinds of territorial units Part A-B-C-D) on the one hand, and growing conflictual pluralism (on the ethnic landscape of the Republic) on the other hand, put considerable divisive stresses on the *raison d'etre* of this newly emerged federation in South Asia, and demanded a territorial reorganization so as to acknowledge and recognize regional distinctiveness and claims of the various ethnic communities. It was in the backdrop of the major ethnic communities' increasing 'rights sentiment' to perpetuate their claims that the federal government at the Centre amended the Constitution (Seventh Amendment) in 1956, followed by the States Recogniza-tion Act of 1956, both of which went into effect on November 1, 1956. The States Reorganization Act had its root in the growing 'conflictual pluralism' which had already threatened the federal *raison d'etre* of the Republic and the federation was recognized along the linguistic-cultural lines. After the reorganization the Indian Republic consisted of fourteen states of equal legal status—the distinction between Part-A, Part-B and Part-C states disappeared—and six federally administered territories were created.

Reorganization of territories along the linguistic-clutural lines, as a matter of fact, sought to: (i) make the federation in India geographically expressive to an extent as it was necessisated: (ii) sustain the pressure of divisive stresses; and (iii) creates a new state idea vis-a-vis *raison d'etre* so as to accelerate the nation-building process for an integrated personality. Since the territorial reorganization in 1956, the Republican Constitution has been amended for so many times with a view to perpetuate the regional distinctiveness of the various ethnic/tribal communities, e.g., Assam suffered several territorial turncation: Meghalaya, Aurnachal Pradesh, Nagaland, Manipur, Tripura and Mizoram were created out of it, manifesting growing conflictual plauralism in the North-East on the one hand and the perpetuation of the major tribal communities' right sentiment on the other hand. Several unions or federally-administered territories were elevated to the status of states because inhabitants (communities) rights sentiment there, increased to an extent as to have sought for the perpetuation of their distinctiveness and the Central government complied with their demands (Adhikari, 1983; Adhikari, 1992).

Notwithstanding, the Republican Constitution underwent several major amendments in the last forty-five years, in an obvious attempt to create new areal patterns in the federal polity, to give expression to political and/or ethnic communities, but the regional claims of the components/federating units of the federalism were not allowed to be perpetuated. The federal-state relations were, therefore, one of pressures and dictates in the formative stages of the political structure rather than of one based on cooperation and coordination. The states in the union were subordinate to the federal government, and the federal polity lacked mutual interdependence between the federal government and state governments. The relationship was, therefore, highly asymmetrical. As the Republican Constitution lists many items on the Concurrent List which necessitates a high degree of cooperation and coordination between the Centre and states, but it was not the case. The centre-state relationship continued to be guided by the principle of dominance on the part of the federal government. The Planning Commission and the National Development Council were the major federal agencies which were created to give effect to cooperative and coordinated development of the political structure but functional at the will of the central government. And as a result of which developed the core-periphery conflict in the federal polity, which tended to make the system highly unstable (Adhikari, 1986a).

Federal government's dominance and its administrative suppression at the cost of cultural-linguistic expression of the major political and/or ethnic communities, during the greater part of the federation, ultimately led to what may be called the political expression of the linguistic-cultural states' rights sentiments for greater political autonomy in the 1970s. It could be exemplified by several conclaves of the opposition-ruled states but the most effective and expressive one of such political expressions of the states' rights sentiments was that of the famous Anandpur Sahib Resolution of the Akali Party in 1973 that sought to make the federal-state relationship more expressive and mutually interdependent, in term of space and time, so that the regional distinctions of each of the linguistic-cultural federating units (i.e., states) might be guarnteed and recognized in the Republican Constitution. It would have been made the federal polity highly flexible and desirable so as to suit the requirements of the time. However, Jammu & Kashmir has been enjoying a greater amount of regional antonomy since its accession. The Christian-dominated states of Nagaland, Meghalaya and Mizoram, and to some extent, Manipur, enjoy more kind of antonomy within the federal framework while rest of the remaining states in the area denied of this. As the linguistic-cultural states rights sentiments increased aftermath of the Anandpur Sahib Resolution, so increased the greater demand for autonomy and a review of the existing federal-states relationships. It was in the backdrop of this persistence demand that the Sarkaria Commission was set up, which recommended certain measures including symmetrical and cooperative centre-state relationships in which neither federal government nor the state government should feel itself superior to other. However, some of the major recommendations of the Sarkaria Commission, dealing with the division of power between the Centre and the states, have not been implemented and the central government still welds considerable power and dominance over the federating states.

On the question of the viability of the Indian federation, it can be said with certainity that it is faced with a persistence crisis of viability since its inception in 1950. Viability is a measure of the effectiveness with which the state can be administered to fulfil the purposes for which it was created. Such purposes seem to have the necessary appeal to command widespread support and which are sufficiently distinct from the purposes formulated by other states. These purposes necessarily constitute the state idea, which the state is created to develop and defend.

Since the Indian federalism was imposed from the above without getting the masses of different backgrounds, involved in its making, the ruling elites of the Congress Party that succeeded the colonial British administration in 1947 could not come out with a clearcut state idea which could have necessarily engulfed the entire dominion vis-a-vis the republic in the years to come. Such an idea was necessary as the dominion consisted of various territorial units with diverse character and background. The accession of the princely states was more of an administrative in nature rather than the units' strict adherence with enthusiasm, to the political idea for which the Indian Dominion was created. The princely states had different traditions, experiences, objectives and *raisons d'etre.*

Lack of a clearcut state idea in the early 1950s, necessitated the territorial reorgnization of the Indian federalism along the cultural-linguistic lines. This was done in an obvious attempt to make the federalism geographically expressive to an extent as suited the requirement of the political and/or ethnic communities. Restructuring was done, but an idea, unique to the territorial reorganization was missing, and once again the ruling elites missed the opportunity to create a new sustainable state idea for the citizens of the Republic. The failure to create a positive state idea unique to the Indian State has badly affected the nation-building process, but a number of competing state ideas emerged in most of the cultural-linguistic federating units of the union, strengthening the centrifugal tendencies. The Indian State miserably failed to control over the means of violence, particularly in its peripheries that resulted in the rise of insurgencies in these areas. Peoples in the peripheries identify themselves with different political (i.e., state idea) ideas, much in contrast to the *raison d'etre* of the Indian federalism (Adhikari, 1992).

Rivalries between the cultural-linguistic federating units, such as between Punjab-Haryana, Maharashtra-Karnataka, Tamil Nadu-Karnataka, West Bengal-Assam, Nagaland-Assam, Manipur-Nagaland and Orissa-West Bengal over the allocation of resources, location of boundaries and ethnic minorities' problems necessarily weaken the federal polity on the one hand and strengthen the states' rights sentiments on the other. Hardly, there is any political idea, at present, sufficiently strong enough to overcome these forces of disunion and/or unity.

Notwithstanding these centrifugal forces of wide vertical and horizontal dimension, restricting the dynamism of the centrifugal forces vis-a-vis the state idea, the federation has not collasped. This may be attributed to what is called the 'political inertia or momentum'.

Chapter 12

Electoral Geography

Electroral geography is the study of geographical aspects of the organization, conduct and results of elections. In other words, it is the study of the spatial voting patterns/behaviours, or the study of the spatial distribution of political phenomena of voting. There are many reasons why voting analyses are especially appealing to geographers, not the least of which is that voting results are best portrayed on a map. Votes cast are measures of attitudes, perceptions and biases. Thus, when vote returns are mapped, the resulting distributions give indications of place-to-place differences in behaviour. The political geographer's task is to explain or account for the variations over space of the voting decision. Many times the task is not easy, because behaviour can be difficult to explain.

If success can be measured by quantity of production, then electoral geography is the success story of modern political geography. In the last two decades there have been hundreds of studies on the geography of elections, so much so that some have argued that the growth has been disproportionate in relation to the general needs of political geography. In fact, ideas on the role of electoral geography in political geography range from those who imply that it is "the very core and substance of political geography" to those who feel that it does not belong to political geography at all! In the political geography of the state elections play a key role at the scale of ideology in channelling conflicts safely into constitutional arenas. The goal of most studies seems to be nothing more than understanding the particular situation under consideration.

There are five major areas of study within electoral geography:

(a) the spatial organization of elections, with particular reference to constituency;

(b) spatial variations in voting patterns, and the relationships between these and other population, characteristics, notably social class;

(c) the influence of environment and spatial factors on voting decision;

(d) spatial patterns of representation which result from the translation of votes into seats in a parliament or similar body; and

(d) the spatial variations in power and in policy implementation which reflect the patterns of representation.

The study of the second and third of these major areas of analysis was advanced during the 1960s as part of the adoption of a positivist approach in human geography, as a result of the quantitative revolution in goegraphy. Voting returns offered a great volume of data whose spatial variability could be analyzed within this 'paradigm', and correlation methods were adopted to investigate the associations, at an aggregate level, between voting and other social characteristics. Deviations from the expected general relationships were interpreted as possible examples of contextual effects; models of these effects were developed, which included a spatial component to the 'diffusion' of information and other voting ones.

Trends in Electoral Geography

One of the earliest works on the geographical study of election was made by the French geographer, A. Siegfried, in 1913, when his book *Tableau Politique de la France de l'oueste* was published. It marked the beginning of the geographical study of elections. In 1916, Edward Krehbiel published an article in the *Geographical Review* in which he attempted to analyze the change in the spatial variation in voting in Great Britain from 1885 to 1910. In the article he tried to associate the voting results with the environmental factors, such as social and economic conditions. A correspondence or association was found between the spatial variation in voting and spatial variation in the environmental factors. Krehbiel, in fact, set forth the paradigm of 'areal association' in the geographical study of elections. Stuart Rice offered a new dimension to the geographical study of elections when his book *Quantitative Methods in Politics* appeared in 1928, which set forth the scientific approach to voting analyses. Rice concentrated on the problem-solving approach in which a hypothesis is stated and then tested through statistical analysis. He used the country data for analysis, and discussed regionalism in voting and diffusion of political attitudes.

However, since Krehbiel's study of environmental influences on elections between 1885 to 1910, geographers have concentrated on the temporal and spatial variations of voting aggregates and their association with environmental, social and economic variables. C.O. Paullin prepared a series of historical maps of voting results in his book, *Atlas of the Historical Geography of the United States*, which sought to indicate regional trends over period of time. In 1932, J. K. Wright, in his article, 'Voting Habits in the United States', published maps to illustrate the results of presidential elections over the period 1876 to 1928. He briefly analyzed these maps in terms of large scale regional contrasts, and more specific factors, such as farming areas and ethnic minorities. In a 1935 study of voting in Chicago, Harold Gosnell and Norman Gill used both correlation and factor analysis—the two complex statistical techniques.

Beginning with Andre Siegfried's classic study of the Ardiche region of France, the French geographers and sociologists since World War II have contributed a wealth of research in which they associate voting behaviour with population characteristics and socio-economic activities. Francois Goguel, for one, has published an impressive number of electoral studies, the best known of which is probably his, *Geographie des elections francaises de 1890 & 1951*. A series of lengthy, excellent regional studies have complemented the more general works of Siegfried and Goguel. Canadian geographers, such as Hamelin and Letarte, in a monograph on provincial elections in Quebec, have continued this French tradition. For the most part, this stream of electoral research has utilized and analyzed areal voting data by means of areal association; nevertheless, the large number and generally high quality of these studies far overshadows the contributions by American geographers.

In 1949, V.K. Dean's article on the geographical aspects of an important vote in Newfoundland was published. Not long after this article was published, R.M. Crisler briefly discussed voting habits in the United States in an article appeared in the *Geographical Review*, and H.R. Smith and J.F. Hart made a contribution in a different direction by looking in detail at regional differentiations in the American tariff map.

Geographical analyses of voting behaviour began to increase in both quality and quantity during the 1950s, largely as a result of the theoretical-positivist revolution in geography. Though most of the works tended to concentrate on the national level but significant advances were also made in studies of regions and individual states. Edward Miles studied New York politics in 1959. Trenton Kostbade studied geography and politics in Missouri in 1959; and Lloyd Haring analyzed voting patterns in Tennesse in 1959. His study was the first geographical analysis of voting to use the multiple-regression statistical technique.

There have been more and more methodological innovations in the study of electoral geography since 1960, and some older methodologies were refined to suit the needs of the situations. Though the trend continues to focus on the national, regional and state levels, but the major focus again turned to smaller unit areas, and the areal association-type studies were replaced by work that concentrated on spatial processes, such as migration and interaction; and how these processes affect voting behaviour. In 1961, Kasperson analyzed the spatial aspects that influenced decision making in Chicago. Pierce Lewis analyzed the impact of Negro migration on the electoral geography of Flint in 1965. In an article on political parties in Burgenland (Austria), published in the, Annals in 1964, A.F. Burghardt examined the spatial patterns of voting behaviour and sought to determine the underlying factors that influenced the voting. The use of one of several techniques of quantitative analysis of voting tallies was done by Roberts and Rumage, dealing with leftist voting in urban areas of England and Wales. Here, use is made of multiple regression analysis, and maps show regression residuals rather than straight data. K.R. Cox, in 1968, studied the spatial contrasts in voting behaviour in the city of London, comparing the suburbs and the central city in terms of voter turnout and party preference. In his article he made use of the factor analysis and correlation techniques. In 1970, Robert Norris analyzed the effect of migration on voting behaviour. It was perhaps the first geographical study to use survey research method; the analysis was concerned with the effect of migration into a city as well as the personal movement patterns of the voters. In India, some people, like Amani, Dikshit and Singh, have contributed to the electoral geography studies. Their works were mostly based on the western models. However, the application of the western models to the Indian situation did not yield any positive fruitful results.

The tendency for electoral geography studies, during the phase of the critical revolution in geography, contrary to the quantitative revolution in the 1970s, seemed to be a return to the analysis of larger areas. States as well as regions were analyzed again and a few new studies appeared on national voting trends. Spatial processes in voting and urban areas also continued to be important research topics.

Most work in electoral geography has been descriptive of various aspects of the conduct of elections and the pattern of voting. Relatively little has been done to link it to other areas of political geography; although, as Taylor in 1978 has pointed out, the function of an election is to allocate power so that if the inputs (the pattern of voting) and the through puts (the transformation of votes into seats) have clear spatial components, so too should the outputs. This point was also taken up by Johnson in1980, and an examination of the geography of public policy as it related to electoral geography was undertaken in a major study of federal spending by him .

More recently, attempts have been made to set the study of elections into a much wider context, through work on geography where various types of elections are held; and of the separate geographies of support and power mobilized by political parties. In this, the goal is to emphasize the roles of political parties and other actors as agenda-setters and manipulators of the electorate; traditionally, electoral geographers have focused on the electorate, adopting an approach akin to the 'consumer sovereignty' that underlies 'neoclassical economies'.

However, the above analysis, illustrating the trend in electoral geography, is not a comprehensive review of the works, done in the field, but it seeks to acquaint the researchers/students to the evolution of research in the field by citing particular examples that exemplify certain techniques, concepts, geographical scales and paradigm which have been used hitherto.

Areal Association Model

It is one of the most common models which has been long used by geographers. 'Areal association' refers to the idea of comparing one set of geographic facts (called a spatial distribution) with another set. Both spatial distributions must be from the same study area. For instance, if a state is considered a study area, then the countries/constituencies within the state are spatially distributed unit areas.

Each county/constituency has a unique location though many are contiguous. Information (data) can be mapped for each unit of country/constituency. The map, so prepared, gives an illustration of a spatial distribution of the data. The process then is repeated with a second set of data, and the first map (spatial distribution) is compared to the second. The comparison is made to determine whether regions in the state with large magnitudes of data set are similarly large for the other data, or whether large magnitudes of one are found when the other is small. In fact, the comparisons are made to determine whether there is an association between two sets of data on an areal basis. This has been the most common approach among the French geographers. Siegfried is believed to have pioneered this areal association model in his 1949 study of voting in the department of Ardeche. However, the map comparison technique was found to be inaccurate largely because of variable perceptions of the people, leading to different analyses.

The statistical/quantitative revolution in geography in the post-war period brought about significant changes to the model, and provided it with a new paradigm. The statistical model 'correlation regression' was found to be more desirable to fit the requirement of the areal association model, because of its preciseness. This model has been used, modified, abused and criticized, but it does illustrate one effective approach to the study of the geography of elections. The application of the 'correlation regression' model marked the beginning for more sophisticated techniques.

The correlation technique is used to compare one set of measures with another. In voting behaviour research, the concern is with 'why' the votes for a candidate are distributed over a space in the manner shown in a map. Thus, the map may be thought of as a 'statement of a problem', the problem being to explain the spatial distribution of votes. The vote returns are the 'dependent variable' for the correlation model. That is, they vary from one place to another and presumably are dependent upon other factors. The analysis begins with the selection of a second measure that may explain the spatial distribution of vote returns. The second measure is called the 'independent variable'. This is done on two-dimensional graph—one scale on the graph is for the dependent variable (the vote returns) and the other for the independent variable (the age of the voters). By tradition, the dependent variable is plotted on the Y-axis, the independent variable on the X-axis. Countries or constituencies are represented by dot, i.e., each dot on the graph represents each county/constituency of the state. The data are plotted by placing a dot at the meeting of the two bits of information (the dependent variable and the independent variable), i.e., the vote returns and the age of the voters. If there is a strong relationship between the dependent variable (the vote returns) and the independent variable(the age of the voters), the dots will tend to form a linear scatter. A hypothesis may be developed that there is a positive relationship between vote returns for the candidate and the age of the voters. The hypothesis is tested statistically, and if it is found to be true, it is assumed that age is a factor in explaining the spatial distribution of voting.

If the hypothesis is false, it is rejected, and age is found to be of no consequence in explaining the return of vote in that particular election. If there is no relationship between the variables, the scatter will be circular. If the scatter is oval or elliptical that the dots are not all in a straightline, then the relationship between the variables does not seem to be strong, though some relationship does exist between them.

If the hypothesis continues to be rejected with the age of the voters having been played no role in the vote returns for the candidate, then another independent variable is chosen and tested, and the process continues until a satisfactory level of explanation is found. There may be a series of independent variables, each explaining only part of the variation in the dependent variable.

Further analysis can be made between the stipulated variables through a correlation, coefficient regression, coefficient and intercept value. Due to the paucity of space here that the formulae cannot be mentioned. These measures describe the degree of relationship, the slope of a regression line, and the point when the regression line crosses the Y-axis, they are represented/denoted by 'r', 'b', and 'a' respectively. The correlation coefficient (r) always ranges between one and negative one, any positive value describes a positive relationships between the variables, while any negative value describes a negative relationship.

Here, in the present analysis, attempts have been made to find out whether or not there exists any positive relationship between (a) the opposition voting pattern and some socio-economic variables (such as urban population, literate population, workers population and scheduled caste population, all drawn from the 1981 census); and (b) the Congress voting pattern and the above variables also. In each case four scatter diagrams with the regression line on each, have been constructed and the value of 'r', 'b', and 'a' has been worked out. The model has been applied to illustrate the spatial voting pattern in the 1989 parliamentary elections in the tribal Chotanagpur region of Bihar where there are altogether fourteen parliamentary constituencies. In India, neither the boundaries of the parliamentary constituency properly coincide with those of the district or administrative unit, nor the boundaries of the administrative units have been carved out in such a fashion to fit with the boundaries of the constituency. As a result, a great effort is needed for the reconciliation of the spatial units (parliamentary/assembly constituency and the administrative unit) and the involved data of the units. The socio-economic data, used in the areal associations or ecological correlations, have been collected from the 1981 census for each district involved in the Chotanagpur region and an suitably and conveniently reconciled for the preperation of the figures. No study of this nature in India would be adequate and fruitful unless the reconciliation between the spa-

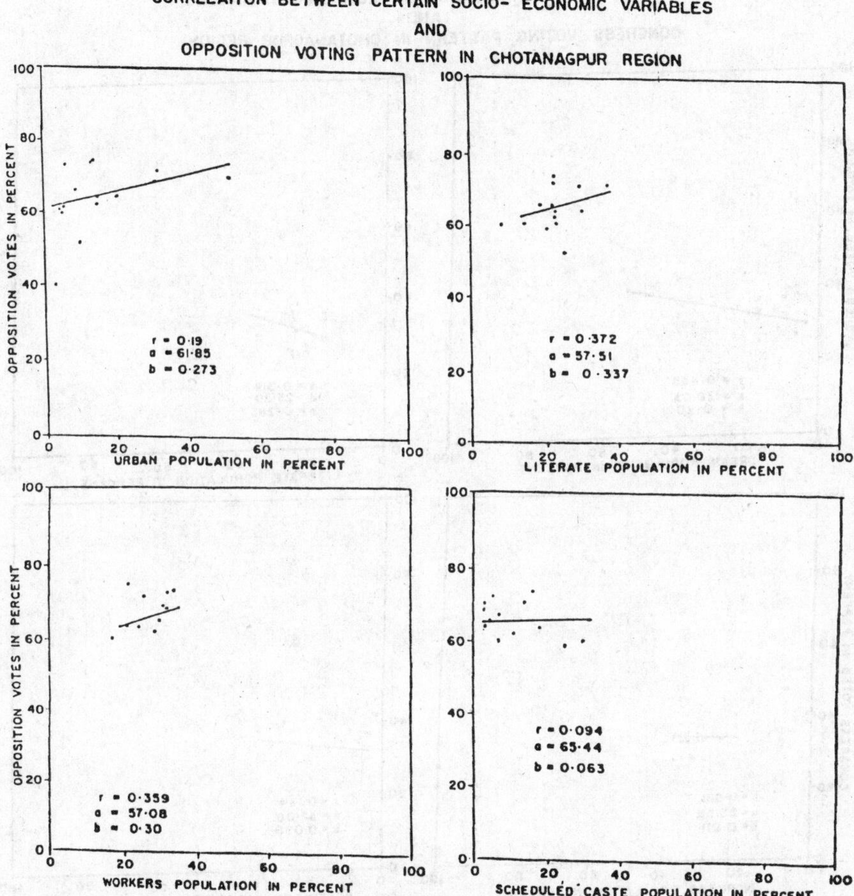

Figure 12.1: Opposition Voting Pattern in Chotanagpur Region (Areal Associaton)

tial units and data, is done/manipulated.

Figure 12.1 shows that the opposition voting patterns reveal a fairly positive relationship with the literate population and the workers population in the Chotanagpur region. However, the opposition voting patterns show a fairly negative relationship with the scheduled caste population and the urban population. While Figure 12.2 explains that in the same 1989 general elections, the Congress voting patterns show a fairly good relationship with the urban population and also with the literate population, but fairly bad relationship with the working populations, and also with the scheduled caste population. Figures 12.1 and 12.2 tend to explain that in the Chotanagpur region of Bihar, particularly in the parliamentary election in 1989 that the vote for the combined opposition

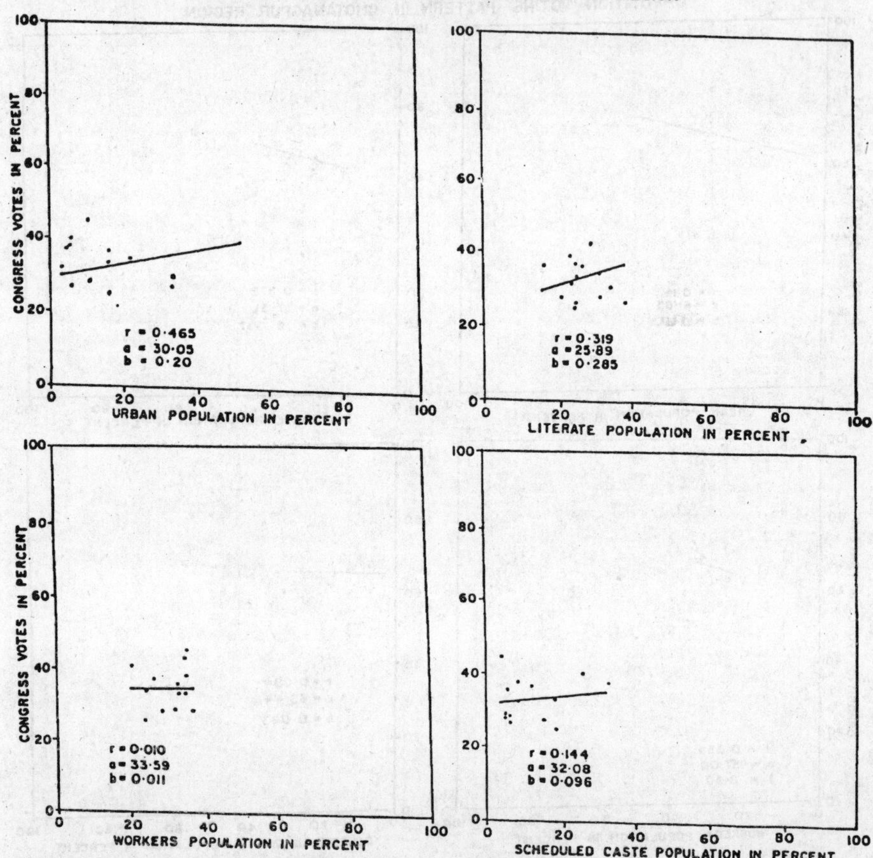

Figure 12.2: Congress Voting Pattern in Chotanagpur Region (Areal Association)

party was higher in constituencies with higher percentage of literate and workers population, similarly the vote for the Congress Party was higher in the constituencies with relatively higher percentage of the literate and the urban electorates. The Congress voting patterns also explain a relatively weak relationship with the scheduled caste population in the region.

The correlation technique discussed above was a refinement of the map comparison technique, and both are part of the areal association process. Statistical methods allow a more precise interpretation of the information gathered about the study area. There are numorous correlation techniques which can be referred to as 'multiple correlation". The basic idea with the multiple correlation is the same as that described for simple correlation. The major difference is that in the multiple correlation, more than one independent variable is used in the same calculation. A series of independent variables can be examined simultaneously as to their relationship with the dependent variable; and, therefore, the calculations are much more complicated. However, the computers have made these complicated calculations much easier.

A wide variety of sophisticated statistical techniques has been used in the geographical studies of election frequently leading to changes to the positivist-led areal association model in electoral geography. The most frequently applied techniques, other than the correlation techniques, are factor analysis, or its related principal components form and estimating equations of multiple regression type. In the mid-sixties itself, Roberts and Rummage made use of multivariate statistical techniques to the geographical study of elections. Cox and others have used the application of the factorial ecology in their studies, wherein the structural dimensions of social and economic characteristics of a population in a designated area can be identified as orthogonal components or factors.

"These sophisticated statistical techniques can be successfully applied to deal with a large number of variables and observations as well. This is mainly true in case of factor and principal components analysis where a large array of data is reduced by picking out those groups of variables most closely interrelated. The most useful quality of these techniques is that the groups of variables ('factor' in factor analysis, 'components' in components analysis) are put in descending order of importance and their significance in each area or constituency is indicated by a value or score. When the variable includes electoral statistics, the factors or components which contain the electroral variables may be regarded as those particularly associated with political viewpoint. However, there are some very serious shortcomings inherent in the use of the multivariate analysis in this context. One of these lies in the fact that these studies must rely on data sources which may not enumerate all the politically significant variables. For instance, the census reports can tell us very little about political history and tradition that are always significant in influencing people's political outlook and perception on politics" (Dikshit, 1982).

The areal association model is sometime called the aggregate data analysis, and the most important criticism of this model is that from such an analysis it is not easy to infer how the individuals themselves or in groups actually voted as they did and why. For example, the percentage turning out for a voting is usually below the average in a scheduled caste constituency. From this it does not necessarily follow that the inclination to vote is low in the case of the scheduled castes. The alternative explanation that in the scheduled caste constituencies many people belonging to upper castes abstain from voting, brings down the overall participation figure for constituency, but this also is no less plausible than the previous explanations. To take another example, the Bhartiya Janata Party (purely a Hindu political party) usually performs better in constituencies with relative higher percentage of the Muslim electorates in western Uttar Pradesh, or the Muslims League does better in the Hindu-dominated constituencies in Kerala, but the correlation in both the cases can be statistically explained by either of the two following explanations: (a) Muslims in western Uttar Pradesh vote for the Bhartiya Janata Party; or Hindus in Kerala vote for the Muslim League; or (b) in areas with large Muslims compositions such as in western Uttar Pradesh the communal issues/clearages dominate the election to motivate many Hindus to vote for the Bharatiya Janata Party and Muslin altogether refrain from voting in western Uttar Pradesh, while the same explanation may be given in the Kerala cases also where the Muslims are motivated to vote for the Muslin League and the Hindus largely abstain from voting. Between these two alternative explanations regarding the performance of the communal parties in the Muslim/Hindi-dominated areas in western Uttar Pradesh and Kerala, the second would be more plausible but not on statistical grounds.

Besides, what is true of aggregate is not necessarily true of an individual. There is a difference between 'total' correlation (based on individual based data) and 'ecological' correlation (based on aggregation) and the 'ecological fallacy' of attributing to individuals' characteristics of an aggregate. An unfortunate, if common, methodological weakness of the aggregate analysis approach or the areal association model is to collect information about individuals and then to aggregate it for analysis. Such an analysis does not permit investigation into the behavioural process. Another kind of fallacy is that of attributing individual characteristics to groups, e.g., from the finding that the 'poor' vote for communists, it does not follow that 'poor constituencies' vote for communists. It is equally possible that 'poor' in developed constituencies vote for communists. Besides, the nature of relationship between two variables is different at two levels of aggregation—at the constituency level with individual as a unit, and at the district level with constituency as a unit.

It has been found that a statistically significant correlation coefficient does not mean that one variable caused the other variable. Urbanism did not cause people to vote for the Congress Party in the 1989 parliamentary elections in the Chotanagpur region. Another obvious problem with the correlation techniques is that the data used for the independent variables were from the population of the entire constituency, and not strictly from those who voted. Thus, it must be assumed that the data (a surrogate measure) represent the actual data that are unavailable.

Besides, any attempt to relate aggregate electoral statistics to aggregate census data always runs the risk of falling into the 'ecological fallacy' which in this context may be defined as the error of assuming that ecological correlations at the constituency or district level are also correlations at the level of the individuals.

Regardless of the weaknesses and the problems, the areal association model, particularly the ecological correlation, is a time-tested and useful technique. It has been used successfully to discover new dimension in voting.

Behavioural Model

For some geographers analysis of voting data by areal units is not considered sufficiently 'spatial' to form a distinctive electoral geography. Standard statistical techniques, such as the regression analysis used by Hechter, and others, ignore the spatial context of the areal units which are treated as separate and independent observations. Hence standard statistical analyses of voting returns were replaced by location models which emphasized the 'local context' within which voting took place. In this way simple 'descriptive geography of voting' would be replaced by a more sophisticated 'geographical influence in voting'. This argument fitted in well the behavioural school of geography which was emerging in the late 1960s.

The behavioural model postulates that the correlation of aggregate data, such as those relating to number of votes and economic status of voters, does not allow any difference or prediction to be made about individual behaviour; further that the geography of election is better explained as a function of nodal characteristics, nodal location and nodal links via an information flow network. The individual elector is conceptualized as a node or a point in an information flow network; this node distributes information from one node to another and links the voting nodes to yet other nodes. The nodes between which information flow may consist of not only individual's but also of households, informal or formal groups meeting at one place, urban places and the sources of mass media. It is also clear that such information flows get influenced, if not distorted, by propaganda of political parties. Cox has made an invaluable contribution to the behavioural electoral geography in an article, "The Voting Decision in a Spatial Context", which was published in 1969 in *Progress in Geography*.

There are four basic processes that may lead to local influence on voting decisions:

I. *Candidate voting* or more commonly termed as 'friends-and-neighbours effect', which has commonly been found to occur in American, Japanese, Irish and New Zealand elections. Friends-and-neighbours effect makes a particular contextual effect in electoral geography, whereby voters favour local candidates (sometimes deserting traditional partisan preferences in order to do so). Some models of the effect associate it with the spatial diffusion of information about candidates away from their home area, so that election result displays a density gradient of support around the candidates' homes, i.e., support decreases progressively with distance from their homes. The process is also known as 'localism' and with the help of 'isovotes' (lines connecting similar percentage of voting for local candidates), the friends-and-neighbours effect for the candidates can be established/found out.

II. *Issue voting* occurs where a particular topic in an election is of more importance to some areas than others.

III. *Campaign effects* reflect the differential influences of the campaign. This may involve particular targeting as in the US presidential election when additional efforts is put into key states or more simply local campaigning differences in terms of resources used.

IV. *The neighbourhood effect* is the most studied geographical influence in voting. It attempts to explain why it is that parties do better than expected in their strongest areas. The neighbourhood effect is a form of local social influence. The characteristics of people's social environments are believed to affect the way they think and act. It intervenes between perceived self-interest and actual behaviour, with the individuals acting not only in their best interests but also on the opinion and images of the neighbourhood population with whom they interact.

The neighbourhood effect postulates the following process. For any individual in an election campaign there are two sources of information. The general information from the mass media available to everybody and the particular information derived from local contacts. The latter will be biased to the extent that the individual lives in a partisan area. Hence general information will go through a partisan filter in the voting decision-making process. The result will be that 'all' classes living in working-class areas will be more likely to vote for the 'natural' party of the area and 'all' classes living in middle-class areas will be more likely to vote for the 'natural' party of that area. It has been found in the survey data, e.g., that working-class voters living in working-class districts are more likely to vote Communists in France, Labour in Britain and Democrat in USA than working-class voters living in middle-class area. In the caste-conscious Indian society, the neighbourhood effect plays the most decisive role in the voting decision of the people. In a communally-surcharged society, it is the communal cleavage which largely affects the voting perception of the fellow-electorates.

In a recent survey, in West Bengal, it has been found that the electorates involved in primary and secondary activities have mostly voted the Left Front, whereas, the electorates involved in tertiary activities, other than the primary and secondary activities, have mostly favoured the Congress. This difference in the voting decision can be illustrated, in part at least, by the neighbourhood effect.

Apart from the above four basic processes, there is one more process, i.e., the *process of relocation effect*, which also leads to local influence on voting decisions. It is the migration of the people which creates the relocation effect and which does have certain decisive effects on the voting decision. Relocation involves alternation in the networks of those who have migrated, and through political propaganda by political parties. Voting habits in most of the constituencies in north-east Bihar have been largely motivated by the relocation effect, largely as a result of the relocation of Bangladesh immigrants in these constituencies. P.F. Lewis has sought to examine the relocation effect on the voting behaviour in Flint, Michigan, during 1932-1962, especially in terms of the impact of Negro migration to it. His study appeared in the *Annals of the Association of American Geographers* in 1965.

The behavioural model in electoral geography relies mostly on survey analysis, involving the compilation of questionnaires and interviews of a sample of electors. This approach does not seem to have been used in any of the studies so far done in electoral geography in India. Probably, it is too early and too costly for a large and populous country like India. Further, it is difficult to have all statewise basic data, and more so for the smaller regions. It is very difficult to test the friends-and-neighbour effect and to draw isovotes, because the voting data are not arranged in such a way so as to measure this effect. Though the neighborhood effect could be measured but that would be very time and money consuming effort, as it relies on intensive fieldwork. Moreover, researchers find difficulties in carrying out survey works, largely because of illiterate electors who are more drawn/inclined to their castes/communal and political loyalties, and would not answer to the quarries.

The behavioural model is yet to make its presence felt as a tool in geographical research in electoral studies. It must, however, be said in favour of this model as it offers venues for model building and theory construction incorporating spatial component in voting behaviour. It is also a complementary method to aggregate analysis of voting pattern and voting behaviour, and therefore, no incompatibility exists between the two models. Though, at the present, the areal association model appears to be more practicable in studying voting behaviour in India, it is necessary to make a beginning in studies based on regional and local samples.

Geography of Voter Participation

Voter participation is the input to the electoral system and results vis-a-vis the seats won by political parties tend to constitute the output of the system. In fact, it is the *raison d'etre* of the election. No election is meaningful unless the people participate in it. There is considerable spatial variation in the voter participation in the state. It may be very high in some constituencies, and very low in the others. Even within a constituency itself, significant spatial variations in the turnout can be seen. It is particularly true in the parliamentary constituency wherein different assembly segments (which together constitute the constituency) usually witness marked spatial variations in voter participation.

Voter participation in most of the states in the world is not mandatory, and as a result, most of the states in the free world register a low turnout. However, in Australia, it is mandatory and fines are levied for non-participation. Participation there approaches 90 per cent of the eligible voters. Sweden also experiences a very high turnout, though it is not compulsory there. In India, if the turnout approaches or exceeds 90 per cent, it is then assumed that malpractices, such as rigging and booth-capturing have occurred. In such cases, however, repoll is ordered.

There are many factors which account for the differences in voter participation from place to place. Even, there is difference in the male-female participation. Surveys and election data have shown that men are more likely to vote than women. This is true not only in the peripheral states but also in the core states, like the USA.

It has been observed that states with homogeneous populations register relatively higher voter participation than those which have heterogeneous populations, leading to various types of 'cleavages' in the society. Lack of literacy among the voters also stands as in the way of the participation. In some peripheral states, the turnout is extremely low because of the lack of political maturity and consciousness among the people that they fail to realize the political significance of the right. Sometimes ignorance on the part of the electors leads to considerable variations in the turnout. Distance to polling booths is another factor, causing to the difference. There are many more factors for differences in voter participation. Thus, there is a geography of voter participation.

Norris and Haring have developed a voter participation probability model with a view to understand some of the factors involved in causing the spatial differences. The model shown in the Figure 12.3 can be put under the category of a 'behavioural model' because of the integration of factors affecting individuals (micro scale) with factors affecting groups of people in an area (macro scale). The micro and macro factors are each divided into (a) 'constant' or long term influences, and (b) 'situational' influences, that occur during only one particular election. The division of voting participation into the 'motivations' for

Scale	*Change from election to election*	*VOTING*	
		Motivations	*Restraints*
Micro (individual)	Constant	A	E
	Situational	B	F
Macro (area)	Constant	C	G
	Situational	D	H

(A+C) (B+D) = Total Desire to Vote
(E+G))F+H) = Total Restraints to Voting
(A+C) (B+D) -(E+G)(F+H) = Voting Probability

Figure 12.3: Voter Participation Probability

voting versus the 'restraints' confronting the political voters completes the contingency-table aspect of the flow chart so that statistical measures such as chi-square analysis could be used to detect the voting probability of an area. Each of the cell of the matrix contains a letter that represent the factor or factors that should be considerd for each situation.

One factor that motivates an individual to vote is his 'constant motivation', which includes his general interest in political matters, consciousness, sense of duty or commitment to particular political party which is contesting the election, and loyalty to particular political ideology which the party is carrying forward. It is the Marxian philosophy which has been, for long, motivating the Bengali voters to vote the Marxist Party in elections. This is a long term or 'constant' influence, which is represented by the 'A' in the model. Another motivational factor for the individual that may occur once (situational) is dependent on the circumstances of a particular election. Possibly there is one issue or one candidate that the person feels strongly about— so strongly that he will make an extreme effort to vote for or against the issue or candidate. In the 1989 general elections, it was the Bofors scandal that motivated the Indian electorates to vote against the Congress Party, or in the 1991 mid-term elections it was the Ram Janambhumi-Babri-Maszid issue that motivated the electorates to vote the Bharatiya Janata Party. It may be the only time some people ever vote, or it may occur at numerous times. Possibly the individual voter knows the political party or the candidate personally, but whatever circumstances, there are elections that are of special interest to some individuals. These may be called 'situational motivation', and are represented by the 'B' in the model.

People do not vote for various personal reasons. The 'constant restraints' might include political alienation. Weaker section peoples in India are not allowed to exercise their franchise. This has been the practice since the electoral system was introduced in independent India. Some people are 'turned off' by anything political and will not vote in any election. Some people are handicapped and are unable to vote regardless of the strength of their motivation to do so. These types of influences are put in the cell 'E' of the model.

The last personal influence (cell 'F' in the model) is the 'situational restraints'. This category includes illnesses that are temporary. A person who is committed to vote, but falls too sick on election day to make it to the polls. Intimidation and terrorism to voters before the polling usually prevent them to vote. This is again a very common practice in India where the weaker section people are intimidated and terrorized before the polling day so that they may not make it to the polls. Sometimes sporadic violence on the polling day prevents the people to vote. The demands of some people's employment may keep them away from the polls. This is the reason that elections are held on weekends in Finland, Sweden, Australia and India. Other people who generally vote but skip a particular election may do so because of the particular candidate involved. The choice between the two candidates may be too difficult for some people, and they simply do not vote, or they may dislike both candidates, and thus refuse to vote one way or the other.

The motivations and restraints to voting affecting everyone equally in a particular area are somewhat similar to the individual influences. Constant motivations (cell 'C' in the model) might include the social pressures in a community. People with a a high interest in politics put pressure on their friends and neighbours to vote on particular issues or for certain candidates. People in Bihar, mostly those belonging to the backward communities, voted enblock to the Janata Dal in the 1995 assembly elections because of the Mandal factor as it stood for social justice, and it sought to emancipate the backward people from the sustainable exploitation perpetuated on them by the upper caste people for long.

The political communication, as a result of the friends-and-neighbours effect, works much more effectively in some areas than in others; thus there are place-to-place differences in the constant-motivational influences.

The situational motivations (cell 'D') that affect groups of people could include the campaign excitement promoted by particular candidates. Debates between rival parties on the electronic media before the elections usually generate much interest in that election, leading to unusually high voter participation. Also, particular issues, especially those related to social tension, economic problems, and problems of taxes, etc., affect people directly, and can generate unusual interest, resulting in the high voter participation/turnout.

The most important macro level constant restraints (cell 'G' in the model) from participation in voting in any country or state are the electoral laws existing there. In India, some legislations are being enacted with a view to making the voter participation meaningful and reasonable. Obviously, these enactments will have decisive impact on the people, e.g., voter registration laws in India are being amended in such a way so as to exclude the illegal immigrants from the voters list. Photo identity cards are being issued to genuine electorates. Moreover, it is like by to the made mandatory that each genuine electorate must have his identity card which he is required at show of the polling booth otherwise he will not be allowed to vote. Lowering of the voting age from 21 years to 18 years has already affected the turnout. The number of voters has increased which has also led to an increase in turnout.

The macro level situational restraints (cell 'H' in the model) include such factors as the weather on election day. In fact, the weather may have more effect on turnout than registration rules. Other factors that retard voter turnout on the macro level include difficult choices between candidates and weakly contested elections. It has been found that, faced with a difficult choice, people tend not to vote at all, and that dull election campaign tend to cause voter apathy.

"The voter participation model presented here is intended to be a heuristic device. It is a general model used to learn about some of the factors involved in the voter turnout. In order to calibrate the model, the letters in each cell of the matrix would have to be replaced with numeric values (measures) of the individual factors. These values would vary from place to place; thus a map of voting probabilities would be developed. To test it, the resulting map could be compared to an actual voter participation map..."

Regional Stability

Voters in West Bengal have voted the Left Front with overwhelming majority in the five successive elections, which were held in 1977, 1982, 1987, 1992, and 1996, and the Left Front is in power there for little more than seventeen years. Voting patterns established in 1977 in West Bengal have persisted to this day. In spite of a number of issues reflecting the successive failures on several fronts, however, there is an extraordinary durability to Bengali voting habits in West Bengal. Regional persistence of partisan loyalties to the Left Front is a feature of electoral geography in West Bengal. Similarly, in Maharashtra, the Marathi voters have always expressed their loyalties to the Congress Party, and also there is an extraordinary stability in the regional voting pattern in the state. These regional stabilities in the voting patterns in West Bengal and Maharashtra seem incredible in light of other changes that have taken place. However, there is hardly any work on this aspect of electoral geography in India.

In the book, *Southern Politics: In State and Nation*, published in 1949, V.O. Key emphasized regional stability in voting habits, especially for the State of Tennessee. The vote on secession from the Union in 1861 established a pattern of voting that has lasted until today. The two regions in Tennessee that voted against secession became areas of Republican stronghold, and the two groups of secessionist counties became Democratic strength. The pattern was established by the distribution of slave ownership. Counties where slaves were owned voted to secede from the Union, and became Democratic. The pattern in Tennessee was a small scale reproduction of the remainder of the United States. The south was known for many years as a stronghold for Democrats. 'Dixie' became synonymous with voting Democrats.

When American westward expansion began after the civil war, the people who moved took their voting habits with them. As they settled in new areas, they established voting patterns that have remained for well over 100 years. The north-south settlement of Oklahama brought Dixie Democrats to the southern part of the state and mid-western Republicans to the north part. Partisan patterns were established in the state, and they have persisted to this day. For instance, compare the Republican counties for the first presidential election in Oklahama with those for the most recent election. The southeastern part of Oklahama is known as 'little Dixie' which is a reflection of the early settlement pattern. In 33 of the 77 counties of Oklahama, registered Democrats comprise over 90 per cent of the voters. In fact, in 20 counties, registered Democrats constitute over 95 per cent of the voters, and in three counties the percentage exceeds 99. Regional stability in Oklahama is maintained by the pattern of partisan attitudes; however, in spite of the larger area and high percentage of Democrats, Republican candidates do win the state. It shows that people that register for the one political party do not necessarily support candidates for that party. In nearly every state in the USA are regions in which voters consistently vote for one political party.

Urban-Rural Conflicts

Another form of regional stability is the pattern established by the 'conflict between urban and rural' interests. People in urban centres have different voting habits from those in rural areas for many reasons. Most urban dwellers have incomes from salaries, whereas formers earn income from what they produce. The source of income is the most important rural-urban difference—even more important than amount of income and that intrinsically reflects in the voting behaviour. Other rural-urban differences include most of the variables commonly associated with voting 'age'—average ages in urban centres are lower than in rural areas; 'females' in urban areas participate in election whereas the rural women disssociate themselves from voting; 'minorities' in urban areas have a greater racial mix than rural areas; 'education'—levels of average number of school years completed are generally higher in urban areas than in rural areas; 'income'—average incomes are higher in cities than in the surrounding rural areas; and 'communication'—facilities are there in urban centres rather than in the rural areas. Practically any other factor mentioned will be different in the city than in the country. These differences cause differences in attitudes that are manifested in voting. The rural-urban conflict has been stable since cities first developed, and thus is a part of the regional stability concept.

Cities dominate rural areas not only by containing more people and merely outvoting them, but also by influencing rural voters. Newspapers and television stations spread the influence of the city into surrounding countryside. There is a distance-decay (decrease with increased distance) to the spread of the urban influence. Conceptually, the influence of a city radiates from its centre in concentric zones, decreasing with each zone outward. Thus, voting would be expected to follow the same pattern; areas closer to the city would vote more like the city than areas farther away. This conceptual pattern is generally true, but the concentric zonation can be interrupted by state boundaries, and can be distorted by transportation routes. In other words, the urban influence on voting is similar to a diffusion process. The ideas and attitudes formulated in the city diffuse outward more easily along transport routes than where routes do not exist; thus, voting is more similar to that in the city at greater distances along routes of interaction than elsewhere. The same ideas and attitudes are stopped by the barrier of a state boundary, thus voting habits change at the boundary.

However, when there is a great deal of interaction across a boundary, the barrier effect will be decreased. In fact, increased interaction will serve to enhance the attitudes in adjacent areas, and thus voting will be more similar than would be expected. This condition exists where cities are located adjacent to each other, but are in different states.

The single most important determinant for regional stability in voting is tradition. Over 70 per cent of those Bengali voters who acquire the franchise right recently as a result of the lowering of age in West Bengal stick to the Communist Party of India (Marxist) as their parents. The same is true for the Marathi voters in Maharashtra who strictly adhere to the Congress political culture. This has been called the 'inherited vote', but attitudes and perceptions are inherited, not political philosophy. Once behavioural patterns are established, they tend to remain constant. Also, in order to be a 'region', an area must have some underlying homogeneity in its resources or production capability. The similarity factor in the economics of an area attracts people who have similar interests, attitudes and goals. Thus, regional stability depends on (a) the homogeneity of the area, (b) the inherited vote, (c) the committed voters, and (d) the common interests of the people of the area. Major realingnments in partisan attitudes are rare. Certain elections are important because realignments did occur, but these are the exceptions to the rule. The same holds true for most regions—they tend to remain loyal to one political philosophy for a long time.

Once a region is established as a homogeneous voting area, new people migrating into it will not necessarily change its political make up. The political philosophy of the area is absorbed by the migrants rather than the migrants changing the area. Migrants change their attitudes to conform to those prevalent in the new region because they are constantly coming in contact with ideas and concepts that may be opposite to those in the area from which they migrated. For example, a Communist who has migrated to Bombay from Calcutta and settled there would definitely move in for the Congress culture because he would be exposed to the Congress culture by new friends and neighbours. Thus, the political homogeneity of a region can be stronger than the inherited vote of the individual. Obviously, realignment of individual does not occur when they move to areas that contain people with political attitudes similar to their own. However, large groups of people with similar attitudes moving into an area can cause a realignment of the area.

Regional stability in voting is mostly in a bi-party system, whereas in a multi-party system, it is not a common phenomenon; for example, in India, there are a number of national parties and numerous regional parties at the regional level, and therefore, frequent changes in the voting habits do occur.

Regional Realignments

Regions tend to remain politically stable, but they can change from one partisan loyalty to another. Usually, the change is gradual, but it can occur from one election to the next. Considerable effort and expense are devoted in modern society to changing the attitudes and opinions of individuals. "All advertising is geared toward convincing people to buy particular products. Political communicators work much the same way; their 'products' are political ideas or candidates. When the ballots are counted after an election, the results can be analyzed, but the effectiveness of the pre-electing advertising can only be guessed, whereas the effectiveness of a television advertisement for a product can be judged fairly accurately by the increase in the volume of sales. Thus, although the methods in product advertising and political advertising are similar, there has never been proof that they produce similar results. In addition, a consumer can try a new product, and discard it, sell it, or exchange it if he is not satisfied. Once an elected representative takes office, however, his constituency is more or less 'stuck' with him until the next election. For this reason, electors are more conservative in their choices than consumers."

Regional realignment means the change in the voting habits of a region. It occurs mostly as a result of (a) migration into an area, (b) conflict in political philosophies from which particular candidates or parties benefit, (c) localism or when a local 'favoured son' is running for office, (d) communal and caste cleavages, and also linguistic cleavages (these are potential factors in India), and (e) groups of people not confined to a particular region changing loyalties from one political party to another. Of course, there are other reasons for regions to experience political changes, such as changes in their political perceptions, increase in their political maturity and consciousness, the neighbourhood effect, and changes in their economics. Although non-change (stability) seems to be more prevalent than change in the core countries where democracy is deeply rooted, realignment (change) is the most common electoral phenomenon in the peripheral countries, including India.

The first regional level realingnments in the voting habits in India occurred in 1967, when people voted the non-Congress parties to power in several states. The traditional Congress votes went to the non-Congress parties effecting a major change in the regional voting habits. Since then change became a more common phenomenon in the electoral scenario in India. It was in 1977 that the first realignment occurred at the national level when people voted the Janata Party to power. Nevertheless, the change was more common in the Hindi belt rather than in the peninsular region of the country. Most of the states in the Hindi speaking region have experienced recurrent changes (realignments) in the voting habits. Castes/communal conscious people in this region usually vote to such political parties which indulge in, or practice casteism and communalism. Here, in this case, some form of neighbourhood effect cannot be ruled out.

Realignment in West Bengal in 1977 set a trend that is still continuing and is rapidly giving way to the stability. Uttar Pradesh witnessed three realignments during 1989-93, the first occurred in 1989 when the people voted the Janata Dal which was a centrist party but soon it collapsed and the second realignment occurred in the year 1991 elections when the voters favoured the Bharatiya Janata Party, and again in the year 1993 election a new coalition, called the SP-BSP coalition was voted to power by the Uttar Pradesh electorates. However, the state is at present under the President Rule as the SP-BSP coalition and then the BSP-BJP coalition in early 1995 collapsed. Fresh assembly elections will be held this year and a new realignment will come up. Frequent realignments in Uttar Pradesh reveal lack of consistency in the voter perceptions and attitudes. However, the realignment that occurred at the national level in 1989 was short-lived, it could not set any trend which could continue further.

Localism

The location of a political candidate's home in most elections, but is essential for third party candidates and in state elections. Third party candidates always find their strongest support in areas close to their homes. This phenomenon is known as friends-and-neighbours or localism (mentioned earlier) voting. People tend to vote for someone they know personally, or perhaps they know the candidate's family, or least know the local area where the candidate was raised. This type of support for the 'home town boy' has a transient nature because of the turnover in the ranks of the people seeking to become representatives or office seekers. Therefore, it is classified as a type of regional realignment. That is, regions will go against their normal voting habits in order to support a local candidate.

The Patna parliamentary constituency had been a CPI stronghold that the electors here used to vote the CPI candidate but in the 1989 elections, the people voted the BJP candidate, which in itself manifested friends-and- neighbuors voting because the BJP candidate was a local resident whereas the CPI candidate lived in the periphery of the constituency away from the urban area. It was found that the polling booths which lay near to his residence, registered unusually higher percentage of vote while the polling booths away from his residence registered a relative decline in the percentage of votes polled to him. The election results reveal a strong distance-decay in popularity away from the BJP candidate's place of residence. The constituency also witnessed a similar phenomenon in the 1993 by-election when the BJP candidate lost to a more 'hometown' boy of the Janata Dal. The results of this election reveal that real realignment has occurred in this case that the Janata Dal candidate was more like a third party candidate (other than the CPI and the BJP). The distance-decay model seems to be in well fitted in this case because there had been appreciable decrease in the number of votes polled to him with distance. It was much less in the peripheries of the constituency.

One of the major realingnments in the Indian electoral politics, in the recent years, has been that of the Mulsims having switched over their loyalty to the Janata Dal. The Muslims used to vote the Congress ever since the electioneering process started in independent India. It was in the 1989 elections, that for the first time, the Muslims changed their loyalty to the Janata Dal, on the plea that the Congress Party had failed to maintain the secular fabric in the country. This realignment had the effect on regions, mostly inhabited by the Muslims where the Congress Party did fairly bad. Another realignment in the voting habits occurred in the 1991 midterm election when the caste-Hindus in the Hindi-heartland voted the Bhartiya Janata Party, discarding the Congress Party which, hitherto, had the support of the caste-Hindus.

Last elections in Uttar Pradesh had revealed that the scheduled caste people, there, have expressed their loyalty to a new political party—the Bahujan Samaj Party rather than to the Congress Party which till recently claimed their supports.

Large scale Muslim immigration to northeast Bihar had its impact on the voting habits in the region. They expressed their loyalty to the political party which did not oppose to their immigration. As they were forced into non-integrated neighbourhood, they became voting blocs rather than being absorbed individually into the local politico-social milieu. Kashmiri Hindu immigrants in the Delhi region who have been registered as voters, have also caused realignment in the voting habits of the region, with their loyalties being expressed to the Bharatiya Janata Party that the party did extremely fair in the recent elections.

Individual migrants tend to change their attitudes to conform to their new areas but when large numbers of peoples with similar political perceptions move into an area they can 'overwhelm' the local political attitudes. Thus, regional alignment can be caused by migration, but peculiar circumstances are necessary, such as the isolation of new arrivals through discrimination or the movement of large numbers of people into previously uninhabited areas.

Urban-Suburban Conflicts

Urban-suburban conflicts also tend to be a potential factor, causing regional realignment in the voting habits/patterns, particularly in the urban regions of the core countries of the world, which have registered maximum urbanization. The exodus from American central cities is a type of migration in which people settle in areas that were relatively uninhabited. This mass movement of people to urbs has changed the voting patterns of urban regions. It can be classified as a type of regional realignment. Suburbs began to appear on the American landscape shortly after World War II. They have continued to grow since then, and they are growing at a much faster rate than the central cities. In fact, there was a net decrease in population in thirteen of the twenty largest cities in the United States during 1960-1970, while during the same period suburban areas of those cities registered growth. The average growth rate for the twenty largest central cities was only 0.59 per cent. While the average rate for the same cities' suburbs was 19.6 per cent. This rearrangement of the urban spatial structure created a spatial dichotomy in the urban voting pattern.

People tend to be situated spatially within an urban area according to age, ethnic background, and lifestyle but the most important factor is the kind of housing they can afford. Thus, resulting urban demographic spatial structures are based on economic considerations. Political conflicts arise because of divergent interests that are rooted in the economic difference. Wealthier and rich people in the USA prefer to live in the suburbs because better housing facilities are found there, and relatively less wealthier people continue to live in the central cities. As a result, the pattern of voting in American cities has been for the people in the suburbs to vote Republicans, and the people in the central cities to vote Democrats. The suburban conservatism in some areas is even more persistent than that in the rural parts of the states.

However, urban-suburban conflicts on the Indian electoral scenario are intrinsically confined to the major metropolitan regions on account of the persistent nature of the fast growing socio-economic cleavages. Metropolitan areas are witnessing areal expansion because of rapid industrialization followed by mass exodus from the rural areas into the suburban areas. Therefore, some kind of 'rural' influence in the suburban voting pattern can be observed. While the residents of the central cities of the metropolis usually stick to the traditional political parties like the Congress, and the inhabitants of the suburban areas with some kind of rural perception and background normally favour the newer political parties. Therefore, within the metropolitan regions, there are political conflicts, which get translated into the variable voting habits, frequently leading to realignment in voting behaviour.

Adherence to the Marxian philosophy, in contradiction to the Congress political culture, by the average people of Kerala as early as 1950s, brought about the first significant regional realingment in the voting habits in the newly emerged state. In West Bengal, the first regional realingment in the voting pattern occurred mostly as a result of the political disillusionment with the Congress culture but the major regional realignment there took place when the average middle class Bengali people enthusiastically identified themselves with the Marxian philosophy and expressed solidarity with it, which got reflected in the voting patterns/habits. It is important to note that these two states have more educated and literate people than the rest, and voters there, on account of being educated, readily understood the inherent concept of the Marxian philosophy, and simultaneously, realized its socio-economic relevance in the contemporary situations. This realization had the impact on the voting habits of the people of the states which finally resulted into the realingment. However, there is correlation (implicit) between the literacy and the realignment in Bengal and Kerala, the measures of which can be statistically found out through the correlation, coefficient, regression, coefficient and chi-square.

Regional realignment is more common in a multi-ethnic/multi-national states, where the political parties identify themselves with the dominant ethnic or national groups. Obviously, these states usually have multi-party system to give effect to the frequent realignment in the voting habits.

Contextual Effect

It is a concept, being used in electoral geography to account for local variations in voting patterns. The basic approach to the study of voting sees the elector responding to the stimuli provided by various candidates and parties on the basis of self-interest. Most appeals for support are made not to the individual voters, however, but to groups within society with which voters associate: hence, the development of electoral cleavages, of which the most common are those based on social class. In addition, however, most voters are influenced by others with whom they have social contacts; these others form the context within which voting decisions (and a wide range of other aspects of attitude formation) may be shaped.

Two processes have been identified as contributing to the development of a contextual effect. According to the first, i.e., the 'acquaintance-circle process', individuals are influenced by the weight of opinion within their contact networks, so that in areas where a majority of individuals are predisposed to a particular view, some members of the minority will be 'converted' by them; information flows through social networks in the same way as diseases.

According to the second, i.e., the 'forced field process', a local political culture is established in an area by the activities of political parties and other key sectors; they mobilize attitudes in a particular way, according to the local class structure, and in some cases around local issues. In some places, a singular local culture may develop, resulting in pattern of voting that deviates from general, national trends. Most places with similar class structure have similar local political cultures and voting patterns, however. Many analyses of the geography of voting have produced results that are consistent with the contextual effect concept. Most of these use aggregate data only, however, they face the problems of the ecological fallacy and make no explicit test of the processes involved.

Geography of Representation

The geography of representation has been a particularly fruitful area of inquiry in countries that use a plurality system of voting such as USA and UK. In this system, a candidate is elected to a legislature on the basis of obtaining most votes in an electoral district. This simple spatial organization of elections has proved to be amenable to some relatively advanced spatial analysis techniques.

Geography of representation has been concerned with the 'districting problems'. This states that different patterns of electoral district boundaries will produce different election results in terms of legislative seats "even if the underlying pattern of voting remains the same". Since there are many different ways of dividing up an area into a given number of electoral districts, it follows that there are many different results even if we hold the actual voting constant. This has led to two types of electoral abuse: 'reapportionment', and 'gerrymandering'.

The spatial manipulation of votes through constituency delimitation is known as 'electoral abuse' which is based on the underlying concept of 'electoral bias'. Electoral bias is measured as the difference between the percentage of seats of a party wins and the percentage of votes polled in its favour.

In the case of reapportionment, the districts of different populations are designed to favour one party over another. The most common form that this takes is to favour rural areas, and hence parties with rural support, which has been reported for Britain, Japan, Australia, South Africa, New Zealand, France, Chile, and Canada. The most notable case, however, was USA before the malapportionment revolution of the 1960s when the courts insisted on equi-populous districts for elections at all levels.

Malapportionment/reapportionment may be explained with the help of the following hypothetical example of a small country divided into five constituencies to elect following five representatives: The eastern region of the country (the main base for the East Party, EP) is divided into three constituencies of 100 votes each, while the western region (the main base for the West Party, WP) has only two constituencies with 150 voters (Fig. 12.4). This apportionment of constituencies would mean that EP has three safe seats out of five, and hence a stable majority, even though the overall numerical supports for the two parties are equal. Under this arrangement of constituency boundaries even a marked swing (say of 10 per cent) in voters support in favour of the West Party (WP) is unlikely to grant her majority since the apportionment provides for a very high margin of support for EP (Fig. 12.4). In most western countries (UK, USA,

WP	120	WP	20
		EP	80
EP	30	WP	20
WP	120	EP	80
		WP	20
EP	30	EP	80

(a)

WP	135	WP	30
		EP	70
		WP	30
EP	15		
WP	135	EP	70
		WP	30
EP	15	EP	70

(b)

Figure 12.4: Electoral Abuse: Malapportionment

Australia, France, Canada) malapportionment/reapportionment has been intimately linked with the issue of a rural overrepresentation so that rural constituencies send a representative for much smaller numbers of people per constituency than the circumstances in urban areas do.

However, it is gerrymandering (named after Governor Gerry of Massachusetts, who, in 1812, established an oddly shaped electoral district in order to favour his party) which has been the main concern of recent research since it has been shown that election results can be easily manipulated without any need to resort to malapportionment. Gerrymandering involves drawing the boundaries of electoral districts in such a way that favours one party or candidate over another. It can also be illustrated with reference to the hypothetical example of a small country with a total of four constituencies, as shown in Figure 12.5. It a reveals a situation where the support areas of the two rival parties (EP and WP) are so distributed as to give a 'fair' election result wherein strength of party support is matched by the number of seats won. In Figure 12.5 the constituency boundaries have been so manipulated (gerrymandered) that even though each constituency is of the same size (in terms of population), the net result of boundary manipulation is one in which the areas of WP support are so divided that it gets an overwhelming majority in one constituency and a clear minority base in all others. Thus, gerrymandering by EP sympathizers has created a situation where three clear victories are assumed to that party while its rival, WP, gets only one clear victory (albeit with a very large majority) even though the overall support for WP (60x3+130=310) is higher than that for EP (90x30+30=300).

WP 130	WP 30
EP 30	EP 130
WP 130	WP 30
EP 30	EP 130

(a)

WP 130	WP 60
	EP 90
	WP 60
	EP 90
EP 30	WP 60
	EP 90

(b)

Figure 12.5: Electoral Abuse: Gerrymandering

There are several strategies which may be adopted. A stacked gerrymander, for instance, is one in which an opposing party's votes are largely concentrated into just one or two districts which they win with a large majority, but which leaves them with few votes and therefore seats elsewhere. The general idea is to make votes as effective as possible in winning seats while wasting the other party's votes either in surpluses in large majorities or else in losing districts. Where the drawing of district boundaries is a political task then governments can help perpetuate their power by careful political cartography. There are many examples of this abuse in the US and French elections.

There seems to be simple solution to this abuse. Why not take it out of the hands of politicians and let a neutral body draw the boundaries? This is, of course, the situation in several countries—Britain, Australia, New Zealand, Canada and South Africa, for example. But in these countries problems remain. Neutral drawing of boundaries does not eliminate the districting problem; it merely removes the intent to discriminate against an opponent. A neutral drawn districting plan will not necessarily be neutral in effect. To think otherwise is to subscribe to what the 'myth of non-partisan cartography'. Such districting is merely 'innocently partisan' and employs "the three monkey's policy—speak no politics, see no politics, hear no politics". This is the most concrete example in political geography of Schattschneider's dictum that "all organization is bias".

But what is the nature of the bias instilled in election result even by neutral commissioners? This depends upon the spatial pattern of voters as reflected in the level of segregation of voters supporting different parties. Since party systems are based upon social class, religious and/or ethnic criterion which are also important in defining residential segregation, it follows that we can usually identify areas of support for different parties. In short, the spatial distribution of support for particular parties is relatively uneven. When district boundaries are added to this map, they produce districts with different mixes of each party's supporters. This process can be modelled to show the possible effects of the procedure. The basic result is that the arbitrary (or neutral) drawing of boundaries will inevitably tend to favour the majority party in the area being districted. In Britain, for instance, this means that Labour Party gets a higher proportion of seats than votes in urban and industrial counties whereas Conservatives obtain a higher proportion of seats than votes in suburban and rural counties. Overall the two biases tend to cancel themselves out although the majority party in the country as a whole (either Labour or Conservative depending on the election) will have a disproportionate majority in parliament. This is sometimes known as the 'cube-law'* and results from the particular mix of social segregation and scale of constituency underlying the spatial organization of elections in Britain.

If the partisan districting (gerrymandering) and non-partisan districting (in-

* It refers to a statement of the electoral bias in a single-member constituency electoral system. The law states that the ratio of the percentage of the seats won by two contesting parties (S_1/S_2) equals the cube of the comparable ratio for percentage of the votes $(V_1/V_2)^3$. (The law applies to two-party contests only). Thus, if $V_1 > 50$, then $S_1 > V_1$, producing electoral bias which can occur without any electoral abuse (e.g., gerrymandering or malapportionment strategies). Recent research suggests a more general law $(S_1/S_2 = (V_1 V_2)^b$, with the size of b reflecting the degree of segregation of suppoters of the two parties.

nocent gerrymandering) are unsatisfactory why not employ bi-partisan districting where parties agree between them on the district boundaries? This solution has become quite popular in USA where both informal and formal bi-partisan commissions have been created so that bi-partisan districting has been widespread since the reapportionment revolution. The problem is that such districting omits one important interest from the negotiations, namely, that of the voter. Bi-partisan districting tends to produce sets of safe districts for each party. This means that there are few marginal seats where voters may effectively cause a seat to change hands. Bi-partisan districting takes the uncertainty out of elections! The classic case of this in the 1974 Congressional election in the immediate aftermath of the Watergate scandal. This hurt the Republican Party in the polling booths but not so much in Congress since the existence of a relatively large number of safe Republican seats insulated the party from the worst effects of its unpopularity. Since bi-partisan districting lessens the influence of voters on election results it is sometimes referred to as bi-partisan gerrymandering. This is the final confirmation that in the geography of representation all organization is bias.

A Systems Model for Electoral Geography

Most of the research works that appeared in various journals and books in electoral geography in the 1970s tended to make the sub-discipline uncoordinated and isolated. The wayout of this impasse was not for more empirical research but for a new synthetic attempt to integrate these various themes. Such an approach was found to be available in systems analysis which had already made its appearance in political geography but with no significant impact in the contemporary scholarship of political geogpraphy. However, the simplest model employed was Easton's political system which could be reduced to just four elements: input, throughput, output plus feedback. Such a framework seems to fit electoral geography—which is, after all, commonly thought of as dealing with electoral systems. This approach has been attempted to integrate studies of elections with administrative systems but without any satisfactory framework.

Taylor has made use of systems concept in electoral geography (Fig. 12.6). Geography of voting and geographical influences in voting become the input to the system. Geography of representation becomes the throughput leaving the geographical effects of the resulting legislature/executive as the output of the system. Three implications of this recording of the literature were identified. First, electoral geography was given a purpose and focus beyond the elections themselves. Second, the current emphasis on one part of the system—the input—seemed excessive in comparison with the other parts. Third, in contrast, the massive neglect of the output was highlighted. This was the reason that electoral geography seemed to have no clear direction. By treating elections as an end in themselves, the actual purpose of election—the producing of legislatures and governments—had been largely forgotten. Hence, the systems approach pointed towards a redirection of electoral geography beyond input and throughput.

Electoral System	*INPUT →*	*THROUGHPUT→*	*OUTPUT*
Electoral Geography	Geography of voting and geographical influences in voting	Geography of representation	Geographical effects of elections

Fig. 12.6 A Systems Model Applied to Electoral Geography

Johnston has taken the argument one stage further and located electoral geography as a part of a systems-oriented political geography. Feedback loops between input and output round off the system and integrate electoral and political processes. This is clearly illustrated by American pork-barrel* politics whereby politicians ensure the area they represent is well treated by government and they expect, in return, the gratitude of citizens to be expressed in their votes. Although this process is difficult to substantiate statistically, there is no doubt that it is an important element of American and Indian politics. Though less recognized, the same process tends to occur in other countries like Britain where there are other explicitly geographical government effects such as in regional and inner city politics. In India, it is a common phenomenon and particularly true of the ruling parties' legislatures in different states that there are numerous avenues for them to become members/chairman of various kinds of spending committees, and they try to frame policies beneficial to their constituencies.

The systems approach has proved to be more important for what it reveals rather than what it solves. It has opened up a real pandora's box.

A Revised Model of Electoral Geography

Every election incorporates two distinct processes. First, there is intra-class competition within the dominant class over state tactics for promoting accumulation. Second, there is inter-class conflict over distribution issues. The former includes state relations with the rest of the world economy, the latter concentrates on domestic issue. Thus, there are two processes—the 'politics of power' and the 'politics of support' respectively. Political parties operate in both these politics by promoting special interests in their policies and mobilizing voters in their campaigns. The activities of the parties in this regard produce 'two' electoral geographies, a geography of power and a geography of support (Fig.

* An American term for activity by elected politicians designed to obtain benefits (usually in the form of public spending) for their constituencies. More generally, the term is used to describe any apparent spatial favouritism by government in the allocation of resources.

12.7).This should be compared to the simple systems model of electoral geography. The single linear sequence is replaced by two loops representing the two politics involved in every election.

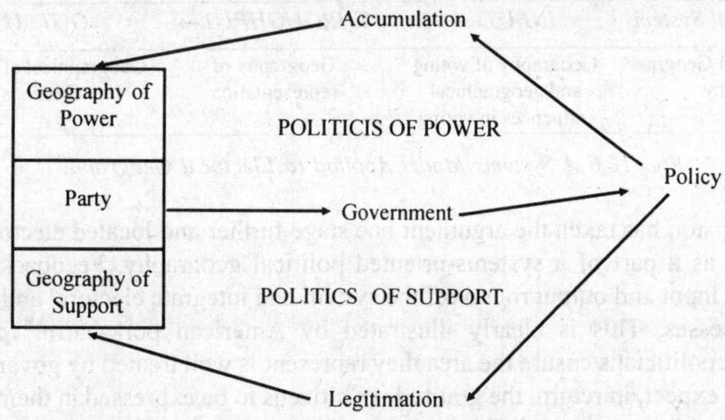

Figure 12.7: A Revised Model of Electoral Geography

The most important feature of this model is that the two processes occur as separate geographies. There is no general relationship between them; there are only particular relations for every state depending upon the class relation within the state, the relation of the state to the world economy, and the history of these two relations. Nevertheless, structural tendencies can be identified. The following five statements provide the basic proposition of the model:

1. There is no structural need for the two processes to provide a single consistent basis for a party's actions. In fact, the contradictions in the state's function will normally translate into tensions within parties.
2. There is a structural need to mystify the dual role of parties. Without this mystification the power function of the party becomes impossible. This is one of the processes of liberal theories of the state.
3. The balance between action based on one or other of the two processes will vary in terms of whether a party is in office or opposition. Opposition parties operate more in the politics of support, for instance, 'social democratic' parties become notoriously 'socialist' in periods of opposition.
4. The prime basis of action in the politics of power is class whereas there will be a variety of bases for the politics of support. In fact, the mystification function is facilitated if the politics of support is not based upon class (i.e., the hegemonic solutions, above).
5. Parties may operate involuntarily to deflect attention on contradictions away from the state by taking the blame for the situation: a potential crisis

of the state becomes a crisis of the party, e.g., Republican in the USA in the 1930s and Labour in Britain in the 1980s.

This revised model of the electoral process enables to make better interpretation of some of the basic problems involved in the system. Hobson's paradox of voting in the 1910 British elections now reduces to a simple contrast between a geography of support and a geography of power. The tariff issue was one fought out between parties and represents a conflict within the dominant class. At the same time voters were being mobilized more and more along class lines so that support reflects inter-class conflict. These two processes have different geographies and hence Hobson's identification of a paradox.

Two normal votes in American elections can be accommodated to this model in a similar way. In the non-sectional normal vote a politics of power with its geography is being mystified by a politics of support with its contrasting geography. In the sectional normal vote the politics of national integration based on northern leadership is accommodating the peripheral south in a safe politics of support. In both cases it is the politics of power which lies behind policy and which insulates the state from the people as represented by the politics of support.

The present chapter has shown that there is large number of factors to consider in the analysis of voting behaviour. Obviously, there is a wide range of techniques that could be used, and there are many examples in the periodic literatures where they have been used to analyze voting pattern and behaviour. However, there is plenty of research potential in electoral geography. Modern political geogpraher is trying towards precise measurement in problem solving through research based on hypothesis testing. However, on the basis of the ideas and concepts, these areas of interest have been identified—the goegraphy of voting, geographical influences in voting (neighbourhood effect), and the geography of representation (cube law, malapportionment and gerrymandering). However, recent researches (systems model and a revised model of electoral geography) have sought to overcome the uncoordinated nature of political geography/electoral geography.

Chapter 13

Global Strategic Models

The word 'strategy' refers to the art of using power, while the twin words 'global strategy' together imply the art of using power in relation to the whole world. The 'global strategic models' in this chapter simply imply the geographical patterns related to global strategic ideas. Political geography has a long heritage to its credit but the 'heritage' that gradually developed with imperialism, witnessed a consistent preoccupation with the world as a political system. An outcome of these preoccupations has been a series of 'global models', each an attempt to describe the world political structure with an equilibrium model on some principal causal basis. With Aristotle and several others the patterns of global political structure was explained by the areal differentiation in environmental condition. Over the last century there have been several spatial models of world power suggested, based on a variety of such factors as historical continuity, shifting balances of power, changing ideological structures and technological innovations in communications and weaponry. Such models are 'ethnocentric' in focus and open to rapid obsolescence, especially in terms of the prescriptions they implicitly contain.

Each of the global model reflects the issue of 'national exceptionalism' that each of the great scholars, strategicians, diplomats, who is credited with the models, seemed to have attempted to fit into his 'model' the particular need of his community and country in global perspective. These models are, therefore, partial views of reality and so are ideological in terms of the contemporary political geography framework.

Mahan's Sea Power Concept

The first really global strategic model is attributed to Alfred Thayer Mahan (1840-1914)—a US naval officer—who held important positions in the US Navy. He was the president of the prestigious Naval War College at Newport, after having retired from the rank of Rear Admiral in the US Navy. He wrote a number of books to his credit, viz., *The Influence of Sea Power upon History, 1660-1783* (1890); *The Influence of Sea Power upon the French Revolution and Europe, 1793-1832* (1892); *The Life of Nelson* (1897); *The Interest of America in Sea Power*; and *The Problem of Asia* (1900).

However, none of the above books truly contain his global model but that has been developed from the main excerpts from these books. To him, the sea is "a great highway; or better perhaps...a wide common space over which men may pass in all directions, but on which some well-worn paths show that controlling reasons have led them to choose certain lines of travel rather than others. Trade is normal for all states and seaborne trade especially so for those states which border the sea". To him, "it is the wish of every nation that this shipping business should be done by its own vessels. The ships thus sail to and fro must have secure ports to which to return, and must, as far as possible, be followed by the protection of their country throughout the voyage. In these three things—production with the necessity of exchanging products; shipping, whereby the exchange is carried on; and colonies, which facilitate and enlarge the operations of shipping and tend to protect it by multiplying points of safety—is to be found the key to much of the history, as well as of the policy, of nation bordering the sea".

Mahan, in his strategic global model, emphasized the land-based importance of sea power by identifying following six fundamental factors affecting the development of the sea power of a state:

1. *The geographical location of the state*, whether it fronts on more than one sea, whether these waters are interconnected or is there any easy communication by water between these seas, whether it also is vulnerable, exposed to land boundaries, whether it can command important trade routes, control strategic base and threaten the territory of a potential enemy with its ships.
2. *The physical conformation of the state* (configuration of its coastline), whether its coastline possesses natural harbors, estuaries, inlets and outlets, an absence of harbor normally prevents the nation from having the own sea trade, shipping, or navy, the importance of navigable rivers to internal trade but their danger as avenues of penetrations by enemies.
   To Mahan, "... numerous and deep harbors are a source of strength and wealth and doubly so if they are the outlets of navigable streams, which facilitate the concentration in them of a country's internal trade, but by their very accessibility they become a source of weakness in war, if not properly defended."
3. *Extent of territory of the state*, implied in it the length of the coastline and the relative ease or difficulty of protecting it.
4. *The size of the population of the state*, a large population is desirable because it will be more capable of building the nation, and maintaining the merchant marine and navy than a state with a small population.
5. *The national character,* in particular an aptitude for commercial pursuits, for sea power is "really based upon a peaceful and extensive commerce".
6. *The character of government* and its policy will determine whether the best of natural advantages and the richest human resources will actually materi-

alize in sea power that it should "take advantage of the physical and human opportunities available within the state".

Two of the above fundamental factors' (5 and 6) tend to refer to the question of the national 'will', which are explicitly reminiscent of Kjellan's 'geopolitical instinct'. Indeed, Mahan's writing in places is quite similar to that of the German geopoliticians, he "was characteristically disposed to view politics in terms of force, whose efficacy was qualified only by inexorable natural and moral laws... only the fittest nation could successfully sustain themselves in the constant grappling. Fitness was measured in terms of national strength. This national strength was characteristically viewed by Mahan, in strategic terms. It depended, in turn, on the moral and martial fibre of the population."

The model of Mahan, that a state with a significant coastline should aim also to possess sea power and that seapower needs to be supported by the possession of overseas military and strategic bases, simply encouraged a competition between sea powers for the possession of such bases, in the early part of the present century, and scramble even continued beyond the Second World War.

Mahan's model had a profound impact on the United State's global approach which could be reflected in the occupation of the Hawaiian islands in 1898, and in 1900 it gained sovereignty over eastern Samoa. In the meantime, extensive territories, including Guam, Puerto Rico and the Philippines had been acquired from Spain by the Treaty of Paris in 1898. The Virginia islands were purchased from Denmark in 1917, and the Panama Canal Zone was leased from the Republic of Panama in 1903. The acquisition of these overseas territories undoubtedly added strength to the contemporary US Navy.

"Mahan's examination of the past and recommendations for the future were well grounded in the geography and technology of his age because he thought in terms of ships propelled by steam power, ...the technology of transportation has changed a great deal... Air power has in large measure replaced sea power, and the air envelops the whole earth, the sea only part of it."

One of Mahan's less known book, *The Problem of Aisa*, published in 1910, also provided a strategic global model which seemed to have an explicit relevance to his seapower view. Here, in the book, he attempted to describe the contemporary Russia "as a vast, uninterrupted mass whose centre cannot be broken". He emphasized Russia's position and its dominance of Central Asia. This view of Mahan simply adumbrates Mackinder's *Heartland*, in the later period. Mahan identified the latitudinal belt of 30° to 40° N as the "unstable zone between British sea power and Russian land power". This resembled roughly the Asiatic part of Fairgrieve's 'crush zone'. Mahan also adumbrated Fairgrieve's 'northern belt of settlement and movement' pointing out that Suez and Panama would mark the southern limit of most active commerce and politics.

Mahan thought that Russian expansion in Asia could be opposed by sea transported power, and he predicted that Britain, Germany, Japan and the United States would find a common interest in containing Russia and controlling China. Surprisingly enough, he advocated providing Russia access to the sea through China, with the view that this would satisfy Russian aspirations for warm water ports, and Russia would be obliged to divert its attention from Europe and the Middle East. But it was a matter of speculation that how could be make such assertion when the bulk of the Russian population was concentrated on the European part?

Notwithstanding Mahan's inherent weakness in his model on Russia vis-a-vis Asia, it formed the basis for the latter global strategic models of Mackinder, Spyokman and others. Mahan's "strategy vis-a-vis the Russian Empire closely resembled in geopolitical conception, the strategy for containing the former Soviet Union actually pursued by the United States during the latter 1940s and 1950s, nearly half a century after his death in 1914". In fact, the policy of containment against the Soviet Union and its continental allies continued till the fall of socialism and the collapse of the Soviet system, and followed by the cessation of Cold War in the early 1990s.

Sir Halford Mackinder was one of those few geographers of the world who had laid down a new tradition in the contemporary political geography through his innovative ideological heritage, which till recently had some relevance in the global political pattern. A Scottish geographer, Mackinder too pondered the 'problem of Asia' and the balance of land and sea power. In fact, he began from the point where Mahan had stopped, and in many respects, he disagreed with Mahan's conclusions, and for some very fundamental reasons. As Stephen B. Jones has put it: "It is not surprising that the United States painfully land minded since the opening of the west and the decline of sailing ships, should have produced Mahan, while Britain, most maritime of great powers, should have produced Mackinder... However... the basic views of Mahan and Mackinder are not as far apart is commonly believed. Mahan outlined in a rough way the Heartland concept. Both men understood that sea power is land-based and that the size, population, and productivity of the land base have much to do with the magnitude of the resulting sea power. Mahan recognized the peculiar virtues of Britain's position, as a large island off the European shore, and one of Mackinder's most scholarly works is called *Britain and the British Seas*. It was in their forecasts that they drew apart. Mahan continued to believe in the greater capacity and flexibility of movement by sea; Mackinder thought the great improvements in land transportation put the shoe on the other foot.

"Mackinder developed his world strategic model at a crucial period in the world economy when Britain was losing her political and economic leadership. In the nineteenth century Britain had been the champion of a liberal world economy when she could dominate. The rise of USA and Germany in the final quarter of the century dramatically changed the situation. He had been a leading member of the Liberal Party—the party of free trade—but about 1903 he began to revise his views. Britain's role was changing and he no longer believed that simple accumulation of capital in London would be sufficient to meet the challenge of Germany's massive growth in heavy industry. He went to a protectionist position which involved changing political parties—the conservatives were the party of tariff reform. This new position emphasized the need to maintain British industry to force the German challenge. These concerns with current power rivalries are directly expressed in his famous world model." He presented this model entitled, *The Geographical Pivot of History* to the Royal Geographical Society in London in 1904, and later it was published in *Geographical Journal*.

The Geographical Pivot (1904)

Mackinder writes: "In the present decade we are for the first time in a position to attempt, with some degree of completeness, a correlation between the larger geographical and the larger historical generalization... We can perceive something of the real proportion of features and events on the stage of the whole world and may seek a formula which shall express certain aspects, at any rate, of geographical causation in universal history."

On the rise of the European civilization, Mackinder remarks: "...it was under the pressure of external barbarism that Europe achieved her civilization...for a moment to look upon Europe and European history, as subordinate to Asia and Asiatic history. For European civilization is, in a very real sense, the outcome of the secular struggle against Asiatic invasion."

"The most remarkable contrast in the political map of modern Europe is that presented by the vast area of Russia occupying half the continent and a group of smaller territories tenanted by western powers."

On the basis of historical evidences, Mackinder points out: "Two groups of states usually divided the country into northern and southern political systems", which roughly corresponded to the north and north-west forest, often broken by marshes and to the south and south-west grassy steppe (Fig. 13.1). "The line separating the two regions, ran diagonally northeastward from the northern end of the Carpathian to a point in the Ural Range nearer to its southern than to its northern extremity. Moscow lies a little north of this line... on the forest side of it."

On the recurrent Asiatic invasions, Mackinder adds: "Through the steppe,on the other hand, there came from the unknown recesses of Asia, by the gateway between the Ural mountains and the Caspian Sea, in all the centuries from the fifth to the sixteenth, a remarkable succession of Turanian nomadic peoples—Huns, Avans, Bulgarians, Magyars, Khazars, Patzinake, Cumans, Mongols, Kalmuks. Under Attila the Huns established themselves in the midst of the Pusstas, in the uttermost Danubian outlier of the steppes, and thence dealt blows northward, westward and southward against the settled peoples of

Europe. A large part of modern history might be written as a commentary upon the changes directly or indirectly ensuing from these raids. The Angles and Saxons, it is quite possible, were driven to cross the seas to found England in Britain. The Franks, the Goths and the Roman provincials were compelled, for the first time, to stand shoulder to shoulder on the battlefield of Chalom, making common cause against the Asiatics, who were unconsciously welding together modern France. Venice was founded from the destruction of Aquileia and Padua, and even the Papacy owed a decisive prestige to the successful mediation of Pope Leo with Attila at Milan. Such was the harvest of results produced by a cloud of ruthless and idealess horsemen sweeping over the unimpeded plain—a blow, as it were from the great Asiatic hammer striking freely through the vacant space... All the settled margins of the old world sooner or later felt the expansive force of mobile power originating in the steppe. Russia, Persia, India and China were either made tributary or received Mongol dynasties. Even the incipient power of the Turks in Asia Minor was struck down for half a century."

The region from which the Asiatic invasions had been carried out from the fifth to the sixteenth centuries, against the Europeans lay, "on the whole a steppe land supplying a widespread, if often scanty pasture, and there are not a few river-fed oases in it, ...the pivot area (Fig. 13.2) is characterized by a very

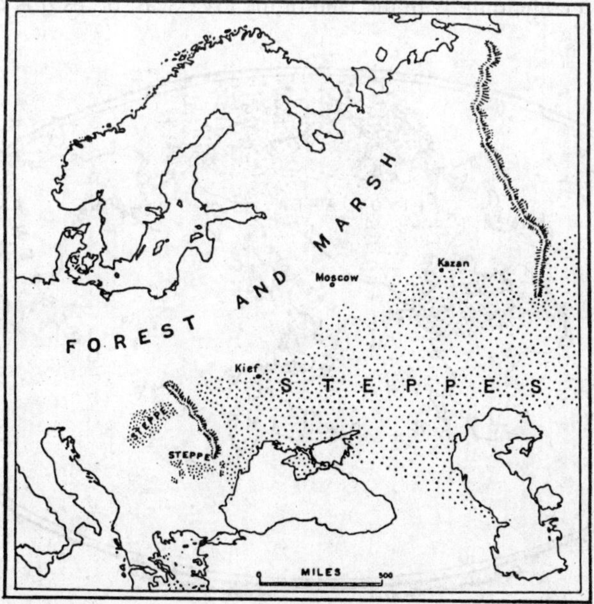

Figure 13.1: Eastern Europe before the 19th Century (after Drude in Berghaus' Physical Atlas)

remarkable distribution of river drainage. Throughout an immense portion of the centre and north, the rivers have been practically useless for the purposes of human communication with the outer world. The Volga, the Oxus and the Jaxartes drain into salt lakes, the Obi and the Yenesei and the Lena into the frozen ocean of the north. These are six of the greatest rivers in the world. Thus core (pivot) of Euro-Asia... is wholly unpenetrated by water ways from the ocean... in this immense area all conditions for the maintenance of a sparce,but in the aggregate considerable, population of horse-riding and camel-riding nomods... For a thousand years a series of horse-riding peoples emerged from Asia through the broad interval between the Ural mountains and the Caspian Sea, rode through the open spaces of southern Russia... into Hungry...the mobility of their power was conditioned by the steppes".

"To east, south, and west of this Heartland (pivot area) are marginal regions, ranged in a vast crescent, accissible to shipmen. According to physical conformation, these regions are four in number, and it is not a little remarkable that in a general way they respectively coincide with the spheres of the four great religions—Buddhism, Brahmanism, Mahometanism, and Christianity. The first two are the monsoon lands, turned the one towards the Pacific, and the other towards the Indian Ocean. The fourth is Europe, watered by the Atlantic rains from the west. These three together, measuring less than 7 million square miles, have more than 1000 million people or two-thirds of the world population. The third coinciding with the land of the Five Seas, or, as it is more often

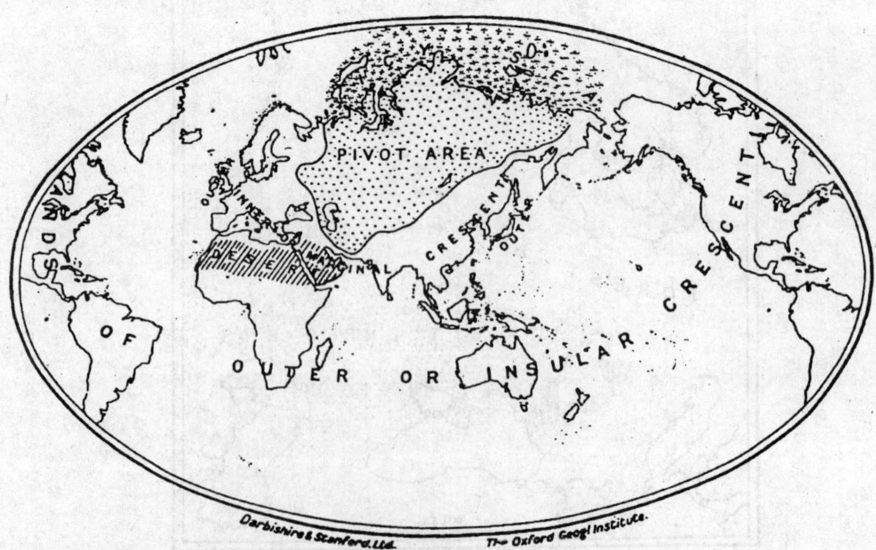

Figure 13.2: The Natural Seats of Power

described, the Nearer East... In some degree it partakes of the characteristics both of the marginal belt and of the central area of Euro-Asia... Dominantly, however, it is marginal, for sea-gulfs and oceanic rivers lay it open to sea-power and permit of the exercise of such power from it."

Outside this marginal crescent, Mackinder continues: "The one and continuous ocean enveloping the divided and insular lands is, of course, the geographical conditions of ultimate unity in the command of the sea... The broad political effect was to reverse the relations of Europe and Asia, for whereas in the Middle Ages Europe was caged between an impassable desert to the south, an unknown ocean to the west and an icy or forested wastes to the north and northeast, and the east and southeast were constantly threatened by the superior mobility of the horsemen and camelmen, she now emerged upon the world, multiplying more than thirty-fold the sea surface and coastal lands to which she had access, and wrapping her influence round the Euro-Asiatic land power which had hitherto threatened her very existence. New Europes were created in the vacant lands discovered in the midst of the waters, and what Britain and Scandinavia were to Europe in the earlier time, that have America and Australia and in some measures even Trans-Saharan Africa, now become to Euro-Asia. Britain, Canada, the United States, South Africa, Australia and Japan and now a ring of outer and insular bases for sea power and commerce, inaccessible to the land power of Euro-Aisa."

Mackinder continues: "... the land power still remains and recent events have again increased its significance... the modern land power differs from the sea power no less in the source of its ideals than in the material conditions of its mobility... trans-continental railways are now transmitting the conditions of land power, and nowhere can they have such effect as in the closed heartland of Euro-Asia... Railways work the greater wonders in the steppe, because they directly replace horse and camel mobility."

On the relationship between the pivot-area and the inner crescent, Mackinder observed: "a certain persistence of geographical relationship." This relationship is one of continuing outward pressures from the pivot-area which is evident from his remark: "Is not the pivot-area of the world politics that vast area of Euro-Asia which is inaccessible to ships, but in antiquity lazy open to the horse-riding nomads, and is today about to be covered with a dense network of railways?"

Mackinder concludes: "If Turkie and Tartar nomads, equipped only with the horse and camel, could so shape the course of history in the peripheral lands of the inner crescent, what might not a modern power, its mobility, enhanced by the railroad, achieve in this respect? This might happen if Germany were to ally herself with Russia." It could also happen "were the Chinese...organized by the Japanese, to overthrow the Russian Empire and conquer its territory." In such an event "France, Italy, Egypt, India and Korea would become so many bridgeheads where the outside navies would support armies" in order to prevent the pivot-area from expanding down to the sea.

Mackinder's thesis that the pivot-area was inaccessible to the sea power, seems to have some relevance in the context of the Crimean War in 1854, in which, though Russia was defeated by the combined sea power of Great Britain, France and Turkey, the effect of the defeat was confined only to the Crimean peninsula, and the sea power could not overrun the pivot-area. However, I.C. Malin puts it: "Formal statements of philosophies of history may come after the event and when such limited validity as they possess has already become largely, if not altogether, obsolete." This is abundantly true of Mackinder's thesis. As Pounds remarks: "Mackinder wrote at the end of the railway age, not at its beginning. The pivot-area had dominated the course of human history at the age of horse and camel mobility; how much more would it dominate if the pivot-area were to become... criss-crossed by railroad lines? This railroad network has still, after the lapse of half a century, not been built. Instead, the aircraft, whose existence in 1904 Mackinder had barely acknowledged, has come in many respects to replace the railroad. Mackinder presented his analysis at a time when the railroad had for some sixty years dominated transportation. Well might he have anticipated further increase in its importance. He also belonged to a nation that cherished the notion that it was made up of sailors and that its prosperity was founded upon sea power. He visualized the naval power of the inner and outer crescents, notably France, Italy, Japan and Great Britain itself, as patrolling the seaways and influencing, if not controlling the powers that encircled the pivot-area. He conceived the range of power of the maritime powers as extending over the basins of all rivers discharging to the ocean except, of course, those which flowed to the frozen Arctic and were thus inaccessible. But to assume that because a river flows to the ocean its basin can, therefore, be dominated by a maritime power is naive in the extreme. Even if the rivers were navigable to their sources—which of course, none of them are—the experience of maritime powers in sending warships up the Chinese rivers would demonstrate the contrary. ...Mackinder's paper was presented at the beginning of the air age and yet failed to take account of this new form of mobility. His map which is in fact a Mercator's projection of the world enclosed within an ellipse, is misleading. It exaggerates the extent of the Arctic Ocean and creates the illusion that beyond the northern coast of Siberia is only ice and yet more ice, when, in reality, only, 1200 miles from Cape Chelyuskin lies the most northerly point of Greenland."

Following fifteen years from the date of the presentation/publication of Mackinder's *The Geographical Pivot of History* witnessed some major political changes in Europe, particularly:

(i) Rise of Germany as a major continental power in Europe, upsetting the contemporary regional balance of power in the continent, and the trouble in the Balkan region, forcing the European powers to accept the dictates of Germany, and some Balkan states, on the other hand, forging strategic alliance with Germany. Russia was ignored in the European states' conference on the Balkan problem.

(ii) Beginning of the war, involving the continental Germany and its Balkan allies on the one hand and the maritime powers of Great Britain, France and others, on the other hand. The navies of Great Britain and her allies greatly failed to force an entry through the Turkish Straits into the Black Sea and German mines had excluded them from the Baltic Sea.

(iii) The German armies advanced into the region of the south Russian steppe in 1917, forcing Russia to come on a term, and the major part of Euro-Asia came under the German domination, while the maritime power had a much less extensive area under its control.

(iv) The collapse of the Russian state followed by the emergence of the Communist system in 1917, which in fact, made peace with Germany almost on the latter's dictates, called the Treaty of Brest-Litovsk in March 1918.

These changes/events/incidents inevitably led to some newer ideas, and Mackinder thought of incorporating them into his earlier thesis, getting it modified and relevant in the contemporary situations. In 1919, he published a somewhat laboured and extended version of his 1904 model, as a small book, entitled, *Democratic Ideals and Reality*. He was led to think that: (i) the possibility of the Japanese controlling the pivot-area (Heartland) and using it as a springboard for control of the old world was almost zero; (ii) if any power outside the Heartland itself could do this, it would be from the West, by way of the steppe corridor (Fig. 13.3) that joins the Heartland with Eastern Europe; (iii) the possibility of the Russian themselves organizing and developing their own vast spaces and great resources, was not convincing but this could be realized most probably by any power that succeeded in approaching it by way of Eastern Europe and the steppe; and (iv) the intention of Germany dominating Eastern, or Slav, Europe, and from this vintage point of aiming at control of the Heartland.

The Heartland (1919)

The word 'pivot-area' was replaced by the 'Heartland'. The Heartland of 1919 was not quite the same as the pivot-area of 1904. "For the purposes of strategic thinking, the Heartland, includes the Baltic Sea, the navigable Middle and Lower Danube, the Black Sea, Asia Minor, Armenia, Persia, Tibet, Mongolia... The Heartland is the region to which, under modern conditions, sea-power can be refused access, though the western part of it has within the region of Arctic and Continental drainage" (Fig. 13.3).

Mackinder emphasized the relative ease of movement through the south Russian steppe from pivot-area (Heartland, a new term used) into East Europe. This he contrasted with the greater difficulty of movement from the Heartland into the peripheral regions of South and East Asia. "There was no impediment to prevent the horsemen from riding westward into regions drained by such wholly European rivers as the Dnieper and Danube. In sharp contrast to this open passage from the Heartland into Europe is the system of mighty barriers (i.e., the Himalaya and related ranges) which separate the Heartland along its eastern and southeastern borders from the Indies... The conclusion to which this discussion leads is that the connection between the Heartland, and especially its more open western regions of Iran, Turkistan, and Siberia, is much more intimate with Europe and Arabia than it is with China and India."

Mackinder was particularly concerned with the explicit German intention of subjugating the Slav Europe, and particularly the location of Germany in response to the steppe corridor vis-a-vis the Heartland. This geographical fact was the reality of which democracy was warned to beware. The events of the First World War, according to him, "were the result of a fundamental antagonism between the German, who wished to be Masters in East Europe and the Slavs, who refused to submit to them". Mackinder, reassured by the contemporary geographical pattern of political developments, particularly in East Europe, urged upon Great Britain and its allies that "unless you would lay up trouble for the future, you cannot now accept a way outcome of the war, which does not finally dispose of the issue between German and Slav in East Europe. You must have a balance as between German and Slav, and true independence of each. You cannot afford to leave such a condition of affairs in East Europe and the Heartland, as would offer scope for ambition in the future, for you have escaped too narrowly from the recent danger... When our statesmen are in conversation with the defeated enemy, some airy cherub should whisper to them from time to time saying:

Who rules East Europe commands the Heartland,
Who rules the Heartland commands the World-Island,
Who rules the World-Island commands the world."

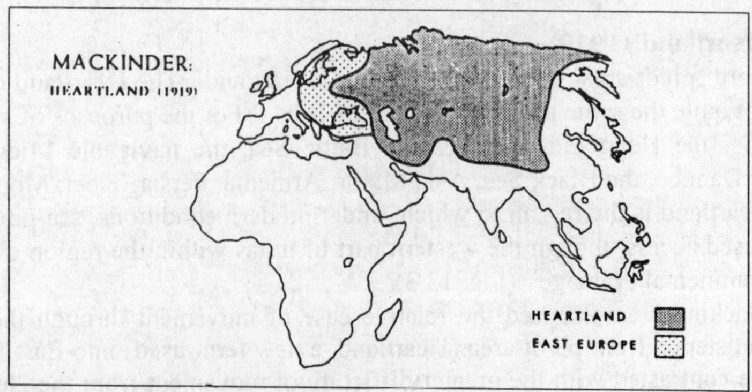

Figure 13.3: The Heartland

(The 'World-Island' is Euro-Asia plus Africa consisting of two-thirds of the world's lands). The message was specifically composed for world statesmen at Versailles who were redrawing the map of Europe. The emphasis on Europe as the strategic route to the Heartland was interpreted as requiring a strip of buffer states to separate Germany and Russia. These were created by the peace negotiation.

Mackinder glorified the strategic situation of the Heartland in relation to the contemporary power potentials. It held the key to world supremacy. The power that could control and manage the Heartland was bound to emerge as the strongest state in the inner or marginal crescent. Hence, it followed logically that "any political power that could effectively occupy and control this Heartland could by definition achieve a dominant world position. Mackinder's Heartland model, undoubtedly, formed one of the basic symbioses which seemed to have special relevance to Germany's post-World War I position, indicating her geopolitical realities and dictating her 'correct' policy in the world, particularly in relation to the form, direction, and chronology of her territorial expansion. "Mackinder's Heartland thesis seemed to indicate to the geopoliticians the necessity for a detente or even an alliance between Nazi Germany and the chief occupant of the Heartland, Soviet Union."

Pounds writes: "The event of two world wars have given some slight measure of support to this conclusion of Mackinder, though one can easily quarrel with his historical judgment. Twice the German armies from their bases in Eastern Europe invaded Russia, and on the first occasion they dictated peace terms to the defeated Russian government. Mackinder would have us believe that these invasions were made possible only by the open nature of the terrain in European Russia. It is more than possible that the determining factor was not the physical geography of the area but the contrasting technical levels of the opposing forces. Yet on both occasions the German armies failed to penetrate deeply—if at all—in to the pivot area as he originally conceived it. The same could be said of Napoleon's invasion of Russia in 1811-12. Are we justified in assuming...that the Heartland is immune to attack from the maritime states? Sea power has nothing to do with the question. Of course, no ships could be navigated from the ocean into the Heartland, but the sea powers of the marginal crescents are all in some degree land powers. Some, in fact, have placed far more stress upon their armies than upon their navies, all are amphibious, and the dichotomy between land and sea power is, in the final analysis, a false one. On several occasions, in the past two or three centuries, armies from states of the marginal crescent have invaded Russia and have failed either to reach or to establish themselves in the Heartland. It would be wrong to assume that the Heartland must, of geographical necessity, always remain inviolate. These invasions took place in the course of wars between states of the marginal crescent. Each invaders from the West had to contend with a second front further West and it was this threat in each instance which prevented a deeper and perhaps more lasting penetration of the Heartland. Conclusion drawn from a comparison of historical events, each of which is unique, are rarely profitable and to allow such conclusions to influence policy is the height of political folly."

Certain events during the Second World War such as those of (i) German havoc in Europe, and its subsequent invasion to the Heartland through the steppe land; (ii) the US involvement in the war, followed by the massive air and naval attack; (iii) Russia responded to the German attack and joined the allied forces against Germany; (iv) the allied powers' insistence on the opening of a second front close to Russia's frontier which Russia disapproved; and (v) the fall of the Third Reich mostly as a result of the successful counter-operation by the Russian army, i.e., the Slav finally resisted the Germans who for long sought to perpetuate their mastery over Eastern Europe and the Slavs.

These events inevitably led Mackinder to offer yet another modification of his own model, which appeared in the form of an article, entitled, "The Round World and the Winning of the Peace", in the *Foreign Affairs* in 1943.

The Midland Basin (1943)

Notwithstanding the perceptible changes in the contemporary power politics, the Heartland continued to be the greatest natural fortress on earth. For the first time in the history it was manned by a garrison sufficient both in number and in quality—the vacuum developed into a power centre following the success of the Communism under the Soviet system.

Mackinder cut short the size of the Heartland, and separated from it that part of the Soviet Union which lay east of the Yenisei river, "a rugged country of mountains, plateaus and valleys, covered from end to end with coniferous forests". This part he called 'Lenaland' without any political significance.

In contrast to Heartland, Mackinder established the 'Midland', consisting of the North Atlantic Ocean, the Eastern United States, and Western Europe. Both the regions on either side of the North Atlantic have identical climate and rich resource base with the abundance of coal, and peopled by the same ethnic stocks.

East-Central Europe or the former German realm separated the Midland Basin from the Heartland Russia, and these two areas, Mackinder described as enveloped and insulated by a girdle of deserts: Saharan, Arabia, Tibetan and Mongolian. This belt of empty lands he extended, through his newly created Lenaland, to Alaska, the Canadian Arctic and the deserts of the American West. In this desert belt, he saw "a practically continuous land-space covering some 12 million square miles... For a long time to come it will break social continuity between major communities of mankind on the globe". Within this girdle of desert and tundra, he thought the Midland Basin and Heartland Russia acting together in amity to eliminate the danger that sprang from the militant Germany that lay between.

Mackinder's 1943 revision was more comprehensive. It reflected the contemporary short-term alliance of Russia, Britain and America what he foresaw, came true that the Midland Basin-Heartland Russia alliance ultimately succeeded in defeating the Nazi Germany. But the subsequent course of events after the defeat of Germany proved Mackinder's forecast in his 1943 revision wrong and superfluous. The Midland Basin and Heartland Russia, soon after the war, got involved, in what was called Cold War rivalries, in areas which enveloped and insulated them. Germany was divided into East Germany and West Germany. The former along with Balkan peninsular went to the Heartland Russia's fold while the West Germany aligned itself with the Midland Basin power. China went communist and got aligned with the Heartland Russia, thus bringing the Cold War on to the Pacific coast of Asia. In no respect have this revision and the forecasts based upon it held up. The fundamental error in this as in Mackinder's earlier revision was his inability to make allowances for technological advance. "At a time when bombers were reducing many of Europe's cities to ruin and nullifying the effectiveness of capital ships, Mackinder could nevertheless write that air power was capable of effecting few permanent changes in the strategical conditions."

Critical Assessment of Heartland Model

Despite its neglect in geography, the Heartland model of Mackinder has remained probably the most well-known geographical model throughout the world. Although first propounded in 1904 it continues to inform debate on foreign policy. It is often said that "the Heartland model stands as the first premise of western military thought". It is argued that the policy of 'nuclear deterrence' in the Cold War period would never have developed but for the Heartland model.

Notwithstanding its global application and the contemporary military-diplomatic relevance, the Heartland model is not free from its inherent weaknesses. These are:

(i) Mackinder had overlooked, in his model, the existence of another Heartland in Anglo-America which was all the time capable of occupying an important place in global affairs as the one in Eurasia. Though he mentioned this Heartland as a part of the Midland Basin, in his last revision of his model in 1943, he failed to follow up the apparently obvious consequences.

(ii) Another weakness in the model relates to its date of publication, 1904. Although time was to substantiate Mackinder's assumption regarding the Heartland to a degree even he himself could probably not have imagined, it must not be forgotten that the original statement of the thesis was based upon data available prior to 1904 . If indeed his model constituted a 'geographical formula' into which one could fit any political balance, as Mackinder himself asserted, and if the pivot-area gave so much power to the possessor, why was Russia in 1904 not more of a world power than it was?

(iii) One of the serious weaknesses is that Mackinder presented his model at the end of the railway age and not at its beginning, and particularly at a time when the railways had for some sixty years dominated the transportation, but surprisingly, railways had not been developed in the pivot-area. Can it be possible when Europe had long been criss-crossed by railroads? How is it that railroads had not been built across the pivot-area? Does it not appear like a dichotomy that railways provided mobility in the rest of Europe while the horse-camel mobility dominated the pivot-area? Mackinder's greatest fault, revealed especially in his 1943 statement, seems to have been his inability to recognize the role of changing technology in the present-day political world.

Mackinder offered his model at a time when the air navigation had just begun, but he failed to take not of this new form of mobility. In his later revision, he did not make any attempt to elaborate the impact of air mobility on the power-potentials. It is clear when he says: "Air fighting will not follow the long history of all kinds of warfare by presenting alternations of offensive and defensive tactical superiority, meanwhile effecting few permanent changes in strategical conditions."

Even in Mackinder's later days the strategy based on the railways swiftly moved into the satellite age. In the present-day geopolitics, the two-dimensional strategic thinking of the past gives way to three-dimensional thinking—for the super powers the enemy is in the 'sky'.

(iv) Perhaps the most frequently levelled charge against the Heartland model is that it constitutes an oversimplification of history and a dangerous determinist prediction—the sea power-land power rivalry, conditioned by the spatial distribution of land and sea, is an endless phenomenon.

(v) The pivot-area/Heartland, in the model, has been shown as an area of permanent difficulties in terms of its inaccessible character, the question is how then could the pivot-area develop into a power centre?

It is apparent in the model that the pivot-area was the home of the inferior quality peoples who were 'cruel and idealess' and who lacked perception, then how could they organize and develop the pivot-area vis-a-vis the vast space around into a power of major dimension, superior or even comparable to those around it? It is the quality of the people which is important in the organization of the political space. With the horse/camel mobility no groups of peoples could develop themselves into a force to be reckoned with. Mackinder seemed to have overestimated the capacity of the Turanian nomadic peoples, in response to the sedentary, superior peoples of the inner crescent.

In spite of all these weaknesses, Mackinder's model (1904) has persisted into the post-1945 era with some revisions. The Heartland model is a part of the heritage of the 'realist' school of international power relations between states.

"Mackinder was much more than the geo-strategist portrayed in political geography. He can be portrayed as more of a political economist with a holistic viewpoint lacking in so many of his followers."

Mackinder's Heartland model laid the foundation of a unique heritage in the field of international relations, particularly the power relations between states. A number of spatial power models, based on the Heartland model, have been proposed/offered which sought to reshape Mackinder's model and to bring it in closer accord either with historical and geographical facts or with existing political realities. One of such earliest attempts was made by Nicholas Spykman, in his *Geography of the Peace*, published posthumously, in 1944. Spykman explicitly perceived post-war American needs as neutralizing the power of the Heartland. As a counter to Mackinder's model he developed his famous 'Rimland Theory'.

Rimland (1944)

As opposed to the land-based power with a traditional geopolitical structure across Euro-Asia, Spykman comes out with the following statement: "The fundamental fact which is responsible for the conditions...of world politics is the development of ocean navigation and the discovery of sea routes to India and America. Maritime mobility is the basis for a new type of geopolitical structure, the overseas empire. Formerly, history had given us the pattern of great land powers based on the control of contiguous land masses such as the Roman, Chinese and Russian empires. Now the sea has become a great artery of communication and...a new structure of great power and enormous extent. The British, French and Japanese empires and the sea power of the United States have all contributed to the development of a modern world which is a single field for the interplay of political forces. It is sea power which has made possible to conceive of the Eurasian Continent as a unit and it is sea power which governs the relationships between the Old and the New Worlds."

Defining the Rimland, Spykman says: "Beyond the mountain barrier, the coast land region, which is called by Mackinder the inner crescent may more effectively be referred to as the Rimland (Fig. 13.4), a name which defines its character accurately. The surrounding string of marginal and mediterranean seas which separate the continent from the oceans constitutes a circumferential maritime highway which links the whole area together in terms of sea power. Beyond lie the offshore islands and continents of Great Britain, Japan, Africa and Australia which compose the outer crescent, to which the terminology 'offshore' will be used...than that of Mackinder."

On the characteristics of the Rimland, Spykman points out: "... the inner crescent of amphibian states surrounding the Heartland consists of those sections: the European coast land, the Arabian Middle-Eastern desert, and the Asiatic monsoon land. The first two regions are clearly defined as geographical areas, but the third is a unit only from the special historical point of view represented by Great Britain. To the Seaman, the Asiatic monsoon land looks like a single region. The similarities of climate and the easy accessibility of the area to sea power contribute to this impression. This territory is also well protected from the Heartland by a string of barriers from the Himalayas and Tibet to the vast desert and mountain regions of Sinkiang and Mongolia. These mountains do not, however, make the monsoon lands behind them a single unit. The ranges of Burma and Indo-China extend down to the sea and interpose a great obstacle

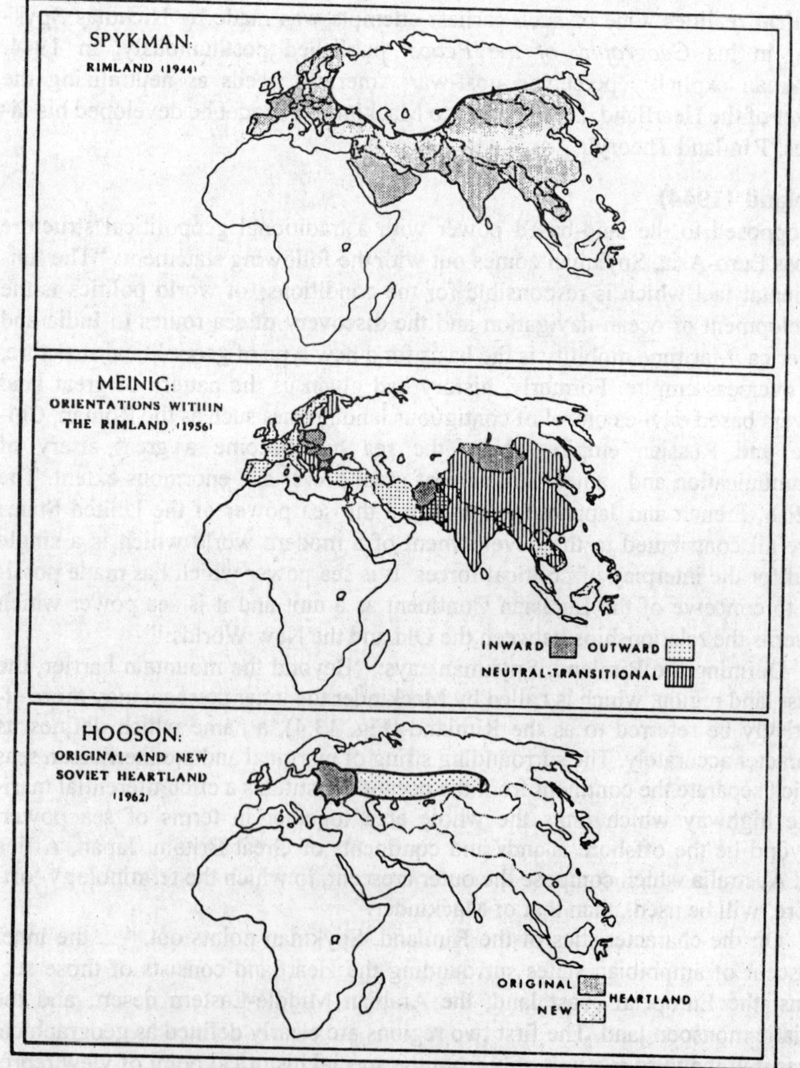

Figure 13.4: Spykman's Rimland and other Variants of Heartland-Rimland

to contacts between the two great states. The fact that Buddhism reached China from India by way of Sinkiang and Thailand points to the difficulty of maintaining direct relations. Throughout their history, these two centres of oriental culture have remained fairly isolated from each other and their only contacts have been of a cultural and intellectual nature."

"India and the Indian Ocean littoral, then, fall into a different geopolitical category from China, and it is scarcely accurate to classify them together as the Asiatic monsoon lands. The future will probably see the power of the two regions expressed on two distinct units connected only across the lower part of the Indo-China peninsula by land or air power and around Singapore in terms of sea power. If this is true, then the Asiatic-Mediterranean will continue to have great significance for the political strategy of the independent Asiatic world even as it has been of vital importance in the era of western sea power encirclement."

"The Rimland of the Eurasian land mass must be viewed as an intermediate region, situated as it is between the Heartland and the marginal seas. It functions as a vast buffer zone of conflict between sea power and land power. Looking in both directions, it must amphibiously and defend itself on land and sea. In the past, it has had to fight against the land power of the Heartland and against the sea power of the offshore islands of Great Britain and Japan. Its amphibious nature lies at the basis of its security problems."

Outlining the inherent weaknesses in Mackinder's Heartland, Spykman points out: "The importance of Heartland... a central position with interior lines of communication made powerful and unified by the development of land transportation to a point where it could begin to compete with sea communication. He (Mackinder) envisaged the transformation of the steppe land from an area of low economic potential to one of high economic potential... The actual facts of the Russian economy and geography make it not at all clear that the Heartland is or will be in the very near future a world centre of communication, mobility and power potential...in the absence of revolutionary developments in agricultural technique, the centre of agrarian productivity will remain in western Russia rather than in the central Siberian region...the actual extent of arable land is only a very small part of the total area of (the Russian State). We must avoid the mistake of identifying all of Russia, or the Heartland, as a region of great potential agrarian productivity. Looking again at the geographic distribution of coal and iron deposits...oil fields and water power...these essential elements of industrial power are located largely west of the Ural mountains."

Commenting on the inherent weakness, in response to the low potential character, in terms of transportation in and around Euro-Asian Heartland, Spykman observes: "The railroad, the motor road and the airplane have certainly created a new mobility in the centre of the Eurasian landmass. It cannot, however, be ignored that this area is ringed to the north, east, south and southwest, by some of the greatest obstacles to transportation in the world. Ice and freezing temperatures for a large part of the year, and towering mountains pierced by only a few difficult passes, form its borders. A large part of the Rimland areas which touch the Heartland have even poorer transportation facilities... The law of the inverse ratio of power to distance remains valid within the same political unit as well as between political units. Within the immediate future, Central Asia will undoubtedly remain a region with a fairly low power potential... In comparison with the interior lines of British naval power running from Great Britain through the circumferential highway around the Eurasian Rimlands, Russia has interior lines of communication. The transportation lines between Russia, Turkistan and Northwest India are certainly interior as compared with the sea route from Southampton to Karachi... unless the raw materials of power in the Central Asiatic regions of Russia turn out to be great enough to balance those of the Rimland regions, Soviet strength will remain west of the Urals and it will not be exerted overpoweringly against the coast lands to the east, south and southwest."

Continuing the debate on Heartland-Rimland controversy, in the light of the dynamic pattern of Eurasian politics and opposition to Mackinder's deterministic production, Spykman argues: "There has never really been a simple land power-sea power opposition. The historical alignment has always been in terms of some members of the Rimland with Great Britain against some members of the Rimland with Russia, or Great Britain and Russia together against a dominating Rimland power." Spykman cites a few examples: "... the opposition between these two states (maritime Great Britain and continental Russia) has never... been inevitable... in the three great world wars of the nineteenth and twentieth centuries, the Napoleonic wars, the First World War and the Second World War, the British and Russian empires have lined up together against an intervening Rimland power as led by Napoleon, Withelm II, and Hitler."

In response to Mackinder's dictum, Spykman argues: "If there is to be a slogan for the power politics of the old world, it must be: "Who controls the Rimland rules Eurasia; Who rules Eurasia controls the destinies of the world."

Continuing his argument, Spykman points out: "...the United States has gone to war twice within thirty years and the threat to our security each time has been the possibility that the Rimland regions of the Eurasian landmass would be dominated by a single power." In this statement, Spykman makes an obvious reference to the Soviet Union (now the Soviet system stands collapsed) which had now in control of East Europe and the Arabian Middle-Eastern desert, as the result of the German defeat by its army. He, therefore, urged that the United States' policy should be directed to the control of the Rimland states or at least to the prevention of their control by the Soviet Union. It is not clear whether the post-war US policy of containment, as advocated by Truman and Kenan and later by Acheson and Dullels, simply manifested the Spykman's dictum on Rimland.

"By the end of the World War II, it was clear that in effect the Heartland could be equated with the USSR (now stands collapsed). Germany's failure to defeat Russia had enhanced Mackinder's reputation. From this point onwards there existed a general model which is known as the Heartland-Rimland thesis involving land power (the erstwhile USSR) versus sea power (the USA) separated by a contact zone (the Rimland). To be sure there were minor variations in terms of definitions and emphasis but this three-tier structure originally derived from Mackinder's 1904 paper persisted into the post-1945 era. Mackinder's initial emphasis on railways seemed pretty antiquated in the age of satellite geopolitics/intercontinental ballistic missiles—but in a sense it does not matter whether the model is an accurate representation of reality; what does matter is that enough people believed it to be true. Therefore, the Heartland-Rimland thesis could become an ideological tool of US foreign policy makers... The world was reduced to two 'super-powers' with the onset of the Cold War (now vanished) and the Heartland-Rimland thesis provided an easy way of conceptualizing the new situation. The original hydrology basis of pivot-area and Mackinder's concern for German expansion were conveniently forgotten and... left with a model in which the enemy, the USSR had control of the fortress, the Heartland, and policy was formulated accordingly."

The Heartland-Rimland model generated considerable speculation in the 1950s and several attempts have been made time to time to reshape the model, so that it could suit more to the needs of the changing political scenario of the contemporary world. In this regard, the name of Donald W. Meining comes more often, because he sought to redefine, reevaluate and reshape the model in the light of its dynamic and functional criteria, in a paper, entitled, "Heartland and Rimland in Eurasian History", published in 1958. He assumed that both Mackinder and Spykman focused too much in their geopolitical time context, and hence, making the model irrelevant to the actual prevailing conditions.

Meining, therefore, addresses: "Our definitions of Heartland and Rimland must be rooted in cultural or functional criteria... which must rest primarily upon the actual functional orientation of the people or state, not upon simple position in relation to land and sea."

In an obvious attempts he traces the physical criteria on the basis of which Mackinder established his Heartland model. Meining redefines the Heartland as follows: "A more stable yet functional Heartland may be defined on that portion of the great Eurasian steppe and desert belt bounded on the west by the Volga basin and the Caspian Sea, on the north by the southern margin of the great northern forest, on the east by the highlands, forming the inner margin of the historic Chinese culture arena, and on the south by the nearly continuous mountainous zone, from Sinkiang, through the Himalayas, Hindukush and Kapet Dagh to the southern end of the Caspian (Fig. 13.5).

The characteristics of this area include the similarity in physical features and cultural development, interior location, "certainly with respect to all the remaining mainland", and the fact that it includes "the nexus of all the historic land routes interconnecting the several Rimland areas of China, India, the Levant and Europe. Thus, Meining's Heartland is smaller than any of those conceived by Mackinder and is surrounded by a broad Rimland (Fig. 13.5). It is with the orientation of this Rimland that Meining is primarily concerned. Both Mackinder and Spykman had this enclosing coastal belt as, by and large, the realm of sea power. To this Meining has objection and holds an altogether different view. He seeks for the division of the Rimland area into (i) Continental Rimland, and (ii) Maritime Rimland. The difference between the two is not geographical but functional. It depends on the orientation of the state and this orientation itself has changed for most parts in the course of time. The orientation is of paramount importance and changes with time.

Since Rimland states have been closely tied to the Heartland in terms of ideology and trade during one period of recent or distant world history; at other times the orientation may have been outward and maritime. Thus, in place of the outward-looking marginal crescent of Mackinder, "there is a Rimland and neighbouring island groups, in part and at times inward-looking toward the Heartland and sometimes and to some extent outward-looking to the oceans (Fig. 13.6). It is difficult to detect any rhythm in these changes of orientation, and thus no predictions possible. In Meining model, there is a scope for certain Rimland states, showing neither continental orientation nor maritime orientation, to function as transitional or neutral states.

Functional orientation of the Rimland states, to a large extent, depends on the perceived needs, in response to the fast changing local, regional and global situations. Rimland states have shown greater desirability and flexibility in their perceived needs, particularly during the Cold War period. China, in its earlier phase, represented an inward-oriented state towards the Heartland USSR be-

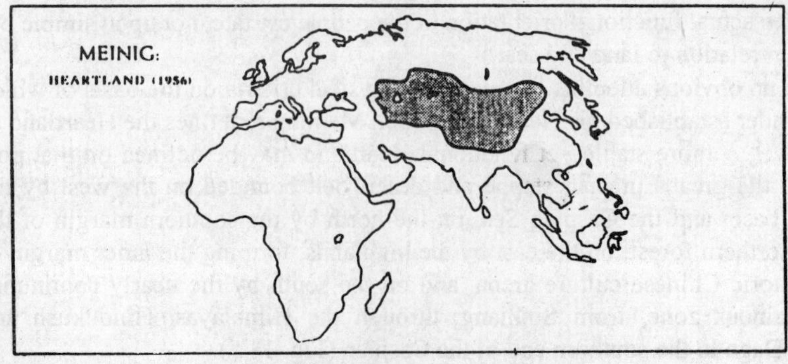

Figure 13.5: Meining's Heartland

cause of the Communist ideology and greater economic link but soon it started to look outward toward the Pacific Ocean as its relation with Heartland USSR declined to a larger extent, in the 1960s, as result of persistent nature of ideological and political conflicts. Yugoslavia (now stands completely disintegrated and is a geographical expression only) was an inward-looking state when it aligned itself with the Soviet Union but soon it turned toward the sea/ocean and for decades it remained neutral. There were a number of Rimland states which have shown alternative phases of their inward and outward orientation, keeping in view of their perceived needs and functions as well as adjustments in the fast changing regional and global situations. Western Europe has generally looked outward to the oceans but Central Europe's orientation has often been fluctuated. For sometime India had been an inward-looking state because of its closer strategic links with the Heartland USSR in the 1970s. Though the Indo-Soviet Treaty was renewed in the 1980s, it abandoned its inward-orientation, once the threat on its integrity disappeared.

Even island states beyond the Eurasian coast need not be necessarily maritime in their interest. An island people is not necessarily a seafaring people though Great Britain ranks as a maritime power, it has not always been so. The Irish have remained obstinately averse to seafaring activities. The Japanese in the early part of their history were a great seafaring people; then in the seventh century, they cut off themselves from outside contacts until the mid-nineteenth century when Commodore Perry discovered Japan and showed how much the

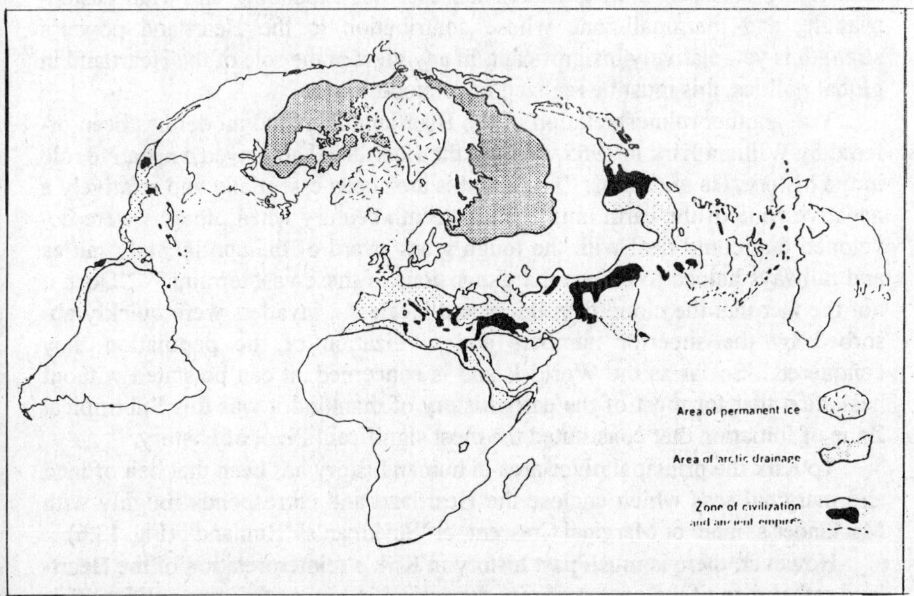

Figure 13.6: Geographical Pivots of History (After William Kirk, 1965)

rest of the world had changed since the Japanese had begun to seclude themselves.

Meining, thus, gives a new lease of life to the Heartland-Rimland model, making it more epistemological, reasonable and meaningful, particularly suited to the changing political ecology, in terms of global strategy.

In the continuing debate on the Heartland-Rimland model, and its contemporary relevance, D.J.M. Hooson, in 1964, attempted to redefine the core of the real Heartland, rather than adding a new dimension to the model in global perspective. With the help of certain parameters such as the rate of population growth, rate of urbanization and urban development, the bulk of the accessible resources, economic specialization, historical association and cohesiveness, and ethnic conditions, he has identified the existence of an established European core around Moscow and the Black Sea—the centre of Russian and Soviet power for many decades—and a significant eastern zone, the Volga-Baikal region (Fig. 13.4). It is this eastern zone which he terms as critical: "... what happens to and in this zone, between the Volga and Lake Baikal, might well have a decisive effect on the fortunes of the Soviet Union as a world power."

de Blij (1972) points out: "If, indeed, this region becomes the focus of the Soviet states—it is presently outstripping the established Moscow core in terms of the rate of development—the point of gravity of the Heartland will be nearer to that suggested by Meining. Just as Meining has pointed out that the term 'Rimland] constitutes an oversimplification so Hooson indicates that the Heartland really consists of long-established core, an expanding and vital eastern triangle, and marginal zone whose contribution to the Heartland power's strength is yet relatively insignificant. In any view of the role of the Heartland in global politics, this must be realized/understood."

Yet, another reinterpretation of the Heartland-Rimland model has been offered by William Kirk in 1965. To him, the Heartland had played a negative role in the history. He questions: "Has not this area been essentially and relatively a negative zone of the earth until the nineteenth century when ploughs were developed that could deal with the tough grass sward of the continental prairies and railways helped to reduce the dimensions of these vast terrains?" "Does it not the fact that the cloud of ruthless and idealess... invaders were quickly absorbed by the superior numbers and civilization of the population they conquered... So far as the World Island is concerned...it can be stated without hesitation that for most of the early history of mankind it was this Subtropical Zone of Initiation that constituted the most significant Pivot of History."

To Kirk the principal pivot-area in human history has been that belt of land and marginal seas which enclose the Heartland and corresponds roughly with Mackinder's 'inner or Marginal Crescent' or 'Spykman's' 'Rimland'. (Fig. 13.6).

However, there is much past history in Kirk's reinterpretation of the Heartland rather than of the contemporary dynamism in terms of power-politics. This re-evaluation of the Heartland-Rimland model does not seem to provide any significant modification in terms of global strategy.

Saul B. Cohen has attempted to carry forward a complete revision of the Heartland-Rimland model. He has questioned the relevance of the model. His basic purpose was to question the policy of containment with its implication that the whole Eurasian littoral was a potential battleground. He exposes, once again, the weakness of the Heartland-Rimland thesis. He points out: "In past global strategic views, emphasis has been placed upon the strategic unity of space, organized through a single arena of movement...A basic premise of these global strategic concepts is that the unity of one arena of movement is indivisible—that the dominant fleet can rule the entirety of the open ocean/seas; the dominant land army can rule all of the land-space; the dominant air power can rule all of the air... But today's realities suggest otherwise. Unity of arenas of movement cannot be complete, and power within such avenues is, therefore, divisible. This is because complete dominance of one avenue of movement cannot be attained unless one power completely destroys another through nuclear warfare."

Cohen's revision of the Heartland-Rimland model consists, therefore, of providing a much more militarily flexible and geographically sensitive model. His revision to the Mackinder-Spykman strategic model comes in two stages, and we will deal with them chronologically.

In his *Geography and Politics in a World Divided*, published in 1973, he offers a hierarchical and regional world model. Using the traditional geographical concept of the region, Cohen tends to distinguish between the 'geostrategic regions' and the 'geopolitical regions'.

"The geostrategic region is the expression of the interrelationship of a large part of the world in terms of location, movement, trade orientation, and cultural or ideological bonds. While it is a single-feature region in the sense that its purpose is to embrace areas over which power can be applied, it is a multi-feature region in its composition... The geopolitical region is a subdivision of the above. It expresses the unity of geographical features. Because it is derived directly from geographic regions, this unit can provide a framework for common political and economic actions. Contiguity of location and complementarity of resources are particularly distinguishing marks of the geopolitical region."

"The scheme for the geostrategic regions, partitioning of the earth", points out Cohen, "rests essentially upon the yardsticks of place and movement. Place includes the location of regional population and economic cores and great carriers zones; movement includes trade orientation and ideological-cultural bonds."

Cohen identifies just two geostrategic regions, each dominated by one of the two major powers which he terms as (i) the Trade-Dependent Maritime World, and (ii) The Eurasian Continental World.

The core of the Trade-Dependent Maritime World is the Maritime Ring of the United States; and that of the Eurasian continental world is the Russian Industrialized Triangle. Thus, both regions can be described as 'nodal'. Maritime Europe and Mainland China have emerged as second power nodes within these geostrategic regions. Cohen visualizes the emergence of a third geostrategic region—the Indian Ocean Plateau realm (Fig. 13.7).

Cohen subdivides the geostrategic regions into various geopolitical regions. The Trade-Dependent Maritime World includes the following geopolitical regions:

(a) Anglo-American and the Caribbean
(b) Maritime Europe and the Maghreb
(c) Offshore Asia and Oceanic
(d) South America

The Eurasian Continental World is subdivided into the following geopolitical regions:

(a) The Russian-Heartland and Eastern Europe
(b) The East Asian Mainland

Between these two geostrategic regions there are two distinctive geopolitical regions which he terms Shatterbelts—the Middle East and South-East Asia. "A shatterbelt is here defined as a large, strategically located region that is occupied by a number of conflicting states and is caught between the conflicting interests of adjoining Great Powers." Shetterbelts are of strategic importance to both great powers and it is here where 'containment' must be practised.

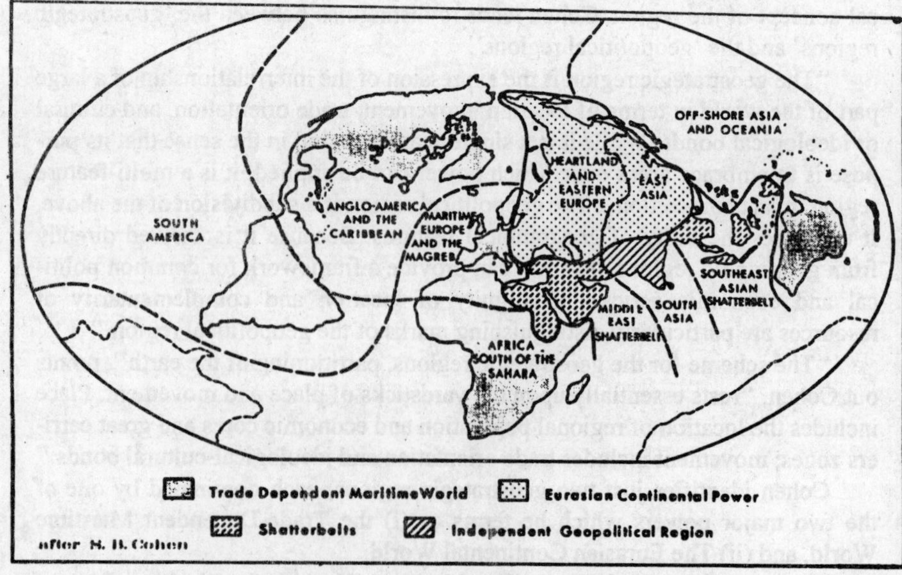

Figure 13.7: World Geostrategic Regions (After S.B. Cohen)

On Africa, south of the Sahara and South Asia, Cohen points out: "South Asia does not possess qualities of geopolitical unity that makes it likely to be recognized, in the near future, as a unit separate from both geostrategic regions. Africa, on the other hand, shows little sign of being able to attain continental geopolitical unity. This does not mean that Africa is not important to the sphere of influence of the Trade-Dependent Maritime World, nor is it outside of it. What it does mean is that Africa south of the Sahara is not likely to find internal geopolitical unity within the framework that has been outlined. If, however, the European footholds in Central and South America should be lost, then the entire eastern half of the continent might gravitate geostrategically to South Asia."

A number of criteria have been used to define the Trade-Dependent Maritime World which include: (1) orientation to the Atlantic and the Pacific Ocean basins; (2) primacy of sea communications interconnnecting this regions; (3) distribution of raw materials and people so as to call for regional specialization and interdependence; (4) a band of white settlement across the temperate lands of the southern hemisphere; (5) trade-dependence with the North Atlantic basins; and (6) highest level of technology.

Communist ideology was the main criterion being used to define the Eurasian Continental World. However, Cohen has noted that "deep ideological rifts such as those over Stalinism, coexistence, and the communism exist between the Soviet Union and China... China has begun to challenge the position of pre-eminence hitherto held by the USSR within the Communist bloc."

Coming down to the Shatterbelts, Cohen points out: "What is peculiar to the shatterbelt is its fragmented political and economic character. Owing to physical, environmental, historical, cultural and political differences, the shatterbelt appears to be incapable of attaining political and/or economic unity of action. Parts of the shatterbelts tend to seek neutrality and to lead the entire region into this path, but other portions are committed to external ties, either because of their self-interest or because of military and economic pressures from the external power centres... A locational characteristic of these belts is that they do not adjoin the core areas of opposing Great Powers... because these (shatterbelts) are easily accessible to adjoining regions, they exhibit many extra regional cultural and economic features... complete control of the shatterbelts is no longer possible for either side...shatterbelt offers footholds to the contending Great Powers. Footholds perform a variety of functions... as bases in cold and hot war situations... maintain the buffer qualities of the shatterbelt... shatterbelts offer the elbowroom for various forms of contention that other areas do not and finally footholds can better enable great powers to encourage friendly neutrals and to discourage hostile neutrals."

Cohen finally points out: "It is unsound to issue blanket invitation to countries of certain areas to enter defense pacts, or to ally ourselves with governments that are totally divorced from their people, when there is the possibility of our becoming committed to countries whose defense is not strategically vital to Free World survival." What he is saying is that not all parts of the Rimland are equally important and policy must be sensitive to this fact. Selective containment, rather than blanket containment, is the policy in line with his geographical realities.

In a revision of his model in 1982, Cohen has further emphasized the divisions of the world strategic system. He has modified some of the details of his initial spatial structure—notably the designation of Africa south of the Sahara as a third shatterbelt—but the major change is one of emphasis on 'second order' or regional centres of power. In the original model geopolitical regions were the bases of multiple power nodes and this comes to the fore in the revised model. Three geopolitical regions have developed as new world powers—Japan, China and Europe—to join the USA and the USSR. Other geopolitical regions have developed second order powers which dominate their region, such as India, Brazil and Nigeria. He assesses 27 states as second order powers and beyond these he defines third, fourth, and fifth, order states. Definitions are largely based on the scope for influence beyond the state's boundaries. The end result is a multiple-node world with many overlapping areas of influence which is much more dynamic than the old bi-polar model. The key difference is the greater inter-connectedness between regions and countries on different rungs of the hierarchy. The influence of both the old major powers has declined to be taken over in part by the rise of the new regional powers. This is a far cry from the simplicity of the Heartland-Rimland model and is returning towards the traditional complexity of regional geography models. Cohen's revised model is explicitly intended to counteract the calls for a renewal of containment policy. His is a very much American view of the world.

However, Cohen's revised model of 1982 requires another revision in the wake of (i) collapse of the Soviet Union subsequent to the fall of communism in East Europe; (ii) unification of Germany, (iii) China becoming all powerful with its maritime economy, (iv) dissension in the Trade-Dependent Maritime World with the European Union taking a stiff attitude towards the United States in the European affairs, and (v) the growing US-Japan rivalry in the maritime world.

Relevance of Heartland-Rimland Model

The Heartland-Rimland model had its maximum application in the post-1945 era, or during the Cold War period. The Heartland Russia was not much involved in the Eurasian geopolitics. Hardly it had played any role in politics before. Throughout history, it was ignored by the inner crescent/Rimland and outer crescent states. On the other hand, it was not much powerful to impose its will on the regions around it. Its repeated attempts in the form of an onward pressure on the Balkan-Arabian Middle Eastern regions of the coastal Eurasia, during the nineteenth and early twentieth centuries had been foiled by the combined sea power of the outer crescent-inner crescent states. The Heartland had never developed into a power centre or region to have dictated/controlled the politics in Eurasia till the fall of Germany. It was simply a fortress with a characteristic of power vacuum, drawing Rimland powers into it. France tried once in the early nineteenth century while Germany tried twice in the present century to fill the vacuum. Their failure was more environmental in nature rather than ethnocentric in character. It was either France or Germany which held the balance of power in most of the period in European history in their favour, placing the Heartland Russia in a relatively disadvantageous position.

The Heartland rose to prominence only after the defeat of Germany in the Second World War and the Heartland Russia was succeeded by the Soviet Union, which emerged as the strongest power in Eurasia. The Soviet system was opposed to the capitalist system in the sense that it incorporated the communist ideology which stood diagonally opposite to *laissez faire*. The outer crescent and inner crescent combine thought it to be a danger to their *raison d'etre*. The post-1945 era witnessed rapid political ideological expansion of communism in the areas around the Heartland Soviet Russia. The whole of East Europe developed into the satellite areas or dependent areas of the Heartland Soviet Russia, while the broad region, east of the Yenesie river including China, witnessed communist upsurge followed by its success in China, thus a contiguous unbroken communist sphere superposed on a vast landmass from the Baltic Sea to the Pacific coast. Thus, communism penetrated into the monsoon lands of China and continental Europe but threatened European inner crescent and the Arabian Middle East-Indian crescent with expansion. In fact, the Sino-Soviet pressure was felt all along the Rimland/inner crescent areas in the post-1945 period. This was the period which made Mackinder's model more relevant and time-tested. This situation necessitated the outer crescent-inner crescent/Rimland combine to resist the outward expansion of the Heartland Soviet Russia into the neighbouring areas.

The Heartland Russia was conceived of a fortress, and required to be surrounded by the ring of anti-Heartland Soviet alliances in the inner crescent or Rimland, and here the Spykman's model found its geographical expression, through the containment policy. The outer crescent-inner crescent combine led by Anglo-America came out with a series of multilateral and military alliances such as NATO in Europe, CENTO in West Asia, SEATO in East Asia and ANZUS in the Pacific, against the Heartland Communist bloc. The Heartland Communist bloc also had Warsaw Pact in Europe and a separate Sino-Soviet military alliance in Asia. Thus, whole of the inner-crescent or Rimland turned into a potential battle ground between expanding Heartland Communist bloc and the opposing outer-crescent-Inner-crescent combine. This marked the beginning of the Cold War making the Heartland-Rimland dichotomy more expressive and relevant.

Some major conflicts took place in Berlin, Korea, the Middle East, Vietnam and Afghanistan in the post-1945 era. All of these conflicts are premised on preventing Heartland Soviet domination of the World-Island. In its wake, it has spawned more limited but equally simple spatial models to deal with particular sectors of inner crescent or Rimland. The classic analogy was domino theory whereby the fall of one country would inevitably lead to the defeat of the US interests in adjacent countries; the loss of Kampuchia puts Thailand and Malaysia at risk and so on. While the domino theory was applicable more to the Asiatic inner crescent, it was the notion of 'Finlandization' which was more relevant in Western Europe, whereby there would be no Soviet military take over but the USSR influence would nevertheless be extended by insidious control of the domestic politics of the countries involved. Finland suffered it.

Whereas containment policy emphasized the Rimland the second policy that reflected the three-tier world model mostly concentrated on the implication of a Soviet Heartland. It was argued that the policy of nuclear deterrence would never have developed but for the Heartland-Rimland dichotomy. Quite simply, it was accepted that the USSR had the superior geopolitical location then nuclear arsenal would act as a counterbalance to Heartland Russia's basic strategic advantage. Despite the Heartland theory, a new balance required to be created on the basis of the nuclear deterrent and the World-Island could be saved, and this necessitated what was called the nuclear arms race, resulting into the armageddon scenario.

However, the events in the late 1980s and the early 1990s have once again put the Heartland-Rimland model on the point of being irrelevant and rejected. The classic analogy of the domino theory can be best applied in East Europe where the fall of communism in the late 1980s inevitably led to the defeat of the Heartland Russia's interest and position in its satellite states, and one by one all its satellites fell to western democracy, renouncing their alignment to the Soviet Union. Germany got unified and United Germany once again emerged as the strongest state in Central Europe. The unification of Germany, subsequent to the fall of communism in East Europe, was followed by the collapse and disintegration of the Soviet Union, which inevitably led to the cessation of Cold War in the World-Island. China has long disassociated itself from the Heartland Russia, and in the Asiatic Rimland politics, it has continued to resist the Soviet pressure and implicit expansion. The Soviet failure in Afghanistan in the late 1980s and early 1990s also reflected its declining power-potential.

Even within the Heartland region there are contradictions; for example, the Russia-Ukaraine rivalry over the control of the Black Sea Fleet, the Russia-Khazakastan rivalry over the question of the possession of nuclear arsenals of the former Soviet Union and the rise of Mulsim fundamentalism in Central Asia vis-a-vis the Steppe region, in contrast to the *raison d'etre* of the Heartland, all these have gone against Mackinder's prescription. Outer crescent state—the United States—has emerged as the master of the World-Island. Even Russia and some of its former republics in the Steppe region have sought for the membership to the NATO. A number of powerful states have emerged in the Rimland around Russia which are capable of resisting any expansion and pressure. The United States has abandoned its policy of containment soon after the fall of the Heartland Russia.

Disintegration of Yugoslavia and Czechoslovakia further weakened Heartland Russia's foothold in its adjoining areas. Growing US-Russia detente and Russia's intention of becoming a member of the European Union on the one hand, and the emergence of the United States as the Master of the World on the other have further weakened the validity of the Heartland-Rimland model. Growing Sino-US cooperation in the Pacific region and the US-Japan rivalry in the World-Island also tend to make the model irrelevant and not applicable. Nevertheless, it should not thought that the Heartland-Rimland model is diminishing in importance. If there is any revival of the interwar German geopolitics in the Unified Germany, then there is every possibility of Mackinder-Spykman again becoming the prophetic genius to stop the Germans.

The Heartland-Rimland model simply reflects a two-dimensional strategic thinking but the massive development in the science and technology, particularly in the field of air navigation and its striking capacity, necessarily, sought for a three-dimensional strategic thinking with the sky above, being the major zone of uninterrupted mobility, much more flexible than the oceanic surface. It is in this background and in contrast to the Heartland-Rimland model that Alexander P. de Seversky, in 1950, argued that the land and sea powers in the world have been subordinated to the greater power of air. As early as in 1942 he remarked: "...the promised command of the sea, through the employment of forces shakes down to a meaningless phrase. It is valid only if preceded by the command of the air."

Though a number of people, such as Edward Warner, Giulio Douhet and Mitchal, had advocated in favour of the geographical necessity of air power in the wake of rapidly declining importance of the land and sea powers, it was not until 1950 that a model to this effect was developed by de Seversky. He advocated the development of massive air superiority as the prime goal for the US policy makers.

In his book, *Victory through Air Power*, published in 1942, de Seversky points out: "...the rapid expansion of the range and striking power of military aviation makes it certain that the United States will be exposed to destruction from the air within a predictable period." He went on to outline how the threat could be met through the development of a superior air force, and listed eleven points on the lessons of modern air power:

1. No land or sea operations are possible without first assuming control of the air above.
2. Navies have lost their function of strategic offensive.

3. The blockade of an enemy nation has become a function of air power.
4. Only air power can defeat air power.
5. Land-based aviation is always superior to ship-borne aviation.
6. The striking radius of air power must be equal to the maximum dimensions of the theatre of operation.
7. In aerial warfare the factor of quality is relatively more decisive than the factor of quantity.
8. Aircraft types must be specialized to fit not only the general strategy but the tactical problems of a specific campaign.
9. Destruction of enemy morale from the air can be accomplished only by precision bombing.
10. The principle of unity of command, long recognized on land and on sea, applies with no less force to the air.
11. Air power must have its own transport.

de Seversky's model appears in his another book, *Air Power: Key to Survival*, published in 1950. The model was specially prepared to suit the American requirement, in the light of the growing Soviet power and pressure in coastal Eurasian areas. The model can be best defined to have come up as a result of the beginning of the Cold War.

The model is best expressed with the azimuthal equidistant projection being centered on the North Pole. The popularity of North Pole projections has been a valuable correction to the overuse of the Mercator's. Mackinder and Spykman used the Mercator's projection for the cartographic expression of their models. The model expressed through the azimuthal equidistant projection sought to view the chief adversaries for global supremacy in the post-1945 world as standing face to face across the Arctic Mediterranean, through whose air space pass the shortest routes between places in the Heartland and North America.

de Seversky advocated that the United States should aim at the development of massive air power as its primary military objective and the superiority in air should be made so complete that no adversary might be tempted to engage in adventures against her for fear of complete destruction at the hand of the US relatiatory forces. He believed that virtually complete air supremacy, not just local or temporary air superiority, was possible. The side that obtained air supremacy held the other at its mercy. de Seversky did not expect this to come without enormous effort and loses but felt that a country such as the USA, with advanced technology but limited manpower, could better pay the price of air supremacy than that of superiority in three media. Since he wished the United States to avoid surface and particularly ground, combat, he thought overseas bases as undesirable, probably untenable, and, in an age of intercontinental flight, unnecessary. He, therefore, advised the US policy makers against involvement in small wars around the Russian periphery, in the Rimland—such as the one in Vietnam—which, he felt, only led to useless expenditure of valuable resources and energy without doing any harm to its arch rival—the Soviet Union.

His model on the azimuthal equidistant projection inevitably carried him to conceive of both the United States and the Soviet Union, separately holding complete air-dominance over vast areas with their respective orbits. The circles marking their spheres of influence overlapped over a vast area in North America and Eurasia. The overlap of the American circle and the Soviet ellipse was the 'area of decision' (Fig. 13.8) where the mastery of the air would be decided.

Besides the Soviet Union and the United States, Great Britain, he argued, alone had the potentialities of great air power. Latin America, within the circle of American air dominance, seemed to be the main reserves of American industry. Much of Africa and all of South-East Asia were within the ellipse of the Soviet air dominance. de Seversky believed that for its survival in the event of a total war, it was necessary that the United States should concentrate all its energies and resources in acquiring complete air dominance in this zone of decision

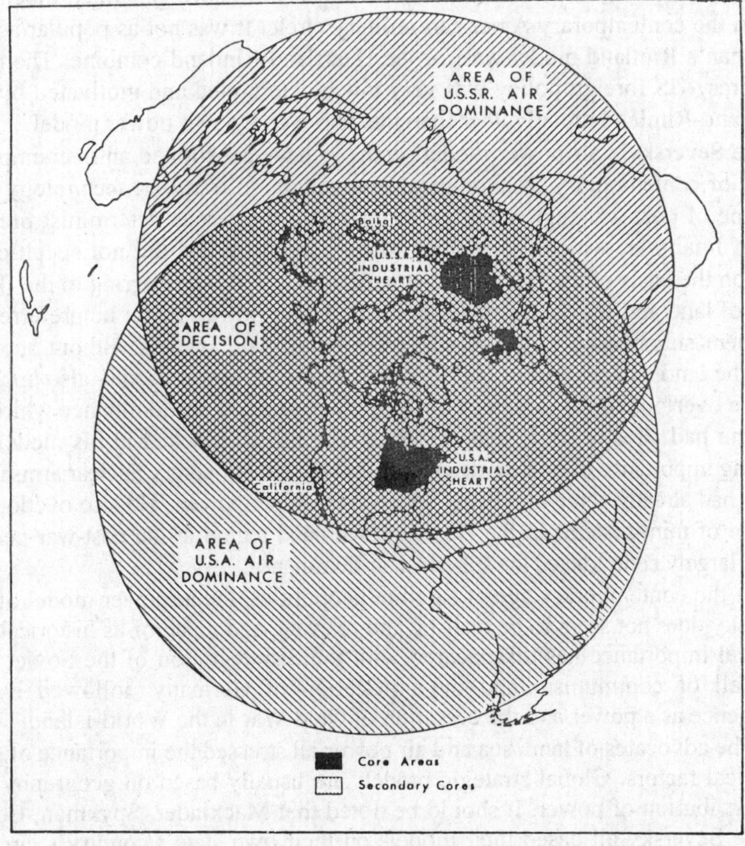

Figure 13.8: The Airman's View (De Seversky, 1949)

it is here that decisive conflicts of the future would take place. de Seversky model simply swings back to the concept of western hemisphere defence, with a north-south, rather than an east-west emphasis.

"The notion of absolute air supremacy based on intercontinental mobility through air, and the juxtaposition of the United States and the Soviet Union as the principal Cold War antagonists standing face to face across the Arctic, tended to encourage in the United States a sense of air isolationism oriented to the western hemisphere."

It was felt by the US Senate Sub-Committee on Strategic and Critical Materials that large parts of the Rimland required to be brought within the defensive perimeter if Latin America were to be secure, because control over the African airfields by the Soviet Union would inevitably make Latin America vulnerable. Thus, "the perception of air isolationism, inherent in de Seversky's model, inevitably led to what may be called 'containment policy'.

de Seversky's air power model does not seem to have generated much debate in the contemporary American military circle. It was not as popular as the Spykman's Rimland model was, or the Heartland-Rimland combine. The contemporary US foreign policy was very much determined and motivated by the Heartland-Rimland model rather than the de Seversky's air power model.

de Seversky's air power model seems to have constituted an oversimplification of contemporary technological innovations in transport technology and the type of post-war regional alignments, and a dangerous determinist prediction of total war, which too seemed to be unrealistic. He did not specifically mention the basis of the US air power superiority, without referring to the flexibility of land and sea forces as a support to the air power, rather he preferred to call them subordinate to it. No air power could gain success without support from the land and sea forces. de Seversky, in his air power model, also appears to have overlooked the existence of the Chinese area of air dominance which by the time had already come into existence. He also overlooked in his model the growing importance of nuclear deterrence and the contemporary nuclear arms race, which had already come into being between the super powers. He also overlooked the rise of mini-systems in the Heartland-Rimland region in the post-war period, which largely contradicted the spherical air dominance.

In the contemporary age of satellite geopolitics, the airpower model of de-Seversky does not seem to be realistic and relevant, and much of its historical and political importance has disappeared with the disintegration of the Soviet Union, fall of communism and the unification of Germany, followed by its emergence as a power and the cessation of Cold War in the World-Island.

The advocates of land, sea and air power all stressed the importance of geographical factors. Global strategic models are usually based on geography and the distribution of power. It should be noted that Mackinder, Spykman, Cohen and de Seversky all based their models on their own state's/country's circumstances during particular eras and times.

Chapter 14

World Organizations, Regional Multinational Associations and Political Regions

What is normally believed that "conflict is almost inevitable between the states". According to the philosophy of Social Darwinism that conflict is necessary and the survival of the fittest desirable on the assumption that a state is an organic entity and must thus obey the laws which define the growth of organism. The organic theory, as we have seen in Chapter 2, has neither empirical nor logical foundation. Nevertheless, the decision makers in sates, despite their countless protestations to the contrary in preambles to treaties and in their public utterances, act as if they had accepted the Social Darwinist's view of state. It is refreshing, then, to come to the study of international agreements, organizations, and instruments that are based on the opposite view that survival depends not on a conflict from which the fittest to survive will emerge victorious but on cooperation and collaboration between nations. The extreme international conflict and international cooperation are, in fact, so mixed that is sometimes difficult to tell which of the two predominates in particular decision" (Pounds, 1972).

Empires, kingdoms, states and nations over many centuries have attempted political and military associations, and about as often as these efforts succeeded. The ancient city states of Greece formed leagues; so did the Hanseatic ports. Kings and princes joined their realms and then fought battles for renewed independence. The Concert of Europe, in the early nineteenth century, may be viewed as a first rational attempt to begin with a regional inter-state organization, but it failed in its aim. In fact, the earlier associations were formed for war strategy, and were a means to maintain the balance of power. It was one of the most geographically expressive political doctrines as it was concerned with 'areal-political differentiation' or based on 'areal-differneces' in military potentials of political regions.

Apart from regional inter-state organizations, there were attempts in the past for extra-regional inter-state organizations and associations. In fact, the twentieth century carried forward the paradigm of inter-state association, and organizations of the nineteenth century, in a more effective and vigorous way.

Therefore, the efforts toward greater international unity as they occur today must be viewed in the light of the past progress and reversal. It is often questioned whether present attempts at inter-state or international unity in various parts of the world are something new—or just another ill-fated version of one of man's ancient feelings?

Expressing his reaction on the relevance of the question, de Blij (1972) remarks: "...the post-World War II era has been one of unprecedented activities in the field of supranationalism. In virtually all parts of the world and practically in every conceivable sphere states are seeking alliances, treaties and other forms of association. And there is something new in this; in their determination to associate, states are doing something they have not been willing to do on such a scale previously. They are giving up some of their sovereignty in return for the security, economic advantage, cultural strength, or whatever benefit they perceive to accrue from their involvement. As these supernational bodies emerge, the world political pattern changes. This appears to be beginning of the period of the superstate, and, although previous efforts of this sort, notably those of inter-war period, have failed and collapsed, the effort is much more universal and vigorous now then it was than. The United Nations is a far more representative body than the League of Nations was."

World Organizations

Most of the inter-state organizations or so-called 'international organizations' in the past and early part of the twentieth century were regional in nature, or necessarily European in nature. Inter-state organizations in the continent that appeared particularly after the Congress of Vienna in the nineteenth century and onwards were a means to maintain the balance of power, i.e., to check/resist a state becoming all powerful to threaten the peace in the region. It was not until 1920 that warring nations in the First World War felt the need for an international forum which could timely represent the world community based on 'areal-political differentiation'. The League of Nations (1920-1946) was first such experiment to come up, and the fundamentals of which had emerged during the years the blood bath of World War I, and which involved every continent and every major nations of the world. In 1919, an agreement was reached among the allies concerning the text of the Covenant, and League of Nations began operating in 1920.

The League of Nations

The United States of America was instrumental in the formation of the League of Nations that could maintain peace. The League of Nations was primarily designed to "curb aggressive war, and was necessarily designed to act as an instrument of collective security through joint repudiation of any aggressor". Although the League was the brainchild of President Wilson, the United States never joined it. The non-participation of the United States, the most powerful core-state of the contemporary world, was a serious blow to the League. Similarly, the non-inclusion of the Soviet Union till 1934 was another serious mistake on the part of the protagonists of the League of Nations.

In all, 63 states were members of the League of Nations, though, in fact, the total membership at any single time did not reach 63: the Soviet Union was allowed to join in 1934, after Germany had abandoned it in 1933. Costa Rica and Brazil had departed as early as 1925 and 1926 respectively. Some eligible countries never joined it. Others remained critical of the Covenant. "But despite these troubles, the League of Nations represented a tremendous leap forward in international relations, for it embodied a principle that up until that time had been a matter only for theoretical discussion among scientists and historians."

The first meeting of the League of Nations was held in 1920 in Geneva. Geneva continued to be the headquarters of the League throughout its period of existence, although the World Court sat at the Hague. Legislative and administrative functions were conducted by an Assembly and a Council, whose main purpose was to solve international disputes, and reduce tension, and armaments. In this goal, the League of Nations was partially successful, which included solution to the problems of German colonies which were put under mandate, the creation of Permanent Court of International Justice, the protection of minorities, the settlement of frontier and boundary disputes, the provision of avenues for discussion of sensitive areas such as Danzig and the Saar, establishment of a number of international agencies and bodies in such fields as health, communications, finance, and intellectual exchange.

However, the League of Nations experienced more failures than successes. Its major weakness was its lack of coercive power. By mid-1930s, it was evident that the League was not in a position to control the threat of aggression. Japan overran the Chinese coast, and Germany occupied the Rhineland and annexed Austria. Similarly, Italy overran Ethiopia, a fellow member and annexed it, and Franco led his troops home from Africa to conquer the government in Madrid, and a host of other such territorial-political problems. In some of the cases, the major powers attempted to ignore and ridicule the League's pronouncements and they showed their disrespect to the Covenant. The outbreak of the Second World War, finally, brought about the collapse of the League of Nations. It was officially terminated in 1946, after United Nations had started functioning.

On the non-participation of the United States or its absence from the League of Nations, Pounds (1972) remarks: "The absences from the League of Nations have an explanation that is partially geographical. The absence of the United States is partly explicable in terms of the isolationist feelings in the United States, itself a geographical phenomenon. The absence from the membership list of many of the very small states was in part a function of their neutrality and in part of their small resources, the explanation of which is again partly geographical. Germany, Italy and Japan left the League because their territorial ambitions could not be realized without war, and conflict between these countries and the League itself was inevitable."

The United Nations

The United Nations, with a membership of little more than 180 in 1995, is probably the most geographically expressive of all international organizations. It is truely expressive of 'areal-political differentiation'; i .e., the variable political character of the earth's surface, as its membership is worldwide. The United Nations succeeded the League of Nations. As World War II drew to a close, the leaders of the victorious allied powers gathered in San Francisco to consider an international organization that could maintain the post-war peace. The result was the United Nations Charter, patterned after the old League of Nations, with an Assembly, Council and a Court.

The *General Assembly* serves as a rudimentary legislature, but it has no power of enforcement. Its membership has exceeded 180 and a great majority of them belong to the Third World. It is the fall of the colonial system in the post-war period that subsequently led to the emergence of nation-states of variable size, from a tiny island-state like Nauru, to a giant state like India, but all sought for the U N membership. As the membership increased, so declined the influence of the Atlantic core-states in world affairs. To all emerging nation-states, the United Nations is a vital geographical necessity as it assures protection to their *raison d'etre.*

Each member-state in the Assembly is assured of a voting right, and it is often felt in the western circle that the proliferation of small states has had the effect of unbalancing the representation in the Assembly; today, representatives of less than 25 per cent of the earth's people can muster a majority vote. In 1978, this belief prompted the United States Congress to temporarily refuse to appropriate funds for the technical programmes of the United Nations, as well as to limit other appropriations in such a way as to make them unavailable under the rules of the United Nations. Voting patterns in the Assembly, since 1970, have shown recurrence of the core-periphery conflicts which necessarily reveal the determined efforts of the periphery to substantially oppose the pressures of the core, and to that of the core, to continue with its ability to make decisions and impose them on the periphery. The fact cannot be denied that in the ongoing core-periphery conflicts for the last two and half decades, the periphery has, to a large extent, lessened the pressure of the core.

The *Security Council* consists of the fifteen members, of which five members are permanent members of it, and the remaining ten members are elected for two years terms by the General Assembly. Five permanent members are the United States, United Kingdom, France, Peoples Republic China (it replaced Nationalist China which was one of the founding members), and Russia (which succeeded the Soviet Union in 1992-93). However, there is a strong demand from the periphery that a periphery state should hold a permanent seat in the Security Council.

The Security Council bears primary responsibility for maintaining international peace, and it may enforce its decisions without the use of arms (by calling for interruption of economic relations, breaks in transportation and communications or severance of diplomatic relations), or it may call on UN members to volunteer armed forces.

The United Nations forces have acted in Congo, Suez Canal Zone, Cyprus, Angola, Campuchia, and Ethiopia, particularly when civil wars broke out in these areas. The UN peace-keeping forces are also active in civil-war-torn Yugoslavia, where they are providing security to the Muslims, and are trying to contain the expansion of the Serbs into the Muslim territories. The major military efforts of the UN forces had been in the repudiation of the communist aggression in Korea in the 1950s, and Iraqi aggression in Kuwait in 1991. Recently, it has achieved some successes in its attempts to treat a cease fire plan on the warring factions of the Serbs, Muslims and Croats in Boshia-Hergegovina, and a durable peace in the war-torn region may be achieved.

The *International Court of Justice* at the Hague is a protomorphic judicial branch of world government. It represents the first step toward international legislation and an international order of law. The litigant states may choose to come before the court, however, and the court has no executive power of enforcement. If any party to a case fails to heed a court judgment, the other party has recourse to the Security Council, which may decide what is to be done. However, the Court had achieved some notable successes in what may be described as 'intrablock disputes' such as between United Kingdom and Iceland over fishing rights in North Sea waters, and between Nicaragua and Honduras over the location of their mutual boundary. In fact, the member-states involved in such disputes have abided by the Court's decision. But the Court failed to offer any solution to the quarrel between Albania and Britain in the Corfu Channel case,and between South Africa and Southwest Africa (Namibia) when the former illegally occupied the latter. But, in most of the cases, the Court has failed to deliver judgments, acceptable to the contending states.

"The two categories of specific functional agencies of the United Nations have proven the most successful international collaborative structures. Some agencies facilitate communications among member-states: The Universal Postal Union, the International Telecommunication Union, the International Civil Aviation Organization, the World Meteorological Organization and the Intergovernmental Maritime Consultative Organization."

"Others encourage international cooperation towards specific economic, social, health or other humanitarian goals, with the hope that such cooperations stimulate political cooperation. This is an appealing theory, but, unfortunately, of dubious validity. These cooperative agencies include the International Labour Organization, the United Nations Educational, Scientific and Cultural Organization, the Food and Agriculture Organization, the World Health Organization, the International Atomic Energy Agency, the International Bank for Reconstruction and Development; and the International Monetary Fund. The United Nations Trusteeship Council today supervises the administration of only a few Pacific islands and these islands are entrusted to the United States."

On the successes and failures, Bergman (1975) remarks: "...of the goals of the United Nations as a political system, the system has not prevented all wars, nor has it won adequate food or shelter for all men. But it has prevented some wars, brought end to others, and its agencies have undoubtedly contributed to the welfare of many of the world's poor citizens and states. Surely the integration of the system is weak, but even to provide any sort of structure linking almost all men is an accomplishment not to be underestimated. Much of the pattern management and tension management among states take place in bilateral or multilateral negotiations outside the United Nations, but most problems in international affairs do not, in fact, involve the world. Toward truly global activities and problems—transportation, communication, population, the sess, the global environment—the United Nations has taken or is taking significant initiatives. And as far adaptation, the United Nations has struggled to promote international understanding of this globe as our only one earth."

de Blij (1972) comments: "The significance of the United Nations, in the present context, lies in the fact that it reflects, however, imperfectly, the continued desire on the part of states for mutual action, open communications, and a maintenance of international peace and security. States that have faced the censure of the United Nations nevertheless continue to participate and contribute. That attitude is an indication that the states of the world are beginning to be prepared to give up a small bit of sovereignty—however minimal—in the interest of international collaboration. This is a completely new phenomenon on the politico-geographical scene... But the world organizations of today mark the greatest achievements of a desire on the part of states to collaborate, a desire that is also reflected by the numerous regional organizations of international co-operation that have recently sprung up. The world organizations incorporates the widest possible range of interests of member-states. The regional organizations, based upon states that are often contiguous and share many historical and cultural experiences and attitudes, have gone further. They may be indications of the political world to come."

Regional Associations or Regional Multinational Political Systems

More restricted than the near-universal United Nations political organizations are numerous regional multinational political systems. Proximate states often form regions of mutual political interrelation. The foreign policy of each state, for example, is largely influenced by those of its neighbours, particularly on the basis of measures of the nature and level of cohesion among states, the nature of communications among states, their level of power, and the structure of relations among states. These regional multinational political systems represent a regional bias. This is natural, as regions not only afford the binding element of spatial proximity among member-states, but also contribute to similar social and physical situations that create similar desires and needs. Independent national states, therefore, have continued to form regional or interregional organizations, or regional multinational political systems while maintaining membership in the United Nations.

Post-war period has witnessed a large number of regional organizations coming up, in different parts of the world, which were necessarily designed to maintain political and economic stability on regional basis, and balance of power, in terms of military potentials, on the world scale. It was during the Cold War period that the functioning of regional organizations became more pronounced, and their impacts on world affairs were far-reaching. However, with the cessation of Cold War in the 1990s, some of the regional organizations and alliances lost their political credibility and had to be abandoned. Few regional organizations of multinational character on continental scale deserve special attention because of their growing global impact.

Europe

Europe has always been a forerunner in regional movements, based on political necessity, economic needs and strategic requirements, and geographical culture. These movements, in fact, reflected the Pan-European movements of one kind or another that have existed in Europe for centuries. But not until after the end of the World War II did any really effective unifying movements develop, particularly in economic and strategic fields. By then, the political forces in the continent were polarized around (i) capitalist-democratic system, and (ii) authoritarian-socialist (communist) system, with contrasting political, economic and strategic requirements.

However, the first such regional organization, which had nothing to do with the polarization of political forces in the post-war period, was that of the BENELUX Union of Belgium, the Netherlands and Luxembourg. Its foundation was laid in 1922 when a custom union was set up between Belgium and Luxembourg and in 1947, it was extended by the incorporation of the Netherlands. Common tariffs were established for many goods, and plans were made for gradual elimination of import licences and quotas. In fact, Belgium, Netherlands and Luxembourg had a long history of regional association and cooperation, which was interrupted by recurrent wars and hostilities in the region, but finally, it was again revived after the World War II, when the demand for greater cooperation was felt by these states.

However, the BENELUX was superseded by a relatively larger union in 1948, that was, the Organization for European Economic Cooperation (OEEC), which included, France, West Germany, Italy, the Netherlands, Belgium and

Luxembourg. It was established with a specific object of coordinating the Marshal Plan funds contributed by the United States "to speed the recovery of Europe from the ravages of the Second World War".

In 1950, Robert Schuman, the French Affairs Minister, proposed a common market for Western Europe in coal, iron and steel and raw materials from which the latter was made. Schuman's plan found its recognition by the six OEEC members, and in 1952, the European Coal and Steel Community (ECSC) was established. Great Britain which earlier showed interest in it, but declined to join it. The ECSC continued until 1959, when the organization was marked with the common market. The object of the ECSC was to diminish the cost of production. It also sought to remove hindrances to the flow of labour and investment capital, so that maximum economic integration could be achieved. In 1957, the European Atomic Energy Community (EUROTOM) was established. This political structure has worked to develop atomic energy for community power needs, but its efforts have met only limited success. Technological problems in planning and constructing atomic power plants have been complicated by military ramifications of the work, but Europe's expanding demands for imported fuels might still invigorate this body.

The six ECSC member-states, however, wanted to create in the shortest possible time a common market for all articles of commerce. They sought for more closer economic cooperation, and a treaty to this effect was signed in Rome in 1958, which created the European Economic Community (EEC), otherwise known as the 'Common Market' (Fig. 14.1)

The tariffs which surrounded the EEC were to be near the average of the previous tariffs of the six states. Internal tariffs were to be progressively lowered until complete freedom of trade within the EEC was achieved. EEC's economic goals include the creation of a custom union with free movements of goods, labour, services and capital, coordination of agricultural policies and integration of national transport systems. The Rome Treaty came into effect in January 1959, when the first reductions were made in the internal tariffs of the community, a process that was completed in July 1968. Since then, the level of external tariffs has itself been reduced following discussions within the framework of GATT (General Agreement on Tariff and Trade). Now, discussions regarding the level of external tariff will have to be done within the framework of a new global organization—WTO (World Trade Organization)—which has replaced GATT in 1994-95.

However, several European countries that did not join the EEC, in 1957, saw the formation of that bloc as a threat to their foreign trade. Thus, in 1960, Austria, Denmark, Norway, Portugal, Sweden, Switzerland (with associated Liechtenstein) and the United Kingdom, soon to be joined by Finland and Iceland, formed a looser and less ambitious grouping than the Common Market, called the European Free Trade Association (EFTA). These countries sought only free trade among themselves in industrial goods, a goal they achieved by the end of 1966. They never sought either a common external tariff wall or abolition of barriers to trade in agricultural products. (Fig. 14.1).

The EEC and EFTA, both, had one each member of the core category: France in the former, and United Kingdom in the latter, and these two core countries spelt out their rival economic interests in Europe. However, both the EEC and EFTA were comprised of non-Communist states and represented political forces that polarized behind the democratic-capitalist system of 'comparative advantages'. Nevertheless, the EEC and EFTA had been rival to each other, but, on 22 July 1972, both the economic organizations sought to create one free trade zone of seventeen countries (the original EEC six, the EFTA ten, plus Ireland). Tariffs on industrial goods were to be abolished over the five year period from April 1973 to July 1977. The merger of the EEC and EFTA together, finally led to the creation of the European Community—a more ambitious multinational undertaking that seeks for greater European unity.

The European Community

The European Community (EC) is truly expressive of a multinational regional political system on a continental scale, and is one of the most significant examples of supranationalism in the World-Island. It has brought about drastic

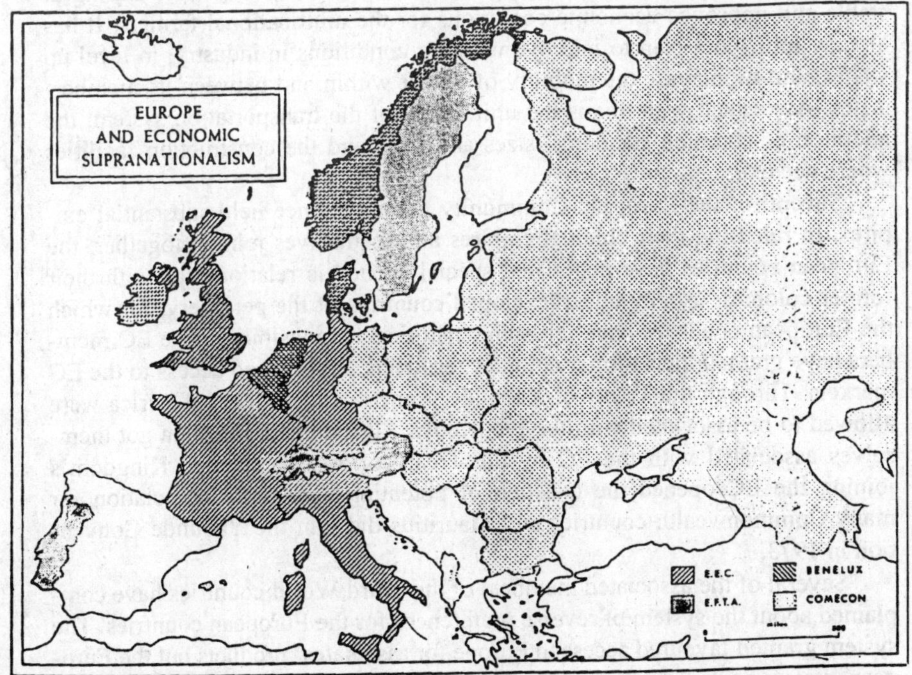

Figure 14.1: Regional Alliance in Europe during the Cold-War Period

changes in the landscape and economic geography of the European continent. Landuse definition and regional specialization now take place not within the limited area of national boundaries, but within the far wider scope of spatial organization of the entire community area.

The political machinery of the European Community includes a Council of Ministers (one from each member government), a Commission (the executive wing, with its members appointed by agreement among member governments, but independent of the national governments in their actions) and a European Parliament. The EC structures include also a large number of consultative bodies. The Economic and Social Committee is the most important, and it is organized corporatively. The European Court of Justice, set up in 1952 with the European Coal and Steel Community, has been remodelled and its authority has been extended to cover the enlarged European Communities. The body of European law applies directly to all Europeans in the community member-states, but generally the national courts adjudicate it. In fact, European law is becoming more forceful in European life, and a European Government appears to be coming up.

The European Community creates a common custom union which seeks to remove all kinds of tariffs and other restrictions for more economic consolidation and integration. It has adopted a common agricultural policy, aiming at stable and improved economic conditions for the multinational farmers. It has already initiated a plan to improve working conditions in industry, in level up wages, and to increase the mobility of labour within and between its member-states. Associated with this is the unification of the transportation system, the adoption of common standards, sizes and rates and the construction facilities where needed.

Several of the European Community members once held substantial empires. In releasing their colonial empires and themselves joining together, the European countries have negotiated special economic relationships with their former colonies, usually underdeveloped countries of the periphery, for which the European countries have felt some historical responsibility. The EC members have granted their former colonies' products a privileged access to the EC markets. Through the Treaty of Yaounde, some nineteen states of Africa were allowed to be associated with the EC. Kenya, Uganda and Tanzania got themselves associated with the EC by the Treaty of Arusha. United Kingdom's joining the EC opened the question of potential community association for many Commonwealth countries and Mauritius did join the Yaounde Convention in 1973.

Several of the associated members of the Third World countries have complained about the system of reverse preferences for the European countries. The system granted favoured access to Europe for associates' products but the European states gained reciprocal faoured access for their products. This has prevented the underdeveloped countries of the periphery from buying their needs in the cheapest world market and has been seen as a perpetuation of the colonial relationship. Also, the United States and other industrial countries, including Japan, outside the European Community, have also complained that reverse preferences closed their products out of EC associates' markets.

Opening negotiations on redefining Europe's relations with the underdeveloped world have clarified a few emerging new principles. The Common Market will no longer demand, nor will it seek, reverse preferences, although it will not refuse them if offered. Also, the EC will help the peripheral countries develop processing of their products rather than export only raw materials. Terms of the Yaounde and Arusha treaties have been redefined in this background so that the trading relations might be more flexible.

In addition to its economic goals, eventual political union is a stated goal of the European Community.

Members of the European Community felt a need of a more 'politically flexible and economically viable' union, in place of the existing structure, on the following two major grounds:

(i) To resist unified Germany's political hegemony in Europe. Unified Germany is an emerging core state in the continent and is likely to be a potential continental power. The break-up of the Soviet Union and the fall of the socialist regimes in East Europe, in the early 1990s, necessarily created a political vacuum in Mackinder's Heartland, with Russia gradually loosing its impregnable status of a continental power. This has given an additional hegemonic superiority to Germany over a vast area of East Europe vis-a-vis Russia. Germany's industrial capacity has far exceeded to that of France, United Kingdom, Italy and others, and this can be measure of its political power. In this changed political scenario, it has now become a geographical compulsion for European nations to contain Germany's growing hegemony and this can be done only through a union with more powers vested in it.

(ii) To contain and resist the growing US, and Japanese economic hegemony in Europe, which has been developing over the past few decades. It has necessarily caused much 'damage' to the sustained economic growth of the European community members. The community members, particularly the European core-states, have felt the need of putting more tariffs and trade restrictions on the entry of certain kinds of the American and Japanese products into Europe, so that the economic growth within the community can be sustained without pressure. The community can decide its own economic destiny.

It is in this background, the members of the EC signed the Maaschtrist Treaty and the European Union came into being. People of some fifteen European nations have, through referenda, acknowledged their countries participation in the European Union. The national legislatures of these nations have already ratified the Maaschtrist Treaty. The national legislatures of few more nations are yet to ratify the treaty while the governments of these nations have already approved of it. Apart from a custom union, the European Union seeks to initiate a common currency for the member-states. It seeks for a greater economic cooperation among the member-states, so that it can emerge as an alternative viable to the United States and Japan in the world economy.

In contrast to the regional multinational political system that came to be developed around the liberal-democratic-capitalist system, across West Europe, the authoritarian-socialist system laid the foundation of the Council of Economic Mutual Assistance (CEMA) in 1949, across East Europe. As mentioned earlier that World War II left much of Europe in ruins, and the United States' famous Marshal Plan initiated economic cooperation in Europe to get the various states back on their feet economically. Marshal Plan aid was offered to all European states, including the Soviet Union, but the Soviet Union and its satellites refused to offer. In 1948 seventeen European nations did join the Organization for European Economic Cooperation and Development (OEECD), and in 1949, Federal Republic of Germany joined in it. The OEECD was formed with twin factors in mind: (a) growing European impoverishment as a result of declining trade; and (b) mounting danger of communism in the wake of impoverishment which might eventually sweep Europe. The United States and Canada became full members of it. From European point of view, it may be said that the OEECD represented a step backward and not forward in the struggle for European unity.

The Soviet Union sharply reacted to the formation of the OEECD by joining with its East European satellites in forming by the COMECON in the same year (Fig. 14.1). The countries that joined the Council of Economic Mutual Assistance (CEMA), beside the Soviet Union, were Bulgaria, Czechoslovakia, German Democratic Republic, Hungary, Poland, and Rumania. However, Yugoslavia refused membership. The CEMA was comprised of nations which were economically so poor as to have been categorized as 'peripheral' in the world economy. The Soviet Union, though, emerged as a super power, was itself a peripheral country, and only in the 1960s and 1970s, it reached to the rank of a semi-peripheral country in the world economy. It was the main reason that the CEMA could not emerge as a viable economic alternative to its West European counterpart.

The CEMA or COMECON countries differed fundamentally from that created in the European Community. The latter was based on private enterprise and guaranteed to the product freedom to sell his products anywhere within the area he could find a market, and with certain limitations, freedom to establish his works, whenever he found it most profitable. The CEMA or COMECON was an agreement between governments which themselves controlled all industrial undertakings and all trade within their respective states. Through the mechanism set up by CEMA or COMECON, some degree of integration was achieved between the development plans of each of the member-states. Trade among themselves continued to be based mainly on bilateral barter agreements negotiated between them. It was designed to centralize and administer trade agreements with the organization. However, CEMA provided opportunities for national planning, and long-term trade agreements. Each member-state drew up its own economic plans and carried them out. Although, the CEMA or COMECON showed a considerable measure of cooperation between them, this partnership was more based upon international treaty. It was more formal and less flexible than the European Community. Nevertheless, a higher proportion of the total trade of its members was with one another than was the case with the European Community.

The CEMA, however, could not create conducive conditions for free movement of goods, labour, services, and capital, coordination of agricultural policies and integrated infrastructural systems. It could not bring about any drastic changes in the landscape and economic geography of Eastern Europe. It was not a potential economic union, like that of the European Community. Since it was comprised of East European peripheral states with the dominance of the Soviet Union, which had, practically, no place in the world economy, the CEMA or COMECON lacked sustainable economic growth over decades, resulting into complete economic depredation in East European states. The Soviet Union, including the satellite states, could not recover from economic depredation, which ultimately led to the collapse of the state-controlled economic policies which pulled down the CEMA or COMECON in the early part of the 1990s. Unification of Germany was a severe blow to the CEMA. Disintegration of Yugoslavia and Soviet Union added further impetus to the downfall of the CEMA, and the member-states denounced it. Large number of East European states, including Russia, have now sought for the membership of the European Union, and the response is positive.

Council of Europe was a political grouping of five West European nations that came up in the wake of Cold War in 1949, when the five western nations met at Brussels, and signed a treaty, establishing the Council. Federal Republic of Germany and Italy latter joined the Council of Europe. Ultimately, its membership increased to sixteen. The aim of the Council was to achieve a greater unity between its members for the purpose of safeguarding and realizing the ideals and principles which were their common heritage and facilitating their economic and social progress. The Council of Europe was consisted of a Council of Ministers and a Consultative Assembly, and in both of which all member-states were represented. The Council was not competent to make political decisions. It had no real political power, and perhaps little political importance, but, undoubtedly, it sowed the seeds of a greater European Union, which now becomes a reality.

United States-Soviet Union rivalry in post-war Europe, in the form of Cold

War, necessitated regional multinational strategic/military organizations. Concerned at growing communist menace in Europe, and its sustained political and military pressure on West Europe, necessarily made West European nations to seek for a greater strategic cooperation. The United States, which too felt the need for such an alliance to contain communism on the periphery of Europe, found a suitable ground to mobilize the West European nations, which were already apprehensive of the Communist threat. It was in this background that the North Atlantic Treaty Organization (NATO) was signed in Washington, in 1949, by the Benelux countries, viz., Denmark, France, Iceland, Italy, Norway, Portugal, United Kingdom, Greece, Turkey, United States, and Canada and Federal Republic of Germany were subsequently admitted to membership. (Fig. 14.2). The member-states pledged themselves to develop their power, both individual and collective, and to resist aggression, and they also agreed that an armed attack against one or more of them in Europe and North America shall be considered as against all of them, and thus they pledged to assist the victim of such attack and aggression. It has political objectives only—the security and well-being of the states which belong to it—which it pursues with the aid of the combined power of its fourteen members.

"The North Atlantic Treaty is more than a defensive alliance. By the very fact that member-states enjoyed the advantages of collective security, they could in terms of need focus their attention upon the development of their resources in a way that would have been impossible had each been compelled to act individually. Hence, the military organization has had considerable effect upon the Western European economy." However, France has withdrawn from the organization but still maintains certain ties with it under special provisions. The German Democratic Republic, which merged with the German Federal Republic in 1991-92, provided additional strength to the NATO.

In contrast to the NATO, which held considerable balance of power in Europe in its favour, the communist bloc or COMECON states in East Europe came out with the Warsaw Treaty Organization (WTO), known as the Warsaw Pact, signed in 1955, and dominated by the Soviet Union, just as the NATO, being dominated by the United States. The Warsaw Pact was a twenty-year defence treaty among the USSR, Albania, Bulgaria, Czechoslovakia, the German Democratic Republic, Hungary, Poland and Rumania. Yugoslavia soon left it. The Warsaw Pact was, in effect, a reaction to the admission of the German Federal Republic to the NATO. It allowed the presence of Soviet troops on satellite states' soils, and greatly increased the effectiveness of Soviet control (or witnessed by the rapid suppressions of the Hungarian-Polish uprisings in 1956, of the Czechoslovakian uprising in 1968, and also of another Polish uprising in 1981). The Warsaw Pact also improved the Soviet bargaining position in Europe. The Warsaw Pact was more effective than the COMECON, and it successfully contested the growing military power of the NATO on the soil of Europe.

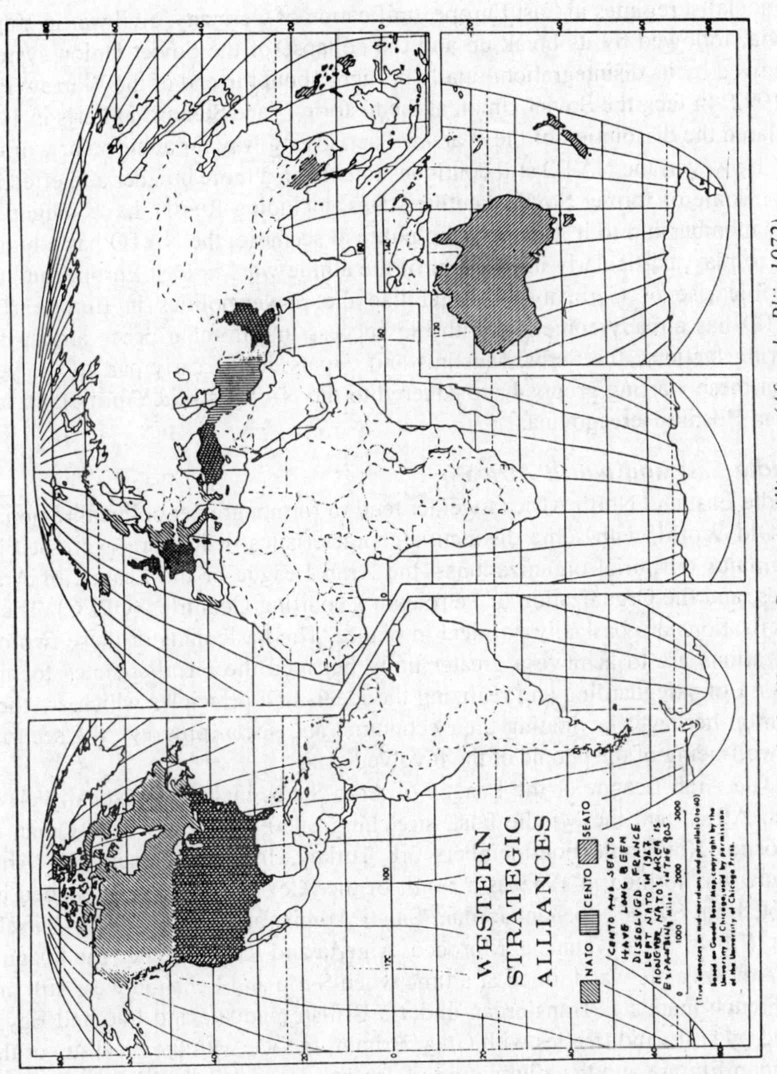

Figure 14.2: Western Strategic Alliances (After de Blij, 1972)

There was the 'balance of terror' in Europe, on account of the presence of the NATO and the Warsaw Pact, and all the time, throughout the period of Cold War, dark clouds of war loomed large over the continent. However, the fall of the socialist regimes in East Europe, unification of Germany, civil war in Yugoslavia, followed by its break-up and the collapse of the Soviet Union system, followed by its disintegration, finally brought about the end of the Warsaw Pact in 1992. In fact, the Soviet Union at the historic Peace Summit in Paris in 1991 declared the dissolution of the Warsaw Pact, giving way for a uni-polar world.

However, the NATO still continues to exist in a more broader and effective way. Some of former Soviet satellite states, including Russia, have sought for their membership to it. In a changed political scenario, the NATO has a bigger role to play, particularly in the light of the ethnic wars in East Europe, and the possible rise of Germany to destabilize the power-politics in Europe. The NATO has already come out with big success in enforcing peace among the warring factions: the Serbs, Muslims and Croats, in the early part of the year when these warring groups have adhered to the NATO's peace formula to end war in Bosnia-Hereegovina.

Middle East and North Africa

Middle East and North Africa together tend to form a greater political region in the Old World, with some distinctive characteristics, which are expressed by two major territorial organizations—the Arab League or the League of Arab States, and the Organization of Petroleum Exporting Countries (OPEC). These organizations are basically political in nature. The basic aims of these two organizations are to achieve a greater unity between the member-states for the purpose of safeguarding and realizing the ideals and principles which are their common heritage, facilitating their economic and social progress, the security and well-being of the people of the involved states.

The Arab League or the League of Arab States includes practically all of North Africa and the Middle East, stretching 8000 kilometres from Oman to Morocco. Noticeable non-members are Turkey, Iran and Israel. The Arab League was formed in 1945 as a result of the Alexandria Protocol, signed by Egypt, Iraq, Syria, Lebanan, Jordan, Saudi Arabia, and Yemen in 1945 itself. Later, Libya, Sudan, Tunisia, Morocco, Algeria and Kuwait joined the League. The Arab League was formed at a time when Syria and Lebanon were still under French mandate, Transjordan under a British mandate and Iraq and Egypt bound by still valid treaties with Great Britain. In fact, with the break-up of the Ottoman Empire and the elimination of Turkish control in the Middle East, the European colonial powers were put in charge of mandates over various parts of the Arab world, which necessarily strengthened the Pan-Arab movement.

To be sure, the establishment of the League with seven members in the years following World War II did not remove potential sources of discord between Arab states but it did provide a forum within which grievances could be considered and direct contacts between high level delegates might be made easier. The establishment of the Arab League was an event of great importance in the modern history of Arabs since it reflected their collective will to project the unanimity of their goals and destiny as one nation. It marked the emergence of a national framework for collective action at that time a remarkable achievement for the loosely knit Arab world.

The British and American were particularly impressive with the establishment of the League since the initiative was a purely Arab one. It was a response to a strong public desire for close inter-Arab cooperation and signalled a victory for moderate Arab nationalism. It was also a victory for secular liberalism in Arab thought. Pan-Islamism and the concept of the Great Arab Empire had lost their relevance, and cooperation and free association had replaced them. To this end, the Alexandria Protocol which had laid down the political, legal and institutional frameworks for the Arab League did not stress on union or federation, leaving it to individual governments to evolve stronger forms of association if they wished to in the future.

Following factors seemed to have played a significant role in the formation of the League, which included: (a) growing Arab solidarity with the Palestinian problem; (b) linguistic homogeneity of the Arabic language which is the language of Syria, Iraq, Jordan, and the Arabian states. It is the normal language of practically whole of North Africa, and it creates a strong bond for the Arabia regionalism; (c) common economic requirements of the Arab states; (d) the increasing role of Egypt in Arab affairs. Egypt was uniquely positioned for this because it had no territorial ambitions and was not involved in the dynastic rivalries that had resisted other unity attempts in the past; (e) growing liberal secularism; and (f) growing threat of Zionism (Israel). British policy-makers at the time who commanded considerable influence in the Arab world saw the virtues of dealing with the area an interrelated whole. The end of the war created a favourable climate for the promotions of economic regionalism.

In the fifty years since its formation, the League's membership has risen to 22 states, including the PLO which it considers the legitimate representative of the Palestinian people. It is often said that no union among Arab states has worked as well in such a broad range of areas as the League has. Though hopes for Arab unity are not likely to be realized in the near future, nevertheless, the League itself is a strong force to be reckoned with, in the Mediterranean region.

At a conference in Baghdad, in 1960, the Organization of Petroleum Exporting Countries (OPEC) formed. Originally comprised of Iran, Iraq, Kuwait, Saudi Arabia and Venezuela, it sought to provide a mechanism to deal with the multinational companies that controlled oil production and distribution in their countries. In fact, it was formed as a special interest group to promote greater economic and political returns from oil production. However, OPEC's membership was not completely regional, i.e., it is not limited to the Middle East and North Africa. Gabon and Nigeria are located in Central Africa, Indonesia in

South-East Asia and Venezuela and Ecuador in South America. Nevertheless, the Arab nations control the entire organization and decide its destiny, and the non-regional member-states simply follow them. OPEC is essentially an international cartel with a virtual monopoly of the surplus petroleum production of the world. It emerged as a dominant political force in international politics. Geopolitics in the Middle East is expressive of a conscious rivalry between the western core countries and the OPEC members of the Arab world and they wield considerable political power in the region to thwart any western move to destabilize them.

The OPEC's action to impose an oil embargo in 1973, on the supply of petroleum to western countries, including the United States, Canada and Japan, had an adverse impact on the economy of these western states for years.

The almost immediate increase in wealth and political prestige of its member-states, particularly of the Arab nations, has been one of the dominant stories of the present century. Its politics has been supportive of Third World policy to a considerable degree, in the wake of the core-periphery conflict, nevertheless some members of it are among the world's wealthiest on a per capita basis. The Arab OPEC members now wield considerable political influence in world politics.

Nevertheless, the 1991 Gulf War started simply because of one of the Arab OPEC members—Iraq—illegally occupied the territory of another Arab OPEC member—Kuwait—and threatened the integrity of Saudi Arabia—one of the founding members of the OPEC. These Arab states sought the help from the world community, and accordingly, the UN Security Council resolved for the military action against Iraq. For the first time, in the history of the Middle East politics, a substantial number of Arab OPEC member-states aligned with the NATO countries (core-periphery military alliance), in the war, against Iraq. The 1991 Gulf War has proved that quite a good number of Arab OPEC member-states are more inclined towards the United Sates and its European allies than with the local Arab states and they have developed bilateral relations with them.

However, much of the OPEC's political importance in world affairs has declined following the oil-boom in the North Sea, and the fall of communism in East Europe with Russia having gone to the fold of the western countries. This will facilitate uninterrupted supply of oil to the Atlantic and the Pacific coasts from the Russian oil fields. Such a situation in the coming years may cause a split in the OPEC. Nevertheless, there is no doubt that in a changed Eurasian political scenario, the six break-way oil-rich former Soviet republics may join the OPEC.

There was a multinational military organization in the Middle East. However, it was shortlived. Growing Soviet pressure and threat necessarily threatened the integrity of Turkey and Iraq in the late 1940s and early 1950s. In the absence of any viable military organization in the Middle East and the Mediterranean region, there was none to resist the Soviet access to the entire region. Concerned at the growing Soviet presence and pressure on their borders, Turkey and Iraq met in Baghdad in 1955 and signed a pact in which they pledged military assistance to one another in the defence of their territory. Iran and Pakistan also felt the need for such an inter-state military organization in the wake of the Soviet threat, and they joined the bilateral Baghdad organization, making it multilateral, in the same year. The objectives of the Baghdad Pact suited the United States' foreign policy requirements which were necessarily based on the principle of 'containment of communism". It gave an opportunity to the US and its allies, to hold on the Soviet expansion into the Middle West-Mediterranean region. The United States and United Kingdom joined the Baghdad Pact, and it came to be known as the Central Treaty Organization (CENTO) (Fig. 14.2). However, Iraq—one of the two founding members of treaty—withdrew from it and its headquarters was shifted to Ankara from Baghdad. It was a collective security system, aimed at resisting Soviet aggression. It also held to cooperate for their security and defence. It also sought to provide economic and technical assistance to the poor Arab signatory states. There was no doubt that the CENTO intensified Cold War in Middle East-Mediterranean region. The Soviet presence and pressure on the one hand, and the western presence (USA and UK) on the other hand to counter the Soviet pressure and vice versa, necessarily created a confused political situation for the local Arab states. They became divided among themselves, and were caught between conflicting interests of socialism/nationalism and capitalism/imperialism. S.B. Cohen (1973) called the region a 'shatterbelt'.

However, the CENTO did not continue for long, but, much before the cessation of the Cold War hostilities, it disappeared or the member-states abandoned it. It was, probably, because of the antagonism between the western partners and the Arab states that the military organization had to be abandoned. Moreover, the region experienced rapid Soviet influence at the expense of the western influence, and the western appeasement to Israel at the cost of the Arab sentiment, further deepened the crisis within the signatories of the treaty, which finally put down the organization. Turkey, then, sought for the membership of the NATO, and it was admitted to it. However, the CENTO was not completely regional, as it was also represented and by the United States, United Kingdom and Pakistan. Pakistan and Iran were non-Arab member-states, and Pakistan, particularly, was not a Middle East country. Similarly, the USA and UK belonged to Mackinder's 'Midland Basin', much away from the region. Nevertheless, the thrust of the CENTO was on the Middle East.

Africa

The 'Dark Continent' Africa did not remain isolated from the pan-movements that have occurred in various parts of the world since the end of the World War II. Here, in Africa, the Pan-African movement in the post-war period, necessarily, revealed the political forces, being polarized against colonialism and imperialism, and a political association of just-independent African states was a political compulsion. Very much modelled on the Council of Europe, the Organization of African Unity (OAU) was established in 1963 with thirty African states, with headquarters at Addis Ababa (Fig. 14.3). OAU, like the Arab League, was viewed optimistically as the embryo out of which an eventually all African governments may grow.

The main purpose of the OAU was to coordinate the policies of these states on certain vital political and economic issues. Foremost among these were the elimination of the last traces of colonialism and imperialism in Africa, safeguarding of the independence of member-states, and opposition to the White-dominated policies of South Africa and Rhodesia. In 1964 Cairo Summit meeting of the Organization of African Unity, all the member-states pledged to respect the borders existing upon achievement of independence. It has since successfully intervened in border disputes between Gabon and Equatorial Guinea, Guinea and Senegal, and Morocco and Algeria. In 1964 border clashes punctuated the Ethiopian-Somali dispute, but the OAU arranged a truce and which was followed by a mutual withdrawal of troops from the border.

Over a period of thirty years since its inception, the OAU has worked with many successes like those of installation of the Black nationalist governments in Zimbabve, Rhodesia, South Africa, liberation of Angola and Mozambique from Portuguese control, withdrawal of South Africans from Namibia (South-West Africa) and so on. It has contributed to the solution of many tribal and other problems, notably the problem of racial segregation (apartheid) and the Nigerian civil war, which were a part of the legacy of colonialism and imperialism. Elimination of White-domination in South Africa was, probably, the greatest achievement of the OAU.

In spite of its successes, the OAU has failed to contain intra-tribal violence in Angola, Somalia and Ruwanda where several lakh lives have already been perished. Nevertheless, the OAU now enjoys the unifying influence of anti-colonialism, but divisive elements have already appeared. While some wish to see the rapid implementation of a United States of Africa project, others desire to maintain their total sovereignty and are reluctant to enter political union. The argument is not entirely dissimilar from which attended the birth of the Council of Europe, and ultimately it goes back to the basic question of whether political unification should proceed or follow collaboration in other spheres. In view of the youthfulness of the participant states, the survival of the Organization of African Unity is matter for satisfaction on the part of those who want to see political divisions, barriers, and hindrances eliminated rather than strengthened.

Pan-Africanism in political sphere may have achieved some successes because of the interrelated nature of political phenomenon in the majority of the states in the continent. Pan-Africanism, in economic sphere, has had its visible impacts, because it has led to several inter-state economic organizations. Attempts to forge some degree of economic unity among states, however, has met with little success, primarily because their degree of economic interdependence

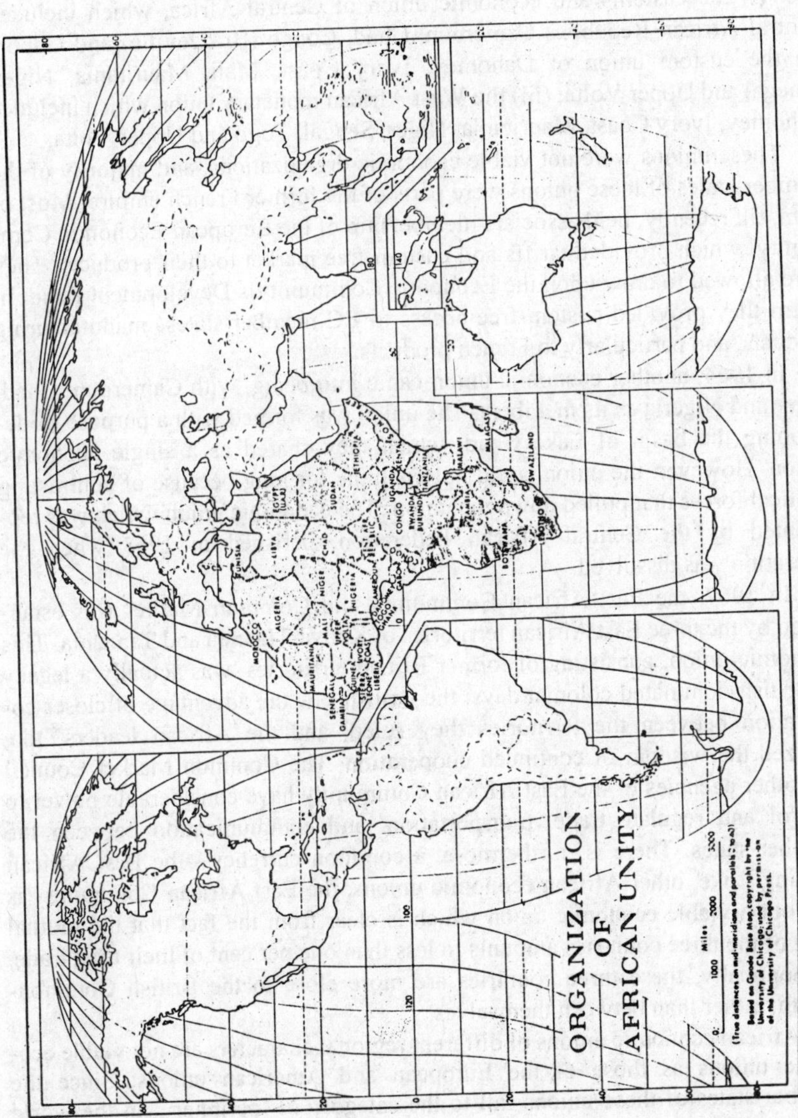

Figure 14.3: Organization of African Unity (After de Blij, 1972)

was slight. Three overlapping groups have emerged from the former French empire: (i) the customs and economic union of Central Africa, which included Central African Republics Cameroun, Chad, Congo (Brazzaville) and Gabon; (ii) the custom union of Dahomey, Ivory Coast, Mali, Mauritania, Niger, Senegal and Upper Volta; (iii) the West African monetary union which included Dahomey, Ivory Coast, Mauritania, Niger, Sengal, Togo and Upper Volta.

These unions were not viable economic organizations, and majority of the member-states of these unions were parts of the former French empire. Most of them, till recently, held associate membership of the European Economic Community, which provided tariffs and custom-free market to their products. They were allowed to draw upon the Economic Community's Development Fund. In return they provided custom-free access to EC member-states' manufacturing products, and particularly to French products.

In 1964, another economic union came into being, with Cameroun, Chad, Niger and Nigeria as its membeis. The union was formed with a purpose of developing the basin of Lake Chad, which they shared as a single economic region. However, the union could not continue for long because of contrasting political forces that pulled down the union. The economic union which was represented by the Central African Federation, perished in 1963 when the federation was dissolved.

In 1967, the East African Community and Common Market was established by the three East African territories of Kenya, Uganda and Tanzania. This economic union, consisting of former British territories, was actually a legacy of British-dominated colonial days; the British saw the advantage of closer cooperation between the territories they ruled, and the African leaders, too, realized the wisdom of continued cooperation. The Common Market Council and other agencies of the East African Community have considerable power to control and regulate trade, transportation, and communication between the member-states. There is, furthermore, a common currency—the East African Shilling. Like, other African economic unions, the East African Community is also not a viable economic union which is clear from the fact that the mutual trade of the three countries amounts to less than one per cent of their total trade. Economically, these three countries are more close to the British Commonwealth, rather than between themselves.

African economic unions of different regional characters are not viable economic unions as those of the European and American unions. Since the member-states of these unions fall to the category of 'periphery' in the world economy, much of their survival intrinsically, depends on the core-states and their unions, spreading over different continents. They are more closely interwined with the extra-African unions, rather than among themselves.

Asia

It is interesting to observe that the continent of Asia does not have political association or organization of continental dimension like those of the European Union, Organization of African Union and Organization of American States. The absence of a large political association of continental dimension in Asia may be attributed to the presence of mutually exclusive nature of interrelated political phenomena, which necessarily restrict the move for a greater political cooperation, union and association. It is only in the 'Asiatic Rimland' of West Asia, South Asia and South-East Asia that a few regional unions or organizations have come up in the post-war period. Since the Asiatic Rimland was a part of the European colonial empires for a long period that it inherited the colonial heritage of cooperation and association, while vast areas of interior Asia and north of the Himalayas remained isolated and separated from European influences for greater part of the history.

West Asia, South Asia and South-East Asiatic Rimlands, with their maritime location, offered greater flexibility towards regional cooperation. One of the reasons of regional cooperation was that of the sustained political pressure from the communist forces, and the other being, the regional impoverishment.

One of the earliest regional cooperations that came to be developed in the post-war period in South and South-East Asia was that of the 'Colombo Plan' which was meant for the cooperative economic development of the region. The draft for the Colombo Plan was prepared in 1950 with the object to pursue in South-East Asia the same kind of objectives that the OEEC (Organization for European Economic Cooperation) had in Europe. A group of South-East Asian and South Asian countries, comprising British Borneo, Cambodia, Laos, Malaysia, India, Pakistan and Ceylone, met in Colombo in 1950 and signed the treaty for the cooperative economic development of the region. Some more countries joined the plan which included Vietnam, Burma and Nepal in 1952, Indonesia in 1953, and Japan, the Philippines and Thailand in 1954. The countries that represented the Colombo Plan were confronted with the problems of low standards of living, inadequate capital, insufficient mechanical and scientific skills, and a population that was growing faster than agricultural production. Japan's economy was ruined and devastated by the World War II. All these countries were impoverished states and had experienced colonial administration and exploitation for centuries. There was imminent danger of the communist coup in these states, as the communist influence was rapidly progressing there.

Concerned at the growing communist influence in the political life of these impoverished states of South and South-East Asia, prompted the United States, United Kingdom, Australia, Canada and New Zealand to become members of the Colombo Plan and to share their economic burden. The first two were the principal source of capital investment and technical assistance. The object of this association of the developed states was to ensure that widest use should be made available of capital and resources in raising the level of welfare of as many people as possible so that, they might not fall in the hands of communism.

However, the Colombo Plan sought to remedy the impoverished situation by raising the output of both agriculture and industry by improving the technical level of agriculture and the industrial development. As these undertakings required heavy capital investment and technical assistance, which the regional states were unable to provide, and naturally, help came from the United States, primarily. However, to a small extent, the Asiatic members of the Colombo Plan also helped one another in matters of technical assistance and expertise.

"The Colombo Plan was primarily economic, like the OEEC and its successor OEDC, but it too had political overtones. Higher productivity and welfare were conceived of an means of achieving greater political stability. Overtly, it was not drawn up in terms of the East-West conflict. Indeed, some of its members, notably Burma, Indonesia, Nepal and perhaps India, were neutralist in their political outlook. It was generally supposed, however, that the ability of the communists to create trouble in South-East Asia varied inversely with the trend in the level of human welfare in that area, and the Colombo Plan aimed to raise this level. The Colombo Plan was also paralleled by a strategic-military organization, called the South-East Asia Collective Defence Treaty.

The South-East Asia Collective Défence Treaty or South-East Asia Treaty Organization (SEATO) was a strategic-military organization, based on South-East Asia, and South-West Pacific area not including north of 21° 30°N, like those of the NATO and the CENTO. The SEATO also formed a part of the grand political strategy of the containment of communism in the Asia-Pacific region that the western world undertook in the post-war period. By a treaty signed at Manila in 1954, Pakistan, Thailand and the Philippines, together with Asutralia, New Zealand, and three other states with military and strategic interests in the Asia-Pacific region, viz., the United States, United Kingdom and France, established South-East Asia Collective Defence Treaty or the SEATO (Fig. 14.2). The parties to the treaty each acknowledged "that aggression... in the treaty area against any of the parties...would endanger its own peace and safety, and agreed that they would take joint action. The United States added the condition that its obligations were limited to resisting communist aggression".

A number of factors seemed to have necessitated the urgency of a collective defence treaty in the Asia-Pacific region which included, besides other factors, constant Chinese threat on South and South-East Asia following British withdrawal, an increase in the area of operation of the Warsaw Pact with communist China becoming a partner to the Pact, and the Vietnam War in which France was involved with the Vietcong guerrillas. There is no doubt that the SEATO had some initial successes in containing communist threats in the region. But, soon its weakness was revealed when Laos and Cambodia fell to the communist pressure and it could not resist it. The communists, then, loomed large over Burma and Thailand. Occupation of substantial part of Ladakh by China in Jammu & Kashmir not only did threaten the integrity of India, but also Pakistan.

The communist influence was increasing rapidly in South-East Asia. As a matter of fact, these small impoverished nations of the region were caught between two contrasting and conflicting interests of the two contemporary super powers, making them divided and politically unstable. In S.B. Cohen's model of world's political pattern, South-East Asia was shown to be a 'shatterbelt'.

The core-periphery military alliance in South-East Asia and South-West Pacific region could not survive long. It failed to protect the integrity of Pakistan in the 1971 war, but its end came when it lost the long battle to the communist forces in Vietnam. It was a personal victory of the Vietcong guerrillas over the US forces, which replaced the French armies in the 1960s. Liberation of Bangladesh and unification of Vietnam were the two major political events in South-East Asia in the early 1970s, which finally led to the collapse of the South-East Asia Collective Defence Treaty or the SEATO. With the fall of the SEATO, came the end of the Colombo Plan.

It was widely believed that the defeat of the American forces, followed by the fall of South Vietnam, would have a 'domino effect' resulting in the fall of successive governments in South-East Asia. Subsequently, Malaysia, Singapore, Indonesia, Thailand, and the Philippines formed the Association of

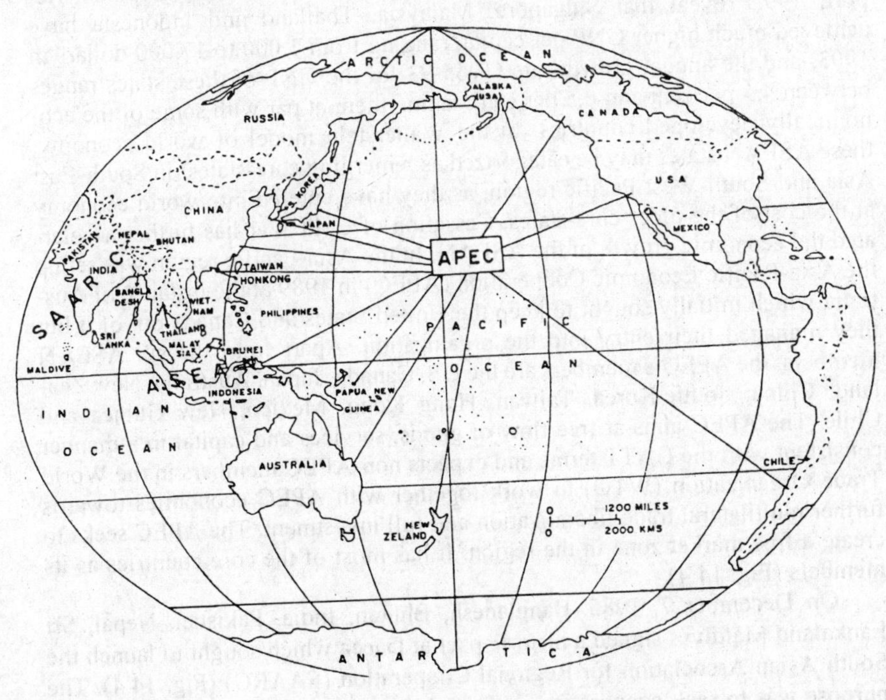

Figure 14.4: SAARC-ASEAN-APEC

South-East Asian Nations (ASEAN) in 1967. Brunei was allowed entry into it in the late eighties. Vietnam has joined the ASEAN while Laos and Kampuchia would be inducted into it very soon. However, the ASEAN member-states are looking forward to Myanmar, becoming a member of it. It is just possible that Myanmar may attain membership earlier than Laos and Kampuchia (Fig. 14.4). Gradually, this regional association grew into prominence. The ASEAN has become one of the political realities of the region. Its members have gained sufficient confidence to feel that they could work cooperatively with the local communist states and also with the erstwhile European and North American members of the Colombo Plan. South-East Asia is no longer a 'shatterbelt' because the forces that used to divide and create political instability to the states of the region have largely disappeared. Moreover, conflicting interests of the super powers have also ceased to influence them. The ASEAN is now a stable political and economic association, and attracts investment from the core countries. The European union has sought for a greater economic cooperation with it. The United States of America has entered into an agreement with the member-states of the ASEAN while China has recognized its political and economic viability in the region, and has sought for a greater economic cooperation with it.

The Asian Development Outlook, 1994 and the World Development Report, 1992 reveal that Singapore, Malaysia, Thailand and Indonesia have achieved much higher GNP per capita, ranging from 1,000 to 17,000 dollars in 1993, and the annual growth rate (1965-93) of the GNP of these states ranges between 4.5 per cent and 6.5 per cent, taking them at par with some of the economically developed countries. In the Wallerstein model of world economy, these ASEAN states may be categorized as 'emerging core-states' in South-East Asia and South-West Pacific region, as they have entered into world economy at the cost of the older core-states. Cessation of Cold War has further accelerated the economic growth of the ASEAN. In the Asia-Pacific region was set up the Asia-Pacific Economic Cooperation (APEC) in 1989 at the instance of Australia which initially sought to keep the United States and Canada out of it but they managed their entry into the organization. Apart from the six ASEAN members, the APEC's members are the US, Canada, Japan, Australia, New Zealand, China, South Korea, Taiwan, Hong Kong, Mexico, New Guinea and Chile. The APEC aims at free flow of goods, services and capital in a manner consistent with the GATT terms and expects non-APEC members in the World Trade Organization (WTO) to work together with APEC economies towards further multilateral trade liberalization and full investment. The APEC seeks to create a free market zone in the region. It has most of the core countries as its members (Fig. 14.4).

On December 7, 1985, Bangladesh, Bhutan, India, Pakistan, Nepal, Sri Lanka and Maldives signed a historic pact at Dacca which sought to launch the South Asian Association for Regional Cooperation (SAARC) (Fig. 14.4). The purpose was to seek cooperation in the field of telecommunications, meteorology, shipping, infrastructure, agricultural rural sector, joint ventures, scientific and technical fields, market promotion in some selected commodities, education and technical fields and also in cultural fields. The SAARC aims to provide a new impetus to the concept of a collective self-reliance in the region.

The SAARC is yet to emerge as an alternative viable to the ASEAN in the Asiatic Rimland because of inherent inner contradictions among the members-states. With regard to the scope of cooperation, there exists considerable confusion among the member-states. While Sri Lanka, Maldives and Pakistan, on the one hand, want it to be more comprehensive, including vital economic and political issues, India and Bangladesh, on the other hand, want it to concentrate on the economic cooperation only. On the issue of the institutionalization, Bhutan, Nepal, Sri Lanka and Bangladesh are in favour of institutionalized co-operation while India, Pakistan and Maldives want the development must be preceded by a greater regional cooperation. There are more centrifugal forces in the SAARC than centripetal forces. It is more akin to the African unions and associations as the mutual trade between the member-states of the associations is much below than what was anticipated at the time of its formation.

Per capita GNP of India, Pakistan, Bangladesh and Sri Lanka, particularly, ranges between 225 dollors and 564 dollors and the annual growth rate (1965-93) of GNP of these SAARC states ranges between 0.9 per cent and 3.0 per cent, according to the Asian Development Outlook, 1994. These statistics, therefore, tend to reveal that the SAARC states continue to be in the category of periphery in world economy. Sri Lanka may go in for the ASEAN membership and Pakistan may simply quit it. India is trying for both the ASEAN and/or APEC but not at the cost of the SAARC.

Recently representatives of Pakistan, Iran, Afghanistan and six break-way Muslim republics of former Soviet Union have met the at Islamabad, Pakistan to discuss modalities of an economic union, very much on the model of ASEAN. The purpose of the proposed union would be a greater economic cooperation and integration which may facilitate economic and social progress in the member-states. Nevertheless, the objective of the proposed non-Arab Muslim union is political, and when it comes true, it will then endanger the *raison d'etre* of the SAARC, which is India-dominated.

However, the ASEAN-APEC cooperation in the Asia-Pacific world is ushering in a new era of peace and stability in the region, and is designed to ensure freedon in the regional states. But if the SAARC is drawn into the ASEAN-APEC cooperation, then it will set forth a new paradigm for a sustainable global peace (Adhikari, 1995).

Americas

Americas, though geographically much isolated, from the Old World and World-island, have long traditions of territorial associations/unions based on 'hemispheric perception'. This 'hemispheric perception' had its origin in the famous 'Monroe Doctrine' which US President Monroe spelt out in 1823 that:

"We owe to it...to candor and to the amicable relations existing between the United States and those powers (of Europe) to declare that we should consider any attempt on their part to extend their system to any portion of this hemisphere as dangerous to our peace." It was this hemispheric perception, arising out of strategic reasons, had led to the movement for the Pan-American unity in the last century. American republics were not only scared of the European involvement in their areas but also apprehensive of the United States' interest in Latin America. The republics felt the need of a greater political unity which would possibly balance the growing influence of any country, individually strong enough, to make decisions and implement them as in Latin America.

It was not only the political necessity of the Latin American republics to seek for a greater political association/union and unity, but also the common heritage of the Spanish language and culture which brought them together on a common platform. However, Brazil is Portuguese-influenced, and therefore, closely related in these respects. The cultural ties between the Latin American republics were thus strong, but their territorial disputes were also vigorous. Though, the process towards a greater regional association started in the mid-ninetieth century, but, it was not until the republics dispelled the fear of the US involvement in the Latin America. That the regional cooperation really acquired some *raison d'etre* of a reasonable dimension.

As a matter of fact, the United States itself took the initiative, because it proved to be the strongest trading and investment partner to most of them. The United States, as a matter of fact, desired to maintain peace between the Latin American republics themselves, with a view to ward off territorial disputes between the republics. The Pan-American Union developed out of the 1890 Washington Conference aimed at greater unity. The Conference proposed for a custom union but that could not come up. However, one of its first acts was to create an International Union of the American Republics, with a central office to handle its affairs. However, the achievements of the successive conferences of the American states and republics lay rather in the field of improving their relations with one another, of setting their own internal disputes, and of improving conditions for trade. There was more antagonism toward the United States at the conferences held earlier in the twentieth century.

Certain developments, such as economic depression, worsening international situations, the failure of attempts at disarmament, and the lack of market facilities to Latin American tropical products, necessarily, compelled the republics and states, to abandon hostile attitude to the United States, at the Montevideo Conference in 1933. By the time of the Conference in 1933, the United States had consolidated its position as an American core country, with global economic and strategic obligations, and the 'peripheral' Latin American republics found in the United States, a saviour to their *raison d'etre*. The possibility of German-Italian intrigues in Latin America was a matter of grave concern and it was assumed in the Latin American circle that if Germany and Italy succeeded in controlling the European continent, the broad Atlantic was not really broad enough to give complete protection to the New World, and a greater cooperation, among the republics, including the United States, was the only remedy.

Political events, in and around the World-Island, before and after the outbreak of the Second World War, compelled the American republics to seek for a tighter union than they had ever known before. At the Havana Conference, republics and states renounced the transfer of any non-independent territory in the New World from the possession of one European power to that of another. In other words, British and French possessions shall not be allowed to pass into German and Italian control. However, the US preeminence was established after the World War II and it took active part in the reconstruction of the global economy which was ruined and shattered in the war, particularly in the Old World, and the formation of the OEEC, with the US aid was an example.

Post-war changes in the world, with the communist threat looming large over the Western Hemisphere, necessarily brought the American states and republics much closer to one another. It was at the Bogota Conference in 1948 that the Organization of the American States (OAS) was formed (Fig. 14.5). All American republics, including the United States, Mexico, Banana republics of Central America, the Caribbean states, and the Latin American republics, that existed at that date became the members of the OAS. However, Canada, on account of its obligations with British Commonwealth, did not join the OAS, and Cuba disassociated itself from the organization, because of its anti-US communist orientation. However, the OAS members have long declared sanction against Cuba. Once in 1961, during the great missile crisis in the Caribbean, the possibility of the OAS members' involvement became inevitable, but the crisis was somehow diffused with the withdrawal of the Soviet warships.

Over the past few decades, since its inception in 1948, the OAS has grown into a much stronger and tighter political, economic, social and cultural union in the Atlantic-Pacific regions. Hardly, there is any regional association or union in the world of such an inter-continental and hemispheric dimension as of the OAS. Some of the OAS members of Latin America, such as Chile, Argentina and Brazil, can, now, be put into the category of 'semi-periphery' in world economy, as they have made their economies partially global, as a result of sustained economic growths in their respective areas.

In economic regionalization, the Latin American republics did not lag behind their Old World counterparts. The first of this kind was that of the Central American Common Market (ODECA), which came into being in December 1960. It was comprised of El Salvador, Guatemala, Honduras (which has since withdrawn) and Nicaragua. These were subsequently joined by Costa Rica. The ODECA sought for closer economic ties between the member-states which

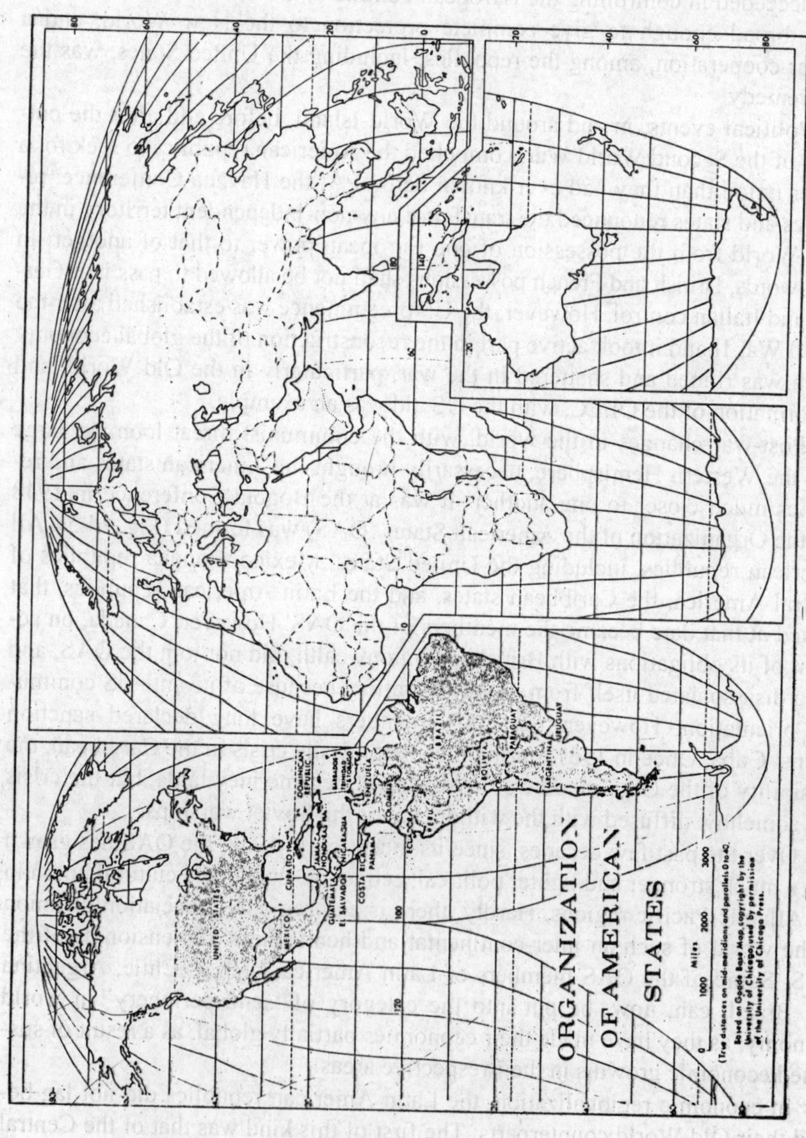

Figure 14.5: Organization of American States (After de Blij, 1972)

could facilitate economic development in the region as a whole. A General American Bank was set up to facilitate the movement of investment capital. But, the ODECA met the same fate as those of other economic unions in the 'periphery', that it could not become a viable economic union. The member-states were so similar in resources and nature of development that their mutual trade was relatively small in volume.

The Latin American Free Trade Association (LAFTA) was formed in 1961 by an association of Argentina, Brazil, Chile, Mexico, Paraguay, Peru, and Uruguay and later joined by Colombia, Ecuador and Venezuela, and some more states. It sought to create a custom free union of Latin American republics, and to remove trade and tariffs restrictions on the movement of commodities within the union. The LAFTA also sought to increase production and a higher level of welfare, notwithstanding the small volume of mutual trade between the member-states. However, the United States has provided substantial aids and loans and other forms of assistance to the association, so that the member-states could achieve sustain economic growth. Land reform, tax reform, improvement in agricultural infrastructure and increase in industrial growth, check on inflation and population control, were a part of the duties of the recipients states of the association. In spite of the massive US aid, the LAFTA could not achieve substantial economic growth, than its European counterpart, the European Community. Drug-trafficing is the major concern for the LAFTA countries, which probably put the major hindrances to its effectiveness. Nevertheless, the LAFTA is the only major economic association in Southern Hemisphere.

Recently, the North American Free Trade Association (NAFTA) has been formed, with the United States, Canada and Mexico, as its members. The basic purpose of the NAFTA is to maintain a custom union, and to put tariffs and trade restrictions on the movement of certain Japanese and European commodities, entering North America. It has been found that in the last few years, the North American market has been flooded with the Japanese and European products, and which have adversely affected the economic growth of the member-states, particularly of the USA. The NAFTA is a vital economic necessity for the United States, particularly, because its global role, as an impregnable core country, is at stake. Nevertheless, NAFTA will maintain greater economic ties with Japan and European Union, rather than, with LAFTA.

Intercontinental Associations

Apart from regional associations and organizations, there are associations spreading across different continents or over vast areas of the globe. These associations are based on cultural and social ties of sufficient strength to unit nations that are quite diverse. These associations and organizations are highly multinational in character. They are designed to promote unity, share information and funds, and foster strength. Contemporary values seem to favour economic interests as a major uniting force for such intercontinental association. Many associations of intercontinental dimension existed in the past, but the more significant ones presently functioning have grown out of the empires of former colonial powers such as the Commonwealth and the French Community.

Commonwealth

Among the World's most enduring and successful international association of nations is the Commonwealth. It has been created out of the vast colonial empire of Britain. Indeed, the British Empire of Elizabeth's great grandmother Victoria, at its peak size in 1900, covered more than one-quarter of the earth's land surface, and at that time the British had already lost the United States. This enormous Empire has gradually and remarkably, peacefully been transformed into a loose association of free and independent nations — the Commonwealth of Nations. Peaceful devolution of the Empire actually began in the nineteenth century when the British feared that, unless granted local autonomy, the Empire's Canadian provinces might follow the secessionist example set by the United States in 1776. In the process, the dominion of Canada was launched in 1867, and system of home rule soon followed in Australia, New Zealand, New Foundland and South Africa.

The Imperial Conference of 1926 defined Great Britain and these dominions as "autonomous communities within the British Empire, equal in status, in no way subordinate, one to another in any aspect of their domestic or foreign affairs, though united by a common allegiance to the Crown, and freely associated as members of the British Commonwealth Nations".

The 1926 Imperial Conference formally brought the organization into being. However, the 1931 Statute of Westminister legally recognized the status of the dominions as defined in 1926. Since World War II, the Commonwealth has grown steadily as the British Empire has shrunk. Almost every former British colony freely retained Commonwealth association upon receiving independence and most have remained members. However, Burma, which became independent in 1948, did not join the Commonwealth. The Irish republic severed its relationship in 1949. South Africa withdrew in 1961 because of criticism of her racial policy. Pakistan withdrew in 1972, protesting against Britain's policy during the Indo-Pak War in 1971. However, Bangladesh which gained independence, subsequently became a member of it. Now, both South Africa and Pakistan are reseeking for their membership to the Commonwealth (Fig. 14.6).

Today, Commonwealth represents one-fourth of earth's population. Most of the Commonwealth nations have become republics, but Queen Elizabeth remains head of state in eleven of them besides Britain. It is multiracial and multinational in character as it has representatives on several continents that existed prior to the post-war period of decolonization, and now incorporates many of the countries that waged a struggle for independence from the British. Despite this struggle, most emergent, British-influenced availed themselves of the opportunity to join the Commonwealth, and the full-scale participation of such

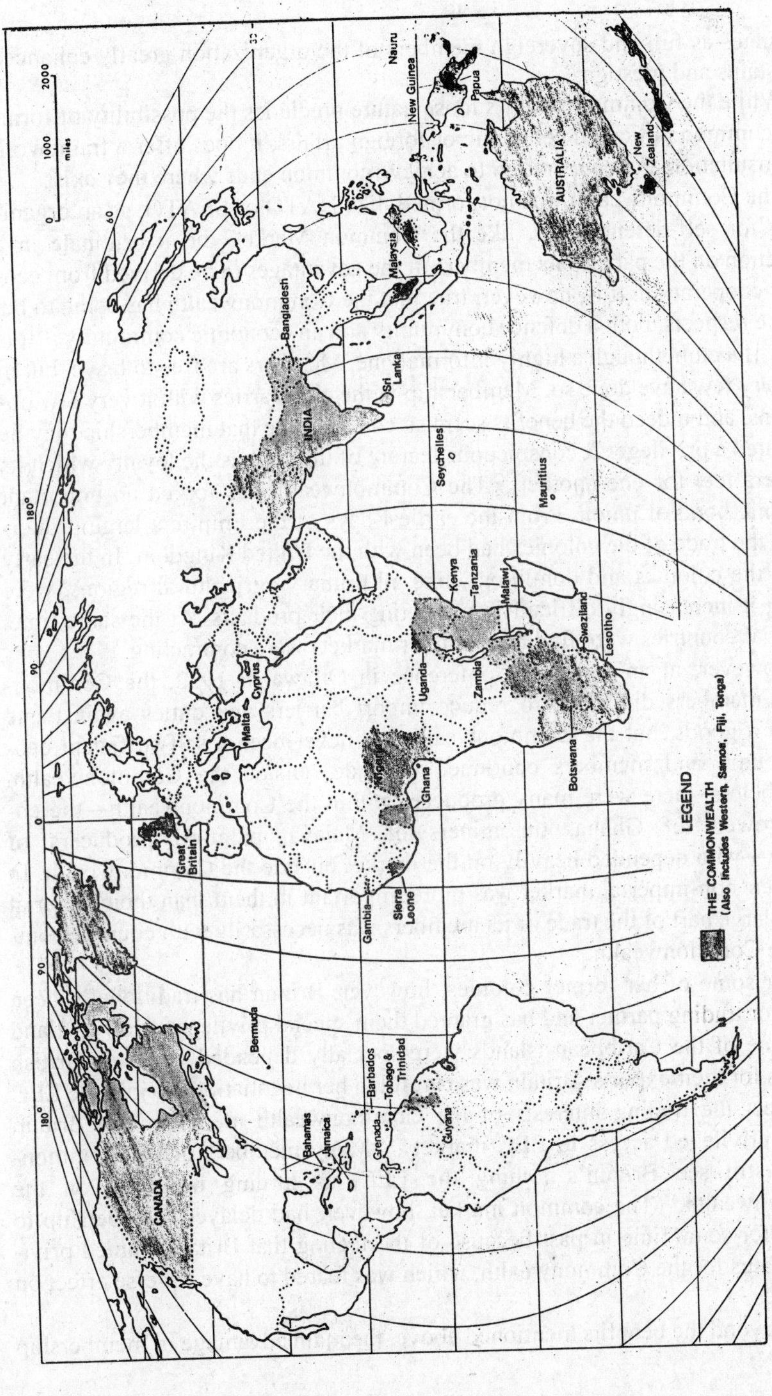

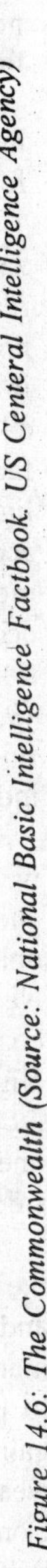

Figure 14.6: The Commonwealth (Source: National Basic Intelligence Factbook, US Centeral Intelligence Agency)

new states as full and sovereign members of the organization greatly enhanced their status and prestige.

While the Commonwealth's loose nature precludes the possibility of forming a common policy on economic or foreign affairs, it does offer a framework for consultation and cooperation to achieve common ends where they exist.

The Commonwealth was not formed, like NATO or SEATO, as an organization for self-defence, nor, like the Common Market, did it originate in a realization on the parts of its members of the advantages to be derived from economic cooperation. It is, however, true that the Commonwealth has come to be, in some respects, both a defence community and an economic community. "It is a kind of a club, though a highly informal one. Members are free to leave, but in fact, very few have done so. Membership in the club carries with it very few obligations, and indeed the benefits seem so considerable that membership may be accounted a privilege. A conspicuous feature of this club is the loyalty which its members feel for one another... The Commonwealth has forged an important economic bond of union. From the earliest days of the Empire a large proportion of the trade of the colonies had been with the United Kingdom. In the early 1930s, the colonies and dominions, like all primary agricultural regions, were finding it increasingly difficult in marketing their products. At the same time, industrial countries were finding that their markets were contracting".

However, at an Imperial Conference in Ottawa in 1932, the Commonwealth members did agree to reduce import barriers and duties against one another's goods, but the Commonwealth has never been a self-sufficient economic unit, and members continued to trade outside the Commonwealth. Nevertheless, there were many producers within the Commonwealth—the cocoa growers of Ghana, tin miners of Malaya, palm-oil producers of Nigeria—who depended heavily on the market outside the Commonwealth. In fact, their non-imperial market was more important to them than their imperial one. A large part of the trade of its members was necessarily with countries outside the Commonwealth.

For some of her former colonies, however, Britain has traditionally been the major trading partner and has granted them special privileges. New Zealand and some of the Caribbean islands were specially depended upon the British markets for their exports. Britain was careful in her negotiations to join the EEC to protect the trading interests of the Commonwealth members and Britain gained privileged access to EEC markets. "Many members of the Commonwealth still see Britain's joining the EEC, as turning her back on the Commonwealth." The common market, however, had delayed membership to Britain for some time in past because of the feeling that Britain wanted privileged status for the Commonwealth, which was feared to have adverse effect on the EEC.

"Beyond the benefits mentioned above, the main advantage of membership in the Commonwealth remains the association with a large body of nations that hold many similar values. Through the framework of committees and delegations, members are in constant contact with each other, exchanging ideas and information. It is not intended that every act of every member will meet the approval of the others, but rather a general concern for the common good will prevail. There is some basis or the belief that, in their quest for international co-operation, other states can learn from the Commonwealth."

The *raison d'etre* of the Commonwealth is the long tradition of historic association, during which certain British imprints were made, through the spread of the English language, in the social and political lives of peoples with diverse geographical character, over a wide and vast areas of the habitable space of the earth's surface. It has brought together nations that are quite diverse under a common sustainable system.

French Community

The French Community is another intercontinental association/organization, of relatively less diverse in nature, and built on the remnants of an empire (Fig. 14.7). France built up one empire in the seventeenth and eighteenth centuries, but lost most of that empire in her eighteenth century rivalry with England. Dur-

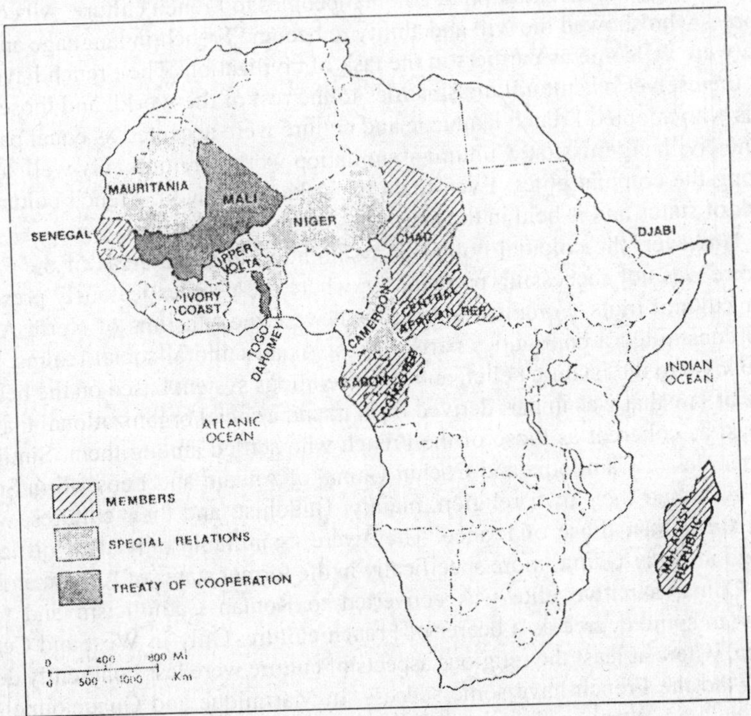

Figure 14.7: The French Community in Africa in 1960

ing the nineteenth century, France built up a second, beginning with the occupation of Algeria in 1830 and culminating in 1919 with the assumption of mandates in Syria, Togoland and the Cameroun.

While Britain's motives for building her empire were often unclear even to herself. France more single-mindedly used the material resources and man-power of her colonies to enhance French power—especially in competition with Germany. France's use of Senegalese troops to occupy the Ruhr in 1923 stingingly emphasized this to Germany.

As compared to the British Empire, the French Empire was more organized and centrally directed. While the British encouraged regionalism in their colonies, the French preferred unified direction from Paris. Political evolution for the British meant eventual independence from London; for the French it meant affiliation with Frenchmen in equal representation in the metropolitan government. French colonial policy reflected French dedication to equality and fraternity, if not to liberty. Segregation was nowhere allowed, and race and colour were never criteria for voting rights or for positions of responsibility.

The greatest boon which France could possibly impart to her colonial territories was, in her opinion, to give them French culture and civilization. The French policy thus became one of 'assimilations'. In fact, fraternity was emphasized through the assimilation of colonial peoples to French culture. All colonial peoples who showed the will and ability to become French in language and custom were welcome as partners in the task of civilization. The French have long felt themselves as cultural missionaries to the rest of the world, and those colonials who adopted French language and culture were accepted as equal partners in the civilizing mission. Cultural assimilation worked remarkably well, at least among the colonial elites. Even today in Dakar or Saigon, French culture is a mark of status and is held in the highest esteem.

However, the colonial policy of assimilation in some areas of the French Empire was not successful, particularly, where the peoples jealously preserved their cultural traits. Foremost among them were the Muslims of North Africa, who constituted a contiguous part of West Asian cultural-social realms. They were loyal to the Islamic belief, and had a religious system based on the belief, a code of law that was in part derived from it, and a social organizational that was at least as coherent as those of the French who settled among them. Similarly, the peoples of Cambodia and Cochin-China, of Annam and Laos, all in South-East Asia had their own religion, mainly, Buddhist, and their cultures, which were older than those of France. They were assimilable only with difficulty, though in 'Indo-China' more specifically in the former states of Annam and Cochin-China, a native elite was converted to Roman Catholicism and today serves in some degree as a bearer of French culture. Only in West and Central Africa, where at least the religious aspects of culture were less coherently developed, did the French have some success. In Martinique and Guadeloupe also, there was no effective indigenous culture—the Negroes were immigrants like the French themselves— to compete with that which the French brought with them.

Thus, the French, politically, attempted to govern their empire in as highly centralized a manner as in France itself. The French conceived of the empire as forming one political and economic unit, so that the subject peoples would politically mature not to independence but, rather, to fuller representation to the government in Paris.

However, the failure to the process of assimilation led the French government to establish in 1946 the French Union—'Union Francaise'—a centralized and uniformly governed empire.The Union consisted of metropolitan France and its overseas departments plus the associated territories. The Head of the Union was the President of France and the Union's political machinery also included a High Council and an Assembly. This highly centralized scheme collapsed under the pressure of the wars for independence in Algeria and Indo-China, and when Charles de Gaulle assumed the Presidency of France in 1958 he proposed replacing the French Union with a new French Community—'La Communaute Francaise'. Though less centralized than the organization it replaced, the Community resembled a very streamlined Commonwealth. To some extent, it was a conscious move in the direction of the latter, but without the Commonwealth's capacity to adapt itself to every shade of local circumstances. The French Constitution of 1958 described the Community as follows:

Title XII "On the Community":

Article 77. "In the Community instituted by the present Constitution, the States shall enjoy autonomy; they shall administer themselves and manage their own affairs democratically and freely."

Article 78. "The Community's jurisdiction shall extend over foreign policy, defense, currency, common economic and financial policy, as well as over policy on strategic raw materials. It shall include...the supervision of tribunals, higher education, the general organization of external transportation...as well as telecommunication..."

Article 80. "The President of the (French) Republic shall preside over and represent the community..."

Article 82. "The Executive Council of the Community shall be presided over by the President of the Community. It shall consist of the Premier of the Republic, the heads of Government of each of the member states of the Community and the ministers responsible for the common affairs of the Community."

With the exception of Guinea, which voted against the proposed association with France and terminated all ties to France in 1959. However, France's

African colonies approved the Community structure in individual referenda. But as these African states proclaimed independence and became members of the United Nations, it became clear already by 1960 that little was left of political ties in the community. These newly-independent African states continued to rely on France for economic aid, however, allowed only for either full association in the community or else total severance of links, had to be amended to allow for independence with community membership.

Article 86 of the French Constitution was amended from:

"...a member State of the Community may become independent, it shall thereby cease to belong to the Community to:

"...a member State of the Community can likewise become independent through a special agreement, without ceasing to belong to the Community."

The Community

President of the Community

Executive Council

Court of Arbitration Senate of the Community

Members

A. The French Republic
   1. The 90 Departments of France
   2. Overseas Departments (French Guiana, Renunion, Guadaloupe, Martinquel)
   3. Overseas Territories (St. Pierre, Miquelon, Oceania, Afars and Issas, New Caledonia, the Comoros)

B. Member States

   Republics: Upper Volta, Dahomey, Ivory Coast, Mali, Mauritania, Senegal, Niger, Chad, Central Africa, Gobon, Congo, Malagasy

C. Associated States

   None

Problems have continued to plague the French Community, but they are perhaps inevitable in an association of one highly developed state (core to the world economy) with several weak and poor ones (periphery to the world economy). The subordinate members generally criticize France for lack of generosity, accuse France of using the association for her own ends, and suspect that the political formula has served simply to preserve French colonialism. Also, the association with France has left the rulers of being more Francophile than nationalistic. If the organization and operation of the community favoured France they would clearly be unacceptable to African nationalists, and yet France would not accept being dictated by a majority of peripheral African states. The popularity of General de Gaulle was important to the cohesion of the Community, but this personal element was necessarily more temporary than, for instance, the English Crown as the symbol of the Commonwealth. De Gaull's successor George Pompidou visited several African Community members which still value their cultural ties to France, but economic links between France and Africa are increasingly bound up in the question and arrangements of EEC (now European Union) links with the African states. These African states will enjoy, as it appears, some economic privileges in European Unions as Britain has secured some concessions to protect the trading interests of the Commonwealth states in the Union.

Apart from the economic benefits that the African members of the Community enjoy, there is a large measure of security. The structure of the French system allows it to move relatively fast to protect allies. In 1978, the Community troops were sent to Mauritania, Senegal, Ivory Coast, Gabon and Chad—all ex-colonies. There also was evidence that the Community may intend to fill the vacuum left by the Belegians in the Congo. In 1978, France quickly sent troops into Zaire, the former Belgian colony, to repulse an invasion from neighbouring Angola. Thus, the French Community extended its military power into a non-community state to counter the military invasion of a communist neighbour attempting to expand in the area of another international 'world'. Today, the Community is basically a contractual system of interlocking alliances rather than a formal organization.

The fundamental difference between the Commonwealth and the French Community is that the former is global in nature and is stable, while the latter is confined only to Africa, that too, and there is a high degree of instability in it. The Commonwealth now consists of some older and emerging core-states and a few emerging semi-peripheral states also, but the French Community is comprised of France, being the only core-state, and the rest belonging to the periphery, which to a considerable extent, depend on France. While the Commonwealth explicitly approved of the idea of home-rule in different parts of its empire, encouraging political regionalism, the French Community renounced political regionalism in its empire, rather, preferred to unified and centralized administration, discouraging self-rule. Today, most of the Commonwealth nations have federal polity, but the member-states of the Community have continued to maintain a unitary polity, expressive of the French political heritage.

Several other political associations of smaller intercontinental dimension, perished in the post-war period, which included the Dutch, Spanish and Portuguse systems. In the early 1990s, the Soviet system collapsed or the Soviet territorial block perished in the wake of the popular upsurge against the 'socialist regime'. However, the 15 break-way republics of the former Soviet Union have formed the Commonwealth of Independent States (CIS) with the purpose of greater economic and military cooperation among themselves. Notwithstanding their (break-way republics) differences with the Soviet system, they still hold the Soviet heritage and tradition, which perhaps motivated them to come together to form the Commonwealth of Independent States (CIS) in 1993. No other intercontinental association is geographically so contiguous as that of the

CIS as it spreads across Europe and Asia. Some member-states of the CIS may have nuclear arsenals under their possession, but they are very poor, and put in the category of the periphery in world economy. Russia has itself relegated to the category of the periphery, and now, increasingly requires western aids and assistance to accelerate its economic growth. The CIS, therefore, seeks for closer tie with the European Union, the United States and Japan.

The muslim World has come up with an intercontinental association, called the Organization of Islamic Conference (OIC), which was founded in 1969, at the initiatives of King Feisal of Saudi Arabia. It was formed at the conference of the Arab states at Rabat in 1969, which had, perhaps, tacit support of the United states. As a matter of fact, the OIC was formed to counter the Arab League, which was then more inclined towards the Soviet Union. The growing Soviet presence in the Middle East-North Africa was a matter of concern to both the United States, and its Arab ally, Saudi Arabia, which, by then, had wielded considerable command among the Arab states. President Sadat of Egypt explicitly supported the move of King Feisal, in his attempt at institutionalizing the creation of a standing Islamic Conference, an idea which both of them had cherished for some years. It became more evident when Sadat expelled the Russian men from Egypt in 1972. The withdrawal of Russia from Egypt, no doubt, weakened the Arab League. However, Egypt, having forfeited its place in the Muslim family, as a result of its separate peace talks with Israel at Camp David, was not invited to the Islamic Assembly of the OIC, at Taif and Mecca in the early in 1981 but that brought together42 monarchs and other heads of states including the PLO, covering Northern Africa-Middle East, South Asia and South-Eastern Asia from Morocco to Indonesia—all along the Mediterranean-Asiatic Rimland, except East Asia. In terms of spatial dimension, the OIC is much more wider and inter-continental than the Arab League, traversing the Euro-North African-Asiatic Rimland of the World-Island, while the Arab League is basically regional confined to Middle-East and North Africa only, and at the same time, it is expressive of the Arab culture, heritage and tradition, but the OIC is expressive of diverse Muslim culture, heritage and historic association.

The Organization of Islamic Conference (1969) has been designed to promote Islamic unity with greater dimension, coordinate policy, disseminate information, share information and funds and foster political strength. The OIC has successfully brought together all the Muslim states, irrespective of their geographical location, political structure, political orientation, and involvement and system, under a common acceptable system. It seeks to protect the interests of the Muslims of the world, irrespective of their racial affinities and ties.

Political relevance of the OIC has increased manifold with the collapse of the socialist regimes in East Europe, break-out of civil war in Yugoslavia (particularly between the Muslims and the Serbs), collapse of the Soviet Union, followed by the cessation of Cold War. Muslim unrest, in West China, in Russia, particularly in Chechniya, in Bosnia-Herzegovina, in former Yugoslavia, and in some other parts of the world including Kashmir, has further enhanced the politico-geographical relevance of the OIC. India, which has earlier denounced the OIC, is now determined to maintain a closer tie with it, because it has the second largest Muslim population in the world. It is more of a political necessity than a cultural compulsion for India.

The number of the OIC membership has increased with the induction of the six break-way Central Asian Muslim Republics of the erstwhile Soviet Union, and a a few Central African states. Gradually, a wider intercontinental Islamic realm is coming up, right from the Kazak in the north uplands in Central Asia, down to the Equator in Africa in the south, across Central Asia, South Asia, West Asia, Asia Minor, South-East Europe, the Mediterranean Sea, North Africa and South-East Asia (between 0° and 50°N and 18°W to 115°E). Here, in this emerging Islamic realm, the political phenomena seem to be so closely interrelated as to provide a fundamental unity. The OIC has to play a big role in this regard. The fall of the communist realm in Eurasia, and the subsequent emergence of an Islamic realm (in which the OIC has to play the most vital role) seems to be a major concern to the United States-dominated western states. The United States of America has already reoriented its foreign policy in the light of increasing role of the OIC vis-a-vis the emerging Islamic realm. The western world is now having the greatest challenge from the emerging Muslim world after the fall of communism.

"Supranationalism, thus, has come to virtually all parts of the world. The time of blocs, the alliances, and the unions/associations has arrived. Inevitably, the progress of politico-territorial organization always having been oscillating one, there will be breakups and setbacks. But the trend appears to have all the earmarks of permanency, and a new politico-geographical map is indeed being forged."

Supranationalism, necessarily, leads to new areal patterns in different parts of the globe, making a rapid process of change on the political landscape of the habitable part of the space of earth's surface, causing more areal-political differences.

Political Regions

It is the popular belief that political region and political association/union are synonymous. But, the word 'political region' implies what it suggests etymologically, that is, a large geographical area wherein exists a set of interrelated political issues in a general setting of geographical uniformity. Political association, on the other hand, reflects regionalism, i.e., loyalty or allegiance based upon a region, or in other words, political association manifests a voluntary grouping or association of three or more states with the ultimate purpose of forming a unified political entity. The word 'entity' is certainly different from the word 'region'. A political region is a stable concept, deeply rooted in areal similarities and differences. A political association cannot be a stable concept and there are examples of political associations having been dissipated and abandoned by the 'involved-states'.

Goblet (1955), while commenting on the (great) political regions, observes: "The great political regions are not necessarily groups of states;their limits sometimes cut across the territory of states, and even of small states. They may be oceanic as well as continental, and some may be intermediate, the marches of land or sea. To be able to explain them, it is essential to take into account their physical elements, but these elements alone do not determine the regions (realms), which owe their formation very largely to ancient historical regions, rarely, however, coinciding with them. They are not, in all probability, the regions of the future, even of the near future, any more than they are regions of the past... The territories of political regions have sometimes for general outline the main features of their physical geography. The basic physical map gives an impression of a sketch of these regions, so that one is tempted to designate them physical names: but we must resist this temptation. However, these regions are fundamental elements of the political map of the earth, and to lead a study of general political geography to a conclusion, a sketch of their outlines at the present time should first be made." Accordingly, Goblet (1955) divides the world into eleven great political regions as under. (Fig. 14.8):

1. The North Atlantic, Atlantic Europe and the Mediterranean
2. Continental Europe
3. The Americas
4. The Pacific Ocean
5. The Insular Far East
6. The Continental Far East
7. The Eurasian Steppe
8. The Indian Subcontinent
9. Africa
10. The Near East and Middle East
11. The Polar Regions

1. The North Atlantic, Atlantic Europe and the Mediterranean

"The North Atlantic, like the Mediterranean in the days of antiquity and the Middle Ages, is today the very heart of human activity. Like the Archipelago in Greek times, it is our foremost sea. Three thousand years of navigation have stamped it with the human imprint...the North Atlantic has become the axis of western civilization. From its European coasts were started the voyages of discovery that marked the dawn of modern times; there the thalassocnacies and the colonial power were born; in the American coast is a magnifying mirror wherein each of them sees in own image enlarged and magnified... The once impassable ocean is now the busiest of the world's route; steamers and aeroplanes have reduced its immensity into the same harmonious relation with contempo-

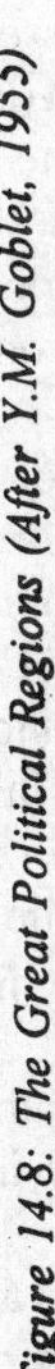

Figure 14.8: The Great Political Regions (After Y.M. Goblet, 1955)

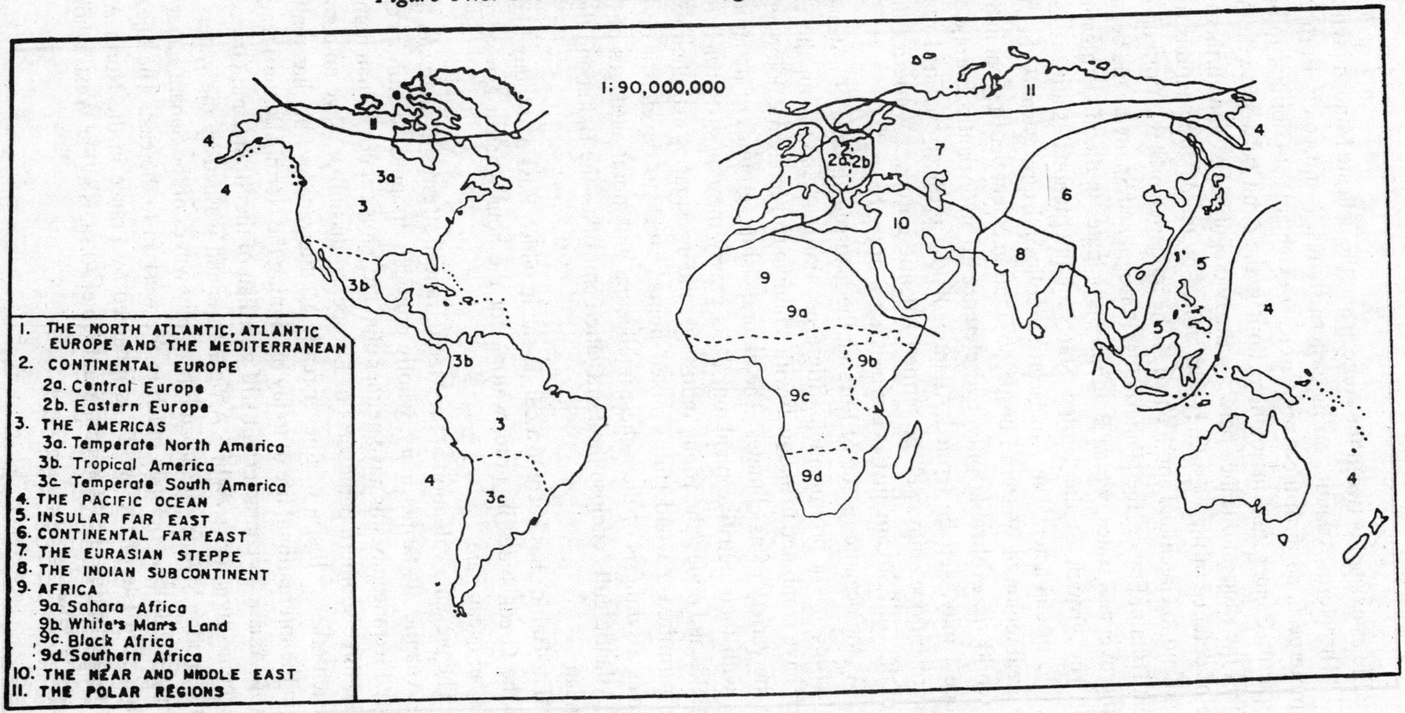

rary life as existed between the Aegean and the delicate Minoan civilization."

"The North Atlantic, on its eastern shores, is not solely European. From Hammerpest...north of the Artic Circle, it extends Past Gibraltar to beyond the Tropic of Cancer, and in southern limit is the strait between west Africa and Brazil, the shortest distance between the two continents. The northern limit is a line of defence of the western world, armed by the Atlantic nations from Newfoundland to Greenland and Iceland... The modern world was born on its coasts. Great Britain, France, the Netherlands, Portugal and Spain are the beggethers of young overseas states, whilst Belgium participates in the modernization of Africa. The growth of the United States in international status is essentially Atlantic in character. The American republics all turn towards the Atlantic... The great region of Western Europe, so small in extent yet so great in the role in the world, is explicable only by reference to its Atlantic Europe...Western Europe... may well be termed Atlantic. It is a presicely defined region...the Western Europe...may well be termed Atlantic Europe... Western Europe is a gift of the Gulf Stream, just as Egypt is a gift of the Nile..."

"As the oceanic facade of Eurasia, the land-sea junction of a world, Western Europe has a prominent maritime position and links with the continent which have combined to endow it with a human and economic homogeneity despite the variety of its climates. The natural fishing grounds of its lepid coastal areas with their nutritive plankton, is its grassy meadows, its tilled lands, its coalfields and mines, the young industries, and its estuaries with their twin ports have permitted a wonderfully mixed human stock to develop a civilization which is a synthesis of the richest intellectual and moral heritages of the past. Two Atlantic gulfs enclose the Eurasiatic peninsula—the Baltia and the Mediterranean."

"The Baltic...has become a cul-de-sac in which Russia of today like that of Peter the Great, bides its time, waiting for the hour when it can seize in the Straits, an ocean gate."

"The present evaluation of the Mediterranean stresses its character as a gulf of the Atlantic. Its farmer unity, wholly political, disappeared with its empires. The Mediterranean basins have neither climatic, physical nor human homogeneity. The three southern peninsulas of Europe, so dissimilar, have no connection with each other. ...Iberia was never really Mediterranean; Italy has realized its place in the international life of today by signing the North Atlantic Treaty; Turkey, now Asiatic in character but still guardian of the Straits, and Greece, have also become signatories. While Africa, an island washed by the waters of the Atlantic and the Mediterranean and the sandy waves of the Sahara ...that southern limit of Europe—belongs much to the west an to the east. The Djezirat el Maghreb, 'the Isle of the West', is included by France in the North Atlantic Treaty Organization and Morocco, Maghreb el Aksa, is a 'Far West' wholly Atlantic in character."

"The abiding characteristic of the Mediterranean is that its waters provide, between its European and African coasts, a seaway from Western Europe to the East, replacing the former Adriatic route; it is a seaway of the world now that the Isthmus of Suez is crossed by a canal whose principal users are the shipping fleets of the West; a route to the Levaut cross-roads where the formerly intense human activity has now returned in a new form."

2. Continental Europe

"The Rhine...forms a political boundary between America and Central Europe. Conteninital by virtue of its geographical position, its climate, and its economic life, Central Europe, with its great river, the Danube, exists within a well-defined frame from the Rhine to the Carpathians and Transylvanian Alps, from the Hereynian Massifs to the ranges of the Alps. Its active commercial relations with the Mediterranean can be maintained through the Alpine passes. The Adriatic shore is separated from its hinterland...and its great days were those of Byzantium and Venice. On the contrary, there is no continuous line of separation between the brokenup country of the centre and the plains of the north. Great rivers flow in parallel southeast to northeast courses to the Baltic and the North Sea. As a result, Central Europe is oriented towards the northern seas rather than towards the Danube, whose waters, emptying far to the east into a closed sea, formed, if one may so express it, a route for a riverine coasting-trade until the nineteenth century when contemporary techniques permitted its development as the southern section of an international route from the North Sea to the Black Sea. But in the northern plains there are neither geographical nor human limits; there is nothing...to indicate the limits of Central Europe, and whilst, in former times, Germany—or rather the Hereynian and Sub-Alpine Germanies—remained for long the domain of numerous small, self-contained states, the north, with no eastern limit, because the seat of one of the most distinctive extensive states of modern times, and a Danubian Empire was established in the South."

"Over and above this lack of territorial definition is the human diversity of this land of invasion and passage. Germanic, Slav and Magyar elements were still distinct in 1919 and the Treaty of Paris attempted to organize 'national' states on the ruins of the dual monarchy of Austria-Hungary and the German Reich. Nevertheless, Central Europe is a definite anthropogeographical region, characterized not only by its physical geography and by its historical empires, but also by its Rhine-Danube circulatory system, its parallel rivers which give it deep-water ports in the north, its Hereynian axis and its Alpine passes opening up routes to the Mediterranean in the east. The Eastern Danube no longer begins at the Iron-Gates but at Bratislava, about thirty-five miles east of Vienna: in the northern plains, the frontier zone along the twentieth meridian is now back on the east bank of the Oder. The political map of 1955 is more arbitrary than, and doubtless just as impermanent as that of 1920."

"To the east, and centred along the twenty-fifth meridian, the longitude of Helismiki and Lvov, Eastern Europe is a region of transition between two worlds. Its geographical environments vary from the glaciated terrains of Finland and the Baltic to the marshes and plains of Poland and the heights of the Carpathian and Balkan ranges. The state frontiers on the map recall those rivers which...(it) is the zone of Soviet satellite states. In the steppe lands, where young industries have been superimposed upon a traditional rural economy, Poland has come under the Russian yoke, its eastern voivodeships imputed and its western boundary pushed westwards to include German lands east of the Oder. Politically, Eastern Europe, by virtue of the Russian occupation, extends well beyond that, as far as the Elbe, absorbing Bohenia and part of what the nineteenth century diplomat knew as the Balkans. As a result, Western Europe becomes more and more Atlantic in character and in all respect, closer to America than to the lands on the other side of the Iron Curtain."

3. The Americas

"For long, the Americas have been regarded as a single region from Alaska to Patagonia, as a continent surrounded by the greatest oceans, in a hemisphere quite separate from that of the old world... In spite of the diversity of their latitudinal climatic belts, the common orientation of the Americas becomes more and more markedly towards the Atlantic."

"Temperate North America...is a land humanized, as it were, by a unique act of will, revealed by the economic currents which cut almost at right angles across the main trends of the physical map. Unity is its human, as well as its physical character. Its population is white (except in a few states of the south-east where a new kind of coloured race is in formation) with an historical Protestant Anglo-Celtic core, and a French Roman Catholic group in Lower Canada. Its political unity, founded on liberal and individualist concepts from Western Europe, has stood firm despite the now forgotten quarrels of youth."

"Two states occupy its entirety, two states with no visibly-marked frontier, no armed barriers : the United States, the greatest republic in the world, and Canada, the type-dominion of the British Commonwealth. Their earliest, and most important centres of intense human activity are grouped in their Atlantic sectors. On the younger Pacific coast...is becoming a region of intense activity. The North—the 'friendly Arctic' of Canada and American Alaska—is being colonized and the Northwest is a zone of common defence on the ocean march of the Pacific."

"Tropical America, continental on the plateaus of Mexico and the Andes, then isthnvian and a region of passage between two great continents, has a whole world of islands in the Caribbean Sea. The diversity of tropical America provides the very antithesis to the unity of temperate North America. The Indian remains in the majority on the continent though evolving in quite a different rhythm from the black states in the USA—and some of the main islands are becoming 'whiter' and 'whiter'. Neither Spanish colonization nor Roman Catholicism has succeeded in unifying a land so physically favourable to particularism; but already some young 'middle power' are coming to the fore—notably Mexico, Colombia and Venezuela."

"Temperate South America, whose cattle-rearing steppes where once herds roamed wild are now coming under the plough, whose railway-networks and industries are developing, recalls, in more ways than one, early twentieth century North America. Its three great states—Argentina, Brazil and Chile—to which, despite its small extent, one should add Uruguay (politically a South American Switzerland) are while republics, Spanish and Portuguese. And, in the tropical north, Brazilian Amazonia is an area of colonization of increasing importance. Clear though the major divisions of the American continent are, the continent as a whole forms, in some ways, a region (or rather a 'super-region' with multiple centres) which its present evoluation and the universal evolution turn towards the Atlantic. The fundamental causes of this evolution are geographical rather than historical or political."

"From the Artic Ocean to Cape Horn the high mountain ranges of the west leave but a narrow plain on the Pacific coast; the interior plateaus and plains descend to the Atlantic, the terminus of the hydrographic systems. And as the Europeans necessarily founded their first settlements on the Atlantic coast, or very soon transferred them there, the political and economic life of the New World developed on that shore. History and geography agree in explaining the sites of New York, Rio de Janerio and Buneous Aires. Economic development over the last century has everywhere confirmed this orientation. Even the Andean states, some with Pacific ports, seek an Atlantic outlet. From 1932 to 1935, Bolivia, the Poland of South America, waged a crucial war to keep the Chaco...for it represents the country's (Atlantic) ocean front. The reason why in 1932, Peru attacked the Columbia village of Leticia...to reach the great river which is its highway to the Atlantic. For western status of South America, the Panama Canal is the open door to the Atlantic; it has brought the whole west coast of South America nearer to New York."

4. The Pacific Ocean

"Still uncharted a century and a half ago, the Pacific has a character different from the Atlantic. Twice as large, with areas of ocean void, almost nowhere does it form the oceanic portion of an anthropogeographical complex; but it is a frontier march where the western world and the Asiatic East have several points of contact. In the extreme north, America, Russia and Japan meet and in the Aleutians, no more than a few miles separate the last American island from the first Russian one—and there the three continents established military bases. In the equatorial and north tropical regions, from 135° E to 180°, is the front between South-East Asia and the South Sea dominions and it was there that some of the bitterest battles of the Second World War were waged."

"...the Pacific as a whole is a great oceanic march...the United States has outputs over the whole ocean as far as the Philippines. And this oceanic march of the Pacific, dotted with British and French archipelagoes, is cleared to the south by a continent—Australia—and two large islands—New Zealand."

5. *Insular Far East*

Unlike the Americas which have Pacific coasts, continental Asia is separated from the Great Ocean by marginal seas outwardly enclosed by string of islands which isolate and watch over the continent rather than protect it. Malaysian and Japanese, these islands are strangers to the continent. The South China Sea is surrounded by Malaysia; Japan, in the Meijii era, expanded gradually from Formoca to Kamchatka, and on the eve of the Second World War, shipping into the South China Sea between French and Siamese Indo-China and the East Indies, established herself on the same valueless islets that mark the axis of that sea, thus controlling, for a while from Singapore to Kamchatka. This insular and peninsular Far East is, in its Malaysian section, a region in course of full transformation; wholly colonial but a short while ago, it is now composed of British Malaya with its independent native states, the Indonesian Republic and the Philippines Republic. Although Japan has lost Formosa, Sakhalin, the Kuriles and its continental possessions, its eclipse cannot be considered and complete or final.

6. *Continental Far East*

"On the continent are the greatest continental powers of the twentieth century : China, Russia and India, each in a domain among the best defined by nature."

"From the Pamirs to the sea of Okhotsk an almost uninterrupted suit of mountain systems marks the eastern limit of Eurasia; from the Pamirs to the backbones (Yoma) of Burma, the Himalayan ranges mark the northern limit of India. Within this mountain are the deserts of the Gobi, Takla Makan and Tibet constitute a zone which caravan tracks and high altitude passes do not lesson the insulating value. To the east of these barriers, as far as the east coast of Asia, the continental Far East has become the Chinese Empire. Peoples originating in Turkestan and settling in the basins of the Hwang-Ho, Yangtse-Kiang and Si-Kiang have been able, sheltered from foreign influences, to become a homogeneous nation, creating a state whose intensive core has hardened inside the mountainous crescent running from the Gulf of Chihli to the Gulf of Tonking. This state has directed its dynanism towards those peripheral regions from which it was separated by no impassable barrier, and it has become the 'Middle Empire' surrounded by vassal states, ruling over the whole continental Far East."

"In the valleys and deltas of Indo-China this region has human, cultural and political extensions; this is a meeting-place of the Chinese, Indian and Malaysian civilizations. Vietnam, Siam and Burma are as continental as China and India. Whilst Malay peninsular is so to speak the first island in the Indonesian archipelago. This Southeast Asia, a secondary region, is the region of contact between continent and the archipelagoes, between 'races' and civilization and, now between policies of East and West."

7. The Eurasian Steppe

"Whilst the continental Far East is surrounded by an isolating relief, the Eurasian steppe suggested no limit to the westward expansion of a Mongol or Russian State. In Asia, it might become the domain of an extensive state which would reach to the limit of mountains and deserts when modern transport liberated in from the tyranny of space...The twentieth-century techniques have opened the steppe to stock breeding and farming. Mineral wealth is exploited, sources of water power are harnessed, and industrialization, under the direction of a totalitarian state, has made of the Russo-Asiatic complex a modern power, materially amongst the most highly developed in the world. Its European territory is the intensive core of a colonial empire which stretches from the Caucasus and the Pamirs to the Arctic Ocean, from 32° to 150° east of Greenwich, and in the far north, as far as 180. From Central Europe to Eastern Asia, the steppe has been transformed and has become the 'termac' for the Far East, thanks to the modern techniques of penetration and domination, techniques far more efficient than the Mongol cavalry."

8. The Indian Subcontinent

"Lying between the Far East and the Middle East, the Indian sub-continent belongs to neither. Apparently isolated—its well-developed circulatory system has scarcely say links with those of its neighbours—India is, in reality, bordered by dangerous zone of contact. Its continental character is as marked in the Deccan peninsula as in the Indo-Gangetic valley, and as in the north in the jungle of the Terai, the heights of the Siwaliks and the ranges of the Himalayas. On its continental front, small-scale maps give the illusion of natural frontiers—but they are of little protective values unless defended by arms and an able diplomacy, whilst the fertility of the plains attracts the invaders. Extremely diverse in its physical structure and human elements, it has nevertheless the unity of a great human end physical region, and also the strength born from numbers and area, whilst its geographical position can make it the centre of gravity of an Asia in course of transformation."

9. Africa

"Seen from outside, Africa with its regular contours and surrounded by oceans has an almost island-like unity; that is why Europeans, approaching it from the sea, attributed a distinct personality to the 'Dark Continent'. But the exploration has changed... and has revealed it as a collection of deserts, forests, mountains and enclosed river basin. There are no great physical regions like those of the continental Far East, nor any great human ones like those of Western Europe.

Setting aside white Africa, north of the Sahara, which belongs to Europe and the Near East, the regions of contemporary Africa are what the Arabs and Europeans have made them."

"Africa, east of the Rift Valley of the Great Lakes, from the mountain of the Drakensberg to those of Ethiopia, belongs to the Indian Ocean and is the world of the Arab traders and of Portuguese and British colonization. The high plateaus of Kenya, Uganda and Tanganyika include in East Africa a "white man's land". Further north, Ethiopia, a Christian country for more than a millennium, is the only historic native—but not black—state in Africa, whilst the young Anglo-Egyptian Sudan may perhaps become the youngest Moslem state."

"In the heart of Africa, in the real Black Africa (Dar-es-Sudan, the land of black men), the Sudanese savana lands, the equatorial forests, the steppes and deserts of Southern Africa succeed each other from north to south. It was these lands that saw the fullest development of the great colonial period of the nineteenth century, where Europeans not only developed the land but also started a western human and economic evolution. Regions grew which must still be designated by the names of their European creators—Belgium, British and French."

"Southern Africa is the great new region on the twentieth-century map. Its temperate part has seen the birth of a white nation, and the Union of South Africa has become the axis of Austral Africa, an axis continued through the Rhodesias to link with the Belgian Congo in the north, and with Indian Africa in the east. Modern economic life and its industrialization have sometimes changed whole countrysides, upset tribal organizations together with the mental outlook of the natives, and posed problems quite different from those in the Sudan—problems more difficult of solution and made more intricate by the Indian element which introduces international complications."

"Isolated south of the great deserts, Africa, where it meets Asia and Europe, enters into a north-south complex, the Near East, which is at the same time a cross-roads and a frontier march and which becomes one of the most uncertain and one of the most disquieting, political regions of the world."

10. The Near and Middle East

"The Mediterranean ends to the east in a cul-de-sac enclosed by deserts and mountains—a heterogeneous region, supposedly of small intrinsic value, but which its position on the globe had endowed with an extensive contact and is known to contain one of the world's greatest reserves of petroleum. This is the Near and Middle East. The division between the two is vague, although one may regard the Syrian desert as marking the separation. The Near East would then comprise: in Europe, Greece, its archipelagoes and Crete, and Turkish Thrace (Trakya) with Istanbul and the straits; in Africa, Egypt and Cyrenaica; in Asia, Anatolia, where Turkey has been regenerated, Armenia and the Caucasus, absorbed by Russia and the Mediterranean facade of Asia—the Levant of the Crusaders—with Greek Cyprus. Arabia, a desert between two busy sea-routes, and Iraq, a zone of transition between Syria and Iran, belong to the Near East rather than to the Middle East with which they are often included. The plateau of Iran, on the contrary, with Persia and Afghanistan, possesses a distinctive personality from both the geographical and human standpoint. But whatever division or name one adopts, these exists between the Mediterranean and the Indian Ocean a definite region of growing importance in a world in course of reconstruction."

"It is a region of passage, where the European transcontinental railways from London and Paris to Istanbul-Haider Pasha join up with the Anatalia-Taurus railway, the trans-Iranian, the trans-Arabian (not, at the moment, operating) and via Syria and Israel, the rail network of Egypt... Although these routes may change at the call of political events, their general direction remains the same; from the West to India and the Far East, their paths always lie across the lands, seas and skies of the Near and Middle East."

"It is a region of direct or indirect contacts, many of them not without friction, and no longer a region of foreign influence alone as it was in the days of the old extensive Ottoman Empire...from its ruins, in the fertile crescent and on the coast rejuvenated by a new economic life are springing up young states with the ambitions, impatience and uncertainties of young beings seeking their path in the grey down of a new day..."

11. The Polar Regions

"The physical map of the Polar regions is not yet complete, and yet their political map is already an indispensable part of any Atlas of the world. Profitable soils and mineral deposits have been recognized in the Arctic lands, deep-sea fishing and whaling are prerogatives of the Antarctica seas; and the shorter routes between the continents line the polar skies. Around the North Pole, the Old World crosses the 70th parallel and the New World the 80th. The history of Iceland and Greenland is more than a thousand years old; for centuries whalers have sailed their surrounding seas. Greenland is a Danish colony with a very advanced native population. In Spitsbergen coal is worked. In Canada, Alaska and Russia, the soil and underlying strata are being exploited far north of the Artic Circle, and Russia is attempting to organize a seaway along the Artic coast where ports are being constructed."

"Antarctica, on the contrary, lies beneath its cap of ice, surrounded by formidable stretches of ocean; it is the domain of the scientific explorer, whilst whalers have their bases on some archipelagoes in the far south of the ocean. However, both Arctic and Antarctica have an economic value and even a 'strategic' importance; several points of their lands have been integrated in the oecumene; both polar regions and now political regions of the world."

However, in 1967, Bruce Russett found correlations between world regions based on physical proximity of capital cities and regions derived on the basis of social and cultural homogeneity, trade, membership in international organizations and United Nations voting behaviour.

Louis Cantori and Steven Speigel have, in 1970, grouped world states into fifteen regional systems subordinate to the global political arena (Table 14.1), on the basis of measures of the nature and level of cohesion among states, the nature of communications among states, their level of power, and the structure of relations among states. Each political region (realm) is further subdivided into a core and a periphery; intrusive systems which impinge on the relationships in each subordinate system are also identified. The table of subordinate international systems published by Cantori and Speigel in 1970 was virtually identical to an earlier classification offered by G. Etzel Pearcy in 1964. These definitions of international political regions are similar in approach, however, in that they focus on actively functioning regions, rather than on static formal political structure. However, Cantori-Speigel model of political regions requires to be modified, particularly, the intrusive systems of it, in the light of the cessation of Cold War and subsequent collapse of the territorial system of the Soviet Union, and the unification of Germany, in the early 1990s.

Table 14.1

Subordinate system of the major political regions of the world and their subdivisions

Region	*Core*	*Periphery*	*Intrusive System*
1. Middle East	United Arab Republic	Israel	U.S.
	Yemen	Turkey	USSR
	Saudi Arabia	Iran	France
	Kuwait	†Afghanistan	Great Britain
	Iraq		West Germany
	Lebanon		People's Republic of China
	Sudan		
	Jordan		
	Syria		
	South Yemen		
	(Persian Gulf States)		
2. West Europe	France	Northern	U.S.
	West Germany	*Great Britain	U.S.S.R.
	Italy	*Ireland	
	Belgium	*Switzerland	
	Netherlands	Iceland	
	Luxembourg	†Finland	
		*Denmark	
		*Sweden	
		*Norway	

Contd...

Contd...

		*Austria Southern *Spain *Portugal †Turkey Greece Malta Cyprus	
3. East Europe	Poland Czechoslovakia Hungary Rumania Bulgaria	*Albania *Yugosdlavia Finland East Germany	U.S. France West Germany U.S.S.R. People's Republic of China
4. U.S.S.R.	U.S.S.R.		
5. North America	U.S. Canada	†Trinidad and Tobago †Jamaica †Barbodos †(West Indies Associated States)	
6. Latin America	Argentia Bolivia Brazil Chile Columbia Coasta Rica Dominican Republic Ecuador El Salvador Guatemala Honduras (British Honduras) Mexico Nicaragua Panama Paraguay Peru Uruguay Venezuala	*Cuba Trinidad Tobago Jamaica Barbados Guyana Haiti (Surinam) (West Indies Associated States) (French Guiana)	U.S. U.S.S.R. Great Britain Netherlands France People's Republic of China
7. East Asia	People's Republic of China	*Taiwan North Korea South Korea Mongolia Japan (Hong Kong) (Macao)	U.S. Portugal Great Britain U.S.S.R.

Contd...

8. South-West Pacific	Australia New Zealand	(Islands of South Pacific) Western Samoa	U.S. and France Great Britain U.S.S.R.
9. South-East Asia	Maritime S.E. Asia Indonesia Malaysia Philippines Mainland S.E. Asia North Vietnam South Vietnam Cambodia Thailand	Singapore (Territory of New Guinea) (Terirotry of Portuguese Timor) Burma	People's Republic of China Japan Australia. U.S. France
10. South Asia	India	*Ceylon *Nepal *Bhutan *Sikkim Afganistan Maldive Island Pakistan †Burma	Great Britain U.S. U.S.S.R. Great Britain People's Republic of China
11. North Africa	Morocco Tunisia Algeria	Mauritania Libya (Spanish Sahara)	France U.S.S.R. People's Republic of China Spain
12. West Africa	Ivory Coast Dahomey Guinea Senegal Upper Voltas Mali Niger Togo	Nigeria Liberia Sierra Leone Gambia Ghana (Portuguese Guinea)	U.S. U.S.S.R. France Great Britain Portugal
13. Southern Africa	South Africa Rhodesia (Angola) (Mozambique) (South-West Africa)	Malawi Malagasy Rep. Lesotho Botswana Zambia Swaziland Mauritius	U.S. Great Britain Portugal
14. Central Africa	The Congo (Kinshasa) Ruwanda Burundi	Central Africa Republic Chad Cameroon Gabon	U.S. Belgium People's Republic of China U.S.S.R.

Contd...

Contd...

		Congo (Brazzaville)	France
		Equatorial Guinea	Spain
15. East Africa	Uganda	Ethiopia	U.S.
	Kenya	Somali Republic	U.S.S.R.
	Tanzania	(French Somali land)	France
			People's Republic of China
			Great Britain

(After Louis J. Cantori and Steven Spiegel, 1970)

(An Asterick (*) indicates a state which is potentially part of the core. Parentheses indicate a colony. Only the most important colonies (in terms of their effect upon the subordinate system) have been listed. A dagger (†) indicates a state which could possibly be a member of a second periphery).

Note: The model has lost its relevance as considerable changes have taken place during the past twentyfive years. Africa is liberated with colonial powers having been disappeared. The 'Black Rule' has been established in 'Meso Africa' and South Africa. A number of islands in the Indian Ocean and Pacific Ocean have been freed. Pakistan stands disintegrated and Sikkim became part of Indian Union. Vietnam is unified and independent. Germany is unified. The Soviet system is collapsed. Czechoslovakia and Yugoslavia stand disintegrated. Cold war disappeared and European Union comes into being. China is gradually moving into market economy and is being treated as the 'Most Favoured Nation' by the US. The peace-process has been initiated in the Middle East and South-East Asia. The gradual replacement of the US hegemony by growing Japanese economic sypremacy has ushered in a new era of 'rivalry' in world politics.

A Critical Evaluation of Goblet's Scheme

A little more than forty years have elapsed since the publication of Goblet's scheme of the great political regions of the world and during this long period have occurred so many changes in the political patterns, particularly in and around the World-Island that political phenomena/issues in each of the great political regions are so intensly interwoven/mutually interdependent as to have manifested the fundamental distinctiveness of each of them. Goblet, in fact, identified larger political regions of continental and/or subcontinental dimension, and, therefore, the geographical boundaries of such larger regions suffered a little variations and changes, except in some cases in Eurasia, during this long period of a little more than forty years.

Goblet's North Atlantic, Atlantic Europe and the Mediterranean Region corresponds with Mackinder's (1943) Eastern Midland Basin and Cohen's (1973) Maritime Europe and the Maghreb, and the boundary of this great political region, therefore, coincides with the Bohenuian-Harz mountains and the

Weiser-Elbe rivers. It was the region that suffered most during the Second World War, and in the backdrop of the communist menace from the east, immediately after the war, the states of the region felt the need of a greater political and economic cooperation, and also a collective defence system. It emerged as a 'liberal-democratic' region and the Council of Europe was established. Though the states in this great political region had variable economic interests but they necessarily subscribed to a common political idea vis-a-vis the socialism and/or communism. A number of economic groupings such as the BENELUX, EEC, EFTA and OECD were set up. However, all these economic groupings were merged together to form the European Community, and that has been finally replaced by the European Union. The states of this great political region are tied up with a Western Defence System (NATO) though, France left it. However, the African part of this great realm had long aligned itself with the Arab League, probably, because of the ethnic-cultural and religious solidarity, that it expressed with the Moslem people. The Maghreb, or the African part of the region has, therefore, got itself politically tied with another areal pattern.

The Continental Europe, in Goblet's scheme, necessarily coincides with Mackinder's Instable/Crushing Zone between the Midland Basin and the Heartland and to an extent, it corresponds with Cohen's Maritime Europe and Heartland and Eastern Europe. Geographically, this great political region is comprised of Central Europe and Eastern Europe and is confined between the Bohemian-Harg mountains and the Carpathian. The Continental Europe was that desirable and flexible strategic region in Mackinder's Heartland model that held the key to the access, and domination /command of the Heartland. The Soviet Union, probably, realized the contemporary reality of the strategic importance of the Continental Europe vis-a-vis its security even during the Second World War, and it was reflected in its reluctance to allow the opening of a 'Second Front' in Bulgaria. After the war, the Soviet Union bargains with the western allies for this great region and finally succeeded in extending its political economic and military hegemony over this vast area. All the states in the Continental Europe including that of the truncated East Germany were made the 'satellite' states, directly under the Soviet control. As opposed to the liberal democracy in the Atlantic Europe was established the totalitarian system within the socialistic/communistic framework, in the Continental Europe. The 'satellite' states in this great political realm were economically and militarily tied up with the Soviet-led COMECON/CEMA and the Warsaw Pact. The Warsaw Pact armies twice suppressed popular revolts in Hungary and Czechoslovakia during the 1950s and 1960s.

The Cold War period witnessed intense mutual rivalries between the democratic Atlantic/Western Europe and the totalitarian/socialist Continental Europe. But the totalitarian/socialist system in the Continental Europe could not sustain its political distinctiveness and it collapsed in 1989-90 because the masses in the satellite states revolted against the Soviet Union and the system it imposed on them. The totalitarian/socialist system was replaced by the liberal democracy. The Berlin Wall was demolished, paving for the unification of Germany. Yugoslavia disintegrated on the ethnic lines, and a number of nation-states have come up in former Yugoslavia, but they are deeply involved in wars. Czechoslovakia has also got disintegrated purely on the ethnic lines, but its disintegration did not involve bloodsheds. The erstwhile Soviet satellite states in the Continental Europe now seek to perpetuate their membership both in the European Union and also in the NATO. The collapse of the socialism, followed by the fall of the Soviet system and the cessation of the Cold War, also brought the downfall of the CEMA and the Warsaw Pact. The political landscape of the Continental Europe witnesses rapid changes creating new areal pattern and once the whole Europe comes within the European Union, a new and more integrated political realm would come into being in the World-Island.

Americas have witnessed minor changes since the publication of Goblet's scheme in 1955. The Organization of American States, founded in 1948 at the Bagota Conference, notwithstanding the cultural/religious cleavages (North American states, except Mexico, are predominantly Protestant and are expressive of the British and the French cultures, and to an extent Germanic culture, while South American states, including Mexico are predominantly Roman Catholic, and expressive of the Spanish and the Portuguese cultures) between the Americas, has provided a unified political outlook to them. The areal pattern, created as a result of intense interest-winning and interweaving of political phenomena over a little more than four decades, has given a new dimension to this great political region. However, Canada is not a member of OAS and Cuba abandoned it. There is some kind of mistakability in the Caribbean because of the US presence but that does not damper the spirit and enthusiasm in this great political realm. Economic organization, like the NAFTA in North America, the ODECA in Central America, and the LAFTA in Latin America have never sought to perpetuate their position in their respective regions at the cost of the OAS. The Americas, therefore, tend to form the world's most 'stable political realm'.

The importance of the Atlantic ocean has long declined and to that of the Indian Ocean declined with the cessation of the super power rivalry as a result of the Paris Peace Summit in 1991 and the fall of the Soviet Union, but to that of the Pacific Ocean, the importance has increased manifold mostly as a result of the greater involvement of Japan, USA and Canada with the affairs of the great realm. The ASEAN is equally involved in this great political realm. A number of island-states have recently come up in the South Pacific, and a great majority of them are members of the British Commonwealth, including Australia and New Zealand. Some of the Andean states of South America do express their interest in the Pacific realm. In order to make an integrated unified political outlook in the general setting of the geographical uniformity of the Pacific

Ocean, an economic organization with political spirit and enthusiasm was established in 1989, called the Asia-Pacific Economic Cooperation (APEC) which in its last Tokyo Summit in November 1995, has sought to create a free-trade zone across this great political realm by 2020 AD, irrespective of political affiliations, attitudes and structures of the littoral states. This would certainly bring about some form of fundamental unity in the political traits of this vast realm.

Goblet's Insular Far East extends from the Sea of Japan in the north to the South China Sea in the south, and included in this great political region are insular states like Japan (and its Russian-occupied Kurileo and Sakhalin islands) and Taiwan; the Philippines, the Republic of Indonesia and Malaysia, Japan and Taiwan are actively involved in the APEC and Japan, particularly, rivals the United States in the Pacific realm. The Philippines, the Republic of Indonesia and Malaysia (Indonesia, Malaysia, along with the continental part of the South-East Asia were defined as the south-eastern shatterbelt by Cohen in 1973) in the latter part of 1960s tended to form the ASEAN, along with the continental states of the South-East Asia excluding Vietnam, Laos and Compuchia. The continental and maritime south-eastern states, during the period of intense Cold War rivalry in the 1960s and the 1970s, tended to form a 'political bridge-head', and were integrated under a defence system, called the SEATO. The 1971 ASEAN declaration sought to create ZOPFAN (Zone of Peace, Freedom and Neutrality) in the South-East Asia. During the past two and half decades, more changes have taken place in the ASEAN, an its membership increased, and its importance has increased considerably, following the cessation of the Cold Was and the super power rivalry. A new areal pattern is set in motion and in December 1995, it sought to create the South-East Asian Nuclear Weapons-Free Zone (SEANWFZ).

The Continental Far East, another great political region in Goblet's scheme, coincides with Cohen's geographical region—East Asia that belongs to the geostrategic region of Eurasian continental power. Goblet's Continental Far East extends from the Pamirs to the Sea of Okhotsk in the north-east, and it also includes in it the Indo-China peninsula. Its western and northern boundaries merge with the Eurasian steppes, besides the Pamirs-Tienshan and the Altai mountains. Historically, the entire Continental Far East concides with the traditional Chinese Empire. Now, this great political region is comprised of the following:

(i) Mongolia, one time buffer state between the erstwhile Soviet Union and China in the 1970s and 1980s.

(ii) The Korean peninsula another 'political bridge-head' in East Asia where, in the early 1950s communist forces put up a strong resistance to the American sea power and a truce was followed the famous Korean War. The Korean peninsula was artificially divided along the 38th parallel; North of it lies North Korea and south of it is South Korea. The totalitarian system was superposed across North Korea and the democratic system in South Korea. Though several attempts at the unification of Korea were made during the Cold War period, particularly after the unification of Vietnam but all went in vain. The attempts at the unification, however, in the post-Cold War period, may yield positive result. South Korea is involved in the APEC and attempts are being made to get North Korea involved in it.

(iii) However, the greater of this great political region consists of modern China which is sometimes called the last bastion of continental communism, which tended to interweave the diverse character of political phenomena into one of interrelated political landscapes in a general selling of geographical uniformity. The cessation of the Cold War, followed by the fall of the Soviet Union, has created a new set of political issues in China, notwithstanding its persistence suppression to the pro-democracy movements since 1989. It has abandoned its 'closed' political system and increasingly inclined towards the Pacific realm. China is one of the founder-members of the APEC, and now enthusiastically looks forward to the market economy.

(iv) The continental part of the South-East Asia—'political bridge-head' and 'shatterbelt' during the heyday of the Cold War—is now rapidly developing into a political unit within the framework of the ASEAN. Vietnam, one time foe of the ASEAN member-nations, has been recently inducted into it. Myanmar (Burma), Campuchia and Laos are likely to be drawn into ASEAN, as the hurdles have been cleared for their entry. All the members of the ASEAN are directly involved in the APEC. The Insular Far East, the Continental Far East and the Pacific realms, in the past-Cold War world, appear to be rapidly moving closer to one another, or in others, an Asia-Pacific realm may come up, as a result of a conscious coalescence of these three great political regions of Goblet, in the near future.

The Eurasian steppe of Goblet's scheme—Mackinder's geographical pivot—the homeland of the ruthless-horse-camel-riding Turanian nomadic peoples, necessarily coincided with the Soviet-Russian State which expressed, until its disintegration in 1992, a complex interrelated political landscape, based on Marx-Lenin paradigm. The political phenomena were so deeply interwoven in the general setting of the geographical uniformity that for decades the totalitarian political system existed. The Continental Europe was tied up with this great political region till the fall of socialism. Nevertheless, the geographical boundary between these two great political regions was clearcut and distinct. It was in the Eurasian steppe the slavs meet the Muslims and the Mongols. For decades since 1917 till 1992, they remained together under a common totalitarian system. Since the system could not sustain the changes in and around the great political region that it collapsed. As a result, different sets of republics have emerged: (i) the Balstic republics or the Forest and Marsh republics; (ii) Forest and Steppes republics of Ukraine and Belarus; (iii) the Russian Federation; (iv) the Caucasus republic; and (v) the Islamic republics of the Asiatic Steppes. The breakway republics have formed the Commonwealth of the Independent States (CIS) in which the Russian Federation plays the dominant role. The Baltic republics and the Steppes republics of Ukraine and Belarus seek to perpetuate their membership in the European Union and the NATO, but the Islamic republics of the Asiatic Steppes are looking forward to the Organization of the Islamic Conference (OIC). Sing Kiang, a predominantly Muslim autonomous region in China, with its location at the cross-roads of the Eurasian Steppe and the Continental Far East, now appears to be more inclined towards the Islamic republics of the Asiatic Steppes. However, the Russian Federation is more inclined towards the western world rather than the Asia-Pacific world. It is in itself has emerged as a 'unique' political realm transcending the European and the Asiatic marchlands.

The Indian subcontinent or Cohen's South Asia is a distinct political region between the humid South-East Asia and the arid and or semi-arid West Asia. Its political distinctiveness lies in its common historical habitation and experience that transcended its geographical uniformity. The Hindu iconography predominates over the greater part of this political realm while the Islamic system of belief is dominant in the western and the eastern marches. British India was divided along the communal lines. The predominant Muslim areas in the west and in the east came to be known as West Pakistan and East Pakistan respectively—a divided state system thus emerged in the subcontinent in 1947. India became the predominant Hindu State, and then, the bilinguial island state Ceylone (modern Sri Lanka). Nepal, Bhutan and Sikkim in the Himalayan region had long served as the buffer between British India and China. These were the 'dependent' and 'protectrate' states to British India, and India inherited this responsibility when the Paramountcy lapsed with the Britsh withdrawal in 1947. In spite of the political differences and clevages, there existed a set of interrelated political phenomena and issues that transcended the political region. However, Kashmir remained and still remains the bone of the contention between India and Pakistan—a source of constant tension and rivalry in South Asia.

In 1917, East Pakistan seceded from Pakistan and emerged as a sovereign state in the name of Bangladesh and in 1973 Sikkim, one of the protectorate states in the Himalayan region, merged with the Indian Union, through a referendum. India and Pakistan fought thrice in 1949, 1965 and 1971, nevertheless, they felt the need for a greater cooperation in the region. Other states in the region also acknowledged the necessity of a regional cooperation and in 1984, all the South Asian nations, irrespective of their affinites, attitudes and outlook, founded the SAARC. The SAARC is all set to give an 'integrated' orientation to this great political region and a common political goal to the member-nations in the future. It is interesting to observe that the SAARC survived the Cold War and persistence arm race between India and Pakistan that probably manifested in geographical compulsion and necessity because large number of similar regional cooperations in other parts of the world could not sustain the Cold War and perished before the cessation of the Cold War. The SAARC is, therfore, expressive of the politico-geographical distinctiveness of Indian subcontinent/ South Asia.

More changes have taken place in Africa since the publication of the Goblet's scheme in 1955. It is now free of the European domination. Namibia has been freed and the White regime in South Africa has been replaced by the Nationalist Black regime. The policy of the racial segregation has been given up, and the most important being the disappearance of the buffer zone south of the equator as the sphere of influence of the Black nationalist expanded rapidly southward from the Central Black Africa. The Organization of African Unity (OAU), created in 1963 with just thirty-three states, has expanded its sphere of operation, and it now transcends the entire continent. The OAU, thus, creates a new areal pattern, crystallizing the political phenomena in such a fashion as to have made this great political region/realm, politico-geographically distinctive. The Mediterranean states of the Maghreb notwithstanding their affinity with the OAU, are more involved in the Arab League and the Organization of the Islamic Conference, probably because of Pan-Arabism and Islamic solidarity.

The Near and the Middle East in Goblet's scheme has long functioned aas a 'zone of contact' between the European ecermene and the South Asian ecumene. Here in this great political region flourished the Mesopotanian civilization in the valleys of the Tigris and the Euphrates, the Nile valley civilization and the Greek civilization in the antiquity. Here in the deserts flourished the Islam with a new system of belief, which, to an extent, is compatible with the Hinduism and Christianity, though there are fundamental contracts between them. It was also the birth place of the Zionism. The Islam engulfed the entire region. In the antiquity Baghdad was the seat of learning. The Ottoman or the Turkish Empire that flourished in the Near and the Middle East in the sixteenth centuries, continued to exist for a long period. It was in this Ottoman Empire the Greek orthodox people met the Moslems, and the communal cleavages were strong enough to weaken the empire. Russia made several attempts to disintegrate the Ottoman Empire but Britain always sought to protect the integrity of the empire because the integrity of its empire in the Indian subcontinent was dependent on it. Once the Ottoman Empire was disintegrated, the Russian would have an easy access to the Red Sea-Persian Gulf vis-a-vis the Arabian Sea and threatened the Indian state system.

However, in 1821, Greece seceded itself from the Ottoman Empire. The secession of Greece had weakened the empire and the Greek orthodox people revolted against Turkish ruler and Russia intervened. The Crimean War broke out in 1854-55 when Russia openly invaded the empire and the Turkish defence system collapsed but Britain and France intervened against the Russian invasion. The Turkish Straits which were under the Turkish control provided access to the British and French fleets and the coalition fleets that assembled in the Black Sea fought the Russian forces in the Crimean peninsula and inflicted defeat on them. It was during the Crimean War that the strategic importance of the Black Sea and the Turkish Straits was realized. The Turkish ruler still controlled a substantial part of the Balkan peninsula north of Greece and continued to suppress the ethnic nationalism of the Slavs who subscribed to the orthodox Greek Christianity. The outbreak of the First World War may be attributed to the suppression of the nationalism in the Near East. Political phenomena in the Near East revolved round the Slav-Muslim rivalry and Turkey was more involved in the Near East rather than in the Middle West. Even today Greece-Turkey rivalry (inherited-historic experience) in the Near East manifests a sustained political cleavage that tends to create a new areal pattern of confrontation. Incidentally, both are drawn into the NATO.

Goblet's Middle East is quite extensive: from Egypt to Afghanistan across the Arabian peninsula and Persia. The Turkish Empire never extended across Persia and Afghanistan. In the modern usage of the term, Afghanistan is not included in the Middle East and if Afghanistan is included, then why not Pakistan? It is more inclined toward the Middle East than the South Asia. The Middle East consists of the Arab and the non-Arab Muslim territories. Persia or modern Iran is a non-Arab Muslim State and experienced a separate historic habitation. It had never involved in the Arab wars. The Arab 'world' indeed remained a part of the Ottoman/Turkish Empire but always maintained a separate historical identity. The Arab territories were mandate territories. The League of Nations approved the British and French mandates over them. Vast petroleum resources and a crossroads location (between Europe-Asia-Africa) in the World-Island enhanced the political strategic importance of the Middle East in the contemporary politics. It was in 1945 that a movement from the Pan-Arabism started that swept across the Middle East but Iran did not join the movement. However, it did support the Islamic cause of it. As the mandatory system lapsed after the Second World War, the Arab territories regained their independence. With the creation of Israel in 1948 in the Palestine followed by large-scale exodus of Palestine Arab refugees to the neighbouring Arab states and/or kingdoms, began the modern history of 'rivalries' in the Middle East. The Arab nations opposed the creation of Israel, but the creation, indeed, accelerated the Pan-Arabism movement.

The Middle East gradually divided into the Soviet and the American spheres of influence and was brought within the framework of the super power rivalry vis-a-vis the Cold War. In the American sphere of influence developed the CENTO but that collapsed soon. The Arab states were reluctant to recognize Israel. To give an impetus to the Pan-Arabism movement the OPEC was created to monitor the oil-flow. To Cohen, the Middle East developed into a 'shatter-belt' as a result of the US-Soviet rivalry. The region witnessed three Arab-Israel wars in 1956, 1967 and 1973, followed by the Arab oil embargo against the western states including Japan. However, the Arab-Israel wars were move of 'national' and 'cultural' in nature but the Iran-Iraq War in the 1980s was more of geographic in nature. Iran in the 1970s experienced an Islamic revolution against the rapid Americanization of the Persian culture. The Shah was deposed. Nonetheless, it maintained a separate identity in the Middle East Muslim realm.

When Iran and Iraq were involved in war, Egypt and Israel agreed on the peace accords at the Camp David in the early 1980s. The Egypt-Israel peace accords were a turning point in the regional politics but not an end to the Arab-Israelis hostilities. The Arab states lifted the ban they put on the supply of oil to the western states and the Suez Canal which was closed for international traffic during the successive Arab-Israel wars was opened. In 1990-91, Iraq invaded Kuwait which was opposed by the majority of the Arab states, including Saudi Arabia. The Security Council of the UNO approved for a military action against Iraq. A multinational army under the US leadership went into action and liberated Kuwait from Iraqi occupation. The UN sanction against Iraq is still continuing. The year 1995 has been a turning point in the political geography of the Middle East because of the cessation of Arab-Israeli hostilities. A number of peace accords between Israel and PLO, between Israel and Jordan and between Israel and Syria marked the beginning of a new era of freedom, peace and stability in this great political region. Granting a self rule to the Palestinian Arabs to the Gaza Strip and the West Bank has already sown the seed of a Palestine State. In a changed scenario, the political phenomena are rapidly getting interwoven in a general setting of the geographical uniformity of the region.

Afghanistan, which was a buffer during the greater part of the present century, witnessed the Soviet invasion and occupation in the 1980s. After the Soviet withdrawal, the tribal factionalism and internal ethnic strifes led to the outbreak of civil wars in different regions, creating a political vacuum in Afghanistan. The Muslim countries are getting involved in the OIC.

The geopolitical significance of the North Pole has declined and to that of Antarctica has increased. It has now become the last frontier in the world system wherein lies the contemporary geopolitical rivalry.

A political geography perspective on world economy organized around geographical scales does seem to offer a fruitful approach to understanding modern world organizations, multinational regional political systems, and intercontinental organizations, as well as great political regions.

Bibliography

Abrahamsson,B.J. 1986: The Law of the Sea Convention and Shipping. Political Geography Quarterly 5: 13-17.

Ackerman, E. 1963: Where is the Research Frontiers. Annals. Anns. Amer. Geogr. 53: 429-440.

Adhikari, S. 1983: Geographical Bases of India's Federal Polity. The Indian Geographical Journal. 2:162-171.

Adhikari, S. 1986a: Indian Federation and Centre-state Relations, Geographical Review of India. 9:21-27.

Adhikari, S. 1986b: Some Aspects of Indian Federation. Tropical Geography. 7:1-11.

Adhikari, S. 1992: Indian Federation: Crisis of Viability Paper presented to the 27th I.G.C. Washington D.C.

Adhikari, S. 1992: Fundamentals of Geographical Thought. Allahabad. Chaitanya Publishing House.

Adhikari, S. 1995: SAARC-ASEAN-APEC cooperation. Paper presented at the IGU/NAGI conference on Environment, Development and Peace. Delhi University.

Alexander, L.M. 1963: The World Political Pattern (2nd Ed.) Chicago. Rand Mcnally.

Alexander, L.M. 1986: The delimitation of Maritime Boundaries. Political Geography Quarterly. 5:19-23.

Alexandrowicz. C.H. 1954: Is India a Federation. The International and Comparative Law. 3:402.

Alland, A. 1972: The Human Imperative. New York. Atheneum.

Anderson, B. 1983: Imagined Communities. London. Vaxo.

Andrey, R.C. 1966: The Territorial Imperative. New York. Atheneum.

Archer, J.C. 1981: Public Choice Paradigm in Political Geography. In A.D. Burnett and P.J.Taylor (eds.) Political Studies From Spatial Perspectives. New York. John Wiley.

Bergesen, A. and Schoenberg, R. 1980: Long Waves of Colonial Expansion and Contraction. 1415-1969. In A Bergesen (ed.). Studies of Modern World System. New York. Academic.

Bergman, E. 1975: Modern Political Geography. Iowa. W.M.C. Brown. Co. Publisher

Berry,B.J. 1969: Review of B.M. Russett: International Regions and International System. A Study in Political Ecology.Geog. Rev. 59: 450-452.

Birch, A.H. 1966: Approaches to the Study of Federalism. Political Studies. 14:15-23.

Blaut, J.M. 1975: Imperialism. The Marxist Theory and its Evolution. Antipode. 7:1-19.

Blaut, J.M. 1980: Nairn on Nationalism. Antipode. 12:1-17.

Boggs, S.W. 1932: Boundary Functions and Principles of Boundary Making. Annals. Anns Amer Geogr. 22:48-49.

Boggs, S.W. 1940: International Boundaries. A Study of Boundary Functions and Problems. New York. Columbia University Press.

Brun, S.D. 1981: Geopolitics in a Shrinking World : A Political Geography of the Twentieth Century. In A.D. Burnett and P.J. Taylor (eds.). Political Studies from Spatial Perspectives. New York. John Witey.

Bunge, W. 1966: Gerrymandering. Geography and Grouping. Geog. Rev. 56:256-263.

Bunge, W. 1982. The Nuclear War Atlas. Society for Human Exploration. Qubec. Victoria ville.

Burghardt, A. 1964: The Bases of Support for Political Parties in Burgenland.Annals Anns Amer. Geogr. 54: 372-390.

Burghardt, A. 1969: The Core-Area Concept in Political Geography. A definition of Term. Canadian Geographer. 4:349-353.

Busteed, M.A. 1975: Geography and Voting Politics London Oxford University Press.

Cantori, L.G. and Spiegal, S. 1970. International Politics of Regions. Egglewood Cliff. Prentice Hall. 8-10.

Carlson, I. 1971. Geography and World Politics (India Ed.) DehraDun. Patil and Datt.

Chandana, R.C. 1989: Population Geography. New Delhi. Kalyani Publication.

Clarke, J.J. 1965/1972: Population Geography. Oxford University Press.

Cohen,S.B. 1973: Geography and Politics in a Divided World (2nd ed.) New York. Oxford, U.P.

Cohen, S.B. 1982: A New Map of Global Political Equilibrium. A Developmental Approach. Political Geography Quarterly. 1:223-42.

Cohen, S.B. and Rosenthal, L.D. 1971: A Geographical Model for Political System Analysis. Geog. Rev. 61:5-31.

Cornish, V. 1922: The Great capitals. London. Methuen & Co.

Cox, K.R. 1968: A Spatial Interactional Model for Political Geography. East Lake. Geographers. 4:58-76.

Cox,K.R. 1968: Suburbia and Voting Behaviour in the London Metropolitan Area. Annals Anns.Amer Geogr. 58:111-127.

Cox, K.R. 1969: The Voting Decision in a Spatial Cotext. Progress in Geography. 1:81-117.

Cox, K.R. 1971: The Spatial Components of Urban Voting Responses. Economic Geography. 47:27-35.

Cox,K.R. and Reynolds, D.R. and Rokhan,S. (eds.) 1974: Locational Approaches to Power and Conflict. Beverly Hills. Sage.

Dean, V.K. 1949: Geographical Aspects of New-Foundland Referendum. Annals Anns.Amer Geogr. 39:70-77.

Dear, M. and Clarke, G. 1978: The State and Geographic Process. A Critical Review. Environment and Planning. 10:173-183.

de Blij. H.J. 1972: Systematic Political Geography. New York. Wiley.

de seversky, A. 1942: Victory Through Air Power. New York. Simon and Schuster.

de Severky, A. 1950: Air Power : Key to Survival. New York. Simon and Schuster.

Deutsch, K.W. 1953: Building Blocks of Nationality. Nationalism and Social Communication.Cambridge. Technology Press of MIT. 23-30

Deutsch, K.W. 1953: Communication and Concept of a People. Nationalism and Social Communication. Cambridge. Technology Press of MIT. 70-74.

Deutsch, K.W. 1953: Nationalities and Nation-States. Nationalism and Social Communication, Cambridge. Technology Press of MIT. 78-79.

Deutsch, K.W. 1953: Growth of Nations. Some Recurrent Pattern of Political and Social Integration. World Politics. 5:168-95.

Deutsch, K.W. 1961: Social Mobilization and Political Development. American Political Science Review. 59:494-95.

Dikshit, R.D. 1970: Toward a Generic Approach in Political Geography. Tijdschrift Voor Economische en Social Geografie. 61:242-245.

Dikshit, R.D. 1975: The Political Geography of Federalism: An Inquiry into Origins and Stability. Delhi. Macmillan.

Dikshit, R.D. 1980: On the Place of Electoral Studies in Political Geography. Trans. Inst. Ind. Geog. 2:23-28.

Dikshit, R.D. 1982: Political Geography. A Contemporary Perspective. New Delhi. Tata-McGraw Hill Publishing Company.

Dwivedi,R.L. 1990: Fundamentals of Political Geography. Allahabd. Chaitanya Publishing House.

East,W.G. 1950: How Strong is the Heartland? Foreign Affairs. 29:78-93.

East,W.G. and Spate, O.H.K. 1950: The Changing Map of Asia. London. Methuen & Co.

Etzioni, A. 1962: A Paradigm for the Study of Political Unification. World Politics. 15:44-74.

Fairgrieve, J. 1915: Geography and World Power. London. University of London Press.

Fawcett,C.B. 1918: Frontiers: A Study in Political Geography. Oxford. Clarendon Press.

Febvre, L. 1932: A Geographical Introduction to History. London. Kegan Paul.

Fisher, C.A. (ed.) 1968: Essays in Political Geography. London. Methuen.

Fitzerald,W. 1946: Correspondence, Geography and its Components. Geographical Journal. 272-273.

Garnier, B.J. 1966: Geography of Population (English Translations. S.H. Beaver, 1978) London. Longman.

German, F.C. 1960: A Tentative Evaluation of World Power. Journal of Conflict Resolution. 4:138-144.

Ginsburg, N. 1957: Natural Resources and Economic Development. Annals Anns Amer Geogr. 3:197-216.

Goblet, Y.M. 1955: Political Geography and the World Map. London. George Philip & Sons. Ltd.

Glasser, M.I. 1986: The New Political Geography of the Sea. Political Geography Quarterly. 5:6-8.

Goquel, F. 1951: Geographice Electorate de l'Ardice. Paris. Armand Colin.

Gottmann, J. 1952: The Political Partioning of Our World. An Attempt at Analysis. World Politics. 4:512-519.

Gottmann, J. 1982: The Basic Problem of Geography: The Organization of Space and Search for Stability. Tijdschr. econ. Soc. Geog. 73:340-49.

Greaves, H.R.G. 1940: Federalism in Practice. London. Allen & Unwin.

Gregory, D. 1986: Distance Decay. In R.J. Johnston and et. al. (eds.). The Dictionary of

Human Geography (2nd Ed.). Oxford. Basil Blackwell Ltd. 110-11.

Hagget, P. and et. al. 1965/1977: Locational Analysis in Human Geography. (2nd Ed.) London. John Wiley.

Hall, P. 1981: The Geography of the Fifth Kondratieff Cycle. New Society, 26th March. 535-537.

Hall, P. 1982: The New Political Geography-Seven Years on. Political Geography Quarterly. k1:65-76.

Hamdan, G. 1964: Capitals of the New Africa. Economic Geography. 40:239-253.

Harring, L. 1959: An Analysis of Spatial Aspects of Voting Behaviour in Tennessee, (unpublished Ph.D. Thesis. University of Iowa).

Hartshorne, R. 1935: Recent Developments in Political Geography. American Political Science Review. 29:758-804 and 943-966.

Hartshorne, R. 1936: Suggestions on the Terminology of Political Boundaries. Annals. Anns. Amer Geogr. 23:56-57.

Hartsharne, R. 1940:: The Concept of Raison detre and Maturity of States. Annals Anns Amer. Geogr. 30:59.

Hartshorne, R. 1950: The Functional Approach in Political Geography. Annals Anns. Amer Geogr. 40:95-130.

Hartshorne, R. 1954: Political Geography. In P.E. James and C.F. Jones (eds.) American Geography. Inventory and Prospect. Syracuse. Syracuse University Press. 167-226.

Hartshorne, R. 1960: Political Geography in the Modern World. Journal of Conflict Resolution. 4:52-67.

Hartshorne, T.A. and Alexander, J.W. 1988: Economic Geography (3rd Ed.). New Delhi, Prentice-Hall of India Pvt. Ltd.

Hechter, M. and Brusteen, W. 1980: Regional Modes of Production and Patterns of State Formation in Western Europe. American Journal of Sociology. 85: 1061-1094.

Herz, J.E. 1957: Rise and Demise of the Territorial State. World Politics. 9:473-93.

Holloway, J. and Picciotto, S. (eds.) 1978: State and Capital : A Marxist Debate. London. Arnold.

Hooson, D.J.M. 1962: A New Soviet Heartland. Geographical Journal. 28: 19-29.

Jackson, W.A.D. 1958: Whither Political Geography. Annals Anns. Amer. Geogr. 48:178-183.,

Jackson, W.A.D. (ed.) 1964: "Politics and Geographic Relationships. Englewood cliffs. N.J. Prentice-Hall.

Jefferson, M. 1939: The Law of Primate City. Geog. Rev. 29:226-232.

Johnston, R.J. 1970: The Electoral Geography of Election Campaign. Scot. Geog. Magz. 93:98-108.

Johnston, R.J. 1980: The Electoral Geography and Political Geography. Australian Geographical Studies. 18:37-50.

Johnston, R.J. and et. al. (eds.) 1986: The Dictionary of Human Geography. Oxford. Basil Blackwell Ltd.

Johnston,R.J. 1986: Electoral Geography. In R.J. Johnston and et. al. (eds.) The Dictionary of Human Geography. Oxford. Basil Blackwell Ltd.

Johnston, R.J. 1986: Contextual Effect. In R.J. Johnston and et. al. (eds.) The Dictionary of Human Geography Oxford Basil Blackwell Ltd.

Jones, S.B. 1954: A Unified Field Theory of Political Geography.Annals Anns. Amer

Geogr. 44:111-123.
Jones, S.B. 1954: The Power Inventory and National Setting. World Politics. 4:421-452.
Jones, S.B. 1955: Global Strategic Views.Geog. Rev. 45:492-508.
Jones, S.B. 1959: Boundary Concepts in the Setting of Place and Time. Annals. Anns. Amer Geogr. 3:241-255.
Kalder, M. 1979: The Disintegrating West.London. Penguin.
Karan, P.P. 1961: Dividing the Water: A Problem in Political Geography. Professional Geography. 13:6-10.
Karve, D.G. 1932: Federation: A study in Comparative Politics. London. Oxford University Press.
Kasperson, R.E. 1961: The Know-Nothing Movement in Massachusetts. 1853-1857: A Study in Historical Political Geography (unpublished Ph.D. Thesis. University of Chicago).
Kasperson, R.E. and Minghi,J.V. (eds.) 1969: The Structure of Political Geography. Chicago. Aldine Publishing Co.
Key, V.O. 1949: Southern Politics in State and Nation. New York. Alfred A. Knopf. Inc.
Kirk, W. 1965: Geographical Pivots of History. Leicester. Leicester University Press.
Kliot, N. 1995: Environmental Migrants: A Threat to World Stability. Paper presented on the IGU/NAGI conference on Enviorment. Development and Peace. Delhi University.
Knorr, K. 1957: The Concept of Economic Potentials of War. World Politics. 1:49-62.
Krehbiel, E. 1916: Geographic Influences in British Elections. Geog. Rev. 2:419-432.
Kriesel, M. 1968: Montesquieu: Possibilist Political Geographer. Annals Anns Amer Geogr. 48:557-574.
Kristof, L.D. 1959: The Naure of Frontiers and Boundaries. Annals Anns Amer Geogr. 3:269-282.
Kristof, L.D. 1960: The Origins and Evolution of Geopolitics. Journal of Conflict Resolution. 4:15-54.
Lasswell, H.D. & Kaplan, A. 1950: Power and Society: A Framework for Political Inquiry. New Haven. Yale University Press.
Lewis, P.F. 1965: Impact of Negro Migration on the Electoral Geography of Flint, Michigan, 1932-1962. A Cartographic Analysis. Annals Anns Amer Geogr. 55:1-25.
Liebowitz, R.D. 1983: Finlandization: An Analysis of the Soviet Union's Domination of Finland. Political Geography Quarterly. 2:275-88.
Livingston, W.S. 1952: A Note on the Nature of Federalism. Political Science Quarterly. 1:81-95.
Livingston, W.S. 1956: Federalism and Constitutional Change. London. Oxford University Press.
Mackinder, H.J. 1904: The Geographical Pivot of History. Geog. Journ. 23:421-437.
Mackinder, H.J. 1919: Democratic Ideals and Reality. London. Constable & Co.
Mackinder, H.J. 1943: The Round World and the Winning of the Peace. Foreign Affairs. 21:595-605.
Mahan, A.T. 1890: The Influence of Sea Power upon History, 1660-1783, Boston. Little Brown & Co.
Mahan, A.T. 1892: The Influence of Sea Power upon the French Revolution, 1793-1813.

Boston. Little Brown & Co.
Mahan, A.T. 1900: The Problem of Asia. Boston. Little Brown & Co.
MeColl, R.W. 1967: Political Geography as Political Ecology. Professional Geographer. 18:143-145.
Mehta, S. 1995: Peace in Plural Societies, Population, Political Economy and Environmental linkage. Paper presented at the IGU/NAGI conference on Environment, Development and Peace. Delhi University.
Meining, D.W. 1956: Heartland and Rimland in Eurasian History. Western Political Quarterly. 9:553-569.
Miles, E.J. 1959: New York Politics, 1860-1958. In R.J. Raybeck (ed.) Richards Atlas of New York State. New York. Richards.
Miliband, R. 1969: The State in Capitalist Society. London. Quartal.
Minghi, J.V. 1963: Boundary Studies in Political Geography. Annals Anns. Amer Geogr. 53:407-428.
Modelski, C. 1978: The Long Cycle of Global Politics and the Nation-State Comparative Study of Society and History. 20:214-235.
Moodie, A.E. 1957/1963: Geography Behind Politics (5th Ed.). London. Hutchinson University Library.
Muir, R. 1981: Modern Political Geography (2nd Ed.) London. Macmillan.
Nanda, V.P. 1986: The Exclusive Economic Zone. Political Geography Quarterly. 5:9-11.
Nairn, T. 1977: The Break-up of Britain. London. New Left Book.
Nairn. T. 1981: The Origins of Nation-States. In L. Tivey (ed.). The Nation-State. Oxford. Robertson.
Neumann, F. 1965: On the Theory of the Federal State. In A. Macmohan (ed.) Federalism Mature and Emergent. New York. Columbia University Press.
Niebuhr, R. 1959: The Structure of Nations and Empires. New York. Charles Scribner's Sons. Pvt. Ltd.
Norris, R.E. 1970: Spatial Interaction and Politicization of Individuals (Unpublished Ph.D. Thesis. University of Iowa).
Norris, R.E. and Harring, L.L. 1980: Political Geography. London Charless E Merill Publishing Company.
Nystuen, J.D. 1966: Boundary Shapes and Boundary Problems. Fourth North American Peace Research Conference-Society Papers 7: Chicago. 108-128.
O'Connor, J. 1973: The Fiscal Crisis of the State. New York. Liberal Arts Press.
Orridge, A. 1981: Varieties of Nationalism. In L. Tivey (ed.). The Nation-State. Oxford., Robertson.
Palmer, N.D. 1961: The Indian Political System. London Houghton Miffins Co. 94-96.
Pandey, H. 1989: Geographic Influences in the Parliamentary Elections in the South Bihar Plain, 1977, 1980 and 1984: An applied Study in Electoral Geography (Unpublished Ph.D. Thesis, Patna University).
Parker, R.S. 19949: Australian Federation. The Influence of Economic Interests in Political Pressure. Historical Studies in Australia and New Zealand. 4:1-24.
Paulin,C.O. 1932: Atlas of the Historical Geography of the United States. New York. American Geographical Society.
Pearcy, G.E. and et. al. 1948/1957: World Political Geography (2nd ed.) New York

Thomas V. Crowell Company.

Philbric, A.K. 1963: The Human World. New York. John Wiley.

Poulantzas, N. 1969: The Problem of the Capitalist State. New Left Review. 58:119-133.

Pounds, N.J.G. 1951: Origin of the Idea of Natural Frontiers in France. Annals Anns.Amer Geogr. 41:146-157.

Pounds, N.J.G. 1972: Political Geography (2nd ed.) New York. McGraw-Hill Book Company.

Pounds, N.J.G. and Bull, S.S. 1964: Core-Areas and the Development of the European States System. Annals Anns. Amer. Geogr. 54:24-40.

Prescott, J.R.V. 1959: The Functions and Methods of Electoral Geography. Annals Anns. Amer Geogr. 49:296-304.

Prescott, J.R.V. 1965: Geography of Frontiers and Boundaries. London. Huchinson University Library.

Prescott, J.R.V. 1968: The Geography of State Politics. London. Huchinson University Library.

Ratzel, F. 1882: Anthropogeographie. Vol.I. Stuttgart. J. Englehorn.

Ratzel, F. 1896: The Territorial Growth of States. Scottish Geographical Magazine. 12:351-361.

Ratzel,F. 1897: Politische Geographie. Munich. R. Oldenbourg.

Reynolds, D.R. 1969: A Spatial Model for Analyzing Voting Behaviour. Aeta Sociologia. 12:122-130.

Reynolds, D.R. 1969: A Friends-and-Neighbours Voting Model as a Spatial Interactional Model for Electoral Geography. In K.R. Cox and R.G. Golledge (eds.) Behavioural Problems in Geography. Northwestern Studies in Geography. 17:81-100.

Reynolds, D.R. 1981: The Geography of Social Change. In A.D. Burnett and P.J. Taylor (eds.) Political Studies from Spatial Perspectives. New York. John Wiley.

Rice, S.A. 1928: Quantitative Methods in Politics, New York. Alfred A. Knopf.

Riker, W.H. 1964: Federalism. Origins, Operation and Significance. Boston. Little Brown & Co.

Robinson, G.W.S. 1959: Exclaves. Annals Anns Amer Geogr. 49:283-295.

Robinson, K.W., 1961: Sixty Years of Federation in Australia. Geog., Rev. 51:1-15.

Russell, B. 1938: Power: A New Social Analysis. London. George Allen & Unwin.

Russett. B.M. 1967: International Regions and the International System. A study in Political Ecology. Chicago. Rand McNally.

Sack, R.D. 1981: Territorial Bases of Power. In A.D. Burnett and P.J. Taylor (eds.) Political Studies from Spatial Perspectives. New York, John Wiley.

Sack, R.D. 1983: Human Territoriality: A Theory. Annals Anns. Amer Geogr. 73:55-74.

Sauer, C.O. 1927: Recent Developments in Cultural Geography. In. E.D. Hayes (ed.) Recent Development in the Social Sciences. Philadelphia. J.B. Lipparicott.

Sawer, G. 1969: Modern Federalism. London,C.A. Watts.

Schaeffer, F.K. 1953: Exceptionalism in Geography. A Methodological Examination. Annals Anns Amer. Geogr. 43:226-49.

Schaffle, A. 1875/1878: Bau and Leban de Sozialen Korpers 4 Vols. Tubingen. H. Laupp (Translation by Lucious Moody Bristol. 1915: Social Adaptation. Vol. 15. Cambridge. Harvard Economic Studies 123).

Short, J.R. 1982: An Introduction to Political Geography. London. Routhedge & Kegan

Paul.

Siegfried, A. 1913: Tableaux Politique de la France de l'Onest Sons la Trois leme republique Paris. Armand Colin.

Siegfried, A. 1943: Geographie Electrorate de l'Ardice. Paris. Armand Colin.

Singh, C.P. 1981: Indian Electoral Geography: Some Methodological Aspects. Annals, National Association of Geographers, India. 2:105-108.

Sinha, S.K. 1992: Spatial Voting Patterns in the Chotanagpur Region. A Geographical Study of Parliamentary Elections of 1977, 1980, 1984 and 1989. (Unpublished Ph.D. Thesis, Patna University).

Smith, G. 1986: Geopolitics. In R.J. Johnston and et. al. (eds.). The Dictionary of Human geography (2nd Ed.) Oxford. Basil Blackwell Ltd. 126-127.

Soja, E.W. 1971: The Political Organization of Space. Washington Association of American Geographers. Resource Paper No. 8.

Soja, E.W. 1974: A Paradigm for the Geographical Analysis of Political System. In K.R. Cox, D.R. Reynolds and S. Rokhan (eds.) Locational Approach to Power and Conflict. New York. Holsted Press.

Spate, OH.K. 1942: Factors in the Development of Capital Cities. Geographical Reviews. 32:622-631.

Spate, O.H.K. 1944: Geography and Federalism. Indian Geographical Journal. 14:24-36.

Spate, O.H.K. 1956: Two Federal Capitals: New Delhi and Canberrra-Geographical Outlook. 1:1-8.

Spencer, H. 1876/1896: The Principles of Sociology. 3 Vols. New York. D. Appleton.

Spykman, N.J. 1944: The Geography of Peace. New York. Hart Court Brace and World.

Tarlton, C.D. 1965: Symmetry and Asymmetry as Elements of Federation. A Theoretical Speculation. Journal of Politics. 27:861-874.

Taylor, P.J. 1978: Progress Report: Political Geography. Progress in Human Geography. 2:153-62.

Taylor, P.J. 1984: Accumulation, Legitimation and the Electoral Geographies within Liberal Democracy. In P.J. Taylor and J.W. House (eds.) Political Geography. Recent Advances and Future Direction. London. Croom Helm.

Taylor, P.J. 1985: Political Geography. World Economy, Nation-State and Locality. London. Longman.

Taylor, P.J. 1985: The Geography of Elections. In M. Pacione (ed.) Progress in Political Geography. London. Croom Helm.

Taylor, P.J. 1986: Political Geography. In R.J. Johnston and et. al. (eds.) The Dictionary of Human Geography (2nd Ed.) Oxford Basil Blackwell Ltd. 178-180.

Taylor, P.J. and Johnston, R.J. 1979: Geography of Elections. London. Penguin.

Vallaux, C. 1935: Le Solet i'et at. Paris.

Valkenburg, S.V. and Stoz, C. 1963: Elements of Political Geography (2nd ed.). New Delhi. Prentice-Hall of India Pvt. Ltd.

Wallerstein, I. 1974: The Modern World-System., Capitalist Agriculture and the Origin of European World-Economy in the Sixteenth Century. New York. Academic Press.

Watterstein, I. 1976: A World-System Perspective on the Social Sciences. British Journal of Sociology. 27:345-54.

Wallerstein, I. 1977: The Task of Historical Social Science: An Editorial Review. 1:3-8.

Wallerstein, I. 1979: The Capitalist World-Economy. Cambridge. Cambridge University Press.

Wallerstein, I. 1980: The Future of the World-Economy. In T.K. Hopkins and I. Wallerstein (eds.) Progress of the World-System. Beverly Hills. Sage.

Wallerstein, I. 1980: Modern World-Systems II, Mercantilism and the Consolidation of the European World Economy, 1600-1750. New York. Academic Press.

Wallerstein, I. 1983: Historical Capitalism. London. Verso.

Weigert,. H. and et. al. 1957: Principles of Political Geography, New York. Appleton Century Crafts Inc.

Wheare, K.C. 1951: India's New Contribution Analyzed. In A Gledhil (ed.) Republic of India, London. 92.

Wheare, K.C. 1963: Federal Government. London. Oxford University Press.

Whittlesey, D. 1935: Political Geography: A Complex Aspect of Geography Education. 50:293-298.

Whittlesey,D. 1935: The Impress of Effective Central Authority upon the Landscape. Annals Anns Amer Geogr. 25:85-97.

Whittlesey, D. 1939: The Earth and the State. New York. Henry Holt & Co.

Wright,J.K. 1932: Voting Habits in the United States. A Note on Two Maps. Geog. Rev. 22:666-672.

Young, C. 1982: Ideology and Development in Afirca. New Haven. Yale University Press.

Zolberg, A.R. 1981: Origins of the Modern World System-A Missing Link. World Politics. 33:253-81.

Index

Index

Index